Globalization

JoAnn Chirico

This book is dedicated to my father, Joseph Chirico, who taught me that all of humanity was my family; my mother, Mary Chirico, who taught me the importance of home; my daughters, Casey Miller and Erin Corrado; and grandchildren, Nathan, Natalie, AJ, Angel, and EJ.

Globalization

Prospects and Problems

JoAnn Chirico

Pennsylvania State University, Beaver

Los Angeles | London | New Delhi
Singapore | Washington DC

Los Angeles | London | New Delhi
Singapore | Washington DC

FOR INFORMATION:

SAGE Publications, Inc.
2455 Teller Road
Thousand Oaks, California 91320
E-mail: order@sagepub.com

SAGE Publications Ltd.
1 Oliver's Yard
55 City Road
London EC1Y 1SP
United Kingdom

SAGE Publications India Pvt. Ltd.
B 1/I 1 Mohan Cooperative Industrial Area
Mathura Road, New Delhi 110 044
India

SAGE Publications Asia-Pacific Pte. Ltd.
3 Church Street
#10-04 Samsung Hub
Singapore 049483

Printed in the United States of America

Library of Congress Cataloging-in-Publication Data

Chirico, JoAnn.
Globalization : prospects and problems / JoAnn Chirico, Pennsylvania State University, Beaver.

pages cm
Includes bibliographical references and index.

ISBN 978-1-4129-8797-4 (pbk. : alk. paper)

1. Globalization--Textbooks. I. Title.

JZ1318.C463 2014
303.48'2—dc23   2013012634

This book is printed on acid-free paper.

Acquisitions Editor: Diane McDaniel
Editorial Assistant: Lauren Johnson
Production Editor: Laura Barrett
Copy Editor: Matthew Sullivan
Typesetter: C&M Digitals (P) Ltd.
Proofreader: Sarah J. Duffy
Indexer: Jeanne Busemeyer
Cover Designer: Scott Van Atta
Marketing Manager: Erica DeLuca
Permissions Editor: Karen Ehrmann

SUSTAINABLE FORESTRY INITIATIVE
Certified Chain of Custody
Promoting Sustainable Forestry
www.sfiprogram.org
SFI-01268
SFI label applies to text stock

14 15 16 17 10 9 8 7 6 5 4 3 2

Contents

Introduction

The title of this book, *Globalization: Prospects and Problems*, suggests that globalization is inherently neither good nor bad. It is what people make of it. Studies of globalization tend to emphasize macro-level forces and events such as the rise and fall of empires, the spread of democracy, increasing volumes of trade, global recessions, and cross-continent industrial processes. It is easy to forget that in one way or another, each force, system, network, or structure is a consequence of individual actions. The world is made and remade every day through the activities of billions of people within cultural and social structural constraints and opportunities that developed globally over centuries. Some people have power to make decisions that affect many people's lives, whether they are acting on the basis of their personal economic or political power or on behalf of interest groups, corporations, organizations, or countries. These decisions crystallize into social structures and institutions—such as an occupational structure or educational system—that limit choices for many people, creating problems, and expand them for others, creating prospects.

Globalization increases the interdependence of people's lives. Today, more than ever, the impact of people's decisions reverberates the world over. Some decisions are very personal, such as when to have a child or how many children to have. Even personal decisions may be shaped by global forces. In many wealthy nations, women are choosing not to have children or to have only one. The cumulative effect of their personal decisions is negative population growth. Twenty countries now have declining populations, which threatens their economic health and global growth. Germany and Japan tried paying people to have children but met little success. In countries that are poorer, it makes sense for women

to have several children. Where infant deaths are high, having more children ensures that some will survive. Living in a poorer or richer nation influences how many children people have, and whether a country is richer or poorer hinges on global forces, some hundreds of years old. Relations like these, between the micro-level activities and macro-level forces, and between the public spheres such as economics and politics and the private spheres such as family and religion, are at the crux of understanding and shaping globalization.

Globalization is characterized by paradox. As in the example of fertility, a strategy that makes sense for one person or country may be detrimental to the whole. This occurs particularly in times of transitions. For example, in the case of fertility, it may make sense for people to have more children to ensure that enough survive to contribute to the family economy and take care of elder family members. This works in agricultural societies. As a society industrializes, this becomes a drain on a country's economy. There is less work for children. They need to be educated and provided with food, and they are more of a liability overall. Until the society is wealthy enough to afford sanitation systems, adequate nutrition, medical care to ensure child survival, higher wages, and a level of social welfare to protect people unable to work or with no opportunity to work, it makes sense for a family to have more children. But this drains the society and contributes to further impoverishment. Higher fertility rates grow out of conditions of poverty as a safeguard for families but end up exacerbating poverty and crippling a society's development. Low fertility rates are characteristic of societies transitioning from industrial to service and information economies and in which women's social positions are gaining parity with men's.

1

Another paradox is that globalization results in more homogeneity across societies—such as the spread of fashions like blue jeans and ideals like democracy—but also creates diversity. One form of diversity results from modifying global elements to fit local contexts. This is glocalization. Glocalization is apparent in most globalizing trends. For example, there is enough homogenization of the general appearance of McDonalds restaurants in the color schemes, arches, and overall family friendly décor to make a McDonalds recognizable wherever it is found. However, the menus are adapted to local custom and taste. This increases the variety available globally. At a deeper level, the spread of McDonalds represents the spread of rationalized social structures—social structures designed for efficiency and predictability. Another example is every country recognizes human rights, but there are now many interpretations, not all of which are harmonious. Homogenization across societies may produce divergence within them as elite classes and working classes become more similar to their counterparts in other societies but more dissimilar to one another within societies, another example of globalization creating diversity.

It is paradoxical that globalization spreads both modern practices and ideas and the reactionary movements that resist them. One of the most striking features of the 1970s was the worldwide rise of religious fundamentalism. Most visible were Christianity in the United States and radical Islam in the Middle East, but versions of fundamentalism arose in nearly every religion. In common is the resistance to the secularization of modern societies— the release of social life from religious grounding and orientation. Fundamentalists see danger in abandoning religious laws in favor of civil laws and in allowing the encroachment of science into religious realms such as the origins of mankind. This is one origin of the so-called culture wars.

Yet another paradox is that the pressures of transborder interactions, systems, and problems require increasing global coordination and collaboration and decision making at the same time that increasing demands for self-determination require more decentralization, local autonomy, and decision making.

Globalization is viewed by some theorists as a centuries-long process, and indeed it is important to understand how the social structural arrangement of societies and global cultural ideals evolved. The Treaty of Westphalia laid the foundations of the system of nation-states—how a state is defined, along with its rights and obligations to its citizens and other societies. Colonialism, through the action of nation-states, cemented a hierarchy among societies that persists, in large measure, today. Other theorists find contemporary events—the independence of economic actors from state control, the rise of global cities as strategic command posts, the cultural revolutions and reforms of the 1960s onward—so thoroughly different than those of any other historical epoch, they argue that globalization is a very contemporary process, arising after WWII, during the 1960s, or as recently as the 1980s.

How globalization forms the structure of constraint and opportunity within which people act and how people's actions shape the prospects and problems of globalization are the subjects of this book. There have been thousands of books and articles written about globalization. Many are narrowly focused on a single dimension of globalization, such as economic, political, cultural, religious, or institutional globalization. This book addresses a broad array of globalization processes and the relationships among them. Understanding the connections is critical because very little results from economic, cultural, or political forces alone. You cannot analyze treaties about the environment (a transborder problem) without discussing governance (polity), trade (economy), organizations (corporations and civil society), and the ideas and values (culture) in play. Cultural constructs, such as human rights, cosmopolitanism, nationalism, and accountability, are important to understanding cultural, political, and civil society globalization. Although we separate these forces for analysis, in life, they are inseparable.

The design of this book encourages you to analyze globalization as you study it. "Consider This" boxes ask you to reflect on a case or example and then decide what you think it means or how it should be resolved. "Check It Out Yourself" boxes direct you to a dataset or study for a quick fact check or consideration about the world, your country, other people, or yourself. Case studies embedded in the chapters examine research so that you understand the variety of strategies that social scientists use to study globalization.

At the end of each chapter, in addition to a debate topic and several discussion questions, there are suggested investigations, more detailed than those found in the chapter boxes. Many investigations take you to databases structured for immediate online analyses or available on spreadsheets for use in Excel or SPSS. Although each investigation suggests a line of research, you can use the investigations to stimulate your thoughts about a topic and develop your questions concerning the aspects of globalization of particular interest to you.

The structure of this book facilitates and encourages many different approaches to globalization studies. The comprehensive coverage encourages a broad overview. The investigations, case studies, and boxes encourage hands-on or in-depth analyses. Taking the latter approach, you may do fewer chapters. Below is an overview of the chapters and what you may expect to learn from each.

Plan of the Book

This first chapter introduces you to the concept of globalization, its major dimensions, and some of the salient scholarly debates. It is necessary for you to get an overview of globalization before studying any area in depth. You'll understand why people started thinking about globalization, why it became such a big deal, and how it affects people's daily lives.

Chapter Two examines select theories of globalization, providing you with analytical approaches to studying globalization. The selection represents a cross-section of globalization theories—some focusing on the cultural, some the economic, and some the political dimensions. Different views concerning the beginning of globalization, whether it is a new phenomenon or centuries old, are also represented. Finally, the theories vary in how they view the importance of individual societies and states—whether they put the state in a major or minor role in globalization processes. Each of the theories provides you with a framework of concepts and ideas. Undoubtedly, you'll find some more compelling than others. It is important to understand the basics of each. As you study globalization, you will find how each contributes a perspective to the overall analysis of globalization.

Chapter Three outlines the foundation of economic, political, and cultural globalization from early phases, roughly from the Treaty of Westphalia in 1648 through colonialism up to about WWII. We

tend to take the social constructs of countries and states for granted. But the world was not always organized in this way. How and why states emerged, and how the cultural, economic, and political relations among them evolved, is critical to understanding the dynamics of the world today and imagining other possibilities.

Contemporary economic relations are analyzed in Chapter Four. The first section of the chapter explains the global economic and monetary policies established at the Bretton Woods conference at the end of WWII. Outsourcing and offshoring, inshoring and reshoring, foreign direct investment, the job structure, and many other topics important to your pocketbook and the economic health of a country and the world are covered. The second section analyzes the global economic recession, why developing societies emerged earlier than developed, the debt crisis that followed it, and why companies may actually like regulations.

The concept of civil society and the possibility of a global civil society are examined in Chapter Five. New groups form as people from around the world interact. Some of these groups, civil society organizations, try to solve global problems—often at great personal cost. The principles that lead to success in challenging and changing the global agenda are illustrated through case studies of the human rights movement in Eastern Europe, the treaty to ban landmines, and the global environmental regime. Although civil society organizations can be successful in bringing change, the degree to which they can serve as a basis for global democracy is very debatable. Chapter Five considers the contribution global civil society can make to democracy and its limitations.

Ultimately, the quality of governance will determine how economic and other forms of globalization are shaped and how global problems are solved. Globalization is forcing dramatic changes in the state system that governed relations among and within societies since the mid-1600s. Whether or not states are even viable as lead actors as we get deeper into the global era is questionable. The challenges globalization presents to the current state system, the range of actors involved in global governance, and the demands and expectations that people have for global governance make it a very fractured and contentious process. The globalization of governance is critically important, and some form of global governance (not global government) is necessary. The problem of global governance and suggestions for systematizing it are the issues of Chapter Six.

The responsibilities and rights of governments are radically changed by globalization. It used to be that what happened within a state's borders was not the concern of anyone outside of those borders. Now, global culture has evolved in such a way that individuals in every country have rights as members of humanity. If states do not abide by minimal global standards with respect to issues such as human rights, other states and the global system—as members of humanity—have the obligation to step in and protect those individuals. Other expectations for rule of law, transparent and accountable institutions, and democratic practice are also demanded if states are to remain vital societal institutions. The limits and potential of state governments are discussed in Chapter Seven.

We are in the midst of a wave of democratization that surged following the fall of the Iron Curtain in 1989 and spurred democratic movements in the Arab Spring of 2011. Whether or not this wave of democratization will establish stable democracies is not yet known. Chapter Eight considers the spread of democracy in the 20th century, the difficulties and triumphs. Like other waves of democracy, the contemporary wave has been forged by globalization and will change the course of globalization. Common wisdom is that democratic societies do not war with one another. Many people also believe that democracy improves economic well-being and can free people from government oppression. If these assumptions are correct, the diffusion of democratic ideals, if not democracy per se, may be the most important achievement of globalization. Greater democratization does not mean the end of history. Other systems, perhaps that overcome the deficits of democracy that plague even the most free nations, are likely to develop from the foundation democracy has laid.

Cultural globalization is a theme running through every chapter. People make decisions, act, and construct economic, social, and political systems based on ideas—good ones and bad ones. How we think about the world is the subjective basis of life and of globalization. Technologies may change the world and the ways in which we live, but ideas—our knowledge and desires—spawn technologies and how we use them. Culture is a structure that shapes our thoughts and our interactions, but it is a very fluid one. Ideas travel the world. The manner in which ideas change as they travel and change the places to which they travel underlies every aspect of globalization. These are the topics of Chapter Nine.

Globalization of culture impacts not just the economy and polity but also how we structure all of our institutions. The turn of the 20th century and the contemporary periods of globalization have been particularly intense periods of institutional reform. Globalization shapes this reform. Chapter Ten examines the institutions of education, sports, and health care. Chapter Eleven analyzes religion. Of particular interest during these periods are the diffusion of science as a legitimating worldview, the multiplication of social problems, the spread of bureaucratic and rational structures, and the influences of Eastern practices on Western traditions—and how religion responded to them all.

Chapters Twelve, Thirteen, and Fourteen concentrate on critical threats to human well-being. While there are many to choose from, I chose inequality, migration, violent conflict, crime, food insecurity, and environmental health. They are among the risks that we face in contemporary life. They are transborder problems because they emerge from global forces; spread across societies, affecting the health and well-being of everyone; and require global collaboration to rectify.

The book ends with a study of cities. The forces of globalization converge in cities, arguably the most global of social institutions. Already, half of the people on earth live in urban areas, and if urbanization continues as expected, this will rise to 70% before the end of the century. Thus, the problems and prospects of globalization for cities will have dramatic impact on the quality of life for the vast majority of humanity.

I hope that you enjoy this book. Every day, exciting and awful things relevant to globalization happen. Each topic covered here has hundreds of books and articles written about it. Having a solid foundation in these component parts of globalization may propel you toward more in-depth study of one or more aspects of globalization. Most importantly, this overview of globalization will help you understand the world in which you live and act.

Acknowledgments

I could not have completed a book of this breadth and scope without a lot of help. I have many people to thank for their support and work on this book.

Many colleagues, friends, and family came to emergency rescue when my computers were stolen. Thanks to Rebecca Butterfield, Christine Putre, Irene Wolf, and Mari Haffner for their help reviewing chapters and checking for lost references.

Some of the photographs in the book were generously donated by friends. Thanks to Barry Ames, Lauren Langman, Kristin Park, and Laura Lucadamo Scott for sharing their work. Photographer Antonio Rosa, from the Secretaria de Formació Sindical i Cultura CCOO de Catalunya, donated the beautiful and moving photographs of Latin American children at work mining, in agriculture, in dumps, in sweatshops, and on city streets.

On the production end, Linda Garlitz, our faculty secretary, was, as always, of valuable assistance in numerous ways. I appreciate the financial support of Penn State University, channeled by our director of academic affairs, Donna Kuga, and the University College Global Funds through Sandra Gleason.

I had wonderful students in my Global Studies class. Shahanna Begay, Rachel Best, Alnycea Blackwell, Theresa Domitrovich, Mark Krechowski, Ronnie New, Victoria Palermo, Brittany Phillips, Emily Winters, and Brandi Wolfe were all good sports working through a draft copy of the text.

I am grateful for the substantive and thoughtful suggestions on various sections from historians Patricia Clark and Bob Szymczak. I benefitted greatly from numerous discussions with Kristin Park and her substantive review of materials. My sister, Lynn Raith, devoted an enormous amount time and energy checking references and reading and reviewing nearly every chapter. I am very thankful for her devoted work. Thanks go also to Barry Ames. His thoughtful reviews, attention to detail, suggestions of readings, discussion of substantive points, and (sometime rather harsh) critiques kept me on my toes.

The editorial and production teams at Sage/Pine Forge were terrific. Thanks to David Repetto for picking up and supporting the project through its development. I am very appreciative of the hard work and patience of members of the production team, who really helped get this in shape.

A number of anonymous reviewers made detailed and helpful suggestions.

1

The World Has Gone Global

Objectives

This overview introduces many basic concepts related to the study of globalization, preparing you for the detailed analysis of globalization in the upcoming chapters. This chapter will help you

- critique the most prominent definitions of globalization and develop and support a definition of globalization;
- evaluate the debates about when globalization began;
- identify globalization forces within and among societies and their effects;
- use a variety of frameworks for studying globalization;
- distinguish among dimensions of globalization and discuss the relationships among them;

- describe the subjective and objective conditions that have facilitated globalization;
- analyze globalization as a continuation of historical thought and events, and recognize new and unique aspects of the contemporary era of globalization; and
- explain how globalization results from human activity and poses a set of constraints for human activity, from local to global levels.

BOX 1.1 Consider This: Global Forces

How have global forces influenced the lives and life chances of these children? Work, rather than school, is commonplace in many parts of the world. Children like these—in mines, on farms, in factories, and on the streets of global cities—are working all over the world.

In contrast, you are in college not only to learn about the world but also to get an education that will lead to a good job. How has globalization influenced your ability to go to college, your choice of a major, or your future career plans?

How did global norms that condemn child labor and stress the importance of education bypass these children? Can globalization help them? Is globalization in any way responsible for their plight?

Do children everywhere deserve similar life chances?

Turn on the television or the radio. Pick up a newspaper or a magazine. The likelihood that you will come across a story about either the potential or the peril of globalization is high. Globalization reaches into nearly every dimension of social life and more deeply than we might imagine into each of our lives. You have probably noticed that your clothes are manufactured in many countries in addition to the United States. But they are not manufactured randomly anywhere in the world. Your electronics come from a lot of different places, but where they are manufactured is not random. Global forces influence where your clothing, electronics, and any other of your possessions are made.

Are you a coffee drinker? Where coffee comes from and what it costs are as much a function of globalization as they are of climate and market forces. Feel like eating Ethiopian or Japanese? What if you are looking for a Tai Chi or yoga class to get in shape? If the right cuisine or type of exercise class cannot be found just down the block, there is a recipe or training as close as the nearest television or Internet connection.

In 2007, over 20 million name brand toys manufactured in China with lead-based paint were recalled from countries all over the world. In 2008, tomatoes contaminated by dirty irrigation waters in Mexico sickened and poisoned people in the United States. In 2009, Americans purveyed poisonous peanuts internationally. The toys, tomatoes, and peanuts reminded the world that danger might lurk in even the most mundane items. Each of these is part of the globalization diorama.

Globalization is more complicated than products and produce traveling to and from places all over the world. People, ideas, jobs, money, bacteria, pests, viruses, plants, and animals—nearly everything flows throughout the world. These flows knit people from all over the world into webs of interaction that change how they work, play, and think. Events in one country can have repercussions across the world. Consider these events: How did protests throughout North Africa in January 2011 raise the cost of gasoline in the United States? Why would the earthquake and tsunami in Japan threaten workers' jobs in the American Midwest? How did the Asian financial crisis impact the Brazilian and Russian steel markets leading to thousands of steel workers in the United States facing layoffs? How does a debt crisis in Europe threaten American jobs? The Islamist movements in the Middle East and the revival of religious fundamentalism in Western societies are also related. A list of globalization impacts could go on endlessly. Ideas, people, products, and money flow through the world connecting people and places with often surprising results.

How does globalization affect your daily life?

Defining Globalization

Globalization is "a promiscuous and unfaithful word" (Eriksen, quoted in O'Hearn 2009, 498). It has become a buzzword with many definitions that often lack analytical specificity. The concept stretches across the social sciences—sociology, anthropology, geography, political science, economics, law, and religious studies all study globalization. The concept is fluid and slippery, sometimes used broadly as a substitute for *international* and *multinational* that do not mean the same thing. Sometimes, it is used narrowly to mean the spread of production processes across countries or increases in trade among nations.

BOX 1.2   Consider This: Is the Globe Becoming a Single Place, a Group?

Belonging to a group means accepting the formal and informal rules of membership. Groups of societies, such as the UN, NATO, and the EU, have rules for belonging. Globalization has forged interdependence among societies that requires at least a minimal degree of adherence to some basic rules that establish some order. Enticing some societies to go along with the global community—to join with the group—is a tricky and often risky business.

China, Iran, Iraq, Sudan, and North Korea are among recent cases in which diplomats have tried cajoling, coaxing, and at times threatening nations to do what the majority of the global community considers "the right thing." Sanctions and constructive engagement are two ways that societies try to get other societies to change. With sanctions, a country might refuse to trade with another. Using constructive engagement, societies continue to interact, hoping that as the country becomes more integrated into the global community, it will change. Whether to exercise sanctions or constructive engagement is among the most consequential decisions faced in international relations.

Russia and China were reluctant to use the threats of sanctions against Iran that the United States advocated (Landler and Levy 2009). Within the United States, General J. Scott Gration, who favors more engagement with Sudan, is criticized by others who want much stricter sanctions (Thompson 2009). The United States expressed surprise and dismay that South Korea offered a package of incentives for North Korea to give up its nuclear weapons (Landler 2009). The United States angered many of its allies and lost favor in world opinion when it attacked Iraq for its refusals to fully cooperate with the International Atomic Energy Agency (IAEA).

What should other countries do when a country refuses to uphold global norms concerning such important issues as human rights or non-proliferation of nuclear weapons? Should they treat their allies differently than countries with which they have poor relations?

There is a substantively important reason for the confusion. There is genuine disagreement about dating globalization. Some theorists maintain that globalization is a centuries-old phenomenon of increasing interactions gradually involving more people in more parts of the world. They argue that periods of intense interaction among societies have occurred before, such as the trade and travel along the Silk Road routes or at the turn of the 20th century, when people, ideas, and technologies flowed East to West and back. Many of the ideas that are diffusing globally originated and began to spread centuries ago. Other theorists argue that the contemporary period is significantly different from the past. For the first time, every person and every society on earth is caught in the same webs of worldwide interaction. They differentiate global from international activity. Economic, cultural, political, and social systems encircle the globe independent and apart from international relations. Contemporary social life has grown beyond its societal moorings, these theorists claim; therefore, globalization is a unique and new set of processes.

Substantive difficulties defining and dating globalization arise because we are in the eye of the storm, in the midst of the process. Nevertheless, there are important areas of agreement. The discussions in this textbook bridge some of these differences by not only highlighting difference but also emphasizing areas of agreement in the approaches to globalization and substantive areas where different analyses reach similar conclusions.

A broad and inclusive definition of *globalization* is a set of processes through which the world is becoming "a single place" (Robertson and Chirico 1985, 220). There are two important concepts in this definition: becoming and a single place. A *single place* does not mean that the globe is becoming one big city or nation. It means that people are increasingly connected in many ways so that they feel as though they are a part of a single place. There is more of a consciousness of the world as a whole and how parts impinge on the whole. Events in one part of the world impact people living far away with a greater immediacy than ever before. Financial transactions on the New York, London, and Tokyo Stock Exchanges can happen from anywhere in the world, and what happens in one exchange impacts the others. High school and college students make friends through social media and video games who live across oceans. There are few products that are made from materials and parts derived solely from one country. Increasingly, there are more common experiences across cultures. As in other eras, technology has helped to spur these changes. Manufacturing and management can move nearly anywhere in the world due to ease of transport and communication. Media and entertainment from news outlets, music, movies, and books help to spread ideas globally. The capabilities of the Internet and social media have accelerated the technological push.

We also have more shared experiences in institutions such as sports, education, and medicine. Institutions globally are adopting similar, standardized models. The medical model developed primarily in Western societies is spreading to the East. Meanwhile, in the West, medicine has absorbed traditional therapies, such as acupuncture, that originated in Eastern societies. People can even have very similar shopping and dining experiences in diverse cities such as Tokyo, Nairobi, London, Rio de Janeiro, and New York. Children in schools—where they are available—progress through a grade-level system studying knowledge neatly divided into disciplines to obtain diplomas certifying their competence.

BOX 1.3   A Closer Look: UN Peacekeepers

The activity of UN peacekeeping forces has accelerated since the the end of Cold War. Increased ethnic violence, more willingness of the UN to get involved, and an increased sense of responsibility for basic rights of people all over he world contribute. While the level of warfare has decreased, ethnic and sectarian conflict continues. In May 2012, heavy gunfights between government and insurgent groups in the Democratic Republic of Congo pushed residents of Bunagana to the Ugandan border. UN peacekeepers tried to minimize conflict by securing the town.

The connections across different parts of the world require coordination and cooperation among societies and individuals to avoid excessive or violent conflict and intolerable chaos. This is what is meant by *becoming*. People must negotiate some basic rights and responsibilities that everyone has toward everyone else—individual, organization, or government—to reduce conflict. To some extent, that is happening. There are international institutions such as the United Nations (UN), World Trade Organization (WTO), International Monetary Fund (IMF), International Atomic Energy Agency (IAEA), and World Bank that were created after WWII to negotiate and regulate various aspects of international relations. However, they are controversial. They reflect power differentials that conflict with developing global norms concerning equality among nations. Also, they are all state-centered institutions. As the globe is becoming a single place connected by systems that transcend state boundaries, corporations, non-governmental organizations, and other non-state actors have significant power to shape social life.

The globe "becoming 'a single place'" may be thought of as the globe becoming a social structure similar in nature to a group. A *group* is a specific social structure, not just a collection of people. The following are characteristics of a group:

- Boundaries: Boundaries define criteria for membership. For example, new countries adopt constitutions strikingly similar to ones of established countries. People are subject to similar norms, such as gender equality, worker safety, environmental laws, and age at marriage. To be considered a legitimate government, countries are expected to abide by norms such as those regarding human rights, environmental protection, and nuclear proliferation.

Minimal standards of good citizenship are being developed for corporations with respect to their social responsibility. Science is acknowledged near universally as a legitimate form of knowledge, although it clashes, for many people, with religion. Boundaries do not mean that all countries, all organizations, and all people will be the same, just that there are minimal sets of expectations to which they should adhere to remain in good standing.

BOX 1.4   Consider This: Negotiating Privacy vs. Free Speech Globally

Values of privacy and free speech are among the most important in nearly every constitution globally. How they are weighed against one another is a point of contention in global negotiations, even among closely related cultures. Rights of privacy take precedence in most European countries over rights of free speech. This tends to be the opposite in the United States. Although both sets of rights are important in both countries, this subtle difference has led to international contests, particularly regarding online speech. Wikipedia, for example, was sued in German courts for violating the privacy of a murderer by printing his name online after he had completed his sentence. In the United States, criminals' names are routinely published. The man's lawyer stated that even criminals have the right to privacy and to be left alone. German law prohibits publishing criminals' names once they have paid their debt to society (Schwartz 2009); U.S. law does not.

Whose laws should take precedence in cases like this that cross international borders? Would you find this case in favor of Wikipedia or of the criminals? What values influence your decision?

- Statuses and roles: Statuses and roles define positions in the world and the expectations associated with them. People, ranging from world leaders to children, and entities such as corporations, organizations, and states are increasingly subject to expectations common across the world. There are standards of accountability for leaders and expectations for children, such as a minimum number of years of school and minimum age at marriage. Countries have many expectations of one another, such as those based on whether a country is a donor or a borrower in the global financial hierarchy.
- Values: Groups have some basic values that are shared. Universal agreement on each value is not necessary. Values, such as environmentalism, are spreading globally. Not every country embraces it to the same degree, and not all individuals within nations subscribe to it. Nearly all societies recognize the rights to freedom of religion, speech, assembly, elections, and the press. Even more importantly, many countries abide by them.

When a value is widely shared, there may be disagreement on what it means in practice. The United States is among a handful of states that have not ratified the Kyoto Protocol on the environment or the UN Convention on the Rights of the Child. Although the United States supports environmentalism and rights for children, the U.S. government has not supported all of the particulars of those international agreements.

Groups often resort to power to cajole or coerce some actors, perhaps a government or corporation, into assuming their share of responsibilities and obligations. This often causes conflict, sometimes violent. There is no guarantee that the world can forge sufficient agreement to create a more manageable globe with less conflict and more satisfaction of human needs.

Here is an example of how boundaries, roles, and values work together. Recognition of extensive environmental damage worldwide, the interdependence of the world's ecosystems, and the fragility of the environment motivates people—in governments and organizations, and as individual activists—to pressure for changes in environmental behaviors. This applies to all levels of action from individuals remembering to turn off lights to municipal laws about recycling, pressure on corporations for environmentally friendly packaging, national laws concerning carbon emissions from cars and factories, and international treaties on reduction of countries' carbon footprints. Globalization of environmental regulation—the organization and cooperation among nations and other actors—is so extensive that people talk of a global environmental regime to which every society and people and organizations within are held accountable in some way.

Increasing interaction and interdependence is likely to increase contention and conflict. Disagreements over boundaries, responsibilities, and values are a major impediment to globalization. Determining who makes critical decisions on the rules of conduct across political borders and who oversees accountability for them are critical global governance issues. People and organizations often resist change. Corporations may contend that environmental and financial regulation or more stringent labor laws would diminish their profits. People may not see the point of conserving energy or recycling. Religious groups may resist the secularization of law, on issues as diverse as abortion or wearing religious symbols in public school classrooms. Governments may argue that financial regulations concocted by intergovernmental organizations limit their sovereignty. States can sanction people and organizations within their boundaries and compel obedience. However, whether states act in their own interest (realist perspective), cooperate to reduce uncertainty (a liberal institutionalism perspective), or act in accordance with global norms (a constructivist perspective), forging agreement among states is a formidable task. Similarly, finding agreement among states, corporations, civil society groups, and other actors may be daunting.

Turning back the clock on globalization, slowing or stopping interaction and integration, is not a viable option. Interdependence among people world over is already too great. Globalization does not negate the importance of countries, localities, or any other smaller group. Globalization coerces a shift in analytical perspective from societies as the largest unit of analysis to the world. Globalization compresses time and space but does not negate them. As we will see in later chapters, location still matters—the local impacts the global—and so does time—particularly our responsibility to the future.

International, Multinational, Transnational, and Supranational

A number of similar terms are often used interchangeably with *globalization*.

International is the most general term. It refers to nearly any type of relationship, governmental or non-governmental, that involves more than one country. There can be international clubs and associations, regulatory agencies, treaties, schools, pirates, criminals, newspapers, and so on. Treaties, for example, are international because even if every country in the world signed them, they are agreements among nations. However, many treaties are part of an emerging system of global governance because they are one way in which a variety of actors, including states, are trying to manage and govern the globe. Many treaties reflect emerging global cultural elements such as concern for the environment, human rights, or an appeal based on scientific evidence. International institutions, such as those mentioned above—the UN, IMF, WTO, World Bank, IAEA—play important roles in global governance.

Multinational and *multilateral* are forms of internationalism but more restricted in their use. Multinational is used primarily in reference to corporations. Multinational corporations have homes in a particular country; they presumably pay taxes to that country and are subject to some of its laws. Multinationals have branches, subsidiaries, or production facilities in at least one other country. They may pay some taxes to the other country or countries and are subject to some of their laws. Multilateral usually refers to affiliations among more than two governments. Alliances of countries—such as the European Union (EU), Association of Southeast Asian Nations (ASEAN), and the African Union—and regional and global financial institutions, along with treaties among countries, are examples of where multilateral is often used as the descriptor. *Bilateral* is used if there are only two governments involved. *International* could be—and often is—used in any of these cases.

Transnational, in contrast, refers to those processes or entities that transcend boundaries of particular countries, such as transnational classes of people. This term is often used synonymously with *global,* most often with respect to issues related to economic concerns. A transnational labor market means that labor shops freely over the globe for jobs and that management can look all over the world for workers. Transnational classes refer to similarly situated people whose interests, values, and lifestyles have so much in common with one another that they have a common identity. Global systems theorists claim that there is a transnational capitalist (elite) class whose interests in maintaining their wealth and power, spending it in specific social interests, and meeting with one another in exclusive business, political, and social gatherings makes them more similar to one another—regardless of their country of origin—than to their own countrymen. State borders have no relevance to transnational processes or entities.

Transnational capitalism is another frequently used term. It refers to capitalism as an economic system that operates freely in the world, treating the world as one source of resources, one market, and one pool of labor. Transnational organizations employ people regardless of country of citizenship who are dedicated to a common interest that transcends a country's interests. *Transnational* or *global culture* refers to values or beliefs that have grown independent of a particular culture and are accepted across cultures—such as the legitimacy of science, the rationalization of organizations, or human rights. However, when people use the term *transnational corporation,* it is really no different than a multinational corporation, even if the corporation is in every country in the world. Corporations have to be registered in states. As of yet, there really is no such thing as a transnational corporation.

Supranational usually refers to an organization that has been delegated authority by governments and exercises that authority across those governments. The Security Council of the UN, the IAEA, EU, and the International Court of Justice, and many smaller, less visible agencies such as the International Telecommunication Union that have a very narrow scope of authority, are supranational. These can also be referred to as *multilateral organizations,* but multilateral organizations do not usually have the right to exercise authority over national governments.

The use of these terms as substitutes for *globalization* can become confusing. Most have *nation* as their root. This seems to describe a condition of being differentiated from the national. While many aspects of the global system have differentiated from the national, others are global in origin. *Global* and *intra-global*—to stress systemic operations of global systems as opposed to relations among nations—are preferred in this text. I use *transnational* when discussing the work of social scientists who use the term. The other terms—*multinational, international,* and *multilateral*—are used restrictively as described above.

The Subjective Dimension of Globalization

Public Opinion and Globalization in the United States

The earliest appearance of *globalization* archived in the *New York Times* was in 1974. The article warned of the likely catastrophic consequences of the increasing power of multinational corporations. Another article appeared in 1981, and another in 1984. During these years, articles on globalization were similarly scarce in the *Washington Post* and the *Wall Street Journal.* Clearly, globalization, while not on everyone's mind in the early 1980s, was beginning to pique interest.

The sum of entries about globalization from the three primary national newspapers in the United States—*New York Times, Washington Post,* and *Wall Street Journal*—along with press releases indexed in *PS Newswire,* was under 20 in 1984. After a slow beginning, globalization gained cache very quickly. In 1998, there were over 800 references in newspapers and similar exponential increases in the publication of books and scholarly articles about globalization (Fiss and Hirsch 2005).

As more people wrote about globalization, the concept expanded and was related to more dimensions of social life. The majority of news articles and press releases in the early years of coverage were found in the financial sections of the newspapers. Over time, articles and press releases diffused across sections of the newspaper and the types of organizations issuing press releases about globalization expanded. People were thinking of more ways in which globalization impacted their lives. By 1995, newspaper and press release coverage spread from its economic aspects to include globalization as it related to topics as diverse as citizenship, crime, disease, poverty, culture, and consumption (Fiss and Hirsch 2005, 42).

As the discourse concerning globalization spread to more areas, the variety of opinions in newspapers and press releases became more diverse. Well over half of both articles and press releases were neutral in 1986. By 1997, fewer than 30% remained neutral. In articles and press releases, positive and negative items replaced the neutral, but the overall trend was more positive. The number of positive press releases, which originate in the corporate and financial sectors, has continued to climb rapidly. In contrast, positive newspaper articles started to decline in 1992, and negative articles increased rapidly and steadily. By 1997, the percentage of negative articles was over twice that of positive articles (Fiss and Hirsch 2005).

As debate in newspapers intensified, people's opinions about globalization tended to develop favorably despite the headlines. In 1993, when a sample of Americans was asked their opinion of globalization, 40% of the respondents said that they were not familiar with the concept and gave no opinion; 14% thought globalization was mostly bad, and 41% mostly good. By 1998, only 11% gave no opinion; 20% thought globalization was mostly bad, and 54% mostly good (Fiss and Hirsch 2005, 47). By 2004, 65% of Americans indicated that they had a positive view of globalization. In a 2004 19-nation poll, only in France did a plurality have a negative view of globalization (World Public Opinion 2004).

What factors influence people's attitudes toward globalization? Consider economic, social, political, and cultural factors.

The diffusion of the concept of globalization is also global. Equivalent terms appear in Italian, Spanish, Dutch, Portuguese, German, Russian, Chinese, Indonesian, Finnish, Nepali, Sinhalese, Tagalog, Timorese, Vietnamese, Thai, Korean, Romanian, and likely many more languages. In each case, the term signifies that people perceive a

new reality (Scholte 2000, 42). The rapid ascent of a word that might have remained a bit of academic jargon indicates that people are struggling to express something new about social life that is not captured by older expressions.

There is no doubt that globalization is a dominant theme of our era. Whether discussing culture, politics, or economics, or the plight of an individual or of entire societies, globalization is likely to be cast as a major player, sometimes villainous and often heroic.

Perceiving a Common Humanity

Every day, through Internet, television, radio, newspapers, and perhaps friends or family, we are exposed to major global events such as wars, famines, and natural disasters. We also learn about the minutiae of people's lives and lifestyles in every corner of the world. We see the food they eat, the clothes they wear, and the music they listen to, both candid and choreographed, and often in intimate detail. Media expands the scope of connections and awareness among people who will never meet or whose lives may never personally touch but who are impacted by the same global forces and who affect one another's lives. Media, probably more than anything else, have made the subjective sense of the world as a single place real. Regardless of their attitude about them, it is impossible for most people to ignore the plight of others in faraway corners of the world, or the impact that events in other countries have on their own lives. People have begun to feel that they belong to something larger than their own society. The World Values Survey found that 77.9% of people in their global poll of over 82,000 people agreed or agreed strongly with the statement, "I see myself as a world citizen" (World Values Survey 2010).

Humanity as a category of existence now has social standing as a status, along with the individual and society, endowed with rights and owed protection of those rights. For the first time in human history, viewpoints that differentiate who is in-group and who is out-group to deny full humanity to an out-group have been universally rejected (Donnelly 2007, 91). With respect to human rights, it is as though there is no other, only us.

BOX 1.5   A Closer Look: The Blue Marble

Pictures of the earth rising over moon vividly portrayed the earth as a single place. This contributed to the deepening of the subjective dimension of globalization.

Two of the most powerful images that drove globalization home for many of the "baby boomer" generation came from the late 1960s and early 1970s, the height of the civil rights and anti-war movements that spread globally. The first photographs of the earth taken from the moon in 1968 left people awestruck at the beauty, fragility, and smallness of the planet, home to humanity. They changed how a generation looked at the planet. Just a few years later, in 1972, from the Vietnam War came another unforgettable image: a photograph of nine-year-old Phan Thi Kim Phúc, her face twisted in horror, running naked from her village after stripping from her burning clothes. She was fleeing to survive the napalming of her village. This photograph became a global symbol of the human horrors in war.[1]

Television news and news magazines with global reach kept people fairly up to date on many world events in the 1960s through 1990s. In the 1980s, Lech Walesa transfixed much of the world as he led the Solidarity Movement in Poland in challenging Communist rule and won. In the 1990s, the world was horrified by the genocides in Rwanda, Bosnia, and southern Sudan, as people watched on television and read about them in newspapers and weekly newsmagazines. Now, Internet communications relay events globally in real time. They peer into the lives of real people, nearly everywhere in the world, from nearly anywhere. In April of 2009, students in Moldova protesting against Communist leadership of their country seemed to appear at rallies from out of nowhere. They were alerted to gather spontaneously, on the spot, through text messaging, Facebook, and Twitter. Students, youth, and sympathetic adults around the world kept vigil in real time through a special track set up on Twitter (Barry 2009). Students from all over the world offered solace, solidarity, and support via Facebook and MySpace to students half a world away whom they would probably never meet. It was one of the first times that people spontaneously choreographed and publicized demonstrations and protests through social media. Flash mobs have since become a staple of political protest, spontaneous "street" events, and, unfortunately, criminal activity as well.

Similarly, messages from all over the world flooded the Internet offering encouragement and support for the protesters of the June 2009 Iranian election. Computer-savvy supporters from all over the world became involved in the protests by ceding remote use of their computers to the Iranians, helping them communicate and organize. Neda, a young and beautiful Iranian, allegedly killed by a government sniper's bullet, became an international symbol of oppression when news of her death was circulated globally through Facebook and Twitter. Despite its graphic content, YouTube was forced to post the video of her death because so many people uploaded it that the tragic scene could not be blocked. It was viewed by millions globally (Putz 2009). Even though governments often try to block Twitter, YouTube, and other social networking sites to inhibit people's right to assemble and speak out politically, people living in other countries step in to offer their servers for relaying information. Social media connected people so intimately to the 2011 protests in the Arab world that many of us felt as though we had a role in the revolutions, watching and supporting prodemocracy dissidents while holding our breath for their safety. Virtual connections are very real in their consequences.

The Objective Bases of Globalization

The objective bases of globalization are the material and factual matters—the observable indicators of globalization. They are in every dimension of social life, such as the volume of trade, rates of migration, mentions of human rights in state constitutions, and the number of social media connections among people in various regions of the world. This is because globalization, like modernization before it, impacts every aspect of social life.

Analyzing the objective bases of globalization is critical in studying globalization. Because social life is so complex, it is difficult to distinguish among globalization forces as they impact the various institutions and systems of contemporary life. If a multinational corporation is subject to regulations concerning its environmental responsibility or its obligation to pay a living wage regardless of where it operates, that is a function of globalization. But is it political, cultural, or economic globalization? It is all three because the values underlying the regulations are part of global culture. The regulations were brought about by global political processes to regulate the global economy. The recognition that globalization emanates from and impacts every aspect of life is handily called *generic globalization* (Sklair 2002, 41).

Economics, politics, and culture are typically analyzed at societal levels. However, every group has economic, political, and cultural systems. Even groups of two produce and distribute goods and services for survival—the economic function. Leaders make or influence decisions that bear on the common good—even though decisions are often made in the interests of the powerful. This is politics. Every group has a trove of meaning, values, norms, rights, privileges, and boundaries—a culture. Historically, the largest entity that could be called a group has been a society. Now, humanity is fast becoming the largest group—a single place. As members of this globe-in-formation, we participate in and are witness to the development of economic, political, social, and cultural systems that span the globe. Many of the things that we do—practice yoga, volunteer for organizations such as World Vision or Habitat for Humanity (global non-governmental organizations), wear Reebok athletic shoes, appreciate reggae music, or eat fruit imported from Asia—are among the objective bases of globalization.

Culture, economy, and polity, however distinct they may appear, are only analytically distinct. Culture permeates both polity and economy, which are so intertwined that they are sometimes referred to as the *political economy*. Each dimension of globalization has an impressive body of theory and research promoting a variety of views. This chapter merely introduces these areas; each is analyzed in more depth in later chapters.

Economic Basis of Globalization

As early as the 18th century, Adam Smith—author of *The Wealth of Nations* (1776/2000) and founder of modern economic theory—argued that capitalism would spread globally and, despite the ravages of colonialism, would eventually lift all areas of the world out of misery.

Part of Smith's prediction has come to pass. Globalization has changed economic systems within states. Not all societies have capitalist economies, but most have some variation. Globalization shaped economic relations among societies, and there is now global capitalist economy. From material acquisition through assembly, production is dispersed globally for a global market for goods, services, and labor. The activities of multinational corporations around the world, moving jobs, acquiring resources, and selling goods, are among the most visible dimensions of global capitalism. Finance, banking, and other economic processes are also global. The electronic flow of money in and out of societies, as it is invested and divested, is one of the most powerful forces of globalization.

People worry about the impact of economic globalization on their lives in the form of employment, wages, and the price of goods. Some fear that global capitalism is so strong that governments no longer have control over their economies, that the power of states has been eclipsed by capitalist enterprises. For these reasons, economic globalization has occasioned both criticism and fear. One of the most contested questions is whether or not a capitalist global system will ever fulfill Smith's promise and improve the quality of life for the billions of poor people. The spread of capitalism for centuries meant subjugation for millions of people through colonialism, multinational corporations, and amassing of debt by Third World countries. Combating poverty is a major objective of global civil society and international governmental organizations.

Like Smith, Karl Marx thought that capitalism would spread globally and would provide an engine for invention, thus driving the human capacity for material progress. But his prediction for the outcome of capitalist expansion was very different than Smith's. Marx thought that an international union of workers would emerge and revolt against capitalism to establish socialism globally so that everyone could enjoy the benefits of prosperity. It does not look as though Marx's prediction will come to pass anytime soon. However, as discussed in the chapter on economic globalization, some theorists maintain that capitalism has created the conditions for its own demise.

If this is correct, what type of system might replace capitalism, both within societies and globally?

BOX 1.6   A Closer Look: Rapid Social Change in China

China may appear to be beyond the influence of other countries, but globalization has had significant impact on all aspects of Chinese life. Since reopening to the rest of the world in the 1970s, China has undergone dramatic change. To become a global player, China changed its economic system, offering "Chinese-style" socialism—a brand that most of us recognize as a version of capitalism.

- China's annual growth rate from 1978 to 2002 averaged 8.1% (Angang, Linlin, and Zhixiao 2003).
- While China is far from what most people call democracy, it has granted many more civil rights to citizens than they had in the past.
- More Chinese think of their government as democratic, rather than non-democratic.
- Centuries-old habits of saving are giving way to spending, although the Chinese still save about 38% of their incomes in contrast to 3.9% of Americans (Richburg 2012).
- The Chinese currently lead the world in luxury spending (DeMarco 2011).
- Consumer culture among teens is as vibrant as in the United States and other Western societies. The savings rate of Chinese 20-somethings is effectively zero (Richburg 2012).
- Manufacturing centers, the export zones, line the seaboard and attract millions of young women from rural areas to city jobs. Despite deplorable conditions, most stay.
- Unions have been flexing their muscles in China, and the government has done little to stop them. Strikes have spread from plant to plant, although primarily in non-Chinese companies, such as Honda.

Unfortunately, rapid social change brings a price. Culture tends to change more slowly than social structures. Writing about the Industrial Revolution, Durkheim found that rapidly changing social structures rendered social norms obsolete. The society has weak and conflicting guidelines for living. Without meaningful social norms, the social structure is anomic, and individuals experience anomie. The reasons are complex, but the costs of anomie are high. Institutions do not function well. The economy may not provide jobs, schools lose effectiveness, and families may break down under the strain. Crime, mental illness, and suicide rise.

Traditional societies generally have low rates of disorder and low rates of suicide in particular. Suicide is increasing more rapidly in China than anywhere else in the world. Unlike more common patterns, suicide is higher among women than men and rural rather than urban areas (Hasija 2011).

Does this disprove Durkheim's theory of suicide, or does it provide further evidence for it?

Does the example of China support or dispute Karl Marx's and Adam Smith's theories that capitalism would eventually envelop the world?

What we know is that thus far, economic globalization has promoted tremendous inequality among societies and within societies. How economic globalization can be made to serve humanity—and not only some humans—is critical for people's survival and for political and economic stability. This question is one of the most important on the global agenda as the world becomes a single place economically.

Political Basis of Globalization

Globalization is creating a web of connections among societies that continues to expand. Countries and actors within countries are becoming increasingly interdependent. Their activities have a near immediate impact on one another. The highest moral obligation among societies prior to the contemporary phase of globalization was through treaty, although domination of more powerful societies over weaker defined more relationships. New considerations are now on the global agenda.

Whether the system of societies was based on pure struggle for power or building international institutions to facilitate cooperation is a debate among political scientists. Regardless of which is more correct, people are demanding more justice in international relations and relations within societies. Because societies are interdependent to the extent that events in the weakest can impact the strongest, these demands have more leverage. They impose constraint and opportunity, rights and obligations on all societies.

This raises a number of political questions on the global agenda concerning the rights and obligation of

- societies to other societies;
- societies to individuals regardless of where they reside and to humanity generally;
- individuals to other individuals and humanity generally regardless of where they reside or their position in the global hierarchy; and
- societies to their citizens, given their dual status as members of humanity as well as specific societies.

BOX 1.7   Check It Out Yourself: News Analysis

Reading the newspapers daily is educative. Challenge yourself or your classmates to find a global angle in news reports. Find articles in each section of the paper—world, national, and local news; sports; religion; style; food; features; and so on.

Use online and foreign news sources and news magazines as well.

Keep a file or log of the articles. Classify each article under political, economic, civil society, or cultural globalization. Do the classifications overlap?

As the term progresses, relate the articles to the material discussed throughout this book and in class.

A second aspect of political globalization is the development of polities within societies. Political globalization results in structurally homogenous states and political processes. Constitutional governments now blanket the world. The constitutions, as you will see, bear striking similarities to one another. The spread of democracy over the last few centuries has been significant and has intensified since the late 1960s.

Global opinion is converging on what it means to be a legitimate state or society. The importance of the rule of law, representative governments, civil liberties, and human rights are now normative. Governments that do not institute these reforms

often face sanction in the global community and rebellion at home.

A third feature of political globalization is the multiplication of layers of governance. International governmental organizations do more now than just mediate negotiations among nations. Increasingly, they have governance functions, particularly as regulatory agencies. Non-governmental organizations, multinational corporations, and financial institutions have significant influence on governmental and multilateral decision making. More strikingly, they make independent decisions and take independent action in the global market and global community. This makes it difficult for states to manage their own national economies and national social life. These multiple layers of governance raise questions that among the most important of our era.

- How is the balance of powers within states changing?

- How will pressures from and involvement of other actors—civil society, corporations, and other societies—affect how states and relations among states are governed?
- How can a global system of power and authority be held accountable? Can it be democratic?

BOX 1.8   A Closer Look: 1893 Chicago World's Fair

World's Fairs promote cultural sharing and national pride as countries exhibit their latest technologies, best art, and other accomplishments. The first official World's Fair was in London in 1851. The Chicago World's Fair was the first to have amusements, including the technically masterful Ferris Wheel.

Cultural Basis of Globalization

Cultural globalization is the most expansive of the globalization processes. The ubiquity of things from the United States, such as blue jeans, cola drinks, and hamburgers, is a striking feature of global life. Foreign movies, foreign food, foreign languages, and imported goods are a regular feature of life almost everywhere.

Things are only part of cultural globalization. There are cultural elements implicated in every dimension of globalization. What people value and believe are at the basis of all of their actions. We collectively construct the reality in which we live—although some people exercise more power and influence in these processes. The economic and political decisions we make stem from values and beliefs that are emerging globally and the norms, policies, and regulations that result from them are all part of global culture.

Lifestyle is also part of culture. People's lifestyles are influenced by their national cultures and the times in which they live. For example, there seems to be an emerging teen lifestyle that is based on similar consumption and use patterns of communication and leisure technologies. The widespread use of cell phones,

YouTube, and other social media creates possibilities for teens that did not exist in less technologically sophisticated times. Whether this will generate a greater appreciation for diversity as youth search out new ideas, or allow them to surround themselves in a cocoon of the familiar, is one subject of globalization study.

The flash mob has become a youth phenomenon. Summoned by social media, people pass the message to congregate at a particular time and place. Thousands of people heed calls to join the gathering for as innocent a purpose as dancing in the streets while a young man proposes marriage to his girlfriend (Pittsburgh), singing a song (*Hey Jude* in Trafalgar Square, London), or engaging in some other sort of fun mass activity. Recently, the flash mob has had a more serious purpose—to stage the protests that led to the downfall of governments in Arab Spring of 2011. Unfortunately, the technique is adaptable to crimes, too, from rioting in London to flash blitzes through stores while youth grab whatever they can get away with. How people express themselves, organize themselves, and make their livings are all part of lifestyle that is impacted by cultural globalization.

Cultural globalization may have profound consequences. The idea that people are not just members of societies, but of humanity, and have human rights is accepted globally. The specific content of human rights is highly contentious. Negotiating human rights affects economic, political, and other institutional practices. The discussion of human rights in the global community is building toward consensus on several points. First, there is general agreement that people everywhere are owed human rights. There is significant agreement that it is the responsibility of the global community to define human rights. Third, there is a growing sentiment that when human rights are not respected, at least in the cases of genocide and other crimes against humanity, the world community is obliged to protect them.

Globalization arouses passionate objections from those who view cultural globalization as Americanization or Westernization forced on the rest of the world. European and U.S. values are spreading. But so are Asian, African, Latin American, and other cultures' values. The incorporation of yoga, meditation, and herbal remedies into the health care and fitness regime throughout Europe and North and South America are examples of the recent influence of the East on Western routines.

Cultural globalization raises a series of important questions. Among them:

- To what degree will globalization foster cultural homogenization, creating a global culture that is an amalgam of diverse cultures?
- Will cultural globalization provoke more protectionism in matters of culture?
- How do ideas and practices diffuse around the world and are they changed by local uses and local culture as they spread?

Globalization and Identity

The social structures in which we interact, along with the cultural beliefs, values, and habits that we learn, shape our personalities. The rational man and the organizational man[2] were among the archetypes of modernity. These concepts acknowledge that we build our personalities in the context of the broad cultural motifs, such as rationalization, and social structures, such as the bureaucratic organizations, in which we live. The impact of globalization on personality does not receive as much popular attention as economic globalization, but globalization has dramatic impact on how individuals think of themselves. The increasing sense of belonging to the globe presents people with a source of identity beyond national society or other loyalties. It alters the sense of responsibility one feels toward people in different parts of the world. Whereas early societies felt a circle of responsibility within a context of their tribe, with globalization, we are evolving toward a concept of the individual within the context of universal humanity. This seems to create two opposite, but not mutually exclusive, forms of identity: cosmopolitanism and identity politics.

Cosmopolitanism and Identity Politics

Cosmopolitanism and identity politics both emerged in the 1960s, in response, at least in part, to globalization. The cosmopolitan personality, in the broadest sense, accepts the validity and value of other cultures and other ways of life. A cosmopolitan outlook may facilitate a person feeling comfortable in diverse settings and situations, with people who are culturally different; the person may even seek them out. Identity politics, in contrast, stresses the experience and circumstances of individuals because of membership in a particular group, such as a race, ethnicity, or religion that has been marginalized by the mainstream of societies or the global systems. Identity politics encourages people to recognize and celebrate their distinctiveness, as well as organize political activity around it. Black power movements, feminism, movements of indigenous people, and gay rights movements are examples of identity politics. Cosmopolitanism and identity politics are global movements, organizing across borders.

Freedom

Concern with freedom has advanced with each successive phase of globalization. In the contemporary period, waves of democratic reforms have swelled the number of countries that are free since the 1960s. Demands for personal freedom have ignited court cases and protests globally. Freedom comes with its own set of conundrums for the personality. Simmel (1908/1971) celebrated how individuals' economic, political, personal, and social freedoms evolved throughout modernity. But he also issued a warning that freedom could become license and could weaken our social ties. Durkheim (1933/1964) insisted that too little freedom stifled individualism, but too much freedom leads to isolation and anomie.

Freedom has expanded exponentially in many parts of the world since the mid-1960s. One of the most famous lyrics of the 1960s music scene in the United States, "freedom's just another word for nothing left to lose" (Kristofferson and Foster 1969), recognized the boost that freedom was getting from the "world wide revolutions" of the 1960s, as well as the inherent dangers. While it may not have been exactly what Simmel, Durkheim, and Kristofferson and Foster had anticipated, the rapid changes that democratization brings, such as in post–Soviet Union states and other countries that have won freedom, often come with high costs, hopefully short-lived, of economic hardship and political turmoil.

Nostalgia

Periods of rapid social change bring many types of fears. Some people fear that globalization is destroying local cultures. Nostalgia, a longing for the past—very often a mythical past—has emerged in the context of globalization (Robertson 1992, 159). It takes on a variety of forms—from the blatant manipulation of political symbols such as the flag and debates over who is or is not a real patriot, to using idealized images to support consumerism, luring people into buying products by suggesting that they can capture a slice of the good old days. Fundamentalist religious movements are widely recognized as promoting America's return to its presumed traditional values.

Appeals to nostalgia are readily visible in mainstream social life. Many new communities are built or older ones revitalized to resemble the idealized image of small town life. Nostalgia tourism has become faddish. In Britain, a poll revealed that nearly 70% of people choose to holiday in the place of a memorable past experience, primarily from their childhood (Davies 2007). In many countries, people romanticize and celebrate vestiges of the past, creating an imagined past in communities that are a step back in time, such as the Amish in the United States. A town actually called Celebration, built by Disney Development Company in the 1990s, uses early 20th century architecture to mimic the perfect small town of an imagined past, befitting the purveyor of fairy tales. In Switzerland, the town of Kandersteg recently started a new tradition by recreating La Belle Époque, a period of lavish living for the upper classes in Europe from the late 19th century to WWI. The entire town dresses in the clothes, plays the sports and the music, hosts the teas, and tries to recreate the atmosphere of the era. Period recreations are a part of nearly every country's national heritage, such as Colonial Williamsburg, Virginia, which exists all year-round as a romanticized version of the 18th century town, representing the birth of the United States. It was conceived and built during an earlier period of intense globalization. Other movements, such as the slow food movement, have gone global to restore traditional growing methods and promote local high-quality produce and slow cooking rather than

BOX 1.9   A Closer Look: Millennial Nostalgia for the Victorian Era

From shopping centers to real towns, people are trying to recapture the idyllic small town of the turn of the 20th century. Renovations in Oakmont, Pennsylvania, included a town square, non-functional train station, and a brick main street lined with gas lanterns designed to appeal to our nostalgia and romanticize our image of the town. Even a development of new homes mimics the Victorian era.

fast foods and convenience foods (Ritzer 2004, 149–151). The longing we associate with nostalgia may reflect a fear of losing an aspect of one's identity.

Although many manifestations of nostalgia conjure a better imagined past, the interest in nostalgia may also be a response to a social life that is increasingly filled with nothing. While people in contemporary societies, particularly in the developed world, are consuming an abundance of products and experiences, they are mostly standardized forms that can be mass-produced and easily globalized. Products, processes, and experiences—T-shirts, education, health care, or a trip to a theme park—follow a routine formula developed for efficiency and predictability that they could be delivered anytime to anyone. Thus, according to Ritzer (2004), people long for an authentic experience of real Mexican food, a home-spun doctor, or a quaint town square shopping experience, something filled with meaning or cultural content, or infused with personalization. Ironically, a commercial response to this longing has been to further commodify and romanticize the past through developments such as shopping malls and resorts that look as though they stepped out of the 19th century, or the search for the authentic in tourism to exotic and less developed locales and the Third World's accommodation in developing cultural heritage tourism industries.

Globalization of Civil Society

Have you volunteered for your local food bank or delivered Meals on Wheels? Are you a Boy Scout, a Girl Scout, or a member of a faith-related organization? How about a student organization, a community group, a club, or a charity? If you answered "yes" to any of these questions, you are participating in a civil society organization (CSO). These organizations are vital to forming a healthy society. When the organization cuts across boundaries of class, race, ethnicity, age, or other social divide, it helps people see the

---

BOX 1.10   Check It Out Yourself: Being a World Citizen

Poll your classmates or friends and families. Do they see themselves as a "citizen of the world"? What does "I see myself as a world citizen" mean to them? What does it mean to you?

Compare your results to the world as a whole and the United States as a whole, based on these World Values Survey results.

"I see myself as a world citizen . . ."

	Global Frequency	Valid Percentage	U.S. Frequency	Valid Percentage
Strongly agree	19,629	30.1	244	20.6
Agree	31,190	47.8	566	48.0
Disagree	10,767	16.5	303	25.7
Strongly disagree	3,630	5.6	67	5.7

Source: World Values Survey Online Analysis WVS 2005–2008, Question V210. This survey round was conducted in 54 countries. The "valid percentage" includes only those who answered this question.

---

interests that they have in common. By creating bridges across groups, they make societies stronger.

Unless you are a hermit, you probably participate, at least indirectly, in a local, national, or global CSO. When you volunteer at or contribute to your local food bank, you are acting as a member of your local civil society. If you pack bandages and medical kits for organizations such as World Vision or Doctors Without Borders, donate blood to the Red Cross, or contribute money to Children International, you are acting as a member of global civil society.

Civil society is the general term used for all of our voluntary associations, both formal and informal. CSOs, or non-governmental organizations (NGOs), are based on people's common interests, values, beliefs, and ideologies. Civil society and CSOs are difficult to define. Governmental groups and organizations are excluded from most contemporary definitions of CSOs. Most also exclude corporations and other for-profit organizations, as well as familial.

The World Bank definition of civil society is

non-governmental and not-for-profit organizations that have a presence in public life, expressing the interests and values of their members or others, based on ethical, cultural, political, scientific, religious or philanthropic considerations. Civil Society Organizations (CSOs) therefore refer to a wide of array of organizations: community groups, non-governmental organizations (NGOs), labor unions, indigenous groups, charitable organizations, faith-based organizations, professional associations, and foundations. (World Bank 2010)

Global civil society has grown exponentially in both numbers of groups and influence since the 1960s. Because there are so many ways of counting them, estimates vary. The World Bank estimates that international NGOs (INGOs) alone grew from about 6,000 in 1990 to 26,000 in 1999. That is almost a 450% increase in a decade of just one type of CSO. As of 2003, there were about 50,000 non-governmental not-for-profit organizations operating at the global level; 90% of them were formed since 1970. In total, they disperse more funds than does the United Nations (Keane 2003, 5).

CSOs can be powerful forces in strengthening a society. Voluntary organizations help people achieve goals collectively that they would be less likely to achieve on their own. These connections build trust, which is an important form of social capital (Putnam 1995). Social capital can be converted to social goods in the same way that financial capital is used to generate profit. Social capital builds efficacy in a community and society, which enhances people's ability to achieve their common and individual goals. Whether or not CSOs can perform the same function at the level of the globe is being tested. Networking among local, national, and global CSOs has emerged as a popular strategy for affecting change.

CSOs have become an important voice in international dialogue at the UN, at international meetings of governments, and in informing the public about important issues. Social movement groups are an important part of civil society because they publicize and spread values and information about issues they see as social problems. Social movements represent myriad diverse perspectives from some of the most conservative ideologies to the most radical. But there are serious doubts that all people are equally represented within civil society.

CSOs play complementary roles to government and business. Governments provide public order and public goods, using their authority to raise revenue. Business works to provide private goods and services through market mechanisms. Civil society actors try to promote the values and purposes of citizens and citizen groups through their voluntary efforts and through the influence that they exert on both business and government. Governments mobilize resources through legislation, programming, and taxation. Businesses mobilize resources though exchange. Civil society organizations mobilize resources through appeals to values and social purposes (Brown et al. 2000, 8). Civil society groups work within societies to strengthen particular societies and at the global level to combat global risks. They

- identify international problems that are not resolved by existing international arrangements;
- help construct international values and norms that can guide future international policies and practices;
- initiate campaigns to formulate and enforce global public policies in response to critical problems;
- create or reform international institutions to improve response to global problems;
- create and disseminate social innovations that affect international governance processes;
- act as mediators or catalysts for resolving conflicts at national and international levels; and
- mobilize people and resources for international action on important public problems. (Brown et al. 2000, 19–23)

There are a number of important questions concerning CSOs and globalization, particularly whether or not civil society organizations can be held accountable for the common good, beyond their group or organization, and facilitate democracy at the global level.

People's activities in each of these dimensions of globalization—the economic, political, cultural, and civil society—contribute to forming global systems. In social action, the dimensions of globalization are not distinct. This brief review of dimensions of globalization is preparation for more detailed analysis of each later in the text.

Facilitating Globalization

In addition to dimensions of globalization, it is important to introduce facets of modern life that facilitate globalization. They are not globalization and do not cause globalization per se. Nevertheless, they make globalization more likely and increase the rate of globalization.

Technology

Development in technology has more than any other single factor accelerated globalization. Improvements in transportation led to the exchange of ideas and objects and the movement of people along the Silk Road over 1,400 years ago. Shipping made trade and migration easier, leading to the Age of Exploration and bringing the American continents into interaction with Europe, Africa, and Asia. Trains and planes accelerated flows of everything that travels—people, products, and ideas—around the world. Nearly everything is mobile. The ease of transportation facilitates the development of global systems.

Improvements in communication accelerate flows of ideas and information. Culture flows through the world wide web, changing people's ideas, influencing their imaginings about each other and other parts of the world, and even leading to the invention of new social forms. Real-time audio and visual communication from almost anywhere in the world to almost anywhere in the world facilitates interaction among people thousands of miles apart. People who have never met may participate in one another's lives through social media. Families separated by migration maintain connections to one another through wireless media and frequent travel. New communications media allow people to gather spontaneously, whether that means a few friends to see a film or go bowling or a few thousand to stage a protest.

Technologically driven changes in the job structure have an immediate effect on people's lives. With each technological advance, people are displaced and have difficulty securing new employment. Many never do. Advances in technology facilitate faster and cheaper flows of people and ideas, of money and products, accelerating economic, cultural, social, and political globalization. These flows are among the objective bases of globalization.

Population Pressures

The world population reached 7,000,000,000 on or about October 31, 2011. The world grows by five or six people every second or so. The earth is not overcrowded, and experts believe that it can support several billion more—although not at the level of consumption currently in the United States. But the global population is not well dispersed. Too many people in some parts of the world and too few in others presents unique problems in different parts of the globe. Two primary areas of concern are population pressures on the environment and on political stability. Generally, as nations get wealthier, women have fewer children. In some wealthy countries, women are having no children or only one child. Women's recent movement out of the family into the workplace has given women financial and social independence. Marriage and motherhood are choices some women are not willing to make. An advanced workforce and child labor laws render children economic liabilities, rather than assets who can be put to work. This encourages small families. In developing societies, children remain potential workers who can help enrich families. Although children may work, large populations degrade and deplete arable land, potable water, and breathable air. Where social safety nets are weak, children are needed to provide for their parents as they age. In cases in which women want fewer children, they may lack access to family planning, due to either a weak health care system or their husbands' or religions' prohibition. Surpluses of young men in labor markets with chronic high unemployment and no social safety nets ferment political instability.

Women's empowerment and economic development slow population growth significantly. Children are economic liabilities in richer societies. Women have more opportunities than being a wife and mother. Where women are reluctant to have children, societies have too low a fertility rate—below the replacement level, which is about 2.1 children per woman—and experience negative population growth. Negative population growth slows economic growth. With fewer youth, there are fewer innovations to stimulate economic growth. Too few workers yield too few taxes to care for an aging population that is moving out of its most productive years and into its most sickly years. Slower economic growth weakens the export markets of other countries.

Population pressures result from global economic and political forces and subsequently create global forces. Four historic shifts will fundamentally alter the world's population over the ne decades: The relative demographic weight of the world's developed countries will drop by nearly 25%, shifting economic power to the developing nations; the developed countries' labor forces will substantially age and decline, constraining economic growth in the developed world and raising the demand for immigrant workers; most of the world's expected population growth will increasingly be concentrated in today's poorest, youngest, and most heavily Muslim countries, which have a dangerous lack of quality education, capital, and employment opportunities; and, for the first time in history, most of the world's population will become urbanized, with the largest urban centers being in the world's poorest countries, where policing, sanitation, and health care are often scarce. Taken together, these trends pose severe challenges to global systems. Coping with them will require nothing less than a major reconsideration of the world's basic global governance structures (Goldstone 2010).

Migration

Flows of people around the world are one of the most effective agents of globalization, whether among or within regions. About 3% of the world's population, about 219,000,000 people, live outside of the country where they were born. People leave societies for many reasons: a better life, a better job, an education, to escape political turmoil and oppression—or all of these. Migrants are one of the most important sources of cultural and economic flows. Immigrant groups are traditionally hard workers and important sources of innovation—about 25% of the U.S. new technology startups have at least one immigrant key founder (Wadhwa et al. 2007). Immigrants educated in Western universities take their expertise home, often to leadership positions in government or industry. Companies that employ foreign nationals have an easier time breaking into foreign markets, where most of the opportunity for growth in markets is located.

BOX 1.11   A Closer Look: Global Migration

The diagram of global migration visualizes the centrality of world regions to migration networks. Regions closer to the center are more pivotal in migration and those farther away are less involved. North America is the most pivotal region and Sub-Saharan Africa the least. The arrows indicate the relative volume of migration by their thickness and the direction of migration flow at the tip, indicating the heaviest flow of migration is from Latin America and the Caribbean to North America.

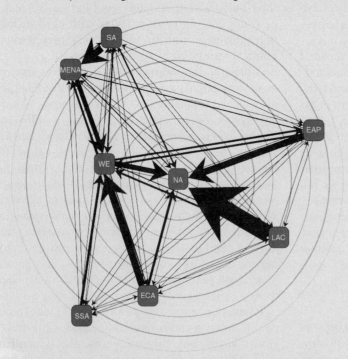

Label	Region
EAP	East Asia & Pacific
ECA	Europe & Central Asia
LAC	Latin America & Caribbean
MENA	Middle East & North Africa
NA	North America
SA	South Asia
SSA	Sub-Saharan Africa
WE	Western Europe

Source: 2009 Civil Society Yearbook: Poverty and Activism, by A. Kumar, J. A. Scholte, M. Kaldor, M. Glasius, and J. Seckinelgin, 2009, London, SAGE Publications. Copyright SAGE Ltd.

Migration can impose costs on societies as well. Refugees fleeing political, racial, ethnic, or religious persecution have a right to asylum, which states are expected to honor. Waves of economic migration or political refugees fleeing to neighboring societies can destabilize the latter, as one country in a region may not be substantially better off than another. Warring parties often stage cross-border skirmishes from refugee camps in a neighboring country. Although some societies welcome immigrants when unemployment is low and their economy is growing, their welcome wears thin during economic recessions. Tolerance may turn to hostility if nationals in the host country think immigrants are taking their jobs or draining their social welfare systems. In some rich societies, the recent intensification of immigration from the Global South has met with hostility. In many European and Asian countries, as well as in the United States, some people feel their culture is threatened. Rigid laws have been enacted to keep immigrants out, even in countries where negative population growth threatens economic growth. The causes and consequences of migration are relevant to many globalization topics.

Dating Globalization

Interaction and connection across societies (and the individuals within them) have existed as long as societies have. The connections are economic, political, cultural, and social, permeating all dimensions of social life. Trade has connected areas of the world for millennia. Imagine trade routes as colored ribbons, a different color for every country exporting to another. As trade increases, regions of the globe are knit more tightly and more colorfully together. People have migrated across continents, spreading ideas and practices while assuming new ideas and practices, creating more bonds of connection. Communication and migration among societies facilitated centuries-long processes of exchange, diffusing ideas, religions, and values along with goods and technology.

Despite the spread and blending of cultures, the rise and fall of empires, and plentiful trade and migration among societies for most of history, societies were more independent than interdependent. Productive processes, financial markets, and communication networks were not as functionally

integrated as they are today. Economic and political actors did not operate as freely across borders. Problems were more contained, or at least seemed to be, within the boundaries of societies or in international relations. Even during La Belle Époque at the turn of the 20th century, when trade and travel were very high, the fates of states were not as mutually dependent as today. The impact of one society on others was much more limited.

Because globalization involves both continuity and change, theorists have tackled it from two different perspectives. Some theorists view contemporary globalization as the most recent period of intensifying patterns of inter-societal connections that have been trending for centuries. World society theorists emphasize globalization as the diffusion of the principle of rationality and of rational organizational forms, such as bureaucratic governments and educational systems. World systems theorists view globalization as a continuation of the expansion of capitalism, cycling through periods of increasing and decreasing economic activity among nations. Robertson (1990) divides the globalization process into five phases, beginning with the early 15th century, although he is reconsidering his dating and proposing an earlier start.

Despite these theorists' depiction of globalization as a centuries-long process, they recognize the contemporary period as a distinctive phase of globalization because of accelerating trends, higher peaks of activity, and waves of activity that have not yet receded. Economic globalization of the contemporary period has surpassed all prior waves of economic globalization. This wave did not diminish with the decline in U.S. hegemony, as some might have expected (Chase Dunn, Kawano, and Brewer 2000). The magnitude of the "organizational explosion" that began post-WWII also defies expectations, and "its ubiquity calls for explanation" (Drori, Meyer, and Hwang 2009). "There can be no denying that the world is much more singular than it was as recently as say, the 1950s" (Robertson 1990, 25).

A second line of theorizing is that globalization is a unique reorganization of social life, altering it in such fundamental ways that globalization should be viewed as marking a new era. Global systems theorists highlight the activity of transnational classes and their differentiation from class structures within societies. Giddens (2003) argues that globalization has created a world of options, of "openness" in social structure. The uncertainty and risk that now confront people have intensified to the point that historical precedent offers little guidance for the present. This holds in the most public realms, from our form of democracy to the most intimate aspects of family life. Appadurai (1996) portrays the globe as a swirl of changing "scapes"—distinct, nevertheless overlapping and interdependent, sweeping continuously among and between people, social life in constant flux. Although communication technologies play an important role in all theories of globalization, Castells (1996) has made it the defining characteristic of globalization. His depiction of the globe as "network society" calls our attention to the exchange of information as the basis of social cohesion. Keohane and Nye (2000) date globalization as recently as the late 1980s because of differences in kind in the processes of political globalization.

Another wrinkle in the debate on dating globalization is the relationship between modernity and globalization. Many globalization theorists see globalization as a continuity of modernity—the social changes brought by the Enlightenment, rationalization, and industrialization (Meyer et al. 1997; Robertson 1990). Others contend that globalization has undermined modernity (Beck and Lau 2005, 526). They argue that before the 1960s, modernity was characterized by a harmony of institutions; societal institutions functioned in coordination with one another. The nation-state, the industrial economy, the nuclear family, the welfare state, and science all supported one other, working in tandem to shape individuals, their actions, and their interactions (527). For better or worse, schools prepared children for citizenship and for work in the industrial economy. The class structure was maintained. Nuclear families taught the lessons of hard work and were mobile and willing enough to move to where they were needed for jobs. Post-1960, the certainty of this arrangement, the logic, and the fit are gone. This has ushered in the second modernity.

This text does not try to resolve the dating debates. There are things that are strikingly new about globalization. Among them:

- Every nation and every person on the globe is involved. This is unmistakable in environmental concerns but is evident in considering the economy, global politics, food, culture, health, and crime.

- Intra-global relations, from the price of oil to fears relative to security, reach into nearly every aspect of how people live.
- The well-being of individuals and societies is much more contingent on the activity of other individuals and other societies than at any other point in history.
- The actions of individuals and societies are also contingent—for better or worse—on people's sense of their common humanity, of belonging to humanity.

At the same time, it is important to acknowledge that "every era builds on others, and historians can always find precursors for phenomena of the present" (Keohane and Nye 2000, 108). Global values such as rationality and science, human rights, and the ideals of the Enlightenment originated long ago, although they were limited in their scope. Understanding the logic of theorists, even when they disagree, helps us to understand different types of globalization processes.

Another reason for the differences in how theorists define and date globalization is that some stress political globalization, some cultural, some economic, and so forth. While different dimensions of globalization are related, they increase and decrease at different times. Some forms of globalization are further along than others.

> Changes in the various dimensions of globalization do not necessarily occur simultaneously. One can sensibly say, for instance that economic globalization took place between approximately 1850 and 1914, manifested in imperialism and increased trade and capital flows between politically independent countries; and that such globalization was largely reversed between 1914 and 1945. . . . However, military globalism rose to new heights during the two world wars, as did many aspects of social globalism. . . . So did globalism decline or rise between 1914 and 1945? It depends on what dimension of globalism one is examining. (Keohane and Nye 2000, 107)

It is only in the contemporary period that globalization reached a tipping point in nearly every dimension. This created differences not just in degree but in qualitative differences in the texture and quality of social life also. Each theorist discussed here, even those who say globalization began hundreds of years ago, highlights the period beginning in the 1960s as more than an intensification of earlier trends but rather as a transformation of them. The convergence of these perspectives on the period of the mid to late 1960s, whether as the beginning or transformation of globalization, is more important than the terminology used to categorize it.

The 1960s mark a point at which world relations changed significantly. Trends and cycles of interaction—political, economic, and social—increased. The volume and intensity of interaction gave rise to the discourse of globalization. The need to find a new word and concept to describe social life signals that something is unique about the contemporary period that is not captured by analyses that focus on the societal and individual levels of social life.

The time frame proposed by Robertson (1992) illuminates the antecedents to contemporary globalization. Although Robertson argues that globalization is centuries old, he recognizes that the concept of globalization "is most clearly applicable to a series of relatively recent developments concerning *the concrete structuration of the world as a whole*" (53, emphasis original). The contemporary period is the major subject of this text. However, most chapters begin with a brief look over our shoulders at the earlier phases of globalization to see how we arrived at our current circumstances. Chapter Two introduces a number of the major theories of globalization and discusses how each dates globalization.

The phases of globalization are as follows:

Dates	Phase	Primary Characteristics and Events
1400s–Mid-1700s	Germinal Phase	This was the Age of Exploration. The Silk Road trade routes wove from China through Asia to Africa and Europe. Along with the spices and silks traded for gold and silver, cultures traveled and blended. Middle Eastern (Near Asian) culture emerged from this blending. Nation-states emerged from the ruins of empire.
Mid-1700s–1870	Incipient Phase	Rights of mankind, an Enlightenment ideal, was expressed in the revolutions at the end of the 18th century and the first wave of democratization. The state system of organizing nations spread. States formalized international relations. In the 1860s, the first international agencies were established.
1870s–1920s	Takeoff Phase	The Industrial Revolution brought trade and travel to unprecedented levels. Land grabs in Asia and Africa named this period the Age of Imperialism. Waves of migrants increased ethnic diversity and populated industrializing cities. Germany tested its rivals, France and Russia and their allies, turning Europe into the battlefield of WWI. World religions became global through imperialism, mission work, migration, and trade.
1920s–1960s	Struggle for Hegemony	Rivalries encompassed the globe exemplified by a series of wars. A global depression caused massive suffering between the wars. The UN and the Declaration of Human Rights gave shape to global governance. The Bretton Woods institutions—World Bank and IMF—and agreements were created to stabilize the global economy. A second wave of democracy rose following WWII.
Late 1960s–2000	Uncertainty Phase	The Iron Curtain fell heavily onto Eastern Europe, and geo-political spheres of influence came to divide the world. African and Asian independence began a third wave of democracy. The cultural revolution of the late 1960s called societies and their institutions to task. Many governmental and non-governmental international organizations were established in response to dramatically increased interdependence of the world. The Iron Curtain rose.
2000–Present	Millennial Phase	The global war on terror engages the world in apocalyptical themes. End-of-time narratives dominate many religions. Secular movements echo similar themes of potential global destruction through climate change, nuclear war, nuclear contamination, pandemics, water crises, and global hunger.

Source: Robertson (1990, 2007).

Globalization as Change

The social dynamics that characterize the contemporary period are much like those of the Industrial Revolution during the takeoff phase of globalization. Rapid social change created chaos within societies. Ways of life and ways of thinking about life in rural agricultural society were useless in the rapidly developing industrial cities. Norms that had governed daily life were meaningless. Rising to the rooster's crow, apprenticing in small craft shops, and other traditional ways of life became obsolete within a generation. People did not know how to "do" urban industrial—how to organize the great masses of people flooding by the millions into large and rapidly expanding cities. How masses of people could be fed, clothed, educated, and employed was excruciatingly problematic.

In *A Tale of Two Cities,* Charles Dickens, the great English novelist, poignantly wrote, "It was the best of times, it was the worst of times, it was the age of wisdom, it was the age of foolishness." The classical sociologists Max Weber, Emile Durkheim, and Karl Marx made similar observations. It was the best because harnessing fossil fuel energy generated sufficient productive capacity to ensure that everyone on earth could have enough food, clothing, and shelter. It was the worst because people could not figure out how to organize themselves well enough to fulfill that potential. They could not create order. Cities grew filthy; poverty and crime increased rapidly, people went hungry, and children roamed the streets.

Now, we ask the same question, not only of societies but of the globe. Violent conflict rages within some societies, and people are starving in a globe of plenty. Since the mid-1960s, several interrelated processes have dominated social life. Any one of these on its own is capable of creating chaos within and among societies.[3]

- Societies are changing their economic basis. Some are industrializing—moving from agricultural to industrial. Some are de-industrializing—moving to bifurcated economies of high-skill, high-pay, high-technology and information jobs and low-level service jobs. Some societies, such as China and India, are developing their industrial, information, and service sectors simultaneously. Transitioning economies require new ways of life—higher levels of education, values related more to creativity and self-direction than following orders. New ways of imagining family and work life, new social positions, hierarchies (or lack thereof), and responsibilities are needed. Each change requires changing how people think about and organize their lives.

- Development also means that a country uses more resources and creates more pollution, requiring more intense global governance.

- Waves of nation building and democratization have accelerated, increasing the number of countries and the number of countries instituting democratic reforms. While most people agree that democracy is the best form of government (as reported in public opinion polls globally), societies in transition are fragile. Establishing a new democracy is difficult, and economic conditions often worsen before they improve.

- It may seem counterintuitive, but globalization has led to both increasing nationalism and increasing cosmopolitanism. This creates tensions within societies as some people want to expand societal life to include diverse lifestyles (such as homosexual marriage, changing roles of women, minority rights, and greater acceptance of immigrants) while others want to maintain their view of their traditional culture.

- Although standards of living improved following WWII, the Cold War, underlying injustices in societies, and the stultifying effects of over-bureaucratized lives affected alienation from the institutions of modern life. These prompted the cultural, social, and political protests that erupted on nearly every continent in 1968. These revolutions rejected the ways of life characteristic of the post-WWII era.

- Improvements in transportation, communication, and mass media technologies spur rapid social changes within and among societies. Technological innovations that increase the volume of interaction across distance also increase the intensity of interaction across societies and advance globalization. The volume and intensity of interaction among societies and among people across societies has made countries' political borders irrelevant in many dimensions of social life.

- Economic, political, and cultural systems operate independently of their societal moorings in many respects. It is legitimate to speak of a global polity that involves many actors other than states in decision making. The global economy stretches production processes, labor markets, and consumer markets across continents. Global culture forces countries to conform to particular standards to be viewed as legitimate. This makes it difficult, if not impossible, for any single state to manage its own economic, political, and social development by itself.

There is nothing deterministic about the course of globalization and how it is shaping the world. It is likely, but not inevitable, that globalization will continue. and it will continue to be fractious and contentious for the foreseeable future, although hopefully less so.

People, corporations, states, and even non-governmental "do-good" organizations conflict as each attempts to navigate its interests in global interactions. Finding common ground among societies and the people within them is difficult. Increasing interactions per se are not globalization. High volumes of interaction necessitate establishing global cultural understandings and social structural forms as a basis for interaction. That is what it means to be a single place, a globe, rather than a collection of societies.

BOX 1.12   A Closer Look: Globalization and Socio-Cultural Change

Social evolution involves continuity and discontinuity. One does not exist without the other. This is analogous to biological evolution. *Homo sapiens* retains many features of much earlier life forms. There is a trend from *Homo habilis*, to *Homo erectus*, to *Homo sapiens*. Despite significant continuity, biologists find points at which they declare difference is significant enough to constitute a different species. Their analytical scheme holds up unless or until new information indicates they need to reorganize their thinking and their theories. This is similar to social change. Social forms retain continuity from the past; at certain points, social forms differ in so many ways from past forms that they are declared a different form.

However, biological evolution could be said to occur "by accident." It is a function of gene mutations. Those mutations that survive are propagated; those that do not are not. Societal evolution is more directed by human agency. For a variety of reasons, such as rapid social change, norms may lose their efficacy, causing a break or change in the traditional or prescribed ways of thinking about and doing things. People scramble to invent new ways of thinking and acting, or copy from another source. Some experiments—those that seem to work well, well enough, or work well for those with power—are repeated and eventually may become normative. They are not necessarily the best possible solutions.

Norms structure life in such a way that we do not have to keep inventing the wheel and deciding what to do in every interaction. Not everything that becomes normative serves the well-being of everyone affected. Colonialism and the Cold War structured relations—the former for centuries, the latter for decades to the benefit of some people but devastated the life chances and opportunities of many more people. Although those eras are over, their effects still limit people's chances today.

Biological evolution produces diversity. It is not a trajectory to a single end. Diversity within and among human populations is also product of societal change or evolution.

Nevertheless, social structure and culture are negotiated in every interaction. Social change takes many forms. Most often, change is slow and incremental, and doesn't challenge the underlying organization of the society. Every so often, however, change is so significant that we think of human societies as evolving from one socio-cultural era to another. With contemporary globalization, the intensity of interaction among societies has reached the point where we have entered a global era, in which intra-global relations are at least as significant, if not more significant, than intra-societal ones in shaping social life.

Summary

Globalization is best thought of as a complex set of processes brought on by increasing interactions of many kinds among people all over the world—the objective bases of globalization. Global interaction, if it is to continue at this high level of intensity, requires creating global systems—economic, political, cultural, and other social systems—that span the globe and exist independently of country borders. This alters every system below—relations among societies, and between societies and the individuals within them. Consciousness of humanity as a whole—the subjective basis of globalization—is informing these changes. This is particularly evident with respect to concern for human rights in creating just political and economic systems. However, vastly unequal power relations and the resurgence of fundamentalisms still stymie their realization.

This cursory review demonstrates that globalization presents an epistemological dilemma for the social sciences. Globalization does not render other levels of social life meaningless or redundant; society, institutions, cultures, individuals, familial, and other sub-societal groups remain important dimensions of analysis. International perspectives that have been stressed in the social sciences are still important. States will still compete, ally, conflict, and at times cooperate bilaterally and multilaterally. But internationalism does not capture the totality of the global era. Social organization at the global level cannot be studied simply through enlarging the societal frame or looking only at relations between societies and states (Hannerz 1990).

Globalization also challenges our interdisciplinary skills. While social scientists cannot be expected to be experts in disciplines beyond their own, they need to integrate knowledge gained from other disciplines to inform their work. Social scientists need to consolidate knowledge gained from diverse disciplines—sociology, political science, anthropology, geography, economics, and so on—into a framework through which the collective wisdom of the disciplines is accessible.

Last, globalization is a charismatic concept (Tsing 2000). It has attracted scholars and inspired popular imagination. Its futurism and newness, its energetic multidimensionality, "its rhetoric of linkage and circulation, of the overcoming of boundaries and restrictions" present us with both challenges and opportunities (328). But, as Tsing argues, in their excitement, analysts need to resist being seduced by the concept. There is genuine advantage to the ways in which globalization challenges disciplines to redesign their boundaries and connections. But it is easy to lose sight of historical connections and civilization lineages—of the connections between time and place. Researchers need to step back and take stock of concrete research questions that detail how globalization is shaping

the contemporary landscape and being shaped by it. Then, globalization promises to illuminate the world as we live in it (332).

Questions, Investigations, and Resources

Questions

1. Debate: Do you think globalization processes are continuations of previous developments in world history, or are they such a significant break from the past that globalization should be thought of as bringing in a new historical period?

   • What kinds of changes would you look for to signify a new era?
   • Would your answer differ for different dimensions of globalization, economic, political, or cultural?

2. Which dimension of globalization do you find most interesting? Why?

   • Which do you think it is most important for people to understand?

3. How does understanding globalization complement a societal perspective on the social and political issues that confront the world today?

4. Develop a list of indicators of globalization. Include cultural, political, economic, and other social dimensions. State why you think each is important.

Investigations

1. Research definitions of globalization. What are some of the components of the definitions that you think are useful? Which are not? Construct a definition that you think will help people understand globalization.

2. How has public opinion about globalization evolved in countries other than the United States?

   a. Investigate foreign newspapers online to find the first mentions of globalization archived. Sample articles from 10-year intervals to document changes. Try to sample from the same section—business, lifestyle, international news—each time. Newspapers have remarkably similar layouts all over the world. (Could this be a globalization phenomenon?)
   b. There are several international polls that ask people's opinions about globalization: Eurobarometer, World Public Opinion, and Pew Global Attitudes Project are potential sources of data.

3. Choose the dimension of globalization that you find most interesting. The databases listed below each are rich with globalization data. Examine the types of information available and form some simple research questions.

Cultural:

- World Values Survey (http://www.worldvalues survey.org) Online data analysis allows for cross-tabulations of many variables for individual countries, sets of countries, or the total sample.
- Pew Global Attitudes Project (http://www .pewglobal.org/category/survey-reports) Access years of survey reports from many countries.

Economic:

- World Bank (http://data.worldbank.org/ indicator?display=map) Online analysis of *The World Development Report*. You can create tables, maps, and graphs of data from 209 countries and 420 indicators over the years 1960 to 2009.
- World Economic Forum Global Competitiveness Report Index 2012–2013 data platform (http:// www.weforum.org/issues/competitiveness-0/ gci2012-data-platform) Analyze the results of the Global Competitiveness Report—the economic performance of countries and factors related to it.
- International Monetary Fund (http://www.imf.org/ external/data.htm#data) A variety of data and databases. Example: World Economic Outlook Databases (WEO)—download time series data for GDP growth, inflation, unemployment, payments balances, exports, imports, external debt, capital flows, commodity prices, and more.

Political: Yearly reports and special reports of these groups are available online.

- Afrobarometer (http://www.afrobarometer.org) Several briefing papers and reports are published yearly along with online data analysis. They track the status of democracy in 18 African countries.
- Eurobarometer (http://ec.europa.eu/public_opin ion/index_en.htm) The European Commission publishes several reports yearly on the political attitudes with the European Community.
- Freedom House (http://freedomhouse.org) Tracks the progress of freedom globally, by country. Issues annual reports and special reports throughout the year.
- Transparency International (http://www.transparency .org) Issues annual reports on corruption.

Social:

- The United Nations (http://hdr.undp.org/en/ reports/) Issues *The Human Development Report* annually. Each year has a specific theme, such as knowledge and culture, environment, or poverty and inequality. Every year, a statistical annex is also issued that reports on human development indicators. The reports are available free online at this website. The development indicators can be browsed or downloaded in spreadsheet form. You may also do your own online analysis using their interactive database to create charts and graphs of the indicators data. Just click the "Statistics" button on the menu from the "Reports" page. From this site, you can analyze data as far back as 1970.
- The United Nations (http://www.un.org/millennium-goals/poverty.shtml) Issues Millennium Development Goals (MDGs) Reports yearly, reporting on progress toward the eight MDGs. Every UN agency issues numerous reports on global topics.

4. Find the Population Reference Bureau interactive maps and tables. Compare regions on fertility, life expectancy, poverty, access to family planning, and so on. What correlations do you find among these variables?

http://www.prb.org/Publications/Datasheets/2011/ world-population-data-sheet.aspx

For detailed information by country, reference "The Population Reference Bureau Factsheet." The 2011 factsheet can be found here: http://www.prb.org/ pdf11/2011population-data-sheet_eng.pdf.

What countries have the largest emigration and immigration (+ or – net migration). Compare and contrast these countries. Why are some of them destinations, while people are fleeing the others?

You can create your own tables, charts, and maps at the Population Reference Bureau.

See their series of interactive U.S. and international data sets: http://www.prb.org/DataFinder.aspx.

Resources

Global Issues http://www.globalissues.org
   (Information on global problems.)

World Values Survey http://www.worldvaluessurvey.org
   (Data and analysis from four rounds of surveys conducted internationally dating back to 1981. Survey covers a wide range of social, economic, and political values. It is very easy to conduct your own analysis using their online data analysis system.)

Pew Global Attitudes Project http://www.pewglobal.org/ category/survey-reports

(Data and analysis from a wide range of surveys on many issues relevant to globalization, as well as globalization itself.)

Freedom House http://freedomhouse.org

(Ratings and rankings of countries based on their development of and adherence to democratic principles and policies.)

Transparency International http://www.transparency.org

United Nations Human Development Report http://hdr .undp.org/en/reports

(Yearly reports concerning the well-being of people in developing nations. Each year concentrates on a particular theme, such as the environment or hunger, but each year has data relevant to important development issues such as literacy, infant death, sanitation, etc.)

The United Nations Millennium Development Goals http://www.un.org/millenniumgoals/poverty.shtml

(Yearly reports on the progress made in developing countries toward the development goals set by the UN in 2000 and which were to be achieved by 2015. The goals are in areas such as education, poverty eradication, gender equality, health, and the environment.)

Video Shorts

The San Diego World's Fair by Mack Sennett http:// memory.loc.gov/cgi-bin/query/r?ammem/papr:@filreq(@ field(NUMBER+@band(awal+2893s2))+@field (COLLID+workleis))

Flash Mob playing "Ode to Joy" from Beethoven's Ninth Symphony http://www.youtube.com/watch_popup?v=GB aHPND2QJg&feature=youtu.be

2

Studying Globalization

Objectives

This chapter reviews major theories of globalization. After studying this chapter, you should be able to

- explain the major features of several theories of globalization;
- analyze theories of globalization for areas of contrast and convergence;
- apply theories of globalization to understanding contemporary issues;
- critique arguments that globalization is a centuries-old phenomenon or, conversely, that it is a new era;

- assess the potential impacts of globalization on individuals, societal systems, and the relationships between societies;
- use the concepts related to social learning and diffusion to analyze globalization processes; and
- explain the concepts of waves or cycles and provide examples of waves in various dimensions of globalization.

Globalization has created controversy on the scholarly scene since its introduction in the early 1980s. The controversy has spread to political and economic circles within governments, corporations, and non-governmental organizations as people struggle for survival or to improve their lives in the face of forces that often seem overpowering and unstoppable.

Despite vigorous debate, there are areas of agreement among theorists:

- Globalization does not mean homogenization. Cultures are not melding into one super culture, with all societies having the same values, beliefs, language, or even foods. Values and beliefs cannot be exported and imported as easily as hamburgers, clothing, or rock and roll. For every cultural import, a local twist is added. Products, ideas, and even global forces are adapted to local contingences,

customs, and interests, or may be rejected as they spread worldwide.
- Globalization is more likely to mean greater emphasis on pluralism and acceptance of diversity, although pluralism is resisted in many quarters around the world.
- Globalization is not likely to result in one world government. There is momentum in two seemingly opposite directions. Countries are breaking up into smaller, more homogeneous states, as with the former Soviet Union, Yugoslavia, and Czechoslovakia, and there are more attempts to form regional political and economic alliances, such as the European Union (EU), the African Union, and Association of South East Asian Nations (ASEAN). These regional alliances are taking on some of the functions of national governments, but they are far from becoming full federations.
- Governments find it increasingly difficult to manage their economies and to fulfill their promises of prosperity to citizens.

- Globalization will not necessarily bring about world harmony or world peace. One of the most striking trends in globalization has been the impressive move away from rule by dictators and military rule to democracy. Despite this, globalization has been accompanied by violent conflict, most visibly in the rise of international terrorism but also present in other forms of ethno-political violence and hate crimes.
- Globalization is not just about economics, the spread of democracy, or the spread of McDonald's and rock music. Globalization involves economic, political, cultural, and social processes. Each is evolving at a different pace, in ways sometimes complementary to each other, but at times in opposition.
- Globalization in and of itself is neither good nor bad. It is a set of processes that have the potential to be shaped by human action. To what ends depends on who does the shaping.

Globalization is a complex set of fluid and dynamic processes. Putting these pieces into a single context so that the "big picture" can be viewed requires a broad theoretical framework. Although there are many good theories relevant to particular outcomes or processes of globalization, a comprehensive theory of globalization needs to work at a variety of levels, taking into account the dynamics of the relationships among societies; the impact of globalization on societal institutions, such as economy, polity, education, law, and organizations; and the influences of globalization on people, why they are doing what they do.

This chapter reviews major theories and frameworks for analyzing globalization. They were chosen to represent the spectrum of perspectives on globalization. Some view globalization as a centuries-old phenomenon, others as beginning in the 1960s or thereabouts. Some are statist, emphasizing the role of states as the central actors and organizers of globalization. Some are non-statist in viewing states as only one type of actor in the global systems and the global system itself as having no central authority—or state. The theories have different focal points; some emphasize culture, some the economy, and some political globalization. Last, some are macro theories that stress processes at societal and global levels, while others examine the micro processes of individual-level action and some strive to capture both. The theories presented here are among the earliest theories of globalization, and each has generated a large body of research. More specific theories focused on

a particular phenomena such as dealing with the economic recession, ethnic war, the development of global regimes, waves of democracy, and so forth, are discussed within the relevant chapters.

World Risk Society

In *Risk Society* (1992), Beck argues that globalization has ushered in the second phase of modernity characterized by risks, reflexivity, and paradoxes.

One paradox is that the advances of science, rationality, and industrialization increase people's standard of living but also create risks. The risks that confront us stem from the uncritical pursuit of rationality, yet they defy rationality because we cannot calculate their consequences. According to Beck, these are new kinds of risks—"*industrialized, decision-produced incalculabilities and threats*" (1992, 22, emphasis original).

Another paradox is that political democratization is globalizing. At the same time, globalization has many non-democratic effects. Humankind has pursued rationality, science, and progress mindlessly, without concern for where it could lead. We pursue progress uncritically. Progress proceeds on the basis of implied consent. People do not question or think about it very much. We assume it is good—or others assume it on our behalf. The uncritical pursuit of progress is undemocratic because there is no public discourse or deliberation. It is not submitted to votes or referendums. Only some aspects of decision making are made part of the democratic process; others escape under the rubric of free enterprise, freedom of investment, and the unquestioned freedom of research and science. Yet, as Beck argues, these have profound consequences for people's everyday lives (1992, 184).

The risks are located along three axes, the ecological, economic, and terrorist. These dangers are "*supra-national, non-class specific, and global*" (2006, 13, emphases original). The people who create the risks are as victimized by them as everyone else; the rich as likely as the poor. Each risk stretches into the future, thereby posing a never-ending danger (23). Environmental dangers do not respect borders and threaten the survival of the human species. Terrorism is "post-national war," not between nations but between groups and nations or groups and other groups (132). It, too, has no boundaries; it could strike anywhere at any time. In the economy, technological progress caused the deskilling of work. If machines do what humans can do, there is less skill required of people. If complex tasks can be divided into such small bits that each bit requires no skill, anyone can do it,

and labor is devalued. Deskilling can continue indefinitely and results in more unemployment at each stage. This can cost jobs at all rungs of the economic ladder. Job loss is a threat to family and loss of identity.

BOX 2.1   A Closer Look: Democratic Governance

Reinforcing global cultural norms pertaining to citizenship in a democracy takes many forms such as teaching the importance of voting. In this Cambodian village, people use drama sessions to teach how to vote and participate in the democratic election process

---

Beck argues that globalization has exposed many of the fallacies of the industrial era and that we are entering a new phase of modernization. Whereas wealth production dominated the first industrial modernity, solving problems of risk production will dominate the second, "reflexive," modernity (1992, 13). Since the 1970s, we have begun to be more reflexive, questioning our notions of progress and how we use science rather than uncritically accepting them. New social movements borrow the skepticism of science and are skeptical about science itself. Beck calls this *second rationalization*. Critiques of science, technology, and progress are not necessarily antimodern but are "expression(s) of reflexive modernization beyond the outlines of industrial society" (11).

Cosmopolitanism is a key dimension of reflexive modernity. The risks we face are global and thus stimulate global consciousness and give rise to global publics—a global group with common interests. Being part of a global public prompts an everyday experience of cosmopolitanism (2006, 23). Genuine cosmopolitanism involves "partaking in the great human experiment in civilization—with one's own language and cultural symbols and the means to counter global threats—and hence of making a contribution to world culture" (21). In this way, the local and cosmopolitan

are complementary, not mutually exclusive. Beck's description of cosmopolitanism acknowledges the importance of national as well as global perspectives. A cosmopolitan culture that uses both facilitates global problem solving.

These are important preludes to understanding global governance, global-local relations, and emerging global cultural themes. Recognizing the global scale of risks is the key. It leads to norms and agreements that benefit the common good, then to "institutionalized cosmopolitanism" (2006, 25). Beck's trilogy—*Power in the Global Age* (2005), *The Cosmopolitan Vision* (2006), and *Cosmopolitan Europe* (2006, with Edgar Grande)—explore globalization and its capacity to reinvigorate politics (2005, xiii) through cosmopolitanism.

Runaway World

Anthony Giddens defines globalization as "the intensification of worldwide social relations which link distant localities in such a way that local happenings are shaped by events occurring many miles away and vice versa" (1990, 64). Unfortunately, globalization is not proceeding in an orderly fashion. It is "emerging in an anarchic, haphazard fashion" (2003, 19). Globalization accelerates the pace of change far beyond our capacity to cope with it. Every social system from the most intimate (family) to the most impersonal (science, the economy, and the polity) is being transformed. Institutions that people depend on—economics, politics, family, education, and science among them—are not working well for most people. This makes the world unlike any other that humans have faced, says Giddens.

The driving forces of globalization, the increasing connections across societies and among the institutions that people need for survival, have put everything in flux, rendering states and institutions ineffectual in providing for people's needs. The economies of nations are so intertwined that national economic policies are not enough to manage national economies effectively (2003, 18). National identities have to be reconsidered because geopolitics are no longer dominated by colonialism or the Cold War. Families are falling apart and, when possible, reconstituting themselves more democratically. Education systems are failing in quantity, quality, or both. Inequality has increased to unprecedentedly high and dangerous levels. Although not all of the changes are bad, the consequences are. No one (including corporations) has control in our increasingly complex and interconnected world.

Many people have lost faith in science, and for those of us who have not, our relationship to science is changing. In an argument similar to Beck's, Giddens says that there is not a realm of nature that science has not touched. We live in a world where the hazards that we create for ourselves outweigh the hazards nature poses, such as tornadoes, earthquakes, and drought—which have intensified due to climate change. Science and technology were supposed to bring the world more into our control; however, the world we live in is more risky—in other words, it is a *Runaway World*, as Giddens titles his 2003 book.

Giddens' approach is similar to Beck's. Our risks are manufactured. Unlike previous risk, where calculations determined how risky something was, our risks are incalculable. For example, we do not know how or in what ways climate is changing, or precisely what the impact of any change will be. We do not know the risks of genetically modified food. Will we create monster weeds and monster pests by using them (2003, 33)? We do not know how to

stop the nuclear proliferation we started, or how toxins in our environment affect us. In addition to the unknowns that we are aware of, we know there are risks yet to be discovered. The world is profoundly different than it was just a generation or two ago. The revolutions in communication and other technologies put globalization on too fast a track for humans to keep up.

Risks do not respect national borders, so we need to collaborate globally on risk assessment and the best responses to potentially dangerous conditions. We also face manufactured risks of incalculable proportions as individuals. It is harder than it used to be to turn to experts for answers. We get conflicting information from different experts, and we get revisions and revocations of previous expert information. Even the simplest matters are subject to conflicting expert advice (2003, 34). How many different scientifically based diets are on the market—high carb, low carb, no carb, no fats, low fats, all fats and proteins? What advice on vitamin supplements is the best? How often can an antibiotic be used before it will not work anymore? What is the danger of becoming addicted to your cell phone, MP3 player, or other electronic device?[1]

How do you resolve these dilemmas when you are presented with conflicting evidence? How would you know which claim is correct or better?

Globalization From Below

Kellner (2002) proposes a critical theory of globalization, emphasizing the contradictions inherent in the global system. He identifies contradictions among economic, political, and cultural factors, and also between the promising aspects of globalization—those that are progressive and emancipatory—and the perilous aspects—those that are oppressive and negative. These contradictions are important because they create openings for "struggle, resistance, and democratic transformation" (16).[2]

The first contradiction is the tension between technology and capitalism. Together, these forces shape the globalized, interconnected world. Technology provides the infrastructure that facilitates the expansion of capitalism. As capitalism expands, it absorbs increasingly more production, distribution, consumption, and other economic processes. Over time, more of the world's economies have become capitalist economies. As technology advances, it assumes more of the role previously performed by the power of human labor. This combination creates tension because people from different countries are brought together as friends, if their interests are in common, while others are brought together as enemies, such as in competing for labor. This forms a class structure that spans the globe (5–7).

Second, the relationships among capitalism, technology, and democracy are wrought with tension. As democracy spreads, it makes demands on techno-capitalism. People recognize that their democratic rights are stifled by the economic system and contest it. Terrorism is one extreme form of contest that has altered the nature of combat. According to Kellner, the abhorrent acts of terrorist networks prompt repressive, undemocratic measures by governments, such as when they restrict the flows of people and ideas and intensify policing. Terrorism and the violent responses of the United States among other societies are both undemocratic. But they are anomalies because both sides are acting in pre-modern and old-fashioned ways. Kellner argues for a newer, more rational politics to take over. If it does not, he fears that the world may face an ongoing battle, an apocalyptic future (7).

Kellner's critical point of view highlights the contested nature of globalization. The crux of the contemporary era is that globalization undermines democracy as it circulates it. Techno-capitalism creates wealth but also poverty, which threatens the democratic principles diffusing globally. The complexity of globalization and its inherent contradictions create spaces for intervention. Kellner compares this approach to Marx's study of British imperialism. Imperialism unleashed productive and progressive forces in India; however, it was highly destructive at the same time.

With respect to the contradiction between global and local, Kellner points out that while globalization spreads culture and thus has a global homogenizing effect, it also produces diversity because local cultures receive and absorb global cultural flows differently. The global does not dominate the local because, in many cases, the local pushes back and alters the global.

Finally, Kellner maintains that because globalization is so complex, an adequate theory requires a model that transcends disciplinary divides. Globalization requires a dialectical model to identify the contradictions within emerging and existing systems, and a historical approach to determine what is a continuation of the past and what is unique (16–18).

Feasible Globalization

Democratic politics, self-determination, and more economic integration cannot all coexist. We can have only two of the three. Markets do not thrive left to themselves; they thrive under the watchful eye of the state. That was the case in Venice in the 17th century, in Britain in the 19th, and in the United States in the 20th. Thus, concludes Dani Rodrik (2002), we cannot have everything.

According to Rodrik, economic globalization, whether measured by trade or economic institutional convergence, is not nearly as significant as domestic growth or domestically engineered reform. Cross-border trade and investment have grown but pale in comparison to national markets. National economies remain very diverse. After the Bretton Woods agreement, nations that found their way out of poverty did it by following nationally engineered plans. China did not base its phenomenal growth on principles developed in the West—or in the East, for that matter. China invented its own mechanisms, such as "the Household Responsibility System, Township and Village Enterprises, Special Economic Zones, and Two-Tier Pricing, among many other innovations" (2002, 8). Nor did it reconstruct any existing legal, social, or political regimes. Likewise, South Korea, Taiwan, Mauritius, India, and Chile all combined existing "best practices" with domestic innovations to achieve their successes (8–9). When the international financial institutions were promoting privatization, free markets, and deregulation, countries such as China and India resisted by protecting their industries and regulating to ensure that the benefits of growth were spread through the society (Rodrik 2011). They fared better than countries that followed the recommendations. Thus, concludes Rodrik, markets thrive best under the watchful eye of government. Strong markets require strong governance.

Convergence in non-market institutions among countries is limited, and this makes deeper economic globalization unfeasible. Countries have different values and different underlying assumptions about how life works. These account for different institutional arrangements, even in culturally similar societies such as the United States and Great Britain. Corporate structure and labor markets, for example, are not highly convergent (Rodrik 2002, 6). Institutions resist change because they are locked in by their relationships to other institutions. Institutional diversity across countries poses transaction costs like transportation and tariffs do. This limits economic integration.

While some economists argue that institutional diversity should be regulated out of existence, Rodrik argues that institutional diversity serves important functions. Chief among them is that diversity supports democracy. When states chase after investments competing through desirable policies for business, they put themselves in a golden straight-jacket.[3] When a country changes to beat the competition, it narrows the range of policy options it can pursue. This impacts many domestic policies, not only investment and trade. Political parties take on increasingly similar positions, and people have fewer real choices. This limits democracy (2002, 13).

The tension between democracy and economic convergence was evident in the Argentina crisis in the late 1990s. Argentina became a textbook case for the failures of convergence—in trade liberalization, privatization, and financial liberalization. Argentina entered a recession in 1998 (in part an effect of the Asian economic crisis) saddled with a large foreign debt. Fear that they could not repay it sent the interest rates on their debt higher, which assured that they could not pay it. To convince foreign investors that Argentina would make good on loans, the administration pulled back from its domestic obligations. People protested austerity en masse. Argentina reversed course and put domestic policy ahead of its foreign obligations. That did not help. The economic minister, Cavello, and President de la Rúa resigned. Foreign money pulled out of Argentina, leaving it in crisis (16).

According to Rodrik, democracy won over globalization in the Argentina case. After defaulting on its debt in 2001, Argentina reversed course and was rewarded with the fastest growth in Latin America from 2002 to 2008, averaging 8.2% annually. Defaulting on debt released it from conditions imposed by creditors. Rather than following IMF directives, it undertook its own macroeconomic policies. It brought its over-valued currency down

to a realistic level and kept it there. It kept interest rates low, weathered high inflation, and focused on growth. Rather than rely on exports, which accounted for only about 13% of its growth during this recovery, it relied on its domestic market. Poverty and inequality have been substantially reduced, and employment has gone up.

Rodrik also considers the possibility of a federal democratic system and continuing globalization under some sort of global democracy. But he concludes this would not work either. Experience in the United States has shown that a federal arrangement with vastly different institutional structures in its component parts is very difficult. The experience of the EU in the recent financial and debt crises also testifies to this. The events in Europe may force Europe toward greater federalism. To prevent the debt crisis from spreading, Europe must dissolve its economic union—do away with the common currency, the common market, the free movement of labor—which not many people seem to want, or develop a greater economic and political union. It is a tug-of-war between globalization and sovereignty. To overcome the crisis, a greater political union within the EU is sought by many European leaders, particularly France and Germany. This stronger union would commit each country to certain budgetary rules and oversight of each country's budget. But, as closely related as EU countries are, there is strong reaction against the loss of sovereignty this implies. People want their country to spend according to their values and priorities. They view the adoption of EU policies in the face of widespread domestic protest undemocratic. The 2010–2011 austerity measures proposed by the EU undertaken in Greece, Spain, and Italy to bring down the cost of their debts were protested in this way. On the other side, people in the EU countries who are likely donors object to bailing them out, imagining them as lazy and spendthrift (the ethnoscape).

Rodrik argues for smarter globalization, not against globalization. He holds that the most feasible political and economic global arrangement is a Bretton Woods compromise, wherein countries take charge of their own economic development policies and thus retain a democratic character. A thin veneer of global regulation that allows states significant latitude to determine their own institutional arrangements according to their needs and values is necessary and sufficient, Rodrik argues.

There are many feasible globalizations according to Rodrik, but there are boundaries to feasibility. Global federalism may be desirable, but national institutions, values, and cultures generally are still too distinct. It is not feasible. It may be possible in the distant future, he believes—perhaps in the next century (2002, 17).

World Systems Perspective

In the 1970s, world systems perspective (WSP) was among the first to argue that individual countries develop as part of a global system. The main premise is that the economies of societies are shaped more by the relations among societies than by internal dynamics. Conflict, competition, domination, and exploitation play critical roles in how powerful societies maneuver others into subordinate positions on a global hierarchy of wealth and power.

Immanuel Wallerstein[4] (1974), Andre Gunder Frank (1969), Samir Amin (1974), and Giovanni Arrighi (1978) laid the foundations for WSP. Although they vary on some details, they agree on fundamentals.

- World systems theorists adhere to Karl Marx's view that economic relations determine others—cultural, political, social, and so on.
- Conflict among stronger and weaker societies (and among the stronger) drives the world system.

- Strong societies benefit from exploitation of weaker societies.
- The world system is the basic unit of analysis.

WSP takes a long-term view of globalization, stressing that globalization has been developing for hundreds of years as capitalism spread through the relations among all societies, although not necessarily within societies. This expansion occurred in relatively regular cycles and waves that transformed relations among societies, some gaining power and some losing it.

From the WSP, the story of the global economy goes something like this:

In the 16th century, mobility by land and sea and technological sophistication allowed for the Europeans to explore and conquer people in territories oceans away from Europe. The modern capitalist world economy emerged in phases as Europeans captured more territory and incorporated the territories into increasingly larger commodity chains. They could use the raw materials from one country, manufacture it into a usable product in other countries, and then sell it in many others. The British, for example, got cotton from India, gold and silver from the Americas, coffee from South America, and so on. They made the cotton into shirts in England and then sold them all over the world, even back to India (until Gandhi led the peaceful revolution in India after WWII).

BOX 2.2   Consider This: Cycles of Hegemony

World systems theorists stress the cycling of nations in and out of power. Here are some of their theories, along with questions to consider how they might apply today.

Arrighi: As profit in trade and production fades, financial manipulations become the source of profit. Profit based on financial speculation rather than real products is unsustainable and leads to decline. This was the pattern in Genoa in the 15th century, the Netherlands in the 17th, and Britain in the 19th.

Is this what caused the economic collapse of 2007—financial instruments?

Modelski and Thompson: "New lead industries," such as information technology or the microchip, give nations advantage across a wide spectrum of economic activity. This creates wealth for political and military uses. As other societies catch up, the new industry loses its competitive advantage, and so does the hegemon.

Think of how expensive handheld calculators, digital cameras, and laptop computers used to be. Did the decline in price of technology precipitate the financial crisis of 2007?

Rennstich: A hegemon may have two power cycles, if the new lead industry emerges from the declining hegemon and is kept sufficiently separate from the declining industry sectors.

(Continued)

(Continued)

If the United States dominates the new lead industry—maybe biotechnology—might it regain its dominant role and maintain it for another two power cycles?

According to WSP, cycles of power last for two K (Kondratieff) waves—about 40–60 years each—before a new lead industry emerges.

As hegemonic power wanes, often due to an overuse and exhaustion of important resources, the system enters a "dark age." This is a time of decreased productivity during which the environment rejuvenates.

Are we entering a dark age? Land depletion, and water and air pollution have reached levels where our environment may need a time out (Anderson et al. 2002; Chase-Dunn 2006; Chase-Dunn, Kawano, and Brewer 2000; Jorgenson and Kick 2006).

As these chains incorporated more territories, they grew increasingly complicated and repeatedly intersected until they formed a global capitalist system in about 1900. The dominant state in the system—the hegemon—is the country that controls raw materials and their transportation, processing, and distribution (Bunker and Ciccantell 2005, 198–199). Portugal, the Netherlands, Britain, and, most recently, the United States have each dominated the world economy. When there is a dominant hegemon, the world system is more predictable, thus more stable, and economic interaction among societies, such as trade, increases. When there is competition for dominance, the world system is unstable, and interaction decreases. This creates cycles.

Core, Semi-Periphery, and Peripheral Societies

Countries are forced into specialized niches in this process and reap rewards based on their position. Together, they form a system. Societies on the fringes of this system, the weakest, are the *peripheral societies*. They tend to supply the raw materials and do very low-level processing. These are the least developed societies. This work, low on the value added chain, does not reap much profit. Societies engaged in higher levels of manufacturing, and some services are referred to as *semi-peripheral*. In the contemporary era, these are middle-income societies, and they realize somewhat greater rewards for their work. Some semi-peripheral societies moved up from the periphery; others fell from the core. *Core societies* are the richest and most powerful. They dominate the high-level services

such as management, finance, marketing, consulting, and product development and higher-level manufacturing.

Control of the highest levels of technology secures the position of core societies in the highest value economic sectors. In the age of imperialism, it was shipping; in the industrial, high-level manufacturing. In the information and service era, design and marketing of high-tech products, supplying information through consulting and media services, and finance reap the highest rewards. Peripheral societies' restricted access to technology concentrates their economies in primary industries, such as agriculture, mining, fishing, and forestry, along with low-level processing. The semi-peripheral societies are a mixture of mid- and higher-level manufacturing, and service with some primary industries. This accounts for the value flow from the peripheral societies. Primary resources and initial production processes offer little opportunity for profit—their prices are easily controlled by dominant countries. Advancing from one level to another is difficult, although some societies are leapfrogging manufacturing and entering the service economy directly.

Hegemonic Stability, Decline, and Rivalry

Hegemonic countries set the rules for trade, currency exchange, and other aspects of the global economy. This gives the system stability, even though they establish rules that favor their own economies. Hegemony is costly because it depends on the economic, political, and military dominance of a core nation. Maintaining the military and political relations required for domination is expensive. This makes dominance inherently unstable. As other nations in the core or semi-periphery improve their economies, they gain influence to challenge the dominant country. If a dominant country has to actually use its military to force cooperation of other countries, it is a sign of weakness and causes further decline. States in the semi-periphery often resist domination by the core. Brazil, India, Russia, and China have all challenged U.S. dominance in international institutions and dominance of the dollar in the global market (Tabb 2009, 46). They have protested the balance of power in the United Nations (UN), the IMF, and World Bank, and on the global stage generally.

A Prognosis for Globalization From the WSP

Critics of capitalism and protests against capitalism and globalization have become commonplace. This began in the cultural and social revolutions of the late 1960s, which Wallerstein (2007) points out was a critical turning point by bringing the struggle between forces for social justice and for continued capitalist domination to the fore. More recently, the decline of the world systemic power of the United States has opened another door for challenges to the existing world system (9). Wallerstein sees two threats to the current world economy: a transition in hegemonic stability and a challenge from within capitalism itself. A challenge to the dominant core could come from coalitions among Russia, China, India, Iran, and Brazil/South America or, more likely, from a Northeast Asian coalition of powers—China (including Taiwan), Korea (unified North and South), and Japan (10). Each potential challenge originates in the semi-periphery among societies that rose in wealth, power, and prestige since the late 20th century. Two or more of these societies have partnered to challenge the influence of the United States, or of the West generally, on issues such as sanctioning Iran, North Korea, and Sudan. Wallerstein believes that this transition in hegemony is unlikely as it depends on a functioning world capitalist economy (24).

A second challenge comes from within capitalism itself. Wallerstein argues that diminishing profits make capitalism less appealing (2005, 1271). Capitalist profit comes from reducing the costs of production and increasing price and sales. Further

reduction in cost is impossible. Corporations will have to bear more costs of restoring environments that they have damaged, such as the Exxon or BP oil spills. Wage laws are forcing higher wages, and many countries and indigenous groups are claiming control of their resources. There is not much room for prices or sales to increase.

Wallerstein thinks capitalism will reach its limit by 2050. At this time, the global economy may become more "hierarchical and polarizing (that is like the present system, or worse) or if the forces of social justice win out, relatively more democratic and egalitarian" (2005, 1275). In other words, it could be the same only leaner and meaner, or something more like the World Social Forum and other civil society organizations (CSOs) advocate. Seymour Melman (2001) also foresees the end of capitalism. He cogently argues, at both micro and macro levels, that the hierarchical, alienating, environment-destroying, military-industrial complex that constitutes American, and increasingly global, business is unsustainable. If not brought down by its own internal contradictions as happened to the USSR in 1989, it will be brought down by internal and external forces of alienation.

Global Systems Theory

Global systems theory (GST) and WSP both emphasize that conflict and capitalism shape the global order. WSP is state-centrist, viewing states as the dominant actors in the global systems, whereas GST is non-statist, viewing states as only one set of actors among many involved in the economy, with no central governing authority. In the place of states, a transnational capitalist class (TCC) is the dominant force in the global system. Membership in the TCC comes from across the globe and controls the economy through the activity of transnational corporations in business, its influence in politics, and ownership of media. It does not matter if the corporate owners, workers, or suppliers of raw materials are in the same country or not. The global economy is a single system across the globe and all classes are transnational. The following are the basic propositions of GST:

- Three spheres of transnational practices—cultural, economic, and political—span state borders yet do not originate in states (Sklair 1999, 4).

- The three spheres are interdependent but distinct processes that develop at different rates.
- Globalization is a new phenomenon, distinguished from previous periods because the most important economic, cultural, social, and political practices now occur within transnational spheres, not within or among countries. This dates to about the 1960s (Sklair 2005, 60–61).

The use of *transnational* signifies that the global system operates independently of national boundaries. People set up production, get their resources, and sell their products from wherever in the world they can make the most profit. Decisions are based on cost and benefit, not on the country in which the owners or workers live or where raw materials or component parts originate. Money flows the same way. People can make and sell investments in any part of the world. Individual national economies became less important as the global ascended into prominence.

Two trends gave rise to the global economy:

- The division of labor and financial investment disperse around the world, releasing production from the constraints of any one country.
- Mass media and transnational corporations spread consumerist culture across the globe, developing the global market. (Sklair 1999, 70)

The TCC, the power elite, comprises four fractions who are the most powerful actors in the economy, politics, and cultural production. They are

- those who own and control the TNCs (corporate fraction);
- globalizing bureaucrats and politicians (state fraction);
- globalizing professionals (technical fraction); and
- merchants and media (consumerist fraction). (Sklair 2002, 145)

The four groups are interdependent. Elite within fractions move from one to another or may hold positions in two or more simultaneously. For example, government officials and corporate executives move back and forth between the corporate and state fractions. Robert Rubin was with Goldman Sachs, secretary of the U.S. Treasury under Clinton, a Citibank officer, and director of the National Economic Council, among many other powerful posts. Dick Cheney was secretary of defense, chairman and CEO of Halliburton, and vice-president of the United States. Within the United States, movement between government, military, and corporate fractions has been common since WWII, provoking President Eisenhower to warn the nation to be wary of the growing power and potential for abuse in the close relationships between the military and industry in the "military-industrial" complex. Now the interlocking relationships occur on a global, not just national, scale.

In the GST view, interlocking fractions can manipulate national and global political systems. Corporate leaders serve on one another's boards where they deal with common problems such as environmental regulation, labor laws, and oil prices. They have motive and opportunity to develop solutions that serve their interests and see that they become global policy through their advisory or official government roles (Robinson 2007; Robinson and Harris 2000). The impact of the TCC is documented in a number of cases where political decision making was deflected from public interest to corporate benefit. Corporate scientists, officers, and industry representatives regularly advise and sit in on meetings of the multilateral commissions and the regulatory agencies that oversee them. They often, if not always, outnumber citizens and consumer group participants, as well as governmental representatives, in these meetings. In case after case, they have blocked public interest regulation that was widely acknowledged as being in the common good in regulatory actions as diverse as rail transport, tobacco, and food safety (Sklair 2005, 151). These conflicts of interest occur because governments rely on experts that come from the very industries they are trying to regulate.

In summary, according to GST, people develop interests based on their class position in the global economy and have the opportunity to form transnational groups regardless of where they live. Individuals are linked to the global system through these groups such as transnational classes, transnational social movements, transnational labor movements, media, professional regulatory organizations, interest societies, and so on. People also participate directly in the global system as consumers of products, media, and culture. The elite transnational capitalist class has more power and control than the global lower and middle classes, or the remainder of the upper class.

Prognosis of GST

GST theorists argue that the global capitalist system cannot survive and that a socialist global economy will emerge. The two primary threats are the polarization of classes and environmental sustainability. Already, capitalist globalization has advanced human rights ideology in the political and civil society spheres. Expanded into the economic and social spheres, it is a threat to global capitalism (Sklair 2004, 47).

Developing socialist globalization depends on extending the culture-ideology of human rights. While capitalist globalization is waning, the world is just commencing on the journey of globalization. WST and GST are in line with most mainstream thought in recognizing human rights and greater democratization as trends in political and cultural globalization. However, the emphasis on socialism as the ultimate carrier of human rights and democratization has less political or cultural support globally.

World Society Theory

Although the names are similar, world society theory is very different than world systems (or global systems) theories. One stresses economics (systems), the other culture (society). One focuses on relations between states (systems), and the other development of a global society apart from states (society).

Did you ever wonder why countries, no matter whether they are rich or poor, democratic or non-democratic, Eastern or Western, have very similar state and institutional structures? Governments have a prime minister or president (sometimes a monarch), cabinet posts, legislatures, and so on. Educational systems also look a lot alike. Most have a sequence of grades across which a curriculum of distinct disciplines is articulated. Even voluntary organizations, whether they are clubs organized around a hobby or an NGO organized around a global cause, have similar structures. They have officers, usually a president, vice-president, secretary, and treasurer, and various committees with committee heads. According to world society theory (and the related world polity theory), there are a limited number of models and principles that serve as templates or models for individual action, legitimate discourse, and organizational structure on which all of these groups and institutions are based. These global models form a world culture. In some respects, world society theory was developed in response to world systems theory, to assert the importance of culture and the development of a world culture as opposed to the economy and the importance of individuals and associations over that of states as the driving forces of globalization.

BOX 2.3   A Closer Look: Citizenship Training

These Hungarian youth are participating in a workshop conducted by the European Commission, reinforcing the global cultural norms regarding citizenship in democratic societies. Hungary was admitted to the European Union, but the government has faced criticisms by the European Commission for violations of the EU Treaty law and erosion of democracy.

The ideas that form the basis of world culture—ideas about the nature of knowledge and of humans (both rational), individualism, state sovereignty, citizenship, and rule of law—arose during the Enlightenment. The ideas spread through social movements, CSOs, intellectuals, the advice of experts, and governmental organizations, among others. People adopt models of individual behavior and of organizational forms—states, education, welfare systems, science, and voluntary organizations—based on these ideas. By the post-WWII era, the models had achieved near global spread, forming a world culture. The process of globalization from this perspective is as old as rationality. However, world society theorists acknowledge that the contemporary period—from about 1960—is unique because of the very rapid expansion and increase in "economic, political, military, social, and cultural interdependence, both actual and perceived" (Drori, Meyer, and Hwang 2009, 22).

World society is another non-statist theory. That means that world society, unlike a national society, does not have a central political apparatus and states are not the dominant actors—individuals and the associations they form are. World culture facilitates networks of communication, association, and organization across societies that span the globe, creating a world society. With no central governing authority, authority resides in the models themselves, which penetrate and shape social life. As a result, national societies have remarkably homogenous structures. States, educational systems, businesses, economies, families, religions, and other institutions follow world culture models. The diffusion and institutionalization of world culture, as opposed to the development of a world state, has driven globalization, laying a foundation of meaning that makes it possible for people, states, and organizations to interact across national cultures. Whereas other theories stress the importance of economic and political power, world society theorists credit "worldwide waves of copying" for shaping national and local structure and policy. Societal homogeneity is not a result of realist politics or economic hegemony but of world culture and the organizational forms it encourages (Meyer et al. 1997 141–147).

This is not to say that world culture is seamless. There is more homogeneity in some elements of world culture, such as state structure and organizational structure generally, than in others such as definitions of human rights, which remain contested. As within any culture, there is conflict among competing perspectives, such as on the meaning or application of individualism in economics or of freedom in politics. There is also opposition to world culture. Many forms of fundamentalisms object to elements of world society. World culture is adapted to local contexts (Robertson 1992). Different societies are individual variations on the elements of world culture, and societies may participate to varying degrees.

World society theory offers a unique perspective on actors. Actors, such as individuals, citizens, states, and organizations, are socially constructed entities. Unlike other entities, such as a species or an ecosystem, only actors have agency—the ability to represent their interests. This presents world society with moral problems and issues. Once an entity is recognized as an actor, world society gains responsibility for them, and they gain responsibility as well. There are proper methods and ways for actors to set and pursue goals, whether they are individuals, states, corporations, or non-governmental organizations (Meyer 2007, 264–265). Awareness of shared problems and risks mandates regulating, negotiating, and moderating pressures among societies. In the absence of a world state, "individual and associations are left to do it on their own, with only modest protection from supra-national authority" (263).

This leads to communities of interests forming around global issues and topics. Through these associations, individuals, organizations, and states are empowered as actors, adding layers to global governance. Global regimes—rules, regulations, treaties, and laws—are created through the networking among these layers. This forms a world polity in which states are the primary actors, assigned with particular rights and responsibilities. When actors step beyond their rights or behave in ways incompatible with a regime—for instance, a corporation that pollutes or another state that uses torture—people usually turn to or pressure states to rectify the wrong.

As a general premise, world society theory argues that mobilizing to develop global regimes occurs first in world society in the context of rationalized discourse among all the layers of actors. The discourse moves to the world polity through the international structure provided by the UN and its multitude of organizations. This creates forums where CSOs bring their concerns to an international audience. Whether or not a world polity, constructed as these theorists envision, can ever be democratic is vigorously debated by many analysts of globalization.

The Global "Scapes"

Imagine a satellite photograph of the globe. Swirls of color intermingle and overlap. The dynamics in time-lapse photography would show constant interchange among them. White cloud cover becomes the blue of oceans. The bright of sunlight becomes the green of vegetation. A snapshot makes these systems look as though they are distinct, but transformation of one to another is constant.

Now imagine that the swirls of color circulating the globe are ideas, people, products, money, and technology. As they flow to various parts of the world, they change the places to which they flow, creating new possibilities, and sometimes problems. Appadurai (1996) distinguishes five such flows of globalization, or "scapes": ethnoscapes, ideoscapes, mediascapes, technoscapes, and financescapes. *Scapes* references the quality of landscapes and seascapes. Although each looks static in at any one point in time, there is constant movement and change.

BOX 2.4   A Closer Look: Tweeting

Social media has been heralded as an instrument to build social capital globally by connecting people regardless of their location on the globe.

Two of the earliest detailed studies of this suggest that it may not be the case.

A study of over 300,000 "tweeters" found that although the networks on Twitter appear very dense, it masks that people keep in touch with very few in the network. The actual network of those who keep in touch is quite sparse. The number of followers grows indefinitely whereas the number of friends eventually saturates. *Friend* in this study was defined as anyone to whom a person directs two posts (Huberman, Romero, and Wu 2009).

University of Toronto researchers found that Twitter ties link users within the same regional cluster (39%), mostly within an easy driving distance. Ties that are over 1,000 km occur much less frequently than if ties were distributed randomly. Also, the number of airline flights is the best predictor of non-local ties. This suggests that long-distance travel and face-to-face contact influences forming electronic ties (Takhteyev, Gruzd, and Wellman 2012).

Flows of globalization change the countries through which they flow and the people within them, and are in turn changed by them. Each flow has a dynamic and logic of its own. They are analytically distinct but impact one another. Trade brings new products to people. New communication technologies bring a taste of freedom to countries where information is tightly controlled and to teenagers who can roam further from home while maintaining the security of home through a full-time electronic tether. Ideas concerning human rights, the importance of education, and medical knowledge flow over the world, often carried by social media and the worldwide web. Migrants spread culture, products, and money as they travel away from home and sometimes back again.

People's imaginations have an important role in shaping global flows. Bonds of social interaction across the globe—beginning particularly with colonialism and accelerating as migration and media flows accelerated—mean that our lives all impact one another. The globe is the field of interaction. Nevertheless, people only catch glimpses of faraway people and places and do not really know them. Their imaginations complete the picture. In this sense, people live in an imagined world. Even within nations, much is imagined because people cannot directly know everything or everyone in all their complexity.

Ethnoscapes refer to the movements of people and the images they develop concerning the possibility and potential of moving. Global migration rates are currently very high. People may move according to the needs of capitalism, the policies of governments, or their own desires. Migrant workers, tourists, religious missionaries, workers for non-governmental agencies, students, and governmental officials are among the many people on the move across the globe. As people migrate, they change the places they were and the places to which they go. Their imagining of other people and places influence where they travel, what they expect to find in their travels, and how they receive travelers in their homelands.

Technoscapes are the flows of machines, of production processes, and of industrial, advanced, and information technologies. Technoscapes are driven by international labor availabilities, transnational financial transactions, political considerations, and the malleability of production processes, among other factors. Industrial technology changed the world system during the takeoff phase of globalization by propelling some societies ahead of others in wealth and power. It is still a vehicle of economic advance. Advanced and information technologies provide a second opportunity for economic and political development. Cell phones and other wireless technologies compensate for weak communication, media, and financial infrastructures, for example, (see Box 2.5). Internet and mobile technologies, for example, were instrumental in organizing the political revolutions of Arab Spring in 2011.

BOX 2.5   A Closer Look: Technoscapes

Access to cell phones can change life dramatically. In the developing world people can pay for goods and services by transferring funds through cell phone technology, bypassing traditional banks. Cell phones and the Internet give people instant access to market information. With money and information flows, small businesses can be started or expanded. Cell phones facilitated the revolution in Tunisia and Egypt as people "tweeted" and used other social networks to spread the word—where to go, when to go, and for what purposes—ensuring that tens of thousands of protestors would show up at rallies.

Financescapes are flows of capital through currency exchange, stock exchange, speculative ventures, foreign investment, and other financial transactions. Financescapes are rapid and complex, making their relationships with the other scapes impossible to predict, and making it difficult for states to manage their economies. The banking crisis that erupted at the end of 2007 brought economic crisis globally; people lost their jobs and homes, and countries entered deep recessions. Countries like Ireland that experienced vibrant growth and labor shortages during the previous decades suddenly had few employment opportunities. The flow of migrants into Ireland reversed course, and the flow of emigration out increased rapidly. The global balance of power shifted as countries such as Brazil, India, and China, which weathered the crisis well, made significant gains in economic power and political prestige. Global financescapes such the flow of foreign investment, the accumulation of sovereign debt, the capacity to manipulate a country's currency, the global market for credit, and so forth, can dramatically alter people's life chances and the overall health of their societies.

Mediascapes are the production and distribution of images and information. Images and information come in many genres, are produced in many modes, are aimed at various audiences, and motivated by many different interests—determined by those who own and control them. They provide an incredible array of images: of other countries, of news reports and recordings, of commodities, lifestyles, foods, and so on. The more removed from direct experience a viewer of the images is, the more the line between reality and fantasy may blur, and the more a viewer is likely to construct an imagined world that is a chimera. People construct narratives from mediascapes with bits and pieces gleaned from this movie or that news report and some other advertisement. How we imagine people's lives in other countries, their feelings and motivations, may be far removed from reality. People may have images of "the Orient" or of "the West" that contain stereotypes, prejudices, and imaginings that bear little relation to reality. They make decisions based on the images.

Ideoscapes are also flows of images and information, although this category is reserved for political scapes, emanating from states or social movements. The Enlightenment ideas of freedom, rights, sovereignty, and democracy have come to dominate global political rhetoric. The human rights movement, the International Criminal Court, the end of apartheid in South Africa, as well as the resurgence of fundamentalisms globally resulted from vigorous flows of global ideoscapes. Different countries have developed different political rhetoric and keywords. Like other flows, ideoscapes interact differently in different parts of the world and convey different meanings. As democracy, individualism, cosmopolitanism, and other politically charged ideas flow globally, they reverberate differently in different cultures, never meaning quite the same thing from culture to culture.

The global scapes are a powerful analytical tool. The flow of the five scapes is driven by interaction, and globalization results from intensifying interactions among the various parts of the world. Analytically distinguishing types of flows and recognizing how they change and are changed by the terrain over which they travel—in sometimes unpredictable ways—are critical in global analysis.

Mechanisms of Convergence

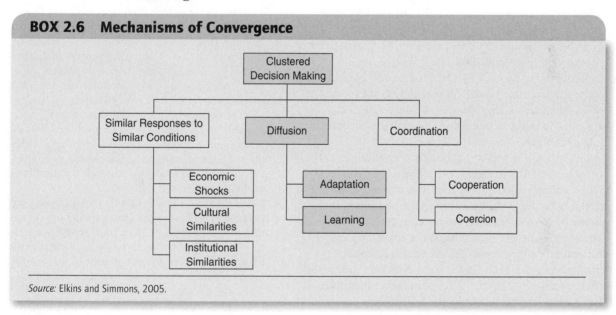

BOX 2.6   Mechanisms of Convergence

Source: Elkins and Simmons, 2005.

Convergence is the process through which societies become more alike or homogenous. Globalization involves convergence on economic policy, political forms and structures, types of laws, values, and of course many other things. Convergence is accomplished by diffusion of innovation from one actor—state, individual, corporation, CSO—or group of actors, to others. A number of theorists have studied mechanisms of policy diffusion. Zachary Elkins and Beth Simmons (2005) consolidated this body of work into a single conceptual framework. While they developed the framework primarily using cases of economic and political convergence, it is applicable to other forms of convergence. The framework addresses some of the ways in which increasing interaction compels convergence, how convergence on a general principle or model can produce divergent outcomes, and how convergence is often mediated by communities of interest and international organizations. Convergence occurs in three ways:

- Societies may make similar responses to similar conditions without coordination, consultation, or copying from others.
- Societies may coordinate because of coercion and conditionality—such as when the IMF and World Bank made privatization and other policies a condition of receiving loans—or cooperation, such as the planning that occurs in the G20 summits.

- Societies may respond similarly because they are interdependent but do not coordinate with one another. This is the special circumstance of diffusion and the most complex convergence process.

The first two are easy to understand, so I will only discuss diffusion here. Diffusion is likely to occur in two situations: 1) adapting to altered conditions and 2) learning. A number of different mechanisms and processes are associated with each, and societies may learn, even when forced to adapt.

Adapting to altered conditions occurs when a country adopts a policy innovation because its environment has changed. When one society institutes changes, it alters the environment of other societies because it is part of their environment. For example, it may make their environment more or less competitive, democratic, fragile, or stable. The altered environment provides an opportunity or necessitates action on the part of other societies (Elkins and Simmons 2005, 40).

Globalizing cultural norms change the environment of societies. Global norms define the conditions of societal legitimacy and thus represent a contingency to societies. Adopting globally accepted norms confers reputational and other benefits. Going along with trade agreements, environmental treaties, and human rights conventions are instances where many societies have had to adapt to conform to new norms. In the event that an emerging global norm is viewed negatively by a country's domestic audience, as is the case with some trade and environmental norms in the United States, a global cultural norm provides a "*cover* from criticism" (Elkins and Simmons 2005, 39, emphasis original). Increasing interaction and interdependence compel convergence on norms in order to receive whatever benefits might accrue. This is how most former Warsaw Pact countries were forced to democratize.

As norms for societal qualities such as education, liberal political processes, and human rights develop and gain global currency, they change the environment of societies by redefining a society's responsibilities to its members. Societies have been forced to adapt, resulting in convergence at the global level. For many nations, adopting goals for providing education, health care, and other social welfare issues has been necessary for legitimacy. Some societies may make commitments to fulfilling these norms well before they are ready or able to accomplish them. This may backfire and cause domestic and international problems when they are unable to fulfill their commitments or fulfill people's expectations.

- Support groups function to facilitate policy diffusion by creating an environment in which there is a network of users. Nations may benefit from adopting the policies of others as the number of adopters grows. As the number of nations applying particular policies increases, expertise within the network begins to grow. Newer adopters have the benefit of the advice, support, and even service of others who have gone before.
- Nations have different thresholds; some adopt sooner and some hold out longer. This happened with policies of economic liberalization. Although societies may have high thresholds and resist change for a long time, few hold out once a majority has changed. In developing constitutions, societies were faced with choices in balancing powers of governmental branches and developing democratic or at least democratic-appearing electoral systems. Each country knew that with each choice, it was joining a network on which it would depend as it implemented and refined its system of government (Elkins and Simmons 2005, 41). Networks within the policy community, including expert governmental as well as non-governmental organizations, facilitate this form of diffusion.
- Competitive advantage is another reason for changing policy to adapt to changing externalities (Elkins and Simmons 2005, 42). At times, countries seem to trip over one another in racing to lower the cost of doing business to secure foreign investment. Countries hope that by altering their tax policies, adopting protectionist measures, and enacting other policies that reduce the costs for corporations, they will attract business that would have gone to other countries. This can also apply with respect to political globalization. Political climate is an important attraction or repellent for foreign investment. Anti-corruption policies, judicial reform, and rule of law are increasingly important to attract and keep foreign investment. This is a much healthier form of competition. CSOs as well as international financial organizations, such as the World Bank and IMF, report on the political climate of countries and advise businesses on the safest places to invest. This compels convergence to be competitive.
- Learning takes place when one society's actions provide information to others as opposed to altering

the external conditions in which a society must operate. Policy makers recognize a problem, try to determine the causes, and then try to develop or find workable solutions. Societies make essentially reflexive choices based on information about what works, what does not, the costs of an action, and various information gained from others (Elkins and Simmons 2005, 43–45). One of the most remarkable features of learning is how often it can go wrong.

- Information cascade (Elkins and Simmons 2005, 43) is a mechanism of diffusion with very little reflexivity. The learning refers only to knowing what others have done. When countries begin to copy what another country has done, the more countries that make the change, the more it appears as though they are making informed choices. A country might assume that it is taking advantage of the collective wisdom of the others. If everyone is making that assumption, there is no collective wisdom. The cascade toward a policy may have begun with one country making a choice when it was forced to act based on little or faulty information. Convergence results as more nations make the same choice. This is similar to simple mimicry or jumping on a bandwagon.

- Availability of models may distort the learning process in a variety of ways. Models and policies of prominent nations are most likely to diffuse because they are the most visible. Spontaneous successes that get high publicity often fuels fad-like adoptions (Elkins and Simmons 2005, 44). The long-term records of success or failure for either of these tend to be less available than the models themselves. Less well-known strategies may have important information related to success and failure that escapes notice. Communication networks of groups involved in policy making encourage the diffusions of select information and models through a process of "channeled learning." The channels have important consequences for information flow and policy diffusion (Simmons, Dobbin, and Garrett 2006, 798). Unfortunately, the best information may not be channeled, and that which is may be defective or inappropriate for some countries encouraged to adopt them.

- Reference groups influence learning as societies tend to adopt policies of others who are similar to themselves in very tangible ways such as geography, religion, language, colonial origins, and other factors (Elkins and Simmons 2005, 45).

Many of these processes are forms of *emulation*. Emulation includes adopting global cultural norms to gain social acceptance in the international community, following the recommendation of experts (an epistemological community) who advocate for a policy or practice, and copying the action of those nations who are similar in cultural heritage (Simmons et al., 2006, 800–801). More than one mechanism of convergence may be implicated in a wave of convergence. During the 1980s, societies adopting policies of privatization of government enterprises were influenced by international norms, conditions set by international lenders, competition for international investment, and the advice of experts.

Mimicry, demonstration effect, bandwagon, contagion, and *policy transfer* are similar terms used by social scientists to describe diffusion. The typology by Elkins and Simmons presented above differentiates specific mechanisms and processes that lead to convergence. As such, it provides an analytic framework for comparative research on convergence processes. This is essential to understanding globalization.

The Global Field

In contemporary social life, the globe is the field of interaction. Robertson and Chirico (1985) emphasize globalization as a set of processes through which the world is becoming a single place. There are two equally important dimensions to globalization processes: 1) *objective*—increasing forms of connectivity and interdependence, the development of global systems; and 2) *subjective*—increasing consciousness of the world as a whole. As interaction and interdependence among individuals and across societies increase, consciousness of people's common humanity increases, and together these constitute globalization. Whereas social relations had been dominated by the relationship of individuals to societies and societies to one another, globalization changed that. The emergence of global systems and new consciousness of humanity expanded the field of action from the dynamic of individuals and societies to include individuals, societies, the global systems, and humanity. Each element of the field is changed by continuing globalization, as are its relations to the other elements.

BOX 2.7   A Closer Look: The Global Field

The Global Field: Trajectories of Globalization

Society
(state, economy,
civil society, all
institutions,
organizations, etc.
within a society)

Global Systems
(global economy,
governance, civil
society, etc.)

Individual
(identity,
personality,
statuses, roles,
etc.)

Humanity
(all the individuals
in the world)

Source: Adapted from Robertson and Chirico, 1985: 234.

Attempts to shape and control globalization come from many sources, including individuals, corporations, social movements, governments, and non-governmental organizations—all of which may be component parts of societies, although their interests may not align with any one society. Social movements and non-governmental organizations may be active at the global level and contain members from many different societies. Global movements may be working for a global goal, for instance, to combat global warming, or may be working to improve conditions in a single society, such as autonomy for Tibet.

What are the global processes they try to shape and control? The answer is essentially all of them. Global processes have significant impact on everyone, everywhere. The global economy spreads riches and creates paupers. Decisions about how production and distribution are organized, the rules that they operate within, the responsibilities inherent in directing flows of money and investment, and the financial tools through which they flow affect everyone, everywhere. Political questions have spilled out over boundaries of traditional political systems and nations. How we combat climate change and terrorism, how we regulate or do not regulate economic transactions, how to stop nuclear proliferation, and many other decisions that impact the world as a whole are global governance issues. Actors who are not traditionally considered political actors have

dramatic input into political decision making. Increasingly, global political norms are converging on democratic principles; however, global governance is not democratic—not all interests are represented, decisions are not made with respect to the common good. Controlling global governance is highly contentious and competitive.

Global culture is also a source of conflict, often violent. Deciding the responsibilities of societies to individuals used to be the sole realm of the state. Now global norms define a good state and what a good state owes its citizen as well as members of other societies by virtue of their humanity. The rights that people have because they are human—as opposed to simply members of particular societies with civil rights—are negotiated in social forums at all levels from the local to the global. Most rich nations have some form of universal health care, although there are a variety of models. There are global norms advocating human rights, equal rights for women, tolerance and respect for diversity, environmentalism, and a host of others. Consumerism, materialism, and cosmopolitanism are also spreading. Each of them brings conflict within and among societies between those who accept and advocate a particular norm and those who resist it. People are vying to control and shape global culture.

Globalization and the attempts to shape it create both chaos and order. The effects of globalization have made the post-WWII ways of life obsolete. The worldwide cultural and political revolutions of the late 1960s testified that many people were alienated from their society. Continuing poverty in many parts of the world and global racism led to protests against the capitalist threat in developing societies. The Maoist revolution in China inspired Che Guevara and other revolutionaries in developing societies as well as many middle-class intellectuals and students in developed societies to work and fight for change. The struggles of minorities and the working classes and the plight of rural peasants inspired protests and revolution in the name of humanity—at least temporarily upsetting the economic, political, and social status quo in more societies than not. Independence throughout colonial Africa and Asia swelled waves of democratic revival and, ironically, increased global instability.

Dropping out of traditional economic, social, and political relationships, people experimented with new social forms they believed more conducive to human happiness. In the United States and Europe, people established communes as experimental movements, testing the waters of new economic, familial, and political relations in a break from 1950s urban and suburban life. New religious movements flourished all over the world reacting against the bureaucratization and ritualism of mainstream religions and turning toward evangelical, mystical, and experimental forms. Reactionary movements followed the frenzy of experiments with new social forms. They promoted traditional and fundamentalist values in religion, education, gender relations, and cultural values along with neo-conservative politics and economics.

From the global field perspective, globalization is analyzed as a set of contests over how we will define and live life, as well as allow others to define and live theirs. The meaning and structure of the individual, society, the global systems, and humanity, along with the relationships—economic, political, social, and cultural among them—are being contested by conflicting and contradictory forces and pressures.

The Elements of the Global Field: Humanity

BOX 2.8   A Closer Look: Celebrating the Nation and the World

In January of 2011, nationalistic fervor swept the Arab world. In Egypt, protestors camped and demonstrated round the clock for 18 days. As they demonstrated and camped, they also cleaned. When asked by a reporter "why" they would do this work, one young man replied, "This is my earth. This is my country. This is my home. I will clean all Egypt when Mubarak will go out" (Friedman 2011).

Being part of the world does not negate the other elements of the global field, specifically not the nation. It changes them. What changes are people in Arab nations demanding of the individual society relationship?

How are global forces implicated in the revolutions sweeping the Arab world since 2011? What global forces will help or hinder shaping its future?

Growing consciousness of the common humanity of all people on earth is, in many ways, the crux of globalization. The concept of humanity as the moral community to which all humans owe their primary allegiance and the related concept of world citizenship date at least as far back as the Stoics, about 2,000 years ago. Stoics thought the political, racial, ethnic, and other boundaries humanity drew within itself were artificial. However, for most history, the idea that one's most primordial belonging was to humanity did not have bearing in the conduct of inter-tribal, inter-societal, or international relations. In the contemporary period, the interdependence of all of humankind has real meaning. That is to say that it influences the action of people, corporations, states, and other actors. Economic, social, political, and other processes are judged, at least superficially, according to their effect on human rights and welfare. Individual, societal, and global relationships are increasingly viewed as contingent on the recognition of the human rights of all people.

Modernity ushered in the age of the individual, during which the individual acquired sacred status, elevating the individual above the group and bestowing individuals with special rights and liberties. Globalization is elevating humanity to equal status. Ironically, the universalizing principle of humanity has intensified the revival of particularistic national and ethnic identities. While the particular and universal may enhance one another, when people feel their identity threatened, fear and conflict often follow. Many times, this fear has instigated very virulent, violent conflict, primarily within societies. This is one of the dialectics that warrants careful analysis.

The Individual

Globalization is affecting the internal life of individuals, impacting their personalities and their relationships to the other elements of the global field. Consciousness of humanity as a social category changes individual identity. Significant numbers of people report feeling that they belong to the globe (World Values Survey 2011). With membership in a common humanity, our rights and responsibilities change. While a lot of attention is paid to rights, less is paid to responsibilities. Responsibility is an ethical and moral obligation. Exactly what the responsibilities of individuals as members of humanity are is debated. Do we, for example have a responsibility to preserve and protect the environment for the future of humanity? Do we have a responsibility to protect the human rights of members of other societies? Do individuals from wealthier societies have a special obligation to those in need? The question of what individuals owe others because of their position in society, in the world, and by virtue of their common humanity looms large on the global agenda.

Globalization changes individual society relationships as well. What is an individual entitled to from his or her society in light of human rights? That question is being asked all over the world. Is access to health care a basic human right that must be guaranteed in all societies? It is not guaranteed in the United States. Access to clean water and air can be considered basic human rights, but who will guarantee them? Are these responsibilities that society has to individuals, the global systems must fulfill, or individuals to individuals though charity and good works? Torture and imprisonment without

due process are both considered violations of human rights in the international community. The United States stands up for these rights, yet some people say that the United States violates these rights. Who is to decide? How do we find common ground? All of these questions are being contested in national and global arenas.

Societies

Globalization presents societies with constraints and challenges, as well as opportunities. Global expectations constrain societies to conform to emerging global standards in the structure of their states, the establishment of financial, judicial, educational, and other institutions, and their treatment of citizens, refugees, and other members of the international community. To participate in international relations, for example, states have similarly structured executive, judicial, and legislative branches of government. Cabinet posts at the national level are similarly structured, with similar duties. For example, heads of central banks or national treasuries meet at G20 meetings. Thus, to participate, a country has to have an official with responsibilities for the Department of the Treasury, Federal Reserve, Finance, or its equivalent. Similarly, in the United States, foreign secretaries and the secretary of state meet to discuss and work through international relations. Countries send ambassadors to every country with whom they have good relationships, and ambassadors enjoy similar privileges in every country.

Globalization has altered the relationship between individuals and their society. Every individual belongs to a society. Our society provides each of us with a sense of identity and belonging. We have civil rights that emanate from belonging to a particular society. With the emergence of humanity as a social entity, there are global pressures for states to grant human rights as well. For example, the U.S. Supreme Court outlawed the execution of people who committed capital crimes while they were juveniles. In rendering their decision, the justices cited evolving views of cruel and unusual punishment not only in the United States, but international opinion as well. Countries are expected to abide by treaties and declarations that articulate an ever increasing scope of rights, of women, of children, of indigenous groups, and so on.

Societies are constrained by the global economy and other global systems. One country, for example, can manipulate the value of another's currency by buying or selling it in the global financial market. The UN Security Council can bring a head of state to trial in the International Criminal Court. Pressures from global non-governmental organizations may coerce states to conform to their demands. Issues of nuclear proliferation, trade policy, environmental policy, marriage and divorce, welfare, and most other aspects of societal functioning, even how to respond to the global economic crisis, are discussed at global, not just international levels, and individual societies are expected to conform to majority views or potentially suffer the effects of sanctions if they do not.

Societies and actors within them, such as states, corporations, and CSOs, can make demands on the global system as well. They have taken on an increasingly influential role in global governance and sit at the table in the negotiations of treaties working in partnership with governmental and international governmental organizations, states, and regulatory agencies. CSOs have put pressures directly on multinational corporations to reform their practices in developing and developed countries. Multinationals have advised on the very regulations to which they would become subject. Societies that are increasing in power, such as Brazil, India, and China, are pressuring for restructuring of international organizations to reflect their new influence. The global system will probably be less controlled by the developed countries and become more democratic or perhaps even dominated by coalitions of newly emerging global powers. This may dramatically change the landscape of global politics.

Sovereignty is increasingly recognized and claimed as a human right, a right that individuals and groups within societies take to the international community for validation. The operative idea is that nations should be self-governing. Separatist movements, the establishment of new nation-states, and demands for more autonomy within states are indications of the importance placed on sovereignty. It is ironic that the demands for sovereignty come at a time when economic, political, and social processes have spilled over their societal borders to the extent that some analysts question whether or not even powerful states can be truly sovereign.

Within societies, institutions and organizations—whether for-profit or not-for-profit, governmental or non-governmental, neighborhood or national—are pressured to become more democratic and transparent, and to produce better results for their members. At the same time, there is pressure for enhanced responsibility of individual societies and global systems to people all over the globe regardless of the society to which they belong—in other words, to humanity.

The Global Systems

The global systems are the relatively patterned relationships that transcend societal boundaries—the global economy, global governance, global civil society, and so on. The global economy is the global system that is most often talked about in the popular press. People have had a tendency to reduce globalization to economic globalization. For example, it took quite awhile to convince the anti-globalization factions that their protests were about the inequalities produced by globalization, not all forms of globalization, nor even all forms of economic globalization. Now people protest for and promote an alternative globalization.

Global governance is another profoundly important global system, very different from just international relations. While international relations will continue to be important, the operation of the global polity is assuming many of the functions of both international relations and national governments in coordination, regulation, and negotiation of economic, political, and social aspects of life. It is increasingly apparent that as economic systems become more integrated globally, individual societies have less control over them. More collaboration across more groups is necessary to harness economic processes, negotiate environmental risks, provide for peace, coordinate the development of underdeveloped societies, and respond effectively to other problems of human security. In contrast to bilateral and multilateral treaties and alliances, global governance implies a system to which all nation-states are responsible and in which many layers of actors in addition to states are involved.

Global civil society is another emerging global system. International non-governmental organizations are increasingly influential, impacting global governance and implementing social policies. Global and domestic groups may be well integrated, pressuring both societies and the global system of societies. Many people look to global civil society to furnish the cornerstone of a democratic system of global governance. The power of global civil society to affect global governance is indisputable. However, it is very difficult to ensure accountability in global systems, and thus, whether a global civil society can effectively represent all of humanity is doubtful.

Global terrorism and global crime networks are also among the global systems. They have no respect for national borders, operating wherever there is opportunity. Failed and failing states provide near lawless lands of opportunity. The developed world's appetite for drugs and trafficking in weapons, counterfeit goods, and other illegal commodities, including humans, feed both of these groups. Each has elaborate trafficking routes and financial flows that literally encompass the globe.

Also in question are the responsibilities of the global systems toward individuals. Is fairness expected in global politics and economics? How is it guaranteed? Who is responsible when a society cannot or will not provide the rights and privileges its citizens are due as members of humanity? Who is the ultimate guarantor of human rights? How may they be guaranteed in the case of countries that refuse to grant the rights increasingly accepted as universally applicable to every person on earth?

None of the questions raised above has an easy answer. Much of the disorder and apparent chaos in the world today—from the rise of fundamentalism as a global force to experiments in alternative lifestyles—results as we negotiate, debate, work through, and fight—sometimes violently—about the processes and outcomes of globalization.

Case Study: Economic Integration and Globalization

Throughout this book, case studies are presented to illustrate some of the ways that theory and research are integrated in globalization studies and the variety of methods used. Waves and cycles are among the most important concepts in globalization. Increasing and decreasing rates of global activity—such as trade, travel, or democracy—illustrate increasing and decreasing periods of globalization. This case study demonstrates how economic waves and cycles can be dated, measured, and related to other social forces. Similar methods can be used to study waves of political, cultural, and other forms of globalization. A common measure of economic integration is trade flow. If you buy a Japanese car, a Swiss watch, African carvings, or mangos from South America, or anything that came in part or whole from another country, you are in the global trade flow. Trade indicates the degree to which a country's economy depends on other countries and is measured by the volume of a country's imports and exports. Many theorists reject simple volume as a measure of trade flow.[5] Rates are generally preferred. Rates may be the volume relative to population, gross domestic product (GDP), or some other measure that can be used for comparison across countries. Standardizing the volume of trade in relation to GDP is common and indicates whether economic integration is growing faster than overall economic growth.

Chase-Dunn et al. (2000) employ a rigorous measure of trade flow to gauge the importance of international trade to national economies. When a country's annual imports increase at a faster rate than its GDP—showing that imports are more important than they were the previous year—it is considered an increase in globalization, regardless of the actual volume of trade (78). They derive a per capita measure by weighting the increase for each country by its population size. Then, the country level measures are averaged for a global measure of the density of international trade. This produces a very stringent measure of integration. Because this measure is so rigorous, there can be a high level of confidence that any patterns of trade flow that emerge in the data are significant. The pattern of trade flow provides a template to compare to fluctuations in other factors to determine which may facilitate or inhibit globalization. It also tests whether or not the contemporary period is a uniquely high period of economic globalization.

Using a sample of 24 countries, they found three cycles of increasing and decreasing trade flows over the last few centuries. This supports the WSP contention that economic integration is a centuries-long historical process in which the world system passes through phases of increasing and decreasing economic integration. Waves of increasing trade flows occurred in three periods.

Table 2.1   Waves of Economic Globalization Measured by Trade

Wave	Years of Rise	Years of Decline
One	1830–late 1880s	Late 1880s–1905
Two	1905–1929 (slight decline at WWI)	1929–1945
Three	1945–1995 and continuing 2009	

BOX 2.9   Consider This: Would a Decrease in Global Trade Mean an End of Globalization?

The recession that began in 2007 triggered attempts to stabilize the global economy. The direct impact on trade was delayed. 2008 was a peak year, but trade declined precipitously in 2009. It seems as though this turned out to be a temporary dip, as trade rose again in 2010. Regardless, trade flow is but one measure of economic integration. If trade flows decrease, but other forms of integration increase, there is no reason to say that globalization is decreasing. Although trade decreased, stock markets continued to fluctuate in tandem with one another. Convergence in policy occurred as countries responded first with stimulus packages and then instituted austerity plans in similar time frames.

In addition to the waves, three trends stand out.

The increase that began in 1945 has not abated.

There has been an overall trend of increasing trade flows from cycle to cycle. Each cycle has reached a higher peak than the ones before.

Economic integration climbs following WWII, reaches an historic high in 1975, and continues to grow.

Even with a number of statistical controls, these trends remained significant, indicating a genuine and significant increase in trade openness over time. Although the current cycle is unprecedented in its height, this study did not argue that it is of a whole new magnitude (Chase-Dunn et al. 2000, 89). This analysis ends in 1995. Global trade continued to climb until, jolted by the uncertainties of economic crisis, it declined 12.2% in 2009. Most of the decline, about 9.5%, was recovered in 2010, and growth in trade continued. This continuation might signify that the current phase of economic globalization may indeed be different, it may be—overall—an unstoppable upward trend or plateau.

Explaining Economic Waves and Trends

This study identified a number of factors related to increasing and decreasing economic globalization. Consider how they may be related to other forms of globalization.

Technology: Communication and Transportation. Falling costs and increasing speed of communication and transportation facilitate the expansion of trade. That does not mean that they caused expansions in trade.

(Continued)

(Continued)

Hegemonic Rise and Hegemonic Rivalry. When there is a dominant powerful country (hegemon), other countries are pretty much forced to play by the rules that they set. This creates a stable environment; trade is less risky, so it increases. In periods of hegemonic rivalry, the environment is unstable, and trade decreases. The first and third cycles found in the study were synchronized with cycles of hegemony. In the 19th century, Britain stabilized global conditions making cross-border trade less risky. In the period following WWII, the United States did. However, the middle wave of economic integration, at the turn of the 20th century, does not fit this pattern. Nor does the contemporary cycle, as discussed earlier; trade has continued to increase long after the presumed decline of U.S. hegemony in 1975.

Political Globalization. Economic globalization needs a sufficient degree of coercion or normative consensus, that is, a sufficient degree of political globalization. Political globalization is not the same as hegemony. Multilateral organizations can establish a predictable environment for trade, stabilizing the global order and providing conditions for sustained economic growth (Chase-Dunn et al. 2000, 93). The continuing rise in the wave of economic integration that began after WWII is exceptional. It may signal a new phase of globalization—or some theorists would argue the beginning of globalization—stabilized by a global political regime rather than hegemony.

Summary

Each of the theories and frameworks offers a valuable perspective on globalization. Some are more suited for the analysis of culture, some the economy, or some politics. On complex issues, such as global poverty, each provides insight on where to look for roots of the problem and prospects for overcoming it.

Beck's world risk perspective, Giddens' high modernity, Kellner's globalization from below, and Rodrik's feasible globalization all emphasize tensions and contradictions within the workings of the global system. World risk perspective highlights the thoughtless pursuit of progress through science, rationality, and industrialization—regardless of the consequences, one of which is poverty. Here is one example from agriculture. The unquestioned assumption that the products of science are better than those of traditional farming methods led to indiscriminate application of green revolution technologies. While they boosted production in some countries, they also destroyed croplands and people's livelihoods, made food more expensive, and exacerbated famine and poverty in others. Overcoming unquestioned assumptions is more difficult than it may seem. But from this perspective, it is the crux of solving global problems. Questioning hidden assumptions, recognizing common victimization, and acknowledging the common good are important to overcoming global poverty and other problems of globalization.

Giddens' concept of high modernity stresses that the world is riskier for everyone because our global systems are out of control and our institutions are failing. This is an important insight because it clearly shifts the burden of responsibility for poverty from poor individuals to social structures—education, job structures, factors that stress families to the point of breaking, and the supporting cultural assumptions about progress that are spreading globally. These problems extend well into the (shrinking) middle classes of developed societies. Solving poverty—or any problem for that matter requires global collaboration.

Douglas Kellner analyzes the tensions between economic and other aspects of social life. Technology replaces human labor, and the global economy robs people of their democratic rights. This leads to poverty and powerlessness. The answer to these according to Kellner is a new more rational politics.

World Systems Perspective (WSP) and Global Systems Theory (GST) focus squarely on economic systems and the benefits they reap for some while impoverishing others. WSP is a valuable guide to understanding how the legacy of subjugation through colonialism and the Cold War and continued domination through international organizations such as the UN and IMF impoverishes countries. But not everyone in poor societies is poor. Global systems theory focuses on the interactions among elites. GST provides insights as to how economic and political elites in all countries collude and through their power are able to influence governmental and international policy for their own benefit—putting their global class interest ahead of their national interests.

World society theory does not address global poverty directly. But it highlights that people have unequal access to global culture and thus cannot develop the capacity for global organization. Without organizing a community of interest to represent their interests to the global polity, little will be done to address their circumstance. A global regime to combat poverty has not been institutionalized through a body of international law and policies—despite extensive statements such as the Millennium Development Goals.

The global scapes of Arjun Appadurai provide analytical insight into how important cultural flows may bypass the poor or how they may be further impoverished by others. For example, the slow flow of technology (technoscapes) and liberal ideology (ideoscapes) to some countries and the contexts of colonialism, among others, help explain limited development. The flows of people (ethnoscapes) in and out of poorer countries—through brain drain, as many of the most talented leave and the influx of refugees from violent conflicts nearby—exacerbate poverty. How poverty is portrayed in the media (mediascapes) influences how people respond. If the poor are portrayed as lazy and irresponsible, there is less willingness to grant aid. If the structural constraints that are responsible for poverty are portrayed, aid flows more freely. This issue divided the EU in the debt crisis that began in 2009. Often, countries with debt crisis are portrayed in the media as spendthrifts and living off the public dole despite facts indicating that many countries with more generous social welfare spending are not in crisis. Thus, many people in other European countries are not willing to loan them more money (financescapes) and argue for more tougher austerity measures in debt-ridden countries, despite the lack of success of austerity in many countries.

Beth Simmons and Zachary Elkins analyze the mechanics of globalization. Their work illustrates the ways that societies converge on particular policies and model programs and the conditions under which they do this thoughtlessly or thoughtfully. Given that so many problems of our era are generated by the uncritical acceptance and pursuit of progress, this information is critical. Models that worked well in one context have deepened poverty in others. Alternate strategies for policy and program diffusion with better chances of success will grow out of this research. It addresses the concerns of many theorists who call for a more reflexive modernity, smarter globalization, or rational politics.

Last, the global field is a framework. It forces us to consider the processes that operate at all levels, from the individual to humanity, how globalization forces alter the field and the relations among the elements. It encourages us to consider how people think (the subjective dimension) about the situation of the poor and their responsibilities to the poor, the benefits they reap at the expense of the poor, and how these are structured in societal and global policies—part of the objective conditions that perpetuate poverty—such as the green revolution, the economic structure of societies, technological impoverishment, and the economic and political legacies of colonialism mentioned above.

BOX 2.10   A Closer Look: Major Propositions of Theories of Globalization

This table summarizes the main propositions of the theories of globalization discussed in this chapter.

Theory	Major or Representative Theorist(s)	Central Propositions, Focus, or Concepts
Global Scapes	Arjun Appadurai	Cultural flows: technoscapes, financescapes, ethnoscapes, mediascapes, ideoscapes circulate globally. As flows diffuse they change and are changed by local contexts through which they flow.

(Continued)

(Continued)

Theory	Major or Representative Theorist(s)	Central Propositions, Focus, or Concepts
World Risk Society	Ulrich Beck	The uncritical acceptance of science and pursuit of progress has led to a world characterized by incalculable risks. Globalization has exposed this and is leading to a new phase of modernity—reflexive modernity.
High Modernity	Anthony Giddens	Science and technology that were to make the world safer have made it more dangerous. Globalization has resulted in systems that are beyond anyone's control and institutions are failing to in important functions.
World Systems Perspective	Immanuel Wallerstein	A global capitalist economy organizes the world into core, semi-peripheral, and peripheral societies based on their position in the economy. Societies rise from below and fall from above in cycles.
Global Systems	Leslie Sklair	A global capitalist economy run by a transnational elite—the transnational capitalist class—dominates the global stage. Global systems exist independently of international systems and states.
Globalization From Below	Douglas Kellner	The contradictions among capitalism, technology, and democracy are wrought with tension and conflict. Globalization is spreading both capitalism and democracy but undermines democracy as it circulates it.
World Society	John Meyer	Cultural ideas and models diffuse globally through interaction and association—rather than state action. This forms a stateless world society based on the authority of the cultural models.
Feasible Globalization	Dani Rodrik	Incompatibilities among capitalism, democracy, and globalization prohibit having them all; only two of the three are feasible.
Mechanisms of Convergence	Beth Simmons and Zachery Elkins	Policies and programs diffuse through societies via a variety of mechanisms varying in their degree of reflection.
The Global Field	Roland Robertson and JoAnn Chirico	Globalization is processes through which the world becoming a single place. It has objective and subjective components. Globalization changes relationships among elements of the global field: individuals, societies, global systems, and humanity.

Questions, Investigations, and Resources

Questions

1. Debate: What are our responsibilities as members of humanity? Do they differ from our responsibilities as members of societies?

2. Which theoretical framework do you think will be most helpful in understanding globalization in general? What are its strengths in comparison to the other theories?

3. Compare and contrast theories that date globalization as a centuries-long phenomenon with those that view it as a break from the past and a new era. What does each emphasize that accounts for these differences?

Investigations

1. Investigate the history of an interest of yours. This could be a cultural interest, such as a musical or entertainment form, a religion, or a food. Do you think that it has globalized? If so, can you trace the path of its diffusion?

2. Investigate the economic position of countries using the World Trade Organization's 2008 report to consider the following questions.

   Do there appear to be sets of nations that comprise the core, periphery and semi-periphery? What criteria are you using to determine this?

   - Gross National Product?
   - Exports in goods and services per capita?
   - Share in manufactured goods by continent/region?

   http://www.wto.org/english/res_e/statis_e/its2008_e/its08_merch_trade_product_e.pdf

3. Investigate countries' patterns of production and trade. Go to Chart 1.5 on inter- and intra-regional trade. http://www.wto.org/english/res_e/statis_e/its2008_e/its08_world_trade_dev_e.pdf

   - Do poorer and richer regions depend on different types—inter-regional or intra-regional—of trade?
   - What type of industries do they house?
   - Is there an apparent tiered system or stratification among them that corresponds to their position in the exchange or value chain?

   http://www.wto.org/english/res_e/statis_e/its2008_e/its08_world_trade_dev_e.pdf

   Compare values of exports by country and region.

4. How pervasive is world society? This is likely to vary by the particular institution and the level of a country's integration into the globe.

   - Choose an institution of interest to you, such as education, health, sports, and so on. Chose two countries that rank far apart on the KOF index of globalization.

   2012 KOF Index of Globalization: Definitions and Sources: http://globalization.kof.ethz.ch/static/pdf/definitions_2012.pdf

   - Compare the institutional structures of the two countries. Which adheres most closely to the dominant global model? What criteria did you use to determine this? (The answer to this would indicate the criteria you used to determine the global model.)

Resources

Some of the theorists or theoretical schools mentioned here have websites with publications, their thoughts of the day, or even links to their twitter feeds.

Websites and Blogs

Immanuel Wallerstein http://www.iwallerstein.com/

Douglas Kellner http://pages.gseis.ucla.edu/faculty/kellner/

Dani Rodrik: http://rodrik.typepad.com/

Collections of Op-Eds (short newspaper articles on issues of the day)

Anthony Giddens in *The Guardian* http://www.guardian.co.uk/profile/anthonygiddens

Ulrich Beck in *The Guardian* http://www.guardian.co.uk/profile/ulrichbeck

Collections of Theory-Related Resources and Institutes for Studying Globalization

World Society Theory Resources http://worldpolity.wordpress.com/world-society-theory-resources/

Johns Hopkins Institute for Global Studies in Culture, Power, and History http://sites.jhu.edu/igs/

3

Setting the Stage

Foundations Globalization

Objectives

This chapter explains the foundations of the global economic, political, and cultural systems. It will help you

- analyze the diffusion of the nation-state from the Treaty of Westphalia to the wave of contemporary nation-state building;
- evaluate constitutions in relation to their conformity to global ideals of state structure, function, and the rights of citizens;
- assess the role of colonialism in shaping a global political and economic hierarchy of societies;
- evaluate the long-term impacts of colonialism and the Cold War on economic and political development;

- understand the emergence of global culture related to sovereignty, nationhood, human rights, constitutionalism, liberalism, and rationality;
- analyze the course of economic globalization from simple patterns of trade to early interdependence in production and markets;
- evaluate the relationship between political and economic liberalization;
- identify the influence of convergence on specific state forms and values in constitution; and
- assess early attempts of global governance related to the global system of states.

Globalization is the integration and interdependence among people across societies. In early stages of contact among societies, resources, products, and ideas were exchanged through trade and travel, but this did not constitute globalization. For example, cultural diffusion occurred regularly along the Silk Road as societies adopted material items and religious beliefs of other societies. This in itself is not globalization because the internal systems of one society were not dependent on the other, even though they were related. In contrast, the decline of religious authority and assertions of national sovereignty, the

influence of political and economic liberalization, establishment of colonies, homogenization of constitutions, and rationalization of institutional structures created conditions that facilitated interdependence and integration across societies, setting the stage for globalization. Even though the global system of states is one system among many systems, it is the foundation of globalization. It was based on the simple ideas of nation and sovereignty. As the system of nation-states came to blanket the world, the structural homogeneity of states, democratic ideals and various rights reflected in their constitutions, the necessity and capacity of capitalism for expansion, and the diffusion of ideas of liberalization, rationalization, and human rights integrated the world more and more tightly.

Although theorists of globalization differ on when globalization as a distinct process began, as discussed in the first and second chapters in detail, the foundations of economic and political globalization as presented in this chapter are important in understanding all of the dimensions and how the variety of theories apply to understanding the current state of the globe.

Waves of Nationhood

The Germinal Phase: The Treaty of Westphalia and the Principle of Sovereignty

A *community* is a group of people who have something in common. Traditionally, that has been a land that they share, from which they derive sustenance and a common set of values and rules that arose as they figured out how they would share the land and its resources to ensure their survival. As the interactions among small communities increased, their interdependence did as well. This enlarged their sense of community and from this grew the concept of a nation. Community remains the basis of a nation, a people who feel they share a common identity and belong together (Weber 1921/1978, 395–398). The idea of nation developed gradually as the way of identifying an "us."

In some respects, nations and states grew out of warfare. Europe experienced near continual warfare, from the Hundred Years War between France and Britain in the 14th century to the Thirty Years War that engulfed all of Europe in the 17th. These were a series of religious and political wars that devastated Europe for centuries. Weakened by its own corruption, the Holy Roman Empire disintegrated as the patchwork of princely dominions in Europe fought against the empire and one another for sovereignty, territory, and freedom. Through these wars, the nation became the protector of its people against the Empire and other nations. National identity became a locus of individual identity. As the wars raged, the idea of empire—one rule or ruler

for all of humankind faded; nationalism—the right of a group with a common heritage to govern itself—ascended.

The modern state and system of global governance arose from the rubble of these wars. By 1648, most European princes and kings were bankrupt by the expense of war. Many had already signed treaties with one another. They met in the Westphalia region of Germany to broker a peace. As a consequence of the Treaty (or Treaties) of Westphalia, secular political power was stripped from religious authorities. The Hapsburg and Roman Empires were diminished, and power was decentralized to ruling or newly elected monarchs. Rather than the empire dictating the official religion of a territory, monarchies gained control over religion within their borders. France and Sweden gained disputed territories. Religious membership became voluntary for most individuals, but state membership became mandatory. Trade and commercial activities usurped power from religious authority and to some extent also from the crown. Religious and political freedoms from empire were established, not for individuals, but for nations. In short, nations gained sovereignty. There was no longer any higher power on earth.

The Treaty of Westphalia gave shape to an association of states, each of which claimed sovereignty within its political boundaries and legitimacy based on the nation within. Sovereignty over a politically defined territory and the citizens within remains the defining characteristic of the modern nation-state (Mann 2003, 137). The Westphalia system of states established the following principles, the foundation of global governance of the time.

- States were all free and equal.
- There was no temporal authority higher than the state.
- States had ultimate authority over the conduct of their internal and external affairs.
- The capacity to exercise rule over a territory bestowed the right to rule—might makes right.
- Whoever gained or seized power had authority to act as the head of state and enter into agreements on behalf of the people, regardless of their constitutional standing.
- How a state maintained its power did not reflect on the state's legitimacy in the view of the world community.

- The activity of a state outside of its own boundaries and the treatment of individuals who were not citizens were not expected to conform to the same standards as a state's activity within its borders or the treatment of its own citizens.
- Groups and other non-state actors had no right to contest territorial borders (Held 2000, 162–163).

Although peace in Europe was not lasting, the Treaty of Westphalia established the principle of state sovereignty and the basis of global governance for centuries to come. Monarchs granted themselves and one another the authority to speak for, make commitments for, and sign treaties on behalf of the people they claimed to represent. In return, they obligated themselves to care for the common good, protecting people's security, economy, and other interests. States granted themselves a monopoly on the use of violence within their borders, and the right to use violence in protection of their people. Without the power to compel people to act, states could not make promises on the international stage. To facilitate international relations and guarantee sovereignty, whoever controlled power within a territory—regardless of how it was acquired—was recognized as the head of state. The state assumed an anthropomorphic character, as the primary actor on domestic and international fronts, providing constraints and opportunities for other, sub-state actors, and one another.

Nations invented state sovereignty to bring peace to Europe. Ironically, the treaty presented the first challenge to sovereignty as well. Recognition as a sovereign depends on recognition by other sovereigns. This always comes with conditions that limit sovereignty at the same time that it grants it. Minimally, "states are required to control their territory and be willing to participate in a system of international law" (Donnelley 2007, 250). This is the foundation of global governance and culture.

Expanding the System of States System to the Americas

Colonialism is the economic, political, and social domination of the people within a territory by another country. The mechanical revolution in Europe gave European states a competitive advantage to reach out and conquer people on other continents. At one time or another, Europeans, and in a more limited number of cases the Japanese, occupied or colonized nearly every bit of land on the globe. Whether colonialism was primarily economically motivated to secure resources, markets, and labor, or politically motivated to secure territory, subjects, and prestige, is an interesting debate. But regardless of which it was, colonialism served both purposes well.

After the treaty of Westphalia, the state model was transposed onto colonized lands. European states claimed land on other continents, drawing boundaries to mark their territory and exercise dominion. During the first wave of colonization (the Age of Exploration) French, English, Spanish, and Portuguese settlers migrated in large numbers, primarily to the Americas. In the Americas, the British treated North American indigenous populations as other sovereign states. Treaties were used to justify and legitimize land grabs from Native Americans. England negotiated treaties with Native Americans, although the treaties never granted equal benefits. The North American colonies and settlers prospered, setting up a plantation system based on slave labor in the South of North America and small farms and industries in the North.

South and Central America, colonized primarily by Spain, were also settler colonies, used primarily for their mineral and agricultural wealth. Rather than being isolated on reservations, indigenous populations were vital, although disempowered, actors in the new economies and polities. The Latin American colonies and southern colonies of North America were similar in critical ways. As in the Southern plantation system, rich landowners and landlords, usually colonists, maintained large landholdings using slave labor and poor tenant farmers. Also like the Southern United States, much of the agricultural product was for export and benefitted a small segment of the population. After independence, this pattern of colonialism on both continents gave way to landed aristocracy and the extreme inequality that persists today.

The distance between Europe and the Americas limited the degree to which the Americas were suitable as colonies. Separated from Europe by oceans, American colonists developed a life of their own and eventual independence in the late 18th and early to mid-19th centuries. This was the second wave of nation-state building. Independence for the colonists in the United States led to a democratic republic, a system of checks and balances among branches of government, and federal and state governments based on a constitution that has proved remarkably resilient for well over two hundred years. In South and Central America, autocracy and oligarchy replaced colonial governments. In most Latin American countries, democracy did not stabilize—often hampered by external interference—until relatively recently, in the 1980s and 1990s.

Colonization of Asia also began during this period, first with Russian incursions in the 16th century and Portuguese incursions in the 17th, followed by the Dutch, British, and French. The early colonization was very limited. Unlike their efforts in the Americas, European posts in Asia were means of facilitating and controlling trade, and were concentrated along the coasts. The Dutch East India Company, British East India Company, and French East India Company competed for control of the lucrative trade in Asian exotics, such as spices, silks, tea, porcelain, gems, and ivory. They were effectively the colonizers and administrators of their countries' colonies. The situation was similar, but more dastardly, in Africa. Europeans interest was primarily in establishing trading posts and routes; unfortunately, it was primarily for slave trade.

Aside from a few colonies in Africa in the 17th and 18th centuries, most notably the Dutch and then British in Cape Town and the Portuguese in Angola, the real colonization of Africa was not until the 1870s, coinciding with the colonial push inland into Asian countries. As the North and South American colonies gained independence and industrialization created a pressing need for resources and markets, competition among Europeans for territory in Africa and Asia—continents of diverse cultures, but few modern state borders—was fierce. The French, English, Portuguese, and Spanish were joined by Italian, Belgian, and Dutch powers, staking out territories and drawing political borders across the continents, ignoring the ethnic and religious identities and geographic boundaries that provided the basis for nationhood throughout Europe. (The USSR did the same as it moved through Central Asia and Eastern Europe in the 20th century.) Most of the colonies enclosed diverse cultures within the same arbitrarily drawn borders. Borders united disparate groups, binding them into a common political territory and bisected cultural groups, separating them into different political units. Border disputes remain today, pitting those who want a return to older, ethnically based areas against those who favor the colonial borders.

Ethiopia, one of the world's oldest nations, was never colonized. Iran, Japan, and parts of China are the only other countries outside of Europe who can make that claim. Liberia, colonized by free black Americans in 1822, was established as a republic in 1847. Ethiopia and Liberia were the only independent nations in Africa at the turn of the 19th century.

With few exceptions, such as Liberia and South Africa, the African and Asian colonies were not settler colonies. Relatively small contingents of administrators from the colonizing country ran government and commercial enterprises, often with the help of one faction of the indigenous population. As in South America, indigenous populations went to work for the benefit of the colonial powers. Only small contingents received educations and experience in business and government. Critical infrastructure for a developing society, such as transportation, communication, education, and sanitation was built to support the transfer of raw materials out of Africa, not to maintain a functioning society. Even India, which had a relatively large British administration,[1] could not be considered a settler colony, as most of the administrative and military support rotated through India, few settling and building a new life there.

This was strategic for the colonial powers and dysfunctional for indigenous peoples. Often, one cultural group, a numerical minority, was chosen for the higher status positions not filled by colonists. They served in the bureaucracy and reaped small share of the profits of colonialism, which represented considerable wealth in comparison to other groups. This was the situation in Rwanda. Hutu and Tutsi were stripped of their traditional livelihoods. The Tutsi, the smaller group numerically, administered the interests of the Belgians; they prospered and controlled most of the country's wealth. This bred resentment among other indigenous groups. Violence began even before the Belgians left Rwanda in 1962, but intensified after independence and the Hutu rise to power. The intransigent inequality and deep divide led ultimately to decades of violence, thousands of deaths, and the genocide of 1994, when over three quarters of a million people were killed in just over three months. Similar playing of one ethnic group against another, giving one privilege

BOX 3.1   A Closer Look: Ethnic Map of West Africa

The abundant ethic mix of Africa stands out in this map. Examine the borders of Nigeria, Ghana, and Cameroon, and you can see how ethnic borders were fractured. While the abundant diversity may prohibit mono-ethnic states, could borders have been drawn differently? This, in combination with unequal treatment of groups, resulted in conflict-ridden and tense political dynamics.

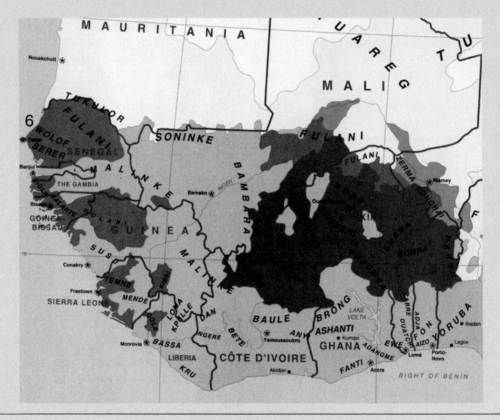

Source: Library of Congress.

over another, was common and left a legacy of ethnic divide and strife throughout Africa.

In 1945, over 750 million people were living in colonial or occupied territories. This was about one third of the world's population. Following WWII, colonization in Africa and South East Asia was not sustainable. Europe's and Japan's energies were occupied with rebuilding their countries. Furthermore, colonization violated the normative standards of the Universal Declaration of Human Rights. However, independence did not follow immediately on the heels of the war. In 1960, the UN General Assembly adopted the Declaration on the Granting of Independence to Colonial Countries and Peoples. This declares that "the subjection of peoples to alien subjugation, domination and exploitation constitutes a denial of fundamental human rights, is contrary to the United Nations Charter, and is an impediment to the promotion of world peace and cooperation" (UN 1960). In 1962, the UN established the Special Committee on Decolonization, and the rate of decolonization accelerated.

Independence movements, some peaceful and many others violent, secured the independence of most of the colonies through the mid-1960s into the 1970s. Left with environments ravaged by colonialism, the education of most populations neglected, severe ethnic and religious tensions, an infrastructure based on the export of a variety of agricultural crops and minerals, and weak or no democratic institutions, most colonies were unprepared for statehood or economic prosperity. Who could or would run the government and the industries? Who could lead the countries into the 21st century? Unfortunately, these questions were answered by continuing patterns of domination determined by the resource and strategic needs of richer countries.

Colonization created a politico-economic system that encircled the globe but was based on forceful domination. It was a system founded neither on normative grounds nor on anarchy among equal and sovereign nation-states. It established a legacy that forms the basis of the global economy by positioning some countries as sources of resources, cheap labor, and markets. It left a political legacy of weak governments run by oligarchies, monarchies, or dictators eager for the rewards that resource wealth and strategic alliances can bring.

Spreading the Nation-State East

Nationalism spread from Europe to the Ottoman Empire. Corruption of the sultanate and economic stagnation fueled nationalistic movements. Monarchies with bureaucratic structures, similar to those that had developed in Europe, evolved within the Ottoman areas of Eastern and Central Europe. Greece declared independence in 1821, but in most of the empire, nationalism did not assert itself until the latter part of the19th and early 20th centuries, marking the beginning of a third wave of nation-state building. The empire attempted to stave off rebellion by modernizing institutions, improving education, and introducing constitutional reforms to grant more autonomy and rights to various populations—modeling Western forms—but they were not enough to hold the empire together. Corrupt, incompetent, and ineffective rule had damaged the authority of the sultanate beyond repair.

Ethnic and religious uprisings among the countries of the empire, which had been gradually disengaging, led to their independence. The Balkan Wars and Russian and European incursions into the empire brought territorial losses and further loss of central control. Following WWI, the remainder of the Ottoman Empire collapsed and was divided as the spoils of war by Britain, France, and Russia. This exacerbated a nationalistic fervor in Turkey that diffused to the Middle Eastern countries.

Mustafa Kemal Ataturk, inspired by ideals of sovereignty and democracy, led the Turkish war for independence from 1919 to 1923. Although Turkey was, and is, Islamic, Ataturk modeled Turkey after the secular European state, encouraging Western-style education, dress, and other ways of life. In other parts of the former empire, such as Egypt and Iran, nationalistic fervor was accelerated by foreign domination. Most other Middle Eastern countries remained under European rule until mid-century.

Diffusion of the nation-state form from West to East stopped at the Chinese border. Although China nominally adopted the nation-state form in the early 20th century and a capitalist economy in the latter part of the 20th, the tradition of empire continues. The Chinese state acts much like an emperor. The government has a very active role in directing economic life, controlling political life, and to a somewhat lesser extent, it also controls religious life. Japan did not adopt a state form until after World War II. Following its defeat, Japanese development was controlled by the West. Then, Japan adopted the state form with a constitution that was largely a work of Western design and a Western economic system.

Early Waves of Economic Globalization

The Silk Road Into the Middle Ages

Economic systems produce and distribute the goods and services people need for survival and to improve the quality of their lives. This has always involved exchange among people within and among societies. Trade can be important for survival. If one person experiences drought and a neighbor experiences plenty, exchange may mean the difference between life and death, providing the person in need has something to trade, money to buy what is needed, credit, or the ability to appeal to the other's humanitarian impulses. Trade over national borders can improve the quality of life by making goods available that are not produced domestically or are available at a lower cost/higher quality.

Trade among societies is ancient. The Silk Road encompassed nearly all the world known to those who traveled it. For close to 2,000 years, from ancient times into the 16th century, it connected Asia, the Middle East, and Europe first by land and later by land and sea. Trade was extensive, extending into Africa as well. Some theorists date globalization to that era. Societies that traded along the Silk Road were not highly interdependent economically, but cultural diffusion was high.

During this period, goods flowed primarily from East to West. Asia—China and India in particular—had developed export economies producing large quantities of artisan goods. Textiles, ceramics, glass, mechanical clocks, paper, gunpowder, compasses, and much more were eagerly sought by Europeans. Asia's agricultural surplus was also valuable to Europe. By some accounts, Asia was producing upward of three quarters of the world's gross national product (GNP), with only about two thirds of the population (Frank 1998, 171, 126–127).

In the Middle Ages, trade expanded rapidly, and nations signed treaties of commerce to make trade more secure. Military exploits expanded feudal territories and enriched aristocracies, but the feudal economic system itself did not encourage or require globalization because feudal systems are self-sustaining economically. Serfs worked the lands owned by the nobility and grew produce for their lords and for their own families. Aristocrats increased their wealth by expanding their territories and raising taxes on serfs and townspeople. It was the unraveling of the feudal system and growth of capitalism that propelled economic globalization. Ever-increasing taxation of serfs, merchants, and artisans ultimately led each to rebellion. Many serfs left the countryside for cities where they became wage laborers. Others bought or rented land to farm. At the same time, towns had grown in influence as merchants gained wealth, artisans organized into guilds, and both protested the taxations imposed by aristocracies. In some cases, new towns sprung up, independent of any nobility and others aligned with the monarchy directly, eliminating the nobility as a middle layer. Contractual labor began to replace obligatory, forced labor. Farm workers, now working for themselves rather than the aristocracy, brought excess produce to market. Money, rather than land, became the source of wealth.

BOX 3.2   A Closer Look: Oil and Coffee

The modern economy runs on oil. It is the most traded commodity. Many a modern person runs on coffee. "Wake- up products," chocolate, coffee, and tea, became increasingly popular during industrialization. Coffee is now the second most traded commodity. The story of coffee on the world market is as intriguing as oil's. It demonstrates how global forces create micro effects. In this case, how you can enjoy a cheap cup of coffee, but at the expense of an agricultural worker.

In 2000, coffee prices fell, pushing hundreds of thousands of small farmers and agricultural workers in Latin America out of business. The entry of Vietnam into the coffee market is at the crux of the downfall. Although its coffee production had been increasing slowly though out the 1990s, Vietnamese coffee production tripled from 1995 to 2000. This flood of coffee dramatically lowered prices of coffee for the 50 countries whose economies depend on coffee exports. Thousands of agricultural workers in other coffee-growing countries were displaced, filling refugee camps.

Although the World Bank has been accused of causing the drop in prices by offering loans for coffee production in Vietnam, there were other forces at work. State loans for coffee preceded the World Bank's. International financial markets determined coffee prices rather than allowing them to be regulated by the Association of Coffee Producing Countries (ACPC). Competition by multinational corporations to get cheap coffee to market resulted in expansion of low-grade coffee cultivation. Farmers overproduced and oversold to pay off their debt. The Vietnamese government endorsed the expansion of deregulation and commercialization in the industry (Greenfield 2004).

Expansion of Mercantile Capitalism

Although many ancient and medieval traders got very rich, the advent of capitalism changed the nature of trade and the nature of globalization. In a capitalist system, it is the obligation of a corporation to make a profit for shareholders. Striving to maximize profit is more than an objective; it is an ethic. Profit accumulation is the goal of every phase of a capitalist enterprise. The first multinational corporations were the Dutch and British East India Companies. In 1600, the British East India Company formed from a coalition of smaller British spice traders. Their intent was to establish a monopoly and drive the Dutch—who had fought the Portuguese for the spice trade—out of business. The Dutch responded by forming the Dutch East India Company two years later. It was the first company to issue stock. Its charter gave it a monopoly and the capacity to coin money, establish colonies, and generally do what was needed to maximize profit, including wage war. Trade routes became militarized. The British East India Company followed suit, acquiring the same powers and a very privileged position in the British economy. The Dutch and British East India Companies are examples of merchant capitalism. The capitalist dimension of their enterprises, aside from a few factories, was limited to trade. The Atlantic, the Mediterranean, and the Indian Ocean connected in a complex web of commodity trading and currency flows financed by merchants and bankers and under the protection of their states.

The quest for new forms of profit was critical to the expansion of capitalism. With extensive colonization, industrialization, and urbanization, the quest for profit could be applied more extensively in economic processes. New ways of generating profit by reducing costs became possible. There are many strategies and techniques to reduce production costs: acquire resources as cheaply as possible, find cheap labor, and locate where taxes are low and laws lax. The search for greater profits sent corporations all over the world. As they expanded, the global capitalist system expanded with them. It expanded over more territory and more phases of the economic system—acquiring resources, buying labor, constructing factories, transporting goods, trade, and securing investment capital. The expansion and integration of economies into a global capitalist economy took centuries, occurring in waves, sometimes increasing in intensity of interaction and integration and decreasing at other times.

The Colonial Wave: Planting the Seed of the Global Economy, 1500s to 1860s

Until the 18th century, every country was pretty much the same: poor and agrarian (Blinder 2006). Cultural and economic factors coalesced to make the colonial period a turning point. With respect to the economy, the capitalist economy began its global expansion in this era. With respect to culture, the era spread both Enlightenment ideals and rational thought. Societies that developed rationalized social structures, including fleets of ships (helped along with compass technology of the Chinese), strong militaries (helped along by the gunpowder invented by the Chinese), and state bureaucracies to support them were more able to explore and conquer territories throughout large swaths of the globe. They found new and fertile lands to settle, plentiful resources, cheap labor, and new markets.

The legacy of colonial systems has been long lived, influencing economic development and the position of societies in the global economy to this day. European immigrants with varying motivations rushed to populate and settle the colonies in the Americas, some to escape their nation and some in the name of it. The sparse population, richness of resources, and clemency of weather made these lands amenable as settler colonies. Patterns of settlements varied. South America and the Caribbean were suitable for large-scale production of cash crops. Plantation systems developed using African slaves. This established land inequality well above the world norms and is reflected in high levels inequality today. Similar dynamics, stemming from the plantation system, slavery, and historic inequalities, have persisted in the southern states of the United States. The northern states, with conditions not as favorable to producing large cash crops via cheap indigenous or slave labor, adopted an agricultural system of small landowners and relied on more favorable distributions of land to attract more immigration. It remains more equal today.

Maintaining the Americas as colonies was difficult. Distance was one problem; another arose because they were primarily settler colonies, and settlers—particularly in the British colonies of North America—were infused with ideas of the rights of man. The American colonies achieved political independence in the late 18th century and first decades of the 19th. By then, the Industrial Revolution was well underway. As industrialization increased, European populations grew, rivalry among European nations intensified, and the demand for food and greater variety of raw materials reached unprecedented levels very quickly (Wells 1920/1956, 804). Demand, along with improvements in transportation and the emergence of international finance capital, doubled international trade from 1870 and 1890, despite adoption of protectionist policies by many European nations (Topik 2005, 3–4).

Europe turned to the Americas to feed its demand. The Americas helped by supplying agricultural and other exports. Europe's need made the plantations particularly valuable and further solidified the power of familial and multinational oligarchies. "The republics of South America, particularly the Argentine Republic began to feel in their cattle trade and coffee growing, the nearness of the European market" (Wells 1920/1956, 804). Brazil expanded trade, becoming Britain's third largest trading partner and the largest in the Americas. Its vast resources were undoubtedly a factor, but more important was the strength of the Brazilian state, which invested heavily in building rail transport and attracting foreign investment (Topik 2005, 15). Brazil dominated two of the hottest commodities of the era, supplying 90% of rubber and half of the world's coffee (24). This was the golden age of Latin America. Unfortunately, some Latin American societies became little more than indirect colonies, too reliant on European trade.

Despite successes, the legacy of colonial oligarchy and slavery in Brazil is at least in part responsible for the prolonged impoverishment of parts of the population and the persistence of great inequality. The colonial legacy of land inequality and subjugation of African and indigenous populations impeded the progress of other Latin American societies, as well as the U.S. South. Sixteen of the 20 most unequal land distributions are Latin American countries. These early and extraordinary amounts of land inequalities have had a lasting legacy in the distribution of non-land assets as well. Public investment in education, for example, runs counter to the interests of land-owning elites. It was in their interest to oppose, not facilitate expansion of public education (Frankema 2006, 8, 15–18). This maintains power but impedes further development. This also is similar to the U.S. Southern plantation states.

Independence in the Americas and the need for materials and markets sent Europeans on land grabs in Africa and Asia. One quarter of the land on earth was distributed or redistributed among the European powers between 1876 and 1915. In Africa, as in North America, a variety of patterns of colonization emerged. Eastern and southern African countries—Kenya, Tanzania, Zambia, Zimbabwe, Namibia, and South Africa—were suitable for cash crops and plantations. They developed high levels of land inequality. They remain very unequal. Central and West Africa, Uganda, Ghana, Sierra Leone, Togo, and Burkina Faso had lower than average land inequality. This region remains relatively equal (Frankema 2010, 427). Most of Northern Africa measured high in land inequality during colonialism and remains unequal (Frankema 2006, 9).

However, much of Africa, in contrast to North and South America, did not present conditions attractive for settlers, large plantations, and cash crops. But there was still money to be made in these colonies.

> In these areas colonists did not intervene directly into the production process but concentrated their rent seeking [seeking money through exploitation or manipulation rather than by adding any value by your own work] efforts on collecting taxes, engaging in the trade and exploitation of natural resource. (Frankema 2006, 17)

The elite class did not develop in the agricultural sector with large powerful landowners. It developed in the urban institutional bureaucracy, through seizing political power to tax and control trade in resources. The urban class grew wealthy at the expense of the rural.

In these cases, the bureaucratic apparatus of administration generated inequality. Small groups were paid well to manage enterprises and maintain a military presence for the colonizing country. They became an extremely wealthy and powerful elite class. Often, ethnic, religious, or tribal lines were exploited by colonizers to divide indigenous populations, one group being chosen to manage the colony and the other(s) to work it. This also explains the somewhat better fate of colonies that were plantations than those that were rent-seeking bureaucracies. Where elites depended on control of the bureaucracy for wealth and power, they have been less willing to give up control and are willing to bear the costs of violent oppression and armed conflict to maintain their power. Their income derives exclusively from coercive political power (Frankema 2006, 16). We are witness to this legacy in the extreme oppression and violent ethnic conflict in Africa today.

In Asian colonies, Europeans were joined in imperialism by Russia, Japan, and the United States. However, on independence, some achieved dramatic success in little time. The Asian Tigers surpassed colonies of Latin America and Africa in development. First among them to develop were the former Japanese colonies of South Korea and Taiwan, and the former British colonies of Hong Kong and Singapore. These Asian societies are now among the most equal societies, known for having distributed the benefits of growth among classes.

What explains their success? Family structure (extended), work values (hard), and sense of purpose (persistence) were critical. But so was their colonial experience with Japan. In cases such as Taiwan, land redistribution under Japanese rule dismantled the power of landed elites. As a whole, the Asian regions—East, South, and Southeast—have land inequality averages well below American and African averages. The maximum degree of land inequality in East Asia is well below the minimum of those regions. While Japanese colonialism was extraordinarily cruel, it brought benefits of modernization, such as schools, railroads, and ports, to its colonies along with the tyranny (Landes 1999, 437, see footnote 23 also). The British also built infrastructure, and those colonies were in better position, through education and administrative training, to expand and maintain the infrastructure, rather than wear it to ruin (434, 438). Economic reforms instituted after WWII, and the geopolitical position of Asian societies during the Cold War bore significantly on their growth. These are discussed later in the chapter.

Interestingly, colonialism accomplished a reversal of fortunes among lands colonized by Europeans. Many of the wealthier territories that were colonized are among the poorest today, whereas those that were poorer at the time of colonization are now wealthier. Indonesia, Brazil, Mexico, and India were all wealthier than the United States in 1700. By 1820, the United States had surpassed them in wealth (Acemoglu, Johnson, and Robinson 2002, 1256). The reversal of fortune thesis is related to the theory of land distribution. A country's current prosperity reflects the types of institutions established during colonization.

BOX 3.3   Check It Out Yourself: Colonization, Independence, and GNP

For a quick idea of how colonization played a role in establishing a baseline for a country's economic health, analyze the relationship between colonization and GNP. Graph the countries of Africa, Southeast Asia, and Latin and South America by date of their independence and their GNP. What does your graph look like? The correlation will not be perfect, but does it appear that more recent dates of independence are associated with lower GNP? What about the outliers? Discovering the ways that outliers have achieved growth may shed light on reducing poverty in the poorest countries.

- Societies that were wealthier and more densely populated had large populations that supplied labor for agriculture and mining. They could also be taxed. These societies developed sophisticated institutions that concentrated power and wealth. European settlers, rather than disturb the system, appropriated it and used it to enrich themselves. This left a legacy in which only a small elite had property rights. This is similar to the legacy of the plantation system and mining in South America and Africa.

- Where societies were less densely populated, many colonizers settled. In these cases, property rights were spread through the society. Institutions that protected the property rights of individuals encouraged entrepreneurship and investment. Policies that granted few rights for most of the population discouraged them. They are both essential for industrialization; the first significant opportunity for societies to enrich themselves. (Acemoglu et al. 2002, 1235–1236, 1279)

A second chance for enrichment emerged following WWII, as industrialization moved from developed to developing societies. A third opportunity arose following the Cold War for those countries able to attract and develop service industries. The Asian Tigers, along with a few other South and East Asian societies such as Indonesia, Thailand, and Malaysia, were able to seize service opportunities as well.

Land distribution and institutional policies are only part of the story. The factors that lead to success for former colonies are complex and involve economic, cultural, and political dynamics, along with population growth and density, international relations, protectionism, international aid, geographic location, access to trade, and human and natural resources. Analyzing the combinations that result in prosperity is critical in determining the most promising paths for globalization. We'll explore some of those in the chapters that follow.

BOX 3.4   A Closer Look: Kennedy at the Berlin Wall

On June 26, 1963, President John F. Kennedy delivered a speech that electrified an adoring crowd gathered in the shadow of the Berlin Wall. As he paid tribute to the spirit of Berliners and to their quest for freedom, the crowd roared with approval on hearing the president's dramatic pronouncement, "Ich bin ein Berliner" (I am a Berliner). The Berlin Wall came down on November 9, 1989, a fitting marker for the end of the Cold War.

Neo-Colonialism and Cold War Strategic Advantage

As colonization was winding down, the Cold War was heating up. Competition between the United States, the USSR, and their allies shaped global geopolitics and economics through the making and breaking of strategic alliances. Decolonization pitted the United States against the USSR in a contest for the hearts, minds, and allegiance of the newly independent nations. In Latin America and in countries that had avoided becoming colonies, such as China, Iran, Ethiopia, and Afghanistan, the Cold War polarized efforts at political, economic, and social change (Painter 2007, 3). In exchange for an alliance with one of the superpowers, the leaders of a nation could expect to reap economic and political benefit.

For the leaders of states, the benefits included financial favor and military support. Many dictators grew wealthy at the expense of their countries and were able to maintain their wealth and position by building powerful militaries. In return for promise of alliance, governments received loans with which they build strong militaries to maintain their oligarchy and lavish lifestyles, exacerbating poverty and inequality within many countries, such as Pakistan, Indonesia, South Africa, Zaire (now Democratic Republic of the Congo), Chile, Argentina, and so on.

The benefits for the Soviet Union and United States ranged from locations for military bases and warheads, to access to valuable raw materials and markets for manufactured goods, and allegiance of a capitalist or socialist economy. Among the most traded goods were arms. The global powers made money by selling dictators arms with which they built strong militaries to protect themselves from rebellion. For decades, the main suppliers of arms to the developing countries have included the permanent members of the UN Security Council, Russia (USSR #1), the United States (#2), the United Kingdom (#3), France (#4), and China (#7) (SIPRI 2010).

Economies throughout South America, Southeast Asia, Latin America, and Africa grew skewed to the export of primary resources and low value-added manufacturing and the import of many foods and higher cost manufactured goods. International financial activity, including direct loans from the Soviet Union, Cuba, the United States, other developed nations, and international financial organizations, facilitated this. Although the World Bank and IMF are declared politically neutral, loans tended to go to countries where significant international capitalist interest was at stake or that were nudging toward political alliance with the United States (Thacker 1999, 46–47). Through these means, the Cold War was responsible for much of the onerous debt accumulated by developing nations (Stiglitz 2006). Third World debt grew to enormous proportions paying for ill-conceived and poorly executed programs and enterprises, arms purchases, and outright cronyism.

BOX 3.5   A Closer Look: Revolutionary Hero

Augusto Cesar Sandino was a revolutionary who tried to throw the United States out of Nicaragua in the 1920s. His name and legacy was claimed 40 years later in 1961 by the Sandinista who fought the dictatorship of Anastasio Somoza DeBayle, a Cold War ally of the United States. Their revolution succeeded in 1979. Images of Sandino, such as this urban art, are plentiful in Nicaragua.

Although called the "Cold" War, real wars were fought by proxy throughout the world. In countries such as Nicaragua and El Salvador, the United States and USSR supported revolutionary movements of the left (socialist or communist) as they tried to overturn dictators of the right (capitalist) and counter-revolutionary movements of the right fought to overturn dictators of the left. Western powers justified their support of dictators by arguing that the stability supplied by a dictator facilitated economic development and that democratic institutions could be encouraged and built gradually. More important, however, was the strategic argument. The United States needed a country to be anti-communist. Communism threatened the power and access to cheap resources that the Western world enjoyed. The USSR used similar strategies to their advantage.

Occasionally, democratic leaders were deposed or assassinated, elections overturned or rigged. Britain and the United States, for example, toppled or assisted in toppling democratically elected governments such as those in Iran and Chile, in favor of dictators more friendly to the West. There are still some scholars who maintain that Pinochet of Chile, one of the cruelest dictators, paved the way toward progress. However, the atrocities through which it was accomplished and the complicity of the superpowers and their allies implicates high-income countries in his crimes against humanity, and others perpetrated against the people of many low-income countries.

In cases such as Korea and Vietnam, competition between the Soviet Union and the United States took the form of civil war, north against south. South Korea is now democratic and a separate country from communist North Korea. South Korea, home of Hyundai, Samsung, and Daewoo, was one of the original Asian Tigers, rising from being one of the poorest countries after WWII to one of the wealthiest by the 1970s. South Vietnam lost its war with North Vietnam and was brought under communist rule. Although still poor, Vietnam instituted economic reforms in the 1990s, diversifying and liberalizing its economy with a flood of foreign investment. It is considered a "baby tiger," one among a larger group of newly industrializing Southeast Asian nations.

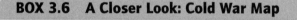

BOX 3.6   A Closer Look: Cold War Map

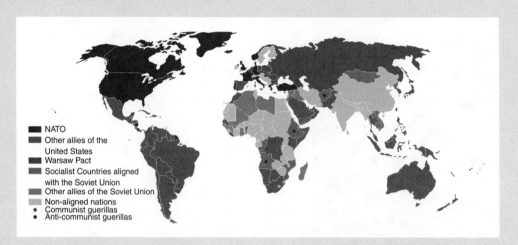

Although many countries switched allegiance through the course of the Cold War, this map is a snapshot of the scope of the allies of the United States and USSR, the major domestic guerilla movements fighting against them, and the non-aligned movement.

Source: Aivazovsky (2008).

During the Cold War, many of the newly independent states were held together, as in the colonial period, by military might and foreign support rather than shared identity based on ideals or heritage. The epidemic of failed and failing states and the proliferation of new states since the end of the Cold War highlight their fragility.

Recognizing the vulnerability of the new states to the power plays of the Cold War, India, Egypt, and Yugoslavia led a movement of non-aligned nations. While membership in the non-aligned movement grew during the Cold War, many of the member states were engaged in conflict with one another, and others did align with one of the power blocs. The non-aligned movement never achieved the status of the super-power blocs or formed a significant counterweight to them. The attempts of the non-aligned movement to strengthen states from the 1960s through the end of the Cold War were, however, early globalization effects. The original goal of the non-aligned movement, to achieve universal human rights through sovereign states (despite some of these being multi-ethnic, such as Yugoslavia and India), has become mainstream, as Kofi Annan emphasized in a speech celebrating their partnering with the UN (UNIS 2006).

A 1985 CATO Institute publication called the U.S. government to task for its Cold War strategy by invoking American's self-image as a model of democracy for the world. While the Truman doctrine of

1947 promised to protect and defend free people fighting subjugation by communism—even against armed insurrection—the United States eventually protected any non-communist regime, in Latin America, Africa, Southeast Asia, and the Middle East, regardless of how morally repugnant they were. Ultimately, this policy worked against U.S. security interests and seriously damaged U.S. influence.

This brief review of colonialism and the Cold War highlights the development of the global economic and political systems leading into the contemporary period of globalization. The Westphalian ideal of equality of states and of non-interference was far removed from the political realities of hegemony and forceful domination. The stability (not peaceful) of international governance was disrupted by the end of the Cold War and increasing demands for democracy, sovereignty, and human rights. However, the conditions for instability of the global system of states were firmly in place: the emergence of weak states with weak economies and deep ethnic divides, along with food insecurity; environmental destruction; population overload; inadequate educational, medical, or democratic infrastructure; and other risks to human security. The Cold War made decolonization more difficult and forestalled development in many countries. Consequentially, the United States damaged its reputation by sacrificing the principles of democracy in its Third World activities (Stiglitz 2002, 25).

A new, fifth wave of nation building began following the dissolution of the Soviet Union, Yugoslavia, and Warsaw Pact in the 1990s.

In each phase, the state system blanketed more of humanity, and the world moved closer to integration as a global system of societies. Blanketing the globe with nation-state forms was arguably the first achievement of political globalization. The number of states continues to expand in the 21st century as some nations within states demarcate boundaries, claiming sovereignty and autonomy. Nation building is an important globalization process, putting nations on a more equal footing as they acquire the recognition and capability to interact with autonomy on the global scene. The global emphasis on human rights—rights owed to everyone on the globe because they are part of humanity—conditions people to demand greater autonomy and self-determination—a state for every nation.

Globalization processes make national identity and self-rule taken-for-granted rights. The ideal typical nation-state guarantees sovereignty for a people who share a common identity and live in a bounded territory. The revival of nationalist fervor within ethno-national groups is also a globalization effect. Nationalist movements arise in response to the challenges that global economic, corporate, cultural, and possibly even civil society and other global systems pose to their autonomy and sovereignty. Nationalism in these cases is an attempt to reestablish boundaries to protect identity and protect or gain self determination.

In 1990, there were over 800 ethno-nationalist movements (Scholte 2000, 167). Some operate within one state's boundaries. Others, such as the

Table 3.1 The Contemporary Period of Nation Building

Waves of Nation Building		
	Dates	**Event**
First	1648	Treaty of Westphalia
Second	Late 18th–19th century	Independence of American colonies
Third	Late 19th–20th century	Fall of Russian and Ottoman empires
Fourth	Post-WWII	Independence of African and Asian colonies
Fifth	1990–present	Dissolution of USSR and dissolution of Warsaw Pact; separatist movements worldwide

Kurds or Roma, exist across boundaries of several states. Many ethno-nationalist movements are demanding and fighting for a "state" and a homeland of their own; others may be fighting for more autonomy within existing states, or just equal rights within the state. In most cases, these groups are indigenous people living as oppressed minorities within their native lands.

Some of these groups have been successful. Status as a state still depends on recognition by other states. This is granted individually by each state—and not every self-declared state is recognized by every other state. Membership in the UN acknowledges the legitimacy of the nation-state form, as well as granting the closest thing there is to a seal of approval on the legitimacy of a new nation-states.

BOX 3.7   A Closer Look: Two Faces of Nationalism

There are two types of nationalism: nationalism based on ideas and ideals and nationalism based on labels (Kaldor 2003). When cast in terms of human rights or democratic values, nationalism is liberating. Human rights are the arbiter of legitimate and non-legitimate states and governments. All states are strengthened by assertions that sovereignty is a fundamental human right. In cases such as Timor-Leste, whose decades-long demand for independence cost from 100,000 to 250,000 lives out of a population of just over 1 million, the support and approval received from the global community with respect to their right to self-rule and their recognition as a state by the UN in 2002 institutionalizes global norms concerning sovereignty.

When nationalism is merely a form of labeling "us" and "them," it is destructive and intolerant. Confrontation with universalizing perceptions regarding humanity has unfortunately exacerbated "tribalism." In the last decades, the world has persisted in an intense and bloody era of nation building. One of the tragedies of our time has been the oppression and violence practiced by nationalist movements who "make claims to political power based on an ethnic label which excludes and is indeed hostile toward others with different label" (Kaldor 2003, 97). Their only concern is political power. Genocides in Cambodia, Bosnia, Rwanda, and the Sudan, and violence against ethnic minorities throughout Europe, Asia, Africa, and the Americas, are the result of the latter, labeling, form of nationalism.

Membership in the UN swelled from just 51 when it was founded following WWII to 192 in 2006 when Montenegro was admitted (UN 2006). Nations were added in waves as colonies gained independence in the 1960s and 1970s and with the breakup of the Soviet Union, Czechoslovakia, and Yugoslavia in the 1990s. Others wrested independence through decades of violent conflict. Regardless of these differences, each of these states confronts similar problems of identity and governance in combining nation and state.

Even though the nation-state form has diffused globally, political equality on the global stage, a centerpiece of the Westphalia system, has never been achieved. As discussed earlier, Cold War strategizing of the super powers and collusion between local elites and global capital effectively controlled many states. Intergovernmental organizations, such as the UN Security Council, the IMF, and World Bank, can maintain the patterns of inequality.

A sense of common interest and of belonging to a common people within a bounded territory has also been difficult to achieve. Inequality within societies based on race, ethnicity, sect, remnants of caste, and other distinctions of assigned identity often prevent a common identity from developing. Many state boundaries, formerly colonial boundaries, continue to defy the idea of nation by dividing national groups across state boundaries and combining others into unequal power relations within states.

Shaping the Modern State

Expectations for the internal shape and dynamics of the modern state developed from the Treaty of Westphalia. It ended the religious and nationalistic wars of Europe and established boundaries through Europe defining the territorial limits of monarchs' powers.

The need for states to act and interact on the international stage influenced the development of similar state structures. States assumed similar institutional matrices, becoming increasingly rationalized and formalized (Weber 1921/1978, 905) as they evolved. With increasing size and complexity, and as knowledge of specialized functions developed, state affairs became increasingly bureaucratized and administered by "professionals." Power was rationalized and divided among administrative, legislative, and judicial offices, which became functionally specialized. Ministers of foreign affairs and secretaries of state became necessary posts for the conduct the business of the state in the global arena. Treasuries, judiciaries, parliaments, and congresses were institutionalized as state forms. Armies became professionalized, requiring a broader base of taxation to arm, and soldiers were no longer expected to carry their own muskets and ride their own horses into battle. States and sub-state institutions developed in tandem, adapting and conforming to the proper model of "actorhood" (Meyer 2000, 45).

Following WWII, recognition by the UN became the seal of approval of statehood. Becoming a state requires conforming to a set of structural norms: A constitution, a head of state, various secretaries or ministers of administrative departments, a parliament or congress, and a judiciary remain the vehicles of statehood. Adopting these structures of government conforms to global norms for external legitimacy and creates parallel channels for societies to conduct international relations. Foreign secretaries or secretaries of state deal with one another. Secretaries of the treasury, defense, commerce, and so on meet with their counterparts from other countries, facilitating dialog among states.

The regulatory powers of the states—essential to the conduct of interstate relations—were strengthened over the course of the centuries following Westphalia. As ideas related to sovereignty gained normative power, states had to legitimize their right to govern through their relationship to their people. In the case of authoritarian regimes, the state claims to *embody* the people. In the case of liberal democracies, the state *represents* the people (Mann 2003, 137).

States and Human Rights Concerns

Among the global expectations of a state are the link between nation and state, the state's responsibilities to its people, the rights due people within states, structures of government, and legitimate forms of governance. In the 17th century, at about the same time that states were emerging from the aftermath of the Thirty and Eighty Years Wars, John Locke, a British philosopher, was expounding on natural rights. His rhetoric, along with that of other social and political philosophers, began to define the expectations of the role of a state. Locke argued that human rights are natural rights, rights that people have as God's creation regardless of their station in life, the country in which they live, the creed they profess, or any other social factor. People have the natural right to anything that God gave them—life, which requires liberty, health, and any property derived from and necessary for one's labor. No one may take any of those away. People thus acquire the obligation to respect the natural rights of others. The duty of government follows from this: to protect and enforce natural rights.

Locke's philosophy provided the basis for rights as they came to be understood during the period of the revolutions of the 18th century. The recognition of human rights unfolded in phases influenced by local culture and events of the times. In the United States' *Declaration of Independence* and France's *Declaration of the Rights of Man and Citizen*, universal human rights are said to be inalienable and adhere to every person, by virtue of their humanity. However, at the time of the American and French revolutions, rights were largely associated with protecting property and voting. Rights for "all" referred in many states, as well as states within the United States, to property owners. It was well into the 19th century before slavery was abolished and universal male suffrage was achieved. It was into the 20th before women got the right to vote in most countries.[2]

The first generation of rights established the protections of the individual from power of the state—such as protection from abuse, oppression, cruel and unusual punishment—and freedoms for individuals—such as freedom of the press, assembly, and religion. The second-generation rights assure protections to particular groups such as women, minorities, and the elderly. Second-generation rights provide for things such as the right to health care, social security, and education. During the post-WWII period and following the 1968 cultural and political upheavals of the global civil rights movements, many of these rights were institutionalized

(Smith 2008, 1820–1821). Still, they remain elusive in many countries for many people.

The Evolution of Constitutions

Constitutions institutionalized the powers and responsibilities of states and of citizens. Toward the end of the 18th century, ideas of sovereignty, liberalization, the power of reason, and the rights of humankind combined to form the constitutional state in Europe. The potentially unbridled powers of monarchies seen in light of these ideas ignited democratic aspirations. Constitutions were the way to institutionalize these ideals. Movements demanding rule of law, a constitution, and perhaps even democracy, arose. These afforded opportunity to wrest authority from the aristocracy.

While democracy as a governmental form was poorly defined at that time, people understood what a "democrat" was: it was an anti-aristocrat (Markoff 1999, 664). A constitution was the tool a democrat could use to rein in the unbounded authority exercised by monarchs.[3] The constitutional state became the counterweight to the power of monarchy. Constitutions replace traditional authority with legal-rational authority. Traditional monarchies give way to constitutional monarchies, presidents, and prime ministers. Rulers, their powers defined by law, became office holders, not simply power wielders.

The U.S. Constitution was the first to be enacted. Poland quickly followed, each country building on its own tradition and heritage. The U.S. Constitution reflected the U.S. tradition of local democracy. In Poland, where monarchs were elected, the legislature negotiated the powers of government with each ruler. France and its satellite states followed. In 1805, Haiti became the second American state to write a constitution after declaring its independence from France. Haiti's constitution became an important model for Latin American nations, as they subsequently wrought independence from Spain. The Germanic states were next (Markoff 1999, 666–668).

Constitutions and democracy developed in tandem. Constitutions derive their authority, as in the U.S. Constitution, from "We, the people," or as in cases such as Poland, from the people and some divine source (Markoff 1999, 666). Although not all nations that developed constitutions became democracies, constitutions themselves offer a degree of liberation from the potentially unlimited nature of traditional authority. Legitimacy as a state now depends on having a constitution or set of laws that rationalize the authority to exercise power and stipulates the people—or God and the people—as source of the state's authority. Even autocrats and dictators justify their exercise of power on constitutional authority entrusted to them on behalf of the people. "What the international community accepts as a state is a state. . . . And that is closely connected with its having a constitution" (van Maarserveen and van der Tang 1978, 234).

A constitution, whether a single document or a number of documents, specifies a society's "fundamental laws, distinguishable by their historical significance, the reverence and esteem in which they are held" (van Maarserveen and van der Tang 1978, 39). A constitution is a body of "meta-norms, higher order legal rules and principles that specify how all other legal norms are to be produced, applied, enforced and interpreted" (Sweet 2008, 219). Constitutions reiterate a country's civil religion, embodying the values and ideals people hold sacred. There is no higher authority than a state's constitution. It has traditional authority emanating from the tacit agreement among states and its acceptance by the people of a state. Constitutions hold such sacred status that to question their values and beliefs is seen in most nations as heresy, and debates concerning the meaning of constitutional clauses are conducted with religious fervor. Other symbols of a country such as its flag, national anthem, and rituals such as a pledge of allegiance also acquire near sacred status, representing as they do "the people."

Not only has the need for a constitution been globalized; the contents of constitutions converge in many fundamental respects. They stipulate the constitution itself as the source of authority, its place in the government, and how it may be amended. Constitutions all provide for central executive and legislative bodies, and most also provide for judiciary, elections, and representation in government. In addition to laying out the structure and function of government, nearly all constitutions delineate a series of civil, political, and democratic rights for individuals. Constitutional homogeneity is a significant globalization effect.

Constitutions are tools for and reflections of major political formation and reform (Gavison

2003, 54). Freedom of conscience or religion, association, expression, and defendant's rights in the judicial system appear as standard content in nearly every constitution. Mentioned frequently, but not as often, are rights to property, equality, and privacy. Constitutions as early as the 18th and 19th centuries provide for these basic rights (van Maarseveen and van der Tang 1978).

Since 1948, the UN Declaration of Human Rights, along with its subsequent protocols and conventions, has proposed universal norms that function as a template for a number of constitutions and international treaties. Building from the elements of national constitutions that preceded it, the Declaration stipulates an international normative model for states in terms of its values and its obligations to citizens. The Declaration serves as an external source of legitimacy. It has the advantage in some quarters of having been conceived by an international body, not by Western governments.

India was very active in the formation of the UN and the drafting of the UN Declaration of Human Rights. Nehru and other political leaders promoted both and were able to invoke them to secure India's position in the world (Bhavagan, 2010). India, trying to extract itself from British rule and declare itself non-aligned during the Cold War, was well served by the UN Declaration. More recently, other Eastern and Middle Eastern governments have objected to the claim of universality, citing the Declaration's reflection of Western understandings and sympathies—particularly with respect to individualism.

However, comparing the values embedded in the UN Declaration with national constitutions written afterward, the influence of the UN is clear.

Nineteen statements of value embedded in the Declaration, ranging from general statements about the "dignity" of humankind to judicial independence, were found in only 39.7% of constitutions written before the Declaration, but are present in 56.1% of constitutions written from 1949 to 1975. As the period from 1948 to 1975 progressed, the rate of incorporation increased, as did the pressures of globalization. From 1967 to 1975, the rate of incorporation of the values was 64.1% (van Maarseveen and van der Tang 1978, 192).

Of the 19 personal and political rights specified in the UN Declaration, the period 1967–1975 stands out as the period with the greatest percentage of adoption in states' constitutions. During the period 1949–1957, the average rate at which constitutions adopted the rights specified in the Declaration was 63.1%. The period 1958–1966, a period of lull in globalization, had an average adoption rate of 55.4%, and in 1967–1975, the beginning of the contemporary period of globalization, the average rate of adoption was 64.1% (van Maarseveen and van der Tang, 1978, 197).

Social rights, in contrast, show their greatest rate of adoption in the period immediately following the UN Declaration. The eight social rights specified in the UN Declaration had an average incorporation rate of 30.8% in the constitutions written before the Declaration. Their average rate of adoption was 57.5% right after the Declaration was adopted, and only 38.1% and 44%, respectively, in the two decades after the Declaration. Social rights did not

Table 3.2   Diffusion of Value and Rights Statements in National Constitutions

As nations developed constitutions and similar values, personal, political, and, to a lesser extent, social values were incorporated. The UN Declaration of Human Rights served as a template.

Period	Pre-1948	1948–1957	1958–1966	1967–1975
Value Statements	39.7%	Not specified		64.1%
Personal and Political Rights	Not specified	63.1%	55.4%	64.1
Social Rights	30.8%	57.5%	38.1%	44%

Source: Van Maarseveen and van der Tang (1978, 192–193, 197, 200).

diffuse to the extent that values and political and personal rights did. None of the former reached above a 70.1% adoption rate in any period (van Maarseveen and van der Tang 1978, 200).

There is a remarkable degree of convergence on the most frequently mentioned values, political rights, and to a lesser extent social rights, which received scant attention in the first generation of constitutions (see Table 3.3).

Democratic innovations from competitive electoral parties, secret balloting, and representative institutions to universal men's and women's suffrage also followed a pattern of increasing diffusion as globalization forces increased (Markoff 1999).

Table 3.3   Convergence in Constitutions

Period	Pre-1948	Number (Percentage) of Constitutions	1948–1975	Number (Percentage) of Constitutions
Top Five Value References (of 19)	Human rights and fundamental freedoms	23 (82.1%)	Human rights and fundamental freedoms	102 (92.7%)
	Equal rights of man	22 (78.6%)	Democratic society	94 (85.4%)
	General welfare	18 (64.3%)	Equal rights of man	92 (83.6%)
	Protection from discrimination, family, will of people, universal suffrage, free or secret voting	13 (46.4%)	Judicial independence	90 (81.8%)
			Protection against discrimination	89 (80.9%)
Top Five Political Rights References (of 19)	Freedom of religion, expression	25 (89.3%)	No arbitrary arrest/fair and public hearing/presumed innocence, etc.	10 (90.9%)
			Freedom of religion	97 (88.2%)
	Freedom of assembly, protection of private life	24 (85.7)	Freedom of expression	96 (87.3%)
			Freedom of association	95 (86.4%)
	Equality before law/equal protection, no arbitrary arrest/ fair and public hearing/presumed innocence, etc.	22, (78.6%)	Equality before law/equal protection	92 (83.6%)
Top Five Social Rights References (of Eight)	Right to work	12 (42.8%)	Right to form and join trade unions	74 (67.3%)
	Right to social security, free choice of employment, education	10 (35.7%)	Right to work	63 (57.3%)
			Right to education	60 (54.5%)
			Right to social security	50 (45.4%)
	Right to form and join trade unions	9 (32.2%)	Right to rest and leisure	39 (35.4%)

Source: Van Maarseveen and van der Tang (1978, 193, 197, 200).

Early Globalization of Liberalism

The links between liberalizing state structures and economic growth as they evolved in the Western European nation-states are important in understanding the development of states. The opening of Atlantic trade routes in the late 15th century factored significantly in the liberalization of governance from 1600 to 1850. Most theories of European development and governance stress factors of national heritage such as culture and religion to explain this. In contrast, economistic theories consider only trade. Some others examine the influence of multiple external global factors in combination with colonialism and slavery on liberalization (Acemoglu et al. 2005, 549–550).

A more compelling explanation demonstrates that global economic factors such as trade interacted with states' political institutional factors (Acemoglu et al. 2005) to liberalize state government. This explanation accounts for differences in the liberalization of states within the regional neighborhood of Western Europe. The two most critical factors turn out to be the nature of trade—the global factor—and the degree of absolutism exercised by the monarch—the internal political factor. Weighing the effect of these factors demonstrates that neither trade nor type of monarchy is significant enough as single factors to explain development in European countries. Together, however, they provide a persuasive account.

Trade had a definitive impact on growth. Countries with access to Atlantic trade had economies that grew more rapidly and became more stable than countries without Atlantic trade. Mediterranean trade produced growth but did not result in a comparable level of growth to the Atlantic trade states. That much is simple enough. But this does not explain liberalization because some countries with Atlantic trade and rapid economic growth liberalized while others did not.

Political factors round out the explanation. In Britain and the Netherlands, the monarchy was less absolutist than in other Atlantic trading states. The monarchy did not exert significant control over overseas trade. This enabled the merchant classes to accumulate wealth and subsequently power. Urban areas became centers of wealth. The rate of urbanization accelerated increasing development and further increasing urbanization. The value of land as a measure of wealth and power began to erode. New institutions that could support these new forms of growth were necessary. The newly wealthy urban classes pressured for more liberal political institutions, such as secure property rights, to support sustained growth (Acemoglu et al. 2005, 550).

International economic activity drove political effects within states, forcing transitions toward liberal and democratic political forms. Normative pressures toward liberalization were a function of internal pressure occasioned by the transition of the basis of wealth and power. Trade acted as an important conditioning factor in liberalizing the polity. Landed wealth gave aristocracy power. As it eroded, so did the power of the aristocracy. This allowed a new class structure to emerge.

Where trade was not as lucrative the effect was different. Venice, Genoa, and other states with relatively non-absolutist regimes did not liberalize. Without access to the Atlantic, growth was dependent on Mediterranean trade, which brought much less prosperity (Acemoglu et al. 2005, 550). The commercial classes were not able accumulate the levels of wealth and power possible in the Atlantic trading states. As global interaction accelerated over the centuries, practical and normative constraints compelled changes in the governance of other states. This is a different sort of globalization effect. States adjusted their internal governance in relation to one another and to their citizens; liberalization diffused, increasing homogeneity. These economic and political neighborhood effects operate in the contemporary phase of globalization, pushing toward greater liberalization globally.

Establishing International Law and Organization

The League of Nations and the United Nations

The foundation of global governance was set with the system of sovereign states. The former League of Nations and the UN are organizations of these presumptively equal and sovereign states intended to facilitate global governance through treaties, resolutions, the activity of its agencies, and the Court of International Justice, which hears disputes between willing nations.

The victorious allies of WWI formed the League of Nations to settle conflicts, maintain peace, and promote their collective security. The League failed to capture the imagination or enlist the enthusiasm of the global community. Despite the League being an invention of Woodrow Wilson, the United States refused to join. Germany was not eligible for admission because it started WWI, and Russia was not eligible for membership because of its communist government. With Europe weakened by the war and three powerful nations on the sidelines, the League was generally ineffective, but its few successes laid the groundwork for cooperative global governance.

The League of Nations advanced international law through a series of multilateral treaties and conflict resolutions.[4] It established sanctions as a mechanism to enforce compliance, although sanctions were not wielded effectively at the time. The League inaugurated the use of sanctions to preserve the sovereignty (territorial integrity and independence) of countries when they failed to live up to their international obligations. Article 16 of the League Covenant required that when a treaty violation occurred, member countries immediately sever all trade, financial, and personal relations with the offending country. The flurry of treaties facilitated by the League and backed by the force of sanctions of Article 16 established a global, self-monitoring system of nation-states (Giddens 1987, 256).

BOX 3.8   Check It Out: International Law

There are international treaties and agencies governing nearly every aspect of international life. In addition to treaties, there are conventions, declarations, resolutions, and other instruments that have moral, if not legal, force.

International agreements are so extensive that they influence nearly every occupation. What is your area of career interest? Are you considering international business or medicine? Trade? The ocean? Human rights? Environmental and human rights treaties alone influence business, medicine, agriculture, and manufacturing. It is hard to imagine any area of human activity that will not eventually come under some form of global regulation, if it does not already.

The UN keeps a database of treaties where you can research laws that may govern your activities someday. See what you can discover about your anticipated career.

http://treaties.un.org/pages/UNTSOnline.aspx?id=2

You'll see that you can search by the title of a treaty as well as by country.

The World Treaty Index is another good resource. It is a project of Center for the Study of Complex Systems and Political Science Department at the University of Michigan.

http://worldtreatyindex.com/help.html

Following WWII, the UN became successor to the League. They share some similarities. The UN is more limited in authority than might be imagined. It is not a world power, a super-state, or a world government. It does not act independently on the global scene as do states. Everything that the UN accomplishes is through the actions of states. It deliberately stipulates "collective measures" and the "principle of the sovereign equality of all its Members" (UN 2010, Charter Articles 1 and 2). The UN is very different from the League in having more expansive functions. The League limited its role to that of an international security organization. It avoided any action that would be construed as interference in the affairs of a sovereign nation (Meyer et al. 1997, 631). The UN was designed with a broad mandate, which gives it flexibility to evolve and respond to changing global conditions. Its objectives include promoting national and international development, human rights, and the global environment (631–632). This agenda invites the UN to develop global norms and work with and within nations to achieve them.

The UN structure contains a General Assembly, Security Council, Economic and Social Council, a Trusteeship Council, the International Court of Justice, and a Secretariat—a rather standard governmental structure (UN Charter Article 7). The General Assembly is limited to making recommendations (Chapter IV). The Security Council decides on actions taken for the resolution of conflict, including the decision to use force (Chapters V–VII). The Economic and Social Council operates the variety of programs and agencies of the UN that promote economic development, education, health care, and the other requisites of human development (Chapter IX). The International Court of Justice hears cases of disputes among states but only if they agree to be bound by the decisions of the court.

Another tool of global governance is the UN resolution. UN resolutions articulate a set of norms that the membership body has approved by a majority vote. A resolution sets a standard of legitimacy. Countries may be motivated to seek greater legitimacy in the eyes of the international community or its domestic audience. A resolution may also lay the groundwork for bilateral or multilateral treaties. One example is a UN resolution calling for a global regime on aquifers. Many parts of the world are water poor or threatened by water shortages. Aquifers, a source of groundwater, may cross the boundaries of several countries. If one country draws too heavily from the aquifer, it deprives the other countries. Many aquifers are running low on water. When the UN called for a global regime, it prompted countries to try to develop their own agreements concerning their specific cases. This has given rise to a series of treaties among countries that draw from common aquifers ("Deep Waters" 2010, 87).

UN resolutions do not have the binding force of international law, but they have power in their capacity to suggest normative guidelines that influence a state's legitimacy in the eyes of the international community and its domestic audience. For violations of its principles and aims, the UN may suspend or expel members or take away voting privileges. The UN, as of this writing, has not expelled a member nation.

Case Study: The Law of the Seas

The earliest international laws were laws of the seas. These developed as customary law and for hundreds of years were not codified. In the 17th century, a country's jurisdiction into the ocean extended only as far as a "narrow belt of sea surrounding a nation's coastline" (UNDOA 2007). This distance was roughly equivalent to what a country could defend—the approximate reach of a cannon shot. The rest of the ocean was free. Countries' main concerns were for international shipping and fishing. Customary law served these well. Most conflicts were limited to disputes between two countries over incidents or circumstances specific to them. The freedom of the seas doctrine persisted into the 20th century.

By mid-20th century, vastly expanded use of the sea beds and oceans for natural resources, laying cables and pipelines, long-distance fishing vessels, and pollution accompanying all of this activity on the seas exacerbated potential conflicts of interest among nations. In 1945, President Truman, conceding to pressure from the oil industry, claimed jurisdiction over all of the resources along the continental shelf along the U.S. coasts.

Other nations followed suit, racing to exploit the ocean's resources from oil to valuable minerals, precious gemstones, fish, and whales. Every nation declared its own standard, from 12 to 200 miles, depending on what they wanted from the ocean and where it was found. Disputes over depletion of fishing stocks, pollution, oil spills, nuclear submarines, and conflicting claims were perilous. There was need for agreement and order among nations. The newly formed UN International Law Commission decided in 1949 to take on the Laws of the Sea as one of its first priorities. UN conferences in the late 1950s and early '60s managed to adopt resolutions but did not gain substantive ground in regulating states. Abuse of the oceans, exploitative fishing to the point of endangering species, and boundary disputes, such as the "cod wars" between England and Iceland, continued.

In 1967, the ambassador to the UN from Malta, Arvid Pardo, declared that international law was "the only alternative by which we can hope to avoid the escalating tension that will be inevitable if the present situation is allowed to continue" (quoted in UNDOA 2007; Nandan, Lodge, and Rosenne 2002). He was right. In his address to the UN, Pardo brilliantly articulated several important principles that would guide future deliberations about the seas. He argued that the oceans and sea beds were the "common heritage of mankind." He advocated for a special body to

(Continued)

(Continued)

oversee the oceans and sea beds as a trustee for all nations. He also maintained that the composition of this trustee body represent all nations equally and not be balanced in favor of more powerful nations (UNDOA 2007; Nandan et al. 2002). Over the next 15 years, an elaborate international regime establishing laws of the sea over myriad issues was negotiated and renegotiated. Although conflicts still arise over a country's claims—China's claims over most of the resource-rich South China Sea put it in direct conflict with Vietnam, Philippines, Brunei, Malaysia, and Taiwan, and threaten to make it the "Palestine" of Asia according to the former secretary general of ASEAN (Bland 2012)—the Laws of the Seas have brought a semblance of order and a court to hear disputes.

The history of the laws of the seas highlights the subjective consciousness of "mankind" as a whole and the earth as commons, for practical purposes and political decision making that crystallized following WWII. It also illustrates the need for global law that eclipses bilateral or multilateral agreements between and among nations. When many nations, or nearly all the nations of the world, are affected by an issue, agreements among only some nations are not sufficient to relieve global tensions and potentially avoid violent conflict.

Despite Pardo's plea for recognition of common interests, countries tend to act based on how they perceive their national interests, as opposed to the interests of the greater community of nations. The United States, for example, has failed to ratify the Convention on the Rights of the Child and the Convention on Landmines (as of June 2010), and has also withdrawn from compulsory participation in the International Court of Justice and reserves the right to participate case by case. It has also refused to be bound by the International Criminal Court. Other countries behave similarly by refusing to sign treaties or going on record as objecting to particular elements of a treaty.

UN treaties now extend into virtually every realm of societal function and international relations. There are two main problems with relying on a UN Treaty as the base of global governance. As discussed, not every nation or every person is bound by any one UN Treaty. Compliance is voluntary. A treaty must be signed by representatives of countries, usually the president or prime minister, and ratified by the country's congress or parliament. In addition, the capacity of the UN to enforce treaties is weak. Only those countries that have ratified a treaty are bound by it. Even when ratified, the power of the UN to discipline countries that violate treaties, particularly powerful countries, is limited. Economic and other sanctions remain the primary mechanism to force compliance.

There is one exception to the lack of teeth in the UN enforcement capacity. In the case of "any threat to the peace, breach of the peace, or act of aggression" where sanctions are not effective, the Security Council may authorize the use of force (Joyner 1991, 6). This responsibility lies with the Security Council, because since the Treaty of Westphalia, nation-states are the only legitimate site for decisions on the use of force and the Security Council represents states. However, the legitimacy of the Security Council is questioned by many states because it is not representative of the entire UN membership. Reformed, it may perform this function with more accountability. Managing the use of force—signaling to states where the "red lines" (designating off limits) are drawn, who is drawing them, and who will enforce them—are related and crucial tasks. Warfare today seems unrestrained by any idea of "red lines" (Picco 1994, 17–18). This same conclusion can be drawn in many areas related to global governance from the global flows of people to the flows of money and finance.

Because the Westphalia principle of equality of states has never been fully respected, the interests of powerful states often dictate the nature of treaties and regulations. The Netherlands in the 17th century, Britain in the 19th and 20th, and the United States following WWII have benefited from periods of hegemony during which their national interest dominated the character and content of international relations. Periods of hegemony tend to be associated with increases in treaties. Hegemony can provide a measure of predictability. A government is more likely to enter into agreements if the effects of the agreements are somewhat predictable. When one country is dominant, it can help create stability that benefits trade, conflict resolution, and international relations generally. Hegemony may also create an environment that is more coercive and thus inductive to treaty making at the behest of the dominant country. But when states enter into treaties with more powerful states or are governed by regulations on which they had little influence, they sacrifice some measure of sovereignty and may be forced into arrangements that are not in their best interest.

BOX 3.9   A Closer Look: International Criminal Court (ICC)

The inability of the UN to enforce international law demonstrates its inadequacy in global governance. The International Criminal Court, established independently of the UN in 2003, may be a step in this direction. It reflects more recent global norms concerning the obligation of the global community to protect human rights. It departs from limits of UN agencies by not requiring voluntary participation. It can order extradition and imprisonment of those charged, regardless of their position in state governments, including heads of state. This gives it more potential for enforcement, but only in a narrow range of cases. As of August 2012, ICC had 121 state parties (ICC 2012).

The ICC is a court of last resort. It hears cases where states refuse to act, cannot act, or do not engage in genuine investigation and prosecution. In 2010, the court held investigations and issued arrest warrants against members of the Lords Resistance Army in Uganda, against individuals in the Democratic Republic of the Congo, Sudan, Kenya, and the Central African Republic.

Although states rise and fall from positions of hegemony, the UN has not been able to facilitate political parity in global governance. Former colonies have not attained political parity with the wealthier nations. International law "bestows rights, obligations, and commitments upon the governments in the international system of sovereign states" (Joyner 1991, 1–2). But the international system of societies can hardly said to be governed through the exercise of legitimate authority. Dominant nations finessed international law to serve their interests with only modest benefit accruing to weaker states. Rather than protecting the sovereignty and equality of nations, international law in practice buttressed the inequalities and indignities suffered by the Third World. International law was shaped by the "priorities of a Eurocentric world, including the legalization of diplomatic and economic relationships, and based on a statist logic that accepted force, war and hierarchy as rational instruments of statecraft" (Falk 2006, 735). As a result, sovereignty for many states remains a fiction and they do not exercise control over their own fates (Mann 2003, 137). Power politics shaped international politics from the drawing of colonial boundaries to determining countries' economic and political fates.

Summary

This chapter discusses the foundations of cultural, economic, and political globalization. The ideals of Westphalia spread globally, but as colonialism and the Cold War ensured, they never attained normative status or were practiced globally. The international system of societies shaped by colonial domination and attenuated by the Cold War continues to cripple states that have not yet recovered from the ravages of environmental destruction and the alienation of indigenous people from their land (Murphy 2009, 8). Inequality and racism, which still associates lighter skin with prestige, is evident in the coloring at the "bottom of the pyramid" both within and among societies. Weak political institutions facilitate authoritarian governments that concentrate power in the military and executive.

To date, states have not exerted equal power on the international stage. The actions of powerful states constrain economic and political development of some states and provide opportunity for others. Despite prohibitions, states frequently intervene in one another's internal affairs, although more or less covertly. Nor have states always represented nations, as testified to by the frequency of autonomy and independence movements within states and the breakup of states such as Yugoslavia and the Soviet Union.

The increasing likelihood that countries' interests will collide is also a challenge to the existing system of governance. As more cross-border interactions occur, whose laws should apply? This was the dilemma faced in deciding on the laws of the seas. Now with intense warfare within nations, global poverty, more cross-country corporate mergers, the global reach of the World Wide Web, and the intensity of other transborder problems, the question of whose jurisdiction and whose laws apply confronts the world daily. The intensity of interaction among states in using the seas led to chaos and then to the law of the seas. Now, global economic, political, and social interaction in nearly every aspect of life has reached such a level of intensity that the current global, political, and economic systems are no longer viable. Even with the establishment of the UN, it is chaotic. Fundamentalist nationalistic movements, ethnic wars, horrible poverty, and environmental, criminal, and other challenges to the quality and survival of life globally demand reform of international relations. For these reasons among others, contemporary globalization challenges the principles of the Treaty of Westphalia and the current systems of societies. These challenges shape contemporary globalization, discussed in later chapters.

Questions, Investigations, and Resources

Questions

1. What cultural values and ideas globalized as the state system spread through Europe and then through Eastern and Central Asia?

2. How did colonialism change the economic and political fortunes of people in colonized lands?

3. What global values are most represented in constitutions? Which were added as new states became incorporated into the global system? How well are they realized today?

4. Did Cold War policies conflict with emerging global values and norms? How did the Cold War change or reinforce the structure of the global economy and polity that emerged from colonialism?

Investigations

1. As new values and ideals became incorporated into states' constitutions, did new treaties and declarations of the UN reflect these same values? What global values are represented?

2. Investigate the ethnic composition of African and Asian nations using the CIA World Factbook or searching the Library of Congress ethnic map collections. How many ethnic groups are contained in the various countries that were once colonies? Which of these countries are experiencing violent conflict or did experience a period of violent conflict?

3. There were many places during the Cold War where warfare was very hot. Go to the Center for Systemic Peace website (http://www.systemicpeace.org). Click on the link to their "War List" Scroll to the 1950s, the beginning of the Cold War. How many countries were at war from then until 1989? Not all, but many of those were "proxy" wars supported by the USSR and United States. Korea, Vietnam, Afghanistan, Nicaragua, Angola, El Salvador, the Congo are a few. Although it is beyond counting, about how many lives were lost in the decades of wars in these countries?

Resources

CIA World Factbook https://www.cia.gov/library/publications/the-world-factbook/index.html

Library of Congress Map Collection http://memory.loc.gov/ammem/gmdhtml/gmdhome.html (Search under the keyword "ethnic maps" to bring up the ethnic map collection.)

UN Treaty Database http://treaties.un.org/pages/UNTSOnline.aspx?id=2

The World Treaty Index http://worldtreatyindex.com/help.html

4

Making the Global Economy

Objectives

This chapter will help you to

- analyze the course of economic globalization from WWII to the present;
- assess the roles of Keynesian and neo-liberal economic policies and institutions in international relations and development;
- evaluate factors that influence the distribution of production processes, outsourcing, offshoring, unbundling, and the impact of the their distribution;

- evaluate benefits and costs of foreign investment to host countries and home countries;
- determine the consequences of economic globalization for workers, for countries, and for corporations;
- analyze the roots of the economic crisis that began in 2007; and
- evaluate the responses of world leaders to the economic crisis.

BOX 4.1   Consider This: Micro-decisions and Macro-policies

The global economy is made of countless individual decisions, from the buying choices of consumers to the decisions of corporations concerning where to locate a factory. All of these are made within the context of macroeconomic policies and programs instituted by countries and international governmental organizations. Policies that encourage subsidies for corporations or tariffs on foreign goods, international regimes of regional and global trade, private property laws, privatization of industry, deregulation, and myriad more form a global social structural system of opportunity and constraint. Together, these macro policies and micro decisions form a complex web of interaction that can encourage prosperity or promote poverty.

If the purpose of an economy is to provide the necessities of life for everyone on earth, then for many people, the global economy is failing. If the purpose of economic growth is to improve the quality of life, the economy is failing even more people.

Using the basic definition of globalization as the world becoming a single place, economic globalization means that how people make a living and how well that living can provide for their needs are dependent on forces operating throughout the globe, not just in their own community or country. Over centuries, the decisions that people have made have increased the density of trade among nations, the activity of multinational corporations, the flow of money and jobs among

(Continued)

(Continued)

societies, and the diffusion of technology from country to country. Economic integration has reached such intensity that we have outgrown the structures that once gave economies order. Economic processes have been freed to go global.

The global economy challenges us to develop new economic relationships to solve contemporary problems of survival. The degree to which individuals, groups, or states can manage their own or the global economy is among the most hotly contested dimensions of globalization. We start the chapter with a brief look at two very active international groups with opposing views of the problems and prospects of economic globalization.

The first part of this chapter looks at the development of the global economy—how societal economies grew to be so interdependent as to form a single global economy. It covers the evolution of trade, finance, and monetary policy. The second section of this chapter analyzes the global economic crisis that began in 2007 and the tugs-of-war among factions of global governance, including national governments, corporations, non-governmental organizations, and international organizations.

The World Economic Forum and World Social Forum

January brings an annual migration to Davos, Switzerland. The world's most powerful economic and political leaders meet in this resort town for the World Economic Forum (WEF). They come from virtually every nation on earth but look astonishingly similar to one another. The near unanimous devotion to the grey-black Western-style suits, white or blue shirts, and subtle tie that compose the unofficial uniform of Davos is striking. There is more variation in the color and style of suits and blouses worn by the few women in attendance. Expensive watches and leather shoes complete the outfits. Adherence to the Davos uniform takes precedence over national styles of dress or styles associated with professions. From Africa, Asia, Europe, and the Americas, not only business executives and politicians, but also media types, entertainers, and even entrepreneurs in the infamously grubby high-tech industry tend to wear the outfit, as if by taking on the uniform of Davos, they seal their membership in a transnational class of wealth and power. They go to Davos to plan the economic life of the world.

BOX 4.2 A Closer Look: Dressing the Part

The clothes people wear convey information. When people dress similarly, it indicates a level of commonality. This is very evident at the meetings of the World Economic Forum (above left) and the World Social Forum (below left and above).

Far from the sophisticated glamour of Davos, the World Social Forum (WSF) meets at the same time. Much less organizational in nature, this forum has publicized itself as the "alter-globalization" or "global justice movement." Not a formal association, the WSF is a loose network of activists and interested parties from around the world—whoever wants and is able to join in. There is no apparent uniform, but there is an obvious dress code. Ethnic and national dress, open-collared shirts, and T-shirts emblazoned with the logos and mottos of local, national, or global activist organizations are the preferred, decidedly informal, attire. It is vibrant. There are many more women and many more youth. Labor groups, academics, and representatives of non-governmental organizations (NGOs), usually of a left-leaning persuasion, dominate.

The WSF motto, "A new world is possible," is a condemnation of the world purportedly created by those at the Davos meeting. The founding principles of the WSF offer a blistering critique of the political and economic policies that shape the global system. The WSF originally presented itself as anti-globalization. Since then, participants acknowledged that global capitalism is only one type of globalization and that they represent another. They come to protest the economic life of the world and plan an alternative.

Each of these groups represents a radically different perspective on globalization and economic well-being. Each forum represents an evaluation of economic globalization that stands in stark contrast to the other.

Which is correct? Is global capitalism a constructive force, having brought at least some prosperity and better lives to all corners of the globe? Or is it destructive, ruining traditional ways of life and enslaving many to enrich very few and spoiling the earth in the process?

Does globalization bring more benefit to workers in newly industrializing countries at the expense of the jobs of more well-paid workers in developed countries? Or does it benefit the richer countries at the expense of the poor?

What do we know about economic globalization and its impacts on people's lives? Is it a race to the bottom, as some claim, or a chance for people in developing societies to rise to the top?

Economic globalization refers to many things: free trade, jobs going overseas, a global market, foreign investment, multinational corporations. Globalization is all of these things, but it is not any one of them. Like other forms of globalization, economic globalization means making the world a single place, a group. Like other dimensions of globalization, economic globalization has the potential to help or to harm. Understanding dynamics of the global economy is critical to understanding the impact of economic forces on the quality of all our lives.

BOX 4.3   A Closer Look: Contrasting Views—World Social Forum Principles

World Social Forum: Globalization for Social Justice

"The World Social Forum is a movement of ideas that prompts reflection and the transparent circulation of the results of that reflection on the mechanisms and instruments of domination by capital, on means and actions to resist and overcome that domination, and on the alternatives proposed to solve the problems of exclusion and social inequality that the process of capitalist globalization with its racist, sexist and environmentally destructive dimensions is creating internationally and within countries." (WSF 2002)

World Economic Forum: Global Corporate Citizenship

"The ultimate role of business in society remains to do business. Global corporate citizenship should not develop from a bad conscience or a feeling that one must give back to society; it should be a feature of this globalizing world that stretches traditional boundaries. Global corporate citizenship is a logical extension of corporations' search for a consistent and sustainable framework for global engagement—and one that adds value for both the companies and the global space in which they engage. It is a form of corporate engagement that can reinforce the positive role of business in society and enhance profitability in the long term. Indeed, global corporate citizenship integrates both the rights and the responsibilities that corporations have as global citizens. And in relying on a multi stakeholder approach to tackling global problems, it can point out the way to new models of effective global governance that integrate business as a key stakeholder." (Schwab 2008)

Waves of Economic Globalization

Globalization and Economic Integration

Integration is a common way of measuring economic globalization. Economic integration includes a variety of forms of interaction. One easily accessible index is the World Bank's trade indicators. Each measure indicates the degree to which a country is open or closed to economic integration. The first two indicators measure the volume of trade. Increases in trade, particularly across longer distances, indicate more openness to globalization. The second two indicators are measures of protectionism. Attempts to limit trade are barriers to globalization.[1]

- Total trade as share of GDP
- Share of trade with neighboring countries
- Index of shipping difficulties
- Average tariffs and custom duties (World Bank 2009, 340, Table A4)

The globalization index published by *Foreign Policy* ("Globalization Index" 2007) measures two forms of economic integration: trade and foreign direct investment. There are more complex strategies as well. The Organization for Economic Co-operation and Development (OECD 2005) handbook has over 200 pages listing and explaining globalization measures. There are four classifications with 10 to 20 indicators each. The four categories are

- foreign direct investment,
- activity of multinational firms,
- internationalization of technology, and
- trade.

How people evaluate globalization relative to these measures is very mixed. Many people argue that more protectionism and less free trade and foreign investment promote domestic growth. They claim that free markets create too much competition with domestic goods and that investments in other nations take away money that could be used domestically. Both free markets and foreign investments, they argue, cost jobs at home. Another argument is that limiting open trade and foreign investment hurts the poor everywhere because it denies them access to cheaper goods (Milner and Kubota 2005). Others have found

that liberalizing or opening the economy promotes democracy and improves people's lives by breaking down elite control over the economy. The reverse is also argued, that democratizing leads to the liberation of markets. Either way, liberalization of the economy and liberalization of the political system appear to be related and mutually reinforcing.

The Keynesian Liberal Wave

First Global Economic Regime: Bretton Woods, 1944 to 1970s

The Depressions of the 1920s and 1930s and the experience of two world wars motivated world leaders to develop a global strategy and infrastructure to provide global economic stability. WWII ravaged and brutalized much of the world and diminished confidence that the powers of Europe could govern colonies, given that they had not done very well governing themselves (Westad 2005). They recognized that the long-term survival of peace depended on reconstructing industrialized nations and preparing the developing nations to move into the modern era. Financial and political leaders both arrived at two important conclusions:

- Economic stability was essential for political stability
- The stability of all countries was interdependent

To avoid a repeat of the chaos and financial instability following WWI, world leaders acknowledged that "*collective action at the global level*" was necessary (Stiglitz 2002, 12, emphasis original). Before the war ended, representatives from the allied nations began planning for peace at Bretton Woods in New Hampshire. International trade needed stimulus, and national currencies needed stabilizing. The primary objective was to rebuild richer nations. Developing poorer countries, although acknowledged, was left up to their colonial powers (11). The agreements forged at Bretton Woods resound with noble sentiment. The summary document of the conference states,

This Conference at Bretton Woods, representing nearly all the peoples of the world, has considered matters of international money and finance which are important for peace and prosperity. The Conference has agreed on the problems needing attention, the measures which should be taken, and the forms of international cooperation or organization which are required. The agreements reached on these large and complex matters are without precedent in the history of international economic relations. (quoted in Army Information School 1946, 31)

This was the first attempt at a multilateral authority for international monetary policy, including mutually agreed rules and an international governmental authority. Bretton Woods established the International Monetary Fund (IMF) and the International Bank for Reconstruction and Development (now part of the World Bank). The International Bank assumed responsibility to coordinate and regulate the international exchange of money to promote worldwide prosperity and political stability. The IMF was to prevent any nation or group of nations from gaining unfair trade advantage, to coordinate ways for nations to help one another through short-term difficulties, and to synchronize each nation's goals with worldwide prosperity. International financial institutions (IFIs) were created to facilitate economic relations among countries, such as loans and investments (Army Information School 1946, 30). Countries pool their contributions in the Bretton Woods institutions to coordinate funding of global objectives. They outlawed practices that might harm worldwide stability.

The goal and strategies of Bretton Woods were macroeconomic stability, import substitution, and governance reform. John Maynard Keynes (Great Britain) and Harry Dexter White (United States) were the principal architects of the Bretton Woods agreement, with White holding more sway than Keynes. This reflected the growth of U.S. power relative to Britain's. Forty-one nations participated in Bretton Woods. The Soviet Union and its allies participated but declined to sign off on the IMF. Instead, the USSR established the Council for Mutual Economic Assistance to facilitate economic activity among Communist bloc nations.

Macroeconomic Stability

The key strategies to achieve macroeconomic stability were the agreements on currency exchange and the insistence that governments act in the interests of the global order as well as their own. A *par value* exchange rate was adopted, in which each country set a value for its currency and promised to keep the value within a range above or below par. The dollar was accepted as the standard, $35 per ounce of gold. This variation on a fixed rate system gave countries some flexibility but eliminated the potential for extreme volatility. Countries were required to maintain a reserve in gold or currency convertible to gold. A global pool of reserves, 25% in gold and dollars and 75% in other international currencies, gathered from all countries was to be held at IMF, available for loan if one country fell short of reserves. The reserve was an insurance fund to stabilize countries when needed. At the time, the U.S. central bank held three quarters of the gold held by the central banks of the world. The dollar was the only currency directly convertible to gold. Thus, the dollar became the international standard and the currency of choice.

BOX 4.4   A Closer Look: IMF Voting

Not all voting systems assume all parties to a vote are equal. The way that voting is conducted in many global bodies is according to some measure of power. In the IMF, every country is given an equal number of basic votes, and additional votes are apportioned according to money contributed. Voting procedures were recently revised to give lower income and fast-growing economies more voting power. Quotas have been increased for 54 growing economies. The number of basic votes was near tripled.

Beginning in March 2011, voting shares changed as member countries paid their increased quota. There are 2,300,394 total votes.

(Continued)

(Continued)			
Some of the richer countries' new voting shares are		A few of the poorer countries are	
Japan	133,805	Comoros	766
Germany	130,759	Dominica	759
France	108,062	Maldives	759
Britain	108,062		
The United States	372,170		

Governments also agreed to stimulate global demand. Keynes argued that the depression was caused by insufficient demand and that governments could act to increase demand through monetary policy such as decreasing interest rates. Where monetary policy failed, governments were encouraged to use expansive fiscal policies such as increasing their own expenditures or reducing taxes (Stiglitz 2002, 11). (This should sound familiar. These stimulus steps were the basis of the G20 agreement in response to the 2007 crisis: decrease interest rates, increase government spending, and—in some countries—cut taxes.)

If markets fail, the IMF provides stimulus money to governments that cannot fulfill their obligation to increase demand. (In the 2007 crisis, IMF funding was increased and the money was used for stimulus money in poorer countries.) Countries also submitted to rules concerning currency exchange and agreed to regulate the flow of speculative—hot money—investments.

Import Substitution

Import substitution industrialization (ISI) builds domestic industries for domestic and regional markets, replacing imports. ISI requires government to finance domestic industry and regulate imports. The strategy is to develop industry internally, moving people from primary industry into manufacturing and better jobs. Better jobs create a domestic market for manufactured goods. Domestic goods are usually more affordable than imports. ISI generated rapid growth in economies recovering from WWII and in some developing nations, such as Brazil, Mexico, Argentina, and some in Africa and the Middle East (Rodrik 2000, 5; Tabb 2009, 117, 270). Financing industrialization was the key to differentiating success from failure. Countries that combined ISI with export did much better than those who did not. This was one factor that helped the Asian Tigers advance so quickly. Countries taxed the agricultural sector to fuel industrialization did not fare as well (Arruda de Almeida 2005, 204–205).

Governance

In addition to establishing mechanisms for organizing and linking economies, Bretton Woods began the debate over a global ethic to govern the relationships among national economies. The charge of the IMF and International Bank is to reconstruct countries, build or rebuild their productivity, and integrate countries in the earliest stages of development into the international economy. Article IV of the Bretton Woods agreement outlines the obligations of member governments to institute and maintain economic policies for stable global growth and avoid policies that give unfair competitive advantage to one country over another. States are to police their own economies and play fair in the international market. This ethic failed most poor countries. Loans to poor countries were contingent on the country adopting the American model—an open economy and capitalist markets—in exchange for capital channeled through the international banks from the richer donor countries, primarily America (Westad 2005, 153). The fledging industries of poor nations needed protection and a more gradual opening of markets.

Another problem that stymies development of poor countries is corruption. Countries often experience corruption while forming and stabilizing their institutional apparatus. For example, in the United States, the period leading up to the Depression of 1929 was one of widespread corruption. Since WWII, corruption has wasted money and led to many failures of World Bank and IMF programs. The practice of handing out jobs and contracts to friends, relatives, and those who can be of benefit is called *crony capitalism*. Among the reforms discussed later in the chapter, the IMF has expanded its role in promoting good governance—"ensuring the rule of law, improving the efficiency and accountability of the public sector, and tackling corruption" (IMF 1997, v). Good governance is, in most cases, essential to economic prosperity. The World Bank also fosters good governance over a range of economic and social issues.

The Bretton Woods regime began to unravel in the 1960s. Import substitution did not overcome the difficulties of all developing nations; urbanization outpaced the rate of job creation. Japan and Europe emerged from two decades of growth following WWII as economic rivals to the United States and became increasingly wary of the power that the United States could wield in their own economies. In the United States, spending on the war in Vietnam and social programs at home depleted the budget. U.S. economic hegemony waned. In 1971, President Nixon ended the Bretton Woods monetary agreements unilaterally by divorcing the dollar from the gold standard (Cohen 2001).

Between the world wars, there was not a hegemon to stabilize the global economic order, and it collapsed. However, following the abandonment of Bretton Woods, the global economy held even though U.S. dominance was diminished.

International financial institutions like the IMF, World Bank, and regional banks continued to manage global coordination. The principles and norms established at Bretton Woods continued to exercise influence over the behavior of national governments. The global social order was sufficiently established that it endured (Cohen 2001, 101). Although the Bretton Woods regime did not achieve the levels of prosperity promised and much of the advice and consultation given did not yield the anticipated results, a global economic order had emerged.

The Neo-Liberal Wave

As Bretton Woods unraveled, a different set of economic principles began to hold sway: neo-liberalism[2] and the Washington Consensus. Many of the economic policies of neo-liberalism were grounded in market fundamentalism. Rather than relying on government to correct the deficiencies of the market in reducing poverty in developing countries, government was seen as the problem. Free markets were seen as the solution (Stiglitz 2002, 13). Neo-liberal doctrine is that the more freedom from government there is—freedom from taxation, freedom from regulation, free flow of capital, freedom of tariffs and quotas—the more prosperity there will be, and prosperity will trickle down from elite to lower classes.

The term *Washington Consensus* was coined in 1989 to describe a set of 10 neo-liberal policies. During the Ronald Reagan (United States) and Margaret Thatcher (Great Britain) administrations of the 1980s, a wide variety of neo-liberal economic policies were implemented domestically and abroad. Neo-liberalism dominated the IMF and World Bank approaches to loans and development after the fall of the Soviet Union and the proclaimed triumph of capitalism over socialism. They were applied in Latin American economic reforms and generally practiced among the world's richest nations (Williamson 2004, 1). They became the focus of neo-liberal doctrine and were applied almost in cookie-cutter fashion.[3]

Whether these policies are appropriate to nations in the very early stages of development and new industries still in need of some protection is doubtful, especially in hindsight. The Washington Consensus favored export to the global market over the Bretton Woods strategy of import substitution, a policy shift reinforced by the debt crisis of the early 1980s and the suc-cesses of the Asian Tigers. Rather than governments taking charge of infrastructure development, structural adjustment policy required that infrastructure be taken over by the private sector. Chile may be the only country where IMF and World Bank policies led to success in the years leading into the 21st century (Stiglitz 2002, 16–18).

BOX 4.5   Consider This: What Makes a Good Economy?

How do we measure the success of a country's economy?

- Economic growth?
- GNP?
- Median income?
- Human development?
- Strength of currency?
- Trade balance?

If we use how well an economy performs its function—providing the means to a healthy life—as the measuring rod, is human development the only criterion that matters in evaluating it?

Trade Liberalization

Trade liberalization, financial market liberalization, and direct foreign investment were the main vehicles of economic integration of this period. Whether for better or worse, economic globalization took a giant step forward. Trade liberalization deregulates trade by removing tariffs, quotas, and subsidies. For example, when the United States puts a tariff on an import from another country, it raises the price of that import in the United States. Other countries find it more difficult to compete in the U.S. market based on price. If the United States subsidizes a commodity, such as cotton, it uses tax payer dollars to lessen the cost of the production of cotton, and U.S. producers can lower the price they charge. It gives them an advantage in whichever markets they want to sell. Quotas limit the number of imports, limiting competition in the domestic market, making it easier for domestic companies to sell in domestic markets. Whether free trade agreements or protectionism results in more cost or benefit, and to whom, has been hotly debated since the Smoot-Hawley Act of 1929 put tariffs on imports to try to spur domestic production for the domestic market.

BOX 4.6   Consider This: Global Trade

Trade is an important form of economic globalization. You can see from the map that the rapidly growing emerging economies of Brazil, India, and China depend heavily on exporting to countries outside of their region. In well-developed economies, the opposite is true. 68% of exports of EU countries and 51% of NAFTA exports stay within the region. 86% of MERCOSUR exports and 75% of ASEAN exports go outside of the region. Is this what you expected?

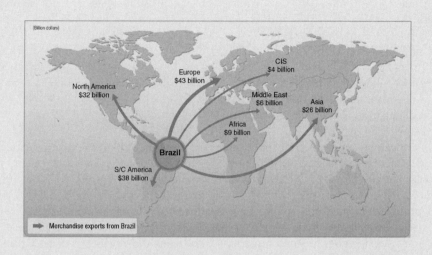

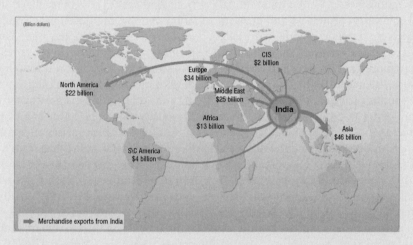

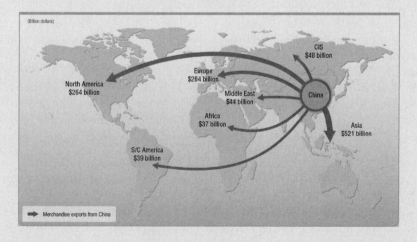

Source: World Trade Developments, 2008. Retrieved from http://www.wto.org/english/res_e/statis_e/its2008_e/its08_world_trade_dev_e.pdf

The World Trade Organization (WTO) (before 1995, the General Agreement on Tariffs and Trade, GATT) sets trade rules, negotiates trade agreements, regulates trade, and arbitrates disputes. The WTO has close to 200 member nations, covering most of world trade. Since its founding, it has fairly consistently worked to liberalize trade. Negotiations have been successful in eliminating many barriers to trade. Gaining most favored nation (MFN) status in the WTO has become a carrot for negotiating political concessions. Trade sanctions are a way of punishing nations for violating treaties or global norms. Nevertheless, the United States and other rich nations have continued protectionist measures, particularly in subsidizing agriculture—corn, cotton, wheat, soybeans, and hay. Some subsidy goes to small farmers, but much goes to agribusinesses, large multinational corporations. In some cases, producers and growers of comparable goods from the developing world are undersold in their domestic markets by subsidized goods from richer countries. This has been the case with corn in Mexico (Relinger 2010).

Although their specific problems vary, many developing nations cannot trade, even when they have products. Infrastructure problems in energy, communication, and transportation make it difficult to get goods to market. Outmoded technologies make production more costly. Political institutions may lack the expertise to develop trade agreements in their country's best interest. Many developing societies are open to competition from other countries but do not have sufficient infrastructure to compete abroad, making them vulnerable. The WTO program Aid for Trade was expanded in 2005 to help developing countries use aid so as to benefit from liberalized markets. Aid for Trade supports the development of policies, infrastructure, production, and other trade-necessary matters. The first *Aid for Trade at a Glance* report published in 2007 found that from the 1970s, as aid for social sectors such as health and education increased—necessary investments, to be sure—aid for trade decreased (OECD/WTO 2007, 22). While markets were liberalized, less aid was given to build capacity to benefit from opening trade.

Trade liberalization can improve economies in developing nations, when they compete on an equal footing with more developed nations. Forging trade agreements to accomplish this has been difficult. The WTO holds global negotiating sessions to develop trade policies and regulations. Issues that arose in the WTO Doha round of trade talks that began in 2000 were still not resolved as of 2012. Environmental laws, intellectual property rights, and subsidies of industries such as agriculture in developed nations have resisted resolution. Developing nations are increasingly demanding fair trade, rather than free trade.

Financial Market Liberalization

Under neo-liberal policies, financial market liberalization became a requirement for developing countries receiving aid. It allows for freer flow of investments among countries. However, it is risky to liberalize financial markets where there are not strong financial institutions in place. European governments did not begin financial market liberalization until the 1970s. Liberalization allowed a rush of hot money into developing countries. *Hot money* is short-term loan money that is intended to win profit through changes in the foreign exchange rate and stock markets. It is not long-term investment in development such as building industries and creating jobs. Hot money is very volatile as it can leave as quickly as it entered, destabilizing markets.

Another problem arises if financial instruments, like short-term loans to businesses, carry high interest rates. The government of the business that borrowed the money is required to keep an amount equal to the loans in reserve (usually in U.S. Treasury bills), earning a fraction of the rate they will be required to pay. The bank making the initial loan makes money on interest. The U.S. Treasury makes money on the funds kept in reserve in its bonds (Stiglitz 2002, 65). The country to which this money was loaned can end up losing. Forcing these policies on nations with weak banking systems was compared to sending them off on a voyage on a rough sea sealing their fate in disaster (17). This contributed to the Asian crisis of 1997 (Williamson 2004, 7). Adhering to the principle of the unfettered market and "expecting the market to be efficient and effective ignored all of the lessons of history" (Stiglitz, 2002, 74).

There was more at work than just pressures to conform to IMF policies. Transitions in financial policy toward liberalization or restriction tend to occur in geographic and temporal clusters, a globalization effect. Purely economic explanations alone fail to capture governmental choices. Culture turns out to be a significant influence on policy convergence. When other variables, such as domestic policy and

IMF pressures, are controlled for, research has shown that the actions of culturally similar countries had a significant effect on whether a country liberalized or restricted economic policy. When countries compete for capital and a competitor liberalizes, it influences liberalization among the others. Countries also liberalize when countries of similar religious orientation liberalize. Religion does not cause liberalization, but religious attitudes affect attitudes toward individualism, materialism, equality, and risk that influence economic attitudes (Simmons and Elkins 2005, 45). Policy convergence research is an important area for political economists and other social scientists interested in governmental decision making. Policy convergence can have disastrous effects when it is not based on careful considerations of policy choices.

Capital account openness can benefit countries that have reached a sufficient level of financial development and sophistication with good accounting systems, creditor rights, and rule of law. Capital liberalization must be part of a larger plan of institutional development (Eichengreen, Gullapalli, and Panizza 2009, 24–25). Unfortunately, this was not the case when these policies became conditions of aid and loans in many developing countries.

BOX 4.7   A Closer Look: Foreign Direct Investment (FDI)

Historically, the United States has been the primary destination for foreign direct investment. According to the OECD (2013), preliminary estimates for 2012 show that China surpassed the United States for the first time, receiving $253 billion in comparison to the United States $175. The chart shows the top recipients of FDI in 2011.

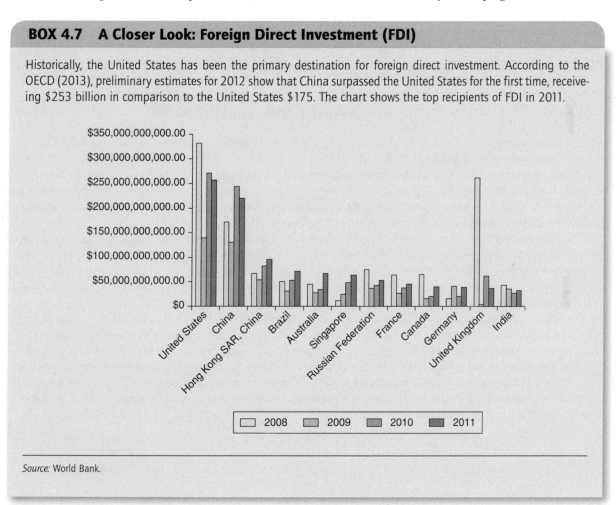

Source: World Bank.

Foreign Direct Investment

Countries and regions within countries compete against one another to attract investment. If a company owns 10% or more of a company in a country that it is not its country of residence, it qualifies as a foreign direct investment (FDI). In the best case, foreign investment is good for the host country and the corporation. The parent corporation gains a new market and is usually able to lower its labor, taxes, environmental regulation, or other costs. Attracting foreign investment is a way for a nation to increase employment without, theoretically, assuming much risk. They gain jobs, new technologies, and expertise. This is happening in the high-tech service industry where a global employment market is emerging and workers' wages in developing nations are increasing (Doh 2005, 697).

Foreign direct investment is a relatively stable form of financial liberalization. But there may be tradeoffs. Consumers in the host country may benefit from cheaper products, a particularly important concern in poor countries, but homegrown domestic industry may not survive the competition (Stiglitz 2002, 68). Foreign concerns may take advantage of

weak labor and environmental laws in developing nations. Foreign investment profit flows back to shareholders of the corporation; these may go overseas to the country of residence of the corporation. Foreign investment, if not carefully managed by the host country, may do little for its long-term wealth accumulation. If governments require accountability for benefits from the foreign investments and liability for any harm caused, foreign (and domestic) investment could make significant improvements globally, not just in the poorer regions. "The Asian Miracle" case study describes how some governments managed and regulated foreign investment.

BOX 4.8   A Closer Look: What This Means to You, the Flip Side of Foreign Investment

U.S. direct investment abroad was not much larger than foreign investment in the United States—$184 billion went abroad in 1990 in comparison to $152 billion brought into the United States (Ott 2002).

- Foreign companies in the United States employed more than 5 million U.S. workers in 2005, providing 4.5% of all private sector employment in the United States.
- An additional 4.6 million U.S. jobs indirectly depend on foreign investment in the United States (2005 data).
- Foreign companies in the United States buy 80% of their inputs from U.S. companies.
- Compensation at foreign companies in the United States is on average 30% higher than the U.S. national average. Foreign-owned firms paid U.S. workers an average of $63,428 in 2004.
- Foreign firms in the United States account for 5.7% of U.S. economic output, as well as 10% of all investment in plant and equipment in the United States.
- Foreign firms generate 19% of U.S. exports ($153.9 billion in 2006). This contribution is greater than their overall percentage of U.S. economic output, which means they are doing more than their share to help improve the U.S. trade balance.
- Foreign firms in the United States generate a disproportionate share of national R&D spending (13%, totaling $29.9 billion). This spending strengthens U.S. global competitiveness in pharmaceutical, high-tech, and other key sectors, and produces innovative products that help to improve the standard of living.
- The economic benefits generated by inflows of foreign capital help strengthen economic leadership. In the late 1980s and early 1990s, some pointed with alarm to Japanese purchases of U.S. assets, fearing they foreshadowed the Japanese overtaking our economic leadership. Twenty years later, the resulting jobs and economic growth show those fears were misplaced.

Source: U.S. Department of the Treasury (2007).

Shaping a New Wave

Bretton Woods Institutions in the Neo-Liberal Era

The multilateral financial institutions of the Keynesian era, institutions designed by activist

governments, were not working in the neo-liberal world that succeeded it. Although international financial institutions expanded their activities and programs, the process of reform has been slow. A 2000 study by the World Bank, IMF, and other international financial institutions highlighted a number of persistent problems in their operations. A follow-up 2001 paper summarized the difficulties.

- The Bank rewards lending for lending's sake, not how well loans worked to stimulate development or alleviate poverty. The report suggested paying more attention to the needs of citizens of client states.
- The roles of the Bank and IMF were not clear; each was doing part of the other's job, and they overlapped the regional banks as well.
- Private sources were doing most of the lending. Countries were relying on short-term loans to finance long-term developments.
- Pegged currency rates (value of currency is based on its relation to a major foreign currency but fluctuates within a range) rather than fixed (exchange rates with nations are enforced) left countries vulnerable to speculation.
- Banks within developing countries were channeling funds to favored industries and companies. Projects were sometimes not completed and reforms not implemented.

Because of these dysfunctions, some countries, in effect, remain in permanent debt to the IFIs (Meltzer 2001, 2–3).

The report found that countries were vulnerable to predatory financial practices and that many programs wasted money. It argued that financial stability does not require that all countries follow the same plan or that the IMF lend for institutional reform. It recommended that the IMF give advice but should not tie the advice to assistance. The World Bank and IMF are working with developing countries to establish context-sensitive best practices, incorporate trade development needs into aid and development programs, and equip developing nations to use trade for sustained growth and poverty alleviation. The *Aid for Trade at a Glance* reports detail some of these best practices as well as plans for monitoring and evaluating them (OECD/WTO 2009). Best practice studies such as the *Aid for Trade* reports facilitate the globalization of policies, often creating more homogeneity among countries.

Case Study: The Asian Miracle and the Rejection of Neo-Liberalism

The Asian Miracle began in the 1960s. Japan grew rapidly from 1950 through the 1980s, creating a strong middle-class society. In the meantime, another wave was sweeping Asia—the rapid economic rise of the Asian Tigers: Korea, Taiwan, Hong Kong, and Singapore.

Joseph Stiglitz, Nobel Prize winner in economics, has studied the Asian Miracle in depth. Their economies boomed, he says, "not in spite of the fact that they had not followed most of the dictates of the Washington Consensus but because they did not" (Stiglitz 2002, 91). After developing import substitution as advocated for developing societies, they switched to focus on strong export economies. Rather than privatizing, their governments took charge of managing their economies and spreading benefits of development throughout the societies. They encouraged savings to provide capital flow for development from stable domestic sources. Some created savings institutions and Singapore went so far as to establish mandatory savings through wage attachments (2006, 32–33). Cultural attributes, such as "fiscal prudence, high savings rates, work ethic, competitive exchange rates, and a focus on education," contributed as well (Williamson 2004, 5). If the market failed to create the industries needed to spur development, governments stepped in. In 1968, Korea created one of the most efficient steel companies in the world, leading to Korea's success in automotives and other industries. The Taiwanese government was instrumental in creating the Formosa Plastics Industry in 1954, necessary for many commodities that are "Made in Taiwan" (Stiglitz 2006, 33).

Successes in other East and Southeast Asian countries followed through the 1980s and 1990s. They relied on two main strategies:

- Careful planning of growth in export industries, including the specification of which industrial sectors they would pursue and restriction of imports to protect their domestic industries
- Liberalizing markets and finance slowly and methodically (Stiglitz 2006, 33)

(Continued)

(Continued)

In instances where selected foreign investment was invited, as in China, Malaysia, and Singapore, firms were required to contribute to the host country's development by transferring technology and training workers. Malaysia used foreign investment to lay the groundwork for establishing its own, government-owned oil company. Keeping a portion of profit from foreign investment inside the host country was also critical to development efforts in Southeast Asia (Stiglitz 2006, 33). While specific policies varied, the common element was governmental oversight of development and investment in human capital. This oversight spread the benefits of growth throughout the society, particularly through educating and building a skilled workforce.

The East Asian miracle has not been all smooth sailing. Recognizing the dangers, the Asian Tigers resisted liberalization for decades. But in the 1980s, they opened to foreign capital—perhaps in response to pressure from the IMF and U.S. Treasury. The newly industrializing countries attracted more foreign money than they could spend wisely. This slowed growth and investors panicked. Lax regulation enabled them to pull their money out quickly. There is widespread agreement that this short-term speculation contributed to the Asian financial crisis of 1997.

Those countries that continued to resist the IMF and put controls in place as the crisis began and removed them when the crisis abated fared much better than those that followed IMF prescriptions. Malaysia and China avoided IMF policies and involvement and came out of the crisis with less debt and stronger financial institutions. The Asian Tigers' first phase of globalization was well managed and brought prosperity. The second phase, where unmanaged, brought the economic crisis of 1997 (Stiglitz 2006, 34–35).

Globalization as Transitioning Industrial Sectors

Improvements in technology—including, but not limited to, improvements in transportation, communication, and energy—enable many types of social systems to expand. This is particularly notable in the expansion of labor markets. As increasingly sophisticated machines replace human labor, demand for one type of labor decreases and generally gets replaced by demand for another type of labor. As long as demand for labor stays stable—increasing as population increases—people remain employed and able to buy the commodities that they need and want. The demand they create for the goods and services of one another's labor maintains the demand for labor and the economy hums along.

For example, the market for jobs moves from agriculture and other primary industries to manufacturing when societies use more efficient agricultural and extraction methods. In 1810, 84% of Americans worked on the land to feed the population. Now, less than 2.5% do (Blinder 2006, 114). As machines improve, fewer people are needed in manufacturing, which is now only 22.1% of the GDP in the United States and under 10% of the labor force. The largest segment of the labor market is services. As technology continues to develop, creating the new industries, increasingly different types of goods and services become available creating more jobs and more diverse types of jobs. Different societies are at different stages of this process. As societies transition, some jobs are lost and some move to other societies, usually those in earlier stages.

New technology is not the only factor that drives the transition in labor markets. Changes in people's desires also contribute. With development, people acquire a taste for the consumption of more services, such as travel, fitness, entertainment, and medical care (Blinder 2006). The loss of manufacturing jobs to lower-cost countries has received a lot of attention. More jobs, however, have been lost to technological advance and changing tastes. Historically, there has been a steady global trend of transition from agricultural to industrial to service economies. Change is now so rapid that some countries are leapfrogging over the industrial transition and moving from agricultural to service or to service and industrial at the same time.

BOX 4.9   Consider This: Transitioning

Labor market transitions take time, and vulnerable populations may bear a heavy cost. What are our choices?

- Do we try to halt globalization and close our markets, prevent outsourcing and offshoring?
- Does every country become an economic island? Is this possible or desirable?
- Do we specialize in services that rely on in-person delivery?
- How do we prepare for a transitioning labor market?
- How do we educate when people skills may be more important than computer skills and creativity will be prized?
- What is the government's role in protecting jobs?
- What kind of safety nets do we need to protect people from economic forces beyond their control?

Unfortunately, transitions in labor markets are not synchronized. Employment in many sectors may decrease significantly before it increases sufficiently in others to return to an acceptable level of employment. People who lost jobs in one sector, such as steel manufacture, may be ill prepared for jobs in newer sectors, such as health care. Furthermore, newer jobs may not afford as high a wage as the older jobs. This is particularly true of the contemporary period in developed societies. While high-income jobs in the information fields are increasing, the largest increases in the number of jobs are in lower paying service jobs.

Societal transitions lead to disruptions. The transition from manufacturing to service and information has caused tremendous dislocation in the labor force. Over the last few decades, jobs in retail, fast food, child care, and other low-pay occupations replaced middle and higher income jobs in the industrial sector. Countries that have strong safety nets, such as unemployment compensation, affordable health care, and meaningful job retraining, spread the cost of economic dislocation across the society and limit the devastation in individuals' lives. People expect countries to invest in social welfare spending to protect them from the worst of the transition. Where there is not an adequate social safety net, people bear the cost of transition through low wages and unemployment. During the contemporary economic crisis, low taxes and concerns over government spending have prevented countries from maintaining safety nets leading to protests, sometimes violent, when governments adopt austerity measures. This is discussed in the chapter on globalizing state governance.

Labor market expansion following transitions is not guaranteed. People, government, and corporations need to be willing to buy more goods and services that they did not have before or the labor market would shrink, rather than expand. There must be sufficient demand. Consumerism functions to increase desire for more products and services among individuals. People, corporations, and governments must also be financially able to buy the goods and services. This depends on people, companies, and the government having excess income to spend. Or they need credit. The trend of decreasing wages in combination with high unemployment and the need for increased spending sounds like a recipe for disaster.

BOX 4.10   Consider This: Spending Money

How much do Americans spend on goods and services? How many do we need? In 2009, Americans had $1.13 trillion in discretionary spending. (This shrank to $1.03 billion in 2010.)

Restaurants	$392 billion
Apparel	$177 billion

(Continued)

(Continued)

Auto Parts and Service	$164 billion
Electronics and Appliances	$99.5 billion
Furniture	$88.8 billion
Hotel and Temporary Lodging	$54.9 billion
Air Travel	$41.9 billion
Jewelry	$27.5 billion (Coster, 2010)

While all of these except auto parts and services declined from their 2008 figures due to the recession, our pets have not suffered.

Pet Industry

2009	$45.5 billion
2010	$48.35 billion
2011	$50.96 billion (APPA, 2012)

How do we manage this conundrum? The Keynesian answer is that monetary policy can be used to stimulate demand. Reducing interest rates, increasing government spending, and decreasing taxes of those most likely to spend the money—those who need more money to cover their basic needs—stimulate the economy by making more money available to consumers. When times improve, governments can then raise taxes and interest rates and cut government spending to prevent inflation.

Transitioning labor markets is one of the sources of growing inequality among and within both developing and developed countries. Globalization is accused of impeding progress in some countries and causing a race to the bottom by locking some countries into the role of supplier of cheap labor, cheap primary commodities, and low-level manufacturing. Others argue that wages are depressed in developed societies as good jobs are lost and wages are forced down in jobs that remain. A third argument is that globalization is a race to the top for developing countries by giving them access to capital investment and technical expertise while simultaneously expanding the labor market in developed societies into higher paying sectors.

How to avoid the first two scenarios and optimize the third is a central concern of globalization research on unbundling—the practices and consequences of outsourcing and offshoring.

Globalization as Outsourcing and Offshoring

Outsourcing and offshoring receive a lot of attention in the popular press. In a search of the *New York Times* archive, the earliest mention is October 14, 1981. Roger Moore, former president of GM, was quoted as saying "that American auto workers had 'priced themselves out of the market' . . . spurring manufacturers to buy more components from nonunion suppliers and overseas automobile companies" (Holusha 1981). That oversimplification became the "common wisdom" about offshoring.

When a company takes a process or task that was performed in house to another country, it is *offshoring*. *Outsourcing* refers to a company or corporation taking a process that was performed within the company to an outside contractor. The original corporation saves money in overhead, benefits, maybe wages, and other costs of production. The contracting individual or company performs the same job or makes the same product at lower cost due to economies of scale, cheaper operating costs in their location, or other factors. When the outside contractor is in the same country, the job has been outsourced. When a job goes out of the company and the country, it is outsourced and offshored.

Offshoring was not new in 1981. The International Ladies Garment Workers Union reported losing 150,000 members beginning in the 1960s, largely due to jobs exported. Workers were worried about losing jobs to overseas competition, which they thought were being used to break the unions. Although there was not much attention paid in the popular press, there was already fear about jobs in the service sectors, as well as in manufacturing (Serrin 1989).

Many corporations offshore jobs to factories that they buy, invest heavily in, or open in other countries. This retains production processes within the corporation and its affiliates. Offshoring is one way that corporations try to garner competitive advantage. Lower wages may be just one part of the picture. Lower taxes, weaker environmental laws, lower land costs, and opening a new market may all motivate a company to offshore manufacturing and other tasks.

Industry argues that offshoring keeps them competitive, lowers costs for consumers, advances poor nations, opens their market to domestic goods, and ultimately increases domestic employment. "'It's not about one shore or another shore,' an I.B.M. spokeswoman said. 'It's about investing around the world, including the United States, to build capability and deliver value as defined by our customers'" (Greenhouse 2003). While customers want a less expensive product, when those customers are in their role as workers, they want better jobs kept in the United States.

BOX 4.11   A Closer Look: "Slicing" the Apple Value Chain

The prices that you pay for the things that you buy reflect the price and profit of every country and person in the value or production chain. An iPod that costs $299 has about 451 mostly generic parts. They account for very little of the value added.

Here is how the price of the iPod is broken down by country.

$163 to the United States

$75 distribution and retail

$80 to Apple conception and design

$8 to component makers

$26 to Japan

$19 for Toshiba hard drive

$7 miscellaneous

$110 to miscellaneous countries for nuts and bolts, very generic parts for which there is little value added. This includes about $47 to Philippines and China (including $4 per unit for a final assembly in China).

By far, the most value added goes to the United States for the conception, design, and marketing (Varian 2007).

In summation, two labor market transformations are occurring simultaneously. First, societies are rapidly transitioning their industrial sectors from primary industry to manufacturing and from manufacturing to service and information/high tech. Some countries are skipping manufacturing. Within high-tech manufacturing and services, new lead industries such as biotechnology, the environmental industries, satellite communication, and new materials sciences are emerging. Nurturing these industries will be critical to a country's success attracting higher paying jobs. Second, jobs in old and new industrial sectors are moving to countries where companies try to gain comparative advantage. They are being unbundled. This is another form of trade.

Globalization as Trade in Labor

Improvements in technology, communication, and transportation enable transitions in labor markets and industrial sectors. As the difficulty and cost of moving goods decreases, production may be geographically separated from consumption, moving production processes farther and farther away from where the product is consumed and taking jobs with them. Historically, "anything that could be put in a box and shipped (manufactured goods) was considered tradable and anything that could not be put in a box (such as services) or was too heavy to ship (such as a house) was thought of as non-tradable" (Blinder 2006, 114). With technological advances in transportation, nearly everything (even components of houses) can be shipped nearly anywhere. This creates a global market for not only goods, but jobs as well.

Consumers generally like the global market for goods. It means that people from all over the world can compete for their business. Consumers can choose from German, Japanese, Italian, or American cars, computers, or cheese. As manufacturers and workers, people are more concerned with the potential downside of the global market. While they enjoy being able to sell their products to anyone, anywhere in the world, they do not particularly like competition in their domestic market. People argue for trade regulations and restrictions to protect their businesses and their jobs.

Improvements in technology, particularly in transportation and communication, facilitate outsourcing and offshoring, because production processes can be relatively easily separated, or *unbundled*, and traded across continents. The first phase of unbundling was from 1850 to 1914. It stalled during the inter-war years and resumed after WWII. The second unbundling began in 1960 and continues into the present. Each unbundling involved progressively more jobs and more countries that were more geographically dispersed, increasing globalization. Each unbundling affected a different industrial sector.

Globalization I: The First Unbundling

The first unbundling was the movement of manufacturing processes from many countries to limited numbers of others. Usually, a manufacturing sector locates in concentrated areas rather than dispersing. The beginning of the Industrial Revolution concentrated textile manufacturing in England. Other industries followed: the auto industry, shoe manufacturing, steel, and more recently the high-tech industry in "Silicon Valley." This is called *agglomeration*. Industries agglomerate in areas where they find competitive advantage. Agglomeration tends to lower costs of production for all the entries in a given market.

The first unbundling occurred in two waves. Here, *North* and *South* refer, respectively, to the Global North, shorthand for developed nations, and Global South, the less developed nations.

Table 4.1   A Closer Look: Waves of Agglomeration

Wave One: 1850–1914	Wave Two: Post-WWII
Industrialization concentrated manufacturing in the North.	Industrialization in the South grew rapidly.
Inequality between the North and the South increased.	Incomes in the South increased with industrialization. The South approached income convergence with the North in some industries.
Trade reached record highs.	Trade rose beyond any recorded levels.
The North grew rapidly.	Economic growth in the South surged.
Inequalities in income and employment increased within societies in the North.	(Eventually, income inequalities grew in the South, during the second unbundling.)

Source: Baldwin (2006, 9).

Agglomeration forces encourage urbanization within countries and within regions of the globe as people cluster to suppliers, manufacturers, and markets. Car manufacturing, for example, agglomerated in Europe because of geographic proximity to suppliers (backward—supply side—linkage) and markets (forward—demand side—linkage). During the second wave, shoe and other leather goods agglomerated in Brazil, near to leather supplies, spurring industrialization in the South. The demand and supply side linkages activate a cyclical feedback loop called *circular* or *cumulative causality*. Industries draw people for jobs. This expands their markets. Then they can expand their production, drawing more people.

Agglomerated industries stimulate learning and innovation. The synergy of specialists concentrated in an area facilitates innovation, growing the industry and spinning off applications. The learning possible within a concentration of specialization creates economies of production and innovation that would not be realized otherwise. The industrialized North, by agglomerating industries as they emerged, squelched the impetus for innovation in the South. This magnified differences in growth, exacerbating the inequality between North and South.

BOX 4.12   A Closer Look: Agglomeration Hump

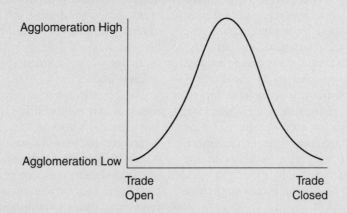

When trade is completely open or completely closed there is no reason to shop for comparative advantage and there is little or no agglomeration. When conditions vary, industries agglomerate.

Source: Adapted from Baldwin, Richard. 2006. "Globalisation: The Great Unbundling(s)." Prime Minister's Office: Economic Council of Finland: Globalisation Challenges for Europe and Finland Project 20 September 2006.

Agglomeration contributes to many of the dynamics of globalization, such as

- the movement of societies through phases of industrial development;
- the movement of industrial sectors from society to society or region to region; and
- the persistence and growth of inequality between North and South, as well as the opportunity for convergence. (Baldwin 2006, 13–14)

Baldwin explains how improvements in technology and liberal or protectionist policy can impact agglomeration. When trade is completely open or completely closed, agglomeration is unlikely. When trade is closed, every country needs to manufacture every product for its own market. When trade is open, or costless, it does not really matter where anything is made. Production could as easily be all in one country or spread absolutely evenly across countries. There is no need to be close to the market. Intermediate levels of trade cost are most conducive to agglomeration because at those levels, it can make a difference in a company's profits. This is the "agglomeration hump" (Baldwin 2006). These dynamics, simple as they seem, are important in deciding economic policy.

Globalization II: The Second Unbundling, 1980s–Present

As with other dimensions of globalization, the contemporary period of economic globalization is strikingly different than prior periods. Unskilled labor absorbed most of the impact of the first unbundling. Firms and industrial sectors left developed countries and moved to less-developed countries and regions. Toward the end of the 1970s, a new economic geography emerged. Ideas and information became quickly and easily portable to anywhere for little cost; manufacturing processes could be unbundled. Instead of a large segment of an industrial sector—such as steel or automotives—or entire factories moving, the production process was disassembled into separate tasks and moved independently of related ones (Levy 2005, 689). The individual task rather than the firm or factory became the smallest level of disaggregation (Baldwin 2006).

Firms now manage geographically dispersed tasks of production and the support services related to them, such as design, bookkeeping, and customer service. Improvements in telecommunications, the rapidly falling price of telecommunication, and readily available organizational skills make this possible. Engineering functions may be in one country, the manufacture of components in several others, accounting in another, marketing somewhere else, and so on. Entire factories need not move or be opened offshore for managers, workers, designers, engineers, accountants, and other workers in the production process to coordinate their activities. Each task can locate to realize the most competitive advantage (Levy 2005, 687).

Fragmenting production processes at the level of the task accelerates the global spread of economic enterprises. Outsourcing and offshoring totaled about $525 billion in 2010, spanning the industrial sectors from low-level manufacturing to the highly technical services (Plunkett 2010a). A global market in highly skilled work, previously thought to be nontradable, has emerged alongside the global market for unskilled labor. The second unbundling or dispersion of tasks increased industrialization of the South. Changing tastes, new technology, and suburbanization stimulated deindustrialization in the North (Baldwin 2006, 14).

The difference between tradable and non-tradable jobs is not, as most people anticipated, the education or skill levels required for the job. The divide between tradable and non-tradable jobs is personal jobs and impersonal jobs, those that require physical presence and those that do not. Many tradable jobs are highly skilled, such as software programming, engineering, and accounting.

They do not require face-to-face interaction or in-person contact. Non-tradable jobs are those that require face-to-face contact. They are personal or location specific. Janitorial staff, plumbers, hairdressers, construction workers, home health workers, and elementary school teachers are fairly safe jobs. Who would have anticipated that engineering, architecture, and computer analysis would not be (Blinder 2006, 116)?

Most current estimates of the number of jobs that can be traded are misleadingly low. The most oft-quoted estimates may be only one tenth the potential job losses. The line between tradable and non-tradable service jobs will keep shifting, just as it did for manufacturing jobs as transportation costs decreased. Any impersonal service job and nearly every goods producing job is tradable. Using this criteria, far more jobs could be lost than the 3.3 million estimate of Forrester Research and the 11% estimates of independent Berkeley and McKinsley studies (Blinder 2006, 116).

We have always considered medicine to be a field that required high skill levels and in-person contact. However even doctors can be traded. Surgeons are beginning to perform surgery remotely. Already, X-rays and magnetic imaging scans are sent abroad for analysis. Doctors can perform long-distance via video and audio conferencing. In addition, medical tourism is gaining popularity as medical costs in developed countries increase. People travel to have medical procedures done at a fraction of their cost in wealthier countries.

It is unlikely that all of the tradable jobs will be traded. Highly skilled, highly educated workers in rich countries are likely to exert considerable political pressure to retain their jobs (Blinder 2006, 7). Nevertheless, no one has a guarantee that their job will not move.

The good news is that wages in many of the personal service jobs are increasing in cases where technological improvements cannot produce major cost-saving measures or displace workers. There are not many ways to increase productivity in personal service as there are with impersonal service jobs. An hour massage will always take an hour. Bathing a patient must be done with care. Education and learning take time and hands-on experience. This is one reason the cost of medical care and college educations have been rising faster than prices generally (Blinder 2006, 5).

Table 4.2 Tradable and Non-Tradable Job Outlook

Potentially Tradable Jobs	Potentially Non-Tradable Jobs
14.3 million manufacturing	22 million local state and federal government
College teaching (many vulnerable)	7.6 million construction and mining
16.7 million professional and business services (many, not all tradable)	15.6 million retail trade (replaceable through online shopping!)
8.1 million financial services (many vulnerable)	15 million (most) health care
3.2 million information services (many vulnerable)	3 million K–12 education
	12.3 million hospitality and leisure (mostly stay)

Source: Blinder (2006, 113–121).

Costs of Offshoring and Unbundling

Unbundling and offshoring are strategies a company uses to gain competitive advantage. It has value to a firm to the extent that it decreases costs and increases the bottom line. The overall cost to societies when their firms offshore is more difficult to calculate.

For every dollar spent overseas, a U.S. company makes 58 cents, saved primarily from wages (Agarwal and Farrell, cited in Levy 2005, 686). Industry tends to present the 58-cent savings as a saving for the U.S. economy. By earning money through overseas investments, offshoring may add to a country's GNP and economic growth. When a company manufactures abroad, it also creates a market there and enhances economic growth. From a worker perspective, economic growth through saving in wages paid to workers is not a source of wealth for the economy as a whole. It is a transfer of wealth from workers who would have higher wages to shareholders who save on the wages that they actually pay. Similarly, when a company sells more U.S. goods abroad, it is primarily shareholders who benefit because a good deal of the production of the goods sold occurs in the offshore locations. Again, workers do not benefit (686).

Different types of offshoring have different impacts on workers. When a company opens an affiliate in Britain, France, or another rich country, its motive is usually to expand the market for U.S. goods. This expansion has little impact on employment in the company's parent country. An expansion into low-income countries tends to be for cost cutting. This expansion does lead to unemployment in the parent country, particularly within the given industrial sector (Harrison and McMillan 2006, 11). In these cases, offshoring may be more about shifting power and wealth than efficiency (Levy 2005, 686, 690; Doh 2005, 700).

Historically, jobs lost in one industrial sector are balanced by the expansion of employment in a new sector. From 1991 to 2001, expansion of U.S. multinationals into developing countries was followed by an expansion of employment, primarily in services and wholesale trade. Jobs in service and wholesale sectors increased, accounting for an overall increase in employment even though jobs in manufacturing decreased (Blinder 2006).

But expansion into new industrial sectors is not guaranteed. One reason for expansion in the United States from 1991 to 2001 was that during those years, the foreign affiliates of U.S. multinationals did not expand into the service sector. Expansion of the service sector remained in the United States. Since then, the expansion of affiliates into service has increased. If service follows the trend in manufacturing, many service jobs will be lost and may not be replaced (Harrison and McMillan 2006, 14).

If there is a transition to new sectors, such as the new lead industries of biotechnology and green energy, job expansion is likely to take more time than job loss. During that time, people lose jobs, lose homes, go hungry, and lose out on education and health care (where there is not universal coverage). When and if employment catches up, questions concerning the types of jobs remain to be answered. Will higher skilled jobs be replaced with lower skilled jobs? Will wages be higher, the same, or lower? Will the workforce be prepared for new jobs?

Of the workers dislocated from 1979 to 1999, 86% were worse off, and 56% were much worse off after losing jobs (Levy 2005, 687). This is despite continued growth and continued production of wealth in the U.S. economy. Dislocation is part of the story of declining wages since the early 1970s.

BOX 4.13   Consider This: The Largest Job Growth in the United States

Transitions in the job structure are anticipated by the Department of Labor. Their projection for 2008 to 2018 is just that—a projection. But if they are correct, what is your prognosis for inequality in the United States? Will most workers be better or worse off? What could be done to change the projections or prognosis?

Table 4.3   Top 16 Occupations With the Largest Job Growth (Numbers in Thousands)

2008 National Employment Title	Employment		Change, 2008–2018	
	2008	2018	Number	Percentage
Registered nurses	2,618.7	3,200.2	581.5	22.20
Home health aides	921.7	1,382.6	460.9	50.01
Customer service representatives	2,252.4	2,651.9	399.5	17.74
Combined food prep and service workers, including fast food	2,701.7	3,096.0	394.3	14.59
Personal and home care aides	817.2	1,193.0	375.8	45.99
Retail salespersons	4,489.2	4,863.9	374.7	8.35
Office clerks, general	3,024.4	3,383.1	358.7	11.86
Accountants and auditors	1,290.6	1,570.0	279.4	21.65
Nursing aides, orderlies, and attendants	1,469.8	1,745.8	276.0	18.78
Post-secondary teachers	1,699.2	1,956.1	256.9	15.12
Construction laborers	1,248.7	1,504.6	255.9	20.49
Elementary school teachers, except special education	1,549.5	1,793.7	244.2	15.76
Truck drivers, heavy and tractor-trailer	1,798.4	2,031.3	232.9	12.95
Landscaping and groundskeeping workers	1,205.8	1,422.9	217.1	18.00

2008 National Employment Title	Employment		Change, 2008–2018	
	2008	2018	Number	Percentage
Bookkeeping, accounting, and auditing clerks	2,063.8	2,276.2	212.4	10.29
Executive secretaries and administrative assistants	1,594.4	1,798.8	204.4	12.82

Source: U.S. Bureau of Labor Statistics (2009, 91).

In addition to thinking about what you enjoy and are good at, how will you select jobs along your career path? Will you try to find a non-tradable job?

Would you follow your dream job to another country?

Here are some other questions to consider.

What are the fastest-growing jobs by percentages and absolute numbers?

Which would appear on a list of tradable or non-tradable jobs?

How many are personal? Impersonal?

How many are high skilled? Low skilled?

How many are high pay? Low pay?

Does economic growth translate to a better quality of life? Always? Often? Sometimes? Never?

Under what conditions do you think economic growth and increases in quality of life for the society as a whole go together?

The Future of Offshoring and Re-Shoring

Dislocation in the labor market is due to many sources, not just offshoring. The deindustrialization of the Global North seems largely a function of internal forces—80% in the United States and Europe, and 90% in Japan. These forces are the shift to services and the increases in productivity, not offshoring (Baldwin 2006, 16). The future of offshoring and outsourcing is uncertain. The benefits of offshoring vary by circumstances. Loss of competitive advantage, lessened credibility with customers, and potential loss of trade secrets are increasing the costs and risks of offshoring. Some firms find themselves bringing home processes that they once had offshored (Doh 2005, 700).

First, foreign direct investment seems to have more impact than domestic investment in eventual wage convergence in developing societies (Doh 2005). One example is how the global market in high-tech and business services has boosted salaries in developing nations. Shortages of workers are driving up wages as well. Developing countries—China and India, for example—face a number of additional problems that lessen their attraction. Infrastructure problems from the physical, such as pollution, roads, and electricity, to the non-material, such as the need for expansion of education and health care, will also increase the cost of doing business there. As costs increase in developing nations, the savings of locating there decreases. Ironically, the success of societies that attracted jobs may cost them their competitive advantage (Plunkett 2012). Another ironic twist is that some of the offshore contractors are opening branches in Europe and America to be closer to their customers. Second, for some companies, factors such as quality control and public relations remain important considerations. This lesson was learned by clothing companies and retailers caught outsourcing to firms that operated as sweatshops. Their products and stores were boycotted. Toy companies whose outsourced and offshored toys contained toxins lost millions of dollars. Violations of labor, wage, and safety laws are still egregious in outsourced offshoring.

Domestically owned offshoring companies are, for the most part, law compliant.

Third, production functions are distributed globally according to their own logic. Many firms are not concerned with owning the overseas firms to which they ship production, services, and thus jobs. Others are very concerned with ownership because of potential costs, such as loss of trade secrets, and of doing business across not just national but also corporate borders. These companies may want to stay close to home.

Growing Economic Inequalities: Within and Among Societies

Economic Growth and Quality of Life

There is not much agreement on how economic openness and integration impact inequality within and among nations.[4] However, nearly everyone agrees that inequality among and within countries has grown over the course of modern globalization. Among those who support capitalist expansion, there is general agreement that by participating in the global market, people are better off than if they do not. Whether they are suppliers of raw materials, unskilled labor, or low-level processing, they have access to trade, capital, and capital investment that they would not have otherwise. As developing societies continue to participate, their standard of living should continue to improve. This was the case in Japan, South Korea, and the other Asian Tigers.

Other societies have not had the same success. Overall, inequality has increased. Statistics on growth, development, and inequality confirm this. At the time of the Industrial Revolution, there was little difference in the mean income across countries. For example, in 1870, the average (un-weighted)

GDI per capita of the 10 richest countries was only 6 times greater than the average (un-weighted) GDI per capita of the 10 poorest countries. In 2002, the ratio was 42 to 1 (Milanovic 2006, 9). The age of development left a majority of the world behind. "Of 108 countries over the 1960–90 period only 11 grew faster than 4.2% per annum (among them Korea, Taiwan and Indonesia), whereas 16 developing countries had negative growth during the period" (Sindzingre 2005, 283).

The extent to which the benefits of growth are shared within countries is also questionable. Rising growth and profits translate to a rising share of wealth going to the richest segments of populations and a declining share to most segments. In the United States, the bottom four income quintiles, 80% of the population, saw their share of the total income of the country decrease from 1970 to the present. The top quintile's share increased, and the higher up the income pyramid, the greater was the relative increase, (Census Bureau 2012, Table 694). In the United States, the value of the minimum wage peaked in 1968 equal to about $10.51 in 2012 dollars. The peak for average weekly wages was in 1973. A study of eight U.S. cities found that on average 30% of families' incomes fall below the cost of a basic, no frills, family budget—figured specifically for the cost of living in each city. That included about 20% of families with a full-time, year-round worker. About 30% fell under 200% of the poverty level (Allegretto, n.d.).

Evaluating economies based on growth masks concerns about the quality of life. The Institute for Innovation in Social Policy (n.d.) has indexed the social health of the United States reaching back as far as 1959. It has found that economic growth was accompanied by growth in social health of the nation from 1959 to the early 1970s. However, from 1970 to 2006, the social health index dropped 17%. In contrast, economic growth has risen by about 302%.

BOX 4.14   Consider This: Index of Social Health

Notwithstanding the recent economic crisis, economic growth in the United States since WWII has been nothing less than phenomenal. However, the quality of life has been decreasing. This index of social health is based on 16 indicators. Six have improved since 1970: infant mortality, teenage drug abuse, high school dropouts, poverty among the elderly, homicides, and alcohol-related traffic fatalities. Ten have worsened: unemployment, wages, health insurance coverage, out-of-pocket health costs among the elderly, food insecurity, affordable housing, child poverty, child abuse, teenage suicide, and income inequality.

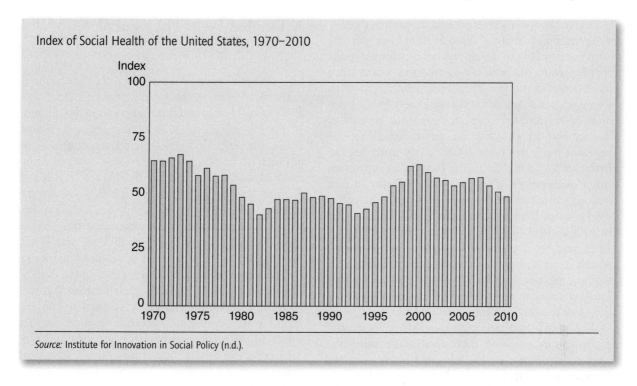

Index of Social Health of the United States, 1970–2010

Source: Institute for Innovation in Social Policy (n.d.).

For these reasons, the economic dimension of globalization has become the most vilified dimension of globalization. The 1999 meeting of the WTO in Seattle, Washington, was one of the first major meetings of an international economic organization to be met with major protests by social justice movements. Protests have continued at nearly every global economic summit since then. Editorials, editorial cartoons, and letters to the editor rarely praise the accomplishments of economic globalization. Declining wages and job loss, low wages, the destruction of the environment, and trade in financial instruments devoid of real value define globalization for many people no matter where in the world they live, in a rich country or in a poor one.

Where Has All the Money Gone?

At first glance, two major concerns about the causes of inequality seem contradictory. Some people argue that globalization transfers money from poorer nations in the periphery to richer nations in the core. The continuing poverty in many parts of the world, despite the wealth of their resources and their volume of labor, supports that claim. On the other hand, offshoring is thought to take jobs and investment from richer nations to the newly industrializing economies. Both arguments have merit. The classic study of Krugman and Venables (1995) found that the world economy must achieve a certain critical level of integration before it differentiates richer from poorer nations. When differentiation occurs, the increase in the rich nations' incomes is partly at the expense of the poor. However, as integration proceeds further, it becomes more costly to do business in the rich nations, and the resulting rise in income in poor nations may be partly at the expense of the rich (876).

This dynamic is reflected in recent statistics on growth reported by the World Bank. From 1995 to 2005, middle- and low-income countries' share of global output increased from 40% to 46%. Low-income countries grew at an average rate of 5% annually, compared to slightly over 4% for middle income. However, much of the growth in low- and middle-income countries was accounted for by a few countries and was not evenly spread (World Bank 2007, 185). Millions have moved out of poverty, particularly in China and other East Asian countries where the millennium development goal of halving poverty has already been achieved (World Bank 2008, 16). Poverty remains entrenched in the most vulnerable societies in Southeast Asia and sub-Saharan Africa. High-income societies grew only slightly over 2%.

Where there is more economic inequality, there is more pessimism about globalization, in both rich and poor nations. Many developed nations have experienced growing disparities in income and wealth since the last decades of the 20th century. In rich nations, where incomes are falling or stagnant, publics are more protectionist. They perceive that the benefits to the winners in globalization are exceeded by the losses of the losers (Coe 2008). In his study for the IMF, Coe found that the rise of India and China coinciding with perceived increases in inequality in rich nations has led to the perception among white-collar workers that their jobs are now at risk and a belief that the benefits of globalization are not shared fairly. They have become more receptive to policy favoring special interest protectionism. Among these same rich nations, the more income is redistributed (social welfare programs) to the bottom 30% of the population, the more receptive people are to globalization.

The policy implication is that where increasing globalization is desired, there needs to be more efficient redistribution of the benefits of globalization. Otherwise, political forces may force a retreat. This redistribution cannot be narrowly defined to workers who have lost jobs but should include those working toward the bottom of the hierarchy. Incentives to continue working must be put into place. These may include education—which tends to be inefficient in redistribution—but more direct measures such as Earned Income Credits and other tax schemes also need to be included at a sufficient level to offset losses of globalization (Coe 2008).

A Tangled Web: The Global Economic Crisis

Like the unraveling of a tangled web, the economic crisis that began in the United States in December 2007 spread havoc and destruction globally. Millions of people lost their jobs; unemployment soared above 9% in the United States, into the double digits in much of Europe, and above 20% in some countries. Millions of people in the United States and Europe lost their homes. By 2009, GDP in the United States dropped to about $1.1 trillion less than its potential and underachieved at this level at least through 2011 (Center on Budget and Policy Priorities 2011). The number of children qualifying for free lunches in the United States increased 46%. The crisis was not caused by globalization, but globalization spread the crisis from country to country. World leaders were quick to evade responsibility for a role in the crisis, pointing out, for example, that "the crisis did not spontaneously erupt in Europe" (Sarkozy, then President of France, quoted in Sanger and Landler 2009). While the crisis did begin in the United States, similar forces at work in Europe, such as inadequate regulation in the finance industry, too much faith in the market to set prices and values, complicated and risky financial instruments, housing bubbles, and reliance on debt to finance growth contributed as well.

If we define economic globalization as increasing foreign investments, density of trade, or any other

---

BOX 4.15   A Closer Look: "The Financial Situation"

Risky financial practices such as those that led to the crisis of 2007 are not new, as this excerpt from the turn of the 20th Century indicates.

There is also the undeniable fact that the whole West is inflated. It has been given too much to wild speculation. Financial methods have been too bold and reckless. The Diamond Match and New York Biscuit episodes are evidences of that. There has been too much money put out on unworthy collateral. Chicago, itself, (is) not sound. The great majority of its securities and its financial institutions are beyond suspicion. But it has suffered from the impositions of many reckless speculators whose wild-cat methods cannot but leave some lasting damage. I fear the West taken generally, will suffer from this inflation, and will be barred from receiving the full measure of prosperity which should result from such natural conditions as...exist.

Source: The New York Times, January 10, 1897.

measure of cross-border economic activity, the crisis slammed the brakes on globalization. As reported in *Euro Intelligence*, a variety of economic integration indicators dropped rapidly:

- Global trade volumes fell for the first time in over 25 years
- Supply and demand for basic shipping fell 90%, although it recovered slightly in early 2009
- Exports from Japan, Korea, Taiwan, and China fell between 10% and 40% in late 2008
- Net private sector capital flows to emerging markets in 2009 were projected to fall to $165 billion—36% of the $466 billion inflow in 2008 and only 20% of the record amount in 2007
- The projected decline in capital flows was about 6% of the combined GDP of the emerging countries. This is significantly more than the decline of

approximately 3.5% of combined GDP in the Asian financial crisis and 1.5% in the Latin American crisis (Das 2009)

While the crisis may have halted cross-border economic activity, the degree to which national economies are woven into a global system became crystal clear by the rapid spread of the crisis. The causes were complex and will be debated for decades. Nevertheless, the housing crisis was a trigger. In the United States, it started simply enough when people started thinking of their houses not merely as homes but as capital investments. In the United States, most people's wealth is in the value of their house, not financial investments. In the 1990s, a number of factors coalesced, tempting people to use their house as an investment vehicle to create wealth.

BOX 4.16   Consider This: Hypothetical Case of Using a Home as an ATM

Original cost of home	$120,000
Down payment	$10,000
Mortgage (5% interest rate)	$110,000
Inflated home value after five years	$180,000
Amount owed on mortgage after five years	$100,000
Home equity loan (75% of equity in the house)	$60,000
Total owed on house	$160,000
Bubble bursts	
Value of home	$120,000 or less!
Homeowner "under water"	$40,000

The Taxpayer Relief Act of 1997 changed the tax code so that people did not have to pay taxes on the profit they made when they sold their homes. Houses became a source of tax-free windfalls. Some scholars think it accounted for as much as 17% of the increase in home sales (Bajaj and Leonhardt 2008). Home sales and home prices rose. A housing bubble began.

Many people tried to build wealth buying a house and selling it at a profit. It seemed a surefire and safe way to make money. The housing bubble grew. When interest rates fell to very low levels,

home buying became an even more attractive investment, making both buying and selling easier. Home prices went higher; the bubble got bigger.

Other tax policies and new instruments also encouraged home buying. Many costs of owning a home are tax deductible. In effect, this makes a portion of the cost income. Through home equity loans, people borrow money based on the value of their house. These loans cost less in interest than conventional loans, and the interest is tax deductible. A contributor to Paul Krugman's blog stated this effect succinctly: "[A] huge number of households in this country, in response to virtually stagnant wages and rising expenses, used the increasing perceived value of their homes and low interest rates to make their homes into virtual A.T.M.'s" (Doug Johnson, in Krugman 2007). It is understandable that people wanted to make money on housing if they could. Many people borrowed a lot of money, up to 80% of the inflated value of their homes.

The mortgage industry was getting creative as well. New financial instruments allowed many people who did not qualify for conventional mortgages to buy homes. People were sold loans at low initial rates that increased after a few years, when they presumably would have a bigger salary. Unemployment was very low in the late 1990s, so this seemed a safe bet. People with bad credit histories and low incomes entered the market. They were sold subprime mortgages that had high interest rates and very low down payments. The bubble grew bigger and bigger.

Homeowners were not being greedy. The real value of wages has declined since 1973. People saw a chance to buy a house—the American dream—and make some money. They believed lenders and real estate agents who told them to "buy up" as an investment and had faith in the fiduciary responsibility of banks. The lenders and agents may have believed their own advice as well. Lenders had little to fear. Many sold the mortgages after they processed them. If they kept the mortgage and a person defaulted, the lender could still make money from the fees and interest on the initial loan and on resale of the house if it was forfeited. When warnings about the housing bubble were sounded, the industry either did not hear them or ignored them. Even Alan Greenspan, Chairman of U.S. Federal Reserve Board, who could have helped avoid the catastrophe, did not heed the warnings issued by many economists.

When housing prices dropped, many people who made a small or no down payment or who had borrowed based on the inflated value of their house were living in houses that were not worth what they owed. Many others were in houses that they could not afford once their low initial loan rates rose. People began to default on their mortgages. Because housing prices were lower, banks could not recoup the risky loans they had made based on inflated values. Hundreds of thousands of people were losing their homes. These homes flooded the market, driving prices further downward. Many people who had never missed a mortgage payment were underwater and lost their homes.

BOX 4.17   Consider This: Are You One of These Students?

Although Canada experienced a recession at the same time as the United States, "more than 9,000 U.S. students are studying at Canadian universities and colleges, up from 2,500 just 12 years ago" (Lewin 2009).

What could be driving U.S. students to pursue degrees in Canada, when so many foreign students are coming to the United States? Are the universities better in Canada, or are other factors at work?

Financial Contagion

How did the crisis spread?

With little regulation during the last decades of the 20th century, the financial industry kept busy inventing new instruments to make even more money from buying and selling financial products. Individual mortgages were bundled into packages of thousands and sold as "mortgage-backed securities" and "mortgage derivatives." In those packages were the risky loans that people would eventually not be able to pay.

Banks owned these toxic assets, bad mortgage loans that had little or no value. Because they were bundled, no one knew exactly where these bad mortgages were or which banks owned them. Banks became risky business partners. Banks stopped loaning to other banks. If banks could not get money, employers could not borrow to meet their payrolls, companies could not borrow money for new equipment, and stores could not borrow money to replace their inventory. Credit, once free flowing, froze. People lost houses and jobs. People without jobs stopped spending. People in fear of losing their jobs, those facing reduced hours or pay freezes, also stopped spending. The freeze in consumer spending froze demand, which froze production, and more people lost jobs.

Within weeks, the misery spread globally. Bank lending linkages were most likely the primary driver of the stress. Some foreign banks had bought the mortgage-backed derivatives. Confidence in those banks dropped. Corporations in the United States and abroad could not buy or sell. With more companies losing business, more workers lost jobs. Spending slowed further, shrinking economic growth globally for the first time in 60 years (Goldman 2009). In March 2011, the number of jobs in the United States was still 7.5 million less than it had been at the official start of the recession in December 2007. The labor market was 11.3 million jobs short of where it needed to be to restore the unemployment rate to 5.5%, the rate at the beginning of the crisis in December 2007. In March 2011, the unemployment rate in the United States seemed stuck at 9% (Shierholz 2011). By the end of 2012, it had dipped to 7.7%. In the 27 countries of the Eurozone, the picture was bleaker. In October 2012, unemployment for most countries was in the double digits. Only four were below 6%, and Greece and Spain were above 25% (Eurostat 2012).

Advanced economies degenerated rapidly. Iceland was among the first casualties. Not because banks had bought the mortgage-backed securities but because Icelandic banks were heavily in debt. Like those people who had bought a larger house than they could afford, Icelandic banks had been on a buying spree from decades of global expansion. When credit froze, they could no longer finance their debt (Pfanner 2008).

The impact was felt by developing nations within weeks. Food prices soared. The ripple effects of unemployment in developed nations were enormous. In India, textile manufacturing has been a route out of poverty for many of the indigent. Salaries of $3 to $4 a day mean a life above poverty, a home, and education for their children. Half of Indian textile production is for export, and 20% of that goes to the United States. When spending dropped, millions of textile workers in India lost jobs or saw wages plunge back to $1.50 a day. Even China lost jobs. This scenario has been repeated throughout the developing world. Growth in some developing nations, including India, rebounded more quickly than in the developed nations, but damage to the poor is longer lived. The IMF estimated that 50 million people were driven into poverty globally, and another 200 million were put in very precarious positions (Goldman 2009).

The roots of the economic crisis run deeply. Some economists believe that relying on financial instruments to make money rather than producing goods and services is a recipe for disaster. The share of the finance sector in total corporate profits rose from 10% on average from the 1950s through the 1980s, to 22% in the 1990s, and an astonishing 34% in the first half of this decade (Friedman 2009).

BOX 4.18   Check It Out Yourself: Confidence

To what degree has a normative consensus on economic values facilitated a spread of capitalism within societies? You can find data concerning people's attitudes, values, and beliefs in the World Values Survey Online Analysis.

http://www.worldvaluessurvey.org

These questions have content related particularly to economics:

V117: Private or government ownership

V142: Confidence in major corporations

V146C: Confidence in ASEAN

V146E: Confidence in NAFTA

(Continued)

Another issue is people's perceptions. Some economists have argued that the objective nature of the crisis did not warrant the severity of the economic experience that followed. A crisis of confidence exacerbated the financial crisis. When people do not have confidence in the system and are anxious or fearful of their economic status, it affects more than just stock prices; it affects all aspects of their economic activity (Freidman 2009).

By 2009, a new phase of the crisis emerged. Debt crises threatened Greece and Ireland. Both of these countries had been fast growing in the years before the global recession. Foreign money was readily available and they borrowed freely. When the recession hit, revenues dropped dramatically and the flow of foreign money dried up. Greece could not pay the service on the bonds issued on its debt. In the case of Ireland, the government paid for the bailout of their banks as a result of the recession. Despite aid packages from the EU, severe cutbacks in government spending—cutting salaries, pensions, and other programs—the debt crisis spread. By 2011, Spain, Portugal, and Italy were in trouble. Because these are national, sovereign debts—unlike regular debtors—no one can force a country to pay. Loaning to these countries became riskier. Therefore, interest on their bonds increased, lessening confidence in their ability to repay and their actual ability to repay their debts. Because debt bonds are traded internationally, banks who own their debts are threatened, jeopardizing economies not only in Europe but everywhere. If one country defaults on its debt, it may panic investors, making borrowing for all European countries more difficult. In many respects, this echoes the crisis that hit Argentina in 2001.

Governing the Global Economy: Responding to Crisis

There are no easy solutions to economic crises like the global recession and European debt crisis. There is a lot of disagreement among economists, politicians, and the public over how they should be solved. Bretton Woods gave governments fiduciary responsibility over their economies and mechanisms to intervene in the economy to fulfill that responsibility. The neo-liberal principles that replaced the Bretton Woods regime transferred that responsibility to the market. The assumption is that the market, comprising people seeking their own self-interests, would act as a responsible fiduciary—that private greed would serve the common good.

The basic tension between government and markets remains at the center of the contemporary debates. At the 2000 UN Conference on Trade and Development, Gerald Helleiner optimistically declared in the prestigious Prebisch Lecture that

> we have learned from the crises in the 1990s and the suffering of so many people globally that [there are] important institutional and legal prerequisites to the effective and socially harmonious functioning of markets, without which free market behaviour can approximate the law of the jungle. (2000, 7)

Again, after the collapse of the dot-com bubble in 2000, there was some support for international solutions such as an expansion of the ability of the Financial Stability Forum to govern flows of money, but there was more support for national sovereignty over economies and national regulation of financial markets (Dore 2000, 15). In many societies, this meant little regulation. There is a fundamental choice in economic affairs. The virtues that are needed if we are to have a free market—prudence, temperance, thrift, promise keeping, honesty, and humility—cannot be optional. If people want loose political bonds and little regulation, they need strong moral bonds, substantial moral capital. We have had neither, which led to the contemporary crises (Gregg 2008).

At a Congressional Hearing on the economic crisis, Alan Greenspan, chairman of the U.S. Federal Reserve from 1987 to 2006, echoed this, admitting those who relied on the self-interest of those in the mortgage industry to "protect shareholders' equity . . . are in a state of shocked disbelief." His ideology, he conceded, had a flaw (quoted in Andrews 2008). Whether or not a better balance between market and government will be achieved in response to the crisis that began in 2007 is not clear. However, as of December 2012, little had been done to balance needs of the market with regulation at national or global levels.

The crises have also raised the question as to whether corporations have any more control over their environments than societies have. This is very different than the situation from colonialism through WWII. Prior to WWII, the activities of corporations internationally were not contingent on any consideration other than market. The intensity of global economic activity has changed that. The challenges that face corporate heads today are more volatile and unpredictable. Challenges of

> the Internet, of globalization, of creating trust in the face of rapid change . . . of balancing shareholders and stakeholders, and of understanding the need for broader vision and leadership in society . . . will be assessed by historians as having been too difficult for most CEOs to handle all at once. (Garten, quoted in Holzner and Holzner 2006, 212)

Given the volatility of their environment, there is evidence that corporations may welcome increased regulation. Regulation creates a more stable and predictable environment. In the East Asian crisis, Malaysia was warned that the strict capital controls it put in place would create an exodus out of the country. Instead, capital controls attracted capital.

Examining the positions of the main groups of actors in the period following the crisis may provide clues to the direction of global economic governance and the shape of the evolving global economy.

The View From the World Economic Forum

The Interests of the Private Sector

The theme of the Davos annual meeting in 2009 was "shaping the post crisis world." Wedged between the 2008 and 2009 meetings of the G20, the WEF brought heads of state, financial ministers, leaders of multilateral organizations, and civil society groups together with leaders of the world's largest private enterprises. A number of themes emerged. The WEF does not issue an official statement, but summaries of the meetings, an annual report, and reports on special topics are issued. The comments summarized below represent a sampling of the opinions expressed at the WEF, emphasizing the opinions of corporate executives.

The private sector worried that the loss of public trust and influence would cause governments and people to overreact to the crisis, by instituting protectionist policies, on the one hand, and fomenting social unrest, on the other. Jeroen van der Veer, one of the co-chairs of the meeting and CEO of Royal Dutch Shell, acknowledged the crisis revealed the "flaws of laissez-faire ideology" but argued that "few [people] would wish to see a return to communism, or to the stagflation of the late 1960s and the 1970s." The crisis, he said, created a rare opportunity to "forge a new consensus and build a better system," implying that nations would avoid drastic change: Change is unpredictable and poses considerable risk (Gowing et al. 2009).

The discussions reverberated with fears that failures to reform the global economy could have unpredictable consequences. The threat posed by deepening inequality and poverty was reiterated by corporate, governmental, and nongovernmental representatives.

- "The time for words is over; this is the time for implementation and action. If we come back in six months or a year and are still talking about the same things, we will have failed. And the social unrest we will have to deal with will be absolutely dramatic" —Maria Ramos, a CEO from South Africa (WEF 2009b, 15).
- "When the economic malaise really begins to affect families and people do not have jobs, that

will have huge political repercussions . . . while 2008 will be remembered as the year of financial crashes, 2009 will go down in history as the year of 'political crashes,' with governments falling in many countries."—Moisés Naím, editor-in-chief of *Foreign Policy* (media) (WEF 2009b, 7).

As it happened, governments did fall. Ireland, Iceland, Greece, Spain, Italy, and France saw governments topple and lose elections, based at least in part on loss of confidence to manage their economies and anger over austerity measures.

BOX 4.19   Consider This: Do You Agree?

"The current architecture of managing global affairs is broken and needs to be fixed."
    Kofi Annan, former secretary-general of the United Nations and co-chair of the WEF Annual Meeting 2009 (WEF 2009b, 17).

Coordination

At the WEF, business and government leaders called upon the G20 governments to coordinate to a greater level than they ever have before. Aside from avoiding protectionism and steps that would raise public ire, there was less agreement.

Global coordination of fiscal stimulus plans, large enough to offset the decline in private investment and consumption and ensure sufficient capital flow to the developing world, received strong endorsements across the board. World leaders agreed to increase contributions to the IMF and other international financial institutions and allow countries to borrow before they are in balance of payment problems (WEF 2009b, 12–13).

Business leaders urged governments to address the immediate and persistent problems of a successor to the Kyoto Protocol on climate change and resolve the Doha round of trade talks. They promised that the WEF would facilitate public and private cooperation on key issues of climate change, clean energy, education, water security, food security, the economic potential in untapped markets, entrepreneurship, and the global financial system through ongoing discussions of the Forum's reports. Getting governments to settle the trade and environmental agreements provides a more predictable context for business decisions.

Effective global economic coordination is inescapably linked to global governance. The meeting's outlook for better global governance was bleak. How can nations agree on a new global economy if they cannot agree on agricultural subsidies, intellectual property, and other issues in the Doha round of trade talks? More democratic global governance to provide a greater role and voice for emerging and developing economies and closer and better monitoring of stability of national economies brought general agreement.

All participants agreed on the need for better global governance. Economist Joe Stiglitz argued that although the G20 was a better instrument for global governance than the G7 because it represented both developing and developed nations, it was still more concerned with interests of the richer nations. Others picked up this thread and argued that if stability requires more oversight of developing nations by international institutions, such as the IMF, it requires more oversight of the rich nations as well, particularly the reserve currency countries (WEF 2009b, 19–21).

Morality and Profit

Industry leaders acknowledged that too much greed and chasing short-term profit, with too little personal morality and ethics, played a large role in the crisis. The possibility of social backlash and strategies for preventing it were high on the agenda (WEF 2009c).

"It's time to challenge corporations to examine their personal morality and ethics and whether they truly believe that what's good for corporations has to be good for society and what's good for society is good for corporations," said Indra Nooyi, Chairman and Chief Executive Officer of PepsiCo. "We have to ask companies to perform with a sense of purpose, not just performing for short-term shareholder interests." (WEF 2009d)

Participants openly acknowledged the failure of the "invisible hand" of the market. "It delivered enormous wealth for the few but not enormous wealth to the masses" (WEF 2009d).

Suggestions for correcting the global capitalist culture were plentiful.

- Turn management into a true and honorable profession that is to serve society.
- Incorporate an oath of ethics into business similar to the Hippocratic Oath.
- Change the business school curricula to emphasize long-term sustainability, not short-term profit.
- Require independent audits of corporate culture and workforce engagement.
- Correct executive compensation to reward long-term sustainability, "measures of the company's reputation, employee morale and customer satisfaction."
- Reduce multiple board memberships so that corporate board members have time for meaningful oversight.
- Prosecute those who had betrayed public trust.
- Reduce executive compensation.
- Improve regulatory agencies by paying higher salaries (WEF 2009d).

There were no definitive regulatory recommendations; most were vague. There was not a call to temper the dominance of the profit motive in capitalism. Whether right or wrong, better or worse, corporate ethics are still thought to demand maximizing profit. Van der Veer stated this unequivocally, pointing out that although employment had to be sustained to maintain political stability, most companies, regardless of the outcomes, would have layoffs. "The behaviour of companies accelerates the crisis," he said, "but we do not really have a choice because we have to do what is best for the company" (quoted in Gowing et al. 2009).

Regulation

Increasing regulation was accepted as inevitable. The idea of a single supra-regulatory agency was rejected as unrealistic, even though Chancellor Merkel suggested that such an agency, similar to the UN Security Council, may be necessary (WEF 2009b, 13). At one meeting of the 2009 summit, the group issued a strong set of recommendations after voting on each one. The meeting had a mix of corporate, university, government, and civil society representatives, therefore not a straightforward representation of corporate officeholders.

An international regulatory framework was voted the top priority, with 40.6% of the votes (WEF 2009b, 13). Among the other recommendations were a complete overhaul of the IMF, World Bank, and other IFIs. The overhaul, it was suggested, would include

- a rebalance of voting rights in keeping with the balance of economic power,
- a greater voice to developing nations (19),
- a more proactive role for the IMF in responding to national situations before they become global crises (20), and
- better supervision of the major reserve currency countries and oversight of the use of financial leverage (21.3%) (13).

Other suggestions for better regulation were to

- ensure greater market transparency and accountability,
- regulate more categories of capital exchanges,
- overhaul bank capital standards and the internal risk models used by banks to implement those standards, and
- review the role of the credit rating agencies in assigning risk. (WEF 2009b, 13)

The View From the World Social Forum: Civil Society Reports

The mood among the civil society organizations (CSOs) at the 2009 meeting of the WSF was cautiously celebratory. With global capitalism in crisis, government and industry were promoting reforms that many of the CSOs advocated. Traditionally, the WSF serves primarily to generate discussion and mobilization. Because 2009 seemed a critical global turning point, many people present at the forum, such as French activist Henri Rouillé d'Orfeuil, wanted to break with that longstanding tradition and promote specific proposals for reform (Estrada 2009).

Charting the best strategy for civil society action was one of the recurrent discussions. The right strategy would mean the difference between success and failure of attempts to change the direction of the global economy. The choices included

- a local approach, focusing on broad range of issues within local areas;
- an advocacy approach, employing single issue networks spanning the globe;

- a state approach, pressuring for national institutional reforms and progressive policies; and
- a shared approach in which they try to coordinate local, national, and global activity. (Pleyers 2009, 2–3)

Many WSF proposals were similar to those of the WEF: regulation of economic activity, sustainable development, and partnerships among government, industry, and NGOs. In its closing statement, the Forum announced some of the broader goals that came from the smaller assembly meetings. These included both economic and political objectives. Some were recognized as more achievable than others, although all, except perhaps for nationalization of banks, were widely shared. The suggestions included

- nationalization of banks;
- maintenance of salaries for workers at enterprises hit by the crisis;
- energy and food sovereignty for the poor;
- withdrawal of foreign troops from Iraq and Afghanistan;
- sovereignty and autonomy for indigenous peoples;
- right to land, decent work, education, and health for all; and
- democratization of media and knowledge. (Kirk 2009)

These proposals were targeted specifically at relieving the suffering of those most vulnerable to the global recession. Of course, some countries, such as Iceland, Sweden, India, Britain, and Ireland (without forestalling crisis), did nationalize some banks. Other banks were put into receivership, taken over by more financially solvent banks, or given bailouts, costing governments billions of dollars. Corporations, such as two of the big three automakers, Chrysler and General Motors in the United States, were also given bailouts. The successes and failures of strategies taken by various governments will be debated for decades.

The View From the Group of 20

The 1997 Asian financial crisis confirmed that the degree of interdependence among national economies had outgrown the capacity of the IFIs or any one country to stabilize. The Group of 20 (G20) was organized as an annual forum for financial ministers and central bank governors to hold policy discussions and make policy recommendations to cooperatively stabilize and strengthen the global and national economies. Its members are 19 of the richest countries and largest emerging economies and the EU. Together, they account for almost all of the world's economic output and about two thirds of the people on earth.

The G20 assumed a greater urgency with the severity of the 2007 recession and began meeting twice a year in response to the crisis. Heads of state inaugurated a G20 Leaders' Conference, also to meet twice a year. Before each meeting, countries issue a set of proposals; after the meetings, policy initiatives of the G20 are published in a series of communiqués. They are posted on the G20 website along with the responses of individual countries. Their agreements, and there are generally at least 100, are not binding, but they establish a normative framework and countries are scored on how well they implement the agreements. These meetings, along with UN initiatives, are a major dimension of global governance.

Affirmation of Capitalism

Although protestors called the April 2, 2009, meeting of the G20 "Financial Fools Day" in reference to their views of the foolishness of capitalism, world leaders remained firm in their support for capitalism albeit reformed and regulated capitalism. There were minor skirmishes along the way to agreement but little talk about the end of capitalism, not even among the formerly socialist societies. Russia's proposal to the summit called for a new international financial architecture; economic reforms focused on more coordination, regulation, democracy, and transparency, not an end to markets (G20 2009c). At the Leaders' Conference, Barack Obama (United States) summarized his position on the American economy and its role in the global crisis. While admitting that America bore some responsibility for the crisis, he did not acknowledge any fundamental weakness in the American model or that American power and prestige was diminished. He proclaimed confidently "that there is a vibrancy to our economic model, a durability to our political model and a set of ideals that has sustained us even through the most difficult times" (Gonyea and Montagne 2009).

Regulation and Stimulus

The twin themes that emerged from the 2009 meeting were economic stimulus and regulation. Angela Merkel (Germany) and Nicolas Sarkozy (France) were adamant in stressing the need for much greater transparency and regulation in finance. Sarkozy threatened to walk out of the summit if there were not much greater regulation of the financial industry. Merkel called for a "change in the world as we know it," not a discussion that has no bearing on practice in the real world. She said decisions had to be made "today and tomorrow," that another meeting would have no purpose without real results in this one ("G20 Summit" 2009).

Obama wanted to focus on stimulus, not regulation, even though many of the regulations sought by the G20 were already included in his administration's plans for the United States. China stood fast with the United States in prioritizing stimulus (Ydstie and Inskeep 2009). China stressed avoiding protectionism and giving the BRIC—Brazil, Russia, India, and China—nations a greater voice in multilateral organizations (China View 2009). Although they stressed regulation, Merkel and Sarkozy each had initiated stimulus packages by the time of the conference and vowed to contribute to help poorer nations fund their stimulus packages.

Despite these variations, the consensus that each country should institute an economic stimulus package to jump start its economies was overwhelming. Governments vowed to "spend their way out of the recession" (Schwartz and Satlmarsh 2009). The United States pledged almost $1 trillion to stimulate its economy. Japan, facing its worst economic times in 35 years, announced a $150 billion stimulus ("Japan" 2009). The European Union, Great Britain, and other developed nations followed suit. About $5 trillion was very quickly pledged for various national stimulus programs. Central banks took action by cutting interest rates and invoking expansionist monetary policies. Banks need to lend, companies need to hire, and individuals need to spend. The national stimulus packages were the tools, although many were short-lived as governments turned to austerity measures within two or three years, putting concern for debt ahead of recovery.

Leaders recognized that the situation was dire for poorer nations. They agreed that stimulus packages financed by richer nations through the IMF would be extended to developing nations. The large developing economies, such as China and Brazil, had sufficient cash to finance their own stimulus packages as well as contribute to others, but most developing countries did not have the capacity and were dependent on the IMF. The "Leaders' Statement" from the April 2009 summit promised to add $1.1 trillion to the IMF and multilateral lending institutions. It suggested an optimistic future for the global economy, praising their agreement as an historic achievement for so diverse a group of nations to pledge to work together for global interests. They also pledged to refrain from nationalistically oriented practices that threaten the global order, such as protectionism or currency devaluations. The statement reiterated support for "open world economy based on market principles, strong regulation and strong institutions" (G20 2009a).

The G20 fulfilled their promises, at least in the short term. The IMF distributed $175 billion in aid to emerging and developing nations and made $275 billion more available through "drawing rights" with set-asides for emerging and developing markets and low-income nations. Multilateral development banks increased money available by $150 billion, and regional development banks increased their commitments, raising them 50% from their 2007 level (World Bank 2010, 5; G20 2009b). Stimulus packages were implemented, but whether they were large enough or implemented for long enough is debated as the recession persisted and was compounded by the sovereign debt crises in Europe. After initial agreements forged at the 2009 meeting of the G20, disagreements on policies to alleviate the recession that began in 2007 and the European debt crisis emerged. The policy debate shifted course from stimulus and regulation to austerity and regulation.

The Debt Crisis

May Day 2009 brought hundreds of thousands of protesters into the streets of Europe demonstrating against unemployment and stagnant wages. In 2010, austerity measures ignited strikes, protests, and riots throughout Europe. In 2011, the world was still grappling with high unemployment from the financial crisis, which was compounded by the European debt crisis. Protest continued. On November 30, 2011, British government workers held the largest strike in Britain since 1979, calling for 2 million workers from 30 unions to participate. Teachers, nurses, doctors, paramedics, cooks, janitors, university professors, and border guards were among those who marched in the streets protesting a proposed six-year extension of austerity measures that included pay freezes, raise caps, and a reduction of pensions. In the United States, both the Tea Party and Occupy Wall Street movements expressed outrage at the increasing fortunes of the wealthy—who triggered the economic crises—and the plight of ordinary people. Occupy Wall Street spread globally to the financial centers of major cities. In India, bankers themselves protested the tactics of other bankers who thrived while the rest of the world suffered and the potential privatization or foreign ownership of India's banks (Sahni 2011). Protests against austerity measures to reign in government debts spread through Europe.

The recession of 2007 was proclaimed to have ended in the United States in 2009. However, a number of indicators suggested that the economy remained weak:

- Unemployment was still over 9% in 2011.
- 213,000 housing foreclosures had backlogged in the banks.
- Property values in many areas continued in their decline and the market for housing was stagnant.
- Cities and states were slashing safety nets and cutting back on services, including health care and education.
- While interest rates remained low, credit was difficult to get.

Europe was not faring well either. According to the OECD, the Euro-area crisis posed the greatest threat to the world economy. Greece and Ireland both fell into severe debt crisis and, being part of the Euro-zone, could not devalue their currency to stimulate exports or take other unilateral measures. Both were forced to adopt austerity measures. Before the crisis, Ireland had one of the fastest rates of growth in Europe, becoming known as "the Celtic Tiger," mimicking the name given the fast-growing "Asian Tigers." Unemployment brought on a wave of emigration from Ireland, whereas only a few years before, workers were flocking to Ireland because of employment opportunity. Austerity measures, such as raising taxes and cutting benefits, were estimated to cost Irish families about 3,000 euros. GDP per capita (inflation adjusted) fell from about $62,000 to $50,767. Salaries of state employees were cut about 20%, and unemployment was 14.7% in 2011. Suicide prevention clinics saw their caseloads rise by a third (Alderman 2011). It may be that by saving their banks, Ireland prevented a worse contagion across Europe. If this is the case, is does not seem fair that Ireland bear this cost alone, as one EU minister suggested at the 2011 WEF Summit (Hutton 2011).

Lack of confidence in European economies spread the crisis. Portugal, Italy, and Spain—all deep in debt—experienced dramatic increases in the cost of borrowing, making it even more difficult for them to repay their debt. The debt of weak countries risks the credit ratings of stronger countries that hold their debt. This can trigger bank failure in the stronger countries as well. How the debt crisis, ongoing in 2013, will play out is difficult to foresee.

Three strategies to avoid deepening the crisis and more contagion emerged: bailout, greater regulation, and greater political union in the Euro-zone countries. Without bailout, countries may be forced to default on their debt, which could bring financial chaos. Economic globalization is so intense that stock markets around the world react to any hint of movement in one of these directions.

Countries were offered various forms of debt reduction and maturity extensions in exchange for greater regulations and austerity measures. Greece's debt was restructured, writing down its debt by 21% in July 2011. For the European Central Bank (ECB) or Euro-zone countries to bail them out, they wanted assurances of further austerity. Many people opposed the austerity measures, particularly in the midst of the recession that has already reduced the standard of living. Not only will they lose benefits in difficult financial times, but they also view demands for changes in their domestic policies as a threat to their national sovereignty. Like many in the United States, they see the financial industry as the culprits and themselves as the victims who are asked to sacrifice more.

In 2010–2011, the IMF bolstered the economies of Ireland, Greece, and Portugal. Italy and Spain, however, were too large and would quickly deplete IMF funds. Other countries could step into these situations by buying debt of failing economies through bonds or channeling money through the IMF. European leaders approached

China, which already owned over $3 trillion of international debt, much of it from the United States, to buy more debt. There is political as well as economic incentive for China. Increasing crisis in Europe and the threat of contagion to the United States may close two of their largest markets. Furthermore, buying debt buys political favors at the same time. They however, remained reluctant to buy debt but have responded by expanding investment and increasing imports. Many German and French citizens resist channeling money through either the ECB or IMF. They resent being asked to pay for what they see as overspending in other countries.

Nevertheless, in 2012, the ECB agreed to buy unlimited amounts of government bonds of countries that agree to strict requirements. They need to apply to the ECB and agree to cut spending, deficits, and debt. Stock markets around the world rallied at the news (Associated Press 2012). Whether Italy and Spain will take the ECB offer is not a foregone conclusion.

Most experts agree that in the long run, saving the Euro-zone requires greater regional political and economic integration throughout the EU. Merkel and Sarkozy announced that even their wealthy economies are better off as a member of the zone than trying to make it on their own. Their proposal, issued in December 2011, called for tightening the treaties that established the EU. In exchange for a larger role for the ECB in protecting individual state economies, they asked for more regulation and enforcement of sovereign debt limits and oversight of national budgets. Questions concerning the extent to which an appointed international body, the European Court, should rule on the activities of a representative national legislature speak directly to the nature of both sovereignty and democracy. France, among other countries, would oppose too great a role. However, debt limits and automatic sanctions on countries that exceeded them would be considered. Merkel and Sarkozy wanted approval for new treaties from all EU countries, not just those in the Euro-zone. As this drama played out in Europe, stock markets worldwide responded with upswings each time the crisis seemed resolved and downturns when the news was bad—a globalization effect. How the debt crisis is resolved will influence the fate of other proposed common regional currencies and the possibility of a global currency.

The emerging economies have weathered the recession better than most developed societies and are playing a more important role in global governance. The BRICS (Brazil, Russia, India, China, and South Africa), Argentina, and Indonesia are growing rapidly. China and Brazil are international creditors and as such can wield significant influence. As the G20 increases its leverage, coalitions of emerging economies block proposals of richer nations, such as France's proposal for global bank levies at the 2010 Seoul meetings. China resisted calls from the United States and Europe to adjust its currency. The United States and France claim China's currency is undervalued on the global market, giving China an unfair export advantage. Ironically, China—still a poor country but rich in reserves—may end up bailing European countries out, directly or through contributions to the IMF. Either way, these moves by China will come with economic and political price tags.

BOX 4.20   Consider This: Changing Our Thinking About the Economy

"What we are experiencing is the birth of a new era, a wake-up call to overhaul our institutions, our systems, and above all, our way of thinking" (Schwab 2009).

This is a quotation from Klaus Schwab, the founder of the WEF. After having read this chapter and the chapter on transborder problems, what changes in "our thinking" would you propose?

The need for a more stable and predictable economy to maintain a high quality of life has never been doubted. Based on the G20 talks, it appears that the foundation of the global economy is likely to remain rooted in the premise that private enterprise can manage individual and social welfare more efficiently than government. However, there is also increasing sentiment for legitimate and reliable governance to provide predictability and stability. A global governance regime seems to be emerging based not only on IMF and World Bank institutions but from multilateral forums such as the G20.

The Circumstances of Globalization

The last section of this chapter is divided into three parts.

- A summary of the objective conditions of economic globalization that were described in detail in the previous chapter
- A sketch of the globalizing impact of these circumstances on individuals, societies, and the global system of societies
- A summary of the attempts to shape globalization in response to the economic crisis of 2007

Nearly every measure of economic global integration has been increasing to unprecedented levels or at an unprecedented pace since the mid-1970s. Economic integration has accelerated during the last half of the 20th century and has undergone significant change in the last 20 years[5] (OECD/WTO 2009, 12). Many researchers pick out one or another of these and determine whether globalization is increasing or decreasing based on that factor. One may be increasing while others are decreasing, or vice versa. No one measure is sufficient, nor probably is there one factor that is a necessary stimulus to creating a global economy. The synergy of the volume and density of economic integration created by them collectively, as well as others not listed here or measured, gives rise to economic globalization.

Global Chain of Production and Consumption

- Technological advances in communication, production, transportation, and organization facilitate disengaging economic processes at the level of the task.
- High-tech products, such as cell phones, robotics, the Internet, and irrigation systems, are diffusing rapidly among diverse parts of the world with economic, political, and cultural development benefits (Galperin and Mariscal 2007).
- Foreign direct investment flows increased rapidly, in both directions between developing and developed societies, among developed societies, and among developing societies.
- The production chain of commodities is fragmented and geographically dispersed over increasingly wide areas.
- Nearly every nation is integrated at some level into global economic activity.

Establishing the Global Market

- Waves of increasing trade density that began after WWII reached unprecedented levels by the early part of the 21st century. "For the entire 1950–2007 period, trade expanded on average by 6.2 per cent, greater than in the first wave of globalization from 1850–1913" (WTO 2008, 15).
- Industrial sector transitions are decreasing the share in manufacturing exports of developed countries from 85% to 66%, while developing societies have increased to 33%.
- Deregulation and financial innovation grew global financial markets more rapidly than any other global market, expanding from $0.1 trillion in 1970 to $6.3 trillion in 1990 and to $31.8 trillion in 2007 (Bhattacharya 2009).
- **The global market has sparked interest in regional currencies and potentially, a global currency.**

BOX 4.21   Check It Out Yourself: The Bottom Line

The Global Competitiveness Report ranks countries on factors thought important in their ability to succeed economically. A color-coded interactive map allows you to view the rankings of countries and their scores on individual factor rankings. The 2012 map can be found at this URL:

http://www.weforum.org/issues/global-competitiveness

Do the countries that show up as "best" on any of the indicators surprise you?

Of the factors listed, can you identify which may be most likely to be affected by globalization? Which are not? How might your home country improve its ranking? Considering these criteria, which countries are likely to benefit from globalization, and which may not?

How can globalization be used as a tool to help more countries benefit?

The 2012 WEF Data Platform allows you to examine the factors of competitiveness and countries that interest you most, and to make comparisons among them. http://www.weforum.org/issues/competitiveness-0/gci2012-data-platform

Globalization of Labor

- More jobs are tradable due to improved communication and technology. High- and low-skilled, manufacturing, and service jobs can be traded.
- Workers are mobile. Net migration to developed countries was 64 million people from 1974 to 2006. Migration among countries of the "South" was also significant. Still only about 3% of people are living outside of their country of birth.
- Remittances from migrants to their homeland became the largest source of foreign aid, topping $400 billion in 2008. (UNCTAD 2009, 19)
- Improved communication and travel allow migrants to maintain close contact with family and friends at home. This has political and cultural consequences as well as economic.

Economic Convergence and Coordination

- Societies have a variety of different economic systems, but most converge on a variation of capitalism.
- While following different patterns in different nations, the overall trend has been toward high levels of inequality within and among nations.
- Growth patterns in China, Brazil, and India no longer reflect those of more developed societies. Their recession was not as deep as in the United States and Europe, and their growth rebounded more quickly.
- Some forms of global economic activity, such as trade in goods and in the financial markets, decreased after the financial crisis of 2007. Other economic activities, such as coordination, regulation, and activity of the international financial institutions globally, increased.
- Alternations between practices of Keynesian economic policy (post-WWII and post-2007 crisis) and neo-liberal policies (1980s) tend to be coordinated globally through the activities of the IFIs.

Each of these forms of integration evolved and intensified over many years. With successive changes, global economic relations differentiated from national and international economic activity. You can think of this process as similar to how the U.S. national economy emerged from the increasing integration of local and state economies within the United States. A national economy developed in addition to the lower levels of economic activity. It developed within a larger political union. Political coordination across the states was, and still is, required.

Globalization of governance is tending to greater coordination, negotiation, and regulation of the economy. Governments and people are demanding more transparency and accountability in global and domestic economies to avoid continuing economic crisis and instability and reverse the trend toward greater inequality.

Summary: Shaping Globalization: The Possibility of a New Order?

Two primary drivers are likely to shape the global economy in the foreseeable future. First is increased regulation, coordination, and demands for accountability. Second is the growth of the emerging economies, some of which are poised to surpass members of the G7, the largest economies. China has already surpassed Japan to become the second largest economy, after the United States; Brazil is seventh.

G20 communiqués pledged regulation, coordination, and accountability. States promised a new set of obligations. With these obligations, they assume new fiduciary responsibility and involve more actors in economic decision making. Institutionalizing these reforms is challenging. Heads of state and finance ministers make agreements at summits; it is up to legislatures to make them real. Many nations, among them the United States and China, placed

"Buy American" and "Buy Chinese" provisions— however briefly—in their 2009 stimulus packages. These are forms of protectionism. Not only do these measures violate the spirit of the reforms the countries agreed to, but protectionism also prolonged the Great Depression of the 1920s and '30s. The new protections were relatively weak but still angered other governments.

As the EU started drafting the legislation and regulations promised at the summit, headlines in the *New York Times* announced, "In Britain, an Aversion to Rules From Europe," alluding to the suspicions of the British concerning adopting foreign rules (Thomas 2009). In the United States, the headlines such as "Bill Shields Most Banks From Review" (Labaton 2009) and "Banks Brace for Fight Over an Agency Meant to Bolster Consumer Protection" (Martin and Story 2009) cast doubt on how well the policies agreed to at the summits would be implemented.

Along with the Euro-zone countries discussed, the United States, Japan, and Britain were also deep in debt in 2011, but not in a debt crisis. They retreated from economic stimulus and adopted austerity measures. Even though most economists agreed that the U.S. stimulus package was too small, paying down the debt through austerity measures took precedence over stimulus in the 2010 Congressional elections. Britain imposed even greater austerity and fewer stimulus measures. Krugman (2011) has persistently argued in his *New York Times* column that to escape from recession, more spending is needed. If people do not have money to spend, government must. If government spends putting people to work, it creates demand that puts more people to work. The debt crisis in Europe was not, he cautioned, a result of spending. Many countries with much larger welfare states, as a percentage of GDP, did fine. Welfare spending in the European nations in debt crisis was actually lower than in Germany and much lower than Sweden. Japan and the United States also had larger debts as a proportion of their GNP than most of the European countries. The European debt crisis, according to Krugman, is a result of the inability of Euro-zone countries to borrow money in their own currency. Countries with much larger debt that pay it in their own currency need not worry about debt until the economy is back on track (2011, A25). This is how Argentina escaped its crisis in 2001 (Weisbrot 2007). It restructured its debt and devalued its currency— and had a stroke of luck in having valuable commodities to sell.

The debate between stimulus spending and paying down the deficits (with no tax hikes) continues in Washington and elsewhere. High unemployment does not offer much chance of relief. Ireland took the path of austerity to pay down debt to no avail. Its unemployment rate in 2011 was 14%. For the 27 members of the EU, it averaged 11.7% in October 2012 (up from 10.4% in October 2011), ranging from a high of 26.2% in Spain and a low of 4.1% in Austria. In Japan, it was 4.2% in September 2012, having peaked at about 5.5% in 2009 (Eurostat 2012).

In the meantime, growth in the emerging economies caught most of the world by surprise. The world GDP shrank 1.1% in 2009; developed economies shrank 3.4%, while emerging economies grew 1.7%. They have made the strongest recovery. How did they manage this? One factor was that none of these countries relied too much on exports, and when the export market dried up with the credit market, each of these countries had huge domestic markets ("BRICs Emerging Markets" 2009). Each of them was very cautious in capital liberalization. None was reliant on foreign capital. These countries are savers as well. Their banks were full of money as opposed to credit. China had large reserves to pump directly into its stimulus package. Brazil and India were able to do the same. Brazil reduced reserve requirements of its banks, allowing them to put more money into the economy, and India turned to the 38% of its GDP in domestic savings.

Indicators point to continued growth for the emerging economies. Consider the conditions related to economic growth: workforce growth, rising educational levels, technological progress, and growth in new capital investment. By these measures, growth in the emerging economies will not only be greater than in the developed economies, but emerging economies will overtake them in size. China could move from second to first by 2025. The emerging economies expected to increase most significantly—the E7—are Brazil, India, China, Russia, Indonesia, Turkey, and Mexico, which could possibly grow to 50% larger than the G7 by 2050 (Hawksworth and Cookson 2008). Forty years is a long timeline, and many events could intervene, but it is likely that many of the emerging economies—which also includes Vietnam, Malaysia, Thailand, Nigeria, Philippines, Argentina, and others—will grow significantly in relation to the developed economies of today.

This is not a bad thing for the developed economies. Increased growth will increase standards of living, improving the lives of billions. This should bring more stability to the world and much less conflict as people will have something to lose through violence. The emerging economies will provide a bigger market for goods and services. As their income and educational levels rise, their consumption of goods and services will converge toward the developed societies today. There will also be more imports available. As with industrial transitions, there will be groups in the developed economies that will be vulnerable to dislocation. They will need social protections, income subsidy and training. With such potent economic transitions looming ahead, it seems a good time to take control of the global economy, to democratize.

Historically, transitions from one social order to another take time, a generation or more. It will be hard to get the global economy under control. The ensuing years may be painful and chaotic, as experiments in establishing order are tried and abandoned. Success for any of traditional lead economies will depend on developments in new lead industries to revitalize their growth. This could happen. However, China has surpassed the United States in manufacturing solar panels, which we now import from them. The technology was invented in the United States.

The November 2010 meetings of the G20 in Seoul reiterated previous strategies and commitments. These included action plans in the following areas:

- Monetary and exchange rates, including promises not to manipulate currency to gain advantage
- Trade and development, including pledges to maintain open trade and oppose protectionism
- Global standards for financial reform
- Structural reforms to stimulate job creation, sustainable development, social safety nets, and tax reform to remove distortions
- Modernization of the IMF, democratization of international financial institutions and other international bodies by giving greater voice to developing nations
- Strengthening, regulating, and supervising financial services
- Limiting the effect of non-cooperating countries on the stability of the global economy through implementing transparent assessments

- Protecting individuals from undue economic risk in financial institutions and predatory loans and other financial instruments
- Pursuing development with respect for environmental contingencies
- Democratizing the activity of international development efforts by ensuring self-determination on the part of borrowing nations
- Enforcing pledges made by states by sanctioning states that do not oblige
- Maintaining sufficient reserves (G20 2010)

There seem to be a number of potential paths.

- Countries agree on greater political globalization—regulation, conditionality, coordination, and so forth—to achieve more economic stability.
- Economic globalization continues under the auspice of a new global more democratic regime.
- A new dominant power rises from the emerging economies—as has happened in other periods of transition—producing greater economic stability.
- The United States or Europe grabs hold of the new lead industries and reasserts hegemony.
- The emerging global economy fails to establish order, and economic disintegration ensues.

What are the potential consequences of each?

Questions, Investigations, and Resources

Questions

1. Debate: Does foreign direct investment do more harm or good for the host country? Does it do more harm than good for the home country?

2. What are the potential benefits and drawbacks of offshoring and outsourcing?

3. Describe the functions of the Bretton Woods institutions. How are they supposed to work to help macroeconomic stability?

4. Why are some countries poor and others wealthy? Consider factors internal to the society and external—individual, cultural, historical, environmental.

5. How did the economic crisis of 2007 impact your hometown? Has it impacted your life in any way, from the cost of college to the availability of jobs?

6. In practical terms, what would be the consequences if the United States or any other developed country took

the advice that you hear commonly and decided to take care of their problems at home and not the world's problems?

7. What factors are most important in determining the economic health of a country? In other words, what differentiates a good from a bad economy? If you were to determine the measures by which a recession/depression were in progress or over, what criteria would you use?

8. Follow up on the economic crisis that began in 2007.

   a. Has the United States returned to economic health? If so, what strategies were employed?
   b. Has the Euro-zone survived? Did any countries leave the union? Was a greater political entity forged?
   c. Were emerging economies able to transfer their greater economic health into political power on the global stage?

Investigations

1. Find an index of Gini coefficients for inequality within nations. Can you find any commonalities among countries with the lowest coefficients and among those with the highest? Do any of the countries' levels of inequality surprise you?

2. Choose five to 10 high-income countries, five to 10 with middle income, and five to 10 low income. Investigate their division of labor. What percentage of their population is employed in each sector: agriculture, manufacturing, and services? What percentage of their GDP is derived from each sector?

   The CIA World Factbook has information concerning industrial sectors in the "Economy" section for each country. More detailed analysis can be found in the World Bank and WTO.

3. Update the forecast for job growth. What are the fastest-growing occupations over the next 10 years? Look at both percentage growth and growth in absolute numbers. What education and training is required for each?

   If they are not on the table, find an estimate for the median annual salary for each of these occupations in the Bureau of Labor Statistics Occupational Outlook and Wage Data Tables.
   Evaluate the changes in the job structure. Are more higher paying or lower paying jobs expected? What does

this mean for the quality of life and economic inequality in the United States?

4. Has your city, state (county, province, parish), or country recovered from the global recession of 2007?

   - List the factors that you would use to determine this answer. Some are unemployment, poverty, homelessness, housing market, health and wellness.
   - Try to find these statistics for one of the levels mentioned above—city, state, or country.
   - Can you find statistics concerning the recovery of the globe?

Investigate the impact of the global economic crisis on developing countries using the *World Bank Global Monitoring Report 2010: The MDGs After the Crisis.*

http://siteresources.worldbank.org/INTGLOMONREP2010/Resources/6911301-1271698910928/GMR2010WEB.pdf

Resources

US Department of Labor, Bureau of Labor Statistics

Occupational Outlook http://www.bls.gov/emp/ep_table_104.htm

Wage Data http://www.bls.gov/bls/blswage.htm

CIA World Factbook https://www.cia.gov/library/publications/the-world-factbook/index.html

World Bank http://www.worldbank.org/

World Bank Database http://databank.worldbank.org/ddp/home.do

World Development Indicators and Global Development Finance: This is an interactive database of economic and a wide range of related data on topics such as education, business, and airport infrastructure. For example, the "Doing Business" category contains information on 183 countries concerning measures of and enforcement of business regulations.

World Bank Global Monitoring Report 2010 http://siteresources.worldbank.org/INTGLOMONREP2010/Resources/6911301-1271698910928/GMR2010WEB.pdf

World Trade Organization http://www.wto.org/index.htm

Forging a Global Civil Society

The activist participation of individuals and NGOs (non-governmental organizations) in debates on global governance has put accountability on the global agenda, and efforts should be made to facilitate greater participation in global governance, particularly through transparency. (Grant and Keohan 2005, 41)

Objectives

Civil society groups have become a major force operating all over the world to advance causes in which they believe. They command billions of dollars and wield considerable power. This chapter will help you

- understand the similarities and differences between civil society and global civil society and important implications for their potential and peril;
- analyze the interactions among local, national, and international civil society organizations, and their engagement with governments, international governmental organizations, and other actors;

- explain the role of global culture in global civil society movements;
- assess effective strategies for NGO and international non-governmental organization (INGO) activity;
- critique the outcomes of NGO and INGO activity in their potential for democracy; and
- evaluate the role of civil society organizations in state and global governance.

BOX 5.1   A Closer Look: Everything Starts With One Person's Idea

In 1968, in Nigeria, a civil war raged as Biafra tried to gain independence. Bernard Kouchner, a doctor with the French Red Cross in Nigeria, witnessed the massacre and starvation of civilians by government forces. In his eyes, complying with the International Committee of the Red Cross's (ICRC) longstanding policy of neutrality was the same as complicity with the government's brutality (Kaldor 2003, 129). ICRC rules prevented medical personnel from delivering services desperately needed by the people of Biafra. Kouchner felt he was part of the war, rather than relief (Brauman and Tanguy 1998).

(Continued)

(Continued)

He founded the International Committee against Genocide in Biafra and called media attention to the horrors there. In 1971, Kouchner joined with a like-minded group of doctors frustrated with the inefficiencies delivering disaster relief in Pakistan. They founded Médecins sans Frontières (MSF/Doctors Without Borders). "By forming MSF, this core group of doctors intended to change the way humanitarian aid was delivered by providing more medical assistance more rapidly and by being less deterred by national borders at times of crisis. Their example changed more than the delivery of medical care. MSF is one of the first documented instances of global civil society action" (Kaldor 2003, 129).

In the early 1960s, Peter Benenson wrote *The Forgotten Prisoner*, condemning the oppression and torture of prisoners. He developed organizational tactics to address global causes. Independence from governments, letter writing, publicizing atrocities, and shaming the nations involved evolved into a powerful strategy, still used to good effect by Amnesty International, the non-governmental organization (NGO) he founded. It is a model for NGOs globally (Keane 2003, 58).

How does one person's vision become a global force? Doctors Without Borders, Amnesty International, and other NGOs begin with a person or small group and gain public attention, financial and moral support, and the attention of governments, international governmental organizations, and even industry. Together, they form a global civil society—people exerting pressure from outside of the economy and state systems and structures to change them. Not every person with a vision is successful, not every human cause represented. Whether or not a global civil society that serves all of humankind is possible is a critical issue on the global agenda.

Civil society, simply stated, is people organizing outside of government channels to meet social objectives. Whereas social movements of the past have focused on communities within nations, today's movements increasingly involve people from diverse parts of the globe to promote human welfare without concern for location and connecting local and global groups' activities.

The Individual Humanity Relationship

Individual differentiation has made us more aware of our humanity. Durkheim (1915/1965) wrote nearly a hundred years ago that increasing social differentiation would lead us to the realization that all we have left in common is our humanity. People would transcend their attachments to only national societies to develop concern for "collective life of an international nature" (474). Humanity is the collective life, the same people who from other perspectives are organized into societies, polities, economies, families, and so on (Simmel 1908/1971, 38).

It appears that Durkheim's prediction is coming to pass. Recognition of membership in humanity is the subjective dimension of globalization. With that recognition comes responsibility, the responsibility shouldered by people like Kouchner and Benenson, but also by those who sponsor a child with $22 a

month, donate blood to the International Red Cross, give money to support those in disaster areas, or participate in any number of activities and organizations in which people help other people, without regard to their class, race, ethnicity, or religion, but simply because they are people.

Recognition of humanity has occasioned a new urgency and paradigm shift, distinguished by the "personalization of commitment" (McDonald 2006, 74). Personalization, called *authenticity*, has two components. First, it means working directly with people on solving problems. Second, being authentic means recognizing that the helper and the victim are in the same boat. Those who help do not approach problems with a sense of pity, but with a sense of shared experience, recognizing that everyone is a victim of global problems and anyone can help. This is the new humanitarianism (73).

Media play an important role in helping people visualize the plight of others and identify with them. "Without television, the new humanitarianism would not exist" (Kouchner, quoted in McDonald 2006, 70). Television brought war, famine, and natural disasters into our living rooms in the 1960s. Today, the Internet and satellite-fed mobile communications intensify the immediacy of people's suffering. We watch one another online in real time and become engaged in one another's struggles anywhere in the world. Whether by donating money, sending messages of support, or actively participating by relaying information around censorship blocks, we join struggles all over the world from our homes.

Globalization changed the relationship between the individual and humanity and the totality of the global field. The global system of societies has a new set of obligations to humanity, and so does each and every society. The global economy, global polity, and global culture all relate people to one another outside of their memberships in particular societies. Global civil society also exists outside of societal bounds, outside of government and the economy. It conjures the image of the global citizen. It conjures the image of humanity, organized differently than in the sum total of societies—an entity of fluid and shifting interactions, people who regardless of "tribal" differences in nationality, race, ethnicity, or gender, have common needs, common rights, and common obligations toward one another.

This chapter starts with a discussion of civil society. It is important to understand civil society before considering the prospects and perils of a global civil society. Next, the processes through which the practical concerns of humanity come into the forum of global civil society and are addressed by states, international organization of states, corporations, and other powerful actors are discussed. Finally, we analyze three case studies of successful global civil society movements: the movement to ban landmines, the environmental movement, and the human rights movement with particular attention to the Helsinki Accords.

Defining Civil Society

When Alexis de Tocqueville, the French political philosopher, visited the United States in 1831, he credited the vibrancy of American democracy to the vibrancy of its associational life.[1] When "several inhabitants of the United States have taken up an opinion or feeling they wish to promote in the world, they look for mutual assistance; and as soon as they have found one another out, they combine" (quoted in Kaldor 2003, 20). Since then, the importance of an active and vibrant civil society for a strong democracy has been taken for granted.

Defining civil society requires normative evaluations. It is first of all civilian. Although civil society organizations very often work with governments, they are not part of them. Everything that is governmental is excluded from civil society. Civil society as a concept repudiates the notion that the state is the society. Second, most theorists agree that civil society should be limited to voluntary associations. That eliminates family. Civil society is not particularistic, as is kinship.

Some early theorists noted that when economic relations differentiated from political and escaped the control of the state (with the advent of capitalism), it created a new dimension of social order based on entirely different principles. They used civil society to refer to these relations. In contemporary life, associational groups exist apart from both the state and the economy, and they protest and critique both. For that reason, this text takes up the position of many contemporary theorists that civil society should be considered distinct from the market. Civil society is the network of voluntary ties that differentiate a community from the state, the family, and the economy. Being an association of people apart from particular interests in the state, kinship, and economy, civil society is in the unique position to lay claim to moral authority from which to judge those institutions. This is the referent for the concept of civil disobedience.

BOX 5.2   Consider This: Competing Definitions

The concept of civil society has been very "glocalized." Its meaning varies not only among nations, but among academic disciplines as well. It has acquired the local flavor of similar concepts that describe non-state actors engaged in varieties of social and social welfare work. The range of definitions will not be reviewed here, but in some countries, being included in the "third sector" or "social economy" and variations of not-for-profit, non-profits, and redistribution of profits may qualify an organization for inclusion into civil society or may disqualify an organization, depending on who is doing the counting and the definitions being using (Roginsky and Shortall 2009).

There are also both more and less radical definitions of civil society. Conflict-oriented perspectives emphasize civil society as a check on the powers of the state. Cooperation-oriented perspectives emphasize civil society as a source of stability. **Can civil society do both? If so, how?**

Cross-cutting memberships in civil society's religious, sporting, community, occupational, and other organizations join people from across social cleavages such as family background, class, and political party. It is "associations in which people's relations are driven by democratic discourse, solidarity, civility, honesty and mutual respect" (Roginsky and Shortall 2009, 474). This builds social capital and extends bonds of trust throughout a community. Civility is a "learned public behavior demonstrating respect for others while curtailing one's immediate self-interest when appropriate" (Anheier 2007, 11).

This brings us to the third characteristic. Most theorists limit civil society to relationships that are civil—non-coercive and non-violent (Keane 2003, 14). When states acquired the monopoly on violence, violence was expunged from the public life of societies. The rule of law and institutionalized means for settling conflicts ascended. Civil society is governed by rules and consent rather than coercion. In the 20th century, Western societies called the Soviet Union and Eastern bloc countries uncivil, coercive societies. They were not legitimated through consent (Kaldor 2003, 1). Their rapid demise after the fall of communism is evidence of their coercive foundation.

In contrast to coercion, civil society is based on trust; when "strangers act in a civilized way to one another . . . rational debate and discussion becomes possible" (Kaldor 2003, 13). This facilitates a society's collective efficacy, its capacity to accomplish its goals and those of the people within. It also provides a source of authority apart from the state that can speak back to the state as a counterweight to the powers of the state. While the stipulation that civil society rejects violence is not included in all definitions, it provides a sharp analytical divide between civil society and groups who claim moral justification for their violence. Use of violence or coercion is antithetical to discourse and respect.

This has been further elaborated by Jurgen Habermas, a contemporary German sociologist and philosopher, who stresses civil society as a check on power and coercion. The core of civil society is made of "those non-governmental and non-economic connections and voluntary associations that anchor the communication structures of the public sphere" (quoted in Kaldor 2003, 22). The communicative dimension of Habermas's definition is critical. Communication is the essence of society; every bond among people, every interaction, is a communication and the essence of civility.

Civil society is not just a Western concept (Anheier 2007, 11). Civility demands that if problems, issues, or conflicts arise, they are not settled by coercion or violence; they must be settled by communication. China, Japan, Iran, and Turkey, among other nations, have distinctive traditions associating public behavior and non-violence.

Combining these perspectives we come up with four propositions for civil society.

- Civil society is a network of voluntary associations.
- Civil society pursues interests that cut across the particularistic fault lines and fissures in society.
- Civil society emphasizes the importance of rational discourse and communication to solve problems.
- Civil society rejects the use of violence and coercion.

BOX 5.3   Consider This: Bowling Alone

Robert Putnam (1995), a political scientist, has proposed that civil society in the United States has diminished over the last few generations. We are less involved in community group activities and pursue more solitary pursuits. Community gatherings such as picnics and parades, organizations such as the Rotary, PTA, Boy and Girl Scouts and religious groups used to be plentiful with boundary-bursting memberships. People used to get together and build ties that built social capital in their communities and the country. Now, Putnam says, we engage in more solitary and fewer group activities. This, he maintains, is a danger to our democracy. Without cross-cutting group ties, trust erodes. Political participation erodes, and democracy erodes. Is this what has been happening? Is this why we do not have high voter turnout?

Has the economic crisis reignited political participation? Are the Tea Party and Occupy Wall Street movements signs that civil society is engaged once again in political life?

You can learn more about building social capital by visiting Putnam's websites, Better Together and the Saguaro Seminar.

http://www.bettertogether.org/150ways.htm
http://www.hks.harvard.edu/saguaro/

Civil society organizations may be not-for-profit groups such as Boy Scouts, Girl Scouts, religious organizations, and community clubs. They can be devoted to a particular cause such as March of Dimes, Race for the Cure, volunteer firefighters, or an environmental group. They can be any one of thousands of similar organizations that gather people together based on their interests—in chess, fishing, playing cards, or bowling. They include interest groups that lobby the government, such as the NRA (National Rifle Association), GASP (Group Against Smog and Pollution), or MADD (Mothers Against Drunk Driving). They can be organized to advocate for groups such as the disabled, the poor, or the imprisoned. Alternatively, they can act directly to alleviate living conditions of marginalized people by providing food banks, soup kitchens, warm winter coats, or Toys for Tots at the holidays. Their money comes from fundraising, foundations, government, or corporate grants. They exercise power through the money they spend and the causes they support.

Defining Global Civil Society

Global civil society is not just national civil society writ large. *Global civil society*

> is the most complex society in the history of the human species . . . a vast, interconnected and multi-layered non-governmental space that comprises many hundreds of thousands of self directing institutions and ways of life that generate global effects. (Keane 2003, 17–20)

Global civil society shares most characteristics with civil society; its fifth makes it fundamentally different. Global civil society is

- composed of only non-governmental, non-economic, non-familial local and global groups and organizations;
- conducted through interlinked social processes, sometimes tightly linked, some linked loosely;
- civil, encouraging non-violence, mutual respect, and compromise;
- pluralistic with strong conflict potential; and
- global, not confined to state boundaries or the interests of any particular nation (Keane 2003, 11–19).

Global Civil Society and Global Regimes

Although global civil society organizations are not part of government, CSOs have to work with governments and international governmental organizations to accomplish their goals. Civil society groups participate in global governance working to establish international regimes devoted to their cause. A regime is a form of governance, an extensive set of "explicit rules, agreed upon by governments that pertain to particular sets of issues in international relations" (Keohane, quoted in Zelli 2008, 2). A regime will have declarations and treaties by governments or international governmental organizations that document their obligations and the monitoring or enforcement mechanisms that hold them to their promises. It is useful to see a regime as a combination of structure, process, and product. Civil society groups participate in all three.

BOX 5.4   A Closer Look: INGO and NGO UN Partnerships

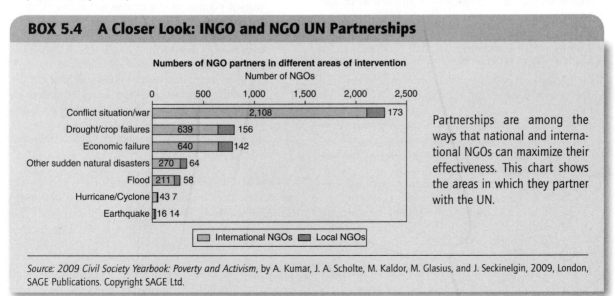

Partnerships are among the ways that national and international NGOs can maximize their effectiveness. This chart shows the areas in which they partner with the UN.

Source: 2009 Civil Society Yearbook: Poverty and Activism, by A. Kumar, J. A. Scholte, M. Kaldor, M. Glasius, and J. Seckinelgin, 2009, London, SAGE Publications. Copyright SAGE Ltd.

- Structure: networks of public, private, and governmental groups
- Process: the modes of discourse and strategies they use to deliberate, debate, and influence governance
- Product: policy, public information, regulation, treaties, laws and other things relevant to achieving their goals (Donnelly 2007, 127–129; Meyer et al. 1997, 623–625)

Whoever can control the cognitive and normative agendas on a particular issue has a good chance of winning the public over to their cause. Civil society groups work to get the public and policy makers to think about an issue as a problem—whether it is pollution, food shortages, or human rights. This is the cognitive dimension. Then they must get people to think about it in a certain way, to care about it. For example, civil society groups are competing to define pollution. Some are promoting it as a health problem and want more regulation. Some talk it about as a jobs or money issue and want less regulation. This is the normative agenda (Rutherford 2000, 78).

Landmines had barely entered public consciousness before the landmine movement. If people thought about them at all, they saw them as military tools. Getting landmines perceived as a problem and then as a particular kind of humanitarian as opposed to military problem was the only way to get the public and key government officials to care about them. In the case of the landmine treaty, INGOs changed people's perception of landmines as weapon to landmines as a killer of innocents. They successfully established landmines as a humanitarian issue rather than as a military or arms control issue, thus setting the cognitive and normative agendas.

A regime is also practical. It includes strategies, solutions, treaties, and protocols that function locally, nationally, and globally. These can be summarized as their declaratory, promotional, implementation, and enforcement dimensions and activities.

- Declaratory activities are public statements that disseminate knowledge of a human condition.
- Promotional activities encourage support for particular policies and programs.
- Implementation activities coordinate national policies and international monitoring procedures.
- Enforcement activities secure binding international agreements and ensure strong international monitoring. (Donnelly 2007, 129)

Global civil society regimes include all of these dimensions. Global civil society organizations have important declaratory functions. In many cases civil society organizations have been among the first to articulate global norms and standards. Many groups issue regular reports. Amnesty International publicizes human rights reports every year. They educate global, national, and local publics on issues to create or sway opinion, often partnering with local organizations to create grassroots pressure from within countries. They establish model programs to implement norms and standards. These programs may be taken over by local or national governments as regimes move into the implementation stages.

Global civil society organizations are active watchdogs, monitoring, investigating, and publicizing the extent of problems from pollution to human trafficking, the progress of states toward fulfilling their obligations with respect to issues such as civil and human rights, and their progress in living up to global norms regarding state functions such as health care, education, and democratic elections. Civil society is strongest in monitoring. Enforcement is the most difficult issue for civil society and for global governance generally. Some civil society groups have imposed sanctions by withdrawing their services. This is difficult because withdrawing services may mean increasing harm to victims.

A measure of the success of civil society organizations is the extent to which a global regime develops that is devoted to their cause and in keeping with their objectives. This can be evaluated along three dimensions of effectiveness:

- The norms that are developed, for example, the various number of UN treaties and declarations on human rights (outcome)
- Changes in the behavior of the relevant actors, for example, the number of states that have signed and ratified a treaty or enacted relevant domestic policies, and their adherence to standards (impact)
- The ultimate effect on their actual objective, for example, the reduction achieved in carbon emissions, the restoration or granting of freedoms, such as freedom of the press, or assembly, or religion (Oberthür and Gehring, in Zelli, 2008, 4)

Global civil society organizations wield power when they take on a role in the name of global public interest. With power comes responsibility. This raises serious questions concerning the accountability of global civil society.

To whom is global civil society accountable, and how can it be held accountable?

Emergence of Global Civil Society

Waves of International Non-Governmental Organizations

A marginal or esoteric topic only 15 or 20 years ago, the potential of global civil society is now one of the most talked about concepts in global studies (Anheier 2007, 1). In one form or another, most of the contemporary definitions of civil society have a global goal or vision (Kaldor 2003, 11–12).

INGOs are the most visible agents in global civil society.[2] The number of INGOs has increased exponentially in the contemporary period of globalization, as has their membership and the flow of funding to them from governments and other non-governmental organizations (Long 2008, 53). There were few INGOs prior to the 19th century, and only six as of 1854. This grew from 163 at the turn of the century to about 1,000 post-WWII, to over 60,000 by 2007 (Davies 2008, 4). There are now over 5,000 world congresses, where INGOs meet, that cover everything from families to sports, nearly every health care field and specialty, and every hobby. Nearly every academic discipline, profession, and social cause has a world congress. Most meet annually and collectively involve the participation of over 50,000 INGOs. Ninety percent of these international groups have formed since 1970 (Keane 2003, 4).

As with other dimensions of globalization, there are waves of growth in the number and expansion of INGOs. It has not been a steady upward trend. The years circa 1948, 1968, and 1989 stand out as periods of particularly intense activity (Davies 2008, 12). Five sets of factors brought on the waves: external political factors, internal political factors, technological, economic, and social factors.

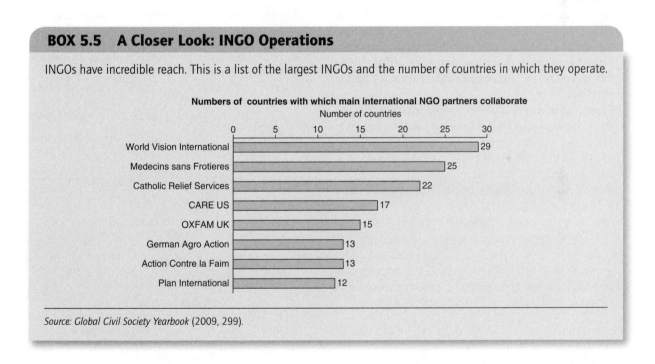

BOX 5.5   A Closer Look: INGO Operations

INGOs have incredible reach. This is a list of the largest INGOs and the number of countries in which they operate.

Numbers of countries with which main international NGO partners collaborate

Number of countries

INGO	Number of countries
World Vision International	29
Medecins sans Frotieres	25
Catholic Relief Services	22
CARE US	17
OXFAM UK	15
German Agro Action	13
Action Contre la Faim	13
Plan International	12

Source: *Global Civil Society Yearbook* (2009, 299).

Establishing the UN was an important external political factor. The UN system provides a global organizational framework for addressing the issues and problems of humanity. This stimulated the formation of INGOs. Not originally designed to accommodate civil society, the UN increasingly includes INGOs in its deliberations and activities. The UN facilitated the environmental and human rights regimes and landmine treaty initiatives of global civil society, among others.

The social conditions of the mid to late 1960s also intensified the growth of INGOs. Social movements denouncing states that used violence or coercion toward other societies or to oppress their own people arose all over the world. These movements differentiated global from national action. Their pursuit of global justice focused on human rights, democracy, peace, civil rights, tolerance, and the environment without regard for where or to whom violations occurred. This accomplished three things. It crystallized the notion of global values that all nations must respect. It established humanity as an entity deserving of rights. And it designated global civil society as humanity's (self-appointed) representative (Anheier 2007).

Advances in communication technology, alienation from state, and disillusionment with international governmental activity also promoted growth of INGOs (Anheier 2007, 5–6). The falling prices and ease of communication among societies facilitate the interdependence of civil society groups and individuals from all over the world. More people have access to information-sharing technologies that until very recently were only available in wealthier societies. People are able to participate in INGO activity, develop relationships among local NGOs, and coordinate spontaneous protests with ease (Keohane and Nye 2000, 117). They also share strategies and obtain support globally.

Last, global culture—forms of discourse and structure—facilitate global civil society. The objective nature of scientific evidence, the verification of arguments through statistics, and appeals for human rights have near-universal acceptance. They are models for discourse and provide a cross-cultural foundation for communication and dialog. Social movements have adopted formal organizational structures and legitimate rhetorical style to be included in UN and national-level deliberations (Kaldor 2003, 87–89).

Global civil society groups have significant successes but drawbacks as well. They have influenced international governmental organizations, such as the UN, World Bank, and IMF. They won important policy changes in areas relating to the environment, human rights, warfare, and so on. They raise billions of dollars in government and private money to implement programs for solving global problems. But the concept of global civil society raises questions and concerns that national civil society does not. The debate about the potential of global civil society poses three main questions. Can global civil society

- be a counterforce to global political and economic systems,
- serve as a global arena of democratic participation and governance, and
- represent the global public? (Berry and Gabay 2009)

BOX 5.6   A Closer Look: Money Is Power

Many INGOs are wealthy, and growing wealthier. Some of the major INGOs and their revenues for 2006 and 2010 (in $US millions) are listed below.

INGO	2006	2010	Cause
World Vision	2,100	2,600	Religious charity
Save the Children	836	1,400	Children's rights
CARE International	624	804	Poverty relief
Doctors Without Borders	568	1,300	Medicine
Oxfam International	528	1,200	Poverty relief

Source: 2006: Aldashev and Verdier (2009, 199); 2010: Slim (2011).

The Challenge of Democracy in Global Civil Society

Global civil society has many of the characteristics of a national society with one important difference. Not everyone is included in global civil society. Many people in national societies are marginalized and not fully included but, in such cases, it violates national or human rights laws. Ironically, there is no law that ensures everyone the rights of representation in global civil society.

Global civil society is often touted as the foundation on which global democracy will be built. These normative claims are not well supported in fact. Most studies of global civil society focus on highly successful cases. The origins and dynamics of their transnational support are neglected. For example, communication and transportation technologies make horizontal ties among NGOs and social movements across countries possible. Nevertheless, some people and groups continue to suffer out of the public eye. Why? There is a lot of competition for the global spotlight, and even if a group is successful, there may be costs associated with the competition for public acclaim and support that go along with it that undermine a group's original intent (Bob 2001, 312).

Global civil society is not always an uncompromised force for democracy, and whether or not a democratic civil society is possible is questionable. Global civil society skeptics claim that global civil society does not live up to its ideals and promises. Their critique assesses often overlooked factors that are important to evaluate the impact and potential of global civil society.

Serious questions arise concerning the degree to which NGOs and INGOs

- represent all marginalized groups by including them in the governance process,
- represent their own goals and objectives to global decision-making bodies rather than the goals and objectives of the people they claim to represent,
- serve powerful governmental organizations and corporations from which funding often flows, rather than be a force for democracy,
- shift the responsibility of governments and international governmental organizations for social welfare into the private realm, and
- engage in truly civil—not just non-violent but inclusive and open—discourse and debate.

Each of these concerns denotes a potential deficit of democratic legitimacy—in representation, goal displacement, interests served, conflict resolution, and accountability. They may influence any activity of INGOs—declaratory, promotional, implementation, and evaluative.

Representation

For all of the good that global civil society has done, there are many groups, millions of people, facing injustices who are never read about in the papers or seen on television. For these groups, global civil society constitutes a "Darwinian marketplace" (Bob 2002, 37). Competition for international support is intense. Rather than radical transparency in which every injustice is illuminated, many groups struggle in obscurity "painfully aware" of the opportunities beyond their reach (37, 46). Securing the benefits of global civil society requires the savvy maneuvering and skillful navigation found in marketing and advertising agencies—not skills handily available to most disaffected and marginalized groups.

Breaking through to the global conscience—or consciousness—is difficult even for very deserving groups (Ayers 2003). How well they can pitch their cause and find the right match among potential donors are two factors that separate winners from losers (Bob 2001, 313). A lot of skill and luck goes into it. Groups who employ similar tactics to those whose attention they seek, who are in more open regimes where it is easier to raise awareness, and who have more resources to create awareness campaigns, have a charismatic spokesperson, a leader with contacts or stature within the global community, the "know how" to present themselves, and the most organizational and mobilization capacity are most likely to be winners (314–315). Those criteria are hard to meet. Groups who meet them and mount successful campaigns are not necessarily the most deserving causes based on need, and many worthy causes get left behind.

Getting notice is particularly difficult if a group is in a low-profile country, if its cause is narrowly defined, of only local interest, or not specifically related to one of the causes of the moment. A group needs to form itself for mass appeal. Framing a cause and universalizing an appeal by connecting it to an issue of importance to one of the large INGOs is critical to success. For example, the Ogoni, one of the many ethnic groups in Nigeria, failed to attract Greenpeace, Amnesty International, and others when they went for help against Royal/Dutch Shell, which was siphoning oil profits from their lands. When they recast their claims as ecological warfare against an indigenous minority, they got support from Greenpeace, Friends of the Earth, and the Sierra Club, among many others. Environmental issues get attention. Indigenous rights also play well, as socialist leaning groups in Guatemala and Zapitista in Mexico discovered when they emphasized their indigenous identities rather than just their complaints (Bob 2002, 39).

Local enemies do not grab the attention of global civil society either. Connecting a cause to a well-known villain can garner recognition for obscure groups, whereas a local villain will not. This connection establishes an important link to broader social movements. Another important qualifier is capturing headlines. Enjoying headlines through protest calls attention to a group and its cause, but protests must be carefully calibrated. The Mexican Zapatista rebels used their indigenous status and anti–free trade standing to broaden and universalize their appeal. They seized a city in protest but were careful not to harm civilians. Although labeled terrorist by the Mexican government, they won the favor of the international community. Most INGOs shun controversial and violent tactics. This happened to Brazilian peasants and poor people's movements who seized land or used kidnapping strategies (Bob 2002, 40). For the most part, the global community favors the *civil* in civil society.

BOX 5.7   A Closer Look: Zapatista "Netwar"

The Zapatista (EZLN) named themselves after Emiliano Zapata, who fought in the Mexican Revolution along with Francisco (Pancho) Villa and Francisco Madero. The Zapatista emerged from an armed guerrilla group (FLN) that fought against the Diaz regime. Although they began with a hierarchical structure, they formed a flatter, network organization (EZLN) as they incorporated indigenous Mayan peasants and took up their causes, particularly land rights and fair trade.

In the1990s, the human rights, indigenous rights, and environmental networks grew globally. The network structure of the Zapatista facilitated aligning with local and global NGOs.

Their methods are not those of the traditional revolutionary. Although they still have an army, their tactics transformed from armed insurgence to netwar. A *netwar* is a mode of conflict using the organization, doctrines, strategies, and technologies of the information age. It is a network-based movement rather than a hierarchical structure. Netwar actors are typically non-state actors, although they may enlist other states in their conflict against their own. Their conflict is waged primarily in cyberspace. A primary tactic is to control the dissemination of information and how conflicts are perceived by their audiences—"who knows what when and where" (Ronfeldt et al. 1998).

Some entire countries are underserved in INGO activities, while in other places, local NGOs are overburdened by trying to manage and administer the largess of INGOs. In Ethiopia, there are five affiliates of World Vision, seven of Oxfam, six of Care International, and 21 of Save the Children. Some small countries, such as Guatemala, Sri Lanka, and Zimbabwe, have over 40 of the 60 largest INGOs, while the much larger Republic of Congo and Central African Republic have only a handful (Koch 2008, 2). Aid earmarked by donors for particular countries may restrict its use. Nevertheless, this is another way in which global civil society represents the interest of money and is not held accountable for the marginalized and neglected.

Global civil society actors engage in debate and influence policies that affect people's lives "without the need for a clear popular mandate" (Long 2008, 55). Only 6% of the board members on the largest development INGOs come from developing countries (Koch 2008, 2). These are all troubling points to many analysts. If global civil society is to achieve democratic ends, it must be inclusive and accountable. Given their power, whether global civil society is "anything more than a collection of advocacy NGOs and social movements with visions and axes

Displaced Goals and Objectives

Capturing public attention is often costly in time, energy, money, and even lives. In the case of the Marxist guerrilla insurgence of the 1980s, international support may have prolonged fighting. The support for guerillas among indigenous peoples and the poor was not as extensive as among international donors. Without international support, guerrillas might have been forced into negotiations years earlier, saving many lives (Bob 2002, 41). INGO success may sacrifice local objectives. Sometimes groups' original goals are subverted in order to achieve international support. Many Ogani, Bob reports, saw their objective of autonomy neglected in favor of the trendier goals of human rights and environmentalism (44).

The strategy of universalizing local concerns may be successful getting global attention but may weaken local channels of communication and rob locals of their voice. The appeals made by INGOs to universal values may not be actually universal. A clash between local and global movements sometimes exposes the particularistic nature of supposed universal values and goals. Seidman (2007) found that workplace complaints got little traction on the global stage in reforming labor laws. Framing the issues as violations of human rights did. "Racist oppression, exploitation of children, legacies of human rights violations and repression" infused the daily minutia of labor grievances with the moral weight of universal concerns" (134). However, the strategy overshadowed local concerns and local priorities were displaced. In South Africa, she found that local activists repudiated the Global Sullivan Principles of corporate social responsibility (developed by Leon Sullivan, an African American) for reflecting American racial concerns (135). Feminist movements in many developing nations were repeatedly stymied when their individualistically oriented approaches to helping indigenous women were not met with much gratitude. Not fully grasping the importance of collective life and family, including male spouses, they often violated local women's ethical and moral understanding of their role in the family and community. The account of the partnership between the Wisconsin Coordinating Council

on Nicaragua and local women's NGOs in Nicaragua poignantly recounts the difficulties, eventually overcome, in establishing global coalitions across cultural and economic divides (Weber 2002).

Some civil society groups' claims to represent the authentic concern of people must be viewed with some skepticism. Local–global coalitions can only be counted as successful if they accomplish local objectives. Strong relationships across borders have to be nurtured to establish a basis for trust and friendship. This can only come from consistent, sustained contact. Otherwise, there will not be open dialog. Local activists have to define the issues on the basis of their concerns and must be involved in interpreting and disseminating information (Seidman 2007, 135). All of this takes time and cannot be accomplished from afar. It requires frequent visits. In contrast, participation and consultation of local groups in global civil society activity is often negligible. Dialog between global civil society organizations and the people on whose behalf they advocate may be scant.

The claim that global civil society functions in a more deliberative way—by getting people's voice heard—than representative democracy does not guarantee its legitimacy in the global arena (Long 2008, 56). Domestic civil society organizations do not make claims of universal values and goals as INGOs do. They advocate for and advance their own particular goals. Their legitimacy is based on free expression and the ability to persuade others to adopt their views. Because they exist in democratic societies, they can ignore what everyone else thinks (Anderson and Rieff 2004, 30). Global civil society groups do not operate within a democratic framework. They do not have the luxury of representing only their interests if they make claims to enhancing global democracy.

Who Is Being Served?

The most obvious answer, the client, is not always correct. NGOs sometimes act as pacifiers, appropriated to legitimize state power or smooth over the roughest effects of transnational capitalism and its exploitation. Social welfare programs, many of which are administered through INGOs, may simply stave off people's dissatisfaction with exploitative economic and political arrangements. They may inadvertently obscure paths to achieving genuine reform of the global political economy or make people more governable by satisfying a baseline of minimal need (Laxer and Halperin 2003).

INGOs may be unintentionally corrupted to buttress the very institutions they want to change. Aid coming through civil society groups (as well as governments) is a form of income and may be competed for among elites either to buy loyalty or for individual gain. In such cases, they contribute to corruption. This can be obscured in analysis of INGO activity. When advocacy is combined with empirical research, the research sometimes fails to critically analyze global civil society groups. When researchers share a normative agenda with the groups they study, perhaps aiding the development of global democracy or some other noble objective, unquestioned assumptions can lead to taking too much for granted. A liberal cosmopolitan perspective often informs both the INGO and its critique. When INGOs are accepted at face value without objective assessment and evaluation, research misses important empirical phenomena (Berry and Gabay 2009, 340). Some of the failings of global civil society, such as misalignment with goals of local groups and neglect of worthy causes in favor of the "cause of the moment," are neglected in many research studies. Uncritical acceptance does not benefit an INGO or the people it serves.

An assessment of an INGO might look quite different from a critical perspective. For example, analyses might question the relationships among INGOs and UN agencies. UN agencies are vehicles of states, and donor funding gets channeled from states through the UN to INGOs. This means that the INGOs are doing states' business. It is couched in the language of good will and development, but it is very clearly the work of the states' development programs (Berry and Gabay 2009, 345–346). In such a case, who are the real clients: the states or the people the INGOs represents? The same criticism may be levied against INGOs that are funded by corporations, including many that contribute to global malaise.

Violence, Power, and Conflict Resolution

Globalization creates diversity as much as it homogenizes; it is unrealistic to imagine a global civil society not riveted with conflict. Social life will never return, barring catastrophe, to an undifferentiated, non-pluralistic state of non-conflicting interests. This diversity poses a dilemma. Even with good motives, there is often disagreement and contradiction among the goals of diverse groups and the means chosen to achieve them. Legitimacy cannot be assumed when equal claims to moral legitimacy clash (Long 2008, 56). Since global clashes are not resolved in an overarching democratic framework, resolution depends on who marshals the most resources of power, money, or prestige.

Contradictory and competing objectives, not only among regimes but also within them, limit a regime's effectiveness. There are many sources of conflict in the legal terms of regime agreements and behavioral conflicts when states act on the basis of these conflicting norms or rules. An example of this is the contradiction between the principle of equal treatment of trading partners found in the Montreal Protocol and the General Agreement on Tariffs and Trade (GATT) division of countries into different groups that receive different benefits (Zelli 2008, 2).

There are many conflicts between trade and environmental regimes. The ozone regime has been stymied in trying to establish trade restrictions on ozone-depleting substances because it conflicts with the World Trade Organization (WTO) rules that prohibit "trade restrictions based on non-product related processes and production methods" (Zelli 2008, 8). Conflicts may arise as a regime is developing norms, after they have been institutionalized in documents, or as they develop over time (3). The conflicts within and across civil society regimes might prevent democratic results depending on the types of leverage that states, civil society organizations, and other relevant actors bring to the political process. The outcome of clashes between groups and regimes tends to be determined by which

- manages to have the conflict ceded to its domain of influence, say, to jobs rather than the environment;
- has more inclusive and stringent norms already in place; and
- has more authority to monitor and enforce their norms.

Power, not democracy, determines the outcome. Global conflict management within and among regimes must be a higher priority.

Global civil society advocates are not blind to the dangers of conflicting interests. Civility does not diminish conflict; civility is the commitment to resolve conflict within the rule of law. Deliberation, debate, discourse, and dialog are non-violent ways to resolve conflict. While there is too little discourse and dialog in the conduct of global events and not all civil society members act civilly, there are global civil society networks that function across lines of conflict and contention. "Horizontal transnational global networks, both civil and uncivil, exist side by side in the same territorial space" (Kaldor 2003, 6).

Thorny Questions of Accountability

Global civil society actors have particularly thorny problems establishing legitimacy in terms of the public they represent. The legitimacy of power is the reasoned consent by those who are subject to the organization or actor exercising it (Long 2008). This does not necessarily apply in the activities of INGOs. For all the good they do, INGOs' capacity to operate democratically and be held accountable is a serious concern. Global civil society groups are in some ways pressure groups. Unlike democratically elected representatives, they are not formally approved of or chosen by all people for whom they advocate. Nor can they be removed from office. They do not operate within a democratic system of governance, as do national civil society groups.

These criticisms regarding lack of representation, goal orientation, who is being served, conflict resolution, and accountability have also been directed at the World Social Forum (WSF). Since 2001, WSF has met annually to promote an alternative globalization. Their motto is "A new world is possible." The forum is an arena for local and global civil society groups to meet and discuss strategies to counter powerful global and local actors (whether corporations, states, other civil society groups, etc.). By creating the opportunity for dialog, groups that seem radically disparate may find common ground in larger collective projects. The visibility of WSF, especially within academic circles, makes them particularly open to critique. Criticisms of the WSF, which may apply to many INGOs, are as follows:

- The diversity of interest represented at the WSF inhibits it from constructing an alternate globalization. Differences between radicals who want to abolish the institutions of power such as the IMF and World Bank conflict with those who want reform. Environmentalists who want to limit growth and consumption conflict with labor unions

who want jobs. The list of juxtapositions and conflict is endless. WSF has not found a way to transcend these differences to find common ground and concrete objectives from which to form a strategy (Worth and Buckley 2009, 650–653).
- The WSF is not representative of the people for whom it advocates. Rather than the forum being occupied with people working at grassroots levels to improve their own conditions, 30% of the people in attendance at the 2005 meeting had post-graduate educations, and 80% had Internet access—hardly representative of the disenfranchised global population. NGOs tend to be running the show, with many academic panels and discussion sessions based on interests of the organizing committees.
- The WSF has been used by states of the "center-left," such as Venezuela, to solicit support by making speeches and appeals at the meetings.
- Many attempts to make attending WSF affordable have failed, limiting participation.
- Funding comes from many foundations (e.g., Ford, Rockefeller, Carnegie) that are the "carriers of US globalization and foreign policy."
- New elites are created in global civil society as NGOs decide what is or is not progressive. European and Latin American NGOs are over represented at WSF, and only those with the most powerful voices are heard. This is also true of the European Forum held in London (655–656).

Despite INGO intentions, critics conclude that there is a wide, perhaps insurmountable, chasm between the radical, counter-hegemonic, transformative voice that the WSF would like to be and its current status. Addressing these issues is essential for INGOs to achieve their normative goals, whether their goal is to become a vehicle for democratization of global governance, a strong voice for oppressed peoples, or to alleviate global problems.

This critique of civil society does not mean that networks of NGOs and INGOs are not important parts of democratic systems, but they in and of themselves are not democratic. If the intent of civil society is ultimately social justice, how it is defined and by whom—the questions of representation and accountability—cannot be glossed over. Seidman's (2007) work on labor rights suggests that INGOs may be a more effective tool of democracy by working to strengthen weak states and institutions than by trying to effect change on their own. INGOs cannot be an effective regulatory regime by themselves. Voluntary regimes, Seidman argues, work only when backed by the power of a state. Local activists' priorities, at least in labor movements, are to make states more responsible and effective in protecting them and the vulnerable. Strengthening states has broader national impact—and potentially global impact through social learning and other mechanisms of diffusion. Learning from the best practices of INGOs and NGOs in global civil society and reconciling them with responsible critique are necessary.

Global Civil Society: Interacting Layers of Governance

Civil society organizations operate in different structures of opportunity. Access and constraints within and among societies influence the pathways and strategies NGOs and INGOs employ to achieve their objectives, pressuring governments, organizations, and international governmental organizations to act.

Channels of opportunity for democratic participation in government and international governmental organizations vary in the degree to which they are open or closed. Institutional openness varies within the international community and within countries issue by issue as well. Civil society groups have to navigate these channels seizing each opportunity to open them. This explains, in part, the differences in tactics and effectiveness of social movements (Sikkink 2005, 154–157). Global civil society groups are critical in domestic reform when national civil society groups find channels blocked.

There are four situations that NGOs and INGOs confront determined by the logical possibilities of openness and closure.

- **Diminished chances of activism** (Sikkink 2005, 156): In this case, both domestic and international channels are closed. This is the situation faced in many countries where groups cannot attract the attention of international governmental organizations or NGOs (Bob 2002). This is not an impossible situation, but some external event or internal vulnerability has to happen to open channels sufficiently to initiate change. In the case of democratization in former Warsaw Pact countries, economic difficulties forced the countries to make concessions to European governments. This created a small opening that activists seized to enlist Western governments and other INGOs in pressuring their governments to democratize.

- **Boomerang effect** (Sikkink 2005, 163–163): Here, domestic channels are closed but international ones open; therefore, activists use international channels to publicize their situation, cultivating an international constituency to pressure their government from above. International organizations, other governments, corporations—any actor who can exert pressure can be used. The collapse of apartheid in South Africa was furthered by pressures on multinational corporations and transnational groups to withdraw from South Africa or risk their own reputation and profits.

- **Spiral effect** (163): This is a version of the boomerang effect but more complex and entailing a longer process. The spiral effect refers to cycles of pressure for change and eventual changes leading to greater pressure and more change. It captures how changes can have a synergistic effect instigating changes in other parts of the society to make way for further activism. Domestic groups may reach out at times or concentrate domestically at others depending on the specifics of the moment. Changes in civil rights in the United States demonstrate a spiral pattern, expanding both the groups covered by civil rights laws and the domains of life where protection is warranted.

- **Insider–outsider** coalitions (165): In this case, both domestic and international arenas are open. Activists work primarily for domestic change, using international coalitions for a secondary support. Change and reform in a number of governments may occur simultaneously in domestic and international arenas. These have been the tactics of the peace movement, landmine movement, as well as the environmental, and similar movements that have brought change to democratic societies.

Global and domestic civil society groups influence governmental bodies through these networks, moving across channels when they confront blockages. They contract with governments, form ad hoc partnerships, lobby them to change their policies, and work with one another. States that are poorly connected, such as North Korea, are hard to reach; there are few paths of opportunity into them at any level. Myanmar (Burma), impervious to international sanctions for decades, suddenly instituted democratic reforms with the new government in 2010. The government has asked for international assistance integrating into the global civil society, political, and economic systems. Channels are now open and pressures are being eased bit by bit with each reform.

Creating structures of opportunity is about building relationships. Myriad relationships are cultivated for global civil society groups to be effective in the multilayered system of global governance. They cultivate the relationships among diverse individuals who are their members, with their external environment which includes other civil society groups, local, national, and global, and with governmental representatives and organizations.

Civil Society Case Studies

Global regimes develop in many areas of social life, from the reduction of inequality, poverty, and hunger, to the frontiers of space and the ocean. The human rights regime and environmental regime were chosen as case studies because they represent two of humanity's common causes. Few regimes are as well developed as these two. The landmine ban treaty in and of itself is not a regime. It is an instructive case because as a global civil society movement, it defied the odds. Although many innocents have been killed and maimed by landmines, they are not planted the world over. They are primarily in the developing world. Nor were they perceived as a global problem when the movement began.

Although there are commonalities among these movements, each had a different trajectory in achieving success, and each case study emphasizes a different aspect of the relationship between civil society groups and the global system of societies. The presentation of the landmine treaty emphasizes the importance of partnerships, alliances, and the strategies that can bring success. The environmental movement emphasizes the importance of framing a cause in a universal rhetoric and making a universal appeal. It also demonstrates the evolution of a regime through early phases of uncoordinated activities, NGO and INGO growth, treaty development, and institutionalization in regulatory agencies. The study of the human rights regime illustrates how in the face of blocked channels, an opening widened them enough so that through the spiral effect groups gradually achieved changes to establish a human rights regime. Each case study illustrates the importance of controlling cognitive and normative agendas and the importance of strong networks to accomplish their objectives.

Case Study: Treaty to Ban Landmines

Landmines killed or maimed 30,000 people annually in Cambodia during the 1990s. In Afghanistan, there are an estimated 10 million mines, vestiges of the Soviet invasion and Taliban insurgency. There are millions of landmines in countries all over the world, concentrated in Africa, the Middle East, and Asia, but also in Latin America and Eastern Europe. In the early 1990s, conventional wisdom was that a treaty to ban landmines was an impossible dream. In 1997, it became reality. The success of the Treaty to Ban Landmines is the story of insider-outsider coalitions. The INGOs and NGOs had the advantage of working in states whose channels were open and through the UN. They took advantage of open opportunity structures, relying on global and domestic groups to influence states to change their policy toward landmines and subsequently use those states to influence others.

What mechanisms worked? Attributing them simply to power plays or states' interests is not sufficient. The United States, a leader in most of the landmine debates, was unsuccessful in seeking the exceptions it wanted in the treaty and did not sign it.[3] Many states that manufactured anti-personnel landmines destroyed their mines and signed. The pressures exerted on states came from changing global perceptions and changing global norms. Ultimately, the INGOs succeeded because they were able to control the ways that landmines were perceived. They were strategically smart. Specific tactics used by the INGOs are emphasized throughout the discussion.

This analysis of the landmine movement and its strategies draws from the case studies "The Landmine Ban: A Case Study in Humanitarian Advocacy" by Don Hubert (2000), including the preface by Neil MacFarlane (2000), and "The Evolving Arms Control Agenda: Implications of the Role of NGOs in Banning Antipersonnel Landmines" by Kenneth R. Rutherford (2000).

Early Momentum

Landmines were not on the agenda of arms control, the military, or governmental policy makers until the late 1980s to early 1990s (Rutherford 2000, 80). There was one relevant international treaty. The 1980 UN Convention on Certain Conventional Weapons (CCW) prohibited the indiscriminate use of landmines and put some restrictions on remotely deliverable (scatterable) mines, but did not ban landmines or impose stringent controls (Hubert 2000, 5).

In the eyes of those who had worked with landmine victims, the CCW did not go far enough. Doctors and de-miners working in the field tried calling attention to the devastation wrought by landmines a decade earlier. The ICRC field surgeons published articles in medical journals condemning the unnecessary suffering and injury caused by landmines. In 1979, a group of doctors working in Cambodia formed Handicap International (HI) to work with landmine victims. Seeing the problem of landmine death and destruction worsening, not only in Cambodia but in the 26 other countries where they worked as well, HI became proactive, writing and speaking out about landmines. The Coalition for Peace and Reconciliation (CPR) was also working in Cambodia in 1979. They became more active. The ICRC continued in its anti-landmine activity. These three groups were soon joined by others. The movement to ban landmines had begun, led by global civil society INGOs.

BOX 5.8   Consider This: Key People Framing the Issue

From the beginning of the campaign, key people involved were experts in the field who had been working with landmine victims and landmines (Hubert 2000; Rutheford 2000). They could speak with authority and credibility. They had credentials to frame the issue both in humanitarian and scientific discourse. These are the universalizing discourses of the global era.

What are other forms of discourse that might appeal to other audiences? In what circumstances might religious, emotional appeals to a higher loyalty, or other concerns, frame the debate or discussion of an issue? Do these ever apply in debate about global issues? What framing devices do you hear with respect to contemporary issues such as welfare, abortion, environmentalism, and others?

1991

The Vietnam Veterans of America Foundation (VVAF) and Medico International (MI) joined forces to combat landmines and enlist other NGOs to call for a global ban (Hubert 2000, 8; Rutherford 2000, 86). In October of 1992, they joined with Human Rights Watch, the ICRC, HI, and CPR to hold a conference at which they would enlist others to the cause. Building a coalition of NGOs and INGOs resulted in the core planning groups with experts from a variety of perspectives. This would broaden their appeal.

1992

Activities of the INGOs and UN agencies to educate the global public and combat landmine devastation intensified. The movement attracted the attention of the UN and its agencies, helping it to gather momentum.

- ICRC issued "Mines: A Perverse Use of Technology."
- Boutros Boutros-Ghali, secretary-general of the UN, spoke out against landmines in "An Agenda for Peace."
- The UN Department of Humanitarian Affairs (UNDHA) was given responsibility for mine-related activities.
- UNDHA and the Department of Peacekeeping hosted a series of meetings of UN departments and INGOs to share information.

The coalition built on partnerships with UN agencies. For example, from October 1992 to December 1993, UNICEF spent roughly $287,000 in mine awareness throughout El Salvador, engaging community groups, schools, and health clinics in educating the broader public about the dangers of mines (Landmine Monitor 1999). These activities extended their networks into intergovernmental governance through the UN to local NGOs and local governance. The INGOs also clarified their focus—a total ban on landmines and commitments to demining activity.

The U.S. Congress passed a one-year ban on the sale, transfer, and export of mines proposed by Senator Patrick Leahy and Representative Lane Evans in October 1992. The EU followed with a five-year moratorium on export of mines. The INGOs could already claim a measure of success. They had changed the perception of landmines. They were now seen as a humanitarian issue, not arms control. As it turned out, this would not be enough.

BOX 5.9   A Closer Look: Personalizing, Partnering, and Setting the Cognitive Agenda

The early steps awakening civil society to the issue of landmines contain the seeds of their eventual success. The committees used horrific victims' stories to personalize landmine statistics in their many reports, public speeches, meetings, and conferences. These were disseminated through the media, giving the issue extensive coverage and riveting the attention of the public and policy makers.

In this way, the INGOs successfully set the cognitive agenda establishing landmines as a serious problem (Rutheford 2000, 91–92).

By couching the statistical appeals as a legal and moral issue within the humanitarian frame, rather than in an arms control frame, the INGOs were able to establish the normative agenda as well (Rutheford 2000, 94–95).

Extensive partnering with other NGOs and UN agencies was an early strategy used throughout the campaign. As the campaign expanded, the expertise of key personnel and the scientific-humanitarian nature of the discourse did not change but was complemented.

Joining Forces and Enlisting Governments

1993

The original five INGOs collaborating on the landmine ban and HRW formed The International Campaign to Ban Landmines (ICBL) at a meeting in London. Fifty representatives from 40 NGOs also attended. Buttressed by the activity of its member groups and Western governments, the NGO membership of the ICBL grew very quickly to over 350 within two years (Hubert 2000, 8).

BOX 5.10   A Closer Look: Landmine Casualties

This chart shows casualties due to landmines and unexploded ordnance in countries with over 100 casualties. Children accounted for about one third of the casualties where age was known. In recent years, there have been over 5,000 casualties annually. This has decreased from the 1990s. There were over 75,000 recorded casualties from 1999 to 2008. Many are unrecorded.

Country	Number of Casualties
Afghanistan	859
Colombia	674
Pakistan	421
Myanmar	262
Cambodia	244
Lao PDR	134
Somalia	126

Source: International Campaign to Ban Landmines (2010).

The ICRC held the Montreux Symposium to bring NGOs, governments, militaries, manufacturers, mine clearance personnel, and victims into deliberations to share facts and ideas. The expertise of the movement grew as it gained better understanding of anti-ban objectors. National campaigns in Cambodia, Sweden, Germany, Britain, the United States, New Zealand, Australia, Italy, Belgium, Ireland, Canada, South Africa, and Afghanistan lobbied political leaders, met with government officials, conducted educational campaigns, and collected signatures in support of the ban. This pressure upward on states was significant in helping to sway public opinion in favor of the ban (Hubert 2000, 9).

- Senator Patrick Leahy continued to push the landmine ban agenda in the United States and internationally. In November, he introduced a resolution to the General Assembly of the UN urging states to put a moratorium on exports of landmines.
- The U.S. Senate extended the previous year's moratorium for three years (Rutherford 2000, 77).
- The U.S. State Department issued "Hidden Killers: The Global Problem With Uncleared Mines." This pressure from peers was effective. Fifteen countries established moratoriums within two years. In

1994, Leahy went back to the UN, asking not only for more states to join the moratorium on exports, but also to work toward "the eventual elimination of landmines" (Hubert 2000, 12).
- The French government declared that it would formally request a review of the 1980 UN Convention on Certain Conventional Weapons (CCW). Sweden called for a complete ban, and the Netherlands destroyed its stockpile.

1994

U.S. President Bill Clinton was the first head of state to address the UN on the need for a landmine ban. Clinton recognized the humanitarian dimension of the problem—he increased funding for de-mining and for victims—but he continued to support military and political arguments to retain a landmine option. This support for exceptions to the ban cost the United States its leadership role on the issue.

ICBL strategy to refrain from attacking the military utility of landmines and maintain focus on illegality of weapons that posed an indiscriminate threat to civilians was successful. No state was able to attack the humanitarian frame. The moral argument stigmatized the mines and any state that continued to use them (Rutherford 2000, 105). The movement pointed out that the mines had only limited utility. This was uncontroversial and allowed them to stick to a straightforward message. Even the states that opposed the ban, such as the United States and the United Kingdom (until Princess Diana assumed a leadership role and the Labor Party came into power) could not ignore the humanitarian argument. They had to address and sympathize with the plight of victims. The result was that their anti-ban arguments seemed incoherent (105). The anti-ban countries ceded the public debate to landmine ban advocates.

The UN General Assembly called for four meetings to prepare for treaty talks. They began in 1994 before the landmine review conference. That is when things started to unravel, a bit. First, China restricted observation status for both the preparatory meetings and the actual conference to the ICRC and UN agencies. People in the ICBL who had the greatest experience were not able to participate. Not easily deterred, 100

BOX 5.11   A Closer Look: Landmine Victims

Rehabilitation programs for landmine victims are critical component of the emerging regime on landmines and other unexploded ordnance.

representatives from 70 agencies lobbied in the corridors where the meeting rooms were and closely monitored the negotiations to compensate for lack of formal participation.

U.S. Senator Leahy and the VVAF, along with other allies, held a conference, "The Global Landmine Crisis." In the meantime, despite their relentless efforts and leadership roles, the Clinton administration continued to pursue landmines as a national security issue.

Spiral Effects

1995 was a definitive year. Coalitions among INGOs, NGOs, UN agencies, and states were growing; more government representatives and organizations attended each conference and meeting. In many ways, everything was falling into place for the ban to be successful. NGO lobbying and educational efforts were effective. By using expert military testimony on the limited military utility of landmines and the unreliable nature of the self-destroying mines, the ICBL and ICRC were making their point. Public opinion was swaying states. Belgium banned the production, purchase, sale, or transfer of anti-personnel mines. By 1994, about 30 countries supported a total ban.

Despite this, little progress was made on landmines in the CCW review negotiations. Even though Sweden called for a total ban on landmines, the first CCW session focused primarily on their military utility and ended early and in deadlock.

- The ICRC ramped up its campaign to stigmatize use of mines. It launched a worldwide campaign working through national and regional levels to pressure states. The ICRC called for a total, immediate, and definitive ban on landmines. An ICRC report, written by a British combat engineer and demining expert, stated unequivocally that landmines were not just ineffective, but counterproductive.
- The VVFA sponsored an open letter to President Clinton in the *New York Times* signed by retired military—including the much admired and distinguished U.S. commander in the Gulf War General Norman Schwartzkopf—denying the argument of the military need for landmines.
- Raising the ante in the United States, Leahy proposed a moratorium on the use of landmines by U.S. troops to begin in 1999. Congress passed it unanimously.
- The day before the review conference opened in September 1995, the ICRC released the VVAF report that issued from the Montreux Symposium, *After the Guns Fall Silent: The Enduring Legacy of Landmines* (Roberts and Williams 1995).

The campaigns were by any measure a success. By then, 40 countries supported a ban. At least that many had declared a moratorium on exports and others were destroying their stockpiles. Little was accomplished in the January or April sessions of the review conference with respect to landmines. But in meeting rooms outside of the convention rooms, eight *pro-ban states*—Austria, Belgium, Canada, Denmark, Ireland, Mexico, Norway, and Switzerland—met quietly with the ICBL to discuss a potential future strategy (Hubert 2000, 14–16).

BOX 5.12   A Closer Look: Policy Diffusion

Enlisting sympathetic experts from every relevant interest group including the military broadened and legitimized the appeal. Policy innovations tend to diffuse from one government to others. One government's policy change can break logjams and change can spread quickly. When countries jump on board after a few make the switch and a policy diffuses quickly, as in the case here, it is called a *bandwagon effect*.

The Ottawa Process Begins

The alliance of eight states forged at the CCW meetings planned an alternative strategy. It was decided that Canada would host a meeting of pro-ban states and grant the ICBL a seat at the table as a full partner. Non-ban states could observe. With this alliance, the insider–outsider pattern of NGO activity solidified. Fifty-six states attended the October 1996 conference as full participants—meaning that they had committed to the ban; 24 states observed. After two days, some participants thought there was little concrete accomplished and considered handing the process over to the upcoming Conference on Disarmament. This would have reversed one of the ICRC and ICBL's most important accomplishments—framing the debate as a humanitarian issue—and put the ban directly into the military arena.

The alliance had a back-up plan. On the third day, the Canadian host, Lloyd Axworthy, surprised the participants by inviting them to return to Ottawa in one year for a treaty-signing conference. Using the fast-track process, the ICBL bypassed the time-consuming UN treaty process. They justified this by the perceived urgency of the landmine problem. After negotiating with Canada, the United States sponsored its annual UN Resolution 51/45/S, "An International Agreement to Ban Antipersonnel Landmines." The final text welcomed the conclusions of the recent Ottawa Conference and called on states to "pursue vigorously an effective, legally binding international agreement to ban the use, stockpiling, production and transfer of antipersonnel mines with a view to completing negotiations as soon as possible." The resolution passed 156–0 with ten abstentions (Hubert 2000, 22).

BOX 5.13   A Closer Look: Controlling the Agenda

Moving the landmine ban from a consensus-seeking forum to a negotiating forum allowed the INGOs more control over the agenda (Rutherford 2000, 113) Consensus forums make every participant a "veto player" empowered to block provisions. That is one of the reasons why the minimum becomes the maximum achieved in some conventions, such as with the landmine provisions of the CCW Convention.

Over the next year, a core group of 11 states—the original eight plus South Africa, Mexico, and the Philippines—prepared for the Ottawa meeting. Much had to be accomplished in a short time. They divided the labor. They planned two major meetings—each with over 100 countries represented—and rounds of smaller conferences, lobbying efforts, and campaigning all over the world. They concentrated activities that ordinarily could have taken years into months. States, INGOs, NGOs, and international governmental agencies all played a role. They also held a series of intense regional meetings. Making use of neighborhood effects, regional meetings were used to build political will among countries and secure commitments (Hubert 2000, 22). By late May, 70 countries had committed to the Ottawa process. New governments in the United Kingdom and France reversed their countries' positions and pledged support for a comprehensive ban.

The last major meeting before the treaty was to be signed was an international conference in Brussels in June. Ninety-seven countries signed the Brussels Declaration. There had been no progress on landmines in the Convention on Disarmament. If something on landmines was to be accomplished, the Ottawa process would have to succeed. States that had been holding out began to convert. In August, the United States signed the Brussels Declaration. The United States signed to be allowed to participate in the Oslo meetings, where the convention would be concluded before it was opened for signatures in Ottawa. This was the first of the Ottawa series meetings attended by the United States. The United States wanted to add amendments to the agreement, including the right to use mines along borders and in the demilitarized zone in Korea, to use mixed system anti-tank mines, and accomplish a nine-year deferral for some of the provisions (Hubert 2000, 25).

Ironically, discussion of the amendments dominated the meetings to such an extent that disagreements over other issues were not addressed. Having no success, the United States finally withdrew its proposals, and the text passed and was signed by 122 states at the Convention in Ottawa. It entered it into force in September 1998, after achieving 40 ratifications. The United States,

Russia, China, and Israel are among the countries that have yet to sign.

The success of the treaty is a success of global governance. An obscure interest of battlefield doctors and soldiers, passage of the treaty was far from guaranteed. Originally, specific interests of particular states overrode interests in the common good. States that used more sophisticated landmines wanted to preserve the right to use them—at least in some circumstances—and restrict the use of less-sophisticated landmines that did not self-destruct. States that had stockpiles of cheap landmines wanted to preserve the right to use theirs and restrict the more expensive and technologically advanced ones (Hubert 2000, 4).

BOX 5.14　Check It Out Yourself: NGO and INGO Publicity

In 1997, the Vietnam Veterans Association took out an advertisement in the *New York Times*. In a child's printing, it read

"Dear Mr. President,

Why can't we sign the treaty to ban land mines?"

The only picture was a stick figure image of the child, missing the bottom of her left leg.

Have you seen appeals from NGOs or INGOs in your local paper or a national paper? For at least a week, keep an eye out for them. NGOs have become very sophisticated in their pubic appeals.

Have you seen TV appeals or heard radio announcements for global causes supported by NGOs or INGOs? Which appeals did you find most effective and why?

The landmine ban owes it success both to the geopolitical context of the 1990s and to the strategic maneuvers of the pro-ban leaders. The end of the Cold War changed the perspective of the world on matters of national security. Whereas the superpower rivalry had been a global national security focus, wars within nations had increased dramatically in the years immediately following the fall of the iron curtain. NATO and the Warsaw Pact were no longer at a standoff. Bringing peace to countries devastated by civil wars and ethnic rivalries was a major objective of the global political community. Light weapons were causing much of the destruction (Hubert 2000, 29–30).

While there is no global regime for security, securing the treaty involved multiple layers of governance: INGOs, NGOs, states, international governmental organizations, and the UN. They worked in different combinations at different times to achieve a turnaround, from disinterest and objection to the treaty expressed by nearly every state in the UN to eventual acceptance and ratification by nearly all of them. The ICBL Committee and Jody Williams won the Nobel Prize for Peace for their work securing the Treaty to Ban Landmines. In 2010, the United States announced it would review its policy on landmines.

Case Study: The Environmental Regime

The environmental regime impacts all aspects of societal function, from the methods and resources that people use to acquire the means of survival to disposing of the waste that they generate in producing and consuming it. It is "a partially integrated collection of world-level organizations, understandings, and assumptions that specify the relationship of human society to nature" (Meyer et al. 1997, 623). Its development highlights the interdependence of issues facing the globe and how interacting layers of governance draw organizations not directly related to an issue into its governance regime.

(Continued)

(Continued)

Environmental ethics extend beyond traditional ethics in transcending time and space in ways critical to globalization generally. Environmental issues demand that people engage across borders as ecosystems do not respect political boundaries. Because environmental resources are subject to depletion and destruction, environmental issues demand that people engage the quality of life for future generations as well as their present concerns. One view of environmental ethics stipulates that they

- encompass not only intra-human obligation among contemporaries, but all people everywhere, animals, and all of nature as well;
- are interdisciplinary, encompassing economics, politics, the natural and social sciences, as well as some religious concerns;
- have competing ideas and perspectives; and
- are revolutionary, challenging anthropocentrism, materialism, consumerism, and capitalism. (Yang 2006, 24)

World society theorists' analysis of the environmental regime illustrates the importance of world polity and culture. According to these theorists, the environmental regime grew from discussions within civil society organizations to more formal articulation in international governmental and economic contexts without being driven by a dominant nation. States in the West that dominated the adoption of international regimes in security and other areas have been not been willing lead the way or even participate in environmental policy and structures (Meyers et al. 1997, 627).

The environmental regime grew without strong domestic programs of environmentalism to diffuse through regions or to other groups of states. States did not create ministries or departments of the environment until the regime was well on its way. The development of the environmental regime demonstrates the importance of global culture, of "a world-level frame within which interaction and discourse about environmental issues could expand rapidly" (Meyer et al. 1997, 629). The growth of the environmental regime was a global civil society success. Global civil society groups worked the connections across governance levels and groups. Emulation, social learning, coercion, and nearly every other mechanism of diffusion played a role in extending policies and practices.

Phases of Environmental Regime

Take-Off Phase: Late 19th and Early 20th Centuries

There are three generations of environmental organizations (Trzyna 2008). *Early environmental groups were primarily* conservation organizations whose goals were to protect wildlife and natural areas. Among the international civil society groups engaged in conservation activities were International Friends of Nature (1895), the International Bureau of Antivivisection Societies (1925), the International Union of Forestry Research Organizations (1891), and the Commonwealth Forestry Association (1921) (Meyer et al. 1997, 635). The number of international environmental organizations increased gradually from 1870 on, reaching 50 in the 1950s (625). Although a number of multilateral agreements were signed during this phase, they were generally limited to the protection of a particular species or habitat. These treaties tended to be motivated more by sentiment than purpose and thus did not extend the environmental discussion beyond the particularities of specific species or treaties (637).

BOX 5.15   A Closer Look: Early Voices of Environmental Science

Many environmentalists recognize Rachel Carson as a, if not the, major figure, stimulating the global environmental movement. The publication of *Silent Spring* in 1962 captured the public's imagination as well as ire. Although the book was scrupulously researched, it was viciously attacked by the chemical and agricultural industries, for its dire warnings of the consequences of DDT (dichlorodiphenyltrichloroethane) use as pesticide in farming. Carson documented death and destruction by water pollution, linking cases nationwide with DDT use. She used science to critically examine the unquestioning use of scientific products. Science, at the time, was seen as only beneficial and benevolent. In 1963, a presidential scientific commission established by John F. Kennedy in the United States supported Carson's findings.

Limits to Growth was published by the Club of Rome in 1972, a "small international group of professionals from the fields of diplomacy, industry, academia and civil society." Its first report elaborated the theme that has become the Club of Rome's fundamental and recurring premise: "unlimited consumption and growth on a planet with limited resources cannot go on forever and is indeed dangerous" (Club of Rome 2009).

The environmental regime began in global civil society, not with states. A number of factors elevated environmental concerns from the realm of sentimentality to a global movement of life and death rhetoric. Increasing pollution from coal-fired plants as industrialization revved up following WWII, the smell of industrial waste discharged into bodies of water, water clouded with algae grown from farm fertilizer run-off, scorched earth, and treeless forests impacted people's sense of something gone awry. But concern for the health of the planet was not enough to effectuate an environmental regime. Two macro-level developments cleared the path for civil society groups to advance international discourse and action on the environment:

- Rational-scientific discourse
- The UN (Meyer et al. 1997)

Rational discourse is accepted near universally as legitimate and authoritative. International norms concerning the application of science to policy decisions influenced development in many areas of international relations. The environmental movement had little traction when its appeals were sentimental (save the teddy bear) or involved competing international interests over resources, as in the early movements to save the whales. When environmental arguments were cast in the universal language of science, they were legitimized by the assumed objectivity and disinterested nature of science. The apolitical language of science stressed the unity of the earth as an ecosystem. Environmentalism advanced through this lofty appeal attracting more media and public attention with much greater currency in influential political circles than sentimentality ever had.

The UN is a global vehicle for dialog and coordination. Before the UN, international governmental agencies were limited in scope and function.

Although bilateral and multilateral treaties were plentiful, they addressed particularistic needs of partner nations. The UN's broad mission provides a platform from which all types of global movements can launch. Its forum facilitated bringing environmental matters to world attention, coordinating global policy and action, and using peer pressure among nations to develop treaties (Meyer et al. 1997, 647).

The timeline of the environmental regime development illustrates how it emerged in global civil society and then moved to domestic governmental levels. Armed with a global discourse and global vehicle, the activity of global and CSOs intensified. INGOs were more numerous and arose earlier than treaties. The number of governmental and intergovernmental organizations relating to the environment lagged behind both INGOs and treaty development.

The pace of international environmental law quickened after WWII, but it was not until the "late 1960s and early 1970s that the extent and intensity of international environmental regulation began to increase significantly, and a nascent international regime emerged" (Held 2004, 133; Biermann, Siebenhüner, and Schreyögg 2009; Tryzna 2008).

The Contemporary Era

Science is a foundation of global discourse, facilitating communication among nations. Science is presumed to be objective and universal, not influenced by nationality, race, class, or any other particularistic interest and relevant to nearly any set of problems. The number of international scientific organizations increased rapidly following WWII. Global environmental organizations were among them. They relied on science to draw international attention to the state of the environment, portraying the earth as a single ecosystem in delicate balance and highlighting the interdependence of every nation's well-being. Global nongovernmental environmental organizations parlayed scientific knowledge and discourse into pressure for domestic and international governmental organization and regulation (Meyer et al. 1997, 635–637).

NGOs grew first in number and then expanded their membership and missions as new environmental concerns came to light. The early organizations' histories mirror the evolution of the regime itself. For example, the World Wildlife Fund was founded in 1961 in London and expanded quickly in mission, membership, and across countries. It has continuously reinvented itself as environmental concerns spread from the realm of scientists to more segments of the general public, growing in membership, developing partnerships, and expanding its mission as new environmental concerns emerge. During the 1960s, it concentrated on conservation of wild species. In the 1970s, it included habitat destruction. In 1986, the World Wildlife Fund changed its name to the World Wide Fund for Nature to reflect its expanded mission. In the 1990s, it expanded further along with the environmental movements concern for the effects of human activity and sustainable development (Hails 2013). During the 1990s, its again-revised mission included biodiversity, sustainable development, pollution, and wasteful consumption (WWF 2012, "1990"). At the turn of the century, it self-reportedly has "vastly upscale(d) its ambition, aiming for transformational changes that lead to lasting conservation, sustainable development and sustainable lifestyles" (WWF 2013a). In 2001, it dropped the words from its name to better translate to its global membership and vastly expanded mission and adopted the acronym as its new name, now simply WWF International (WWF 2013a, 2013b).

BOX 5.16   A Closer Look: The Progression of the Environmental Regime

This graph shows the evolution of the environmental regime. INGOs developed first. That was followed by international treaties, then international governmental organizations. National environmental ministries were the last to emerge.

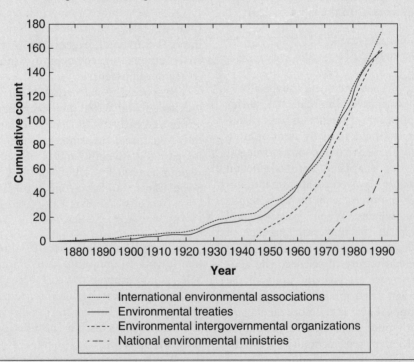

Source: The Structuring of a World Environmental Regime, 1870–1990 by John W. Meyer, David John Frank, Ann Hironaka, Evan Schofer and Nancy Brandon Tuma. *International Organization*, Vol. 51, No. 4 (1997) pp. 623-651 Copyright © 1997 The IO Foundation and the Massachusetts Institute of Technology.

Global environmental organizations pressured for environmental treaties. Rather than the narrow treaties such as the 1911 Fur Seal Convention or sentimental such as the 1933 Convention Relative to the Preservation of Fauna and Flora in their Natural State, treaties after WWII reflected the scientific discourse of the NGOs (Meyer et al. 1997, 637). Once treaties were signed, international governmental organizations multiplied. As they increased in number and expanded their scope to regulation, the need for treaties diminished, and the rate of treaty development slowed. As more environmental issues arose, international governmental organizations expanded the scope of their missions. New concerns were added to existing agencies, rather than developing a new agency for every new issue or concern. International governmental organization growth then slowed.

The UN Environmental Programme (UNEP) is a good example of the growth and mission expansion of international governmental organizations. UNESCO held an international conference in 1969 to stimulate global cooperation on environmental issues. UNEP opened for business in 1972. It now has offices all over the world; some are regional headquarters, and some are issue specific (UNEP n.d.-b, 36–40). UNEP oversees the global environmental regime, recommending policy, monitoring the environment, coordinating among governments, civil society, and the private sector, developing regional programs, providing expertise in developing countries, formulating environmental policies and programs, and helping to develop international laws (18). It also administers a number of environmental conventions (21).

As international governmental agencies expanded their missions, the rate of INGO formation slowed. Another interesting development was that from the late 1960s to early 1970s, even international organizations without an environmental mission, such as the International Maritime Organization, Organization for Economic Co-operation and Development (OECD), World Trade Organization (WTO), World Bank, and North American Free Trade Agreement (NAFTA) expanded their functions to consider environmental impacts in their policies (Biermann at al. 2009, 5). Last came national ministries, departments, and cabinets in the 1970s.

The environmental regime remains vibrant at local, national, and global levels. Local NGOs have grown in number and size. 1,400 civil society organizations participated in the 1992 Earth Summit in Rio de Janeiro. In 2002, in Johannesburg, there were over 15,000 registered. These included business organizations (Biermann et al. 2009, 10). The *World Directory of Environmental Organizations* (discontinued in 2008) estimated that there were about 100,000 NGOs engaged in environmental issues at local, national, and global levels (Traer 2009, 173).

The environmental regime consists of thousands of NGOs and INGOs at every level, international governmental agencies, treaties, and national and local laws on everything from industrial emissions to curbside recycling, and plans for monitoring and implementing them. **How was it accomplished?**

Strategies of Diffusion and Growth

Governmental and Non-Governmental Organization Links

By the 1980s, developed countries were addressing environmental problems, but the environmental crisis was spreading. As developing nations industrialized and raised their standards of living, their energy use, their industrial waste, and use of fresh water and other resources increased dramatically. So did pollution. Using many cheap, highly polluting energy sources, such as soft coals and few clean modern technologies, the pollution and environmental devastation in the developing world caught up to and in some instances surpassed the pollution of wealthier nations. Although they have improved since, dark clouds of pollution shrouded satellite photographs of Mexico City and Beijing.

Tension between development and environmental depletion and degradation inspired the sustainability movement, which began around the 1980s. Sustainability describes an ideal relationship between the lifestyle of humankind and its use of nature; a symbiotic relationship that can be maintained indefinitely, improving the quality of people's lives without straining the capacity of the ecosystem.

The WWF expanded its mission to develop a holistic approach to conservation. It also adopted

BOX 5.17   A Closer Look: Smog Visible From Space

This NASA satellite photo shows smog over Eastern China. Similar photographs of smog could be taken over nearly any global or mega city.

the strategy of partnering with international governmental organizations. In conjunction with UNEP, it published *World Conservation Strategy*. Thirty-four nations adopted suggestions from the strategies when they were launched, and there are now 50 nations that use them in their national conservation plans (WWF 2012, "1980"). Other civil society organizations lent their expertise to international governmental agencies, jointly developing plans and programs. *Our Common Future* (WCED 1987), *Caring for the Earth* (IUCN et al. 1991), the 1992 Rio Earth Summit Conference, and the blueprint of action that came from it, *Agenda 21* (UN 1994), were among the partnerships that highlighted a successful wave of environmental protection campaigns (Andonova 2009).

International organizations positioned themselves to become the "managing core of environmental regimes" (Andonova 2009, 198). One of the largest partnerships to evolve from this wave of environmentalism is the Global Environmental Facility (GEF), created by the World Bank in 1991. It has 182 member governments, as well as partnerships with other international governmental organizations, NGOs, development banks, and business. It provides funds to governments and civil society organizations for projects with a broad mandate to "address global environmental issues while supporting national sustainable development initiatives" (GEF 2013).

Since about 1997, international governmental organizations and civil society organizations have been forming public–private partnerships (Andonova 2009, 206). Agencies are more likely to pursue partnerships with private organizations when under pressure from financial constraints or from the public for greater effectiveness. The partnerships benefit from being very flexible. They are small and non-bureaucratic, and often take a "let's see what works" approach. Unlike the international organizations themselves, which are dedicated to broad areas such as climate change or desertification, partnerships generally focus on a very specific issue or problem, such as carbon financing or technology transfers. They may undertake any governance function from providing financing, to lobbying, or simply giving advice.

International organizations do not have absolute control over the type and extent of partnerships they develop. Those that are more technically oriented and those with more "agency slack" have greater capacity for innovation. When an agency's mandates are more tightly drawn—such as with the international treaty secretariats—there is less room for innovation (Andonova 2009, 201–204). Treaty constraints also restrict the capacity of many agencies to innovate using private–public partnerships. But they make INGOs more responsive and prevent the goals and objectives of international governmental organizations from being driven away from a project's stated goals and mission (204).

This public–private partnership brings civil society and business organizations squarely into governance roles (Andonova 2009, 196–197). It forces civil society organizations to be more accountable than if acting only on their own accord, responsible only to their funders. Accountability is an important if civil society organizations are to play an increasing role in global governance.

The Human Rights Regime

Defining Human Rights

To study human rights with analytical rigor, it is necessary to adopt a definition that distinguishes human rights from other concerns such as justice, equality, civil rights, or human dignity. Human rights, first of all, are equal rights; every human has the same ones or none at all. Second, they are inalienable in that a person cannot stop being a human, no matter how badly they behave. Third, they are universal, in that all members of the species hold them (Donnelly 2003, 10).

BOX 5.18   Consider This: Are There Levels of Being Human?

A 19th century issue of the *British Medical Journal* offered a spirited defense of "dum dum" bullets: While accepting that the bullets should not be used in European wars, an article argued that "civilized man is much more susceptible to injury than savages . . . the savage, like the tiger, is not so impressionable, and will go on fighting even when desperately wounded" (Hubert 2000, 2).

How did this British author view human rights? Did his definition of *human* put people from colonized lands on the same plain and the British and other Europeans?

Human rights do not include everything that is good, nor are they simply abstract values; human rights are social practices. They represent the claim of highest resort when other claims to various levels of legal rights fail. Human rights are a standard of legitimacy for nation-states. States that protect human rights are legitimate, although no state lives up to all of the standards of human rights. That is why they are so important. They demand the political and social changes "required to realize the underlying moral vision of human nature" (Donnelly 2003, 12–15). Although all societies acknowledge the concept of human rights, there is disagreement on the specific elements of what constitutes a human right.

Conceptions of rights that preceded those of the modern West do not qualify as human rights. Rights in Islam, China, India, and the pre-modern West fail to meet the three criteria that distinguish human rights from others. Early statements of rights did not grant rights to every human. Most were based on a particular role or legal status. In most cases, rights were stated as general values, often a version of fairness or distributive justice. For instance, when *fairness* is defined as giving "everyone his due," as in the Indian caste system, what is due varies dramatically by caste (Donnelly 2003, 79).

Conceptions of specific human rights usually evolve from an affront to human dignity, although not every affront becomes a human right. That is a political affair (Donnelley 2003, 58). Colonialism did not arouse sufficient outrage as to awaken sentiments of human rights. Even following the atrocities of WWI, the League of Nations did not mention human rights. It took the inhumanity of WWII to set the stage for human rights by conceptualizing "crimes against humanity"—crimes committed by states against individuals including, but not limited to, their own citizens in the Nuremberg and Tokyo trials. The umbrella of crimes against humanity has continued to expand and evolve.

The South Africa Example

Struggles for freedoms have engaged dissidents against repressive regimes for centuries in Europe, Latin America, Asia, and Africa. Apartheid in South Africa ended only after decades of struggle as people fought for rights and were rebuked and massacred by their own government. Decades of constructive engagement from the 1960s through the 1980s by the United States and Great Britain, during which minimal negative sanctions were applied and rewards to South Africa were often plentiful, strengthened apartheid.

NGOs had been involved in South Africa at least since 1912 (Donnelly 2003, 131). South African NGOs were able to use INGOs to exert pressure on states and corporations. In the late 1970s and 1980s, both NGOs and INGOs increased indirect

pressure on South Africa by lobbying their own governments to apply meaningful sanctions and lobbying multinational corporations to divest. Corporations responded. In the end of 1982, direct U.S. investment in South Africa was $2.8 billion; by the end of 1986, it had diminished to $1.3 billion (Mangaliso 1997, 225).

NGOs and INGOs offered financial support to the African National Congress. The South African government was condemned by religious leaders. The credit for ending apartheid belongs in the end to Nelson Mandela and William DeKlerk. South Africa had resisted external pressures for decades. Each realized that apartheid's time was over. Together, they led the country through a peaceful transition in power and reconstruction of its institutions. Ironically, but understandably, some of the same activists who once pressured multinationals to leave are courting them to return. Although they think that divestment was necessary to force the South African government to concede, they also recognize the need for investment if South Africa is to thrive (Thurow 2000).

Case Study: The Helsinki Effect

Unraveling the impact of civil society groups within the emerging layers of global governance is difficult. It requires discerning the relevant players, tracing the historical threads of interaction among them, and weighing their influence on one another to determine which produced real effect and which dead-ended. Daniel Thomas's (2001) intensive study of how the Communist states in Eastern Europe and the former Soviet Union were forced to abide by the human rights provisions in the Helsinki Accords is an impressively thorough analysis of national and global civil society at work. Through extensive interviewing and analysis of hundreds of documents, Thomas captures the myriad roles and interactions of individuals, governments, intergovernmental organizations, and civil society groups in achieving this world-changing breakthrough.

His conclusion: International norms matter, but only if they are made to matter. It was "the persistent shaming and lobbying efforts of a transnational network combining dissidents and human rights groups in the East, sympathetic private groups in the West, and the specialized agency within the U.S. Congress that they helped create" that ultimately forced the world to pay attention to human rights in Eastern Europe and the Soviet Union (Thomas 2001, 155). The Helsinki Accords alone would not have had that effect. Against all odds and despite the resistance of the two superpowers, an international human rights regime emerged in the mid-1970s. This was among the most powerful factors establishing the global human rights regime and effecting the disintegration of Communist rule that just a few years earlier seemed invincible, protected as it was by the powerful iron curtain.

The Helsinki Accords

The Helsinki Accords themselves were an accomplishment of international governmental endeavors. They began with a proposal in the 1950s by the Soviet Union for a Conference on Security and

Cooperation in Europe (CSCE). The Soviet Union wanted to solidify their sphere of dominance in Eastern Europe, gain recognition of East Germany as a sovereign state, and reduce the influence of the United States in Europe (Thomas 2001, 29).

It took decades of intense negotiations before the conference actually took place. By the time the preparatory talks began in 1972, the interests of all the parties to the talks had shifted. The European Commission (EC) wanted to expand and strengthen their union by showing a united front in foreign policy matters and establishing their collective identity on the forefront of human rights, both domestic and international (Thomas 2001, 40). A multilateral meeting on European security could satisfy their domestic audiences and establish the legitimacy of their voice in world affairs. The Warsaw Pact and Soviet Union needed to stimulate their economies through scientific, economic, and technological relations with the West. Economic progress would legitimize their taking greater political control. Ironically, the opposite occurred.

No party, other than the EC, wanted to include human rights in the meetings. Every country's agenda was determined solely by its interests, in keeping with realist political theory. The United States, brought into the meetings at the insistence of NATO, resisted including human rights. The United States had already refused to ratify a UN treaty on human rights. Some U.S. allies and NATO members had poor human rights records; human rights treaties would bring pressure and potentially sanctions to bear on these allies. Throughout the meeting process, the Soviet Union and Eastern bloc countries repeatedly dismissed human rights appeals by issuing vicious and violent reprisals on dissidents in their countries. Despite the resistance of the Warsaw Pact countries and both superpowers, the Europeans prevailed.

The Helsinki Accords were signed on August 1, 1975. Consideration of human rights was the most contentious issue. Basket III, which addressed human rights, and the seventh principle that called for "respect for human rights and fundamental freedoms, including the freedom of thought, conscience, religion or belief," required 761 negotiating sessions (Thomas 2001, 86). By signing the Accords, the world was on its way to creating global norms for states' obligations to their people. The relationships among and between states became contingent on how well states fulfilled human rights obligations. This was a major development in establishing the globe as a single place, with a common normative boundary. However, the Warsaw Pact countries had no intention of abiding by the human rights norms. No country that signed the Accords even expected them to try.

Reaction of Civil Society

Writing human rights into a treaty as a contingency in international relations, although symbolic, does not have real meaning if it is not enforced. No one, not even EC delegates who fought so hard to include human rights, thought the socialist states would grant rights to their citizens. The Warsaw Pact countries heralded the Helsinki Accords with great fanfare—a resounding victory for the Eastern bloc, they proclaimed. Eastern bloc officials emphasized the economic, technological, and scientific benefits, and the promises of sovereignty, equality, and non-interference by the West in their affairs. The human rights provisions were not mentioned in their celebratory remarks.

The well-oiled propaganda machines of the Eastern bloc managed to define the Helsinki Accords for the whole world. The *New York Times* and the *Economist* in Great Britain both condemned the Act. They accused the Western powers of handing Eastern Europe over to the Soviets, betraying the dissidents who were fighting for rights and depending on the West to alleviate their persecution (Thomas 2001, 97).

The dissidents themselves were not disappointed. This was their opening. They seized upon the Accords, determined to force the agreements on human rights to the forefront of international diplomacy. The dissidents adopted an "as if" strategy. They acted "as if" the Accords were a sincere expression of intent on the part of Soviet bloc governments. They acted "as if" Western governments would hold the socialist states accountable if they did not enforce human rights. They exerted pressure upward on the Soviets and outward to the West any way that they could (Thomas 2001, 99). They convinced the world to expect and respect human rights in the Eastern bloc.

In Czechoslovakia, Poland, and the USSR, dissident groups mobilized quickly.[4] They formed an international network, a global civil society. In Moscow, Norway, Poland, Great Britain, and the United States, Helsinki watch groups formed to help them. Dissidents in the Eastern bloc countries monitored and reported human rights violations to the Western groups. They made direct appeals to Western government officials and anyone who would carry their cause to back to their governments. They formed bonds laterally across the bloc countries and out to groups and individuals in the West who seemed sympathetic (Thomas 2001, 218).

The vitality of the dissenters and their burgeoning international support made it impossible for the Western governments to ignore their pleas and petitions. The wave of dissident activity changed the course of Western governments. The United States was the first to change its view and use the Helsinki Accords as an instrument of change. After pressure from the public and from Congress, the Carter administration pursued vigorous enforcement of human rights norms at the CSCE meetings in 1978. Ironically, the EC and NATO did not engage the enforcement issues and protested the United States' action. Warsaw Pact countries refused to be held accountable and NATO refused to cooperate.

The meeting ended in a non-negotiable standoff and led to a severe crackdown on dissent from 1978 to the mid-1980s. Across the Warsaw Pact countries, governments increased repression in attempts to squelch the movement. The dissidents were persistent. Helsinki watch groups kept records of abuses and reported out to the West. Underground dissident groups continued to grow, to inform their public, and gain domestic and international legitimacy. Western governments continued to condemn human rights abuses within the Eastern bloc. The global human rights agenda continued to grow and adherence to it became a central feature of the legitimacy of a government.

For the next decade, dissidents participated in an intense and personally costly game of cat and mouse with their countries. The protest and watchdog groups tested governments on both sides, East and West, of the issue. Years of peaceful protest by Charter 77[5] in Czechoslovakia gradually strengthened civil society there and established guidelines for human rights implementation. People increasingly identified rights that they should, but did not, have. Eastern bloc nations were under severe pressure from an increasingly restive public within and international opinion and potential sanctions externally. The spiral effect—dissidents reaching out to international actors who pressured their own governments to pressure the Eastern bloc nations over and over again, making bits of progress at a time—weakened the stature and resolve of some Eastern bloc countries.

The Demise of the Eastern Bloc

Although the Brezhnev regime had little respect for human rights, the Helsinki Accords set two dynamics in motion. A robust civil society network developed within the Eastern bloc that was well integrated into the global human rights regime. Human rights performance became a critical criterion of East–West diplomacy (Thomas 2001, 221). When Gorbachev took office as General Secretary in the USSR in 1985, he commanded "a powerful army, a vast network of secret police, and the levers of economic policy" (222). No visible sign suggested that the Warsaw Pact had weakened its political monopoly or considered human rights norms relevant to its self-interest or its internal or external legitimacy (220). Nevertheless, the Soviet Union and Warsaw Pact disintegrated within five years.

Gorbachev was elected to reform the economy, but he proceeded on a trajectory of political, rather than economic, revolution. Eduard Shevardnadze, a very complicated political figure and Gorbachev's foreign minister, wrote to Gorbachev in 1984, "'Everything's rotten. It has to be changed'" (quoted in Thomas 2001, 228). And so it was. Gorbachev's governmental appointments included many who shared sympathies with the dissidents and protestors. He brought Len Karpinsky and Roy Medvedev to Moscow, both of whom had been expelled from the Communist party and had become part of the activist network. Zdenek Mlynar, a signatory of Charter 77 in Czechoslovakia and law school friend of Gorbachev; Aleksandr Yakovlev, ambassador to Canada; and Anatoly Chernyaev, a dissident sympathizer took government posts in Moscow. Gorbachev surrounded himself with advisors with a dissident streak who questioned the repression of the Brezhnev era rather than bring in loyalists, who could buttress his position in the party. With this change in direction, others in the Gorbachev government who had cooperated with Brezhnev found a need to compensate, at least partially, for their complicity in repression.

The continued pressure of civil society groups—including a demonstration of 15,000 workers in Poland six weeks after Gorbachev's election—convinced the party leadership that political repression was not sustainable. The 1986 Vienna meetings of the CSCE reinforced this, the West wanted concrete action. Gorbachev began a program of liberalization throughout the bloc, framing it as compliance with Helsinki and "universal human values." The United States called it "Westernization" (Thomas 2001, 251).

Over the next few years, Gorbachev released hundreds of political prisoners, including Andrei Sakharov. The Eastern bloc opened to foreign judges, prosecutors, psychiatrists, and NGOs specializing in human rights. Moscow television broadcast Ronald Reagan's criticism of Soviet human rights violations. Dissidents—emboldened by swelling ranks of activist groups, increasing concessions of the bloc, and ongoing CSCE talks—intensified protests and political party organization throughout the bloc (Thomas 2001, 246). Although there were violent reprisals, they were for the most part the last gasps of a dying regime. One by one, governments in the Eastern bloc sat down to negotiate with opposition parties and legalize them. In the spring of 1989, Solidarity, the Polish labor union, was reauthorized. In June 1989, it won landslide electoral victories (247). In June 1989, Hungary commenced roundtable talks with the opposition. Presidential elections were held in November, and parliamentary elections followed in 90 days (249).

The government of East Germany held out. In June, thousands of East Germans headed to Hungary and did not return. Because Hungary opened its border in keeping with Helsinki, many East Germans moved through Hungary to Austria. On November 9, 1989, in an attempt to quell unrest, East Germany declared that East Germans could travel freely. The wall that had divided Berlin since the beginning of the Cold War came down that night.

The Communist leadership in Czechoslovakia resisted for a month after the Berlin Wall fell. On November 17, they ordered police to beat protestors. Rather than backing down, the opposition organized strikes and created a political party to replace the loose network of Charter 77 dissidents. The party began negotiations on November 21. Although still considering escalating force, the Czech government recognized that further violent reprisal could be disastrous. More violence would escalate protest and would delegitimize the government domestically and internationally. International human rights treaties could no longer be taken lightly. In exchange for assurances against reprisals by a new government, the Communist leadership relinquished power on December 10 to a transition coalition headed by the new Civic Forum Party. Václav Havel, former Charter 77 leader, was elected president by the end of the year.

Protests forced the Bulgarian Party to relinquish exclusivity on January 15, 1990. They agreed to hold free elections in six months. Romania was the sole exception to non-violent revolutions. Second-tier government and military leadership led a week of violent protests, ending with the execution of Nicolae Ceaușescu and his wife in December 1989. Warfare-level violence continued. Altogether, over 1,000 were killed in that month.

BOX 5.19   A Closer Look: Helsinki Echos

It would be great to report that human rights abuses in the former USSR and Eastern bloc nations had ended. In Georgia, public discontent swept the government of Eduard Shevardnadze from power in the Rose Revolution of 2003. In 2007, opposition protesters took to the streets accusing the government of corruption and political oppression (left), forcing early elections. In 2008 Russian troops invaded Georgia to reassert domination, ostensibly to protect citizens of two Georgian breakaway regions, South Ossetia and Abkhazia, who want unification with Russia. Although establishing their democracy has been difficult, Georgians seem unwilling to settle for less.

Summary: The Helsinki Effect

Any course of human events has a variety of contributing factors. Change any one of these and the course of events could change. This said, Thomas's analysis establishes the importance of linkages and interaction among national and global civil society groups. Dissident groups within oppressive regimes can enlist global and other national groups who have access to open channels. They, in turn, can pressure their governments to push other governments for reform. At the same time, dissident groups continue to pressure from within by educating their publics, despite frequent reprisal. This spiraling effect democratized Eastern Europe.

Domestic forces alone could not have accomplished this (Thomas 2001, 111–114). Although they contributed to the vulnerability of state socialism throughout the Eastern bloc, they did not suffice as explanations for the dramatic mobilization of human rights activity (Thomas 2001, 118). Similarly, domestic events cannot explain how states in the West, particularly the United States, adopted human rights as key elements of their foreign policy. Although the EC was influenced by its own identity work to include human rights in Helsinki, they did not expect that the accord would have much effect. Human rights language had appeared in the Universal Declaration in 1949 but had been dormant for nearly 40 years. The example and pressure of activists in Eastern Europe and their interaction with NGOs and government officials in the West elevated human rights to global discourse. The protests throughout the Arab world that began in January 2011 are eerily reminiscent of the protests that brought down the Iron Curtain.

Summary: The Global Field

This chapter has focused on one global system—civil society. Global civil society is, in limited respects, a social structural crystallization of humanity. It unites people apart from their membership in any particular country. It is not antithetical to or opposed to national civil societies. It often complements and partners with them. Although comprised of organizations and groups, it is not an organization or a group. It is a network; thus, it is not a global society as such.

The activity of global civil society demonstrates the connections between and among the elements of the global field. Each element was implicated in the pathways to success for each of these movements. The passions and work of individuals, forming various levels of association—apart from any particularistic interest based on nationality, race, class, or religion, and on behalf of humanity—outside of state or intergovernmental activity exerted pressure on societies and their states, as well as international governmental organizations to achieve CSOs' objectives. The dependence of states on one another for economic, political, and social benefit, and their reputational and identity concerns, determined their responses, opening and closing opportunities for CSOs in consideration of their interests. The global system of societies through the work of the UN and its agencies facilitated the coalitions of states and intergovernmental and non-governmental organizations—domestic and international—necessary to accomplish goals on a global scale.

Global civil society is a very fluid web of associations among individuals and organizations formed on the basis of their activity. Global CSOs claim their activities are in the interests of humanity—although, as we have seen, all of humanity is not included. Simmel defined humanity as the elements of all of the societies in the world but in a different combination. Global civil society is also a different combination of the same elements, but not all of them. However, considerations of what it means to be human and of the rights and obligations that accrue to individuals as members of humanity, generate the core of global civil society arguments on behalf of the various CSOs and their activities.

This is not to say that there is or ever will be agreement among civil society groups on the specific rights or obligations that are in the interests of all of humanity. This remains a contested field. Global civil society represents the interests of humanity to the global systems, to individuals, and to individual societies. As long as humanity is diverse and unequal, its interests may be as well. Global civil societal groups are not assured to have complementary interests. In complex associations, conflicting interests are likely. One assumption of the most ardent global civil society promoters, is that through genuine deliberation common interests of humanity can be discerned.

Global civil society is not, and may never be, a perfect representation of humanity. The limits of its capacity to be wholly inclusive and truly democratic are problematic. As global norms develop and global law clarifies, a broad level of consensus may emerge. It is not likely that consensus will be complete, but may attain a sufficient level to serve as the basis for a tolerable level of social order. Who is included in global civil society and who has a voice loud enough to be heard are important determinants of accountability. Without concerted effort on the part of INGOs and NGOs to be more inclusive and less influenced by factors other than global norms of justice, global civil society is not likely to be representative of humankind.

Questions, Investigations, and Resources

Questions

1. Debate: Can civil society organizations represent the global populace democratically?

2. What role should civil society organizations have in global governance?

   - Consider both domestic and global civil society organizations.

3. Compare and contrast the power and influence wielded by civil society organizations with economic organizations such as corporations. What types of power and authority are exercised by each? How can civil society organizations leverage their power and authority to better achieve their objectives?

Investigations

1. Investigate a global civil society network, such as a labor movement, health-related movement, or development-related movement. Generate a network diagram of local and global connections. What governmental and international governmental organizations do the groups try to influence? How successful have they been?

The UN and World Bank have directories online that are good resources to help you get started.

There is a *Directory of Development Organizations* organized by region.

The *Global Civil Society Yearbook 2009* has an interesting chronology that provides information on civil society activities throughout the world.

2. Most cities, towns, counties, or provinces have directories of civil service organizations. Are there local affiliates of global civil society groups in your town or in the town where you attend school?

   - Judging by the array of civil society organizations, which problems or issues seem most important to people in your area?
   - Are there groups that tackle the problems that you think are most important?

3. Investigate a local or global civil society organization.

   - How are they funded? Does their funding seem adequate?
   - How effective are they at helping people at the individual level?
   - Do they partner with any governmental or other non-governmental (domestic or global) agencies or organizations?
   - Do they work strictly at the individual level, or do they work also for systemic change at the local, national, or global level?

4. There are many investigations of civil society that can be completed using the World Values Survey. You can look at one country over time, compare variables within a country, or compare and contrast two or more countries. There are questions concerning people's membership and activity in organizations in the category "Perceptions of Life." There are questions concerning their political activity and confidence in various dimensions of government in "Politics and Society." Below are some suggestions to get you thinking.

   - Choose a country for investigation. Determine the relationship between voluntary activities and demographic factors such as age, education, and gender.
   - Which demographic factors do you think are related to attitudes about the environment? Test your hypotheses.
   - Compare the political or voluntary activity of people in two or more countries that vary by their level of freedom.
   - Compare countries on their level of voluntary activity. Are those that are high in voluntary activities also high in political activity?

Resources

UN: New Online Directory of Civil Society Organizations http://social.un.org/index/CivilSociety/tabid/62/news/42/Default.aspx

UN: Directory of NGOs Engaged in Partnership With the Division for Social Policy and Development http://social.un.org/ngodirectory/ngosdirectory_list.asp

World Bank: Civil Society Organizations http://web.worldbank.org/WBSITE/EXTERNAL/TOPICS/CSO/0,,contentMDK:20127718~menuPK:288622~pagePK:220503~piPK:220476~theSitePK:228717,00.html

Directory of Development Organizations http://www.devdir.org/index.html

London School of Economic: The Global Civil Society 2009 http://www2.lse.ac.uk/internationalDevelopment/research/CSHS/civilSociety/yearBook/contentsPages/2009.aspx

The Patrick J. Leahy War Victims Fund: Portfolio Synopsis http://pdf.usaid.gov/pdf_docs/PDABW491.pdf

Who Gets What, When, and How: Global Governance

Objectives

This chapter reviews the processes of global governance and evaluates its potential. This chapter will help you

- analyze the challenges posed by globalization to the current system of global governance;
- identify the multiple layers of global governance;
- evaluate problems of accountability at the level of global governance;
- assess the obligations of actors such as corporations and non-governmental organizations when they take on roles in global governance;

- understand the problems and prospects of democracy in global governance; and
- assess propositions and potential structures of global governance.

Many of the activities within one country endanger others far beyond its borders. Over the past decade, toxic emissions, unsafe products, substandard nuclear power facilities, counterfeit medicinal drugs, and other dangers created in one country crossed borders into others. Poor governmental coordination across borders, among other factors, gives international criminals free space in which to operate. The only way to ensure that countries and other actors within them abide by global norms, reduce or eliminate their dangerous practices, and coordinate effectively with others is through good global governance.

For better or worse, globalization has disrupted the system of governance within and among societies, a system of governance driven since the Treaty of Westphalia by the power of states. Since WWII, the

structures of global governance have multiplied, and the processes of political globalization have intensified. Globalization has changed political relations across societies so much that one scholar (Keohane 2001) has suggested that the field of "international relations" change its name to "world politics," as a way of acknowledging challenges to the monopoly of state power.

Globalization is forging a dramatically new political world order. The contours are only dimly understood, but they are highly contested. Who makes the rules—both laws and informal norms—that govern the globe? There are myriad ways in which countries need to coordinate if international and global processes, from vacation travel to financial transactions, are going to run smoothly. Who decides the proper use of the seas, including the resources housed there? How close to a country's shore should another country extract resources such as fish or oil? Increasing demand on these limited resources requires increasingly sophisticated management. Is dumping waste into the seas, nuclear or otherwise, a good or a bad idea? Who decides? Can countries decide these issues independently of one another? The list of situations requiring global governance is extensive, and it gets longer as global interactions and risks increase.

State-centric globalization began as states formalized intricate networks of relationships through bilateral and multilateral treaties, such as the Treaty of Westphalia in 1648, and established international regulatory organizations beginning with the International Telecommunications Union in 1865.[1] Since then, the number of treaties and intergovernmental organizations has grown exponentially. These are joined by thousands of non-governmental entities—primarily civil society organizations, philanthropies, and corporations—that also participate actively in global governance. The density and architecture of global economic, political, cultural, and social interaction has become so large and complex that many theorists wonder whether the power of states to govern the globe has been eclipsed by these other actors.

Political globalization processes alter the global field. The political landscape of domestic and global governance is shifting, in some times and places creating seismic ruptures and voids in governance. How the globe should be governed is not an empty academic question. The answer has the potential to improve or worsen the quality of life for everyone in the globe.

Harold Lasswell defined *politics* as deciding "who gets what, when, and how." His question is a good guide for a discussion of governance in the global era. It is devoid of common presumptions about states, corporations, the UN, other institutions, or any other actors doing the decision making, and it leaves a clean slate to analyze who is deciding, who should decide, and how to establish workable and legitimate systems of governance.

Many new actors play a role in the field of political globalization. Multinational corporations with budgets dwarfing some national economies exert significant power in national and international policy concerning issues as diverse as financial regulation and environmental law. Civil society organizations working locally and nationally intersect and partner with global organizations to exert pressure on states, corporations, regulatory agencies, and international governmental organizations. In such a complex global network, it is not sufficient to talk of government. Rather, we should talk of governance, which includes the myriad actors involved in decision making. Local and global networks of governmental and non-governmental actors exert pressure on states from above and below, changing the nature of the relationships between states and their societies, the individuals and institutions within the global systems, and humanity. Political globalization raises a number of questions for both for global and state governance.

There are normative questions for citizens to decide:

- What constitutes good governance?
- Which decisions should be made locally and which globally?
- What or whom should representatives represent: territorial divisions, interest groups, religions, classes, some other category, or all of the above?

There are also analytic questions for social scientists to answer:

- How can a system of governance function effectively and legitimately with the variety of actors in the political field?
- Who are the significant political actors, and how do power and influence flow among them?
- Governance is for the public good, but how is the public defined in a globalized world?
- Are norms of governance emerging globally? If so, what are they? Whose values and worldviews do they reflect? Are there any universals?

There are evaluative questions for citizens and social scientists:

- Who benefits from governance, and who does not?
- Are the criteria for governance appropriate, that is, fair and functional?
- Who should watch over the decision makers? How should they be made accountable?

The first part of this chapter reviews challenges to state-centered politics. These are forces, systems, and structures operating within and across countries that require negotiation, collaborative action, and settling conflicts of interest among people at local and global levels. In addition to those presented in this chapter, there are other challenges discussed in the chapters on threats to human well-being, the global economy, and emerging global culture. These challenges cut across state borders. Since few people or state governments accept domination by one country or group of countries to settle these issues, some system of global governance that people perceive as legitimate is needed.

The second section analyzes the possibilities for global governance. There are qualities that most people in most parts of the world seem to want and expect in governance, and there are propositions for systems of global governance that try to satisfy these criteria. The chapter does not draw conclusions for you or promote a model of global governance. It does urge you to assess, evaluate, and decide what you want from global governance and then become involved in activities that give you a voice in shaping the programs and policies that will determine who gets what, when, and how.

Globalization and the Challenges to Westphalia

The spread of similar state structures, without the corresponding granting of sovereignty on which they were based, cemented a global hierarchy of power and wealth among societies and domestic hierarchies of power and wealth within societies. It was an international order forced on the world by colonialism, strengthened by the Cold War, and legitimated by the UN. Although it never conformed to the ideals of Westphalia, it persisted through the closing decades of the 20th century. The pressures of globalization, such as the growing regimes of human rights and democracy, the global economy and culture, and globally shared risks, challenge the Westphalia order.

Developing nations and civil society organizations are demanding that non-democratic forms of international governance and state governance be reformed. The global economy and international organizations challenge the monopoly on international power that states have held. These conflicts reflect the themes emerging in global political culture that are influencing economic and civil society globalization as well. A legitimate global forum to resolve long-standing problems is needed. Among the issues to be resolved are greater equality and autonomy for developing nations within the global system, increasing democratic qualities both within and among states, greater accountability of decision makers (elected and otherwise), greater transparency for decision-making processes, as well as rectification of and compensation for ravages to the economies and environments of countries on the bottom rungs of the global hierarchy.

The Challenge of Government Failures

The demand for better governance at the global level stems in part from the failure of governments to fulfill their functions. If everything were satisfactory to all or even most people, the status quo would not be so mightily challenged. The roots of many state failures (as well as failed states) are deep in colonial and Cold War history. Three causes of governments' failures shared among wealthy and poor societies alike are

- transborder problems impacting quality of life within countries,
- material or organizational resource deficiency, and
- refusals to admit or address or problems (Koenig-Archibugi 2002, 49).

These factors may exist independently or in combination. The threats to human security are transborder problems. For example, pollution does not respect boundaries. Resource depletion of forests, for instance, impacts atmospheric quality and global warming everywhere. Waste disposal into oceans washes up on distant shores. Civil wars and oppression create refugees who spill across borders, destabilizing their neighbors. No country can solve these problems alone.

Resource deficiencies—such as lack of medicines and medical facilities, food, energy, roads, education, and so on—aggravate hunger, poverty, and epidemics in poorer countries. Depleted water levels lead to food scarcity in many countries. Lack of clean water, soaps, and medicines raised the death toll due to the cholera epidemic in Haiti. Cheap building materials, poor design, and inadequate regulations increase death tolls following earthquakes. All of these problems hinder economic and political development. Many countries do not have the organizational resources or the infrastructure of social institutions or rule of law to function effectively. This is true from the former states of the USSR, through many Asian societies, to Africa. Somalia, for example, has no central government. Although Somalia's north is relatively stable and acts independently, the south is in turmoil. Years of civil war destroyed its judiciary, health care system, and other institutions. Drought destroyed harvests and land for grazing. High food and fuel prices create dire insecurity. Somali pirates, most former fishermen operating off the Horn of Africa, claim that there is no other way to feed themselves, their families, and their villages. Hundreds of thousands of Somalis are under the protection of the UN High Commissioner for Human Rights. The action of other societies had a major role in creating these troubles, and Somalia and countries in similar straits cannot solve them on their own. With the help of international aid agencies, Somalia is trying to stabilize.

Within wealthy nations, states fail to protect or grant equal opportunities to large segments of their populations. Women and ethnic and racial minorities often lack political representation. The rule of law does not reach everyone; so justice is not equally distributed, and minorities are more likely to find themselves convicted of crimes and imprisoned. Rates of illness, infant and maternal death, and educational attainment all reflect unequal opportunities of minorities. These are but a few examples of state failures among the wealthier societies.

Sometimes states will not acknowledge problems. People warned government overseers, notably Alan Greenspan, former Chairman of the Federal Reserve, about the housing bubble and the insecurity of the mortgage industry in the United States. Their warnings were ignored (Bartlett 2009; Grim 2010). AIDS spread through South Africa while President Mbeki refused to acknowledge the problem, causing as many as 300,000 needless deaths (Boseley 2008). Environments were ravaged and water supplies ruined because people refused to acknowledge their fragility. While international norms were written codifying human rights in the 1948 UN Declaration on Human Rights, most governments, including the United States, ignored many of them until the civil rights movements of the late 1960s erupted across the world. In the Middle East, ignoring human rights issues and concerns with unemployment kept resentments simmering until they exploded in the Arab Spring of 2011.

BOX 6.1   Consider This: Kosovo and the Right to Rule

One of the most violent intrastate conflicts was the move for independence on the part of Kosovo, a primarily Albanian province in Serbia. Slobodan Milosevic rallied Serbians to unity as Yugoslavia was breaking apart; he made an emotional, provocative appeal to Serbs to protect their identity by preventing Kosovo from separation.

On July 22, 2010, the International Court of Justice ruled that Kosovo did not violate international law when it declared its independence (ICJ 2010). Milosevic went on trial in 2002 at the ICJ for crimes against humanity in Croatia, Bosnia, and Kosovo.

When a people declare themselves to be independent, who should decide whether or not they should be allowed? Should it be by a vote of the people who want independence? Should it be the decision of the state that they live within to give them their freedom? Should they have to go to war to fight for independence? Should some international governance body decide?

Each of these is a route to independence traveled in the last decade of nation-state building.

Most issues involve two or more of these factors. Terrorism, nuclear proliferation, environmental degradation, and many more social problems spill outside of societal boundaries. Concerns relative to biotechnology (such as genetically modified foods), energy, intellectual property, and copyright require coordination across countries. Borders are not boundaries for economic activity of either legitimate or criminal enterprises. International crimes related to trade in arms, drugs, and even humans grow out of interactions among rich and poor societies. Overcoming the failures of states to manage these problems effectively requires widely coordinated action and governance.

The Challenge of Nationalist Movements

We know that a state is only a state if recognized by the international community. This is a particularly thorny problem for governance. The ideal-typical nation-state remains an aspiration for many of the world's peoples. It should not be surprising that as the state form spreads, people begin to make demands when they gain a voice loud enough to proclaim that they are not represented or treated justly by their state.

Indigenous, marginalized, and ethnically or religiously distinct groups within states are demanding representation. They usually pursue, sometimes in courts and sometimes violently, one of three different goals:

- Federalism: incorporation into the state but as a distinct territory with more autonomy and self-governance
- Separatism: the establishment of a new and independent nation
- Revolution: taking over the government

Claims to sovereignty are claims to a human right, although some groups sacrifice the rights of others while arguing for their own. Regardless of the legitimacy of a group's claims, the result often depends on their appeal to global culture. Unfortunately, attracting the interest and attention of influential civil society groups and of other governments capable of pressuring their own government often determines whether minorities or nationalist groups will receive support from the global community.

The trend toward conflict within states is a common argument for the view that globalization is causing the demise of the nation-state, destroying it from within. However, because people are fighting for a right to have a state, or be empowered by one, the case is probably quite the contrary (Gilpin 2002, 239).

BOX 6.2   A Closer Look: Haiti

Fragile political. economic, social, and natural environments have kept the UN involved in Haiti, the poorest country in the Western hemisphere, for decades. The UN was called in to supervise elections in 1990 and quell a subsequent coup in 1991. UN peacekeepers have deployed on a number of missions to establish legitimate governments, settle armed rebellions, and maintain stability following earthquakes in 2010 and 2012, and the cholera outbreak that persisted for years. Here, UN peacekeepers are distributing food and water following the 2012 earthquake.

Among the challenges for political globalization are determining criteria for recognition as a state and avoiding violent conflict in nation building. One determinant as to whether or not there is violent conflict is the willingness of an existing state to allow separation of a people within that state. When East Timor declared independence from Indonesia in 1975, Indonesia immediately occupied it. In 1999, after many UN Security Council and General Assembly resolutions, Indonesia finally withdrew in a fury of bloodshed, massacring thousands of Timorese and burning towns. The UN administered East Timor until it was recognized as a state in 2002. From declaration of independence in 1975 to statehood, over 200,000 lives were lost (Chopra 2000, 27–28). In the breakup of Yugoslavia, some republics separated without violence, but Serbia fought viciously in Croatia, Bosnia-Herzegovina, and Kosovo, resulting in charges of crimes against humanity in all three wars and an additional charge of genocide in Bosnia against Slobodan Milosevic, the president of Yugoslavia and also of Serbia, who directed and inflamed the fighting.

Global governance must find a way to allow for the negotiation of autonomy and statehood or fair and equal treatment within states. States must be willing to offer equal rights, protection, and representation to all citizens. Establishing a new state or other sovereign entity requires stable institutional structures, from courts and legislatures to the laws that shape them to satisfy people's needs for justice, and economic infrastructure to fulfill their needs for food, clothing, and shelter. Avoiding violence and building adequate political structures—as we've seen in the states in transition from the former USSR and Arab Spring—can be difficult and requires global assistance.

The Challenge of Global Systems

The contemporary period of globalization differs from previous periods in many ways. One of the most profound among them is the release from state control of non-state actors. During the latter half of the 20th century, multinational corporations, financial institutions, communications media, military alliances, and non-governmental organizations (NGOs) multiplied in number and broadened the scope of their influence beyond state boundaries. This weakens, or minimally modifies, the central power of states (Tilly 2004,[2] 101).

Even wealthy nations have difficulty managing their economies. Using tax deductions, Starbucks paid no taxes in Great Britain in 2010, 2011, and 2012, despite £398 million in revenue in 2012. Protests forced them to offer to pay £10 million for 2013 and 2014, assuming the role of the state in determining its tax burden as though taxes were

voluntary like charitable contributions (Pfanner 2012). Other corporations behave the same way in Britain and in other countries. Billions of tax revenue are lost to the United States, whose multinational corporations (MNCs), including Apple, Google, Microsoft, and Hewitt-Packard, avoid their true tax burden by shifting money overseas (Gongloff 2012).

The global economy links economic problems across countries. When stock markets dive in one, they dive in others. Stock markets fell sharply in 2012 all over the world in response to the European debt crisis. Interactions in global political, economic, cultural, and other social systems—social media, the World Wide Web, flows of finance, corporate decisions, operations of civil society organizations, and so on—impact states' functioning, but states have little capacity to shape them. Threats to human well-being transcend borders but are beyond any single state's capacity to solve. The developing world is most buffeted by these forces, but everyone is affected.

These global systems make global governance necessary and condition how state governance functions. They also create discord. If a country looks out for its own interest, it affects the welfare of other countries—and could intensify its own problems (Keohane 2002, 325). This is evident when countries pursue short-term economic growth regardless of the environmental costs. These costs, in depleted or polluted resources, contributing to greenhouse gases, cause hardship in the most vulnerable countries and eventually limit growth in the offending countries as well.

The Challenge of Multiple Actors

Global governance and a considerable degree of state governance is unplanned and haphazard, affected by a complex mix of often uncoordinated local, regional, national, and international governmental and non-governmental actors. Thousands of new actors have taken to the global political arena. Layers of governance are emerging within, among, and apart from states. Some are granted authority by states to regulate activity within and across state boundaries. Others are delegated authority to perform state functions. Many are run by technocrats, presumed experts in their fields, who make decisions with economic, political, and social consequences for people's lives globally. Others are composed of non-governmental actors, such as corporations and NGOs. They exercise power politically—indirectly through their influence, and directly through their activities.

State-Related Layers of Governance

In addition to states themselves, there are a variety of state-related governance bodies. Because these layers are associations of states or state agencies, they may advise, exert indirect influence, regulate, or perform some state functions. International governmental organizations—the UN (and its subsidiaries such as UNICEF), the International Monetary Fund (IMF), the World Bank, the International Maritime Organization, the Universal Postal Union, among others—have power delegated by states who participate. They infringe on sovereignty by demanding policy changes as conditions of participating in their programs.

BOX 6.3 Consider This: The Unresolved Case of the Leap Second

Some problems of global governance would seem easy to solve. Whether or not to continue the leap second appears to be more difficult than may have been expected. It has been so difficult that rather than make a decision, world leaders have decided not to decide until 2015.

The world's time is determined two different ways, by atomic clocks and by the earth's rotational cycle. Because the earth's rotation is slowing, a second must be added to the atomic clocks every few years to keep the clocks in line with the rotation. If seconds are not added, sooner or later—actually much later—high noon could occur in moonlight. A study panel for the UN International Telecommunications Union (ITU) has been working on this since 2002 without reaching agreement.

How should this issue be decided? Should the panel of experts vote? Should the ITU members vote? Should every country in the UN cast a vote? Should the most powerful countries decide? Should each country do it its own way?

If the system of global governance cannot reach a decision on leap seconds, how will it fare on issues of the environment, nuclear weapons, or any of the other issues confounding the world?

- International regulatory agencies: Specialized agencies such as the International Organization of Securities Commissions, the International Atomic Energy Agency (IAEA), and the World Trade Organization (WTO) have authority to establish standards and regulations for the activity of member states in the areas of their specialization.
- International courts: The International Court of Justice (ICJ) is part of the UN, and the International Criminal Court (ICC) is independent. Each has a specific area of authority. Participation in the ICJ cases is voluntary. The ICC cases are brought by governments or the UN Security Council. Its power is in holding individuals criminally liable for crimes against humanity.
- Regional inter governmental alliances such as the EU, NATO, OAS, ASEAN, African Union, and Mercosur serve a variety of economic, political, welfare, and security functions. They also have qualifications and conditions for participating and thus can have impact on holding states accountable for respecting international laws and global norms.

Within these organizations, the conflicting interests among states and among groups within states must be negotiated. Global norms demand that these be settled in keeping with standards of legitimacy. Greater transparency is demanded and, along with transparency, accountability.

Non-Governmental Layers of Governance

Other actors without official standing as representatives of governments exert political power through popular support or economic strength. Powerful civil society organizations (NGOs and international NGOs [INGOs]) have popular support, and many have significant economic clout as well. Most civil society organizations (CSOs) are devoted to a particular cause, such as hunger, disease, peace, or the environment. Thousands are religious organizations. Through virtue of their reputation, money, and publicity, many are seated at the table and participate actively in political decision making. The UN now has a process for including groups that qualify in their deliberations. By carrying out operations within countries, particularly developing countries, their activity has potential to change the social, economic, and political landscape of that country. Because there is little accountability, their operations are a subtle but powerful form of governance.

INGOs and NGOs forge pathways between society and government, setting norms and acting as agents of change (Steans 2002, 102). NGOs and INGOs serve as counterpoint to multinational corporations and international governmental organizations, typically exerting pressures on states and corporations and sometimes on behalf of states. Most INGOs, like the Red Cross, Habitat for Humanity, or WWF, claim to act on behalf of the common good through particular causes. NGOs from different countries often interact, sharing information, strategies, and resources, forming global networks of grassroots organizations. Domestic and international organizations also interact, forming vibrant networks that reach into international governmental deliberations. But no one NGO nor INGO can represent all of humanity, and their interests often compete. Since NGOs and INGOs exert power and influence through lobbying and direct action, there is no guarantee that the outcomes of their activities are democratic. This is discussed in detail in Chapter Five.

(MNC) have economic strength and significant power. They use foreign investment, lobbying, and contributions to political campaigns to influence local and national government policy and regulation. Their advertisements and public relations campaigns influence and shape public opinion. As in the military industrial complex, people may move from high-level positions in industry to government office (elected and non-elected) and back to industry again. Industry representatives often request or are invited to sit on regulatory deliberations. By participating in intergovernmental organizations, often giving expert testimony and advice despite their conflicts of interest, they influence and shape global policy and regulation. If their involvement is extensive, it can lead to regulatory capture, whereby a regulatory agency comes to serve the interest of the industry it is regulating. Despite such significant political power, public interest is not their first concern. They are accountable to their stockholders and in some cases to the clients to whom they offer products and services.

The participation of corporate interests and NGOs as experts and specialists in inter governmental organizations is frequent enough to undermine democracy in governance. Domestically, extensive lobbying distorts perceptions and undermines democratic processes.[3] MNCs also exert power internationally when their operations fall outside of regulated activities. The National Rifle Association, an NGO, and Pharmaceutical Researchers and Manufacturers of America, an association of corporate interests, are among the largest and most powerful lobbyists in the United States. Both effectively influence domestic legislative process, and their influence extends into global governance as well. Global gun trafficking, trafficking in illegal drugs, the course of AIDS in Africa, the cost and availability of medicines in the United States and developing countries, and regulations regarding U.S. citizen purchases of prescription medications from other countries—all are within their spheres of influence. (More detailed discussion of multinationals and NGOs is in Chapters Four and Five, respectively.)

BOX 6.4   Consider This: Layers of Governance

People have different levels of confidence in different layers of global governance. What do you make of these data? Which layers do people trust the most? Should they have more power in governance? If so, what should their role be?

How much confidence do you have in:	A Great Deal	Quite a Lot	N
Parliament	8.9%	25.6%	76,140
National Government	14.1%	33.5%	78,378
Political Parties	5.4%	18.6%	77,110

How much confidence do you have in:	A Great Deal	Quite a Lot	N
Major Companies	7.5%	35.1%	80,142
Charitable/Humanitarian Groups	18.3%	45.0%	76,972
United Nations	12.3%	36.0%	81,621

The 2005–2008 wave of surveys was conducted in 57 countries from every region of the world. *N* = number who were asked each question. Not all questions are asked in every country.

Because these actors are already very engaged in governance, finding ways to make them accountable is critical. Myriad questions and concerns must be resolved. Central among them are the following:

- How can the source of their authority and legitimacy be extended beyond stockholders or donors to the general public and social welfare?
- How can they be made transparent and accountable since they are not subject to election?

The Challenge of Accountability

Accountability is a dominant theme in global political culture. Governance requires the same level of accountability at the global level as at the domestic. States are demanding more accountability of intergovernmental organizations, and people within states are pressuring for more accountability for decisions made and money spent at domestic and global levels.

Because there is no elected body to hold accountable, global governance functions differently than state governance. Authority in global governance is fragmented and parceled among competing actors, agencies, and organizations. Power wielders acquire power through different channels and are accountable to different audiences. Layers of global governance are linked through internal and external accountability, but there are gaps in accountability (Grant and Keohane 2005).

Civil society organizations run a deficit on accountability—beyond obeying laws—to anyone other than their donors. They have some market and reputational accountability. They need to attract public favor to continue receiving funds, and they need to attract local groups as clients. There are no mechanisms to ensure that their activities represent or serve the neediest or the common good. Their lack of formal accountability is a public liability. At worst, their public statements and claims have an aura of legitimacy that could enable deception and fraud (Grant and Keohane 2005, 37).

Corporations have little formal accountability outside of the laws of the countries in which they are chartered and operate. Where these laws are weak, they have little accountability at all. They do have market and reputational accountability (Grant and Keohane 2005, 38). These forms of accountability work fairly well in the marketplace. When Toyota lagged in its safety recall of millions of Lexus and Prius autos, allegedly leading to deaths, its reputation suffered significantly, especially after a rarely issued "do not buy" warning from *Consumer Reports* magazine (Consumer Reports 2010). This also affected its market and reputation.

Hyundai, side-stepping Toyota's mistake, issued a cautious recall of over 1,300 Sonatas in the United States and 46,000 in South Korea due to a faulty door latch, well before any trouble befell consumers (Sang-Hun 2010). Perhaps not coincidentally, this recall was on the same day that Akio Toyoda, president of Toyota, tried to repair Toyota's reputation with his testimony at a U.S. Congressional hearing (Maynard 2010). Accountability mechanisms need to work before human suffering occurs rather than after. Whether Japanese recall standards are not as stringent as those in the United States or South Korea, or Hyundai responded quickly because of Toyota's dilemma or because Hyundai is a better global citizen, the reluctance of Toyota to issue an immediate recall was a deadly (or potentially deadly) lapse in global accountability.

Holding states accountable is also difficult. Regional organizations, such as the EU, may hold states accountable to their peers. But in the debt crisis of 2012, Greece argued repeatedly that its internal accountability to its citizens outweighed external accountability to the EU. (Eventually a majority of citizens voted to acquiesce to the EU's demands.) For democratic states, internal accountability is based on a "higher" authority, the "most virtuous source of power," that is, the people. States can use this to avoid external accountability (Keohane 2005, 51). This is the same claim made by authoritarian regimes, such as China and Russia, when they imprison and label those who speak out as enemies of the state, thus of the people.

Weak or poor states are held accountable to stronger and richer ones in return for beneficent treatment. This did not work well for many states as they conformed to IMF requirements to receive loans. States can be held accountable through sanctions, although their effectiveness varies by situation. The most general form of accountability for a state is based on a country's or organization's reputation, its soft power. While this is the weakest form, it tends to be the most successful in constraining the United States (Keohane 2005, 51–52). Nevertheless, it is not always successful. The United States has risked its reputation, sacrificing soft power, by acting unilaterally, as when it launched the war in Iraq. This cost the United States support of some allies on later issues such as when it required cooperation early in the issue of harsher sanctions against Iran.

Intergovernmental institutions such as the UN, the World Bank, the IMF, and the WTO are accountable to the sources of their funding, the states. Externally, however, they lack accountability to their clients, the poor in developing states who are affected by their policies (Keohane 2005, 49).

Accountability is particularly problematic in a globalized world. The institutions of the state cannot just be supersized to fit a global society. "Who guards the guardians?" Who prevents power from becoming tyranny in a globalized world (Keohane 2002, 325–326)?

Propositions for Global Governance

"Ordinary citizens share a common interest in making globalization work" (Stiglitz 2006, xiv). Establishing a functioning system of global governance does not guarantee that the world will be problem free, but it does mean that there will be a better chance of managing problems, whether the problem is a rogue state refusing to abide by global norms of civility or extreme weather disasters. Globalization is as full of promise as it is peril. Global issues necessitate global governance, "not just effective governance but the *right kind* of governance" (Keohane 2002, 325).

There are three main questions we need to consider to solve the problem of global governance.

- Which functions of governance are best carried out at the global level, and which should be left to national and local levels?
- What is the normative basis of good governance, the qualities people want?
- How can global governance be structured to minimize the inequitable or destructive use of power and coordinate the variety of actors and levels of governance?

Functions of Global Governance

There are many areas of global governance that work well, but in others, the need for improvement is obvious. Global management of time zones, calendars, communications, postal service, among many others, all function well. Where global systems are working well, they should continue. The global problems and issues that challenge human security are potentially devastating. These areas we are not managing well. Problems that no country can tackle alone need to be on the agenda of global governance. The level of involvement of global governance in each of these areas may vary. Minimally, each must be coordinated globally. Global governance must manage

- environmental stewardship—regulating the pollution and destruction of natural resources on which we all depend;
- fair distribution of the benefits of global economic growth, ensuring access to the resources needed for survival—food, clothing, and shelter;
- the potential for widespread violence—nuclear and other weapons of mass destruction, genocide, terrorism, and warfare;
- international crime fighting;
- protection from oppressive governments and human rights abuses; and
- global financial health—regulation of flows of money and prevention global financial crises coupled with protection when crises do occur.

These functions need to be analyzed, coordinated, and distributed among regulatory bodies and agencies. (The variety of functions global governance must perform are discussed at length in Held 2007; Keohane 2002; Kuper 2007.) One may, of course, disagree with this list, but at least it is a good starting point for discussion. The functions and goals of global governance will ultimately need to be negotiated in a global forum.

A Normative Basis for Global Governance

Governance, to be considered legitimate, has to be based on widely accepted principles and values. The first and most basic is fairness. If people think a system is fair, they will trust it and act accordingly. Many studies demonstrate that both politicians and citizens act within norms of reciprocity and fairness, just as people do in other realms of social life. People evaluate institutions on procedural fairness, not just their own success in them (Keohane 2002, 327–329).

People may be evolutionarily equipped for cooperation and reciprocity (Bloom 2010). Research on the moral development of babies shows that they recognize acts of helpfulness in puppet shows, even when geometric shapes are the actors. This does not mean that everyone will buy into and support a global system of governance any more than it means that everyone in a society obeys national laws or that there are not people who will cheat every chance that they get. But those people seem to be the anomaly, not the rule.

There are principles emerging in global culture that capture the essential fairness and cooperation that we expect in human behavior. They offer a promising basis for global governance. The UN Declaration of Human Rights and related protocols, conventions, and treaties (Held 2004) embody them. Operationally, many are articulated in the Millennium Development Goals. Global governance, construed as an honest expression (not just pretense) of these values and principles, has a good chance of success even though there are still cultural conflicts concerning fairness, particularly when individual rights conflict with a perceived collective good or secular rights conflict with religious doctrine.

Infusing Accountability Into Global Governance

The value of democracy is that it ensures, ideally, that those who govern act in the interests of their public and that their publics have regular and ongoing control over their activity (Kuper 2004, 9). If a global democracy is not likely—at least not in the near future—can we capture this essence of democracy in global governance?

A main source of democratic deficit in the current system of global politics is a deficit of accountability. Layers of global governance and the inequality of power in governance bodies result in too many "veto players." As in domestic politics, the more veto players and the more polarized their positions are, the less likely it is that innovative policies will be adopted (Ames 2002, 12). Groups and individuals can block action for the common good based on their own interests. In the case of multilayered governance, where there is little accountability for the global level, this problem is compounded. We have seen that forceful global action has been very slow to materialize even when badly needed, as in Zimbabwe, Sudan, Iran, the violence in the Arab world, nuclear proliferation, and a host of other atrocities and threats. This occurs with the one-country veto in the UN Security Council permanent membership, and when one or several countries refuse to honor sanctions effectively negating the sanctions applied by others. Countries that block action or new policies have little accountability. While some pundits—such as David Brooks (2008), a *New York Times* columnist—argue that this is because "globally, people have no sense of shared citizenship," international polling concerning feelings of global citizenship and willingness to work within global international organizations reveals that this is not the case. Accountability is a realistic functional alternative to electoral or direct democracy. Even within representative democracies, people demand more accountability. Accountability constrains power and ensures that governance responds to the needs and desires of those governed. It has two dimensions:

- The responsibility of political actors to report (transparency)
- The ability of those governed to impose costs based on what is reported (Grant and Keohane 2005, 30)

Governance must be structured so that accountability for the global good can be enforced. Mechanisms of accountability exist in the global system already, but they are disconnected and uncoordinated (Keohane 2002, 339).

Improving Global Accountability Mechanisms

To improve global accountability, we need to identify who has a role in governing and what their roles and responsibilities are. Unless roles and responsibilities are clearly defined, people cannot be held accountable—what would they be accountable for? States and the national and international agencies that act on their behalf, civil society groups, corporations, and citizens have roles in governance at all levels—from global to the most local. Some people and groups are formally involved in governance, and some informally involved through their influence. They all must be brought into the formal governance process. Acting informally, they cannot be held accountable (Kuper 2007). Furthermore, political actors need to be subject to standards of global citizenship. Good behavior should not be assumed, it should be transparent and demonstrated by any person, group, or organization participating in governance.

Corporations and INGOs need to report on their political activities and the activities of associations to which they belong. The market exercises some accountability based on this information. This is not enough, and it has been weakened. Irrespective of constitutional issues, the 2010 U.S. Supreme Court decision *Citizens United v. Federal Election Commission* undermined transparency and accountability in corporate and union campaign contributions. This decision was a blow to accountability.

Corporations and INGOs are involved in governance structures—regulatory bodies, international governmental organizations, and so on—without qualification other than their assumed expertise in an area. They act as advisors and influence what regulations are passed or not passed. Greater transparency does not impose an undue burden, and bringing them formally into governance structures is important. Corporate and INGO reports could be used to deny or grant their representatives participation on decision-making bodies. If they do not adhere to standards of social responsibility, they could be denied the opportunity to participate in political activities. For example, in the case of economic regulatory agencies, corporations should be encouraged to pursue social justice goals as a regular part of their business function (Kuper 2007, 226–237). Good global citizenship could be demonstrated through evidence of environmental stewardship, fair prices paid for resources, good wages, safe working conditions, and so on.

Qualifications for INGOs could also be established. Licensing based on professional standards is a check on the members of some INGOs. This could be strengthened and introduced across more organizations. Whether or not licensing can be applied to multinational corporations and a broader range of INGOs should be considered. Adherence to standards of being a socially responsible global citizen would become an important part of a corporation's or INGO's identity if their ability to influence decision-making was directly dependent on it. One proviso is that the criteria for licensing would have to be carefully calibrated so that it does not turn into a cooptation and control mechanism.

International governmental organizations such as the WTO, IMF, World Bank, European Commission, and UN are accountable to the member states that supervise and fund them (supervisory and fiscal accountability). Their accountability has been compromised because of the undue influence of the most powerful states. Their accountability to the people affected by their decisions is minimal, although it is strengthened when they open more dialog with NGOs and use websites to communicate with broader publics. This also enhances their reputational accountability (Grant and Keohane 2005, 37). If they continue to function in global governance, they must respond to demands for more fairness. People whose lives their decisions affect should have a greater role in their decisions than the powerful states less directly affected.

States' domestic accountability to their citizens can transfer to their governments' performance in global institutions. Weak states need to be accountable to other states and international agencies if they are to reap benefits from them. Powerful states present the most resistance to external accountability. Efforts to make them more accountable can result in less benefit than they usually gain in multilateral organizations or bilateral agreements with less powerful states. They may withdraw from these institutions rather than accept more responsibility (Keohane 2005, 53). Constraining their power is not an easily solvable problem. Global relations based on fairness, accountability, and fulfilling of obligations need to be strengthened.

BOX 6.5   A Closer Look: Lessons From the First Gulf War

The international community responded nearly universally to impose sanctions on Iraq following its invasion of Kuwait, even though it was potentially costly for many. Studying how countries came to support the sanctions provides a lesson for future global efforts.

- Self-interest: Sanctions may be invoked against states if they do not join in.
- Pressure of public opinion internationally and domestically to be on the side of the good: Saddam Hussein's brutal parade of prisoners horrified the world.
- An appeal to ethical and moral international standards: Sanctions following Saddam Hussein's aggression on a weaker neighbor and his mistreatment of hostages and other atrocities were an opportunity to condemn such acts under international codes of decency.
- Legitimacy: The action of the Security Council gave states a strong basis of legitimacy. They were not pursuing an economic war against Iraq on their own behalf but in accordance with their obligations under the UN Charter.
- Mechanisms at the domestic level: Each state's participation in the sanctions had to be legal under its own domestic laws.
- Compensation fund: Where states have much to lose by complying, the international community may mitigate the damage. Romania stood to lose about $2.9 billion dollars by applying the sanctions.
- Clarity in the goals and objectives: Because sanctions may impose significant costs, there must be clarity. In the case of Iraq, the withdrawal of troops was a clear objective.
- Belief that the sanctions will actually work.

Source: Joyner (1991, 29–33).

Ultimately, in Iraq, sanctions did not work or were not given the time to complete their work. Economic and political sanctions were continued until the 2003 invasion.

Two things may influence the reluctance of powerful states to be more accountable. As citizens become more sensitive to world politics, they may demand greater accountability for the obligations that go with power or greater responsibility for exacerbating problems suffered in other parts of the world. Different administrations may respond differently, depending on their constituency. An administration supported by a more cosmopolitan contingent of voters, as Obama was in 2008 (Jackman and Vavreck 2010), may accept more external mechanisms of accountability than past administrations. Another inescapable reality is that global power is shifting. As the emerging economies grow, the developed economies will need to share power more democratically. Even powerful nations like China experience pressures for democracy from within. These forces, with pressures from other states and international organizations, may

affect their behavior more significantly in the future. Globalization increasingly forces powerful nations such as the United States, China, and Russia, and pariah ones such as Myanmar (formerly Burma) and North Korea, to recognize that they need the support and assistance of other nations. Despite the December 2012 missile launch, Kim Jong Un declared better ties to South Korea and extending electricity to build North Korea's economy to be among his top priorities in his New Year's Day 2013 address (Yoon 2013). This will require concerted assistance from more nations than China, North Korea's strategic ally. Globalization may be the most effective force to increase states' accountability.

Technology has made accountability easier to enforce. Communication technology, electronic record-keeping, and interactive databases provide easier access to the information that people need to make informed decisions about whether or not their interests are being represented. Using them inventively for citizens' forums and the like can make participation in governance easier.

Deciding what global governance is for and how parties involved can be held accountable are the first steps. Determining the structure through which this is possible is harder.

Global Participation

If all the stakeholders—everyone in the world in one way or another—do not have the opportunity to participate in global governance, it is not legitimate. Direct and individual participation—such as in the village meetings that inspired Nelson Mandela, the town hall meetings of New England, or the referenda customary in Switzerland and some states of the United States—is desirable but unrealistic given the size, territorial dispersion, and cultural diversity of the global polity. Connecting individual stakeholders to the agencies of accountability is important.

How do we ensure that everyone has access to participatory opportunities?

Although there is a lot of talk about how mobile people are, many are still only mobile to where they can walk. Participation in global governance can take place close to people's homes or from their home, through participation in small groups, as long as the channels of communication to the global level are intact. The smaller units may be dispersed globally but unite people with common interests (Appadurai 1996). They may be geographically consolidated in neighborhoods, where people share local interests that need resolution at a global level.

The key is that participation should start in smaller units, where participants can understand and communicate effectively with one another (Keohane 2002, 340). Smaller units of governance feed into larger ones where discourse continues, bringing the consensus and interests of the smaller units to bear in decision making at more inclusive levels.

Making participation meaningful is also important. This pertains to participation in all political levels—local, national, and global—and within all bodies that have roles in governance, including NGOs and INGOs, governmental agencies, and corporations. One method of participation particularly relevant to problem solving and decision making in a group context is democratic deliberation. It is a method of discussion following explicit rules and structures that facilitate meaningful participation—although nothing can guarantee it.

Democratic deliberation assumes that if reasonable people discuss governance issues from a variety of perspectives, they should be able to reach satisfactory solutions. Deliberation has been a central tenet of democratic thinking, although it is not the same thing as democracy (Fishkin 2002). Deliberation has the character of the ideal speech situation that is part of communicative competence, an essential component of democracy. The ideal speech situation has three simple rules:

- Everyone is allowed to participate in discussion.
- Everyone is allowed to question everyone else's assertions and ideas, to introduce their own assertions and ideas into the discourse, and to express their needs.
- No one may be prevented by any form of coercion from asserting his or her right to speak. (Habermas 1984)

BOX 6.6   A Closer Look: Community Meeting

Giving everyone a voice through meetings close to home or within a community of interest may be an effective way to structure global governance.

One of the questions that arises about deliberative discussion is why people would discuss honestly instead of more usual methods of persuasion where people twist what they say to support what they think is best for themselves. One answer is that the global age presents a unique opportunity for people to engage in more legitimate discussion and decision making. The global age is an age of uncertainty. No one knows the future, and thus everyone is equally in the dark about what course will work best for them or be in their interest. In situations of uncertainty, the best strategy—that is, the most legitimate one—is open and honest dialog (Keohane 2002, 342). Another answer is that easier access to relevant information (including information concerning the records of organizations and corporations participating in the discussion) makes it possible for anyone to question the validity of assertions and ideas that others bring into the discussion. This dampens people's ability to cheat, if uncertainty does not reduce the desire.

Structuring Global Governance

The structures of most contemporary governments comprise executive, legislative, and judicial branches, and the institutions that compose them. Their responsibilities and the balance of power among them vary among countries as specified in their constitutions and everyday practice. No equivalent exists for global governance. One of the first aspects to consider in structure is the role and place of states relative to the many other actors now involved in governance. It is a multifaceted debate. Minimally, the structure of global governance must be sufficient to fulfill the essential functions in ways perceived to be fair, to hold decision makers accountable, and to accommodate full participation.

Proposals for global governance run the gamut from essentially stateless systems to ones in which states have the central roles. In the stateless models, there is no overarching central authority, and state governments are merely one type enmeshed in a network of political actors. The network includes a variety of groups and organizations—some with functional specialties, some with territorial interests, and some civil society organizations. Each is empowered through its constituency to negotiate in the global arena.

Most of the stateless—or globalist—models subscribe to a multilayered conception of global governance. World society theorists maintain that a global polity is already at work. The defining characteristic of an SOA is its capacity to generate compliance. States are one SOA. Cities, neighborhoods, and regions may be others. Interest groups would also qualify as SOAs, as would corporations, unions, and civil society organizations.

> The global stage is thus dense with actors, large and small, formal and informal, economic and social, political and cultural, national and transnational international and sub-national, aggressive and peaceful, liberal and authoritarian, who collectively form a highly complex system of global governance. (Rosenau 2002, 72–73)

In state-centric models, states retain their position as the primary actors on the global field. They exert sovereignty internally with respect to their societies and externally in their relations with other states and wider environment. International institutions remain rooted in the interests of those states who manage to hold onto the most power. But governments and international governmental organizations are not the only actors in global governance. These models of global governance rein in the layers of global governance that have spilled over state boundaries. States retain the significant governance functions, and other political actors act through states and inter-governmental organizations in the global arena. Civil society organizations or corporations, for example, may desire policy changes, but they have to lobby states to create those changes at the global or domestic level.

Another state-centric model proposes a global state in which individual states or regional alliances of states such as the EU would be constituents. This global federation would be similar in structure to the EU or the United States, depending on the number of functions that would be assumed by the global supra-state.

The models and proposals that follow operate somewhere in the globe today, but not as a global system of governance. We can borrow loosely from Falk's typology of global paradigms to structure this section. He describes five paradigms—civil society, regional, imperial, corporate, and apocalyptical (although he limited it to al-Qaeda)—in his article "Reimagining the Governance of Globalization" (2005). To those five, we add the UN model.

The UN as a Model of Global Governance

The UN has some advantages as a forum of global governance. The current UN structure is organized roughly around the rights owed people and the global problems thwarting these rights. Most of the participants and stakeholders necessary for decision making are already at the UN table. It also implements and helps coordinate programs to fulfill obligations to enforce rights and solve problems.

A series of polls summarized in *World Public Opinion* (2005, 2006, 2007) shows widespread favor for broadening the powers of the UN and widening the scope of its responsibilities. Majorities think that the UN should have a standing peacekeeping force, be able to go into a country to investigate human rights abuses, regulate the international arms trade, and stop a country from supporting terrorist groups, among other powers. People reject a single country dominating global politics and favor deciding most global issues among states rather than unilaterally or by a core state or group of states. Even though disillusionment is high, people report that the UN should have a larger role in governance. Polls suggest that people do not think that working through the UN detracts from the power of their state; indeed, it may enhance the sovereignty of states, enabling states to act in areas where it would be difficult to act alone.

The UN, despite its problems, has a significant degree of legitimacy. When UN decisions are based on principles that people agree are legitimate—such as collective opposition to aggression—people voluntarily support policies without requiring material inducements (Keohane 2001). This requires states to put the collective interest ahead of what they perceive to be in their self-interest when or if conflicts of interest arise.

BOX 6.7   Check It Out Yourself: Who Should Decide?

Who do you trust to decide these important global issues? Compare your responses to the world sample or go to World Values Survey online analysis to compare the United States to this world sample.

	Total	Who should decide?					
		National governments	Regional organizations	United Nations	National governments, with UN	Non-profit/ Non–governmental org	Commercial enterprise
Protect Environment	63,666 (100%)	51.5%	26.9%	20.0%	1.4%	0.3%	*
Aid to Developing Countries	62,608 (100%)	24.4%	20.6%	52.9%	1.7%	0.3%	0.1%
International Peacekeeping	63,464 (100%)	37.2%	12.4%	48.9%	1.5%	*	*
Refugees	62,210 (100%)	32.0%	18.3%	47.8%	1.5%	0.3%	*
Human Rights	63,167 (100%)	43.6%	13.2%	41.8%	1.3%	0.2%	*

Source: World Values Survey Online Analysis (2005–2008).

The UN, however, still has a democratic deficit. Accountability, transparency, and equality of representation are all weak.

For example, one of the most important UN agencies is its Human Rights Council. Freedom House, a respected INGO, gave the council a failing grade in many of its functions. It reported that the work of the Council was thwarted by

> a small group of rights-abusing countries that employ bloc voting to eliminate some country-specific special procedures, weaken the language of condemnatory resolutions or prevent them from being introduced, make a mockery of their own reviews under the new Universal Periodic Review process, and threaten the independence of the Office of the High Commissioner for Human Rights. (Freedom House 2009, 2–3)

The Security Council is another vital UN organ. It is compromised by the size, composition, and power of its permanent members (the winners of WWII), who can veto actions unilaterally by voting "no."

BOX 6.8   Consider This: UN Security Council

On July 19, 2012, the UN Security Council voted on measures to end Syria's civil war. If you look closely at the hands raised, you will see the representatives from Russia and China have their hands down. They are both permanent members of the Security Council, and as such, each has veto power. Russia has a naval base in Syria and is its major supplier of arms. China has no particular interest in Syria, but a vote against Syria might set precedent for more measures against China. Also at the table is the representative from Syria. Even though the members of the Council sit at a round table to symbolize their equality, is this equal and democratic global governance?

Perhaps, with reform, the UN could provide a structure of global governance compatible with suggestions concerning accountability. Various stakeholders in global governance could be organized into functional groups, as appropriate to their interest and expertise. Their participation in governance would depend on their qualifications as determined by sets of standards—such as in the Global Compact for corporations—to which they must adhere. The right of participation would follow from responsibilities to demonstrate adherence to standards.

A Civil Society Model and The Question of Global Democracy

The overall upward trend of state democracy indicates that in most countries, there is a demand for democracy. The main criticisms of global decision making concern deficits in democracy: legitimate authority, accountability, and transparency. Deficits of efficiency and effectiveness are also widespread.

What measures would be necessary to establish global democracy? As discussed earlier, the most important is that all stakeholders—those people influenced by decisions and those who have the responsibility for accomplishing the goals of governance—need to be identified and given the opportunity to participate equally. Is global democracy possible? One group of theorists asserts that it is; another is very doubtful.

"Yes: Civil society can be the locus of democracy."

Civil society is hard to define. Generally, it is the connections among and between individuals that are voluntary, everything except governmental, economic, and family ties, although some definitions include economic relations. Civil society is important because it provides bonds that cut across memberships of class, ethnicity, and race. With a vibrant civil society, its proponents argue, trust diffuses through a society and strengthens democracy. When people are involved in civil society, they become more involved in political life (Putnam 2000).

This agenda of those who advocate a civil society paradigm in global governance argue that CSOs can resolve the problems of accountability and the democratic deficit in world governance. From this point of view, INGOs and NGOs can pressure states and international governmental organizations to hold multinational corporations and governments accountable and reverse the harm done related to working conditions, environmental damage, wage disparities, and other social ills associated with impoverishment. CSOs bring the voice of humanity into governance. They can also help establish peace, the rule of law, and international agreements regulating the use of force (Falk 2005, 222).

Mary Kaldor (2003), one of the foremost scholars of civil society, argues that civil society groups need to lead in advancing global governance. Local, national, and global NGOs can generate global discussion and debate on which democratic global governance can be built. In this model, global civil society substitutes for representative democracy. Deliberation takes the place of representation, and authority can be delegated on the basis of issues. Global civil society can monitor the institutions created for global governance and ensure participation in decision making for those who wish to participate.

In addition, civil society must promote nonviolence. Kaldor argues that civil society groups should work toward five objectives:

- Strengthen humanitarian law and the International Criminal Court and apply law impartially.
- Enforce international law and protect civilians in time of war, with multilateral efforts on the scale of Kosovo and Bosnia-Herzegovina.
- Condemn violations of both sides in wars of terror and provide sufficient moral and material support for moderates who offer democratic alternatives to extremism.
- Support local political constituencies to bring about change and give preference to regional and local solutions.
- Commit to global social justice. Increase global aid through global taxes or similar mechanisms. Poverty and inequality are used as justification and incentive for war. International criminal networks feed off them. (2003, 156–158)

However utopian, Kaldor argues, the only alternative to war is through "global rules based on consent" (2003, 156).

World society theory, also called *world polity theory* (see Chapter Two), is compatible with a civil society governance structure. Both emphasize the spaces apart from states as the locus of global culture. States respond to norms that develop in global culture rather than independently enact the norms through which they operate. World society theory maintains that civil society organizations are among the primary vehicles of global culture, but it does not have any theory of power and governance. The civil society paradigm complements world society theory by promoting civil society—as advocates of the world's people—to a central role in the exercise of power and authority over states and global governance.

"No: There is no global public, which is a necessary component of global democracy."

Globalization challenges democracy by exposing the disjuncture between democratic states and the deficits in international governmental organizations and NGOs (Goodhart 2005, 3). Unlike a state and its people, the globe lacks "a coherent and well-defined global public" (Grant and Keohane 2005, 33; Sikkink and Keck 1998).

Global civil society is not a model for democracy. Rather, an active and vibrant civil society is *necessary* for democracy. But although global civil society has fostered democratic transitions, it is not *sufficient* for democracy (Bob 2002; Goodhart 2005, 6). Despite the best intentions, publics may be left out of democratic processes if they rely on civil society groups for their voice. In this way, democratic processes can have non-democratic ends at the global level (Bob 2002; Goodhart 2005; Roginsky and Shortall 2009). These difficulties are discussed at length in Chapter Five.

In sum, for a global public to function politically, there has to be a political structure to define who can participate and on what issues (Grant and Keohane 2005). Enough people have to participate to be representative. Participation also has to be free and open. None of these conditions apply to the globe. There is neither a juridical global public—a public defined by an institution with the global authority to define it—nor a sociological public in the sense of a people who identify as a community, communicate, and keep up on world events (Grant and Keohane 2005, 34).

Which is correct? Is global democracy necessary? Is it plausible? If so, how would it be structured? If not, what characteristics can global governance assume to uphold democratic ideals, if not a democratic structure?

The Imperial Paradigm: A Benevolent Hegemon

Those who advocate an imperial model of globalization justify it on the grounds that the world needs a benevolent hegemon to maintain order, defend human rights, and build democracies. Opponents of this view maintain that the imperial model is a subterfuge for efforts to dominate other countries, particularly poorer nations, rather than liberate them (Falk 2005, 223).

The imperial view notes that some core values of Western societies are becoming universal aspirations, including individual rights, democracy, and free markets. Since at least the 1980s, the foreign policies of the United States and Great Britain have been designed to encourage the normative diffusion of these values and institutionalize them in the structure of markets and governments (Etzioni 2004, 1–3). In the United States, proponents of the imperial model divide into two factions. The neoconservative faction favors the use of American military, that is, "hard power." The liberal faction favors the use of American "inspirational and organizational capabilities," that is, "soft power" (Falk 2006). U.S. economic and military power could be used preemptively and unilaterally to spread freedom and democracy, protect the world from evil, or prevent evil. They view this use of power as a form of benevolence. The United States would be assuming responsibility for national and global security. Military intervention could be used for humanitarian causes and democratic aspirations. Hard power also protects America's economic interests and helps other countries reap the benefits of free markets.

Democracy, development, free markets, and free trade are repeatedly associated in the imperial rhetoric of American foreign policy. The imperialist argument is that as the American model spreads, the zone of peace and prosperity expands. After the attacks on the World Trade Center and the Pentagon on September 11, 2001, a new era of U.S. fervor was unleashed. Democratization efforts and nation building (Iraq and Afghanistan) took on a militaristic character.

The Corporate Model: Allow the Market to Govern Globally

The model of corporate globalization favors a world order based on free market principles. It emphasizes the importance of the economy in providing for people's basic needs, improving their quality of life, and thus paving the way for a healthy society. The corporate model inspired the neo-liberal agenda that dominated the 1980s and 1990s creating a web of economic interests that influence political systems in order to facilitate economic growth (Falk 2005, 221). Corporate models of global governance minimize the role of the polity and enhance the role of the market. A *polity* is a group of people governed by consent. In the corporate model, consent is filtered through the market. In one version of the corporate paradigm, global economic interaction dominates the global systems. Although governments and intergovernmental organizations may establish rules and regulations, those that impact economic functioning would be determined directly or indirectly by a self-regulating global market.

The structure and activity of the transnational capitalist class that exercises power in the global economy have been studied extensively. Composed of corporate actors, state bureaucrats and politicians, high-tech professionals, and consumer-oriented merchants and media, the transnational elite class, some theorists argue, already controls global governance by using its economic power to wield political power (Tabb 2009, 145; see also Sklair 2002). The role of the military, whether deliberately or as a by-product, in expanding the zones of capitalism or capitalist control over resources such as oil reserves is a component of this vision less often admitted or discussed openly (Roberts, Secor, and Sparke 2003).

Thomas Barnett, a former Pentagon consultant, is one of the most vigorous and visible promoters of the military-reliant version of the corporate model. Barnett (2006) argues that the dangers of globalization lie in "the wild zone" or "the gap"—the regions and people not connected to or benefitting from the global economy, technology, and communication. They are the areas of chronic poverty, conflict, crime, and political repression, the conditions that spawn global terrorism. They do not buy into the rule set of globalization—democracy, transparency, and free trade. The gap, generally the poorest areas of the world, including most of Africa, West Asia, Central Asia, a lot of South and Central America, and most of Southeast Asia, is the locus of violence, disorder, and of the U.S. military engagements since the 1990s. Barnett argues that the key to global governance and creating a secure and peaceful world is to integrate the gap into the core—into the global economy. His "new map" or blueprint to integrate the gap relies on the United States because of the threat its military poses. However, while he favors the military as a necessary and very efficient tool in ridding the gap of its evil rulers—as it did in Iraq—the United States wasted its victory, he asserts, because it did not prepare for waging peace (3).

The U.S. military needs to be split into a much smaller leaner warring group that Barnett calls "the Leviathan" and a much more expansive and expensive "Systems Administrative" (Sys Adm) peace- building group. The Sys Adm agencies do the job of closing the gap. Its budget should be funded by cuts in the Leviathan budget. Barnett believes that the threat of war will stimulate regime change by most dictators in the wild zones. They can be toppled, as in Iraq, in weeks with few American casualties. For the others, regime change will be forced as expediently as possible perhaps through special ops. Barnett believes that when other core countries see the capability of a newly designed U.S. force, they will join the effort (Barnett 2006).

This is similar to arguments that integration of all societies into the global economy is the best way to expand zones of peace. But in this perspective, capitalism, rather than democracy, is the glue of integration. The corporate model also overlaps the imperialist perspective. The theme of both is that America is not simply able to make a difference in the world; "America *is the difference*" (Barnett 2006,

xiv). Assertions like Barnett's that other countries of the core will join the United States' action is what differentiates his vision from imperialistic ones (Dalby 2007).

But from the corporate perspective, global governance depends on America's strength in the global economy, not imperialism. This is a common neo-liberal assumption about the power of the market. While some, like Barnett, believe that the United States should compel other states—by force if necessary—to enter the global economy, neo-liberals assume that, once in, the interdependence of the market will bring peace and prosperity (Falk 2006, 731). Their underlying assumption is that the free market and democracy are intrinsically linked and dependent on one another. Thus, democracy follows the free market. A test case of this is China. China is watched closely to see if democracy will follow as it becomes more integrated globally.

The Apocalyptic Paradigm: The Struggle of Good vs. Evil

In bustling cities, the sight of a man or woman on a street corner hoisting a "the end is near" sign or passing out pamphlets with that message is fairly common, more common at times of rapid change than in more calm times. While most people pass street corner messengers without much thought, the messengers are harder to ignore and their impact is more deeply felt when they are a religious in a pulpit or a politician in a bully pulpit. Apocalyptic beliefs—that the end of the world will come with a cataclysmic event or battle—appear throughout history in many societies, both East and West. They contain the seeds of revolution, and timing is everything. Thinking the end of the world is near, believers may become disruptive to the

---

BOX 6.9   A Closer Look: Aggressive Apocalypticism in the United States

In the United States, politically oriented militias, racist groups such as Aryan Christians, and various religious groups have all agitated violently against the existing social order. For many, the troubles of the times mean that the end of the world is imminent. They find proof in a host of end-of-world prophecies found in nearly every religious tradition. Racism and anti-Semitism also figure importantly in Christian and Muslim apocalyptic belief (Landes 2004,

353). Many of these groups are preparing in one way or another for the end of the world. Non-religious militia and survivalist groups have an end-of-the-world-as-we-know-it mentality, even though not all accept the prophecies. They hole up, hunker down, fortify their positions with artillery, and plan to survive the turmoil that accompanies the millennium.

David Koresh led an offshoot of the Branch Davidians. As their prophet, he sought to lead them to the millennium. They prepared by heavily arming themselves in their compound in Waco, Texas. For them, the end did come in 1993, with two fierce gun battles with the Bureau of Alcohol, Tobacco, and Firearms and a fire that devoured their compound. Koresh and over 80 of his followers were killed.

Christian Identity is a biblical literalist militia group identified as domestic terrorists by the FBI. Their vision is of a racial apocalypse. Jews and blacks are the forces they battle (Barkun 1990).

These combinations of apocalyptic views with theories concerning U.S. government policies to destroy white America, hand the United States over to the UN, or similar conspiracies are called *aggressive apocalypticism*.

point of violent revolution if they believe human action is required for the apocalyptic transformation (Landes 2004, 334–335, 348).

There are a number of religious fundamentalist groups with apocalyptic worldviews. Some work to substitute religious law for secular law. They tend to be intolerant of other world views and seek world conversion. Apocalyptic Islam is among these movements; al Qaeda is one faction and the most violent of contemporary apocalyptic groups (Falk 2005, 224). Apocalyptic movements in Europe, Latin America, Africa, and the United States are also trying to transform the global order. The encroachment of capitalism and modernity deep into their traditional cultures is threatening and, in some cases, seen as outright evil (Landes 2004, 338).

The political realm is imbued with a secular version of apocalyptic sentiment. The imagery following tragedy of September 11, 2001, resounded with appeals to a colossal battle on which the fate of the world depended. When George W. Bush proclaimed that "every nation in every region now has a decision to make. Either you are with us or you are with the terrorists" (Bush 2001), he divided the world into two distinct and well-defined factions of good and evil. He pledged every resource within U.S. command. He pledged to follow terrorists from place to place, to pursue any nation that helped them, and to fight until they were defeated. He continued that "this is the world's fight, this is civilization's fight, this is the fight of all who believe in progress and pluralism, tolerance and freedom."

The fervor of his speech and the intensity of the applause of the joint session of Congress confirmed that this was, at least for then, a fight to the finish, and everyone had to choose a side—the good one or the other one.

Although much of Bush's rhetoric was drawn from his religious identity as a born-again Christian, he represents a secular version of the millennial vision inherent in American national identity—that America is reinvigorated and renewed as a republic of virtue that will lead the fight against the evils in the world. The anti-Islamist rhetoric is strikingly similar to Cold War rhetoric.

Real-world dangers may inflame religious apocalyptic fervor. Another layer of the secular apocalyptic vision is the doomsday end-of-world narratives. The nuclear bomb, nuclear energy, the population explosion, AIDS and epidemics generally, rogue states and terrorist groups, the ozone hole, climate change, and increasing numbers of extreme weather events have inspired speculation of the end of the world—or at least the end of the world as we know it. While these movements are based on real dangers, the apocalyptic urgency still places them in this category.

The popularity of waves of apocalyptic movies signals a general anxiety about imminent danger. Although not religious, the fervor of many groups who divide the world into the white hats who attack the enemies of humankind, and the black hats, is religious in its intensity. It is another version of the apocalyptic paradigm, broadly interpreted.

BOX 6.10   Consider This: Global Governance

How would you interpret this data from Eurobarometer 76, taken in Autumn 2011? When asked the question, "In your opinion, which of the following is best able to take effective action against the effects of the financial and economic crisis?" Europeans responded as follows:

The European Union	23%
The National Government	20%
The G-20	16%
The International Monetary Fund	14%
Other	1%
None	1%

The Regional Paradigm: Following the EU Lead

The EU represents regional globalization. It is a middle ground between independent states and a global political order. Regional globalization creates political entities that are politically and economically stronger than individual states and presumably better able to manage and control the forces that impact it. The agenda of those who promote regional globalization is usually to facilitate economic progress and regional security, two traditional state functions. Transgovernmentalism is a similar proposition (Gilpin 2002, 245).

BOX 6.11   Check It Out Yourself: Get to Know the EU

The EU has held the peace among western European nations since World War II. The EU has now extended the zone of peace in Europe to include countries formerly in the Eastern bloc. Whether it continues is a test of regionalism as global governance. Countries in green belonged to the EU in July 2012; those in dark gray were candidates at that time. This online map is interactive and by clicking on a country you can learn something of its culture and its development, and listen to its language. You can find the map at http://europa.eu/about-eu/countries/index_en.htm.

Regional actors emerge through increasing integration, requiring coordination among states. As more realms of state function are coordinated and subsequently regulated, a bit of state sovereignty is eroded. However, when the regulation is accomplished through a treaty among equal partners, although every state is more regulated, each has imposed more regulation on others. States gain more control over their environment and they create a more predictable environment. Sovereignty is enhanced.

As integration progresses, coordination may require expanded regionalization. This is how the evolution of the EU proceeded. Hoping to end the wars that had plagued Europe, Germany, France, Belgium, Luxembourg, the Netherlands, and Italy formed the European Coal and Steel Community in 1951. These nations believed that a common market would make war among the states impossible. The community continued to expand its membership and its functions from the 1960s to the present. It became the EU in 1992, when European citizenship came into force. A common foreign currency was adopted in 1995, and euro coins and banknotes were introduced in 2002. Security policy and the role of the European Parliament have also expanded over the decades.

The success of the EU, though far from perfect, is significant. In the course of increasing integration, Europe became a zone of peace. Europe has had no wars since WWII. The 2009 Eurobarometer showed that a majority of Europeans believe that membership in the EU is a good thing, while only 15% view it as "a bad thing" (European Commission 2009, 86). The economic union gives countries greater economic power than each would have alone.

One weakness is in the widespread use of a common currency without an overarching political framework (as the United States has among its 50 states) or central financial body (such as the U.S. Treasury). Lack of central coordination intensified the economic crisis that struck following the recession. Countries like Greece and Ireland could not manipulate the value of their currency (because it is not theirs alone), nor was there a single economic body that could act quickly in the common interest of the union. Each country's parliament had to move through its own approval process for any plan to be activated. French and German credit ratings were threatened by weaknesses in Greece, Ireland, Spain, and Italy. Many French and German citizens expressed frustration with bailouts, arguing that they were paying for the spendthrift ways of other countries. Spain and Greece resent domestic policies becoming subject to EU regulation as a cost of assistance. All parties appear committed to preserving the union, but whether reforms will weaken the union or build a stronger federation, with authority to create common fiscal policy, may take years to settle.

Nearly every country is involved in one or many regional alliances that have cross-cutting memberships. There are four major trading blocs: NAFTA, the EU, Mercosur, and ASEAN; 133 regional trading blocs have formed from the creation of the WTO, bringing the total to over 180 in 2004 (Chase 2005, 4). Some alliances, like NAFTA, focus on economic issues. Others, such as the African Union, have broader ambitions similar to the European Union (African Union 2010).

Most regional alliances have stayed rooted in their original functions. The North Atlantic Treaty Alliance (NATO), established originally for defense against the Soviet Union, expanded its membership to include states formerly in the Soviet sphere of influence. Its mission remains stability in Europe. Multiplying and expanding regionalism can possibly be an avenue to global peace as bonds of trust and bonds based on interest extend from one group to others through their common members.

BOX 6.12   A Closer Look: Summary of Global Governance Paradigms

Paradigm	Central Focus
The UN Model	The UN structure is a forum to negotiate among conflicting state interests and interests of non-governmental bodies. In current structure, states are responsible for decision making. Other groups sit in sessions and offer testimony.
Civil Society	Civil society groups represent people to global governance bodies, establishing global democracy.
Imperial	A single powerful state is needed to compel or enforce the spread of democracy. Democracy within states will create peace among states.
Corporate	Market mechanisms should be freed to expand participation in the global economy. Increasing economic integration of societies will increase prosperity and peace.
Apocalyptic	The world is divided into good and bad. Defeating the bad is the basis of achieving global good.
Regional	Expanding alliances among states makes the world more manageable by establishing larger zones of cooperation, interdependence, and thus peace.

Each of these five approaches to global governance is being pursued by someone, somewhere in the world today. **How do you assess the potential of each for global governance? What are weaknesses of each? Could one of them be the answer to global governance? Are there other possibilities?**

Summary: Global Governance

The forces and processes of globalization challenge the system of states and the nature of the state established in the Treaty of Westphalia. Relationships among elements of the global field are altered, opening opportunities for change. Finding new formulas for determining who gets what, when, and how, at both global and national levels, is the critical issue of political globalization.

Changes in the Global Systems

- The state form of governance and ideal of statehood now spans the globe. Statehood—sovereignty—is viewed as a right.
- Political and economic power differentials between developed and emerging economies have shrunk. New global powers have emerged, particularly China, India, and Brazil.
- International governmental organizations perform a variety of state functions. Some are very powerful, such as the UN Security Council, IMF, World Bank, and NATO. Democratic deficits at all levels of governance have undermined the legitimacy of many of these bodies.
- The power and influence of MNCs have reached into all levels of governance, often shaping global policy. Gaps in governance also allow multinationals to operate outside of the boundaries of political processes with little accountability.
- INGOs have multiplied rapidly. Many exert significant influence in the political process in international governmental organizations and state politics. Many have assumed governmental functions, particularly in the conduct of social welfare programs.
- Global culture has determined that humanity is a protected category. The global systems collectively have the obligation to protect the human rights of all individuals.

Changes in States and Societies

- Many ethnic and racial groups are claiming the right to self-rule and are fighting for a state of their own or more autonomy within states.
- Not every head of state is recognized as legitimate, even though they have secured the power to rule. Heads of state commit crimes against their own people. Some have been indicted by international tribunals or the ICC or deposed due to actions against their people or the international community.
- Global challenges to the common good within societies and globally are beyond states' individual capacity to confront.
- The global economy—decision making in financial and corporate sectors—constrains states' capacity to control their internal environments, thus requiring global political strategy.

Changes in Individuals and Humanity

- Individuals from every country, although not all individuals, are linked through a network of local, national, and global NGOs.
- Gaps in governance result in individuals who are unrepresented in global—and often local—governance arenas.
- Global migration, increased communication, and travel have given rise to greater feelings of connection among individuals from different societies and feelings of belonging to a common group, that is, humanity.
- The rights and status of individuals as members of humanity are increasingly recognized and enforced.
- Global climate change, human rights abuses, and other transborder problems are perceived as threatening to species survival (the future of humanity) and quality of life (the present generations of humanity).
- Global media—material culture—facilitates participation in and knowledge of political activity anywhere from anywhere in the world.

Global problems and global interaction have moved beyond the ken of international relations. Bilateral and multilateral agreements are insufficient when a multitude of actors is engaged in making decisions that have global impact. Governance involving and binding all actors is necessary. International relations are still important; states undoubtedly will continue bilateral and multilateral relations, but it is intra-global relations that will dominate global governance.

Prescriptions for global governance abound. Only a few are sampled in this chapter. Clearly, the old formula, the formula that granted more capacity to wealthy and militarily strong states to manipulate international relations in favor of their interests, is no longer acceptable. That is not to say that it does not occur, but that it is no longer perceived as legitimate. As testament to their growing clout, President Lula of Brazil and Prime Minister Erdogan of Turkey visited Iran on their own initiative in 2010 to broker a deal on behalf of the UN Security Council (Quinn and Ellsworth 2010). Although the deal brokered was not very meaningful, it was a potent symbolic gesture. As non-permanent members of the Security Council, they rejected their lower status on the council, each of whose five permanent members has the ability to veto any recommendation brought to the council. The richest and strongest of the developing nations are no longer going to take a back seat to Western Europe and the United States.

What do you think are the most important qualities of global governance? How would you institutionalize them?

Questions, Investigations, and Resources

Questions

1. Debate: Should a government sacrifice its own interest for the sake of global order?

2. Debate: Can global governance ever be democratic governance?

3. To what extent are treaties necessary in global governance? Can you think of some areas that need more or better treaties?

4. What prescription for global governance do you think holds the most influence today?

5. Given what you now know, how would you design a system of global governance?
   - Consider short- and long-range plans.
   - Consider the prospects explained at the end of the chapter.

6. Who needs to be represented in global governance? How do we insure that they are represented in keeping with democratic ideals?

Investigations

1. One measure of globalization of international law is treaty ratification. The *Civil Society Yearbook 2004–2005* contains list of humanitarian, environmental, and human rights treaties and the dates that they were ratified by various countries. (These are found in Record Eight of the Data Program, page 265 in the book, or page 22 of 57 online.)
   - Based on ratification of these treaties, which 10 countries are the most globally integrated? Which 10 countries are the least?
   - What may account for the differences in ratification?
   - Are there countries that stand out as having ratified most or all of the treaties in some categories, but hardly any in another category? What may account for these differences?
   - Which set of treaties do you think is most important for international law?

2. Some countries add notes to the treaties. Choose a treaty that you believe is important and find out what notes various countries have added to the treaty. What points are the various countries trying to make with their notes?
   - What factors do you think would keep a country from signing and ratifying a treaty?

3. There are many regional political and security alliances. Choose one of these to investigate. When was it formed? Who are its members? What is its purpose? What is the extent of integration, such as mobility across borders, open markets, military integration, or common currency?
   - North Atlantic Treaty Organization
   - Treaty of Mutual Cooperation and Security (between the United States and Japan)
   - Commonwealth of Independent States
   - African Union
   - European Union
   - Bolivarian Alliance

Resources

Global Civil Society Yearbook 2004–2005 http://www2 .lse.ac.uk/internationalDevelopment/research/CSHS/civil Society/yearBook/contentsPages/2004-2005.aspx

UN Treaty Collection http://treaties.un.org/

Transparency International http://transparency.org/

Transparency International Global Corruption Barometer 2010 http://transparency.org/policy_research/surveys_indices/gcb/2010

Transparency International Global Corruption Barometer 2010 (Results Booklet) http://transparency.org/research/gcb/overview

Transparency International Global Corruption Barometer http://transparency.org/policy_research/surveys_indices/gcb/2010/interactive

Transparency International Global Priorities http://archive.transparency.org/global_priorities

7

Globalizing Political Culture and State Governance

Objectives

This chapter analyzes the diffusion of political culture and global standards to which states are expected to adhere. This chapter will help you

- analyze the forces of globalization that influence state governance;
- understand the indicators of state legitimacy and their various measures;
- evaluate enforcement mechanisms of global accountability on states;
- understand the influence of non-governmental, international non-governmental, and intergovernmental

organizations, along with other actors, on state governance;
- recognize the impact of political globalization on the relationship of states to citizens; and
- understand the dynamics of globalization waves, particularly neighborhood effects on political culture.

BOX 7.1   A Closer Look: China

"In the past, there would have been no doubt that the Chinese government would have punished Google," said Xiao Qiang, director of the China Internet Project at UC Berkeley (quoted in Barboza and Helft 2010). Instead, the Chinese government compromised. After a six-month standoff, the Chinese government renewed Google's license to operate in China. According to the deal, the Chinese government continues to censor content delivered through Google China. But instead of the usual automatic transfer from Google China to Google Hong Kong, users must click on a link to be redirected to the uncensored Hong Kong site (Barboza and Helft 2010). In China, where information is tightly controlled, newspapers are restricted on what and how they may report, and censorship is a way of life, this was an important concession to freedom of information, essential in a democracy.

Perhaps this exercise of goodwill on the part of the Chinese government will spread to Chinese workers. China is developing quickly. GDP increased tenfold from 1978 to 2009. Its economy grew about 8.7% in 2009, and per

(Continued)

capita income in 2009 was about $6,600 (CIA World Factbook 2013). Workers have not shared equitably in the wealth; most are paid at the minimum wage rate of about $160 per month.

To forestall worker discontent and acknowledge international norms, the Chinese government enacted worker laws in 2008. The laws established arbitration courts and guaranteed workers' right to contracts, among other reforms. The strategy backfired: Rather than quell unrest, it ignited it. The laws reenergized worker consciousness. Labor cases in Chinese courts increased 94% from 2008 to 2009, reaching 280,000 cases for the year. In the first half of 2009, there were 170,000 cases and China was heading toward another record. Workers became emboldened not just to sue but also to strike (Han 2010).

Chinese labor, traditionally quiescent, continues to rise in protest. Strikes at manufacturing plants in China sprung up throughout the spring and summer of 2010. Perhaps because they were directed at foreign-owned plants, the government allowed the strikes to continue. Nevertheless, however inadvertently, in responding to globalization pressures, the Chinese government stimulated workers' consciousness of their rights. As a 19-year-old striker at a Honda factory said, "We heard about the new labor law, but we don't know the details. We know we should fight for our rights" (quoted in Wong 2010).

Whether or not the Chinese government will continue with more liberalizing reforms will test the strength of political globalization.

Globalization affects internal changes in states through external and internal pressures. External pressures on states compel conformity to global normative standards, as in the case of Google in China. Globalization pressures confront states with a variety of potential costs if they refuse to comply and the promise of benefits if they do. States conform to global standards to gain admission to regional and interest-based alliances, such as NATO or the EU, to receive loans, attract investment, gain trading partners, or simply to maintain a good reputation and legitimacy in the eyes of their domestic audience, their allies, and the world generally.

Bestowing legitimacy on a state government is an important function of globalization. The need for international legitimacy for governments was minimal until recently. Under the terms of Westphalia, whoever held power was recognized by the rest of the world as the government, regardless of how they attained their rule. During the Cold War, the legitimacy of rulers was bolstered by the support of one or the other of the superpowers. As countries become more autonomous—less subject to control by superpowers—and interdependent demands for legitimacy increased on all nations, those that had imposed their will on others and those whose governments acquiesced.

Internal pressures for change come from citizens as well as other actors such as corporations, institutions, and non-governmental organizations (NGOs). Workers in China, and around the world, are now acutely aware that they deserve more rights than they are given. Access to information from other countries and the possibility of change offered by the Chinese government by enacting new worker laws emboldened workers to fight for their rights. Rationality crisis—the incapacity of a state to perform its key functions—and crises of legitimacy—declining faith or trust in government—create pressure and necessitate change if a state is to remain viable.

While the examples from China, a society in the throes of rapid development, are used to open this chapter, it is a mistake to think that globalization pressures mean forcing developing societies to adopt Western or modern standards. Developed societies are also affected by globalization. Maintaining legitimacy on the global stage and internally to citizens is an issue facing all states.

Over the course of globalization, the structure and dynamics of governance within countries has continued to evolve. Pressures to develop the structural mechanisms and normative principles on which governance is judged have never been greater. Now there is no state function—from providing for welfare, granting and protection of rights, to security and the conduct of foreign affairs—that is unaffected by globalization. Many of the challenges faced by global governance also challenge the governance of countries:

- More non-state actors involved in state governance
- Trends toward greater democratization as well as changes in the meaning of democracy

- Norms requiring transparency and accountability in government and institutions, such as the economy and education
- The human rights measuring rod for citizens to gauge their states' performance

Globalization of Normative Criteria for Governance

The Treaty of Westphalia did not impose criteria for the internal legitimacy of states. Various models—monarchies, republics, democracies, autocracies—all interacted with equal recognition by other states on the international stage. States had sovereign power to control what happened within their borders and their relations to other states. With rare exception, this continued through the colonial period and into the post-WWII era. States did not look too deeply into the inner workings of other states, except as befitting their interests, nor for that matter did anyone else.[1]

The intensity of countries' interdependence and the breadth and depth of global systems has put governance within and among countries at the center of globalization debates. How countries govern matters to other countries and to the mechanics of the global economy, polity, and social community. The pressures on states to conform to global standards result from the diffusion of emerging global political culture and participation in global systems.

Among the most widely cited sets of criteria for governance is the World Bank's Worldwide Governance Indicators (WGIs). A country's score on these measures may determine the likelihood of its attracting investment, tourism, financial and other forms of aid, its global reputation, and myriad other factors both official and informal. The World Bank criteria include six broad categories. Its scores are based on data from wide-ranging sources. In 2008,

---

BOX 7.2   Annual Corruption Scores, 2010

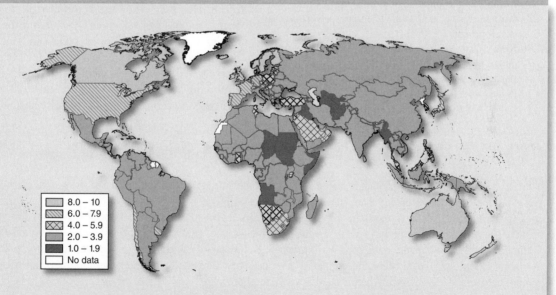

Countries' 2010 scores on the Corruption Perceptions Index, in which 10 equals the least corruption and 1 the most. The Index is constructed by surveying business leaders and others who work in each country, asking them how much corruption they perceive. In the most corrupt countries, bureaucratic rules are rarely followed, producing less equality under law and less efficiency in government.

Source: Transparency International Corruption Perceptions Index Scores, 2010, http://www.transparency.org/policy_research/surveys_indices/cpi/.

data from 33 organizations on 441 variables in 208–212 countries were included (Kaufmann, Kraav, and Mastruzzi 2009, 16). The categories are as follows:

- *Voice and accountability,* the extent to which a country's citizens are able to participate in selecting its government, as well as freedom of expression, freedom of association, and free media
- *Control of corruption,* the extent to which public power is exercised for private gain, including both petty and grand forms of corruption, as well as "state capture" or control by elites and private interests
- *Political stability and absence of violence,* perceptions of the likelihood that the government will be destabilized or overthrown by unconstitutional or violent means, including political violence and terrorism
- *Government effectiveness,* the quality of public services, the quality of the civil service and the degree of its independence from political pressures, the quality of policy formulation and implementation, and the credibility of the government's commitment to such policies
- *Regulatory quality,* the ability of the government to formulate and implement sound policies and regulations that permit and promote private sector development
- *Rule of law,* the extent to which agents have confidence in and abide by the rules of society, and in particular the quality of contract enforcement, the police, and the courts, as well as the likelihood of crime and violence

The variety of sources that the World Bank data set draws from include organizations that poll and survey businesses, NGOs, and households, but is focused primarily on the accountability of government and related public services, not the many types of governance actors. Thus, the discussion of governance below is organized by these dimensions, although the discussion is not limited to the World Bank data and evaluation. In each section, there is data to suggest what the specific norms mean in practice and the extent to which the norms are globalized—accepted or adhered to globally

Accountability

One of the most important aspects of political globalization is accountability. *Accountability* means that power wielders have to answer for and justify their actions. They should answer to those who are affected by their actions and those who gave them their authority. In the age of the expert, many individuals and organizations entrusted with important decisions affecting many lives are neither elected nor subject to recall. This may erode the autonomy of "the people" that is the basis of self rule. The demand for accountability is high in developed states and increasingly demanded in developing countries. It is a necessary element of internal, as well as external, legitimacy. Enforcing accountability within states is somewhat easier than accountability on the global stage.

BOX 7.3　Consider This, Then Check It Out Yourself: Confidence in Governments

It is in the institutions that mediate between states and their citizens, between politics and polity, that globalization has produced the most convergence (Herkenrath et al. 2005).

In what capacities do states relate to their people? Consider the institutional connections between governments and citizens. What is expected of a state in education, health care, autonomy, and civil and human rights? How are states judged? How do you judge their performance? Why do you think confidence in governments is so low? You may investigate to find out how the ratings of countries vary. Do wealthier nations score better than poorer? Do more democratic societies score better than less democratic?

BASE = 82,992 Weight [with split-ups]	How Much Confidence in Government	
	Frequency	Valid Percentage
A great deal	10,593	14.1
Quite a lot	25,245	33.5

BASE = 82,992 Weight [with split-ups]	How Much Confidence in Government	
	Frequency	Valid Percentage
Not very much	27,542	36.6
None at all	11,895	15.8
Don't know	2,233	n/a
No answer	871	n/a
Not applicable	56	n/a
Not asked in survey	4,558	n/a
Total	82,992	

Source: World Values Survey Online (2005–2008).

Grant and Keohane (2005) differentiate four types of accountability: whether those with power acquired it through election or delegation, and whether they act based on the will of those on whose authority they act or use their own judgment as to which is the best course of action. In an electoral democracy, officeholders are to reflect the interests and beliefs of those that elected them. Frequent elections, widespread participation in elections and referenda, and term limits are direct mechanisms of accountability. Popular opinion and referenda are checks on the leader's performance (31–32).

Where authority is delegated, it is more difficult to hold the power wielder accountable. Many governmental agencies, corporations, and civil society organizations fall into this category. Where there is regulation, regulation holds them accountable. In the myriad of decisions for which there are no regulations, a corporation is to act in the best interests of their shareholders. This may not be in the best interests of the majority of the population. In both cases, where authority is delegated, technocrats may operate with little oversight, making decisions that have very significant impact on people's lives.

Holding government accountable depends on citizens having accurate, up-to-date, and complete information concerning government activities. Civil society groups can play a valuable role in gathering information, communicating it to the public, and conducting meetings with public officials in which citizens can deliberate and voice approval or disapproval.

Control of Corruption

Transparency International has a simple definition for corruption. It is the abuse of an entrusted power for private gain. Corruption has serious consequences regardless of whether it involves public officials or private enterprise, or whether it is petty, such as fixing a parking ticket for a friend, or major, such as the governor of Illinois trying to sell a seat in the U.S. Senate. (Rod Blagojevich was convicted on 17 corruption charges, among them offering the vacated Senate seat of Barak Obama for sale.) Corruption in a country erodes the legitimacy of economic and political systems both. Ultimately, citizens and consumers pay the costs of corruption in increased costs for goods and services and decreased quality of government. Corruption erodes rule of law and increases security risks. If a culture of corruption develops within countries or within industries— several of the top offenders in the United States held defense contracts—security risks increase because of less transparency or outright corruption of security officials (Holmes 2009, 394).

Until very recently, corruption was considered a cost of doing business. Many multinational corporations figured the costs of bribes into the costs of their contracts and, in some countries, legally deducted them in their tax returns. Corruption is so entrenched in some countries and in some regions or cities that citizens accept it as normal. Almost three quarters of the 178 countries indexed by Transparency International scored below 5 on a scale from 1 (very corrupt) to 10 (very clean) (Transparency International 2010).

Countries that have the highest levels of corruption tend to be those where violence and conflict are high. Violence decimates the infrastructure of law—legislature, courts, regulatory and enforcement agencies. Helping these societies rebuild institutional structures is a priority for the international community. It is a first step in resolving conflict and nurturing fragile and failed states to recovery. In contrast, states that score low in corruption—New Zealand, Denmark, Sweden, Singapore, and Switzerland—are among the wealthiest (Transparency International 2010). Note that although these states are rich, not all are democracies. Singapore, which is among the five lowest in corruption, was rated only "partly free" in 2009 by Freedom House.

Transparency International also measures citizens' perception of corruption in the Global Corruption Barometer (GCB). GCB gauges citizens' opinions of corruption in six key sectors: political parties, public officials, parliament, business, the judiciary, and the media (Transparency International 2009, 5, 20). As seen in Box 7.4, measuring by both the percentage of people and the percentage of countries, people chose political parties and public officials as the most corrupt sectors (6). The similarity between first choice among people and among countries indicates that globally the trends in people's perceptions of corruption are similar.

BOX 7.4   A Closer Look: Most Corrupt Institutions

Over 73,000 individuals in 69 countries and territories were polled for this survey.

Barometer of Corruption 2009: Most Corrupt Institutions

	Percentage of people choosing this institution as most corrupt (page 5)	Number of countries in which this was chosen their most corrupt institution (page 6)	Percentage of people indicating corruption affects this institution (page 6)
Political Parties	29	22	69
Public Officials	26	19	N/A
Parliament/ Legislature	16	4	61
Business Private Sector	14	13	53
Judiciary	9	11	49
Media	6	N/A	44

Source: Transparency International (2009).

Individual measures vary widely by region. The likelihood that a person has paid a bribe ranges from 40% in the Middle East and North Africa, to 10% in Latin America and Asia Pacific regions, down to 5% in the EU, 4% in the Western Balkans and Turkey, and 2% in North America (Transparency International 2009, 7). In sharp contrast to this, 61% of people in North America believe that their government is vulnerable to "state capture," the influence of bribes by business to influence policy. The only region reporting a higher suspected rate of state capture is the region of the newly independent states of the former Soviet Union, at a rate of 70% (15–16).

Whether correct or incorrect, distrust of business in relation to state policy, perhaps exacerbated in rich countries by the global financial crisis, is further evidence of a serious crisis of legitimacy. It

was the lowest in sub-Saharan Africa, but still significant at 41% (Transparency International 2009, 16). In the regions polled, with the exception of sub-Saharan Africa, one third or fewer people believed their governments are effective in fighting corruption (18).

BOX 7.5   A Closer Look: The Australian Wheat Board Case

The Australian Wheat Board (AWB) case was brought to light when Canadian and American farmers complained to the UN that AWB was violating both free trade laws and UN imposed sanctions against Iraq. The independent Cole Commission, appointed in Australia to investigate, found that AWB paid about $US221.7 million in four years in excessive transportation fees to Iraqi officials (a cover for kickbacks and bribes), deceiving the Australian government, violating UN sanctions, and engaging in unfair trade. The Australian tax office claimed that because the Cole Commission did not say that AWB had bribed Iraqis, AWB activity was legitimate and they could claim the alleged bribes as tax write-offs (Holmes 2009, 387). News accounts of the scandal question the degree to which Australian government officials bore culpability for not adequately reviewing AWB contracts or simply overlooking the violations (Whitton 2007).

In the late 1990s, sweeping changes across many states made it a crime to offer bribes in foreign business transactions. The Organization for Economic Co-operation and Development (OECD) 1997 Convention on Combating Bribery went into force in 1999. The convention binds the signatory nations to pass laws that prohibit bribery. By the May 2011 update, there were 39 signatories, including all 34 OECD states and Argentina, Brazil, Bulgaria, Russia, and South Africa. As new members are brought into the OECD, they are expected to act on the convention. Other countries such as China, India, Thailand, and Indonesia are working closely with the convention (OECD 2010a).

The convention establishes an important set of global norms. They certify that the signatory countries are safe environments for international business. Bribes, kickbacks, and the like are unfair trade practices. They undermine the playing field for corporations from countries where bribes are illegal, who cannot afford bribes, or who cannot afford to defend themselves in court against charges of bribery. States submit annual reports detailing their anti-corruption activities. These, along with the corruption scores of countries, serve as a report card indicating which countries are good for business and which are not.

Government legislation and enforcement are viable strategies for fighting corruption. Corporations are presumably rational actors acting on

calculations of self-interest. Holding individuals accountable and making sanctions greater than benefits may decrease corruption. However, from 1999 to 2009, there were only 77 entities (corporations or organizations) and 148 individuals who have had sanctions brought against them by signatories to the treaties (OECD 2010b, 26). Global norms notwithstanding, states may still pursue what they perceive to be in the best interests of their national corporations acting abroad (Holmes 2009, 396). Of the 38 participants (in 2009), only seven states were actively enforcing the convention, nine enforcing it moderately, and 20 having little or no enforcement. Even in the most diligent countries corruption may occur. Australia, whose companies are among those least likely to offer bribes, had its reputation seriously tarnished in case of the Australian Wheat Board (AWB), detailed in the Box 7.5.

Intergovernmental and non-governmental organizations can play important roles in combating corruption. Intergovernmental organizations are becoming more democratic and reflect interests of countries more equally. The World Bank has acted against a large Canadian corporation, and the EU has acted to permit debarments, excluding corrupt corporations from operating there. The media and civil society organizations can also play important roles by exposing corruption and pressuring states to take corruption more seriously (Holmes 2009, 395).

BOX 7.6   Consider This: Election Turnout

© M. Tafs-Morales, USAID, 2007

Elections are considered the most basic element of democratic governance. In many developing nations, people brave the effects of bullets for the privilege of casting a vote. Indifference and poor weather keep many people in some established democracies from the polls. Is poor voter turnout in many established democracies a sign of maturity or decline?

Violence leading up to the 2011 Guatemala elections did not keep these voters away.

Free and Fair Elections

Elections establish representative government and a measure of accountability for local and national governments. Elections can help stabilize a peace among conflicting parties, conduct referenda on national and local issues, and establish legitimacy for a government. Nearly all constitutions provide for the election of political leaders, and nearly all countries hold elections. However, not all elections are free and fair. Being in a region where neighbors have fair elections and belonging to international organizations that promote fair elections increases the likelihood of a country having democratic elections, but does not guarantee it (Donno 2013). Promoting free and fair elections became a global project in the late 1980s. Reducing or eliminating the intimidation of voters, ensuring the safety of voters getting to the polls, the efficiency and effectiveness of the process, and peaceful transitions after elections are essential for a functioning democracy, but they are not easy to achieve.

Most international monitoring is focused on developing countries. Still, election fraud can occur in any country, and confusing ballots and mistakes on ballots result in faulty vote counts regardless of how well established the democracy—but usually within an acceptable margin of error. A litany of abuses and ways to thwart the electoral process, from denying candidates access to media leading up to the election to intimidation tactics keeping people away from polls, have been practiced and refined in many countries. In the 2008 presidential election in the United States, students at the University of Florida received e-mails the morning of the election stating that due to the high volume of voters expected, the voting day for

Obama supporters was switched to the next day, the day after the election. Similar notices of changed voting dates occurred in other states (Common Cause 2012). The *Washington Post* published a list of voter suppression attempts by both parties in the 2012 election (Beard 2012).

National groups, international governmental groups, and NGOs, devoted in whole or in part to election monitoring, cooperate to try to make elections safe and free of fraud. The 1992 election in Ghana illustrates the global energy devoted to elections.

Before the 1992 elections in Ghana, both the US International Foundation for Electoral Systems (IFES) and DANIDA conducted pre-election appraisals. Administrative and logistical support *(sic)* were provided by Canada, Denmark, France, the EU, Germany, Italy, New Zealand, Sweden, Switzerland and the UK. Following the contentious outcome, international interventions sought to enhance the legitimacy of the electoral process. Arguing that 'credible elections are the sine qua non of the democratic process', USAID deployed IFES to ameliorate the credibility of the Ghanaian Electoral Commission and the voter registration process through Project STEP (Supporting the Electoral Process). The German political foundation Friedrich Ebert Stiftung (FES) and Electoral Commission also conducted training in communication and public relations for the political parties and guidance to media outlets on the coverage of elections. FES also promoted exposure to Western (neo)liberal models of democracy through intra-elite exchanges and study tours to Germany. (Ayers 2006, 326)

BOX 7.7   A Closer Look: Ways to Win an Election

"Stuffing ballot boxes" and balloting frauds are primitive ways of winning an election. There are many others. Some incumbents use state violence to repress opposition, steal votes, and continue oppression, including assassination, after the election (Saine 2008, 455). A favored strategy of autocratic rulers is amending constitutions to suit their interests, for instance, by abolishing term limits, age requirements, and run-off elections.

Other means to thwart democracy are arresting or disenfranchising opposition leaders and voters, denying opposition candidates access to media outlets, intimidating journalists and campaign workers, using state media to help the incumbent, and intimidating voters on election day, resulting in near empty polling stations.

A well-developed set of global norms exists. The Declaration on Criteria for Free and Fair Elections was adopted in March 1994, by the Inter-Parliamentary Union (IPU), an international governmental organization of 155 member parliaments and nine associate members. These are necessary, if not sufficient, conditions:

- Universal suffrage for adults, although people may be declared ineligible on explicitly defined lawful grounds
- Equal opportunity for voting including such things as design of the ballot and location of the polling places
- Equal opportunity for candidacy and to run a campaign
- Access to information
- Access to media channels to express views

These guidelines are followed by every civil society and international organization that works on election procedures. They also typically include the obligations of states to grant political and civil rights such as freedom of speech, assembly, and media, without which democratic elections are impossible.

The Carter Center is one of the most active and respected global civil society organizations involved in election monitoring. Carter Center representatives go only where invited and welcomed by all the political parties involved. A stamp of approval from the Carter Center legitimizes an election and the government established by it to domestic and global audiences. The Center's work begins with establishing election rules and procedures, mediating disputes among parties, and assessing registration and voter education campaigns. During the election, they monitor polls, survey voters concerning the process, and observe ballot counting. They aid in achieving a smooth transition of power and they

may continue working in the country to establish democratic institutions such as an independent judiciary, parliamentary processes, civil rights, and a free press. In the 20 years from 1989 to 2009, they monitored 77 elections in 33 countries (Carter Center 2009).

There are many other NGOs that monitor elections as well as international governmental groups such as the African Union, EU, and UN. Regional groups such as the Asian Network for Free Elections also hold frequent workshops on election processes. Country-level civil society groups, such as the Election Working Group in Bangladesh, use similar criteria. These global norms validate a government's legitimacy to global and domestic audiences.

Rule of Law

Governance is not simply a matter of designing an optimal system and then putting it in place through whatever mechanisms are available (including coercion if necessary). Rather, it should be thought of as a communicative and consultative *process* through which disputes are resolved, consensus is built and performance is continually reviewed. No less critical to its success than its policy instruments is the forum that a governance arrangement must provide for the expression of claims, review, and discussion of continuing reform. (Helleiner 2000)

"Rule of law" has multiple meanings. On the one hand, it is used to refer to specifically political phenomena. Rule of law keeps public officials in line. Presidents and prime ministers need to act within the boundaries of their office; police obey procedural laws that protect citizens' rights; building inspectors refuse bribes; and so on. This classic definition has two components: constraint on the state and protection of individuals. In the 1990s, rule of law took on new significance as an economic principle. The Asian economic crises of 1997–1998 revealed that the institutional basis of countries in crisis was in disarray. While policies might have been acceptable, the institutional setting that they operated in was not. Rule of law came to mean securing property rights and laws that would protect investment and encourage growth ("Economics and the Rule of Law" 2008).

Although there is ambiguity over whether rule of law facilitates growth or growth facilitates rule of law, the push to implement rule of law reforms in Latin America began in the 1980s. The World Bank uses a combination of political and economic indicators, from statistics on various types of crime, confidence and in trust police and courts, to property rights, enforceability and security of contracts, protection of intellectual property, protection of financial assets, and the impact of crime on business (Kaufmann et al. 2009, 76–77). There are measurements for 212 countries.

Recognizing Human Rights

Many freedoms or rights once considered civil rights—granted by states to citizens—are now global and considered human rights—unalienable and owed to everyone regardless of their country. The change with respect to the global field is profound. Until the human rights regime began to take hold, states had little concern for the internal legitimacy of other states. The rights and privileges that states granted to citizens, or whether rights were distributed justly or unjustly, were treated as matters of state sovereignty. Strategic and economic advantage, not concern for human welfare, determined most international relations from WWII until the end of the Cold War. When the EU and NATO negotiated human rights provisions with Eastern Europe, they were secondary to trade, environment, migration, and other concerns. If civil society organizations had not pressured to make those rights real, states may not have bothered.

BOX 7.8   A Closer Look: How Much Respect for Human Rights in Your Country (WVS Wave 5)

BASE = 82,992 Weight [with split-ups]	Respect for individual human rights nowadays	
	Frequency	Valid Percentage
There is a lot of respect for individual human rights	10,600	15.1%
There is some respect	31,211	44.6%
There is not much respect	21,569	30.8%
There is no respect at all	6,664	9.5%
Don´t know	2,584	N/A
No answer	660	N/A
Not applicable	21	N/A
Not asked in survey	9,683	N/A
Total	82,992	N/A

Source: World Values Survey Round, 2005–2008.

Despite the recent worsening rights record of some countries under the guise of the war on terror, a global human rights culture is taking hold.

Human rights have advanced in practice as well as theory. The focus on human rights changes the relationship between individuals and societies and the system of societies. "We are in the midst of a bloodless revolution in values and most importantly institutional practice that is transforming above all else our understanding of global justice" (Falk 2002).

Global efforts of national and global civil society groups and international governmental organizations established a global human rights regime that can claim successes on every continent, from the release of political prisoners such as opposition leader Aung San Suu Kyi from house arrest in Burma, to better working conditions and family policies in both rich and poor nations. The human rights regime grants individuals an identity and a social status based on their common humanity, nothing more but nothing less.

Conceptions of human rights, embodied in treaties and conventions now operate as a set of global laws, used to exert pressure on global actors, states organizations and individuals, to reform in the areas of human rights abuses (Held 2004, 125). States increasingly include human rights in their constitutions (discussed in Chapter Three) and have extended them to include rights for women, children, and minorities as well as regarding issues such as cultural identity and diversity (Smith 2008, 1821). Human rights straddle a global fissure. Nearly all of the members of the Organization of the Islamic Conference (OIC) signed the UN Declaration on Universal Human Rights (the exception being Saudi Arabia) and most signed the two related conventions—International Covenants on Civil and Political Rights, and Economic, Social and Cultural Rights—that followed. However, after the 1978 Iranian Revolution the Declaration was frequently criticized by Islamists. In 1981, the Iranian ambassador to the UN called the document "'a secular understanding of the Judeo-Christian tradition' that could not be implemented by Muslims without trespassing the Islamic law" (quoted in EuropeNews 2007).

BOX 7.9   A Closer Look: Worst of the Worst

Freedom House winners of the worst human rights records of 2011 all had perfect 7s—the worst possible score—for civil liberties, political rights, and their combined score.

Equatorial Guinea	Sudan
Eritrea	Syria
North Korea	Turkmenistan
Saudi Arabia	Uzbekistan
Somalia	

Territories: **Tibet, Western Sahara**

Also on the worst-of-the-worst were countries with 7 in political rights and 6 in civil liberties:

Belarus	Cuba
Burma	Laos
Chad	Libya
China	

Territory: **South Ossetia**

While this looks grim, the data show improvement looking at it historically. In 1984, there were 38 countries on the worst-of-the-worst list.

The OIC issued the Cairo Declaration of Human Rights in Islam in 1990, glocalizing human rights doctrine. It proclaims the religious law of Islam, *shari'a*, as the final arbiter of human rights. While it recognizes general rights to freedom and equality of all people, the limits of *shari'a* contradict the Declaration with respect to the actual freedoms afforded to women and people of other religions (EuropeNews 2007). This effectively denies women and minority religions many human rights recognized in the UN Declaration.

In 1994, the 22 members[2] of the League of Arab States adopted the Arab Charter on Human Rights. This reaffirms the principles of the Universal Declaration, the two international covenants, and the Islamic Declaration. But it is also glocalized. Part I, Article 1 (b) explicitly states, "Racism, Zionism, occupation and foreign domination pose a challenge to human dignity and constitute a fundamental obstacle to the realization of the basic rights of peoples. There is a need to condemn and endeavor to eliminate all such practices" (Council of the League of Arab States 1994). This opens the door for continuing the war with Israel. It also forbids the death penalty for anyone under the age of 18, something that the United States did only in 2005.

China also interprets human rights differently. Officially, the Communist leadership has resisted the concept of universal human rights as a Western invention coercively forced on the rest of the world. Chinese values, they argue, are based Confucian principles of social harmony. Values like individualism are anathema to the strong authoritarian single party electoral system in China. The tension between emerging global values and China's "socialism with Chinese characteristics"—a Chinese-style euphemism for capitalism—is widening a rift between Communist party hardliners and members bent on reform. Prime Minister Wen Jiabao argued in a public address that "China 'had to resolve the issue of excessive concentration of unrestrained power' and 'create conditions for the people to criticize and supervise the government'" (quoted in "Change You Can Believe In?" 2010, 35). He acknowledged that "science, democracy, rule of law, freedom and human rights are not unique to capitalism but are values commonly pursued by mankind over a long period of history" (quoted in "China" 2010, 43). The 2008 *Charter 08* manifesto, signed by thousands of Chinese citizens through circulation online, called for democratic reforms and landed Lui Xiaobo, one of its organizers, in prison with an 11-year sentence. When Lui was awarded the Nobel Peace Prize in 2010, China refused to allow him to travel to accept the prize and refused exit visas for his family members, preventing them from accepting it in his place. As when the Dalia Lama won the Peace Prize in 1989, China interpreted his prize as a Western plot to undermine Communist party rule.

Decentralization

Since the mid-1980s, decentralization has been a key policy to improve state functioning in both richer and poorer countries. It is near universal in appeal, favored across the political spectrum in new and mature democracies and in autocratic and transitional regimes (ICHRP 2002, 5). Decentralization has a role in reforming institutions as diverse as education, management, and even religion. It aims to mitigate the dysfunctions of bureaucracy. As with de-bureaucratization efforts generally, decentralization restructures power and authority by moving them closer to the people whose lives they affect. In governance, it fortifies municipal-level democratic process. In developing countries, it helps build stronger states by integrating rural areas into the central government.

Expectations for decentralization are high. The World Bank (2003) favors decentralization to transfer power to citizens or their elected representatives, giving them more influence in forming and implementing policies and making governance more inclusive and participatory. USAID favors decentralization to mitigate against conflict by building trust in and commitment to government if people see improvement and innovation in their lives. Decentralization can promote efficiency and the stability necessary for both democracy and development (Connerley 2009, 22, 94).

The success of decentralization depends on the degree to which local communities are empowered. De-concentration and devolution are two distinct forms of decentralization and overlooking the differences can turn a potential success into failure—for governments or any organization. De-concentration turns managerial responsibility over to local leaders, but not necessarily authority or funds. In contrast, devolution assigns resources, functions, and authority to local governments (Connerley 2009, 22–23).

For example, if a local area cannot raise its own funds by levying taxes, national fiscal crises will bear directly on the programs it can offer. The goal of stability in conflict-prone states requires both autonomy to raise resources and the authority to distribute them. Where territorially based minority groups have been left out of decision making, devolution may ensure that their priorities will be addressed. However, in Uganda, the opposite occurred. Decentralization created new minorities, whose needs were overlooked by local majorities and human rights abuses at the local level escalated. Many small "nation-states" were created through decentralization (ICHRP 2002, 25). In very fragile states, if local governments are absent or ineffective, de-concentration would be the more suitable alternative (Connerley 2009).

Democratization increases pressures for decentralization. With decentralization, people have more opportunity to participate directly in governance. This makes government more transparent and accountable. If local government has the authority and autonomy to act on people's needs and suggestions—such as for schools, roads, or health care—vigilant citizen monitoring usually results in better direction of resources or improves the delivery of services. Strong local civil society organizations are important for decentralization to facilitate bottom-up innovation and eventual diffusion of innovation through a country or among countries.

Although decentralization is a strategy of democratization and development, it is not always successful. Decentralization is highly context dependent—glocalized. Determining the conditions under which decentralization is likely to accomplish its goals—strengthen states, dissipate conflict, or promote democracy and development—is critical. Characteristics of the specific country and how decentralization is structured have significant impact on what decentralization can accomplish as the case studies below illustrate.

Case Study: Decentralization

Case studies of Mexico, South Africa, and Brazil illustrate how global initiatives have different effects depending on the local terrain over which they flow. While many factors help or hinder decentralization, the interactions of local actors—civil society, political parties, and the national governments in these cases—impact the success of decentralization efforts to transform local innovation into institutional change (Baiocchi and Checa 2009). Comparing policy successes and failures across similar contexts is a method social scientists use to pinpoint criteria for successful innovations.

Decentralization is typically measured by two factors: the percentage of total governmental expenditures that are spent locally and the autonomy of local governments in generating local revenue and borrowing from foreign and domestic banks. From 1988 to 1998, Brazil, Mexico, and South Africa shared several features; each was coming out of an authoritarian period, each had elected authorities at national and local levels, each had a strong tradition of civil society, and each increased funding at local and province levels significantly (Baiocchi and Checa 2009, 137–138). In each country, local actors had the opportunity for policy innovation, but only Brazil accomplished significant institutionalization.

Mexico was the least successful of the three countries. In some cities, such as Xico and Veracruz, administrators worked with civil society and had successes but the innovations did not diffuse for lack of national party coordination (Baiocchi and Checa 2009, 143). The lack of cooperation between political and civil society actors also hampered innovation. None of the major parties "made it a priority to empower municipalities." Taking advantage of ambiguities in the constitution and national policy, state officials overruled local mandates. The Institutional Revolutionary Party (PRI) came into power with the support of civil society but subsequently neglected local urban issues.

In South Africa, the 1994 Reconstruction and Development Program and 1998 Integrated Development Planning provided an institutional basis for direct citizen participation and planning. But little bottom-up

(Continued)

(Continued)

innovation was accomplished. The structure of the acts authorizing the programs prevented meaningful participation. Municipalities were required to adhere to an exacting set of codes and guidelines calling for consultant-driven processes, but few resources trickled down to municipalities to help them pay for generating any plans. In Johannesburg, the plans of locally elected officials became secondary to national plans for Johannesburg to become a world-class city. By way of contrast, in Durban, where a wide variety of stakeholders were involved in planning, including those in the informal economy, such as the street vendors, there was more success in generating bottom-up innovation (Baiocchi and Checa 2009, 138–140).

Another problem in South Africa was the extreme discipline of the African National Congress (ANC). Party discipline is important, but the ANC reportedly became increasingly centralized. It expelled members of parliament or provincial legislatures who dissented from their "top-driven" objectives. Foreign funds intended for civil society organizations were channeled through the National Development Agency. To get funding, civil society organizations had to follow state directives (Baiocchi and Checa 2009, 140).

Brazil is the most successful of the three in both the vibrancy of citizen participation and the diffusion of innovation. The keys to successful decentralization in Brazil were the cooperation of social movements and civil society organizations at the local level and the relationships between civil society and local political parties.

In 1989, the National Forum for Urban Reform declared citizen participation a right (Baiocchi and Checa 2009, 143–144). While lack of coordination between local and national party structure hurts national innovation (Ames 2002), it helped in this case of local innovation. Opposition candidates were able to use close ties to local civil society groups to win office and institute programs. With more funds and more autonomy to use them, ties between local politicians and civil society led to innovations in many cities. Unlike parties in Mexico, Brazilian parties focused on the local levels. Parties—the Partido dos Trabalhadores ("Workers' Party," PT) in particular—were able to govern innovatively and also diffuse successful innovations horizontally through party apparatus, bypassing national channels. This accommodated glocalization; the basic model of innovation was easily adapted to specific local conditions. Brazilian innovations such as participatory budgeting (used now in 250 Brazilian cities) and Bolsa Familia, stipends for families to keep children in school, are innovations that have diffused internationally (Baiocchi and Checa 2009, 144).

Decentralization has had similarly mixed results in West Africa. In integrating rural peasant societies with the central core, the states encountered various challenges: rural social structure, political dynamics, willingness of institutions to devolve power, and the spatial structure of state governance—governing from the center or from local "outposts" (Boone 2003, 357). Whether a rural community is tightly or loosely structured, whether they have capacity for collective action, how powerful the rural elites are, the legitimacy of the local hierarchy, and how their interests are shaped by agrarian policy all influence the outcomes of decentralization (359–363).

Confidence that decentralization can succeed if implemented correctly motivates decentralization. Programs are tried and revised, not only in politics, but also in education, agricultural extension, health care, resource management, and economics.

Providing for Social Welfare

Globalization pressures demand that states provide for social welfare. Globalization creates vulnerabilities for workers. Even if the benefits to a country are greater than the overall costs, shifting patterns of production result in losses for many people. The declining wage-share of national income declines for business owners in many sectors, and job loss exacerbates inequality within societies. In democracies, protections from want are now normative. Governments are expected to compensate for economic declines by providing programs such as education and retraining to address worker insecurity and a safety net such as extended unemployment benefits, food, health care, and housing assistance (Ahearn 2010). Unfortunately, countries have limited budgets for welfare spending, particularly if they are also lowering tax rates and providing incentives to corporations to attract investment and jobs. This is the source of a lot of anti-globalization fervor. It creates democratic pressures to restrict the expansion of world commerce and institute anti-economic globalization protectionist trade and financial policy.

Does this mean that globalization and democracy are incompatible? One side of the debate is the neo-liberal economics thesis that maintains that for societies to attract foreign investment (as well as maintain domestic investment!), they need to absorb some of the cost of doing business for corporations. One way to keep corporate costs lower is to keep taxes low (Ha and Tsebelis 2010, 5–8). Thus, economic globalization results in less money to spend on social welfare programs, producing anti-globalization forces in democracies. In contrast, the other side—the compensation theories—maintains that economic globalization increases social welfare spending. States are pressured to compensate those whose wages and profits are

reduced or whose jobs are lost. This creates a constituency for left-leaning parties more likely to expand social protections (8–10). This could result in the expansion of both economic globalization and social welfare by neutralizing any anti-globalization effect.

Analyses of the relationship between welfare programs and globalization have produced contradictory results; some studies show an increase in welfare spending with increasing globalization, and others show a decrease. Both of these theories use globalization as an independent variable, as the cause of social welfare spending or lack thereof. But, according to Ha and Tsebelis (2010), it makes sense that people need to be prepared to accept globalization. They may need to be assured of their security through the expansion of social welfare programs *before* globalization, not as a result of it. In this case, globalization is the dependent variable, the result of social welfare spending, not the cause. If people are assured that they will be protected from ill effects of globalization, such as economic instability and inequality, they are more likely to support globalization policies to reap the benefits, such as cheaper costs for many products.

BOX 7.10   A Closer Look: Globalization and Social Welfare Spending

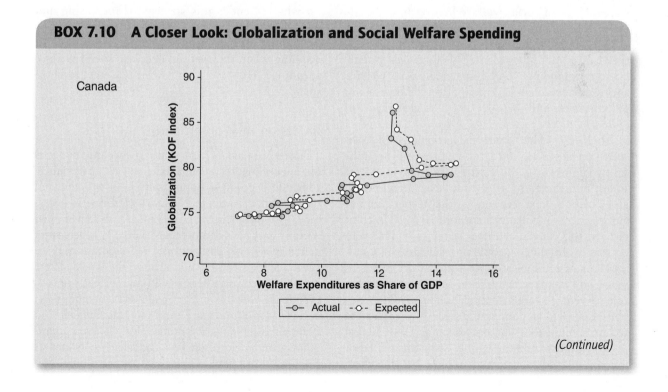

(Continued)

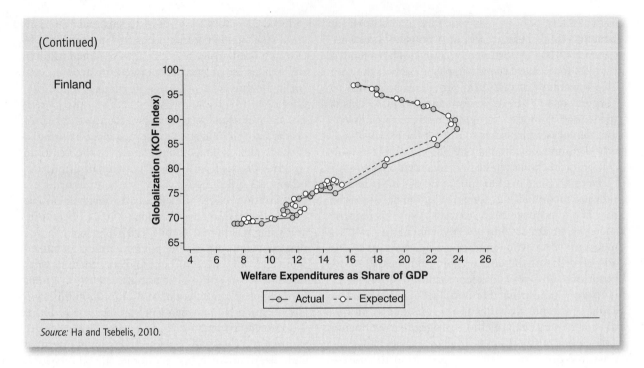

(Continued)

Finland

Source: Ha and Tsebelis, 2010.

Ha and Tsebelis (2010) analyzed the effect of welfare on globalization, as well as the effect of globalization on welfare from 1970 to 2000. They found a distinctive curvilinear correlation; states invest in social welfare before they globalize. They then pull back on social welfare to absorb some of the cost of production so that they can attract investment. This increases globalization, expanding world commerce. Social welfare spending increases in anticipation of increasing globalization and then decreases as globalization increases.

Another finding is that the percentage of GDP spent on social welfare programs trends significantly higher in corporatist states than in liberal states, and therefore so did the level of economic globalization. This accounts for the steeper climb of globalization in Finland, a corporatist state, in comparison to Canada, a liberal state. The more veto players in the state—people or levels at which policy changes could be stopped—the harder it was to make any changes in welfare, consistent with the role of veto players in political change. While globalization was a dominant factor in establishing welfare policy, local factors—such as GNP, liberal or corporatist economy, and strength of labor unions—played a significant role in shaping them

(Ha and Tsebelis 2010, 17–18, 30–31). Globalization and democracy are not incompatible when the state is able to fulfill its social welfare function.

To what extent is this strategy of increasing and then decreasing social welfare programs wise or pragmatic? What criteria should states use in deciding when they should decrease social welfare spending? How do they determine the level of spending?

Inclusion of Women and Minorities

The legitimacy of democratic governance depends on including the full citizenry in governance. Expanding political opportunities for women and racial, ethnic, and other minority groups is necessary. The problem is not confined to developing nations and new democracies. There is a persistent deficit of women and minority representation in the United States, Europe, and around the world. There are few African Americans in the U.S. Congress, despite the election of a biracial president, and Asian and African ethnics are scarce in the English and French parliaments (Reynolds 2006, 5). New immigrant groups, including Turks and Kurds, as well as smaller ethnic populations such as the Roma, and internally displaced persons are disenfranchised throughout Europe by denial of citizenship, lack of representation, and overt discrimination. This is true in Asian and African democracies as well.

In 2012, women composed only 19.8% (up from 18.4% in 2010) of the representatives in parliaments globally (Inter-Parliamentary Union 2012). In many countries, quotas ensure that women hold a set level of political offices. Reserved seat quotas guarantee a set number of seats for women, whereas legal candidate quotas only guarantee a certain number of women on the ballot. These forms of quotas are typically legal, set through legislative process or written into the constitution. Quotas set for the candidate lists of political parties are typically voluntary. The use of quotas is growing because it is recommended internationally and is diffusing across countries as countries emulate each other's practices (Dahlerup and Freidenvall 2009).

Not every country with a quota for women has achieved adequate representation—a threshold thought to be about 30% to 40%—and some countries without quotas have accomplished it. In secular countries that are less bound by traditional or religious values that undervalue women, and in countries where economic and social resources are more equitably distributed, women have been able to achieve threshold levels incrementally (Leyenaar 2008, 2).

Further improvement cannot be taken for granted. Even where women have made substantial gains, gains are threatened by fundamentalism, generational forgetting, goals becoming limits, and individualism.

- The revival of religious fundamentalism is associated with feminist backlash and a return to traditional values in which women are subordinate.
- There is danger of the 30% threshold turning into a ceiling if protections are removed, as has been suggested in some countries.
- It can be difficult to recruit young women who have not directly experienced the discrimination of the 1960s and '70s to mobilize for women's issues.
- The rise of neo-liberal parties that value individual reliance over expansion and support of public welfare programs and state regulation diminish support for programs to benefit groups. (Leyenaar 2008, 2–3)

Representation of minority interests is critical to stabilizing fragile democracies. Not much attention was paid to ethnicity in drawing colonial maps or in establishing new states following colonialism and the end of the Cold War. This has spawned tragedies of nationalism expressed as ethnic hatred, violence, and genocide.

For good reason, quotas for ethnic and religious minority groups are much less common than for women. Women are spread throughout social classes, racial, and ethnic groups. Ethnic and racial group boundaries are class related. Quotas are more likely to reinforce rather than diminish barriers among groups. To win and keep a political office where there are quotas can discourage elected officials and candidates from working across class, ethnic, and racial lines for the common interest or common good. This is true of majority and minority candidates. They are much more likely to win office by concentrating only on the needs of their constituents. As of 2003, no established democracy had quota laws for the protection of ethnic minorities. Most often, representation is solicited by political parties expanding their base among minorities and recruiting minority candidates. Some countries have reserved parliamentary seats for indigenous minorities (Bird 2003, 3).

It is not clear that quotas are a good thing. Quotas were used in some colonial states (India, Kenya, Tanganyika, and Nyasaland) in midcentury to dilute the power of minorities rather than share power with minorities. Although the danger of division and disenfranchisement through the use of quotas is real, quotas now are more often viewed as progressive (Reynolds 2006, 15). Despite the obvious problems with quotas, global norms demand greater inclusion, and some variation on quotas is the current favored policy choice.

Are quotas just justice in determining which ethnic minorities receive preferential treatment and which do not? Do they exacerbate and cement divisions or diminish political accountability? Are there other, better alternatives?

Another strategy is reform of the electoral system to reduce anomalies. Well-designed electoral systems avoid the disadvantages of quotas, reserved seats, and other legislated methods that work by dividing ethnic groups. Electoral systems can be designed to reward candidates who forge alliances across groups rather than polarize them (Reynolds 2006, 20). An electoral system influences how candidates behave to gain and maintain their office. Varying electoral systems may provide vehicles for increasing minority representation without the problems imposed by required identification with a group. Inclusion in electoral systems is critical for minority representation, but equally important is considering how they can be best used to dissipate ethnic conflict and maintain peace following ethnic war.

Although there are many variations in electoral systems, they can be classified as one of three broad types: plurality-majority systems (about 46% of nations use this), proportional systems (about 36%), and hybrids (15%) (Reynolds 2006, 8). The new democracies of Asia, Eastern Europe, and West Africa seem to be converging on "parallel" systems in which "two separate elections are held for different parts of the legislature at the same time" (11). Some representatives are elected by plurality and others are proportioned by party according to the proportion of votes the candidate list of each party gets.

Which specific electoral system will actually work best in any particular country depends on the characteristics of the country, such as the number and size of the minority groups, their geographic dispersal, and who is likely to vote. Ballot design, voter literacy, and how district lines are determined all impact which type of electoral system is likely to work best to get adequate representation and avoid polarization. Reynolds acknowledges that minority women pose a particular problem and that special measures for minority women need to be taken into account when designing electoral systems. For example, simply alternating male and female names on a party list increases the likelihood of electing more females within that list.

As globalization pressures for greater inclusion mount, the innovations will be tested and adopted, hopefully following carefully considered analysis.

If you could design an electoral system, how would you develop it to include likely representation of all minority groups? (Representation may mean office holders, but may also mean responsive to the needs of all groups. Include how people would be included on candidate lists and how voting would be structured and tallied.)

Governance Deficits

Polarization, Deadlock, and Identity

Globalization has created conditions of uncertainty. In uncertainty, many people and organizations react in extreme, orthodox, or fundamentalist ways. This polarization can put a deadlock on democracy. People close their minds to the other side, do not look for common interests, negotiate, or compromise. Nothing gets accomplished.

Polarization is a global phenomenon within, as well as among, many countries. The polarization of parties has created deadlock in places other than the United States. It took Belgians nine months to form a coalition government in 2007, a result of extreme partisanship. In the 2010 elections, half of the vote went to separatist candidates. The nationalist New Flemish Alliance party received 30% of the votes; the far right separatists, Vlaams Belang, got 12.5%; and a smaller populist party got 4%. That is, about 45% of the vote in Flanders went to separatists. Whether or not Belgium will remain a nation-state or split into separate nations is not a moot question (Castle and Erlanger 2010).

Separatist movements spring from some of the same issues as polarization. The location and strength of national identity is the difference. For example, in the United States, belonging to a state does not interfere with the larger context of national identity. Even in Europe, conflicts arise among those with differing views of national identity. Basques in Spain, Flemish in Belgium, and some Scots in the United Kingdom are among those pressing for separate statehood. Greater unification within the EU and the current economic crisis may have exacerbated the sentiment, but they are not the root. On the one hand, nationalism in Europe was originally a response of nations subsumed into empires. Multi national states have been problematic since, as Nazi Germany, Yugoslavia, and the Soviet Union demonstrated.

The Scottish white paper on independence proclaims Scotland's need for separate representation at the EU. The Basque white paper for independence cites the more robust Basque economy in comparison to the rest of Spain (Motha 2010). Economic crisis seems to have heightened choices between the interests of nation, the larger state, and Europe to the fore. Unlike U.S. citizens, Europeans do not yet share a strong sense of being a single people (Freidman 2010). Although there is a common currency, there is not a single polity.

New Modes of Suppression

Where there is action, there is an equal and opposite reaction. The National Endowment for Democracy (NED), a private non-profit funded by the U.S. government, supports civil society groups that work for democratic reform and transformation globally. The 2006 NED publication for the U.S. Senate Committee on Foreign Relations details backlash throughout the world against democratic reform efforts, civil society groups, and dissidents working for democratic reform. Countries resisting democratic reform have been inventive in enlisting legal as well as illegal measures to thwart democratic process. Crackdowns on freedom of the press, assembly, religion, and other more novel tactics to weaken and intimidate civil society and government opposition often arise when an authoritarian government feels threatened.

NED (2006) highlights the hybrid illiberal democracies for their efforts in democracy perversion movements. Russia is the master, running its own democracy promotion agency that provides aid for pro-regime civil society groups to counter U.S. assistance programs to build parties. Using the democratic revolutions in Eastern Europe as precedent, they condemn the U.S. efforts at party building in Russia as regime change assistance (11–12).

The objectives of aid lie in the eyes of the beholder. For the past few years, the Russian government seized the computers of civil society organizations and newspapers, claiming to be looking for pirated Microsoft software. Computers are often confiscated for months whether or not they have pirated software. Records of the organizations are destroyed in the process. This is one of the newest tactics to suppress dissent (Levy 2010).

NED (2006) also cites other movements in petro-states that donate money to suppress democratic movements. Funding from Iran and Syria supports Islamist groups. Venezuelan oil money has supported the "Bolivarian" parties throughout Latin America. This sort of claim and counterclaim is reminiscent of Cold War rhetoric.

NED cites other groups that have had restricted access to democracy promotion activities. The British Westminster Foundation for Democracy has had licenses to operate denied, travel restrictions and censorship imposed, computers and files seized, and some agents detained. Zimbabwe, Thailand, Bangladesh, Cambodia, Nigeria, Kazakhstan, Uzbekistan, Azerbaijan, Ethiopia, Algeria, Egypt—altogether, at least 20 countries are instituting restrictions that weaken civil society and have taken action against civil society groups, including Human Rights Watch. Among the strategies are

[r]estrictions on the right to associate and freedom to form NGOs, impediments to registration and denial of legal status, restrictions on foreign funding and domestic financing, ongoing threats through use of discretionary power, restrictions on political activities, interference in NGO internal affairs, harassment and deportation of civil society activists and establishment of false NGOs. (4–5)

The 2009 Freedom House report *Undermining Democracy* focuses on China, Iran, Pakistan, Russia, and Venezuela. Each of these countries, they maintain, is ruled by a small group that uses the state to maintain its oligarchy, undermining democracy. In Russia and China, democracy is redefined and broadcast through state controlled media, confusing public understanding and inhibiting genuine public discourse. Each of these regimes invests heavily in sophisticated broadcast platforms. Venezuela's *Telsur* is a 24-hour news cable channel. Iran, China, and Russia employ high-tech solutions to restricting Internet communications. They flood the Internet with their own commentators who disrupt democratic exchanges. They use the Internet (including in the United States) to recruit for extremist causes and spread ideology, increasing the likelihood of "self radicalization" of terrorists. Independent media in Russia has shrunk from over 30 to under 10 affiliates. International news outlets such as the BBC, Radio Free Europe, and Voice of America are routinely blocked or subject to interference (Freedom House 2009, 3–10).

Education in any country is used to foster national identity and socialize children into citizenship. In

China and Russia (and in some states in the United States), the educational system is a tool of extreme nationalism fostering very deliberately skewed views of history. Elements of authoritarian repression are omitted or misrepresented and human rights are presented as a tool of the West (Freedom House 2009, 6).

Case Study: Are Global Norms Effective in Improving Elections?

This is the central question of Daniela Donno's (2013) detailed analysis of election norm enforcement. The study uses a new dataset, Enforcement of Democratic Electoral Norms (EDEN). It includes information concerning 670 presidential and legislative elections from 1990 to 2007 in 119 countries; the enforcement efforts of international actors, the UN, the United States, and 12 regional organizations (in Latin America, Europe, and Africa); and the results of the enforcement efforts.

Her answer: Yes, global enforcement works, when applied. The work of election monitors is demonstrably important to improving election democracy. Enforcement of global norms helps to define and delineate the boundaries of good government behavior. Over time, monitoring and enforcement may strengthen and clarify the criteria of legitimacy to such an extent that an adherence to global norms gradually increases as the demand for democracy increases.

Unfortunately, election norms are not always enforced. Less than half of flawed elections in the EDEN dataset were followed by enforcement measures. Flawed elections tend to breed more flawed elections. The EDEN data show the 79% of the flawed elections were followed by another flawed election. Not surprisingly, the more flawed elections a country has, the less likely a clean election becomes. They rarely repair on their own.

Election monitoring and enforcement are necessary interventions. The Donno study examines how organizations and governments decide whether or not to enforce norms and what enforcement efforts are most effective.

International and civil society groups use a variety of criteria to determine whether or not they enact enforcement measures. First, when election monitors provide compelling evidence of misconduct, the likelihood of enforcing election norms increases. This applies to both pre- and post-election enforcement. Objective observers supply an important element of legitimacy to the application of sanctions.

Second, autocratic states were more likely to be sanctioned than states that had made more progress toward democratization, as signified by more democratic scores on the Polity scale. International actors tend to choose the harder rather than easier cases for sanctioning.

Third, strategic interests play a role. Regional organizations and the United States adopt slightly different perspectives on when to enforce norms and which method of sanctioning to use. Regional organizations are less likely to sanction states with strong economies or strong militaries. They are likely to engage in shaming and diplomatic measures, but the more often a government holds flawed elections, the more likely enforcement measures will escalate to sanctions. Whether or not a nation is a fuel exporter does not seem to factor into the decision. Regional organizations with established enforcement protocols are more likely to apply sanctions than regional organizations that have to adopt enforcement measures on an ad hoc basis.

In contrast, the United States is more likely to act than the regional organizations. In the cases of states where it has a strategic interest, such as fuel exporting, strong militaries, or economies, it is most likely to use shaming and diplomacy rather than imposing conditions. Donno suggests that the reliance on diplomacy and shaming allows the United States to promote itself as a guardian of democracy while acting strategically by not imposing sanctions. The UN is not very engaged in election norm enforcement. The UN tends only to get involved in enforcement in post–civil war situations or where they have had a peacekeeping mission; in other words, where they have an interest in maintaining peace and security.

How effective are sanctions in improving electoral performance? The study measured future electoral conduct by the intensity of misbehavior in the following election and changes in the judgments of monitoring agencies. Each measures the same behaviors but in complementary ways. The study also controls and considers domestic variables to isolate the effects of global enforcement.

Donno found that all the strategies of enforcement by the international community—diplomatic engagement, shaming, rewards, punishments, or conditionality—improved election behavior. There are significant effects on both future electoral conduct and post-election outcomes, such as repeating a disputed election, power sharing, an overturn in the next election, or, much more rarely, concessions. Specific findings include the following.

- Conditionality works better than shaming or diplomatic efforts.
- Post-election conditionality, particularly applied over time, tends to have the greatest effect.
- Effective reform requires sustained effort, not one-shot fixes. It requires regular monitoring and specific suggestions for reform.
- The more international groups that are involved in the enforcement, the greater its effect.
- Regional international governmental organizations tend to be the most effective enforcers. They are perceived as the most credible.
- International enforcement efforts can buttress post-election protests by domestic opposition forces.

Concessions after fraudulent elections are another important factor, and international actors have significant influence on whether or not offending governments can be removed from power. The results are very encouraging. Both the United States and regional organizations influence post-election concessions. Again, the more international actors join in, the greater the likelihood of concession. International actors are much more likely than domestic opposition and protest to achieve a concession. This effect is so strong that it appears that "simply the number of international voices taking part" is the factor that determines immediate post-election concessions. Concessions, however, are rare.

Whether or not the cheating government will be tossed out of office in the next election is also an important consideration. Post-election protest and enforcement can result in reformed election processes and a government being voted out of office. Conditionality, particularly "punishment," is the most effective enforcement in this process as well. International enforcement has more significant effects than domestic opposition strategies of protests and coalition building, which are usually touted as critical. These two widely cited domestic strategies were actually found to be insignificant in producing regime change. Regional international governmental organizations were the most effective agents of enforcement in regime change as well as increasing the supply of democracy in elections.

In summary, the Donno study supplies ample evidence that enforcing global norms make a difference in increasing the supply of democracy in a country. Having objective and reliable information concerning electoral abuses from independent monitoring organizations is the first step. International actors need to be involved within countries, bolstering opposition parties, who are unlikely to be able affect change on their own. While domestic groups are critical, they are not effective without the engagement of international actors. Negative conditionality is the most effective method of enforcement, particularly applied post-election and over a period of time in combination with specific recommendations for change. Changing the cost benefit ratio for cheating governments is the most likely strategy to get them to stop.

The lessons of decreasing the democratic deficits in elections are important to transfer to other democratic reforms.

Wave Effects in Globalization

Globalization effects often assume a wave pattern, as in waves of democracy. Wave patterns form when many societies change in the same direction at approximately the same time, over a period with an identifiable beginning and end. Isomorphism, convergence, clusters, homophily, and homogeneity[3] are similar concepts (Elkins and Simmons 2005, 37). All these concepts refer to structural and policy changes that cluster among a number of countries at the same time or within a relatively short period. In one way or another, countries appear to take one another's actions into account whether they are responding to forces as diverse as the need for capital investment, governmental innovations, liberalization, or human rights.

Wave Shapes and Clusters

Waves have different shapes. Convergence often appears as threshold behavior when most states withhold from adopting an innovation until a tipping point is reached. At this point, many jump on the bandwagon, and the wave crests very quickly (Elkins and Simmons 2005, 39–40). Waves may arise slowly or abruptly depending on whether countries join the trend a few at a time or many adopt the change or innovation over a short period. The most common wave pattern is an "S" curve: a slow start, a rapid rises, and then a leveling (Simmons, Dobbin, and Garrett 2006, 783). Waves within different clusters of countries in the same time frame may vary dramatically. After the start-up phase, some clusters may increase gradually over a number of years and others at a rapid rate.

Waves may also recede if countries are unable to sustain the change or if they do not reap the benefits expected from the change. Some countries are poorly equipped to support the innovation. They may lack a strong, independent judiciary, an important element of a strong democracy. Waves of democratization, until the most recent beginning in the 1970s, rose and fell, only to rise again. Wave of democratization within the contemporary period of globalization are different than prior waves. The current wave of democratization has not yet declined significantly, although some countries struggle. Hungary, one of the stronger democracies in Eastern Europe and which assumed the presidency of the European Union in 2011, has shown signs of weakening democracy by placing new restrictions on media and taking steps to consolidate power in the office of the prime minister by replacing the head of the central bank and limiting judicial powers (Westervelt 2011). A wave of democratization began in a new cluster of countries in 2011 with the advent of the Arab Spring.

Sometimes, waves increase indefinitely. Commitment to education seems have followed this pattern. Countries develop public mass schooling programs regardless of their internal characteristics. Many countries built educational systems far beyond their needs for development. Perhaps these countries were building educational systems that they would need for future development, but the evidence supports the contention that mass schooling was seen as an indicator of being a modern state. The desire to be seen as modern is more related to the diffusion of educational expansion than internal factors (Meyer, Ramirez, and Soysal 1992).

Wave Mechanics

Waves may be globalization effects or globalization processes. In cases where the wave is caused by simultaneous responses to an external global event, the wave may be a globalization effect. When a wave results from coordinated policy changes, when societies learn from and copy from one another, are pressured by one another or by the changes made in other societies—this is a globalization process (Herkenrath et al. 2005, 364). In either case, the policy choices of nations cannot be explained by domestic factors alone.

How policies and practices diffuse across countries is an important dimension of globalization analyses. Throughout other chapters, we have examined how international organizations require policy changes and how civil society organizations work to bring policy changes about. We know that changing values can also lead to policy changes. Many researchers have found that neighborhood effects are also important. We see this every day when people are influenced by what they see their neighbors do. If something worked for their neighbor, they think it might work for them. Government interdependence in policy change and innovation is well documented.

What is surprising is that the effect of interdependence seems to be more significant than internal factors such as level of economic development, internal ethnic or social strife, and interactions within and among classes, including elite classes (Simmons et al. 2006, 787). However difficult it is to conceptualize and execute, the study of domestic policy change must be situated in a global [or at least regional] framework (Simmons et al. 2006, 804).

The points made below about globalization are specific to political globalization. However, the processes and mechanisms are applicable to other dimensions of globalization and provide insight into how the world is going global.

Waves of liberalization tend to coincide.

Democratization and economic liberalization have mutually reinforcing effects. Democracies trade more than dictatorships. Mature democracies trade more than newer democracies. Democracies are more likely to remove capital controls (except in the Bretton Woods era). Not only do economic and political liberalization tend to rise and fall in tandem, but whichever moves first, the other follows (Eichengreen and Leblang 2006, 10–11). Positive and negative shocks to the system produce similar results: rise or decline, in each wave, political and economic.

BOX 7.11   Consider This: Arousing Liberalization Sentiments

Does exposure to other societies through media, travel, and education create the desire for more liberalization in the economy and polity? People see material affluence. They see others exercising rights that they do not have and read about governments that are more responsive and accountable than theirs. Does this lead to pressure for political and economic liberalization?

When a system remains stable, a decline or rise may continue indefinitely, pending a destabilizing shock to the system. The recent economic crisis saw an abrupt decline in trade. Democracy has experienced setbacks. Political and economic contractions in former Soviet societies are leading the reversals. Whether there will be significant reversals is not yet evident. So far, the evidence is that trade is increasing and that a new wave of democratic reform is beginning.

Other forms of globalization appear associated with these well-tracked forms. For example, increasing materialism, a cultural globalization effect, accompanies economic liberalization. People develop expectations of a more affluent lifestyle. Similarly, demands for rights and more accountable and democratic governments accompany economic and educational advances.

Stability varies across different forms of convergence.

Where social learning occurs, there is likely to be more stability of newly adopted policies. Where there is normative pressure for an adoption, the change may prove to be dysfunctional. It may not be a good fit with the society, or it may be that too many others have already adopted the solution. This happened with the East Asian development export model. In that case, the more societies that adopted the model, the more saturated the market became and the less rational the solution to adopt the model became, despite the pressures (Herkenrath et al. 2005, 369). Pressures for democratic reforms before prerequisite supports are in place may lead to reversals or failures of democracy.

Convergence among some countries may produce greater divergence with others.

Forms of regional convergence, such as the formation of the EU, result in divergence at the global level. While the countries within the region become more alike, they differentiate from countries in other regions (Herkenrath et al. 2005).

This occurs not only among adopters and non-adopters, but also within clusters of adopters whose pathways of change vary. The supply of democracy in sub-Saharan Africa and South Asia was very similar in 1980. Their patterns of development diverged in the mid-1980s as South Asia embarked on a very rapid path of democratization, and sub-Saharan Africa a much slower path. In 2002, they were in convergence once again (Simmons et al. 2006, 785).

BOX 7.12   Consider This: Dynamics of Neighborhood Effects

Neighborhood effects do not work through contagion as bacteria do. They work through social dynamics. What are the processes behind neighborhood effects that account for convergence? In what ways do neighbors interact that might require or influence some convergence? In what ways are they alike that might lead them to copy one another or respond similarly? Consider how each of the following might be related: trading partners, similar ethnicities, movement of people across borders, and similar physical environments.

Can you think of research methods that would allow you to investigate your ideas?

Increasing flows of information hasten and intensify globalization waves.

The sophistication, power, and accessibility of communication technologies, migration, and travel provide people with more opportunities to learn about what others are doing and initiate processes of convergence. This makes greater diffusion more likely and more rapid. There has been a rise in the number of media-transferring ideas across national borders. Media have become much more efficient in the amount of information they deliver and in their ability to target information to relevant audiences (Herkenrath et al. 2005, 374). Demonstration effects—seeing how innovations worked in other countries—had a much greater role during the contemporary wave of democratization than in the first two waves (Huntington 1993, 101).

Convergence patterns may result from similar responses to similar conditions and coordination of policy making.

Sometimes, societies are struck at the same time by the same shock or other phenomenon. They may respond similarly, forced into a particular path of action. Societies' similar internal characteristics may push them along similar paths to convergence. Sometimes, countries coordinate policy making. In the case of the economic crisis of 2007–2008, G20 nations met to coordinate domestic policies. They pledged to stimulate their economies, not "beggar thy neighbor," and contribute to international funds to mitigate the crisis in developing nations. Stimulus packages were enacted. Later, austerity measures were put in place as debt grew. Treaties are another common way for governments to coordinate policy. Human rights, the environment, and trade are all subject to treaties that coordinate policy and produce convergence.

Powerful nations or international organizations may coordinate (coerce) policy making, and epistemic communities (experts) may facilitate cooperation (Elkins and Simmons 2005, 35). This is how the green revolution in agriculture spread, although it was not equally suited to all countries and had more costs than officially recognized. By offering funds and advice for decentralization, political party development, and other policy choices, the United States and a number of other governments are facilitating convergence.

Neighbor effects are influential in determining the degree to which societies will move toward democracy.

What is the relationship between income and democratization? Research shows that countries need to achieve a threshold level in wealth before they democratize. There is also a level above which nearly all societies are democracies. In between, the relationships are not linear.

For example, the higher a country's GDP, the more stable it is. A 1% increase in annual growth will increase regime longevity by 8%. Despite this, political systems surrounded by ones that are very different than it will "expire three times as fast" as an identical polity surrounded by similar ones, regardless of income growth (Gates et al. 2006, 902).

The greater the difference between a country and its next-door neighbors, the more likely change is. Where a country's neighbors are very different from one another, some democratic and some autocratic, there are cross-pressures. The net effect of these pressures on a country is an average of them all. In a study that included every country from 1966 to 1972, it was found that neighboring countries tended to move toward or away from democracy, converging to a shared level of democracy (Brinks and Coppedge 2006).

BOX 7.13   Neighbor Effects

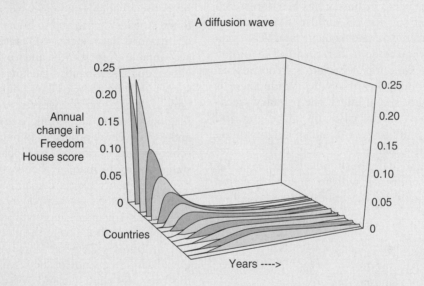

A diffusion wave

Annual change in Freedom House score

Countries

Years ---->

Source: Brinks & Coppedge, 2006.

Note: Simulation of impact of three democracies on 13 countries starting at FH = 2. Each country has 2 neighbors on each side. The diffusion coefficient is .229. For clarity of presentation, only countries with positive changes are included in the figure and the largest changes are truncated at 0.25.

Neighborhood effects are also influential in determining the degree to which societies may change.

Transitions to democracy are more likely the higher the global proportion of democracy is, but this does not negate regional effects (Gleditsch and Ward 2006, 925). Since 1815, the likelihood of any randomly chosen country being a democracy is 0.75 if its neighbors are democracies, but the probability drops to 0.14 if a majority of its neighbors are autocracies. However, the likelihood that an autocracy will be replaced by a democracy is much greater than the likelihood that a democracy will revert to authoritarianism (916).

Thus, neighbors exert significant influence on regime change (Brinks and Coppedge 2006), but the type of effect can differ in different cases. Social learning, mimicry, coercion, or any other of these may apply in specific cases. The neighborhood effect was also evident in data on regional variation in paths of liberalization (Simmons et al. 2006).

Patterns of change in South America during the last decades of the 20th century and the opening of the 21st may also offer anecdotal evidence of this neighborhood effect. The wave of democratization in the 1980s in South America has been followed by a wave toward the left, beginning with Venezuela and spreading through the formation of the Bolivarian Alliance for the Americas. The member states, although regional neighbors, are not contiguous or next door neighbors.

In this case, the spread of the Bolivarian Alliance, Venezuela's influence has been bolstered by the power of its oil industry. Cuba and Venezuela bartered oil and medical care. Venezuela forgave Nicaragua's debt in return for it joining the alliance. Honduras received a generous oil subsidy for coming into the fold. While there is clearly a neighborhood effect, the primary mechanisms involved in the cases of Nicaragua and Honduras appears to be a financial carrot, to get the benefits of alliance. According to the studies of neighbor and neighborhood effects, how far any of these countries will go in any direction will be mitigated by the combination of all of these forces.

Conversion patterns are caused by a variety of mechanisms and processes of diffusion.

The literature on policy diffusion is extensive. A concise definition of *diffusion* is "the process by which the prior adoption of a trait or practice in a population alters the probability of adoption for remaining non-adopters" (Strang, quoted in Elkins and Simmons 2005, 36).

A wave of diffusion may involve many different processes of diffusion (Elkins and Simmons 2005, 37). Determining which types are involved in any particular country requires case study analysis of each adoption within each wave. The most important lesson, though, is that some types, those that involve the most analysis in decision making, are much more likely to work better than simply mimicry or jumping on the bandwagon.

Summary

Some of the most dramatic effects of globalization are within states. Far from being sovereign within its own borders, the contemporary state is held to a set of global standards that identify a good state. The standards, at this point, reflect Western cultural traditions but are not anathema to most civilizational standards. They are likely to be increasingly glocalized and modified to accommodate more Eastern philosophical ideas, particularly regarding individuals' responsibilities to the collective.

Globalization has changed the nature of the relationships in the global field: the relationships of states to individuals and other elements of its society, to the global systems, and to humanity. The demands of citizenry have increased. States must be more accountable domestically and in the global arena. Global culture demands that states provide a greater supply of democracy; civil and human rights; autonomy and inclusion for women, indigenous groups, religious groups, and ethnic and other minorities; and social welfare programs to mitigate the effects of economic globalization. The global economy affects states' ability to manage their own economies, and the global polity exerts demands on them as good global citizens. States that do not live up to their obligations are increasingly subject to interference, sanction, and rebuke from the global community.

How states will emerge from this current phase of globalization depends on how well they respond to the pressures and demands of their society, their internal environments, and the global systems. It is a time of challenge, but also of opportunity.

Questions, Investigations, and Resources

Questions

1. Debate: Would you sacrifice elements of democracy for economic well-being or more economic equality?

2. Evaluate the concept of universal human values or universal human rights. Are there such things? If so, what is their foundation, and what are they? Are they constant or have they evolved—and will they continue to evolve?

3. What challenges do you think are the most pressing for states to address? Can meeting the challenges in one area help meet challenges in another?

4. What are the three things that states could do that would most strengthen their ability to manage a globalizing world?

   • What do you think states should do that would have the greatest impact on the quality of life for its citizens?

5. Is it likely that most people in China will demand more democracy as they get wealthier?

   • What about people in Russia and other countries that were part of the Soviet Union or Communist bloc?

6. What factors do you think are most likely to make decentralization work? Remember, there are a number of objectives: making domestic governance more democratic, stabilizing conflict-prone countries, development, diffusing innovative policies and programs, and so on.

   Consider both devolution and de-concentration aspects of decentralization.

Investigations

1. Investigate the Freedom House Reports and find five countries that are rated free and five not free.

   a. For those countries rated free, are there any variables in which they do not receive a score of 1 (meaning free)? If so, what are they?

   b. For those countries that are not free, what are the areas in which they score most highly?

   c. Is there any pattern as to the variables on which countries have the most difficulty implementing freedom?

2. The World Values Survey is an excellent source of data concerning people's attitudes toward governments in general and their government in particular. Using the most recent database, investigate the relationship between people's attitudes toward their government, such as confidence in institutions of government and demographic factors such as education and age.

   a. Select a sample. You may look at one country, a cluster, of countries or the entire sample.

   b. Create five hypotheses using the question index and the variables age, sex of respondent, education, employment status, race, and religious practice.

c. Test your hypotheses with a cross-tab analysis.

d. Compare two or more countries or clusters with respect to these hypotheses. Do the results hold up across countries? How might you account for any differences? (How would you test these?)

3. Where does the United States fall in Transparency International's Corruption Index? What dimensions of corruption pull down the U.S. scores?

4. Transparency International has an interactive corruption barometer that allows you to investigate each of the corruption indices. You can page through the booklet that summarizes their results.
   Has corruption increased or decreased since 2006?

   a. How well do the public's perceptions align with the opinions of experts?

   b. What areas of public life seem to have the most corruption?

   c. Whom do people trust the most?

   d. Choose one country and discuss their corruption results in detail.

   e. What would you like to see done if you were a citizen of that country?

5. Transparency International also collects data in a number of thematic areas such as health care, climate governance, and education, among others. These can be found on their global priorities page. Choose one of the areas from their global priorities page. If you click on that topic, you will find booklets detailing their program overview in that area.

   a. What is Transparency International doing in the area?

   b. How successful have their efforts been?

   c. Do you think that there are other things that may be done?

Resources

Freedom House http://www.freedomhouse.org

Ranking of all countries on variables related to freedom. A total score is given along with sub-scores for civil liberties and political rights.

Quota Project: Global Database of Quotas for Women http://www.quotaproject.org

Transparency International http://transparency.org

Transparency International Global Corruption Barometer 2010 http://transparency.org/policy_research/surveys_indices/gcb/2010

World Bank Worldwide Governance Indicators http://info.worldbank.org/governance/wgi/mc_countries.asp

Interactive database allows you to produce world maps for each measure, investigate measures by region, or obtain detailed country data reports.

World Values Survey: http://www.worldvaluessurvey.org

World Justice Project http://www.worldjusticeproject.org

A rule-of-law index that measures how well countries conform to the rule of law in practice. There are eight dimensions broken into 52 factors: Limited Government Powers, Absence of Corruption, Fundamental Rights, Open Government, Effective Regulatory Enforcement, Effective Civil Justice, Effective Criminal Justice, Informal Justice. The 2011 Index included 66 countries and jurisdictions. You can obtain detailed country reports as well as the full report.

8

Trends and Transitions in Democracy

Objectives

This chapter will help you

- identify global waves of democracy;
- understand the difference between procedural and substantive dimensions of democracy;
- assess the supply of democracy according to the greater demands on democracy;
- understand how neighborhood factors affect the diffusion of democracy;

- assess the progress toward democracy in various regions of the world;
- evaluate the fragility of governments in transition; and
- understand the problems and prospects of democracy in regions of the developing world and ways that democracy can be thwarted in established democracies.

Democracy is not a static system. It is not the case that a society is or is not a democracy. Societies may have more or less democratic features. Some may have elections—procedural democracy—but do not give people the civil liberties to participate meaningfully in governance. They do not have a substantive democracy. In some places, people want more democracy—the supply does not meet the demand. Either way, the moves the world is making toward democracy may be the most important achievement, thus far, of globalization.

"The one thing that most clearly distinguishes the Globalization Era is that, for the first time in human history, the world has become a predominantly democratic one" (Marshall and Cole, 2009, 12)—at least in a formal sense.

Box 8.1 A Closer Look: 2011, A Banner Year for Democracy...or Not?

Passion for democracy lit the world in January 2011. Beginning with a referendum in Sudan, the grip of authoritarian regimes in Arab nations was loosened. On January 11, 2011, the primarily black-African southern region of Sudan began voting to decide if they would give birth to a new country or remain united with the primarily Arab north. The referendum took a week and it was near unanimous: freedom for South Sudan.

People were jubilant. Children came to bear witness and taste the flavor of democracy. Church choirs sang. Celebration, dancing, and music testified to people's joy.

(Continued)

(Continued)

After waiting in long lines, these Guatemalan women proudly display proof of their vote.

Freedom for South Sudan followed decades of struggle for independence marked by oppressive governments and genocidal wars, much like those ongoing in Darfur in western Sudan. Despite independence, violent conflicts between Sudan and South Sudan continue. Many are over the oil located in South Sudan, which was the major source of wealth for Sudan. There is also conflict over boundaries. Ethnic rebels conflict with governments within both Sudan and South Sudan. Each set of rebels is supported, at least allegedly, by the other's government.

In the Arab world, January protests bled into the Arab Spring. Dissidents wrested power from dictators across the Arab League nations. The wave of democratic protests had been swelling for decades, and active planning of protest was underway online and in secret for months. The leaders of the "April 6" youth movement in Egypt and "Progressive Youth" movement in Tunisia had been collaborating and actively organizing strikes in their respective countries since 2008. But one man's death brought the plans to life. January 14 ended Zine El Abidine Ben Ali's dictatorial rule in Tunisia. Mubarak fell in Egypt within a month.

In Burma (Myanmar), democratic reforms that led to the release of Aung San Suu Kyi in November 2010 continued as more political prisoners were freed and promises of civil liberties, worker rights, and free elections—that had been suspended for half a century—were extended. In Guatemala (above), people queued for hours despite at least 35 people being killed in pre-election violence.

Yet, overall, the supply of democracy in the world diminished in 2011.

2011: A New Democratic Wave?

Whether 2011 turns out to be the beginning of a new wave of democracy or a swell in the wave that swept through Eastern Europe after the fall of the Iron Curtain, it was a momentous year. Beginning with the independence referendum of South Sudan in January and continuing as dictators fell from power and kings held new parliamentary elections in the Arab League countries, democracy was in the headlines. A peaceful transfer of power in Congo and the release of political prisoners in Burma closed a remarkable year of monumental change. The demand for democracy is intensifying within countries that are among the most repressive in the world.

Transitions to democracy are exciting, but they are also extremely fragile. Despite the momentum of democratic gains, the supply of democracy diminished in some countries. By one index, the Economist Intelligence Unit Index of Democracy, democracy declined in most regions of the world that year.

Democracy is hard work both in preparing a country for freedom and maintaining it after the revolutions, referendums, and reforms are over. In many countries, efforts of domestic and global non-governmental organizations (NGOs) and international governmental organizations are prominent among the forces stabilizing democracy. Normative requirements for rule of law, transparency, accountability, citizen participation, and multiparty elections supported by institutions such as an independent judiciary, political parties, and media able to protect civil and human rights are key to political stability and development. The poorest nations have felt the effects of the global recession most dearly. Their plight, along with widespread unemployment and large populations of young adults with no clear route to prosperity, may ignite democratic revolutions more broadly. But if democracy fails at fulfilling expectations, democratic waves may reverse. Since the global recession, democracy overall has stalled. Even well-established democracies experience setbacks in tough economic times—good reason not to take democracy for granted.

BOX 8.2 A Closer Look: Tahrir Square

Tens of thousands protested and camped for weeks to topple the Mubarak regime in Egypt. This was taken on the day Mubarak resigned.

Like other forms of globalization, democratic reform efforts change the landscape over which they flow and are changed by it. Procedural and civil rights, decentralization, accountability, and transparency function differently depending on the local contexts. Establishing the rule of law and institutions to uphold it and stabilizing economies and spreading their benefits after decades or centuries of dictators and rent seekers is an arduous process. Democracy takes on a different character as it is cultivated in different regions. It travels different trajectories and encounters different obstacles. Nevertheless, the global demand for greater democratization is clear.

Diffusion of Democratic Ideals

Arguably, the most pronounced achievement of political globalization is the diffusion of democracy and the increasing number of stable democratic regimes. For the time being, no system of governance has close to the broad appeal. No system of values can contend for legitimacy with democratic ideals.[1] Internal and external pressure for greater liberalization, both within and among states, has become a defining characteristic of contemporary globalization.

As countries achieved independence following WWII, most adopted democratic constitutions and structures. Explicit mention of democracy as a value appears in only 42.9% of constitutions before 1948, but it is specified in 70% of the constitutions drafted from 1949 to 1957, 78.5% of those written from 1958 to 1965, and 93.1% of those written from 1967 to 1975 (van Maarseveen and van der Tang 1978, 197). Since then, particularly in the surge of constitution writing after 1989, constitutionalism has had a distinctively democratic flavor.

Three types of constitutions have developed over time, differentiated by the locus of authority.

Absolutist constitutions "reflect the absolute power of those who govern," such as the constitution of the former Soviet Union and Warsaw Pact countries. Very few other governments adopted this form. The second type, *legislative supremacy constitutions*, grant authority to legislate to the parliament or congress. The legislature has supreme authority and is not subject to judicial review. Britain, New Zealand, and former French republics are examples of these. The third type, *higher law constitutions*, mandate that the institutions of the state derive their authority exclusively from the written constitution and that people have ultimate power by way of elections or referenda. Public authority is only legitimate insofar as it conforms to the constitution, a charter of rights, and has a method of protecting those rights. A process for amending the constitution must be provided. The higher law constitutions are now the only type "*considered to be 'good' constitutions*" (Sweet 2008, 221–222 emphasis original).

A charter or bill that delineates the rights of individuals is also normative. One hundred eighty-three of 194 countries have a catalogue of rights. Of 106 constitutions written since 1985, all showcase a catalogue of rights that includes the traditional civil and political rights, as well as social or positive rights (Sweet 2008, 233). Unfortunately, many states fail to live up to the obligations that they declare in their constitutions. Without adequate political infrastructure or sufficient pressure to fulfil them, the documents remain inert. However, constitutions provide a legal framework that sets the stage for further globalization processes to have meaningful impact. Constitutions are not just the result of political globalization. In the latter part of the 20th century, they became tools of political globalization used by citizens and international organizations as measuring rods for state legitimacy.

Establishing democracy in a constitution does not make it normative in practice (Halliday 2009, 269). The trend toward democracy continues, although unevenly. Unfortunately, many democracies fail and devolve to anocracies—a hybrid of democratic and autocratic tendencies—or full-blown autocracies. Waves of democracy grow as countries reform and recede if the reforms do not stabilize. Different regions have had different paths to liberalism and arrived at different styles of democracy dependent on their cultural—including religious—heritage.

BOX 8.3   Global Trends in Governance, 1946–2010

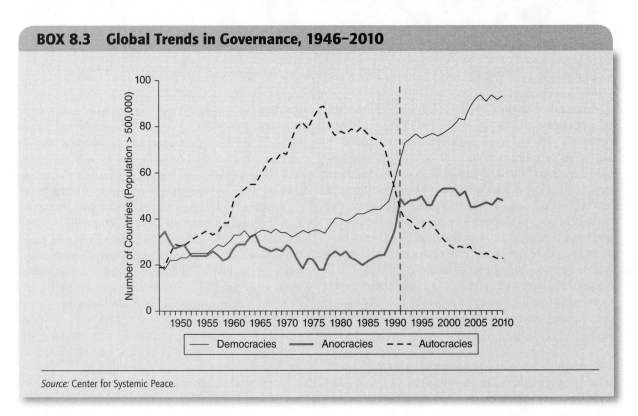

Source: Center for Systemic Peace.

Huntington (1993) first conceptualized waves of democracy. He defined democracy as a political system in which the "most powerful collective decision makers are selected through fair, honest, and periodic elections in which candidates freely compete for votes and in which virtually all the adult population is eligible to vote" (6). This definition is minimal, focusing on democratic procedure, but implies a number of substantive political freedoms: If a group is denied the vote, it is undemocratic; if elected leaders are mere figureheads and not the real power wielders, it is undemocratic; if it is too difficult to mount opposition in elections by being denied access to media and assembly, it is undemocratic (6).

With this definition as a measuring rod, Huntington identified three waves of democratization. No democracies existed before 1760. The first wave of democratic practice swept over North America and Europe from 1828 to 1926 (with 33 democracies at the end of the wave). Although these democratic revolutions took place in the late 18th century, establishing democratic institutions and suffrage for over 50% of Caucasian males took longer (Huntington 1993, 16). For women and minorities, it has been considerably longer.

Democracy receded leading up to WWII, with some nations turning toward totalitarianism. The second wave, from 1943 to 1962, brought the number of democracies to 52. Beginning in the very late 1950s, the democratic wave receded and authoritarian regimes arose, particularly in Latin America and Africa. The third wave began in 1974 and brought the total to 65 by 1990 (Huntington 1993, 18). This wave swept through Latin America, Asia, Eastern Europe, and Africa. Although some countries have since experienced reversals, a reverse wave has not occurred. This is not to say that every new democracy will succeed. Many do not. The overall trend since the late 1970s has been upward, without a significant downward spiral. The most recent wave of democracy has been global. It "moved across southern Europe, swept through Latin America, moved on to Asia and decimated dictatorship in the Soviet bloc" (25). The revolutions and protests of Arab nations extended this wave. The outcome of Arab Spring is not yet clear.

As with other forms of globalization, the contemporary period stands out from other periods in the intensity of waves and in their continued rise beyond the point where a receding wave would be expected.

The wave of democracy in terms of numbers of democratic countries has continued through into the 21st century.

The measures of democratization used by Freedom House, a watchdog NGO, include a variety of political rights and civil liberties. Political rights are those related to the electoral process, including factors like the quality of elections, multiparty elections, and official corruption. Many of these are related to procedural democracy. Civil liberties are freedoms granted people such as freedoms of speech, assembly and religion. Overall, the Freedom House index is one of the most stringent measures of the quality of democracy. Using their measure to compare the supply of democracy is reliable and valid.

Freedom House has documented a wave of freedom extending from 1972 to 2012, during which the number of free countries increased from 44 to 90—an increase from 29% to 46% of the world's countries.[2] By 2012, 43% of the world's population was living in a free country (Puddington 2013, 4).

The overall trend hides the fact that from 2005 through 2012, the global supply of freedom declined. 2012 was the seventh year where the overall declines in freedom exceeded the gains (Puddington 2013, 4). In calculating the global supply, Freedom House determines how many countries made overall advances in freedoms and how many became more restrictive. In each of these years, more counties declined in procedural rights or civil liberties than advanced, although each year there was movement in both directions.

The number of electoral democracies in the world rose from 69 out of 167 countries in 1989, to 117 out of 195 countries in 2012, continuing the third wave. The surge immediately after the Cold War brought the number of democracies to 113. Since then, it rose as high as 123 in 2005 and 2006 (Puddington 2013, 29). At 117, democracies representing 60% of countries, the number and percentage of electoral democracies, well exceed their 1990 levels, although both are below in the 2005 and 2006 peak. This vacillation does not yet constitute a significant reverse wave.

The Changing Meanings of Democracy

Globalization effects on democracy extend beyond the creation of new democracies. Change and reforms within established democracies are part of contemporary globalization. During the first century of multiparty democracy, from about 1880 to 1980, there were few changes in electoral systems. Now, global pressures for greater democratization and new forms of democracy have generated dramatic reforms in the electoral process in both new and established democracies (Reynolds 2006, 10).

Since the mid-1960s, as global civil and human rights movements intensified, even well-established democracies have been accused of having a democratic deficit, resulting in demands for

- greater inclusion and accommodation of minorities;
- greater accountability of individual representatives;
- increases in party and system stability;
- revision of electoral systems to correct anomalies;
- full inclusion in a variety of democratic processes, not just elections;
- elimination of privilege (except age and citizenship for voting and office holding) in determining inclusion; and
- more direct processes of participation to complement representation.

Each of these expands the meaning of democracy to include a more active and engaged public in all aspects of civic life, in keeping with liberal trends for economic, civil, and political rights.

Full Inclusion

Pressure for inclusion of the full society in democratic processes is one of the most important demands. Early versions of democracy did not grant the citizenry full participation. Before being amended, the U.S. Constitution allowed individual states to limit participation to landed males. Other national constitutions limited suffrage to males, to specific religious groups, to ethnic groups, or property owners, among other criteria. Universal suffrage was not achieved on a significant scale until the 1920s (Doorenspleet 2000).

Economic independence was one of the most common considerations as a requisite quality to the practice of democratic deliberation. In some countries, this resulted in females or other minorities getting the vote earlier than non-propertied males. Over the centuries, as rights to participate expanded, states found strategic methods to restrict suffrage, from disenfranchising criminals to strategically locating polling places, constructing difficult to understand ballots, and stringent voter qualifications. Where power, privilege, and other factors of social location limit participation, democratic process may be used for social control rather than liberation. That the United States needed the Voting Rights Act of 1965, and that it encountered fierce opposition when it was last renewed in 2006, demonstrates the extent to which full participation in democracy had been thwarted.

The contemporary ideal of democracy, emerging in the late 20th century, is different from older versions in that participation at any level is not constricted by prerequisites. "It makes participation (and its particular expressions in deliberation, legislation, and governance) a right without regard to current capacity, and thus it eliminates altogether the idea of any sort of privileged group of citizens" (Appadurai 2007, 32). Contemporary demands for inclusion, although not necessarily suffrage, extend beyond citizens to everyone living in the country, whether they are permanent residents, temporary immigrants, or nations within nations.

Full inclusion makes the democratic process less predictable. The Bush administration learned this with Hamas victories in Palestinian elections. In an inclusive democracy, elections cannot be predicted as easily as when participation is limited to certain groups. In the Arab states experiencing protests for democracy in 2011, victors were unpredictable. In some countries, such as Libya, there are not political parties or an organized opposition. Nearly every institution was destroyed during Qaddafi's regime, especially political ones. In Egypt, institutions are stronger, but many opposition parties were driven underground. Aside from the religious, whether or not other groups can organize sufficiently well and quickly enough to mount viable political parties capable of competing in elections or representing a constituency effectively remains questionable. Without competitive parties, authoritarianism is a danger. Equipping these countries for full democracy will be an extensive process.

BOX 8.4   A Closer Look: Mapping Freedom From 1980 to 2012

1980

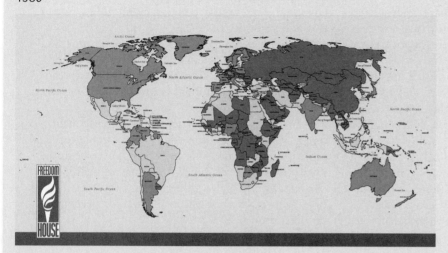

2010

Survey Findings

Freedom Status	Country Breakdown	Population Breakdown
FREE	87 (45%)	3,016,566,100 (43%)
PRRTLY FREE	60 (31%)	1,497,442,500 (22%)
NOT FREE	48 (24%)	2,453,231,500 (35%)
TOTAL	195	6,967,240,100

Source: Freedom House.

Direct Participation

Not only do global norms promote full inclusion, but people's definition of participation in democracy is expanding beyond representation. Social movement literature differentiates old from new social movements. "'New' social movements are those that sprang from the student revolutions of 1968 and focused on human rights, gender, the environment and peace . . . a demand for radical democracy" (Kaldor 2003, 84). As rationality crises develop, governments seem less in control of their economies, and distrust in government grows. Distrust exceeds people's confidence in government.[3] In this circumstance, radical democracy expresses people's dissatisfaction with representative democracy.

Radical democracy advocates favor direct and participatory democracy, in which people assume much more active roles.

Decentralization, discussed in Chapter Seven, and referenda are tools that allow people to express their views outside of the traditional representative party structure. Increasingly, people are turning to referenda, to at least make their voice heard, if not create binding laws. In the United States, referendum (*proposition* or *plebiscite* are other terms used) frenzy during the last few decades, for better or worse, stunned a public amnesiac with respect to their capacity to govern. Proposition 13, passed in California in 1978, cut property taxes by more than half. It set off a tax revolt that spread across the country. Referenda in other states on issues as diverse as education, assisted suicide, gay marriage, medical marijuana, and the decriminalization of marijuana followed.

Few countries have national referenda, although more are considering instituting them. In Germany, referenda in all states and municipal governments assert popular sentiment. Eighty percent of Germans want to institutionalize referenda at a national level. The Swiss use national referenda the most. They have voted on hundreds of issues, and, according to one expert, taxes are lower and productivity higher as a result ("Direct Democracy 2008," 60). Whether or not these forms of direct democratic rule are wise, they change democracy. [The Swiss also voted to ban the construction of more minarets, lest it ruin the Swiss character of their landscape ("Swiss Minaret Ban" 2009).]

The trend toward greater and more direct participation is evident in the movement toward decentralization, intended to make government more responsive and accountable by bringing decision making to local areas or allowing for public hearings at local levels. Decentralization can be an asset in state and nation building by integrating rural areas into the state apparatus.

Monitory Democracy

A *monitory* is a letter warning that something is wrong, as well as recommendations for correcting it. Democracy is being revitalized by the hundreds of watchdog institutions created since WWII that monitor the use and abuse of power (Keane 2009b). Representative democracy changed the nature of governance, subjecting the power of the aristocracy to scrutiny. Monitory democracy changes representative democracy, humbling power through scrutiny.

Applying democratic procedures to groups and organizations other than states can support representative democracy. The culture of voting is spreading into many institutional contexts. "One person, one vote" is giving way to "one person, many interests, many votes." By participating in many institutions, people vote often—for officers, platforms, lobbying, and so on. This gives people a voice in the institutions that scrutinize, monitor, influence, and participate directly in governance. However, these organizations are not electoral, party, or parliamentary institutions.

The pressure to reduce corruption and abuse of power is bringing more actors and processes into decision making (Keane, 2009c). These changes are captured in public discourse and reform movements. The language of democracy has many new terms, some of which are *high energy*, *stakeholders*, *communicative democracy*, and *deliberative democracy*. The changes are not only in the richer countries. Innovations in matters of handling, controlling, and restraining power come from many parts of the world. These include

- "participatory budgeting" from Brazil;
- "integrity bodies" that monitor behavior of police and prosecute them for corruption and wrongdoing come from Australia;
- "constitutional safaris" that examine constitutions around world and come from South Africa;
- "satyagraha" or non-violent resistance, from India;
- "talkaoke," or live-on-Internet filming of events of deliberation, originally from the United Kingdom; and
- "citizens' juries," "railway courts," "public interest litigation," "bioregional assembles," "public memorials," "teach ins," "citizens assemblies," and "global associations of parliamentarians." (Keane 2009b)

Each attempt to expand the practice of democracy relates to increasing the autonomy and rights of individuals as members of humanity; they recognize the obligation of the state to take on the responsibility of making proclaimed rights actual rights. Accountability, transparency, and autonomy are all values characteristic of emerging global cultural norms.

Case Study: Deliberative Democracy in China

Deliberation is a form of participation in civic life. The assumption is that people can govern themselves, arriving at solutions to important public questions when they are informed and have the opportunity to understand all sides of the issue. A number of NGOs, such as the National Issues Forum Institute, provide materials and training in deliberation so that communities may practice deliberative democracy. While some people argue that deliberative democracy is an advanced form of democracy, it is very much like the best town meetings of direct democracy as practiced in colonial New England or the villages of southern Africa.

China has instituted two democratic innovations, public consultations and deliberative polling. While they did not invent these techniques, they are one way that China is developing Chinese-style democracy. Since the mid-1990s, the Chinese have held public consultations in local areas. Village meetings to deliberate and decide important local issues are regular practice in many areas. Public deliberations started in villages and have diffused to cities, townships, governmental organizations, schools, and businesses, all the way to the national level (Fishkin et al. 2010, 436). Some laws in China, such as the 1997 "Law on Price," demand public consultation on the price of public goods and the 2000 "Law on Legislature" requires public consultation before passing any law or regulation (Fishkin et al. 2010, 436).

Public hearings everywhere tend to suffer from the same maladies. They are often unrepresentative and dominated by those with the most direct interest in the issues. Public knowledge about the issue may be limited and shaped by the information provided by the most interested parties. There is usually too little time for discussion. Although public hearings are well intentioned, they often do not produce democratic results. The larger the forum, the less representative and less deliberative the consultation is likely to be. Public hearings often reinforce the position of the most interested or powerful parties to the debate, rather than being an exercise in democracy. This may even lessen people's trust in government or democracy.

Deliberative polling tries to correct this deficit. China held four deliberative polls under the direction of the Center for Deliberative Democracy (formerly the Center for Deliberative Polling). Deliberative polling uses random sampling to select a pool of citizens to represent the public at large. This eliminates self-selection by the most interested parties who are typically the majority at public hearings. Participants are provided background information, and expert panels educate them about the pros and cons of the issues. Participants are given ample time to engage in deliberation. Deliberative polling applies the methodology of the social sciences to democratic decision making, bringing the legitimacy of science into democratic function. This method of soliciting public opinion overcomes some of the problems of traditional public hearings. Deliberative polling events are evaluated along these criteria:

- Representation of the sample
- Magnitude of attitude change
- Observed quality of the deliberation, such as absence of undue influence by people with more social status or other personal quality, absence of polarization, the public spiritedness of the discussion, the magnitude of learning, and degree to which attitude changes resulted from learning
- Influence of the deliberation on public policy (Fishkin et al. 2010, 437)

The results are promising. Evaluation of a county-wide process to select the top 10 projects from dozens of potential projects in China was judged successful by the measures listed above. For some of these criteria, China may be an exceptional case. Being selected in an authoritarian country may be more conducive to participating than in a country where voluntary participation would be perceived as truly voluntary. In China, local party officials were given a lot of authority on these projects and were ready to move ahead quickly on the results of the polling.

(Continued)

Other factors, however, are not likely to be a result of China being a particular case. There was no observed influence of higher status participants, no polarization, and a keen interest in finding projects that would benefit the widest swath of the county. People did not look out for just their village. Learning influenced the process profoundly. Furthermore, local party officials were pleased that the process was educational for people. Whereas the officials thought people would choose projects that improved the appearance of the county, but added little value, people chose environmental and sewage treatment projects (Fishkin et al. 2010, 446).

From 1994 to 2002, 22 deliberative polling experiments were conducted in the United States, Britain, Australia, and Denmark (Fishkin 2003). Polls in Canada, Italy, Bulgaria, Hungary, Northern Ireland, Brazil, Greece, Poland, and trans-nationally in the EU have been added (Fishkin et al. 2010, 436). In August 2011, deliberative polling was conducted in South Korea on the question of the unification of Korea (Fishkin 2011). The reports available on the Center for Deliberative Democracy's website from these and other countries have similarly impressive results. (See http://cdd.stanford.edu/ for more information.)

The Question of Islam and Democracy

Whether or not democracy could flourish in Roman Catholic countries was doubted by many political observers. The centralized authority of the Roman Catholic pope was thought to be anathema to democracy. Similar arguments circulate today concerning the capacity of Islam to accommodate democracy. Majority-Muslim countries have had a difficult time with democracy, but many Muslim societies are democracies or are making the transition to democracy. There is ample evidence that democracy and Islam are not incompatible.

The influence of Islam on political life varies across countries and within different sects, as it does with other religions. Islam spread from the Middle East to Central Asia, through the subcontinent and onto the Malay Peninsula and then islands of Southeast Asia. In Southeast Asia, Muslim identities interact with "equally potent forms of ethnic identity" and have overlapping ties with non-Muslims (Bajunid 2001, 178). This is true in Central Asia and the former Soviet republics as well. During the period of Soviet rule, Islam was consistently under attack and removed from public life. Secular ethno-national identities emerged, along with "political and cultural elites firmly committed to such identities" (Khalid 2007, 2). Islam remains vitally important in these countries, but its place in the political realm is tempered by the value of secular states and ethnicity. The presence or absence of ethnic (or religious sectarian) strife may have more to do with democracy than religion per se.

Democracy is advancing in many Islamic countries. In 2007, there were eight democracies in Muslim countries (scoring +6 or more on the *Polity*[4] scale). Democracies in majority-Muslim countries, such as Indonesia, Senegal, Turkey, and Bangladesh dot the periphery of the Islamic region. Mali, a stable democracy since 1991, suffered serious setbacks after a rebel coup in March 2012 and subsequently prolonged warfare among rebel groups who took control of the north, Islamist extremists, and government troops bolstered by French forces and other African nations who had pledged to help (Nossiter 2012, 2013).

Malaysia and Nigeria have also made progress over the long term. Malaysia's 2008 election was remarkable for meaningful opposition party participation. The losses suffered by the governing National Front, losing its two thirds majority in Parliament and the government of five states, did not promote fraud or violence. Pakistan, hardly free, took steps toward democracy, forging a coalition civilian government after election results were unfavorable to the ruling Musharraf government. Pakistan rated partly free in 2012.

A survey of Muslims in four African countries (Mali, Nigeria, Tanzania, and Uganda) found that

BOX 8.5   A Closer Look: The Importance of Religious Authorities' Interpretations of Governmental Law in Democracy

BASE = 11,677 Weight [with split-ups]		United States	Turkey	Indonesia	Egypt	Morocco	Jordan	Iraq
Democracy: Religious authorities interpret the laws.	Not an essential characteristic of democracy	41.0%	21.5%	11.4%	2.8%	12.6%	13.3%	14.7%
	2	10.0%	8.9%	5.6%	0.7%	5.8%	2.3%	5.0%
	3	7.9%	7.7%	7.1%	1.7%	9.0%	1.7%	6.2%
	4	8.1%	6.2%	5.7%	3.1%	5.8%	1.0%	6.8%
	5	17.5%	13.5%	15.2%	9.3%	15.6%	6.5%	11.3%
	6	6.4%	7.8%	8.3%	7.3%	8.7%	6.9%	8.1%
	7	3.7%	10.5%	8.5%	9.1%	11.3%	8.1%	9.5%
	8	2.3%	8.6%	10.1%	11.0%	10.5%	9.2%	11.3%
	9	1.3%	4.8%	6.8%	7.1%	5.9%	7.1%	8.4%
	An essential characteristic of democracy	1.8%	10.7%	21.2%	48.0%	14.8%	43.8%	18.8%
	N	1,185 (100%)	1,279 (100%)	1,779 (100%)	2,976 (100%)	945 (100%)	1,049 (100%)	2,464 (100%)

The World Values Survey 2005–2008 round included 57 countries. This chart compares the responses of people in several majority-Muslim countries to the United States. The latter was chosen because it has a high degree of religious adherents, as do Muslim countries.

Source: World Values Survey (2005–2008).

they (71%) are about as likely as non-Muslims (76%) to agree that democracy is the best form of government. In keeping with global trends, attitudes favorable to democracy stress the importance of civil liberties, especially free speech, over the electoral process. Muslims differ from non-Muslims in valuing democracy more for social justice than for governing by the people (Afrobarometer 2002, 2–3). Critical in interpreting these findings, Muslims had significantly lower educational levels than other religious groups. Education in these surveys is more related

to attitudes about democracy than religion (6). This suggests that education is potentially a more important driver of attitudes about democracy in these countries than religion.

In their study of Afrobarometer data, McCauley and Gyimah-Boadi (2009) found that Muslims and Protestant Evangelicals place greater importance on religion, incorporate religion more into their lives, tend to have more trust, and have more interest in public affairs than other religious groups in these countries. However, there does not seem to be a difference in more or less support for democracy. None of the countries in the Afrobarometer surveys are members of the Arab League. However, Nigeria, Mali, and Senegal, majority-Muslim countries, are in the sample.

A Pew Global Attitudes Project (2012) study of six majority-Muslim countries indicates that majorities in Lebanon (84%), Turkey (71%), Egypt (67%), Tunisia (63%), and Jordon (61%) want democracy. These are increases from 2011 for Lebanon and Turkey, and declines in Egypt and Jordan. In Pakistan, it was only 42% in 2011 and 2012. Majorities in Pakistan, Egypt, and Jordan also think that laws should strictly follow the Qur'an. Many others think that laws should at least follow the values and principles of Islam. The incompatibility of Islam and democracy is an illusion, according to Sulami (2005). Distinguishing democracy as a system of governance that is supportive of religion, not antagonistic, and Islam as a religion not a system of governance is important to allowing for their compatibility. Seeds of democracy are present in Islam, and the contemporary rejection of democracy in some Islamic societies, he argues, is more related to the experience of colonization by Western democracies than to features of democracy itself. Among the elements of Islam that support democracy are the following:

- The critical approach to *shura*; Islam is against despotic rule
- Social justice; Islam legislated *zakah* (obligatory charity) one of its fundamental pillars, urges Muslims to pay *saddaqah* (voluntary charity) to the needy, to prevent a deep rift between the rich and the poor in the Muslim community
- The establishment of *bait al-mal* (the treasury) to finance the community's needs
- The electoral process ('Umar bin al-Khattab, the second Rightly Guided Caliph, set up the first electoral process in Muslim history in the 7th century to choose his successor)
- The concept of *al-Bay'ah* (pledge of allegiance) which is understood as a social contract between the ruler and the ruled
- The right of the people to criticize an unjust ruler; this stems from the doctrine of *al-'amr bil-ma'ruf wa al-nahi an al-munkar* (the duty of the believers to enjoin good and forbid evil). (Sulami 2005)

BOX 8.6   A Closer Look: Democracy in Majority-Muslim States

Region	Free	Partly Free	Not Free
Arab League	0	4	18
Sub-Saharan Africa	1 (Mali)	7	2
Asia	2 (Indonesia, Turkey)	4	1 (Iran)
Former Soviets	0	1 (Kyrgystan)	5

Source: Freedom House (2012).

Kuran (2012) pinpoints several elements of traditional Islamic law that inhibited the growth of democracy in the Middle East. As reviewed in Chapter Three, liberalization in Western Europe was related to the development of powerful commercial trading companies, unions, religious orders, and other organizations that could counter the power of the state. In brief, Islamic economic rules concerning inheritance, commercial partnerships, and so forth inhibited powerful economic interests and private organizations. This also prevented a strong civil society. There was no counter to the power of the state or mechanisms to prevent state corruption. These conditions no longer exist.

Nevertheless, democracy has been problematic in majority-Muslim societies, but is it any more difficult than in other countries? As evident in Box 8.6, the difficulty with democracy is primarily in the Arab League states and former Soviets.

majority-Muslim countries in sub-Saharan Africa and Asia have a much better rating than those in the Arab League or former USSR: 18% are rated free, 65% "partly free," and 18% "not free" (Freedom House 2012).

Vacillation occurs in majority-Muslim countries as it does in all countries in transitions. The 2001 figures are even closer to global figures. In 2001, 11 countries were rated "free." It is doubtful that Islam alone is holding these countries back politically.

Deficits of Democracy

No society is a perfect democracy. All experience some degree of democratic deficit. Democracy is difficult. As societies transition to democracy, most experience serious deficits in democracy until they establish and stabilize democratic institutions—political parties, electoral systems, a judiciary, governmental watchdog agencies, and so on. Established democracies may pull back on democracy depending on political, economic, or other factors.

A growing threat to democratic governance within and among nations is the increase in decision making by organizations and groups not directly accountable through elections. These include international civil society groups, and for-profit and not-for-profit enterprises, such as corporations and the global health industry. The impact of these actors on people's lives has increased because of their ability to act independently and the power they exercise on policy making and regulatory intergovernmental agencies and organizations. Because profits in the financial industry have soared back to pre-crisis levels before national economies and most individuals have recovered is a sign for many critics that there has not been any ground gained in the quest for responsible private decision making, at least not in the financial sector.

The global trend to expand governmental bureaucracy has resulted in many governmental functions being delegated to non-elected governmental and international governmental agencies. Governmental agencies, such as federal reserves, are self-regulating. This is another layer of governance that has no direct accountability to people. Delegating and exercising power responsibly in ways that are accountable merits careful consideration, particularly in light of the economic crisis that began in 2007. How to mandate transparency and accountability has been a major feature of economic reform efforts.

BOX 8.7   A Closer Look: The Right to Rule

In June 2009, President Manuel Zelaya of Honduras was overthrown in a military coup. Zelaya had been legitimately elected although he was trying to abolish term limits so that he could continue to rule. He was facing abuse of power and embezzlement charges. Despite his abuse of power, governments throughout the region and the globe condemned the coup and demanded Zelaya's return to power (Romero 2009). Fearing that recognizing the government would inspire coups in other countries, the Organization of American States (OAS) suspended Honduras until Zelaya was returned to power. It was the first time in its history that it invoked its "Democratic Charter."

Even after peaceful elections in November 2009, turmoil continued. The nation, the region, and the world became divided on the legitimacy of the newly elected president, Porfirio Lobo, as the election was held by the de facto government set up by the coup (Blair 2010, 32). Human rights groups reported extreme government violence against opposition during the year following the coup, and seven journalists were killed. Four judges who questioned the legality of Zelaya's "ouster" were fired (Lacey 2010). The truth and reconciliation commission of the OAS found both Zelaya and the coup leaders at fault. On the one hand, Zelaya defied Congress by planning to proceed with a referendum to remove the term limit of the presidency. On the other, there was not means to settle the conflict nor could Congress or courts authorize a coup ("Honduras Truth Commission" 2011).

Honduras was not readmitted to the OAS until 2011, after Zelaya was permitted to return to the country. In January 2013, Romeo Vasquez, who led the coup, and Xiomara Castro, Zelaya's wife, both announced that they will run in the November 2013 election.

Receding Waves

Democracies do not always survive. Most waves recede, although usually not to their starting point; most do not stabilize at their crest. Globalization plays a significant role in spreading democracy, in whether or not a wave of democracy recedes, and in the extent to which it recedes—globally or in a particular country. 2012 was the seventh consecutive year that the number of states rated "free" in the Freedom House rankings declined.

One factor is the role of shocks to the system. Destabilizing shocks may emanate from the global economy or polity, but a decline in one form of liberalization is likely to cause a decline in the other. The attacks on the World Trade Center in New York and the Pentagon outside Washington, DC, in 2001 motivated many countries to pull back on civil liberties. The recession of 2007 has been accompanied by declines in democracy, particularly in Eastern Europe and Russia.

The toppling of four Arab dictators (Tunisia, Egypt, Yemen, Libya) may shock the world into another crest, giving synergy to continuing protests for democracy in many parts of the world. But herein lies a danger. Inconsistent institutionalization of political liberalization is another cause of democratic decline. Institutional consistency has a significant effect on the stability of a government. How a head of state is recruited, institutional constraints on the head of state, and political participation of citizenry are dimensions on which consistency can be gauged. Where all three of these are in line with democratic functioning—open executive recruitment, constraints on the executive, and the maximum of political participation—a polity has the longest life span. As any one of these moves away from the ideal, it introduces an element of inconsistency and the durability of the regime decreases. Transitions are generally periods of inconsistency. It takes time to establish the institutions of democracy and vacillation should be expected.

Inconsistent regimes are less stable than either their autocratic or democratic alternatives. Autocracies have a median survival rate 1.7 times longer than inconsistent polities, and democracies have a survival rate 3.8 times more than inconsistent polities (Gates et al. 2006, 901). Elected heads tend to have their power constrained by law and other governmental institutions. Non-elected heads have little constraint and rule autocratically.

The least durable polity is one with an elected executive, extensive constraints, and little participation. On average, these governments last less than a year. Pressures on the regime to expand participation are extensive, and this polity generally moves toward more consistent democracy (Gates et al. 2006, 906). In cases where the ruler is not elected and there is no constraint, as in a dictatorship or kingdom, it is highly unstable when political participation is high. One of three changes is likely in these circumstances: The government might crack down and form a more consistent autocracy, pressures for reform might lead to more democracy, or there could be revolt and a new political order. Civil society typically has an important role in all polity types as a challenge to the authority of the regime or a source of further stability.

Level of development, growth, and political character of the "neighborhood" also influence regime stability. Wealthy countries tend to be stable, but countries with GDP of about US$1,000 (1995) below the mean are more stable than countries at the mean (Gates et al. 2006, 902). Growth is also important. An average growth rate of 1% increases survival by about 8% (906). Neighbors count, too. Governments surrounded by those with different polity types expire 3.5 times faster as those surrounded by similar regimes. Furthermore, inconsistent regimes tend to move "toward the nearest consistent ideal type" (906).

BOX 8.8   Consider This: Is It Democratic to Ban Anti-Democratic Political Parties?

In the Czech Republic, the Communist party membership received about 13% of the vote in the 2006 parliamentary elections. They are the third strongest party. Nevertheless, there is vehement public sentiment and a movement in the Senate to ban it. Is it democratic to ban a party, even if they advocate regime change? Unlike other former Warsaw Pact countries, where the Communist party moved to the left of center, the Czech party has remained firmly entrenched, faithful to Marxist doctrine, although it has renounced violence (Bilefsky and Krcmar, 2009).

Communist parties participate in politics in the United States, many European countries, Latin America, and Africa. Do you think it is democratic to ban a party from the democratic process? On what grounds? In what circumstances?

In May 2010, with elections approaching, young Czechs took to YouTube to advertise against the Communist party. The video encourages young viewers to be sure that their parents and grandparents do not vote for the communists. Although the party has not been banned, there is still strong sentiment that it has no place in a democracy for a party that advocates regime change and has not renounced its ties to Marxism (Bilefsky 2010a).

There is precedent for the banning of a political party. The Czech Republic banned the the far-right "Workers' Party" in February 2010. It was deemed xenophobic and anti-democratic. In Eastern Europe, fears that the financial crises will be used to scapegoat minorities and exacerbate the already rising hate crime rate drove this move (Bilefsky 2010b).

Where globalization effects push a society toward greater democratization, it is important to move simultaneously on all fronts. Consolidating institutions of newly independent states needs to become a priority. Irregularities create instability. Ironically, as democracy progresses, the expectations for democracy increase. Changes in expectations increase the likelihood of inconsistency, put a greater burden of proof on democracy, and make success more difficult. The same features of frail states that challenge human security also challenge democracy. They are major insurgencies, ethnic and communal violence, extreme poverty, severe inequality, chronic inflation, external debt, terrorism, and extensive state involvement in the economy (Huntington 1993, 254). Global actors can take lead roles in ameliorating the conditions that threaten democracy, slowing or mitigating its degradation.

Global support for democracy is necessary for its success. Support for the electoral process is important, but it is not enough. Global support for the development and strengthening of political parties, legislatures and judiciaries, professionalization of the armed forces, and promoting civil liberties such as freedom of speech, the media, and assembly help strengthen democracies. Stimulating and training civil society organizations in political dialog and participation in the political process are important. In the long run, consistent democracies are more stable than consistent autocracies. This bodes well for the continuing overall increase in democracies, despite periodic waves of decrease (Gates et al. 2006, 906).

Illiberal Democracy and Liberal Autocracy

Although they are often used interchangeably, political *liberalization* and *democratization* are independent phenomena. Elections constitute procedural democracy. This is distinct from free speech, free practice of religion, a free press, and freedom of political assembly—the civil liberties. Not all procedural democracies are liberal. This is one source of inconsistency.

BOX 8.9   Consider This: The Price of Order?

"It is a crucible full of explosives that nations watching from a comfortable distance have no idea how to handle. War itself is redefined when it is waged within countries rather than between them; when the environment—soil, water, scarce natural resources—become the spoils that cause neighbors to kill neighbors; when economic development fails to guarantee stability; and above all when ethnic enemies use the outbreak of fighting to settle scores that can stretch back for centuries." (Gibbs et al. 1994)

In 1994, Rwanda was emerging from one of the cruelest, deadliest genocides of the waning, bloody 20th century. Over 500,000 people were slaughtered, many hacked to death by 50 cent machetes imported from China.

(Continued)

(Continued)

Rivers ran red with the stink of decaying body parts. Skulls by the hundreds were displayed as grim reminders of the inhumanity suffered but not survived.

Paul Kagame, in exile during the genocide, assumed the presidency afterward. He quickly restored order, making Rwanda "one of the safest, cleanest and least corrupt nations on the continent." There is health insurance, and computer and transportation infrastructure—at what price? Gettlemen (2010) reports that opposition members have been attacked and jailed, and the local BBC has been shut down. Talking "wrongly" about the genocide is a crime. There is no free press, no critical civil society. The homeless are swept up and sent to "the Island of No Return" for rehabilitation. "It is only you, the international community, who is showering them with praise," one dissenter lamented.

How do you weigh the price of order in cost to liberty?

Global norms concerning democracy extend beyond procedural democracy. A country may hold elections, but people may not be free. Two global movements, one for establishing procedural democracy and another for human rights and civil liberties, are both affecting change. In some countries, they have had success in the same place at roughly the same time, as in Western Europe and North America. Sometimes, one set of reforms proceeds without the other. In Madagascar, for example, people have moderate civil liberties, but there are not elections. In Morocco, there are parliamentary elections, some civil liberties, and a king.

Democratic reform since WWII has increasingly stressed establishing civil liberties and liberal institutions, not just elections (Bujaric 2008, 198, 202). In the new democracies of Eastern Europe, where constitutions and constitutional courts are established, some governments still abrogate power of other institutions without explanation. As recently as 2006–2007, constitutional courts in Hungary, Poland, and Slovenia have been ignored, disbanded, or in other ways been rendered impotent. Populism empowered through election has turned on unprotected minorities, and legislatures in some countries have rewritten law to control media and politicize civil service. Protection of minorities and challenges to the concentration of power seem difficult at best, if not impossible, when democracy is not tempered by liberty (194–195). As Hungary prepared to take its turn at holding the presidency of the EU, Prime Minister Orban came under attack for his populist politics and new laws restricting freedom of the press (Castle 2011). Ten countries from the former Soviet Union and its allies declined in media independence ratings from 2008 to 2009. Half of them are among the new EU members. There were declines in eight countries in "national democratic governance," as well as six declines in judicial independence, elections, and corruption (Walker 2010).

Even established liberal democracies violate civil liberties of people some of the time. Although the United States is counted among the freest societies, there has been criticism from many watchdog organizations due to the passage of the Patriot Act, questionable wiretapping, the treatment and retention of prisoners at Guantanamo Bay, and other activities related to the war on terrorism. More long-standing concerns about the status of minorities and other restrictions on the full benefits of living in a free society, such as health care, the expense of higher education, and capital punishment, also garner criticism. In Western Europe, the first half of the 20th century was marked by competitions among socialism, liberalism, and, most tragically, fascism and Nazism. In the latest wave of globalization, increasing migration to Europe has raised anti-immigration sentiment and harassment of immigrant communities. France's democracy score declined from 2009 to 2010 for its treatment of ethnic minorities and the expulsion of the Roma (Puddington 2011).

Democracy without liberty is dangerous. Russia is an electoral democracy, but people have few liberties. Freedom is secure in theory but not practice. Freedom House calls this inconsistent governmental form that has elements of democracy and elements of autocracy an *anocracy*. *Illiberal democracy* and *unconsolidated democracy* are other terms for these hybrids that may sway between democratic and autocratic practices. These unstable governmental forms are the most subject to reversals to autocracy and the most vulnerable to civic and ethnic conflict.

The rush to electoral democracy without the institutional infrastructure supporting liberty may lead to political and economic failures, as in Africa following decolonization. It was not until the 1990s that some African nations began to recover (Stigliz 2006, 40). Many still face uncertain futures. The states in transition following the dissolution of the Warsaw Pact and the Soviet Union face many of the same difficulties. They have a very mixed record on elections and civil liberties. Those in Eastern Europe are performing the most democratically, while those in Asia suffer under autocratic rulers. Democratic and liberal achievements remain very fragile.

BOX 8.10   Consider This: Afrobarometer Demand for Democracy,

Diffuse support: Democracy is preferable to other forms of government	70%
Specific support: Satisfaction with how democracy functions in [own] nation	49%
Commitment to democracy	50%
Demand for democracy (11 countries)	47%
Reject "one man" rule	79%
Reject "one party" rule	73%
Reject military rule	75%

Source: Afrobarometer (2013).

This 2008 Afrobarometer data is very mixed. How would you rate the status of supply and demand for democracy in these nations as a whole? What statistics are hopeful? Which are troubling? You can look at individual country data online at the Afrobarometer website (http://www.afrobarometer.org).

Civil liberties are an important component of democratic life. In the World Values Survey (2005–2008), 55.1% of people rated civil liberties in the top three categories of "essential to democracy," and 67.4% rated free and fair elections of this same importance. The Pew Global Attitudes Project reports that 5% more people believe that it is very important to live in a society where people can openly criticize the government (71%) than where there are honest two-party elections (66%). Without a knowledgeable public that has reliable and valid information, achieving genuinely free and fair elections is impossible, regardless of the sophistication of the established electoral process.

The relationship between electoral freedom and civil liberties in leading to a fully functioning democracy needs much more research. Whether the United States and other Western nations may be making a potentially tragic mistake by pursuing elections where there are not strong institutions of civil liberties needs to be fully investigated. Elections without civil liberties restrict the knowledge and information that people bring to the polls. Election of autocrats rather than democrats is as plausible, if not more so, because they already hold power. Elections in such contexts, even without outright fraud at the polls, can be easy to control through limiting the capacity of opposition to campaign, limiting information, or even using scare tactics. In Kazakhstan, President Nursultan Nazarbayev, who took office in 1991, was reelected again in 2011 with over 90% of the vote in an election boycotted by the opposition. One of his tactics has been to distort the upheavals in other former Soviet states, convincing people that stability is preferable than change or democracy. People have not shared in the oil wealth of Kazakhstan, but they are better off than before. New leaders, many people think, might have more motivation to steal. Current leaders already have more than they need ("Seven More Years" 2005).

There does seem to be a bright spot: the pattern of change in outcomes for regimes that have a mix of democratic and autocratic features—anocracies. Since 1992, there have been few failures of anocratic regimes—reversion to autocracy or onsets of war (Marshall and Cole 2009, 12). Three effects of cultural and political globalization seem responsible for this achievement:

- Notable increases in proactive global engagement (particularly, conflict mediation, election monitoring, accountability guarantees, NGO activity, direct investment, and foreign assistance)
- More educated and active publics with more competence and higher democratic expectations
- More professionalized armies that are less likely to intervene or support forceful repression (Marshall and Cole 2009, 12–13)

Overall, democracy is rated a "very good" or "fairly good" political system near universally, by over 90% of the respondents in World Values Surveys. Afrobarometer data, which covers 18 of the world's newest democracies, many of which are struggling, offers evidence that people continue to reject non-democratic forms of government and support democracy, even though satisfaction with and commitment to democracy are not robust (see "Consider This: Demand for Democracy," on the previous page). Experiments in democracy continue. They are demanded internally and increasingly by external actors, making them truly global events.

The Development of Democracy Around the World

The first wave of democracy started with the American and French Revolutions and established democracy in the United States and some Western and Northern Europe countries. Like other waves, it was not stable; military coups, dictators, and reversals of civil liberties plagued countries. Although all of the societies of the first wave are now considered stable democracies, even they experience democratic setbacks, such as reversals in civil liberties.

It is not possible here to review the state of democracy in every country, but there are several online sites where you can. Freedom House and the Center for Systemic Peace are two good sources. This chapter reviews the struggles with democracy of some of the world's regions. It is organized roughly by continent; however, in some cases, countries are grouped together because of a shared history or culture. For example, the section on "states in transition" discusses the states formerly part of the Soviet Union or Warsaw Pact. Some are in Eastern Europe and some in Western Asia. Arab League countries are discussed as a group. Some are in North Africa and some in Western Asia.

The Long Road to Democracy in Latin America

Democratization is firmly established in most of Latin America. Even though it was the first of the developing regions to consolidate democracy, the process took nearly a century. It was generally expected that Latin America would follow the development path of Western Europe and North America—the modernization path. It did not—nor has any other region. Latin America struggled with vacillation between elected governments and military coups. The narrative of how democracy ultimately unfolded illustrates the impact of globalizing forces—both in the waves of democratization and authoritarianism—as well as the mitigating forces of local characteristics and conditions.

Following WWII, South America seemed well on its way along the modernization path pioneered in the industrial north. Integration into the global economy using an import substitution model, financed with foreign capital, had generated wealth and growth. Economic development, according to the thought at the time, would lead to political development and democratization. Instead, in the 1970s, the most economically advanced South American nations, Brazil and Argentina, reversed course politically. Military dictatorships grabbed power from the civilian governments through coups. Chile and Uruguay soon followed, and by the middle of the 1970s, nearly all of South and Central America had succumbed to the wave of militarization (E. Silva 2004, 148). By the middle of the 1990s, they were democratic again, although in the recent decade, some have experienced democratic declines. Peru, which had declined, returned to democracy in 2000 (Marshall and Cole, 2009, 11).

South and Central America were buffeted by countervailing forces of economic and political globalization and Cold War strategizing. Democracy, authoritarianism, capitalism, and socialism, in every combination—democratically elected left-leaning governments, democratically elected right-leaning, authoritarian regimes of both the right and the left, military and civilian governments—each had a turn in Latin America. The overthrow or decline of any government through resignation, revolution, or coup was possible with backing of one of the superpowers or Cuba. Altogether, hundreds of thousands lost their lives, hundreds of thousands were imprisoned, and countries were impoverished by civil strife, violent conflict, and dictators. While the Cold War strategists capitalized on Latin American vacillation and facilitated it when in their interests, they did not create it.

The movement to democracy, then to authoritarianism, and then back to democracy occurred in clearly defined waves. How Latin America succumbed to authoritarian rule and how democracy was reestablished warrants a country-by-country analysis; however, there are common themes relevant to the discussion of the dynamics of globalization and local context.

Domestic variables on their own do not offer compelling explanations for democratization. Mainwaring and Pérez-Liñán (2003), for example, test a number of development variables, such as GNP, education, and percentage in agriculture, and find little to support a relationship between democracy and internal development factors.

- "Several comparatively wealthy countries have had long periods of authoritarian rule" (1050).

- "Some poor countries have sustained democracy for a considerable time since 1978" (1051).
- "Declining standards of living in the 1980s prompted fewer authoritarian involutions than any of Latin America's previous waves of democratization" (1051).
- Since 1977, Latin American democracies and semi-democracies have rarely reversed even at low levels of development, whereas in the period from 1945 to 1977, there were 21 reversals (1057).

A convincing pattern with respect to external variables, consistent with research on waves of economic and political liberalization, does emerge from the data.

The first phase of contemporary globalization begins in the 1960s. Democracy had been growing since WWII, with about two thirds of the countries achieving democratic or semi-democratic governments by the early 1960s (Pérez-Líñan 2006, 42). In economics, the international financial institutions promoted import substitution: favoring manufacturing for the domestic market over exports. By the 1960s, growth generated through the import substitution model had run its course in Latin America. Although it had generated rapid growth in the early phases, it could not be sustained. This contributed to the reversal of democracy. Stagnation and inflation threatened the economic order. More investment was needed to advance to higher levels of development through more sophisticated manufacturing. This required capital infusion.

BOX 8.11   Consider This: 1973 in Chile

"Many people didn't come back after September 11 [1973, the day of the coup].... They were arrested in their factories or in the streets, and herded like animals into detention centers... they heard the shooting at night and the cries of the people who were hit, how the ground was covered with blood and the smell was unbearable. Soldiers wearing boots jumped on people until they were nearly dead and then shot them" (quoted in Politzer 1989, 188). This scenario was repeated throughout Latin America through cycles of revolution and counter-revolutions.

At the same time, the cultural revolutions of the 1960s challenged the social order (Wallerstein 1995). Labor unions, social movements, civil society groups, and political parties with left-leaning ideas were gaining political muscle, threatening the interests of business, capital, and the propertied classes. Socialist leaning governments were elected or seized power in several societies. The upper classes viewed

these governments as threats to creating attractive business environments for foreign investment. The military doctrine of national security was used to call on military power to restore order and forcefully direct "material and human resources for national development" (E. Silva 2004, 148).

Democracies tumbled. Experiments in populism and socialism gave way to a wave of authoritarian military governments, of the right and of the left, some through violent coup, some through resignation. João Goulart, elected in Brazil on promises of land reform and nationalizing the oil industry, was overthrown in a military coup in 1964, probably with the support of the United States. Argentina had democratic reversals in 1966 and again in 1976, Bolivia in 1966, Peru in 1968, Ecuador in 1972. In 1970, Salvadore Allende was elected president in Chile and began nationalizing foreign companies. In 1973, he was assassinated and replaced by the brutal and criminal military government of Augusto Pinochet, supported by the United States. In 1973, President Juan Bordaberry dissolved the legislature and ceded control of the government in Uruguay to the military and became a figurehead for the authoritarianism of the military. This has been called "the lost decade" (Larrain 2000).

Military institutions historically are among the first to modernize in developing countries, globalizing along the lines of the rational models that informed all types of institutional structures. Legitimacy for the military depends on highly bureaucratized chains of command, well-defined roles, and loyalty. This form of militarized government is "bureaucratic authoritarianism" (O'Donnell, quoted in E. Silva 2004, 148). The bureaucratic governmental form lent the dictatorship an aura of legitimacy based on rationality, in contrast to dictatorships based on monarchy or personality.

BOX 8.12   A Closer Look: Waves of Democracy in Latin America

Decade	Political Model
1958–1964	First wave of democracy Elected civilian governments
1964–1976	Military authoritarianism
1974–early 1990s	Second wave of democracy Elected civilian governments
1990s	Consolidation of democracy Elected civilian governments

---

The military took a firm hand using brutal political repression. In most countries, the military was responsible for the first wave of neo-liberal economic policies instituted to attract capital investment by assuring investors of the safety of their capital (E. Silva 2004, 148). A new "booming consumer society" was built, benefitting only a few and increasing inequality. Democratic institutions were abolished, civil society groups were persecuted and disbanded, human rights were violated brutally and on a widespread basis, and many social sectors were excluded from the economy (Larrain 2000, 27).

Following a common pattern during the Cold War, governments favored socialism or liberal republicanism. Each type was capable of dictatorship and repression. Neo-liberal policies of economic growth globalized through activities of the World Bank and IMF in the 1980s, for the most part under the watch of the military regimes. South and Latin American countries, unlike many of their counterparts among the Asian nations, adopted these policies. Privatization of industries, abolishing protectionist policies, freeing flows of capital in and out of nations, and opening trade doors to imports promoted growth and economic inequality along with it. Consumerism, another globalizing trend, took hold as well.

The global mobilization of civil society groups was instrumental in maintaining active resistance to dictatorial rule, whether of the right or of the left. The cost in human life and well-being of these years of vacillation cannot be overemphasized. But even before the Cold War had ended, most Latin American countries were able to accomplish transitions in power and establish stable democracies. In 1977, there were only three democracies in Latin America: Colombia, Venezuela, and Costa Rica. By 1995, there were 18 (Pérez-Liñán 2006, 41–42).

Pérez-Linán (2006) cites two important globalization effects in addition to the extension of suffrage and elections of presidents and legislatures. First, the military was forced from its involvement in civilian affairs, and second, civil rights came to be respected (42). The global context brought about both of these changes. Both military dictatorships and unrestrained civilian dictators have little room to exercise power the contemporary global situation, resulting in more balanced polity throughout Latin America. Democracy has stabilized in Latin America, regardless of economic vacillation. When military rule is perceived as illegitimate, rule of law is strengthened.

Among the facilitating factors were

- The end of the Cold War facilitated negotiations among conflicting parties within Nicaragua and El Salvador.
- The OAS took up the protection of democracy and voted to suspend any members whose government was overthrown by force.
- Countries with military turmoil were to be cut off from U.S., European, and IMF aid.
- Military governments had lost legitimacy in the new climate of human rights due to their brutal violations of human rights (186).
- Only institutional means of correcting political conflicts are recognized as legitimate globally (Pèrez-Linán 2006, 189).
- Civil society groups have became increasingly vibrant combining protest across political sectors, becoming the new "moderating power" (Hochtetler, quoted in Pèrez-Linán 2006, 187).
- Privatization required to acquire global investment helped to speed freedom of the press and keep it free from presidential control. State-controlled newspapers have smaller budgets, and anyone can buy newsprint.
- Revolutions in communications technology stimulate free speech and a freer press.
- Competition among newspapers, television news, and other news sources has made them more attentive and diligent watchdogs.

- Popular protest was legitimized on the global scene.
- State repression had been delegitimized.

The second wave of democratization in Latin America was in most cases negotiated among military and democratic forces (P. Silva 2004, 161). Mainwaring and Pérez-Líñan (2005) analyzed the wave of democracy from 1978 to 1999, independently of the prior wave starting after WWII. In this study, the regional political environment of a country was measured by the number of democracies in the region (minus the country itself) and the priority of democratization in U.S. policy. They found that a favorable regional political environment was more significant than any other variable, including domestic GNP per capita and the international political environment, in explaining democratization (26). They find three causal mechanisms that may explain the strength of regional effects:

- International channels of dissemination regarding norms for political behavior such as the dissemination of anti-communist ideology, how people perceive their interests, or willingness to support coups or fight for human rights may be stronger at regional than cross-regional levels.
- Some international actors, such as the Catholic Church in Latin America, may operate in all or most of the countries in a region.
- External actors, such as the United States, can influence regime change in many ways from conspiracy against or overthrow of regimes to public statements that embolden some actors and give pause to others (29–30).

When democratic governments emerged, in the second wave, they continued privatization policies begun by the authoritarian regimes. This is the paradox that has continuously confronted transitions in power. Domestic change is limited by external environmental forces. In these cases, domestic economic policies dictated to military regimes by forces of economic globalization remained the vehicles for acquiring capital, aid, and other World Bank and IMF benefits, even after governmental transitions. "The social and political forces who fought against the military regimes . . . [resisted] accepting the neoliberal model as being the economic engine sustaining the democratic fabric for the coming years" (P. Silva 2004, 158). Nevertheless, they were stuck with it.

BOX 8.13   Consider This: Mexico's Stolen Election?

Summer 2012 brought tens of thousands of people—uniting the left and right of the political spectrum—to town squares in dozens of cities to protest election fraud by Mexico's Institutional Revolutionary Party (PRI).

PRI ruled Mexico for over half a decade, until 2000, gaining fame for corruption in elections and how it ran the government.

Did people voluntarily return PRI to power, perhaps given their dissatisfaction with economic uncertainty and uncontrollable crime? Or did PRI win only because of corrupt election tactics?

See if you can find newspaper or election monitor reports of the 2012 Mexican presidential election.

How likely is the democratic trend to continue? Thus far, most Latin American countries have maintained strong democracies, but democratic decline has been aggravated in some countries. Freedom House identifies a "beltway" of countries—Guyana, Venezuela, Colombia, Ecuador, Bolivia, and Paraguay—facing critical challenges to defining their political futures. If Mainwaring and Pérez-Líñan are correct in their finding that U.S. and OAS policies were effective in preventing democratic breakdown, the mechanics of this need to be studied in much more depth to try to prevent breakdown in these and other neighbors in the region.

Fukuyama (2008) warns that democracy in Latin America will remain fragile until it effectively solves its chronic problem of inequality. Inequality depresses educational levels of large segments of the population and makes for less competitive labor forces. It also makes way for populist candidates to be elected on the basis of social welfare programs for the poor. In Venezuela, Hugo Chavez was able to deliver on his promises, at least temporarily, using oil wealth. Other countries will not be able to emulate his strategy.

In 1992, Chavez rose to prominence leading a failed coup against the repressive government of Carlos Andres Perez. He was elected president of Venezuela in 1998 and managed to continue his controversial rule, surviving two elections, a failed coup, and recall referendums. Among the findings of a Freedom House study were that Chavez bought allies using petrodollars to export corruption (Corrales 2009, 75–76). Chavez formed the Bolivarian Alliance (ALBA) of populist regimes (Cuba, Bolivia, Ecuador, Nicaragua, and Honduras, under Zelaya) regimes that exercise excessive control and have undermined several democratic tenets. Freedom House scores Venezuela, Colombia, Ecuador, Bolivia, Paraguay, Guatemala, Honduras, and Nicaragua as only partly

free. While Latin America may no longer be vulnerable to military coup, the populist movements in the Bolivarian alliance can be viewed as a regression to strong man and personalistic rule.

In Central America and Mexico, where democracy is generally strong, democracy is threatened by crime, corruption, and the economic downturn of 2008 (Blair 2010, 31). There were relatively few coups or attempts from 1991 to 2011 (Center for Systemic Peace 2011). However, in Guyana, Honduras, Mexico, Belize, Peru, El Salvador, Nicaragua, and Guatemala, a majority of those polled by AmericasBarometer support military coup under conditions of high crime. Ecuador, Brazil, Bolivia, Dominican Republic, Venezuela, and Uruguay did not, but their support ranged from 36.3% to 47.4%, not an insignificant proportion (Pérez 2009, 2).

Brazil is the country that people are watching. Brazil has been democratic since 1980, without reversal. Brazil is among the fastest-growing economies and will be exerting more power, economic and otherwise, to shape the global scene. Brazil navigated the economic crisis smartly, helped by a diverse economy including a significant high tech sector and oil revenues.

Still, historic problems of Brazil's "permanently divided government" are not yet resolved (Ames, Baker, and Renno 2009, 8). While this problem is not confined to Brazil, it may make Brazil a poor model for Latin America. A plethora of parties, parties that have yet to grow deep roots and loyalties or offer tickets coordinated at local and national levels; national congressional candidates oriented toward local issues, patronage, and pork barrel; and the necessity of forming elaborate coalitions that may vary from the time of election to actual governance are all liabilities. In short, the number of "veto players," people with the capacity to stall or stop legislation in such systems, has the potential to mire Brazilian national politics in gridlock (11–12, 18). While the regime effectively represents diverse interests, bridges social cleavages, and maintains policy stability, it is less effective at policy innovation, priority setting, resource targeting, and coordinating conflicting objectives (Ames 2001, 228).

Party and electoral systems need reforming if innovative policies to fight endemic problems are to be passed and implemented without depending on patronage and pork barrel. How parties and elections are structured can impact the capacity of a government to govern well. Ames' (2001) study of democracy in Brazil provides insight into this issue and offers potential reforms. While open list proportional representation systems (where voters select candidates and the party gets the percentage of seats as votes its candidates win) work well in some contexts, they have not in Brazil (284). There has been a recent trend globally toward mixed electoral systems. Specific schemes vary in their details, but the model awards a proportion of the legislative seats through closed list balloting and some through open balloting within a district. This model has been adopted for purposes such as fighting corruption (Japan), increasing minority representation (New Zealand), reducing party fractionalization, and increasing stability (Italy) (284–288).

Reducing party numbers could be instigated from campaign finance reform or public financing of campaigns. One-round rather than two-round presidential elections might reduce the number of parties by absorbing some of the smaller parties, who do poorly in round one balloting into like-minded larger parties (Ames 2001, 284). Whatever innovations are tried, strengthening parties and party loyalty without negating the need to negotiate is key to better governance.

Whether or not other regions will have the success democratizing that Latin American has had and whether or not Latin America can stabilize its successes remains to be seen. One thing that has been learned is that there is not one path to democracy. How forces of globalization play out in regions depends not just on when and how they arrive there, but also on the terrain over which they flow. Perhaps new democratic models will emerge from Latin America. As their democratic experiments evolve, Latin models may prove to be more adaptable than northern models to the rest of the developing world.

Perspectives on Democracy in Asia and the Pacific

BOX 8.14   A Closer Look: Is Democracy Coming to Burma?

Since 1962, the fate of Burma (Myanmar) had been determined by coup (1962 and 1988) and military rule, at times thinly disguised as civilian rule—despite periods of violent protest. For decades, Burma resisted the sanctions of the international community and ASEAN, which it joined in 1997. A new constitution in 2008 and a fraudulent 2010 election seemed just more charade. U Thein Sein, the ruling party candidate, a former general who is reportedly the son of peasants, ascended to the presidency. Despite his having risen to power within one of the world's cruelest military regimes, Thein Sein was never personally associated with that cruelty. Surprisingly, moves toward democracy quickly followed his election, beginning with the release of political prisoners. Nobel Peace Prize–winner Aung San Suu Kyi, the opposition party leader who had been under house arrest or jailed for 15 of the last 20 years, was among them. Since then, more prisoners have been released; countries have begun to lift sanctions. Thein Sein continued with democratic reforms and programs to help the poor, including a minimum wage and universal health care. The motivation behind these sudden changes and how far the reforms will extend remains an open question at the time of this writing.

In many ways, Asian societies have been puzzling to the powers of the Western world. Many Asian societies have defied conventional wisdom and achieved economic and political successes on their own terms. Others remain mired in poverty and autocracy where civil and human rights have little meaning.

India, according to Keane (2009a), is a model for the democratic wave into the future. India demonstrated that democracy was viable in a poor country. It is also the world's largest democracy. India is the

> most compound, turbulent and exciting prototype. Defined by various older and newer means of publicly monitoring and contesting power and representing citizens' interests, at all levels, it reinforces the conviction . . . that democracy can be improved by changing people's perceptions, and by humbling those who exercise power over others, and that the seeds of greater public accountability can be planted everywhere, from the bedroom and the boardroom to the battlefield. (17)

South Korea is another counterpoint to Western democratic theory. South Korean leaders did exactly the opposite of the prescriptions of the international lending agencies, the IMF and World Bank. After a political coup in 1961, military leaders were determined to achieve economic and political liberalization on their own terms. They consolidated power, centralized decision making, curtailed political pluralism, and gave little regard for the participation of civil society (Schraeder 1995, 1163). It was a circuitous route, but it arrived at democracy.

Stabilizing and deepening democracy are the challenges for Southeast Asian countries. The relationships among the quality of democracy, its deepening, and democratic legitimacy are key. These relationships are not as simple as is commonly believed. Support for democracy depends on both long- and short-term factors. The "amount" of democracy delivered, the quality of governance, the expectations and demands of citizens, changes in values, and economic performance all influence democratic legitimacy. In East Asia, economic performance weighs in to support for democracy but people generally differentiate political and economic "goods." Where there are sufficient political goods, economic sluggishness is better tolerated (Chu, Huang, and Chang 2008, 23).

The Asian Barometer gauges democracy in 13 East Asian political systems[5] and five South Asian countries.[6] Together, this regional survey network covers virtually all major political systems in the region, systems that have experienced different trajectories of regime evolution and are currently at different stages of political transition. Democracies in East Asia are classified as established (Japan), emerging (South Korea, Taiwan, Philippines, Thailand, Mongolia, Indonesia), semidemocratic (Singapore, Malaysia, Hong Kong), and transitional (Vietnam) (Chu et al. 2008).

Assessing the quality and legitimacy in East Asian democracies, Chu et al. (2008) find that

> all East Asian democracies desperately need more serious attempts to strengthen legal deterrence against the corruption of elected politicians. More rigorous regulations on campaign finance and financial disclosures would help to arrest the encroachment of money politics. The independence and integrity of the judicial branch need to be reinforced making the judiciary less susceptible to political influence. Without these reforms, corruption and unethical conduct are likely to continue. (24)

China has allowed more public demonstration and civil liberties. "Mass incidents [in China] rose from 10,000 in 1994 to 74,000 in 2004" ("China" 2008). China is responding to pressures for greater participation in government, adopting a "consultative style of rule," incorporating more expert advice and public opinion into decision making and more reliance on law in policy implementation. "In 2007, nonparty ministers were appointed to the government for the first time since the 1970s, and draft legislation . . . was changed to reflect input from society" (Freedom House 2008).

One of the more interesting efforts in Chinese democracy is the increase in public consultation. China, while democratically deficient in most areas, made public consultation a rather regular feature of rural village politics beginning in the mid-1990s, and it is spreading now to urban areas. One of the disadvantages of public consultation is that the meetings may be dominated by a particular interest group. Another is that often there is not enough time for deliberation. As discussed earlier, China is mitigating some of these problems by experimenting with "deliberative polling."

Central Asia, containing several former Soviet nations, is not doing as well, as discussed in the section on nations in transition. Western Asia contains some Arab League states, Turkey, and former Soviets. These are discussed in other sections. Iran, at the border of West and Central Asia, merits a brief discussion on its own.

Iranian-Style Democracy

Oil led to the overthrow of a democratic government in Iran in 1953 and the reinstatement of Mohammad Reza Shah Pahlavi allegedly by the U.S. CIA and British Petroleum (British multinationals were permitted under British law to act like countries through the colonial period). Pahlavi was as cruel a potentate as any of the other dictators such as Saddam Hussein in Iraq or the House of Saud in Saudi Arabia, or any of the Eastern European dictators.

The 1979 Iranian revolution that deposed Pahlavi was led by an amalgam of secular and religious groups. Ayatollah Khomeini, a radical Islamic cleric, became a hero by over a decade of exile and he returned to Iran in time to help lead the revolution. A moderate liberal democracy held office for several months following the revolution. However, Khomeini managed to repress and edge out more moderate groups and emerged the supreme leader of Iran and established a radical Islamist theocracy.

Iran considers itself a democracy. The Supreme Leader, the leading cleric of Iran, is appointed by the Assembly of Experts. There are presidential and parliamentary elections every four years, and opposition parties are permitted to run for election and hold seats. The Guardian Council, whose 12 members are chosen by the Supreme Leader, choose the candidates for president and approve candidates for legislative seats, after the candidates have been vetted and many have been dismissed by the Interior Ministry. According to Human Rights Watch (2012a), candidates are dismissed for arbitrary reasons such as "propaganda" or "acting against national security." Opposition party candidates are routinely jailed or put under house arrest for similarly vague reasons and thus cannot run for office.

Sub-Saharan Africa: A Mixed Record

African nations are among the most recent to democratize. Colonial status through to the 1960s and 1970s followed by Cold War dictatorships and oligarchies left most countries impoverished with weak political and economic infrastructures. This legacy haunts them into the present.

Africa is a continent of contrasts, in terrain, ethnicities, and religions. It is also almost universally poor, and most of the continent is struggling with democracy. Every part of Africa, with the exception of Ethiopia, was colonized. Nearly every African country adopted a democratic constitution at independence, most with separation and balance of powers, multiple parties, and human rights. However, at independence, democracy did not stand much of a chance. Nearly every country was handicapped by weak infrastructure in their political institutions, economies, transportation, education, sanitation, agriculture, and every other institutional realm.

Not long after democratic constitutions were adopted, country by country across the continent, constitutional guarantees were curtailed, and democratic hopes succumbed to military rule or civilian dictatorship. Civil and personal freedoms were curtailed. The United States and the USSR were able to use this to their strategic advantage during the Cold War, supporting dictators in exchange for their allegiance.

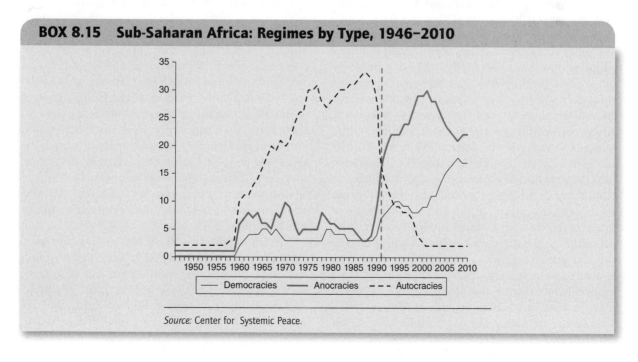

BOX 8.15   Sub-Saharan Africa: Regimes by Type, 1946–2010

Source: Center for Systemic Peace.

Despite civil rights movements, it took until the 1990s for the second wave of democracy to hit Africa. The end of the Cold War reverberated through Africa as it did in Eastern Europe. Marxist governments and single-party systems were discredited. "Such countries as Benin, Cape Verde, Ethiopia, The Gambia, Ghana, Madagascar, Malawi, Mali, Mozambique, Senegal, Tanzania, Uganda and Zambia all got rid of dictators, moved to a multiparty system or cleaned up their act in other pro-democracy ways" ("Bloodless Regime Change" 2006). This was accomplished, for the most part, peacefully through strikes, demonstrations, and other civil society activity. African countries employed several transition models: "national conference, guided democratization, co-opted democratization, and the authoritarian reaction models" (Saine 2008, 455).

Benin was one of the early successes, accomplishing a peaceful transfer of power from the Marxist dictatorship of President Kerekou to multiparty democracy convening a national conference (Schraeder 1995, 1161). In the Gambia, President Dawda Jawara reigned corruptly for 30 years, surviving multiparty elections and a coup attempt in 1981. In 1994, a successful coup brought Lt. Yahya Jammeh to power as chairman of the Ruling Council of the Alliance for Patriotic Re-Orientation and Construction party government (Saine 2008, 455).

West African countries did not all share similar results. Governmental institution-building strategies are shaped by the rural societies over which they govern. Different societies had very different outcomes across West Africa, even though the rural societies may have appeared to be very homogenous. The critical differences were in the capacity of rural actors to bargain with, constrain, or challenge central governments and the degree to which the regime or central government was able to co-opt, manage, circumvent, or accommodate rural interests (Boone 2003 357). For instance, the fragmented peasant structure of coffee and cocoa producers in rural Ivory Coast made it unnecessary for either the French colonial power or the post-colonial state to interfere in traditional local authority structures. Migration to the forest and savannah where land to support production was plentiful allowed them to benefit from increasing yields saving them the costs and political risks of the heavy-handed approach taken in most sub-Saharan countries (Boone 1995). This strong beginning did not prevent Ivory Coast

from a military coup in 1999, followed by rigged elections and disintegration into a brutal civil war in 2002, and again following the refusal of the incumbent president, Laurent Gbagbo, to leave office when he was defeated in election in 2010.

Guinea, by contrast, has been ruled by dictators since independence from France. In the three years from 2007 to 2010, Guinea has had general strikes, military uprisings, and a coup. But the order issued from the interim president, General Konaté or "El Tigre," was that on June 27, 2010, Guinea would have peaceful, legitimate elections. Keeping his promise not to run, he backed his word with 16,000 troops to keep order at the polls ("Guinea's Elections" 2010). Guinea held its first free and legitimate elections in the 52 years since its independence from France and people danced in the streets feeling empowered for the first time in most of their lifetimes. Cynics lamented that corruption cannot be escaped because Guinea is a culture of repression (Nossiter 2010). In this case, maybe one person made the difference, ending decades of authoritarian and military rule; Konaté appointed a civilian prime minister when he assumed power in 2009. Under his watch, the army stopped its massacres and kept the polls secure rather than intimidating voters. Under the new president, Alpha Condé, a democracy campaigner who came back from exile, the country is battling corruption and trying to regain control of its vast resource wealth. It has already cost the life of Aissatou Boiro, the treasury minister who ruthlessly tracked corruption through money flows. She was gunned down in November 2012. This battle puts them up against lawyers in major cities of the West who set up shell companies and bank accounts transferring money around the world to escape the scrutiny of the Guinea government. Encouraging democracy in Africa has to mean more than supporting elections. Cooperation on battling corruption through mutual legal assistance will help Guinea win the struggle for democracy, help Western companies who cannot compete against corrupt ones, and help win the "critical struggle of our generation" not of economics but of values (Collier 2012).

African democracies have had a hard time consolidating, experiencing similar vacillation to Latin America's. Nigeria, for example, has had 13 governments, and only four have been civilian. The president elected in 1997 served for two terms, and the 2007 election marked the first time that a civilian government transferred power to another civilian (Tar 2009, 67). That election, however, was tarnished by accusations of fraud, weakening its legitimacy. The current head of state, in power only from May 2010 until elections in 2011, claims to be determined to make Nigeria's next election fair (Reuters 2010).

Africa's history is also similar to Latin America in being plagued by "strong man rule" and coups. While Latin America has seen very few coups since the end of the Cold War, there have been 22 coups in 16 African countries, from 1990 to 2008. The coups resulted in 10 countries moving away from democracy while 10 remained relatively the same. Only two made progress toward democracy (Center for Systemic Peace 2009). Some African countries regressed away from democracy but have returned to democratic governance since 2000, including Burundi, Comoros, Ghana, Guinea-Bissau, Kenya, and Liberia (Marshall and Cole, 2009, 11). Most African democracies remain unstable and unconsolidated. However, Guinea-Bissau (never stable), along with Mali (was thought to be stable), suffered coups in 2012.

Both external globalizing factors and the internal terrain over which they flow that have shaped the contemporary democratic context in Africa. The external forces of globalization are

- "the new world (dis)order," the disappearance of a socialist alternative to unipolar Western hegemony;
- dominance of international organizations by developed nations and their policies;
- the forceful export of democracy to global South, particularly on the part of the United States; and
- the collapse of economic, social, and civil boundaries.

BOX 8.16   A Closer Look: The Meaning of Democracy in Africa

What, if anything does democracy mean to you?	Percentage 1st	Percentage 2nd
Civil liberties/personal freedom	30.5	10.6
Procedures	6.5	4.4
Government by the people	5.3	2.3

Source: Bratton and Cho (2006). This data is from a survey of 12 countries. Responses were from open-ended questions, to which subjects could give up to three responses. Responses were coded to fit categories.

Internal contexts of Africa include

- structural and economic crisis evidenced by dependency, inequalities, infrastructure decay and internal failures;
- crises of legitimacy of repressive authoritarian states; and
- mass protest and struggles against domestic failures and conditions imposed externally. (Tar 2009, 60)

As in Latin America, the military has been an important political force in Africa, usually for worse but sometimes for better. The military is often the most modern institution, and certainly the strongest and most enduring protectors as well as exploiters of the citizenry. Despite democratization, they remain important political actors. "No African country democratizes without the consent, either tacit or explicit, of the military" (Houngnikpo, quoted in Saine 2008).

Although the wave of the 1990s receded, it seems to be rising again. Despite the struggles of democracy building, Afrobarometer surveys of 19 democracies in Africa demonstrate that "diffuse"[7] support for democracy is high, as is rejection of non-democratic forms of government. The "demand for democracy" has risen to its highest level since 1999, after declining from 1999 to 2002 according to the latest round of Afrobarometer surveys (Afrobarometer 2009, 8).

Commitment to democracy is lower. When asked whether the current democratic government should be given more time when it cannot deal with problems or whether another system should be tried, 50.1% said it should be given more time, and 40.8% said something else should be tried. Support for specific democratic regimes is also low. Only 48.8% report being very or fairly satisfied with the way democracy works in their country. That varies greatly from 25.2% in Zimbabwe and 26.7% in Madagascar, to 83.3% in Botswana. Only 29% reported that they feel as though their country is a full democracy, and 55% a democracy with major or minor problems. Most rated their most recent presidential election as free and fair, or free and fair with just minor problems.

When considering the broad features of democratic governance that reduce corruption and increase accountability such as the separation of powers, a multiparty system, and term limits for presidents, a majority across the countries surveyed agreed that these were important and favorable to less-democratic alternatives. However, there was not a majority in every country.

BOX 8.17   Consider This: Democracy Undone?

Kenya

In 2007, Kenya was one of the most prosperous countries in Africa. It had a high growth rate and democratic elections. Disputed elections in 2007 set off a round of violence (Gettleman 2008). Five years later, waves of ethnic violence have taken over a thousand lives, displacing over 60,000, and Kenya, once one of the most stable countries, has not regained its footing.

On August 4, 2010, Kenyans voted on a new constitution with more safeguards for democracy. Despite this, inter-ethnic violence continues in Kenya, complicated by Islamic militant attacks occasioned by Kenya's incursion into neighboring Somalia. The 2013 elections were relatively peaceful and the results declared fair by the Kenyan Supreme Court. However, the victors, President Kenyatta and his deputy, Ruto, are under indictment by the ICC for the violence following the 2007 elections.

Zimbabwe

In the1980s and through the mid-1990s, Zimbabwe (until then Rhodesia, after Cecil Rhodes) was a rising star. It had just elected its first black African government. It established one of the finest educational and health care systems, not just in Africa, but in developing nations overall. Although the government was accused of political oppression, including murder and less than fair elections, the country was thriving. Advertisements in international magazines and newspapers proudly heralded Zimbabwe as a sure bet for international investment and cutting-edge location to advance an international business or political policy career. In the mid-1990s the tables turned. The Mugabe regime is now one of the most brutal and corrupt in the world.

People perceive that the supply of democracy in their country is less than their demand for democracy. Personal liberties continue to be more important to people than procedures and government by the people (Afrobaromter 2009, 4). This is hopeful in that it reflects a changing emphasis from procedure to freedom. If civil liberties now overshadow procedures through which governments are formed and function, satisfaction with civil liberties may help to stabilize developing democracies. Governments generally are perceived to be performing poorly on economic issues such as jobs, poverty, and hunger, and better on social and infrastructure issues.

Every African case is interesting. Kenya and Zimbabwe have been emblematic in their vacillation. Each country's struggle wrestling with democracy

from one-party rule or authoritarian leadership shows how long struggles may continue and how fragile democracy can be.

The violence following the 2007 elections in Kenya was far from the first round of ethnic violence. In 1991, the government of President Moi sent militias, Kalenjin and Maasai, into unarmed villages of Kikuyu, Luo, and Luhya to prove that tribal clashes prohibit peaceful functioning of a multiparty democracy (Carver 1993, 12). The violence lasted for years, spreading from rural areas to cities, and was more demonstrably politically rather than ethnically motivated (Carver 1993, 17).

Democracy wanes, or already has failed, in Zimbabwe. It may be due to the inability of people to exert their will over Mugabe, perhaps due to lack of sufficient international support for democracy. Abundant Chinese and South African support has dulled the effects of international sanctions. Afrobarometer (2009) measures of diffuse support for democracy were among the highest in Zimbabwe, and Zimbabwe had the largest gap between the demand of citizens for democracy and the supply they perceived coming from their government. Commitment to democracy in Zimbabwe was the lowest among the 18 nations. Only 31% of people said that democracy should be given a longer chance to achieve economic results. Yet, in Zimbabwe, many fought, risking and meeting death to restore open elections.

Robert Mugabe, once hailed as a hero of Zimbabwe's struggle for independence, has ruled autocratically for over 30 years. After losing by a slim margin in the general election in March 2008, he launched a campaign of violence against the supporters of the opposition candidate, Morgan Tsvangirai. Dozens were killed, and scores of others fled Zimbabwe; Tsvangarai finally had to drop out of the runoff election to quell the violence. After months of mounting international pressure, protests over human rights abuses, and negotiations, Mugabe formed a coalition government, and Tsvangarai took the post of prime minister. Mugabe plans to maintain power; in January 2013, he announced he would be running for president in the upcoming elections. Tsvangarai expressed some hope that the elections would result in a peaceful transfer of power and that Zimbabwe could not revert to one-party rule but said he would prepare for worse. A high-ranking military commander, although censured for the remarks, said that he would ensure Mugabe was re-elected. In the meantime, there has reportedly been an escalating campaign of harassment, intimidation, arrest, and prosecutions against opposition supporters, journalists, and civic groups (Chinaka 2013).

In Senegal, a run-off election in March 2012 resulted in the incumbent President Abdoulaye Wade conceding defeat to his one-time political protégé, now rival. While there had been violence in the general election, the run-off was unmarred, at least in preliminary reporting. A peaceful transition of governments is a good sign.

In summary, Africa has a mixed record on democracy. In an extensive study of elections held in Africa from 1990 to 2003, Lindberg (2006) found that there was no overall decline in the number of countries holding elections or the frequency of elections. Most importantly, using 10 indicators of democratization to analyze the 232 elections held in the period, Lindberg considered about half of elections in Africa to be free and fair. Although Lesotho, Sierra Leone, and Senegal moved to "free" in 2013, Freedom House rated only 13% of sub-Saharan Africa's 50 countries free (Puddington 2013).

Nations in Transition: Eastern Europe[8] and West/Central Asia

After decades of brutal oppression, when the Iron Curtain finally fell, it fell surprisingly suddenly and softly, beginning a new wave of democratization. Liberalization, provoked by civil society, changed the complexion of Eastern Europe. Nationalism split some countries along ethnic fault lines but unified others. Following the "velvet" revolution, Czechoslovakia dissolved peacefully, and the Czech and Slovak Republics gained sovereignty. The Berlin wall fell in November of 1989, leading the way for German reunification. Communist rule was rejected immediately in Poland, Hungary, Czechoslovakia, and Bulgaria.

In the first round of democratization, Romania and Yugoslavia failed to escape violence, as Communist dictators resisted giving up their power. In Romania, whether the violence was caused by a spontaneous populist uprising or planned by an opposition party is still subject to speculation. On December 15, 1989, water cannons were turned on demonstrators in Timişoara who were protecting their popular pastor from exile. Violence spread, and over 1,000 people were killed in less than two weeks of fighting so chaotic that 48 cadets were killed in a misguided attempt to capture an airport already in army possession. Nicolae Ceauşescu, arguably the most brutal of the Soviet bloc dictators, was executed along with his wife. They were shot repeatedly and their bodies displayed on December 25, 1989 (McNeil 1999). The revolution was led by second-tier government, military, and Communist party officials, who then assumed power.

In Yugoslavia, Macedonia was able to declare independence without resistance. The Communist party, under Slobodan Milosevic, resisted in other republics. Violence in Slovenia and Croatia was relatively short-lived, although brutal, and Croatia filed suit against Serbia for the crime of genocide. But the war that erupted in Bosnia-Herzegovina led to protracted war and genocide with between one quarter and one half million deaths. Kosovo was also subject to violent repression, leading to over 10,000 deaths in its failed 1998 fight for independence from Serbia. Montenegro declared independence in 2006, came under the protection of the UN, and was not resisted. After 10 years of administration by the UN, Kosovo again declared independence in 2008 and gained near-universal recognition, under protest of Serbia. Its independence was finally verified legal by the International Court of Justice in 2010. Milosevic was arrested in 2001 for crimes against humanity but died before his trial at the International Criminal Court was completed.

Motivation to join the EU has been an important globalizing force in Eastern Europe. Criteria for membership include economic and political liberalization and adoption of EU law. This creates greater homogeneity among states in standards of governance. Poland, the Czech Republic, Slovakia, Hungary, from the former Warsaw Pact; Estonia, Latvia, and Lithuania, the Baltic states of the former

USSR; and Slovenia (formerly part of Yugoslavia), Malta, and Cyprus joined the EU in 2004. Bulgaria and Romania joined in 2007. Although admitted to the EU, several countries still have trouble meeting all of its criteria. Romania, although rated free, has had particular trouble meeting anti-corruption standards (Walker 2010).

Croatia, Serbia, and Macedonia are also in process of joining, as is Turkey. While not part of the states in transition, Turkey is also pressured to globalize and conform to EU standards and law in such areas as the status of the Kurds and of women, social protections, social inclusions, and labor law.

The Soviet Union also dissolved peacefully. The republics declared autonomy, and the Soviet legislature ratified it, releasing them en masse from the union and recognizing their independence. Elections were held, constitutions written. "The seeds of democracy were being planted across the Soviet plains." Expatriates living in democratic countries returned home to help nurture them. It was a romantic time. Unfortunately, it did not last long. The legacy of the past casts a long shadow. Despite resistance of many civil society groups, many former republics seem to be following "ancient gravity to its source in Russia" (Hovannisian 2010).

Former soviets have not fared as well as the Eastern European nations. Joined as the Commonwealth of Independent States (CIS) in preparation for the dissolution of the Soviet Union, they have not been able to stabilize their transition to democracy, sliding backward rather quickly. Many elected their former authoritarian leaders. Most remain not free, although there is a great deal of vacillation.

At the turn of the century, beginning in about 2002, a "rainbow" of protests and revolutions marked the beginnings of a hopeful second wave of post-Soviet democratization—an orange revolution the Ukraine, a rose revolution in Georgia, and a tulip (Islamic symbol of hope) revolution in Kyrgyzstan (Kirgizstan).

The 2002 orange revolution in the Ukraine came to a head in a massive protest of the 2004 election. Exit polling done by the Democratic Initiatives Foundation, a Western election monitoring INGO, declared the election fraudulent. Viktor Yushchenko and Yulia Tymoshenko, among the leaders of the protests, became president and

BOX 8.18   A Closer Look: A Rose of Revolutions

The 2003 Rose Revolution in Georgia brought independence from Russia and hope for democracy to the new republic. A peaceful transition, however, has been difficult.

prime minister in a new election. Their victory was celebrated in the Ukraine and globally. While plagued by troubles building stable administrations due to infighting and weak political parties, elections have been free and civil liberties robust. Civil society and media are active watchdogs. The country gained its "free" rating in 2006. Transitions in power have been peaceful, if not smooth. Corruption at high levels within business and a weak and sometimes corrupt judiciary remain problematic. As quoted in the *Washington Post,* "'The problem is our politicians,'" said Bystritsky, head of the International Renaissance Foundation a pro democracy INGO in Kiev. He maintains that aid from Western nations should be more firmly attached to democratic results. Others disagree arguing that conditionality almost never works (Pan 2010). The Ukraine slid to partly free. Although still counted as an electoral democracy, flawed elections threaten that status. Corruption remains a serious problem (Walker and Habdank-Kotaczkowska 2012).

While some countries have continued democratic advances and may be consolidating, the records for others have not lived up to their initial promise. In many of the nations in transit, democracy is waning. It is receding only slightly in some areas, more dramatically in others. According to Freedom House, scores for 18 of the 29 countries in this grouping dropped from 2007 to 2008. The countries in this category cluster into three general neighborhoods, with very similar scores within each group and very little overlap in scores. In the overall "democracy score," EU member states scored the most democratic with an average of 2.39, ranging from 1.93 (Slovenia and Estonia) to 3.36 (Romania). The scores for Bulgaria, Czech Republic, Romania, Hungary, Latvia, Lithuania, Slovakia, and Slovenia all increased slightly, becoming less democratic (Shkolnikov 2009, Table 9). Nevertheless, all but Romania and Bulgaria, which are considered "semi-consolidated democracies," are considered "consolidated democracies" (Table 10).

BOX 8.19   A Closer Look: Democracy Scores of States in Transition

Non-Baltic Former Soviets	Balkan States	Former Warsaw Pact, EU, or close
5.92	4.04	2.39

Less Democratic ———————————————————————————— > More Democratic

Source: Shkolnikov (2009).

The Balkan states averaged 4.04, ranging from 3.82 in Albania to 5.11 in Kosovo. This score for Kosovo was a slight improvement from 2008, and reflects a trend of improvement from 2004, the first year of recordkeeping in the former Yugoslav states (Shkolnikov 2009, Table 9). With the exception of Kosovo, they are all considered "semi-consolidated democracies," or "transitional" or "hybrid" regimes (Table 10).

The non-Baltic former Soviet states averaged 5.92 (Shkolnikov 2009, Table 9). Three are "semi-consolidated authoritarian regimes" (Moldova, Kosovo, and Armenia). Eight of the countries are now listed as "consolidated authoritarian regimes" (Table 10).

Faulty elections—including non-competitive elections in Azerbaijan and Russia, dangers to journalists, corruption, divisive ethnic politicking, and "outright irresponsibility among political leaders"

(Shkolnikov 2009, 3)—erode democracy across the region. In Russia, it appears that democracy is losing popular support. Although Russia enjoyed "boom times" when the prices of commodities soared, making it oil wealthy, commitment to democracy failed to sustain democratic reforms in the face of the severe economic strife that followed.

The Pew Foundation's Global Attitudes Project (2009) found that popular sentiment in Russia favors a "strong leader" over democracy. In 2009, Pew found that while most people in the former Soviet republics and Warsaw Pact countries favor a multiparty system, the enthusiasm is dimming in six of the nine countries surveyed. From 1991 to 2009, those who approved of the change to democracy dropped from 61% to 53% in Russia; from 74% to 56% in Hungary; and from 72% to 30% in the Ukraine. It only increased in Slovakia (from 70% to 71%) and Poland (from 66% to 70%). It remained constant in the Czech Republic at 80%. Approval of the market economy dropped in all nine. A majority of Eastern Europeans remain in favor of these reforms, but support is waning. In all but two countries, more people said that they were worse off now than they were under communism, although in the Czech Republic and Poland, more said they were better off now than they were under communism. They did not reach a majority, however.

This sentiment was confirmed in the 2008 presidential election of Dmitry Medvedev, Vladimir Putin's protégée, and Putin's move to prime minister. Promising to stabilize Russia after a tumultuous decade, Putin consolidated control of government, business, and media. The election was not fair. Coverage of Medvedev's election opponents was sparse. Western election monitors refused to participate due to heavy restrictions on their activities. A Russian monitoring group, even with severe restrictions, documented hundreds of abuses (Nichol 2011, 2–3). Although there was widespread acknowledgement of the election abuses, many Russians offered support of Medvedev precisely because he would carry on Putin's policies. Support for Putin and hardline policies is diminished in the large metropolitan areas, but support within small cities and rural areas continues in his favor, albeit perhaps not indefinitely.

This applies to Azerbaijan as well. In 2008, it held elections in which the incumbent president won a landslide victory, close to or over 90%. Laws governing the election were far from fair, campaign time was limited to 28 days, and the opposition was excluded from demonstrating and most media coverage. The opposition party boycotted the elections. But not many people seemed to care. Azerbaijan had the fastest-growing economy in the world from 2005 to 2008. It was oil money rich. Azerbaijanis, like the Russians and increasingly across the post-Soviet societies, 20 years after people experienced the euphoria of new freedoms, "have grown cynical about democracy and are so tired of chaos that they would vote for stability in any package" (Tavernse 2008).

The decline of democracy in that region has had consequences. Instability is aggravated as demonstrated by the breakout of war between Russia and Georgia. Civil liberty and human rights violations continue. On January 31, 2010, Russia refused permissions for peaceful demonstrations, in disregard for its own constitution and the International Covenant on Civil and Political Rights (Freedom House 2010). Russia has remained one of the most aggressive opponents of universal standards of human rights, arguing instead for traditional values, often used to justify repression and discrimination against minorities and women (Schriefer 2010, 16, 23).

Kyrgyzstan is characteristic of another type. Kyrgyzstan dropped again to "not free" in 2010, after having risen to "partly free" after the revolution (Walker 2010). It is unsteady, vacillating between some democratic reforms. Local governments have considerable autonomy from central government, but elections on the whole remain riddled with fraud. Corruption in the judiciary and educational system is widespread. Unions operate relatively freely, but there are new restrictions on religion and civil society organizations. An estimated 2,000 people were killed in one month of ethnic violence following the ouster of President Kurmanbek Bakiyev in April 2010. A June referendum gave Kyrgyzstan a new constitution, making it the first parliamentary republic in Central Asia. As quoted in the *New York Times,*

Madina Musina, a 24-year-old ballroom dance instructor, said she voted for the new constitution because she favors a parliamentary system, after seeing two presidents—Askar Akayev and Kurmanbek Bakiyev—so anger their citizens they were overthrown. "We had a bad experience with presidents." (Kramer 2010)

BOX 8.20   A Closer Look: Revolution 101: How to Stage a Nonviolent Revolution

From Bosnia-Herzegovina to Zimbabwe, with stops in Burma, Estonia, Egypt, and Tunisia, the booklet *From Dictatorship to Democracy* has been studied and implemented by dissidents trying to overthrow oppressive regimes. It has been translated into 33 languages (Hirshman 2009).

The International Center on Nonviolent Conflict also uses the paper "198 Methods of Nonviolent Action" in its trainings, one of which was conducted in Cairo and attended by activists in the Tunisia and Egypt revolts. The Muslim Brotherhood is said to have *From Dictatorship to Democracy* posted on their website.

The author of these works, American Gene Sharp, now in his 80s, was active in the United States in civil rights sit-ins to integrate lunch counters. He hasn't gone unnoticed by the regimes that his students oppose. He has been denounced by Iran and Hugo Chavez, autocratic President of Venezuela.

He is passing the torch of freedom from one generation to the next and is witness to it being carried across the globe (Hirshman 2009; Stolberg 2011)

North Africa and Arab League Nations

Tunisia and Egypt

When the Berlin Wall fell, symbolizing the end of communism in the Eastern bloc nations, it fell quickly. In Tunisia, the frustrations of too few jobs, too expensive food, too little freedoms, and too much corruption led to the December 17, 2010, self-immolation of Mohamed Bouazizi that ignited a revolutionary protest that in just under one month—with no apparent help from outside—overthrew the 23-year dictatorship of Zine El Abidine Ben Ali. At least initially, Tunisia's transition seems to have been relatively stable. Tunisia relies heavily on its liberal reputation to attract tourists, a major revenue source. In Tunisia, people have an interest in patience. Elections in October 2011 in Tunisia brought Ennahda, a moderate Islamic party, to power in coalition with secularists. Tensions between Ennahda and secularists over the place of Islam in Tunisia politics have not been resolved. Attacks on some bars that serve alcohol that have gone unpunished, a police crackdown on protesters, and a ban on rallies in 2012 are evidence of some instability. Economic problems remain challenging. Nevertheless, as of early 2013, Tunisia seems to be a success story. The fruits of Tunisia's "Jasmine revolution" will take years to unfold, but it is unlikely that there will be a return to the status quo in Tunisia and perhaps not in any other Arab state. A wave of suicides and suicide attempts by self-immolation spread outward from Tunisia, intensifying exponentially within hours of the news that Tunisia's dictator had fled.

Across the Arab world, hundreds of thousands of protestors organized spontaneously through social networking. In Egypt, these were different than the protests that had become an annual rite. These protests involved everyone: university students, the middle classes, labor, all religious groups and genders. Tens of thousands took to the streets seeking reform. President Hosni Mubarak's weak attempts to mollify them were rejected, and within days, their demands escalated to insistence that Mubarak step down (Bamyeh 2011).

When Mubarak's promises to dismiss his government and make other reforms but retain his presidency failed to satisfy people, he increased repressive measures by outlawing public gatherings and ordering the police force to turn tear gas and fire hoses on the crowds. The "Day of Anger" erupted into weeks of violent confrontations between police and citizens who took over public squares, ripping down posters of Mubarak and proudly hoisting their own placard messages. The Egyptian Army, historically hailed as the protector of the people, refused to turn on them to save Mubarak's regime. He had been among the strongest dictators in the Arab world, ruling since 1981. On February 11, 2011, he was forced, by the will of "his" people, to resign and was imprisoned to stand trial for violence against the people. In June 2012, he was sentenced to life in prison.

The Difficulties of Transitions

The Egyptian case, followed carefully in the news, exemplifies the difficulty of transitions. When

Mubarak stepped down, the Supreme Council of the Armed Forces (SCAF) dissolved Parliament (which was reinstated by court order) and suspended the constitution to take temporary control, apart from the courts, of Egypt for six months until elections. After a period of jubilation, the difficulty of building a new government and managing the transition set in. Egyptian sectarian strife, primarily between extremist Muslims and Coptic Christians, intensified and unleashed some of the worst sectarian violence in a half century. Economic conditions, as might be expected during such a monumental transition, deteriorated. Parliamentary elections and subsequent election by Parliament of members to the Constituent Assembly became mired in protests over their constitutionality. The Supreme Court ruled the election processes for some of the seats unconstitutional. The SCAF dissolved the entire Parliament, sending thousands into the streets protesting, where they were met with violent reprisals.

BOX 8.21   A Closer Look: Democracy Workers Arrested

In December 2011, more than 40 democracy workers, including 16 Americans, 14 Egyptians, two Serbs, two Germans, and a Palestinian, Jordanian, and Norwegian from the International Republican Institute, the National Democratic Institute (NGOs associated with the Republican and Democratic parties who routinely work around the world helping people establish political parties and democratic processes), Freedom House, the International Center for Journalists, and the Konrad Adenauer Foundation were charged with illegal activities. They were accused of working with the CIA in trying to destroy the Egyptian state by inciting Muslim–Christian violence and supporting Israeli interests. The prosecution is led by a former official within the Mubarak regime but has garnered the support of others within Egypt who would like to reduce the influence of the West.

The military engaged the newly elected civilian government in a struggle for power. After they dissolved the Constituent Assembly, they rewrote the constitution, giving themselves much more power. Presidential elections went forward—the first in any Arab country—fraught with tension as the military watched the Muslim Brotherhood gain strength. June 30, 2012, brought the inauguration of Mohammed Morsi, the Brotherhood's candidate. Although he was recognized as president by the SCAF, they stripped the presidency of most of its power days before the inauguration. Morsi pushed back at the military and reconvened the Constituent Assembly and called for the release of people imprisoned by the military to face civilian rather than military trials, and ordered the pardon of 572 people convicted in military courts. The courts postponed a hearing on the constitutionality of the Parliament until September 2012, leaving them time to draft a constitution. The economy is weak. Sectarian violence and crime are high. All of these threaten stability. As the government forms, cabinet and other posts are being filled with civilians from Mubarak's regime, the Muslim Brotherhood, and military. Some of the other political parties complain of being left out of government. There is much work to be done to stabilize democracy in Egypt.

What has transpired in Egypt since July 2012? Is Egypt more or less stable? What evidence can you find of a continuing democratic transition?

While there were hundreds of deaths during the protests in Tunisia (about 300) and Egypt (about 900) (Rettig 2012), other regimes did not topple or reform as quickly.

Libya

Libyan rebels were victorious but only after a long and bloody war and NATO's help protecting their rebel forces with air strikes. February 17, 2011, is celebrated as the beginning of the revolution in Libya. Eastern Libya was won quickly by the rebels, but the battle for Western Libya raged for months. The National Transition Council, a coalition of dissidents, was recognized by France as the sole representative of the Libyan people in March 2011. While Muammar el-Qaddafi was in hiding and fighting still raged in his strongholds, the rebels were being greeted warmly at the UN by the leaders of most countries. The government of Qaddafi—who had ruled since 1969—fell in September 2011, at the cost of over 30,000 lives. In November 2011, Qaddafi was captured and brutally beaten to death by mob violence—a death reminiscent of the cruel dictator Ceauşescu's spontaneous execution in Romania when the Iron Curtain fell.

Libya has been full of surprises. Daily life in Libya resumed a veneer or normalcy after Qaddafi's death. Shops reopened. People went to work. Oil production surpassed pre-revolution levels within months. With no real political structure in Libya, the government had a more difficult time establishing itself. Workers and rebels have not been paid; rubbish has not been collected. Although most militia groups are engaged trying to maintain order, others participate in crime and kidnapping to make a living. Militias in the west have not accepted the legitimacy of the National Transitional Council that grew out of the revolution in the east. They agreed however, to accept the government formed following the June elections.

The Libyan elections held in July 2012 went very well. With no real history of voting, no strong parties, and scant government in place to run elections, nothing about the event was predictable. Country flags far outnumbered displays of party colors in an atmosphere that celebrated the nation. Violence was thin, scattered mostly through rural areas. Voters determined to have a successful election formed human shields around polls in some places to prevent attacks. People were enthusiastic about the right to vote and citizen participation was high. The elections were heralded as free and fair ("Libya's Election" 2012). The National Forces Alliance (a coalition of 58 parties), a centrist secular party led by Mahmoud Jibril, a political scientist educated in the United States, won 39 of the 80 seats reserved for political parties. The Muslim Brotherhood came in second, winning 17 seats.

Sporadic violence continued in Libya. Training camps established during the revolution continued on afterward, training fighters who continued attacks against suspected Qaddafi supporters, among others. In 2012, groups and individuals linked to Muslim extremists, including al-Qaeda, became more visible, staging attacks in Libya. In September 2012, al-Qaeda affiliates attacked the American consulate in Benghazi, killing four Americans, including the Ambassador to Libya, Christopher Stevens. Islamist militants who spent decades in a bloody war against Qaddafi say the revolution that they started has been stolen by the West and Qaddafi's former henchmen, and that they are not getting a fair share of the revolution's benefits (Al-Khalidi 2012). The new government will have to bring many parties to the table to establish legitimacy.

How has Libya fared? Has the violence continued or quelled?

Across the Arab nations, most governments, including Algeria, Iraq, Jordan, Kuwait, Oman, and Morocco, made some concessions to quell unrest. Granting more liberties, dismissing cabinet ministers, and reforming constitutions to make governments more representative or voting more free have been common among them. In Syria and Yemen, protestors were not satisfied by such offers. Violence continued through Fall 2011. In Yemen, the 33-year rule of Ali Abdullah Saleh ended with his agreement to step down and transfer power to his vice president, Abed Rabbo Mansour Hadi, who stood for election to the presidency in a one-man race in February 2012.

The Syrian Revolution

Syria's revolution began on March 15, 2011, and quickly became a very brutal war, with over 60,000 deaths by 2013. Interviews with over 200 individuals confirmed the details of brutal torture of men, women, and children in torture centers throughout western Syria (Human Rights Watch 2012b). The UN declared the Syrian government, led by President Bashar al-Assad, and military guilty of crimes against humanity for the barrage of shelling, mass executions, and illegal imprisonments.

Although most of the Arab League has called for Assad to step down, a universal global voice condemning Syria was late coming. U.S. Secretary of State Hillary Clinton blamed China and Russia for the failure of the UN effort to negotiate peace. China and Russia vetoed two UN Security Council plans to increase pressure on Assad through threatening sanctions and possibly military action if Assad did not comply with UN peace plan.

The longer the conflict continues and more brutal it becomes, the more hatreds and resentments build, and the more difficult resolving a post-Assad

Syria is likely to be. Foreign fighters and al-Qaeda are fast a growing presence there, and they have issued calls for Sunni extremists to join them there (Temple-Raston 2012). This not only escalates the violence with the introduction of suicide bombers but also makes any transition efforts aided by Western democracies more difficult. It changes the nature of the conflict from a battle for democracy to a battle to establish an Islamist state.

According to some voices in Syria, the Assad regime and outside interests are playing up and exaggerating sectarian divisions to divide the populace and prolong the conflict. The regime has justified itself as the only way to maintain order. Others—China, Russia, Saudi Arabia, Israel, among others—have a strategic interest in the regime maintaining power or for prolonged fighting to weaken Syria. According to a Syrian journalist, small destructive sectarian groups have a big impact that obscures the message of the revolutionaries, which is that there is room for every ethnic group and religion in a new Syria. The groups have co-existed for decades, despite the regimes promoting sectarianism as a way of dividing them and instilling fear of one another. If the world wants to see the conflict in black-and-white terms, there are two groups in this conflict: those who want to bring down the regime and its supporters. There are people of every ethnicity on each side (Nachawati 2012).

Whether ethnic divides in Syria are prolonging the conflict or the reluctance of the rest of the world to become involved is responsible, the longer it persists, the more difficult a transition and establishing order will be. The more extremists are able to establish a foothold, the more difficult it will be to extract them, as happened in Iraq and Afghanistan.

What can we learn from these revolutions that will help guide them into the future? Bamyeh (2011) outlines five contextual factors that contributed to the uprisings: marginality, spontaneity, civic character, political single-mindedness on the part of the revolutionaries, and autocratic deafness on the part of the dictators. Although he concentrated his analysis on Egypt, they hold for the other revolutions as well.

- Marginality: The revolutions occurred all over the countries, not just in capital cities. This inspires people with the evidence that revolution can happen anywhere. The death of a street vendor in Tunisia and the leadership of youth also reflect the power of marginal force.
- Spontaneity: No central authority coordinated the activity. People organized themselves as needs arose to take care of the wounded, call for protest, and make demands. In this way, the revolution had the character of everyday life, with little detailed planning.
- Civic character: None of the protests have had a religious flavor. Even protestors with strong religious beliefs have called for a civil, not religious or military, state. There was a definite appeal to civil rights—the dignity of the citizen, the rights to participate in government. This also reflects the emergence of the public as a people a civil society, acting spontaneously toward a common objective.
- Political focus: Economic and other grievances were shed in favor of concentrating on political objectives that united all of the protestors. The common sentiment that evolved was that if the political system were fixed, other problems could then be solved.
- Autocratic deafness: Deliberately ignoring or refusing to understand the severity of people's frustration with government kept the people's resentment simmering for decades. Even during the revolution, the refusal to recognize the extent of people's demands pushed people to extend their demands. Mubarak's attempts to end the revolt by making concessions were woefully too little and way too late.

Could restoring the first four qualities in the context of a responsive interim government, perhaps under a coalition of third parties calm the conflict among groups in Egypt and Syria? Will these revolutions warn dictators across the Arab League, Africa, and Asia that they cannot ignore people's demands for democracy?

How much should Western governments get involved in the revolutions of the Arab Spring and any that may follow? Is there a moral obligation or strategic interest in trying to ensure their success? If so, how?

The Prognosis for Democracy in Arab League Nations

Until the 2011 uprisings, the prognosis for democracy in the Arab League nations was negative. The new wave of revolutions and protests did not begin as ideological, ethnic, or religious. They are very practically rooted. Youth have been very active in organizing protests of the Arab Spring. The enormity of youth unemployment—both educated and uneducated—was the final undoing of the regimes that fell. The problems, although groups suffer differently, cut across religious, ethnic, and ideological divides. Although it may wax and wane, as other democratic waves, it is hard to imagine that the momentum of the Arab Spring will not bring permanent changes, even if not democracies, to the Middle East, North Africa, and other dictatorial regimes.

BOX 8.22   Middle East: Regimes by Type, 1946–2010

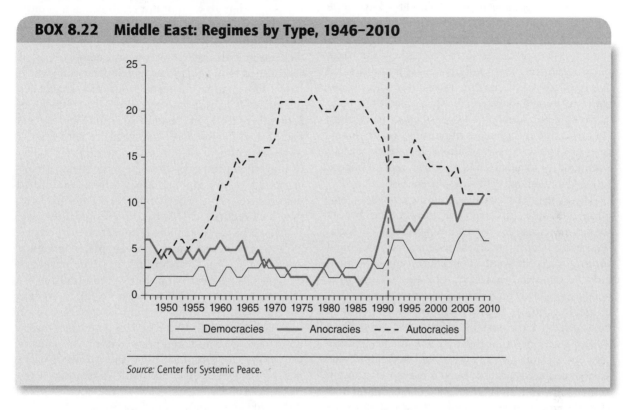

Source: Center for Systemic Peace.

The sectarian divide is a constant tension that plagues most of the Arab League. Like many other ethnic and religious competitions, the rivalries within and between Shiite, Sunni, and Christians date back hundreds of years. Outbreaks of sectarian violence have been frequent throughout the histories of these countries. Sunni-led states, such as Saudi Arabia, have supported Sunni rebels in Shiite states and Sunni governments whose power is being threatened. Shiite states such as Iran behaved similarly, supporting Shiite rebels and Shiite-led states. Often, a coalition can hold together while the fighting is raging but then falls apart when it is time to divide the spoils of war. These rivalries may be resolved as new governments form and stabilize. Lessons from other parts of the world, such as Bosnia, Afghanistan, and Somalia, may be more a primer in what not to do, rather than what to do.

However, other countries have accomplished transitions to democracy. USAID, the UN, and myriad agencies will need to rebuild these societies. Like the Marshall Plan that rebuilt Europe, it will take monumental international effort.

Oil and Resource Wealth

Control of valuable resources is another factor that can complicate the picture for democracy. Whereas coal has been credited with promoting democracy in the West—by fueling mass industrial society and providing workers with the power to strike—oil may have had the opposite effect in Arab nations. Oil has been a curse and blessing. From its discovery in 1908, oil has brought conflict to the Middle East beginning with the British-German-Turkish conflict as WWI commenced.

Oil and resource wealth have been blamed for the historically firm grip of autocracy in the Middle East. The rents coming from resource wealth may tempt elites to tightly control how resource revenues are distributed, enriching themselves further. Certainly, many of the monarchies used wealth to buy loyalty. With revenue coming in from oil, elites have little interest in pursuing other strategies of economic development. When the revenues go directly to the state, they may be used to strengthen the state bureaucracy and control. Ross (2001) found that oil and resource wealth have the most effect where countries are poor and where they account for a large share of GNP. There is much less effect in wealthy countries, and the influence of resource wealth diminishes as a country grows wealthier. Income-producing commodities that do not produce rents enhance rather than damage democracy (342–344).

There are three mechanisms through which oil and resource wealth can make democratization harder. Governments use low taxes and spending on social services to dampen pressures for democracy, they build security forces to ward off pressures for democracy, and the industrial or service jobs that would make people more likely to push for democracy do not materialize. In contrast, mineral-rich societies seem only to be effected by the first of these mechanisms (Ross 2001, 356–357). Although Ross found the relationship between oil and democracy to hold beyond Middle Eastern countries, he also found a robust relationship between the Arabian Peninsula and democracy that he attributes to the historical and cultural factors of the countries, not accounted for by income, resource wealth, Islam, or non-Western status (346).

There is a significant difference between resource rich and resource dependent in accounting for damage to democracy (Dunning 2008). South American oil-producing nations have democratized, although Venezuela's rating slipped in the latter years of the Chavez administration. Some oil- and resource-rich exporting Asian and African nations are democratizing. Depending on variables specific to the local context, being resource rich can contribute to either dampening or facilitating democracy (115). Economic diversification over time and development of the private sector diminishes the impact of oil and allows for regime change (288).

How new governments ultimately deal with the oil curse may determine their stability as more democratic or more authoritarian regimes.

Summary

Since the 18th century, the world has been on a decidedly upward trend of increasing number of democratic countries, percentage of people living in democracies, and an expansion of the rights and privileges that go with it. But establishing a democracy is not easy, and a state in transition is at its most fragile.

Even in states where procedural democracy was established long ago, the supply of democracy vacillates. This happened throughout the established democracies in response to the terrorist attacks of September 2001, in London in 2005, and so on. Established democracies also vacillate with respect to their treatment of minorities. Privacy, treatment of minorities, and crackdowns on the press or concentrated ownership are areas where established democracies are likely to fail. New voter ID laws may well reduce the U.S. freedom scores if they are shown to have a detrimental impact at the polls.

Where democracy is in short supply, as in China, events such as the Arab Spring can create pushback and even more restriction. In response to Tunisia's Jasmine revolution, China went so far as to censor the word "jasmine." Other forms of repression took a heavier toll. Arrests and detentions based on little or no cause, and press and Internet censorship followed. Despite China, the former Soviets, and North Korea, Asia has made substantial progress over the last years: 41% of the countries and 44% of the population are now rated free (Puddington 2012). Burma's election of President Sein Thein and subsequent dramatic reforms add energy to the region's progress and are likely to have effect beyond its borders. Thailand, Singapore, and Bhutan also improved.

Backsliding in all regions in countries as diverse as South Africa and Ukraine demonstrates how difficult it is to establish stable "tamper-proof" institutions. Despite the overall decline in the supply of democracy of the last seven years, the number of free countries held at 87 from 2010 to 2011 and rose to 90 in 2012.

Whether or not the democratic progress around the world will lead to stable democracies (or stable governments of another sort) or have prolonged instability will be influenced by how hard the global community works to mitigate sectarian division, fight corruption, help countries manage oil and resource wealth, facilitate economic diversity and development, and solve the other problems that keep people scrambling to get a fair share of democracy and the resources they need for a life of quality.

Questions, Investigations, and Resources

Questions

1. Why is the transition to democracy generally difficult?

2. Choose one or more countries. Update the status of countries that began to democratize after the fall of the Iron Curtain in 1989 or since the Arab Spring of 2011.

    a. Have they held elections?
    b. What hurdles have they encountered in this country?
    c. How did they deal with them?
    d. Did they solve the problem?

3. Using this chapter and Chapter Seven on state governance, assess the waves of democracy.

    a. What were the major factors that provided the impetus for each wave?
    b. What countries democratized during the wave?
    c. Try to determine which countries slipped somewhat after the wave peaked?

Investigations

1. What problems of democracy have you read about in this text, or in other sources, that rich countries have? In 2009, Amnesty International launched a campaign to fight discrimination in Europe. You can read many of the abuses of human rights that they have documented on their website.

2. Investigate the relationship between demographic variables and attitudes about democracy using the Afrobarometer Online Analysis.

3. Select a group of countries that are newly democratizing. Investigate people's attitudes toward democracy over time using the World Values Survey. Not all countries are included in each round. Start with the first round, then move to the second, and so forth, adding newly democratizing countries as they appear in the survey years.

    a. How have attitudes toward democracy changed overall for this group?
    b. Create a timeline for each country. Do the countries differ from one another in their trends?
    c. If so, what may account for this?

4. Investigate the problem regions discussed in Dennis Blair's 2010 "Annual Threat Assessment" (see Chapter Twelve). How do democracy and governance contribute to global stability and the security of the United States?

5. Investigate the countries that Freedom House considers the Worst of the Worst. What commonalities exist in these countries? Do they have similar levels of development, education, resources, religions, or cultures? What do you think might account for the repression in these societies?

Resources

Regional Barometers and Online Data Analyses

AfroBarometer http://www.afrobarometer.org

Asian Barometer http://www.asianbarometer.org/

East Asian Barometer http://www.jdsurvey.net/eab/AnalizeSample.jsp

Latin American Public Opinion Project http://www.vanderbilt.edu/lapop

Freedom House Reports http://www.freedomhouse.org

World Values Survey http://www.worldvaluessurvey.org

Amnesty International Report on Discrimination in Europe http://www.fightdiscrimination.eu

Select Books by Gene Sharp

From Dictatorship to Democracy

The Anti-Coup (with Bruce Jenkins)

The Politics of Nonviolent Action (3 volumes)

Waging Nonviolent Struggle: Twentieth-Century Practice and Twenty-First Century Potential

Documentary Film

How to Start a Revolution (2011), based on the writings of Gene Sharp

9

Globalizing Culture: Change and Continuity

Objectives

Cultural globalization includes the emergence of new ideas, values, and norms, the global diffusion of ideas from one part of the world, and the changes in local cultures driven by people's experience with globalization. This chapter will help you

- understand culture as a fluid system that exists in interaction, not places;
- analyze the objective conditions stimulating the emergence of global culture;
- explain and assess how global culture impacts different local and national cultures, and vice versa;
- apply principles of the mechanics of cultural globalization to world events and changes;

- analyze how cultural globalization facilitates both convergence and divergence in cultural content and form; and
- recognize enduring elements of cultural diversity and support viable arguments for both their continuity and change.

BOX 9.1 A Closer Look: Defining Mental Illness

American definitions of mental illnesses are becoming global standards, along with the pharmaceuticals to treat them. For the medical establishment, mental illness is not much different than biological disease. Diffusing treatment for depression across countries is viewed in the same way as diffusing anti-viral medications. The World Health Organization has developed protocols for "evidence-based interventions" to address psychiatric disorders. These include recommendations for pharmaceutical and psychosocial modalities (WHO 2008, 11–12). Along with media and travel, the medical establishment, perhaps unavoidably, has helped to globalize symptoms of mental illnesses. Although origins may be biological, mental illnesses are also cultural constructs, and as globalization has progressed, the symptoms of mental illness that people present with have changed.

This is not surprising from a social scientific perspective. While the distress of mental illness is very real, culture provides us with many of the symptoms to present. As cultures spread globally, people learn new ways of expressing mental illness. "Hysterical-leg paralysis," for example, spread as an epidemic through middle-class women in the 19th century giving expression to the distress associated with the social restrictions on their roles (Watters 2010). This may be the first instance of a globalizing mental illness. Now, the diffusion of mental illness across cultures is much more common.

Anorexia, or food refusal, in Hong Kong had traditionally been very rare and presented as feeling bloated. That changed very rapidly in the 1990s. In Hong Kong in 1994, a young girl died from self-starvation as a result of anorexia. Her death was featured prominently in the media. While she was not the first, by the end of the 1990s, anywhere from 3% to 10% of young women in Hong Kong had the American version of anorexia. People learned eating disorder pathologies, and anorexia patients now present as fat phobic like their Western counterparts (Watters 2010).

Meaning in the Global Age

Globalization forces "new transnational forms of living and communicating, new ascriptions and responsibilities, new ways in which groups and individuals see themselves and others" (Beck 2004, 430). Put more simply, globalization changes culture. The globalization of culture is implicit in all forms of globalization. Culture provides a basis of meaning for people's actions. Globalization changes how people view themselves—their needs, desires, goals, and motivations. It changes what people expect from their society in its obligations to them, its legitimacy as a society, and its obligations around the world. Globalization changes how individuals view their relations to humanity, that is, their responsibilities to other humans in light of their common humanity. Some changes are obvious, such as the global adoption of time zones or a common calendar. Others are subtle, such as gradual changes in meaning, such as of freedom or justice. As with every form of globalization, we must consider both the emergence of a global cultural system and the impact of the global system on societies and the individuals and institutions within them.

Each of the preceding chapters addressed cultural globalization. As economic, political, and social policies and practices diffuse, culture diffuses. When global problems, such as climate change, are tackled, or global social movements emerge, such as the movement to ban landmines, cultural globalization informs them. Thus, we have already discussed globalization of political culture, economic culture, and civil society culture. This chapter examines the central questions of cultural globalization.

- What are the processes and mechanisms of cultural globalization?
- Does globalization create new cultural elements? If so, what are they?
- Is there a global culture emerging from the diffusion or fusion of cultures?
- Will cultural globalization be homogenizing, making all cultures the same?
- Can cultural globalization fortify national cultures?

The chapter opens with a brief discussion of the possibility of global culture and convergence and divergence in cultural change. The next section analyzes cultural themes that are diffusing globally as well as resistance to global culture.

Who Puts Italian in Italian Food?

Nearly everyone loves Italian food. What's not to like: ripe tomatoes, rich pasta, zesty spices, great cheese? It's simple and elegant. Harder to capture, however, is the essential quality that makes it Italian. Is any food prepared in Italy—say, for instance, a hamburger you bought on a lunchtime stroll to the Trevi fountain—Italian food? Is food Italian when it is prepared by an Italian-born immigrant now in the United States? What if the chef uses pasta from a box and sauce from cans, all made in America? In Italy, controversy over the essence of Italian food has intensified, particularly since 2008 when a chef from Tunisia and a chef from India took first and second place in a contest for Rome's best carbonara (Fisher 2008).

BOX 9.2   A Closer Look

Southern Italian food reflects the sunshine and zest of high-spirited Italian life.

Food is a cherished cultural tradition in all societies. Food speaks to people's sense of belonging and identity. The taste, texture, and particularly the smell of food evoke powerful memories. Food is very concrete and highly abstract. It is experienced concretely, using all of a person's senses. Yet it is ephemeral, disappearing when eaten. Food is an important part of the material and cultural heritage of a people (Tschofen 2008, 29).

Global flows of people, commodities, and technologies challenge national cuisine and national culture generally. So far, Italian food has resisted many of the fusions of foreign and native that transformed other national cuisines (although, as pointed out to me, neither tomatoes nor pasta originated in Italy). In the opinion of one of Rome's premier restaurateurs, the birthplace of the cook does not matter in the creation Italian food; only the training matters. As long as his chefs are well trained in the flavors of his mother's kitchen, he believes that where the chef was born does not detract from the food. But for other Italians, it seems impossible that a foreign-born person can *understand* Italian food. They believe that the only hope for Italian cooking to maintain its unique character is for it to be carried forward by Italian children (Fisher 2008).

Similar issues arise when deciding who has the right to call a sparkling wine product champagne, whether a minaret on a horizon in Switzerland threatens the Swiss character of the landscape, if Muslim headscarves undermine the secular integrity of European classrooms, or which languages should be spoken in schools (Cumming-Bruce and Erlanger 2009; Erlanger 2010; Ouane and Glanz 2010). Although these issues appear trivial, each of these controversies has been the subject of international headlines.

Does opening culture to global forces, allowing them to be influenced and altered, risk a more monochromatic world, devoid of its most interesting variations? Is cultural protectionism dangerous in a world with increasing flows of people among countries?

These and similar issues penetrate to the crux of globalization controversies, whether the subject is dress, architecture, and cuisines, or civil and human rights, the roles of women in society, granting homosexuals the right to marry, the role of religion in government, and the responsibility to preserve the environment for future generations. Cultural globalization reorients meaning, raising uncertainty about the traditional answers to questions from what it means to be Italian (or Brazilian, Japanese, or American) to what is good or bad, moral or immoral.

Globalizing national culture creates bridges facilitating communication and interactions across cultures. If there is a bit of Northern African flavor in restaurants in Italy, it may make Italy more comfortable for Northern Africans. It may also help Italians be more comfortable with North Africans and more comfortable in North Africa. Global culture also bridges diverse groups. Common respect for human rights, common adherence to rules of rational discourse, and tolerance facilitate building a global civil society, extending bonds of civility and, subsequently, trust. Conversely, antagonism to even minor influences of globalizing national cultures and global culture may increase fractiousness and escalate conflict.

Creating and Negotiating Culture in Interaction

Confusion about the concept of culture has hectored talk about global culture. Analytically, a place, such as a society, is most often viewed as the locus of culture, as in the example of Italian food. This perspective on culture is misleading. National cultures are built over generations of interactions in shared experiences. Traditionally, those people would also have shared a space. However, interaction is the critical component. To sustain a culture, interaction must be of sufficient quantity and duration for people to develop some common understandings—even if there is disagreement over the particulars. Interaction is the locus of culture. Second, cultures are not homogenous. Every person has a unique perspective and thus at least a subtly different understanding. Cultural patterns are also fluid, changing as people change, merging into and dropping out of interaction, and as interactions change. Variation is endemic to culture, not an anomaly.

Loosening the conceptual grip that places and societies have on culture liberates it to inform our understanding of the globalization of culture. A simple definition of culture that captures its essence—social meaning—circumvents these difficulties and provides analytic power appropriate to the global situation. To understand the globalization of culture, it is necessary to recognize the following:

- All systems of intense, sustained, interactions develop culture.
- No culture is homogenous.
- Cultures overlap. No single element of a culture needs to be exclusive to it alone to make the culture unique. It is the constellation of elements that make it particular.
- Individuals are unique amalgams of the cultures—from the smallest to the largest—to which they belong.
- Culture is fluid. It is negotiated in every interaction.
- People use culture to think about, decide on, and manage their social relations. It provides structure for individuals, lending some predictability to life—an idea of what to expect of self and others in various contexts. No one has to invent how to behave over and over every day.

The concept of milieu (Albrow et al. 1994) also frees culture from place. *Actual milieu* is the situational reality of daily life in which people live. It is meaning in context. Individuals create their own *structural milieu* as they move through the flux and flow of life. Travel and communication allow a person to extend his or her structural milieu through experience in a variety groups, organizations, and societies. People acquire local and global cultural competence by broadening their milieu, developing familiarity and experience within many different spheres of life. A person's milieu is a dimension of personality.

Culture divorced from place and seen as milieu mitigates the argument that a "global culture" is an oxymoron, a contradiction in terms. Some theorists argue since a culture identifies an "us," a global cultural cannot exist without an external "other" to highlight boundaries (thus, in the case of global culture, it would have to be something like an extraterrestrial threat or impending planetary ecological disaster) (Featherstone 1990, 11).

Anomie and Globalization

Culture is fluid and always changing to some degree, but it is not always a smooth flow. Globalization produces rapid social change; values, norms, and ideas may become outdated before sufficiently strong new ones have emerged to take their place. This produces social structural anomie or normlessness in many aspects of life. Much of the disorder of contemporary life results from this deficiency of shared meaning. In other words, in many contexts, many people are "winging it, struggling with the effects of globalization (among other things) in their everyday lives" (Robertson 1992). For example, as economies shift from agriculture to manufacturing or manufacturing to information, the knowledge relevant to many occupations becomes outdated. As educational levels rise, the restrictions of an authoritarian regime on speech or action may become unacceptable. A life of hardship in a land of increasing bounty may not seem inevitable. Anomie is difficult to remedy as it requires negotiating new cultural patterns. People often conflict on new norms.

Globalization confronts individuals with diversity. They may question the values and beliefs of their culture or take measures to protect their culture. Each of these globalization effects can dilute the confidence that people have in their culture. Without the confidence that shared meaning provides, many individuals suffer anomie[1]—the discomfort of not having a solid bearing on appropriate conduct and whether or not they are doing the right thing. Anomie is evident in the struggles of individuals in indigenous cultures who must navigate and negotiate between living in traditional ways and assimilating into mainstream culture.

Anomie impacts all realms of life, even the most intimate. For example, family roles and structures are changing. As educational levels and job opportunities for women advance, family size grows smaller. Fertility rates are dropping all over the world. Traditional family roles have lost their appeal now that women are advancing in education and the economy, and children can no longer contribute to raising a family's economic status. Many European and Asian countries have shrinking, aging populations. Women are avoiding marriage and children in favor of earning money and remaining single. Tough economic times exacerbate this. In Spain, the birthrate, already low, dropped 7% in just two years in response to the global financial crisis. With Spain introducing austerity measures, generous stipends and paid leave policies instituted to promote more childbirth are disappearing. Women are responding by staying in the workforce, not financially capable of time off for children (Kim 2009; Livingston 2011).

How would you rate the confidence of people in the United States in their culture? Are there cultural elements that seem to have lost their significance in contemporary life? When people use the phrase *culture wars*, to what are they referring?

Could global contingencies that stimulate global discourse—such as environmental threats, economic crisis, scarcity, crime, terrorism, and so on—unite people enough to form a relatively stable and long-lived pattern of interaction—a global culture?

Flows of Cultural Diffusion

The earliest forms of cultural diffusion resulted from migration and trade. The Silk Road was an early globalizing influence across Eastern and Western civilizations. During the germinal phase of globalization, the East to West flow dominated. China, India, and Japan were the largest producers of goods. Asian societies, particularly China and India, developed extensive export economies. The Silk Road transported Asian influence along with goods, technology, and culture. Europe bought the exotica of Asia with silver imported from the new world. Products from the Asian empires—silks, cotton, tea, porcelain (china), spices, and metals, among many other goods—made Asian nations the largest producers of wealth. Early manufactured goods and Chinese science and technology far exceeded European (Frank 1998). The Ottoman Empire, spanning three continents over the course of two centuries, was a product of East–West cultural blending.

Power shifted in the incipient phase of globalization. Industrialization cemented the reverse flow of influence. By the take-off phase of globalization, the West had gained hegemony, going so far as to establish standards of civilization that non-European nations had to adopt to be included in international society. Despite their indignation, most of the world abided. Lenin was prompted to adopt the Gregorian calendar in Russia, and the revolutionary father of nationalist China, Sun Yat-sen (Sun Zhongshan) vowed to "carry out the duties of a civilized nation" so as to be recognized and treated as civilized (Robertson 1992, 121). Despite its origin in arrogance, the standards advanced a global political culture and discussion of what a modern society should be.

To discuss Westernization and Easternization as dichotomous processes perpetuates a misleading cultural divide. It suggests that the European, African, Middle East, and Asian cultures developed independently of one another. This was never the case. There have been periods of hegemony of one region over another, periods of increasing and decreasing connections of one sort or another, and periods where one region or country went into self-imposed isolation. One of the most dramatic aspects of globalization has been the rapid economic development and growth in Japan and other East Asian societies post-WWII (Robertson 1992, 85).

Japan has had particular influence in the contemporary era. Who has not heard of Godzilla? The wave of Japanese and other Asian horror films—which, interestingly enough, depicted real-life risks, such as the environment and nuclear weapons—continue to influence Western films. The Hollywood movies *The Ring*, *The Grudge*, *Dark Water*, and *Audition* are all remakes of Japanese horror flicks (Biodrowski 2008). In the meantime, another film genre—anime—has made its way west from Japan.

A friend brought a "Hello Kitty" pencil case from the Philippines in the early 1980s. It was very cute and clever with more secret buttons that opened more secret drawers than it looked like the case could hold. It was not long before "Kitty" was made in every conceivable type of children's item and was starring on television. The items didn't even have to be clever any longer. Kitty was "branded." Hello Kitty introduces young Westerners to Japan early in life and can accompany them through elementary school—if someone is a bit "campy," Kitty can go to college, too.

A more significant influence from Japan is Japanese management. In the 1970s, Japanese competition and competence in manufacturing led American business to jump on the bandwagon and redesign manufacturing models to conform to Japanese best practices. These practices ranged from "just in time" ordering so that companies do not build up inventory and other methods to improve efficiency and an emphasis on quality control at every stage of production. The influence of Eastern religions, philosophies, medicines, and therapies have been profound. Discussed in detail in Chapter Ten, they have changed Westerners' thinking about their mind and body and the relationships between

them. East and West have been interconnected from the earliest migrations outward from the birthplace of civilization. East and West have influenced one another over centuries of interaction.

Flows of cultural globalization have had many effects. They have been resisted, resulting in resurgences of nationalism and fundamentalisms. They have been adopted and adapted by local cultures, a process of glocalization. They have resulted in the emergence of global cultural forms and themes that originated in specific contexts but have achieved almost universal adoption. There are also cultural forms that have arisen out of global interaction. These last two form the global cultural system.

The Endurance of Diversity: Civilizations, Nationalism, and Fundamentalisms

BOX 9.3   Consider This: Map of Civilizational Cultures

Researchers with the World Values Survey Project found that civilizations vary along two main dimensions: whether their immediate concerns are more for self-expression than survival—a difference related to socio-economic status—and whether they use traditional values and religion more than secular values as guides for life. If you examine this "map," you'll see that as you move on the diagonal from the bottom left corner to the upper right, the societies increase in wealth. Where is your country of citizenship? How would you explain its position using examples from your national culture?

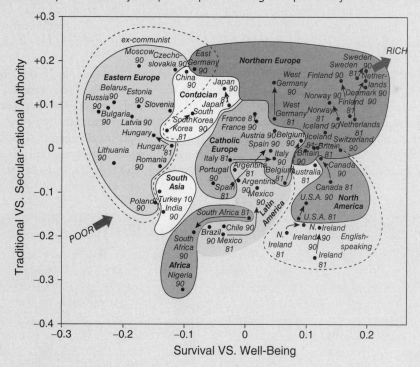

Source: World Values Survey.

Despite cultural globalization, cultural diversity endures. Before we look at ways cultures are spreading, it is very important to acknowledge that there is resistance to global culture. It is ironic but not surprising that nationalism and fundamentalism are revitalized by globalization. Cultural protectionism is as much part of globalization as economic protectionism. Individuals, organizations, and countries vary in their degree of acceptance or rejection of cultural globalization. Nationalism and fundamentalism are vehicles for protecting cultural and personal identities.

Civilizational Identity

A civilizational culture is the broadest and most enduring frame of meaning. Civilizational identities are comprised of deep meanings: the perceived relationships between "God and man, the individual and the group, the citizen and the state, parents and children, husband and wife . . . rights and responsibility, liberty and authority, equality and hierarchy" (Huntington 1993, 25). These are so deeply held that they seem part of the natural order; they are part of a person's identity. Huntington delineated eight major civilizations in the contemporary world: Western, Japanese, Confucian, Islamic, Hindu, Slavic Orthodox, Latin American, and African. The lines that divide them are flexible but real. Consciousness of one's civilization and awareness of the differences among civilizations heighten as people from different civilizations interact. Consumerism, materialism, liberalization, human rights, and the rule of secular law, are viewed differently in different civilizations and resisted in many.

Civilizational divides are so deep that Huntington (1993), among others, says that homogenization, on issues like human rights and individual liberties, may not be achievable in the foreseeable future. Furthermore, the lines of civilizational divide are increasingly the lines of war. Clashes over meanings—of good and bad, right and wrong, virtue and sin, and how to construct a good life or a good society—have erupted worldwide. The line through Europe that Huntington identified, marking the Western boundary of Christianity, passing through Yugoslavia (united during the Cold War and now divided) and along the former borders between the Hapsburg and Ottoman empires, have seen near-constant warfare since the dissolution of the Iron Curtain. The Western–Islamic fault line; China's line of demarcation with its neighbors; and the lines dividing Muslims, animists, and Christians in Africa have all been the site of contemporary vicious, genocidal conflicts (33–34). These wars are discussed in Chapter Thirteen.

Nationalism

It is not hard to imagine how globalization creates conflict across cultures. Even within countries, cultural conflicts arise on religiously tinged issues such as homosexual rights, abortion, and euthanasia. People are protective of their identity. Threats to cultural identity can be paramount to threats to their survival as a people. In the United States, people have been accused, by national political figures and commentators, as well as everyday folk, of not being "real Americans." They talk about "taking America back," as if America were being hostage by foreign powers, not democratically elected representatives or Supreme Court decisions.

BOX 9.4   A Closer Look: Finnish Music, a Cultural Bridge

The Finns tried to protect their musical culture but had very limited success. Having been occupied by both East (Russia from 1809 to 1917) and West (Sweden from the 16th century to 1809), Finnish culture has long been an amalgam of many others, as expressed in its music. Music reflects a perception of reality, sometimes a national or ethnic collectivity. Each occupation of Finland left a cultural imprint on Finnish music. In response, the Finns threw up barriers of cultural protectionism in the 1930s. They tried to block outside influences and develop a purely Finnish national music. Nevertheless, cowboy music in the 1950s and the English rock invasion in the 1960s penetrated Finland. Finally, perhaps inspired by the Cold War surrounding them, Finns accepted and embraced their musical amalgam. They stand out as a "bridge" from East to West forged from their history. This makes them unique and, as such, has become an important part of their national identity (Mäkelä 2007, 52). Their syncretic—amalgamated—culture is a tribute to their heritage.

The revival of nationalism is a globalization effect. States, ethnic groups, and classes use identity and nationalism as ways of finding a place in a shrinking world (Anderson, quoted in Robertson 1994, 124). From the time nation-states were established in the 17th century, history records less and less of the "schemes and ambitions" of this or that king, and more and more about the "Designs of France" or the "Ambitions of Prussia" (Wells 1920/1956, 663). It is as though nations assumed personalities as they became the actors through which people connected to the global stage. In the mid-19th century, European states competed to establish historical identities that extended their heritage as a people back into ancient times. In the late 19th to early 20th centuries, states developed ceremonial and symbolic rites and objects, imbuing the state with sacred qualities and giving birth to civil religions.

Nationalism is also a way that people fight against globalization (Nye 2008, 169). When the nation was the most absolute of all associations (Niebuhr, quoted in Scholte 2000, 159), the local community was the particular. In the global era, the nation is the particular. "Nation-saving" efforts to preserve cultural distinctions abound in both developing and developed nations. The following are some examples of nationalistic reform efforts:

- French, Icelandic, Russian, and Philippine governments have all taken measures to preserve the purity of their "native" tongues.
- The curriculum of the United Kingdom has been reformed to give more attention to British history.
- China, Malaysia, Saudi Arabia, and others have at one time or another outlawed foreign satellite broadcasts. Other countries have tried to block foreign satellite broadcasts by adopting different technical standards.
- In Vietnam, advertisers were warned to enhance the Vietnamese nature of their advertising. They removed billboards that were deemed to have "poisonous cultural items."
- State-owned and regulated media in many countries have used programming to promote national consciousness (165).

BOX 9.5   Consider This: Culture Wars

Ironically, both "cultural dilution" and culture wars attract big headlines. Battles over ideas aren't limited to East versus West or conservative versus radical. The "Google wars" in Italy represent a battle over rights. Free speech and privacy are both respected in the United States and Europe. In the United States, free speech is enshrined in the First Amendment to the Constitution. It has primacy over almost everything else. But in Europe, after decades of "Big Brother" surveillance through regimes of Nazism and Fascism, privacy trumps free speech. People are not free to infringe on others by publishing private concerns.

European regulations are inspired by the conviction that data privacy is a fundamental human right and that individuals should be in control of how their data are used. "American companies often trip up on data-privacy issues because of 'their brimming optimism that the whole world wants what they have rolled out in America,'" says Jennifer Stoddart of Canada, who took Facebook to trial for privacy violations ("Legal Confusion" 2010).

International regulation of data and ownership of personal data put on social networking and other sites is a critical global cultural issue. Do you have the right to control what happens to your data if you quit Facebook, LinkedIn, MySpace, or other networking sites?

- State-owned and regulated media in many countries have used programming to promote national consciousness (165).

Malaysia, Singapore, and Indonesia accused Western countries of trying to impose individualistic values on their culture, where the highest value is the welfare of the society as a whole. This assertion of Asian values along with similar ones, is an assertion of regional identity and the right to develop distinctive political systems in the face of globalization (Nye 2004, 84–85).

Fundamentalism

The worldwide revival of religious and other forms of fundamentalism is one of the most striking features of the global era (Robertson and Chirico 1985). In the United States, the Moral Majority revived fundamentalism in the 1970s, bringing it squarely back into politics. Although the Moral Majority organization lasted only through the 1980s, fundamentalist Christianity remains active and vocal into the new millennium. The Iranian Revolution in 1979 marked the entry of Islamic fundamentalism onto the world political stage. Religious fundamentalist Zionist and Hindu movements also want to restore the primacy of their religious worldview—the fundamentals or orthodoxy. (Religious fundamentalism is discussed in Chapter Eleven.)

Fundamentalism is not confined to religious movements. It flourishes in times of rapid social change. Secular political movements urge that laws and government action return to the intent or the language of the founding fathers. Educational movements promote getting back to the basics. Fundamentalism reduces uncertainty and banishes anomie. It provides definitive answers to life's questions, definitive rules to serve as a guide through life's ambiguities.

People may experience the diversity of values, morals, and points of view wrought by globalization as a siege on their personal and cultural identity. Fundamentalisms assert distinctive, well-defined identities in response to universalizing values, lifestyles, and beliefs. Fundamentalism is not just adhering to orthodoxy; it has an element of rejecting or reacting to modernity, particularly its relativism.

Fundamentalism, cultural protectionism, and nationalism respond to globalization by protecting cultural identity, but we are all trying to figure out "how to negotiate national identity and the rising 'global imaginary,' the growing awareness of an emerging global community" (Steger 2009, 65).

BOX 9.6   Consider This: Preserving Culture

UNESCO works to increase cross-cultural understanding and to preserve cultural diversity. The underlying assumption is that cultural diversity is a benefit rather than a threat or challenge to the international community and that it is of benefit to the people whose culture they preserve. Among the objectives of the 2009 UNESCO World Report is to demonstrate the benefits of cultural diversity. Among them are that cultural diversity

- can renew our approaches to sustainable development by developing knowledge and techniques of indigenous cultures;
- is a necessary component for "the exercise of universally recognized human rights and freedoms"; and
- "can strengthen social cohesion and democratic governance" (2).

The issues are more complex than they appear. For example, what is the cost of educating students in their vernacular language rather than the "vehicular" languages, such as English, Spanish, Arabic, Hindi, and Swahili, which are more commonly spoken around the world? What is the cost of preserving traditional ways of life? Who should be responsible for preserving them? Do some people become the vehicles of nostalgia, stimulation, or entertainment for others?

Governments can succeed in economic protectionism. It is relatively easy, although controversial, to protect an economy with quotas and tariffs. Is it possible for a nation to protect its cultural purity? If it is, how could they accomplish it?

In contrast to cultural protectionism, many people view adopting elements of global culture as prestigious. Incorporating foreign words, foreign foods, foreign articles of clothing—whether a Nehru jacket, as was popular in the 1960s in the West, or U.S. denims in the East—are ways of demonstrating that you are connected and cosmopolitan, not simply parochial or local.

In sum, cultural globalization challenges people with values and norms that are emerging from global interaction. It challenges people with a diversity of meanings from other national cultures. It calls into question cherished ways of life, and the relationships among individuals and between individuals and their society. No one can take for granted the previously taken-for-granted aspects of life; some people embrace this, others resist.

Conversion and Divergence in Globalization

Global Forms and Local Content

Culture has content and form; the distinction helps us assess cultural convergence and divergence. Form is observable. Content is harder to discern, particularly cross-culturally. Content is meaning and must be interpreted. If content adheres to the form, then the implications for homogenization are much greater. If homogenization of form provides new opportunities to diffuse local culture, the diversifying effects of globalizing culture are enhanced (L. Adams 2008, 616).

For culture producers such as artists, using a global cultural form as a vehicle can get their own work recognized on the international stage and gain status for themselves as artistis of international quality. Universal forms used in this way advance local and national artistic content and cultural productions. Using the universal forms generates a wider audience for local culture and local artists on the global scene. Housing local culture in global forms helps a culture attain legitimacy. (L. Adams 2008, 618). Global cultural fields operate throughout various cultural realms, with shared aesthetics and global status hierarchy. Genres of music, dance, film, and other artistic mediums are vehicles for moving local culture into global arenas; so are institutional structures and modes of discourse.

Convergence in form may mask divergence in content. Global and local meaning may both be nested within global forms. Even homogeneity at minute levels of specificity, such as the tilt of a head in a dance or the beat of a tune in music, may convey different meanings. With the spread of hip-hop and rap globally, there is considerable homogeneity of form. The content, however, varies at the most immediate level of the overt message and converges at the deeper level as an expression of teenage angst. The same is true of ballet, in which technical perfection conveys a beauty that arises from the mastery of nature in the West and the capacity to combine traditional culture with modern sensibility in the East. In Central Asia, the development of the performing arts made broad use of global forms of music and dance to celebrate national holidays—and nested local meanings within. The

Olympic spectacles are a good example (L. Adams 2008, 632). Within the global form of spectacle, local cultural fields using folk dance and music from many cultural traditions have been used to express global themes such as concern for nature, material well-being, and patriotism (631).

Science and rationality are global forms generally viewed as objective and unbiased sources of knowledge. Packaging ideas in a scientific and rational appeal bestows them with an aura of legitimacy facilitating cultural content diffusion across borders. This is how the environmental and anti-landmine movements gained global momentum. Money is another example of a universal form. Countries recognize one another's currency as the bond of the issuing country. Therefore, money can be exchanged globally for items and services of widely varying types—allowing for the expression of very diverse local content.

Form may transfer across cultures without content, but the opposite is true as well. Content can travel with form. Material items may carry a large degree of "soft power" or attraction that adheres not only to the object, but also to the values that it symbolizes (Nye 2004, 44–53). Blue jeans on teenagers, electronic gadgetry, movies, and some genres of music symbolize freedom, liberty, and modernism. They may be chosen for their content and carry values with them as they diffuse. Lest this sound insignificant, the soft power of material culture played a role in the downfall of communism in the USSR and Eastern Europe, the end of apartheid in South Africa, and the demands of freedom and political rights presented by the new generation of revolutionaries in Iran (50–51).

Diffusion of material culture may facilitate a global teen culture. Similarities in materialism, styles of dress, and decorative use of cell phones as personal appendages all suggest that teens across cultures are headed toward more similarity than in their parents' generation. Whether the homogeneity in this age cohort is confined to their adolescence or will progress as they age will be interesting to watch—as will its effect.

Convergence on global forms actually produces a feedback loop in which convergence often leads to more convergence. As people perceive more similarities among themselves, they are more likely to copy or model other aspects of culture, continuing and even accelerating the cycle of convergence. This is welcome by some people and unwelcome by others.

Sources of Diversity in Globalization

Despite people's fears that cultural globalization will produce a world of sameness, there is now a world of cultures "marked by diversity of organization rather than by a replication of uniformity," and it does not seem likely that there would be global homogeneity of meaning anytime soon (Hannerz 1990, 237). Global homogeneity seems even less likely 20 years after Hannerz made that statement. It is more likely that globalization will produce more diversity than sameness for the foreseeable future. Fundamentalism and nationalism heighten divergence when people reject global culture. Divergence can also come when people embrace it.

Divergence Within Societies, Convergence Across

Divergence develops within societies as the diversity of cultural experiences accessible to people increases and they make different choices. Many communities of interest, such as professional organizations, voluntary associations, and hobby and interest groups—everything from vegetarians, environmentalists, "new age" devotees, and stamp, coin, and butterfly collectors—are disengaged from specific territories and develop shared meaning across societies that is not broadly shared within.

Economic class is another source of difference within national cultures. When different classes within societies adopt material culture that is diffusing—for instance, the sagging pants, baseball caps, and baggy T-shirts of hip-hop—it creates more global homogeneity across groups but more intra-societal diversity. As economic inequality within and among countries increased, a transnational elite class emerged that is becoming more homogeneous globally—in its tastes, leisure activities, and interests—while its members are diverging further from their fellow nationals. Working classes and marginalized groups are also interacting globally. Economic globalization creates homogenization of classes across societies and divergence within societies along class lines.

Interaction through social media extends a person's milieu resulting in greater homogeneity across cultures, but perhaps greater diversity within. People at their home computers in Europe and the Americas participated in civil disobedience and protest in Africa, the Middle East, and Eastern Europe, supporting protestors with encouraging messages and helping them to maintain open communications when governments tried to block their networks. Muslims in America may become active, even radicalized, participants in Islamist movements through Internet involvement. Personal milieu can expand far beyond what has ever been possible (Albrow et al. 1994).

Glocalization, Hybridization, and Creolization

The interpenetration of the global and the local is one of the most fascinating and critical sites of globalization study. As global culture flows, it changes and is changed by the people and the local contexts in which they live—the scapes through which it passes. This facet of globalization, "particularizing the universal" and "universalizing the particular," is referred to as *glocalization* (Robertson 1992). The infinite variety of cultural elements and the infinite variety of combinations make increasing heterogeneity more probable than increasing homogenization.

BOX 9.7   Close Up: Glocalizing English

American slang is hot among trend-setting Japanese teenagers. Like other jargon, you need to be in the know to understand it. Parents and other hostile forces aren't. Being cool, such as wearing *roozu sokusu* (loose socks), is important if teens want to avoid *disareru* or being dissed, as their American counterparts would say. It is much better to *disu* someone else. But, as for teens everywhere, they must be vigilant because *denjarasu* (danger) could be anywhere.

Using American slang is cool, according to teens. They say it's less rigid, sounds better, and is more fashionable than Japanese. You should *chekeraccho* or "check out" *ko-gyaru-go*—high school girl talk.

English is also creeping into the workplace. To open an *ai-kon*, for example, you need to *daburu-kurikku* the *mausu*, or double-click the mouse. Reporting that the government health and welfare ministry banned excessive use of English in documents, a reporter noted that how much *foro-uppu* or follow-up there would be was not known (Kristof 1997, 3)

Engaging global culture reorients our views of self and collectivity, and changes frames for determining correct action. Reaching into these layers of meaning nearly always involves some degree of glocalization, adapting the global to local traditions and concerns. Cultural content, such as the meanings of individualism, democracy, human rights, and justice, are changed as they diffuse. They are abstracted and interpreted by other cultures, often with the mediating effect of a broker—perhaps a international governmental or non-governmental organization—adding another layer of interpretation in between the originator and the potential adopter (Herkenrath et al. 2005, 368). Consider, for example, how far removed the practices of yoga and meditation in the United States are from their Eastern religious roots.

Hybridization, creolization, and syncretism also refer to cultural blending. Hybridization (Pieterse 1994) and creolization (Hannerz 1992) blend two national or sub-national cultures. As Hannerz has noted, all cultures are "creolized," amalgams and mixtures. Glocalization very specifically refers to blending of local and global. Bringing Asian spices to bear in European foods blends cultures and creates a hybrid or creole. Meditation as a method of relaxation as opposed to its Buddhist use as a method to the "middle path" is a blending. These forms of blending are important in understanding cultural globalization. Cultural blending occurs much more often during waves of intense globalization. Glocalization and hybridization may be evident in the same cultural phenomenon. Musical forms often become global forms, carrying global meaning. Rap, jazz, and reggae, along with Western classical music, have spread globally. In Burma, rap is glocalized. It uses the global form to express adolescent angst with a particularized content, reflecting the respect given mothers and sisters in Burmese culture.

BOX 9.8   Close Up: Barbie Hybridized, Not Born, in America

The ubiquity of Barbie, like McDonald's, has been a symbol of rampant Americanization. Barbie's 50th birthday in 2009 was marked by both celebration and commiseration by women around the world. Interestingly, Barbie was born in Germany, as the Bild Lilli doll—modeled after the cartoon character Lilli, infamous for her dalliances with men. Lilli was copied and manufactured by Mattel as Barbie, who was quickly naturalized and socialized as an American. She became iconic. For many girls all over the world, Barbie was symbolic of the modern, independent, Western woman, spreading ideas of style and fashion globally. While many girls came to love her and emulate her, others rejected the image.

Seen as a victim of male chauvinism in the 1970s and 1980s, attempts to reform Barbie have largely failed. Although her careers span the spectrum and she is truly a global citizen—a model in every ethnicity—her exaggerated body shapes and general style remain virtually unchanged.

Singapore developed a hybridized educational system by studying and merging U.S. and British models. The importance and rationalized nature of education, however, is a global element. Singapore globalized and hybridized. In many cases, with respect to the adoption of new technologies, Singaporeans globalized, adopting new technologies with little or no adaptation. Biotechnologies, however, raise a plethora of ethical issues. Absent universal ethics in the use of biotechnology, biotechnologies require glocalization. Singapore adapted biotechnology to its own cultural context. National ethical standards are being negotiated as the technologies are adopted more broadly (Khondker 2004, 19). Global ethical standards are emerging as increasing interaction across cultures demands more common understandings of acceptable and unacceptable practices.

Mc Donald's: Global or Glocal?

BOX 9.9   Consider This: McDonaldization and Hyper-Rationality

McDonald's is emblematic of the United States in more than its ubiquity. *McDonaldization* (Ritzer 1993) refers to a process of hyper-rationality, arguably most advanced in the United States. Increasingly, more realms of life, from dining experiences to leisure in theme parks and shopping in chain stores and malls, are arranged to meet needs for efficiency, predictability, calculability, and technological control over human activity. This ensures that people know exactly what they are going to get whenever they are in one of the chain operations. It lowers the cost of production and increases profits. Unfortunately, it might also extract personalization and spontaneity from the experience and stifle human creativity and initiative. This is the dysfunction of rationalization, related to alienation.

To what extent is rationalization alienating? Is the experience different for the worker than the consumer? Is rationalization alienating in other spheres of life?

For better or worse, fast food is quickly becoming a staple the world over. Fast food began to enter the markets of less developed societies as their middle classes grew. Fast food franchising came as sustained economic development and economies of scale made the franchises profitable. McDonald's alone has over 30,000 restaurants in 118 countries, and they are still expanding. It has a global supply chain and a global market that served over 58 million customers in 2008. Its 2007 packaging featured ethnically and racially diverse children and adults from 15 countries who were recruited through a global casting call (McDonald's 2007).

However, no matter where they are found, you can expect a high degree of conformity to the global forms. The general style of the restaurants, arches, menu, and packaging all help to make a McDonald's restaurant instantly recognizable. The global presence of the brand, the rationalized procedures of fast food preparation, the extensive global supply chains, and their adaptations to local cultures make McDonald's fast food an excellent example of cultural globalization.

McDonald's in the Philippines would be familiar to customers all over the world.

> Customers are greeted by a life-size Ronald McDonald replica as they enter the premises. The well lit interior gives the place a family friendly atmosphere. Beyond food, the restaurant also offers consumers amenities like an indoor playground, children's birthday parties, clean restrooms, and a stylish design. (Matejowsky 2006, 151)

Beyond the surface similarities, there are deeper elements of homogenization, for instance, the adoption of rational food preparation processes and "efficiency and standards that consumers expect from the fast food giant" (161).

Does the ubiquity of McDonald's bring more homogenization, or does it create more diversity? Is it possible that it creates more global homogeneity and more intra-societal diversity?

McDonald's encourages diversity to fit local markets but within carefully circumscribed boundaries. Seventy-five percent of McDonald's restaurants are owned by local residents. They approach their customers differently in every country. Menus in Asian countries feature more fish. In India, there is no beef. Instead of a Big Mac, you get a Maharaja Mac. Order a koroke burger in Japan and you'll get mashed potatoes and cabbage. In Germany, they serve beer. In Hong Kong, you can have a bun made of rice. Salmon, lobster, shrimp, rice, beans, and avocado sauce all find their way into McDonald's in various parts of the world (Adams 2007). Moreover, the shapes of the arches vary from country to country.

Local conditions each present different challenges. McDonald's' success, particularly in developing areas with poor market integration and fragmented supply chains, depends heavily on the cooperation of local firms and receptivity of the local population. Opening fast food eateries in developing countries highlights the interdependence of global corporations and local interests, how globalization and localization complement one another (Matejowsky 2006, 147). Far from being passive victims of cultural imperialism, local populations are very actively involved in bringing fast food restaurants to their communities and helping them adapt to local tastes. McDonald's is exacting when it comes to "quality control and automated style of service. Yet, managers are able to exert considerable autonomy when it comes to advertising, distributing profits, and adaptations to specific changes in the local market" (149–150).

Even more importantly, the McDonald's form has a different meaning in many developing countries than in developed countries. As the middle classes expand in developing countries, they proudly become the clientele for fast food restaurants. Two working heads of household makes preparing family meals at home more difficult, but provides a bit of supplemental income to spend out. Like other displays of adopting modern culture, eating at a fast food restaurant has come to symbolize the family's upward mobility and cosmopolitan attitude (Herkenrath et al. 2005, 364). The longer term effects of McDonald's and similar fast food chains on people's attitudes toward food and nutrition raise a plethora of questions. Whether or not other aspects of meaning associated with fast food— such as super-sizing and eating twice as much unhealthy food for only a slightly higher price—will carry over to developing nations remain to be answered.

Case Study: Selling Soaps in Egypt

In Egypt in the 1970s, companies did little to adjust their marketing strategies to consumers. In the 1980s and 1990s, however, economic change in Egypt brought foreign direct investment. Ironically, it was the presence of multinational corporations that forced Egyptian companies to pay more attention to local consumer-based marketing strategies (Kehrer 2007, 155). The multi-local geography of multinationals gives them opportunity to develop competence in responding to diverse cultures in their markets. Multinationals don't necessarily produce the same goods for every market. Their products, marketing techniques, and communications to potential customers are adapted in accordance with local custom (152). For example, soap operas that aired in Egypt assiduously avoided topics of political interest, such as minority rights, that might bring disapproval of the government. These are common in U.S. soaps and are the lifeblood of daytime TV.

Multinationals also realize that even within countries, there needs to be a diversity of appeals. Urban and rural women in Egypt have very different lifestyles and concerns. Products must be adjusted. Proctor and Gamble's *Ariel* detergent is manufactured with more foam for washing in rural areas than the detergent sold in urban areas because urban women have washing machines and most rural women do not. The products in rural areas are sold in smaller, less expensive quantities than in urban areas where women have more disposable income (Kehrer 2007, 156–159). Marketers make deliberate use of entertainment to lure rural women to their products at the weekly markets. Marketers set up booths and demonstrate products, provide information, and entertain—*Persil* has colorful clowns touting the advantages of all color detergent. Rural women tend to be in the house six days a week and go out shopping once. Shopping is an event for them. At the market, advertisers will "show you some of the nice things that you have never seen in your life. That's why you love *Ariel*" (brand manager, quoted in Kehrer 2007, 159). Marketers are among the most successful glocalizers.

Global Culture: Compromise and Clash

Cultural globalization revived fundamentalism, nationalism, and cultural protectionism. It brings increasing diversity through glocalization and blending of local and global cultural elements. A global cultural system has also emerged. Global culture is the global forms, ideas, and themes accepted near universally that used to convey international and global legitimacy. Global culture consists of models for social structures, such as government, education, and health care systems; ways of thinking about the world, such as rationality and science; and expectations concerning such themes as human rights, consumerism, and cosmopolitanism.

Rationalization and Alienation

Rationality

Rationality is a reasoned approach to life. Supplanting guidance through religion or tradition in secular domains of life, rationality is, in contrast, objective, based in expertise, scientific understanding, or logic. Enlightenment thinkers proposed that "the more we are able to rationally understand the world and ourselves . . . the more we are can shape history for our own purposes" (Giddens 2003, 2). This line of thought has influenced philosophy, science, and the social sciences from the Enlightenment to the classical sociologists, including Max Weber, for whom its application too rigidly to too many areas of life was a central concern.

Rationalization as a way of looking at the world that engages

> continuing efforts to systematize social life around standardized rules and around schemes that explicitly differentiate then seek to link means and ends;
>
> the ongoing reconstruction of all social organization—subject to increasing systematization. (Jepperson, quoted in Drori, Meyer, and Hwang 2009, 22)

The underlying assumption is that everything—whether part of the natural or social world—can be measured, thus manipulated and controlled, even if it defies our current capability. Rationality quantifies, reducing qualitative difference to quantitative. It is the basis of science, the social sciences, and the expert systems on which modern life depends (Giddens 1990). Rational action is goal directed, with measurable goals and means to achieve the goals chosen on the basis of their efficiency. Experts are the people most adept at measuring, manipulating, and finding the most efficient means to achieve the goals determined possible and desirable—desirability also based on well defined and measureable criteria (Drori et al. 2009).

Rational Organization: Bureaucracies

Bureaucracy is the rational form of organization. The iron cage of bureaucracy, Weber's image of bureaucracy, came to dominate social life throughout Europe during the take-off phase of globalization. Organizations develop in response to their environments and rational organizations develop all over the world regardless of very diverse social, political, economic, and religious, contexts. This suggests a force external to societies produced the homogeneity, not forces within them. Societies and the organizations within them conformed to the global cultural model of the "modern proper formal organization" (Meyer et al. 1997).

Conforming to the rational organizational form is necessary for legitimacy in the global arena, for business, economic, governmental, non-governmental, and political organizations. This aspect of world culture is rarely challenged (Boli 2005, 385). A person's position in the organization is based on expertise and qualifications, not family, friendship, or strategic political reasons. People must follow policies and obey rules. They must keep records and increasingly are expected to operate "transparently." Rational organizations are to operate efficiently. Rational structures dominate education, medicine, science, government agencies, voluntary organizations, and international organizations. The World Trade Organization, for example, has "organizational goals, an internal authority structure, decision-making processes, and officers . . . regular communication with members, periodic meetings, a mission statement, double-entry bookkeeping, auditors, a human resources department, and so on" (384).

Professionalism

A professional is a rational form. Being a professional distinguishes a person as an expert and limits entry into a field of practice. Professionalism standardizes. It involves delineating special qualifications, trainings, knowledge, and skills that someone must have to claim to be a professional in a particular field. When a person is given the designation as a professional, it is a sign that the person can be trusted to perform the duties with a certain level of mastery and that the person will adhere to the ethical standards of the profession.

An example of adapting to the expectation of professionalism is the development of NGOs in China (Chan 2008). To legitimate themselves in the global NGO community, staff at the two religious NGOs, China Agape and ServeChina, felt compelled to adopt global cultural norms. Staffers were put through training programs in participatory methods (as opposed to more communist-type authoritarian styles) and project evaluation. The effect of the trainings was efficiency and better communication—rational goals. At China Agape, most of the staff studied English in college and had to take an English test before being hired. Training in techniques, and advanced English enabled the staff to interact on a professional footing and be recognized as professionals to the broader national and global audiences (247).

The folk dances of Central Asia were professionalized to win a larger audience and global legitimacy as an art form. This was engineered under Soviet direction in the early 20th century (Adams 2008). The choreography of the dance and the posture of dancers were standardized by copying European ballet stylistics to appeal to a generic modern audience. Dance was no longer performed in traditional ways but in keeping with the modern techniques. In this case, professionalization helped legitimize not only the dance but also the Soviet incorporation of the Central Asian nations. It demonstrated that the Soviets were allowing nations to maintain national identity through encouraging folk dance but universalizing and elevating it by incorporating it into international cultural forms.

Professionalism replaced traditional practitioners in most fields. In a world of strangers, professional credentials substitute for more informal ways of knowing. In a family business, a relative may be expected to give a job to another relative, regardless of more credentialed people being available. In a publically owned company or government position, this is corruption. In the developing world, traditional ways of handing out jobs and contracts are increasingly rejected. So, too, is the habit of passing the presidency of a country through a family dynasty. However, as recently as 2008, Fidel Castro's brother, Raúl Castro, assumed his rule. Until January 2011, when he was forced from office, Hosni Mubarak—and nearly everyone else—thought that his son would be the next ruler of Egypt. George W. Bush, in some respects, inherited his presidency from George H. W. Bush, although Bill Clinton held the job in between them.

Alienation

Rationalization remains an important element of global culture. Whereas rationality is certainly functional in many ways, the hyper-rationality of modern life is not. The near-global revolution of 1968 changed people's ways of thinking about rationality. It introduced anti-rationalism (Wallerstein 1995, 117). People reacted in the 1960s to the image of the organizational men, or as Weber called them, interchangeable "cogs" in machines.

The personal alienation and inefficiencies that result from hyper-rationality—rigid structures and modes of thinking based on quantifying quality and repressing individual creativity and judgment—have undermined some forms of rationality. This trend has been bemoaned for over a hundred years, from Max Weber's condemnation that bureaucracies turn people into "specialists without spirit and sensualists without heart" to Ronald Takaki's condemnation that rationalized environments were akin to prisons where the self is placed in confinement. Hyper-rationality of heavily bureaucratized social organization, where people have to adhere rigidly to rules and there is little room for them to exercise judgment, has been challenged. The absurdity of cost benefit analysis in situations where the costs are immeasurable is being challenged more frequently. In the aftermath of the World Trade Center tragedy, people protested deciding insurance benefits basing the worth of each person's life by their salary and the likely amount of pain they experienced. Both Anthony Giddens and Ulrich Beck (see Chapter Two) base their theories of globalization on the danger of the uncritical pursuit of rationality and the irony that we face having to manage the risks that the pursuit of rationality created. This is a major dimension of cultural and social structural reform in the contemporary period of globalization. It is discussed in Chapter Ten.

Liberalization

The 20th century closed with a wave of liberalization. In its broadest sense, liberalization is freedom. Globalization of freedom impacts other spheres of life, political, economic, and social, changing the relationship between societies and the individuals within them. While scholars debated whether or not particular cultural and religious traditions could or could not support freedom, people took the debate to the streets and democracy spread into Eastern Europe, expanding its reach. During the second decade of the 21st century, citizen uprising swept the Arab world, forcing limited democratic concessions in some countries and liberating Tunisia, Libya, and Egypt from dictators.

Economic liberalization, the opening of markets, also occurred in waves, concentrated both in years and regions. From the late 1960s to mid 1990s, region waves are evidence in liberalizing capital accounts and current accounts, adopting unifying exchange rate systems, and and liberalizing foreign economy policy. Mechanisms of learning, including the influence of the policies of the highest growth countries, of new information, and changing payoffs—the necessity to change policies when the old ones no longer work well—all affect the clustering of waves. Governments also change economic policy along the lines of those with similar cultural orientations (Simmons and Elkins 2004, 172).

BOX 9.10   A Closer Look: Save or Spend?

The United States wants the Chinese to buy more American products. On a trip to China in 2005, U.S. Treasury Secretary John Snow urged the Chinese to develop more financial instruments to encourage more consumer spending and borrowing on credit. This is despite Chinese leaders being "keenly aware" of the debate in America regarding the use of "risky new home mortgages to finance homes that people otherwise would not be able to afford" (Andrews 2005).

We may not have to wait too much longer to narrow our trade deficit with China. Chinese youth do not seem to have inherited the "savings gene" from their parents or grandparents. Chinese twentysomethings seem eager to adopt the culture of consumerism. Their savings rate in comparison to their parents is effectively zero (Richburg 2012).

The European model of liberalization seems to have the most globalizing effect. Eastern European countries modeled their domestic laws and policies after European Communities. The South African Constitution was modeled after the European Convention on Human Rights. European laws and policies on "capital punishment, gun control, climate change, and the rights of homosexuals" appeal more to youth globally than policies of the United States (Nye 2004, 76–79). European precedents are even having impact in the U.S. courts. Recent U.S. Supreme Court decisions on the execution of the mentally retarded and of children reflect a sensibility to world opinion of "cruel and unusual" that originated in Europe (Lane 2005). Turkey may serve as a model for the new governments in the Arab world that seek a secular state in a majority-Muslim society.

Consumerism

Everyone is a consumer, not just of food but of products as well. We consume necessities and things to make life easier and more pleasurable, such as music, art, and toys. The things people own from cars to clothes help them define themselves to the world. Consumerism connotes more than simple consumption; it is people's fascination with acquisitions above and beyond what they need in order to satisfy vague needs that have nothing to do with the intrinsic nature of the product (or service) they are buying.

Consumer interests emerged among warriors and nobility in 10th-century Arab territories and 13th-century Europe—often along with a decline in concern for the public good (Stearns 2006, 3). Goods were made by artisans and, through the material used, design, or quality, bore the mark of their origin. Goods from Asia, particularly China and India, flooded into Europe; silks, cottons, porcelain, and other consumer goods were of a higher quality than Europe could produce. Many Eastern goods, such as Kashmir shawls and Chinese porcelain, became fashions and fads in Europe. They symbolized sophistication and worldliness. European wools became objects of desire for Eastern royalty. Poverty and status distinctions kept the masses from developing consumer culture. Even when peasants had cash from the sale of surplus produce or artisan crafts, their focus on solidarity of the group prevented consumerism from developing (4–5).

BOX 9.11   Consider This: Commodity Fetishism

One of the most ingenious concepts of Karl Marx is commodity fetishism. When people make things for themselves or for another—regardless of whether the relationship is fair or exploitative—the relationship of the producer, the product, and the other, if applicable, is direct and obvious. When people produce for the market, the product becomes a *commodity*, an item of indirect exchange. The relationship between people is replaced by the relationship between things. The products become autonomous, disassociated from the people whose labor made them. This was Marx's meaning of *fetishism*, the appearance of independence to objects created by humankind. The fetish disguised the exploitative conditions under which commodities in capitalist systems were made. After all, when we buy commodities at those too-good-to-be-true prices, how often do we think of the conditions under which they were produced?

Modern consumerism diffused with capitalism, industrialization, urbanization, and the middle classes. In the 18th century, mass production increased European production, and people had money to spend. Advertisements and promises of remarkable benefits lured customers into buying things that they had not even imagined they needed. Objects embodied and fulfilled new needs. Even in the earliest arcades (malls) and department stores, shopkeepers used lighting, smells, and attractive displays to entice shoppers.

The traditional social hierarchies broke down under urbanization. But people still needed a form of self-location. Objects became "badges of identity in a rapidly changing social climate" (Stearns 2006, 34). This spread beyond urban areas as rurals traveled into the cities for supplies, and suppliers ventured into rural areas looking for raw materials and markets (33). In the 1860s, "China mania," a craze that developed for the blue-white Chinese porcelain as a status symbol, overtook Europe. The craze was so rabid that doctors said parents cared more for their china than their children. Whistler, the flamboyant American painter who lived primarily in England during his adult life, collected over 300 pieces. He also wore a Chinese robe when entertaining (Stamberg 2010).

BOX 9.12   Consider This: Group vs. Individual #1

A market economy needs people to buy "things," many of which are unnecessary. They are manufactured products for largely manufactured needs. But buying them keeps people employed making them. It also makes profits.

The media need to make us want things, by advertising them. They make their money selling advertising time. Spending money keeps a capitalist economy growing.

In the economic downturn of 2007–2008, people in many developed nations were given "stimulus" checks. One of the flaws in our economy—in the United States at least—is that people spend too much money and do not save enough. Nevertheless, we were told not to save the stimulus check (even though unemployment was soaring) and

(Continued)

(Continued)

not to use the check to pay down debt that we already had. Both of these options made sense for consumers. Instead, people were told to spend the check to stimulate the economy. Is there a better way to stimulate the economy and keep it growing?

Which should consumers have done? If you had gotten a check, what would you have done with it?

In 2011, people started receiving a tax cut that gave them a little more money in each paycheck, rather than a lump sum, believing that people wouldn't notice the small monthly increase and would spend it.

Consumerism did not appear until somewhat later in the Americas. In Latin America, the elite class adopted consumerist orientations in the 18th and 19th centuries, importing and copying the goods and styles of Europeans. In the United States, a small commercial class and resistance to European habits staved off consumerism until the 19th century. By then, the desire to shake the image of being backward expanded consumerism and copying European fashion (Stearns 2006, 44–45). Wealthy areas of major cities in the United States began to resemble the shopping areas of Paris and London. Held back by poverty, the poor became producers of goods for exporting to consumer markets. As the middle class developed in the early 20th century, consumerism spread (111).

Africans were also attracted to European goods, but many were held back by slavery and poverty. Beautiful African products were traded for centuries. European quality was no better than African, but they were valued for their unusual design and style. Although priced higher than African goods, not just the elite but also artisans, merchants, traders, and farmers who could afford it paid the price to be different and to stand out. They were able to elevate their status by having more (Stearns 2006, 116). These early experiences developed the basic characteristics of consumption consumerism: false needs, acquisitiveness as a marker for status, the skill of merchants in marketing, and an extreme emphasis on fashion that renders last year's items out of date and unsellable.

Consumerism came later to China and Japan. Asia had less interest in European goods. More people were poor in Asian societies, but, more importantly, the Buddhist, Hindu, and Confucian values that emphasize the spiritual and public good moderated materialism. Cultural identity and traditional styles had more appeal (Stearns 2006, 94). By the late 20th century, acquisitiveness and status seeking through possessions had spread globally. Japan, South Korea, Taiwan, and smaller East and Southeast Asian economies grew rapidly in the closing decades of the 20th century. Set back only slightly by the economic crises of 1997 and again in 2007, they became well entrenched in the ranks of consumerism. One of the more interesting features of Chinese consumerism is the rapid development of the cosmetic surgery industry. China is the third largest market for cosmetic surgery, following the United States and Brazil. Surgeries are given to high schoolers as graduation presents. The surgeries requested are uniquely Chinese: creating larger-looking eyes by adding a crease to the upper eyelid, making the nose more prominent, and lengthening the jawline (La Franiere 2011).

BOX 9.13   Check It Out Yourself: Too Much Stuff?

People in the United States own so many things that their stuff is spilling out of their houses! Self-storage facilities, like these in Pittsburgh, are a booming business. I know that you are thinking, "This doesn't apply to me! I don't own too many things!" How many pairs of shoes do you have? How many do you need? How many cell phones have you had? Did you really need a new one?

Individualism

The most global use of individualism is based on the concept of individualistic democracy where one person has one vote and constitutions give rights to individuals. There are many glocalized varieties. European models are more influential than the U.S. model. South Africa, in adopting its new constitution, rejected the "extreme" individualism of the United States, which grants "legal protection of press misbehavior and of racist and other forms of hateful speech. [Another objection] is the unwillingness of the US to treat race-based affirmative action as explicitly constitutionally permissible" (Schauer, quoted in Nye 2004, 79). In the case of South Africa, overcoming the horrors of apartheid allows for practices that are unconstitutional by recent court decisions in the United States. Democracies developing in Eastern Europe temper individualistic reforms by preference for the safety nets of Western European countries.

BOX 9.14   Consider This: Group vs. Individual #2

There are many examples where the rights of individuals and those of the group may collide. This has been a major sticking point in globalization. Often, the consequences of past wrongs extend into the present and will extend into the future if not addressed. To what extent should they be addressed by allowing advantage to be given to the members of a group that has been discriminated against in the past? Should groups be protected from the continued spread of prejudice and discrimination by restricting freedoms of speech, assembly, and protest associated with civil and human rights today?

In 2010, Google, which had been compliant with Chinese censorship laws in their Chinese search engines, threatened to stop compliance in response to Chinese hacking into Google accounts. Although many Chinese liberals protest Chinese censorship, Chinese government officials insist that Chinese ideology, which puts collective interest above individual, be respected by Google and others doing business in China (Jacobs and Helft 2010). Similar views temper individualism throughout the East. Human rights and democratic reforms were resisted in Malaysia, Singapore, and even Indonesia "on the grounds that the West was trying to impose alien values that favor individual rights on an ancient culture where the highest value is placed on the welfare of society as a whole" (Nye 2004, 84–85). Middle Eastern societies react similarly, developing and invoking, for example, the Bill of Rights adopted by the Arab League, in place of the UN Bill of Rights.

The Demise of Americanization

The diffusion of American material culture such as blue jeans, the reach of American multinational corporations and cultural products such as music and movies, the might of the American military, and the attempts to spread "brand America" globally have been formidable (Steger 2009, 66, 76). Even those who recognize that the United States is not universally admired as a model nation admit that for most of the contemporary period, the United States dominated globalization. The size of America's economy; the dominance of English; the diffusion of legal, accounting, and technical practices; and liberal economic principles give the United States an advantage in getting its way with globalization (Hubert Vedrine, quoted in Nye 2004, 169).

BOX 9.15   Close Up: Minami, the Management Guru

After years of importing Japanese management techniques, *The Economist* reports that the tables have turned. A new heroine has Japanese managers are rushing to buy up Peter Drucker's classic 1973 treatise on management—scooping 300,000 copies of the book in six months, in contrast to the 100,000 in the previous 26 years. The catalyst? A wide-eyed, fringed-hair fictional teenage girl, drawn in classic anime style who uses Drucker's techniques to transform her losing high school baseball team into winners. Hopefully, Japan's new heroine will not only transform management, but give women a boost into positions of power as well. Japanese women make up only 1% of executive boards in Japan ("Drucker in the Dug-Out" 2010).

The United States is "globalization ready." It already accommodates multi-ethnicity, and ideas flow freely in and out. America formed from many cultures—a natural laboratory for the global cultural experiment (Nye 2004, 170). America's soft power, the model of its successes, and the generosity of U.S. philanthropy spread America's influence globally. American universities are among the best in the world. Students who study in America often return to their own countries to positions of power where they have a direct effect on far-reaching policies. For example, Alexandr Yakovlev studied at Columbia and returned to Russia a key liberalizing influence on Mikhail Gorbachev as he dismantled the Soviet bloc, and Mahmoud Jibril—the interim prime minister of the post-revolution Libyan government—received his Ph.D. in political science from the University of Pittsburgh. Scientific and cultural exchanges spread American ideas of rights and freedoms along with the technology and art (Nye 2004, 45–46). American soft power has been the greatest source of its influence, particularly in diffusing its values.

As globalization progresses, America's influence is likely to diminish. European political influence is on the rise. As mentioned earlier, European pathways to peace and prosperity—until the recent economic crisis—are often preferred above the United States' as a model for "economic growth, equality, democracy and individual freedoms" (Nye 2004, 77). Beyond Europe, rapidly growing economies, particularly China, India, and Brazil, are competing for soft power. Already, China and Brazil are investing heavily in other countries. In the case of China, investments often support their own interest by financing infrastructure to develop its investment opportunity and market. Brazil's aid is more direct, without an immediate self-interest. Either way, aid is soft power and buys influence.

The World Wide Web is becoming more diverse. Chinese users of the Internet will outnumber Americans, and Chinese content will increase, extending Chinese reach and influence. As Internet use increases, the architecture of the Internet changes. America is less of a hub for connections as direct connections among areas that are now marginalized are increasing. All of these mitigate America's global influence, giving people more models, more options, more freedom to choose.

Case Study: Popular Art: "What's Burmese About Burmese Rap?"

Exported from African American teenagers to teens wired into the Internet, hip-hop and rap are accessible cultural forms near globally. An online search demonstrates that rap and hip-hop are a universal language of global youth culture (Gilroy 2008, 196). The case study of rap in Burma (Myanmar) by Ward Keeler (2009) illustrates the complexity of cultural globalization and glocalization. It also illustrates the attention to ethnographic detail necessary to study cultural globalization in varying contexts.

Burmese rap appears to be a thoroughly globalized form, nearly identical in form to its American counterpart. Older generation Burmese claim to have indigenous rap based on eight-syllable word play. However, contemporary Burmese rappers have either never heard of it or proclaimed it obsolete and irrelevant to what they do. American rappers have a similar attitude toward "signifying," a distinctive word play contest among African Americans, primarily males. Burmese rappers go out of their way to make their sound and style American, not Burmese, and use the global form without deviation.

Form

Pronunciation and rhythm: Tonal qualities and syllable lengths in Burmese speech are very precise and convey meaning. In Burmese rap, capturing the rap form is so important that the qualities of Burmese speech are sacrificed to imbue the lyrics with an American sound. The rhythmic form takes dominance over pronunciation. The words of the rap are barely intelligible; however, the rap is imbued with an overall American effect (Keeler 2009, 5).

Performance: Burmese rappers' performance is virtually identical to their American counterparts. The rapper acts energized and enraged, as though he (but sometimes she) can barely keep contained. Arms flailing, face twisted and contorted, the rapper is barely in control. A troupe of complementary performers usually accompanies the rapper onstage, break-dancing or cavorting in other ways, true to the standard American form.

Clothes: Clothes play an important role in the rap performance. Clothes convey status and identity, and hip-hop style is no exception. Baggy pants, ball caps, sunglasses, necklaces and chains, tank tops and T-shirts are the Burmese rappers' uniform—the same uniform in the United States. Although the clothes and jewelry connote a rapper's status and costume changes are common in any contemporary musical performance, one Burmese rapper took this to an extreme, with changes between each number. While the style is copied American form, it is in keeping with the Eastern emphasis on elaborate costuming (Keeler 2009, 6).

Topical Content

Lyrics: The content of American rap did not diffuse with the form. The lyrics of Burmese rap vary dramatically from American rap. One difference is theme. Burmese rap is very tame. It does not engage the vulgarity, misogyny, and violence common in the U.S. rap. It focuses on romantic themes—love betrayed, love lost, and love scorned. Rappers offered two explanations. One was censorship. Even the mildest suggestion of political matters could get a song banned and recordings confiscated. Second, as one rapper responded, "We're Buddhists, we know shame." As their sisters may be in their audience, they would not want their sisters, or other people's sisters, to hear that kind of material (Keeler 2009, 4).

Although American rap is criticized for its violence and vulgarity, some commentators see it as subversive. (Would this be true if it were shown to contribute directly to the black-on-black violence within African American culture?) These critics think that Burmese rappers are missing the chance at subversive expression (Keeler 2009, 7). While free speech does not have much cost in the United States, in Burma, the cost is very high.

Meaning: Burmese rappers strive to appear rich, modern, and cosmopolitan in ways they learned through mass media. This is the same motivation documented by Adams (2008) in her ethnography of dance in Central Asia. By taking on the stylistic qualities of African American youth, Burmese rappers enhance their status by showing that they are like the Americans. This is an interesting contrast to American middle-class rappers who take on rapper style to go against the aspirations of American mainstream. White American rappers make a very different statement—of rejection of status and the status quo—than the Burmese aspire to modern status rather than reject it (Keeler 2009).

And Yet, Convergence at a Deeper Level

Underneath the style, Keeler (2009) found significance often overlooked. He argues that the universal appeal of rap is not its association with the protest of the oppressed but the angst of the adolescent male. Whether upper, middle, or lower class, East or West, black or white, modern adolescent males face similar life events (10). Rap celebrates radical individualism and stereotypical versions of masculinity. The powerlessness modern adolescent males feel is expressed in a masquerade of agency

and power, a contemporary version of an old theme from James Dean's *Rebel Without a Cause* to *The Outsiders* and *The Breakfast Club*.

Cultural Flows Emerging From Global Life

New global cultural forms and content are emerging due to the intensity of global interaction, new technologies used globally, and the experience of common problems. They are emerging not from diffusion from one culture to another but primarily from people's common experiences with globalization. For example, as mobile technology spreads globally, a global teen culture is developing in which cell phones are expressions of individual identity. Teens, seemingly everywhere, keep cell phones on them at all times. They have become a personal appendage and are treated as modes of self-expression (Castells et al. 2007). Cell phone decoration, ring tones, away messages, and even the post-scripts at the bottom of texts—such as "Out skiing—sent from my black and blueberry"—have been co-opted by teens and young adults as vehicles for self-expression.

BOX 9.16   Close Up: Technology-Driven Culture

Memes

Evolutionary biologist Richard Dawkins used the term *meme* to signify a small but a meaning-packed unit, such as a bit of information contained on a gene, that facilitated biological or cultural evolution. A meme passes from person to person, evolving and mutating as it does. Some memes have staying power, some do not. Meme itself has now mutated. On the web, a meme could be an enhanced or animated video clip featuring cartoon or commercial characters, set to music. People add new movies to the same music, mutating it. A meme could be a question on a blog that others pass around, adding questions.

Kitten memes may be the most popular: photos or cartoons of cats, captioned with funny (absurd) sayings. Memes are global and now so mainstream that Yahoo! has a meme site.

Cell Phone Novels

In the meantime, from the land of the haiku where cell phones are more cherished by teens than computers, teenage girls are writing and reading novels on their cell phones. Appearing in 2000, the cell phone novel is a distinct genre of flat characters, lots of dialogue and little description: much the tone of a diary. It has become so popular that the novels are printed out and sold as books. The novels did not originate with the desire to write, encouraging teens turned to the cell phone; the cell phone stimulated the desire to write.

Die-hard fans claim to be able to tell the difference in the rhythm of the lines between a cell phone novel and a copy-cat written on a computer (Onish 2008).

Some emerging global culture is unique to this era, and other aspects have gained particular salience in this period of globalization, the period of uncertainty. These cultural themes are arising simultaneously in many parts of the world. Each one is likely to be highly glocalized. Another precaution is that global does not mean universally accepted. No one motif is likely to be ascribed to by everyone in the world or even everyone within any single part of the world. Some themes conflict with one another, such as those that value universals to the exclusion of particulars and those that value particulars at the expense of universals. These contrary positions are debated and negotiated within small groups, organizations, societies, and in global relations—sometimes violently.

Interconnectivity[2]

The capability to be continuously available 24/7, made possible by mobile technology, has become a norm—where possible. The expectation that people are constantly available when we need or want them has become an issue of etiquette. Among some groups, being out of touch or unavailable is considered impolite or insulting. There is no excuse not to instantly return a call or text. The capability for interconnectivity has also become a need for many people to be continually in touch. Even in the presence of face-to-face interaction, many people need to be connected technologically to the larger world as well (James 2004). Social life is transformed as the imperative for interconnectivity allows us to engage in a "full time intimate community" staying close to our inner circle regardless of distance and time (Castells et al. 2007, 91–93).

Does the capability of being in touch with our closest friends keep us from expanding our friendship circles and forming new close friendships?

BOX 9.17   Check It Out Yourself: Evolving Technology Talk

Perhaps no culture changes as quickly as high-tech culture. Not too long ago, beepers were the latest gadgets. Having only numerals to work with, beeper talk had to be very inventive. Can you translate these beeper messages from a decade or so ago?

007	0001000	911
100-2-1	1-8	1776
10	54321	121

The emoticons are probably more familiar.

(@@)	:-?	:-X
:*)	:-<	:-D
%-)	(:-$	:/

(Answers are at the end of the chapter.)

(Continued)

You are probably familiar with elaborate text messaging codes? Lol, brb, and gtg—the grandchildren of FYI—are familiar to most people. While they vary by language, these codes started simply and have become increasingly complicated. Many of them are indecipherable by older generations. Is there a new tech talk that you and your friends use?

Micro coordination of daily activities is also a feature of daily life. Often the unpredictability of life often makes changing plans necessary. The capacity to change plans spontaneously makes it an opportunity rather than contingency. Family and friends, professionals maintaining contacts with their clients, migrant workers keeping in touch with family or job opportunities, even demonstrators being called to a protest keep in touch so that plans can be adjusted and changed instantaneously anytime someone has a new idea or a prospect arises. Being disconnected is so unhip that youth who are not connected are left out of communication loops and miss many events (Castells et al. 2007, 128).

Being continuously online and in demand may reflect someone's importance. In the United States, and maybe elsewhere, texting during meetings is within the realm of good manners in many contexts. Politicians, business executives, and busy people text message voraciously in contexts where anything other than undivided attention would have been seen as dismissive a decade ago. Now, it is interpreted as a sign of dedication to work or to clients to be texting, showing that there are important things to which you must attend. Some psychologists have suggested that these changes in norms result from addiction. The surge of adrenaline from being connected and getting near-instant feedback may be driving the increasingly evident cultural imperative for interconnectivity. Another possibility is that the demands of contemporary life are such that one's dexterity for multitasking is another sign of being modern and global.

Imagining Mobility

The world is one place, and people are increasingly forced or want to travel. Both actual and anticipated migrations have globalization effects. Mobility has cache as an indicator of cosmopolitanism, another growing global ideology. The elite classes are highly mobile. Capital is highly mobile. Jobs are mobile. Not all people are mobile. Some are mobile only to places where they can walk. Imagining mobility—that one might have to move—may be frightening to many people and exciting to others. The imagining that everyone is clamoring to live in the West has shaped public opinion by contributing to intolerance, because many people believe that their way or life or financial security is threatened. With open borders in the European Community, many Europeans are finding it difficult to imagine that migrants could enhance their country or culture with the youth, higher birth rates, and fresh perspectives that they bring. In many aging Asian and European societies, the imagining about migrant groups and fears associated with them may hurt their own welfare.

Forced migration—due to war, oppression, or economic need—and voluntary migration contribute to the globalization of culture. Mobility and concern for mobility are part of globalized culture and a stimulus for global culture (Appadurai 1996).

The UN Educational, Scientific and Cultural Organization (UNESCO) reports that there were about 190 million migrants—people living outside their country of birth—in 2005 (2009, 31). A large portion of contemporary migrants are women, working in electronics and clothing industries, in low-level service occupations, as prostitutes, and as domestic workers, often taking care of other people's children while having to have left their own behind. Many are enslaved as well. Students, missionaries, and NGO workers are also migrants.

Migrants establish global communities that transcend territorial location and boundaries. They

BOX 9.18   Consider This: Networks of Student Migration

Students are important carriers of global culture. In the map of student migration, a region's position in the hierarchy indicates its standing with respect to volume of in and out flow. Judging from this map, which region is the most isolated?

Global International Students network

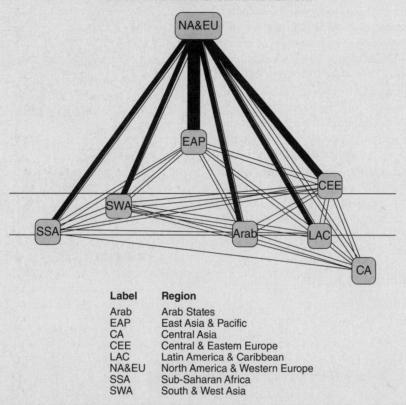

Label	Region
Arab	Arab States
EAP	East Asia & Pacific
CA	Central Asia
CEE	Central & Eastern Europe
LAC	Latin America & Caribbean
NA&EU	North America & Western Europe
SSA	Sub-Saharan Africa
SWA	South & West Asia

Source: 2009 Civil Society Yearbook: Poverty and Activism, by A. Kumar, J. A. Scholte, M. Kaldor, M. Glasius, and J. Seckinelgin, 2009, London, SAGE Publications. Copyright SAGE Ltd.

make the local global. Developing countries in particular work hard to keep close contact with their émigré communities. Migrants change both the cultures of their origin and residence. They carry new foods, values, habits, and art forms to their new country. They serve as sources of cheap and—much too often—slave labor. In some cases, the best educated and hardest-working citizens migrate, leaving those less able at home. Remittances migrants sent home to their families totaled $318 billion in 2007, most of which went to developing countries. This money dwarfs the official development aid sent by governments. It can alleviate the effects of poverty for millions and promote cultural development by enhancing educational opportunities, health care, or the acquisition of material things. Through communication and returning home, migrants bring new ideas, new values, and new ways of life. Tourism is another global flow of people. It is a major industry and serves as a significant source of income in many developing countries. UNESCO estimates that 25.3 million tourists traveled internationally in 1950, 800 million in 2005, and an expected 1 billion in 2010 (2009, 16). The glimpses of life in other countries that people glean from migrants and tourists form part of the global ethnoscape, our imagining of the rest of the world and people in it.

Security

Concern for security is imperative in a world full of risk. Risks do not respect borders; therefore, the need for security knows no boundaries. Security challenges have grown beyond the traditional concerns related to defense. A variety of very distinct threats, including terrorism and crime, the environment, poverty, health, housing, and literacy, reach into nearly every dimension of social life—the economy, family, culture, politics, gender, and so on. How some of these risks are viewed varies from society to society, but the expansion of security concerns and the expansion of state function and global cooperation in security are common globally. The sense of insecurity and concern to be more secure is a global theme. Just as it emanates from nearly every dimension of social life, it also has implications for people's decisions and actions in every dimension of social life. From survivalists to people combating climate change, securing security is a major preoccupation of contemporary life.

Humanity and Human Rights

The crystallization of humanity as a concrete orientation in individuals' lives is a defining element of both the objective and subjective dimensions of globalization (Robertson and Chirico 1985). Another aspect of humanity as a global cultural theme is that many of the conditions of modern life force the individual out of conventional social categories and into the realm of universalistic and ultimate concerns. Possible species extinction, abortion and end-of-life debates, devastating poverty, and monstrous forms of oppression confront people with the question of what it means to be human. This question extends from asking when human life begins to when it ends and what our obligations to one other are as humans at every point in between.

Changes in the global field—within individuals, societies, and the global system of societies—now occur in one way or another with reference to humanity. Humanity "underlies the structure and discourse of the world economy, world society, global markets, worldwide telecommunications, and so on" (Boli 2005, 391). Humanity is becoming a near-sacred category. Appeals to human rights have gravitas globally. Violating human rights is so egregious a crime that the International Criminal Court (ICC) was established to hear these cases.

BOX 9.19   Consider This: Group vs. Individual #3

Another area where the interests of the group and the individual may conflict is in due process. In the U.S. court systems, the presumption of innocence and the extensive due process rights are to guarantee that if the courts err, they err on the side of releasing individuals who are guilty, rather than imprisoning someone who is innocent.

In some other countries, the reverse is true. The choice is to protect the group first, individuals second. Thus, imprisoning the innocent is thought to be a lesser mistake than letting a guilty person go.

Which mistake do you prefer? Should the United States and other countries pressure societies to implement the same rules and procedures of courts that we have in the United States? Where do we draw a line between human and civil rights, preserving national culture and adoption of global culture?

The contemporary architecture of human rights was formalized in the 1948 UN Declaration of Human of Rights and the two protocols on civil, political, economic, social, and cultural rights that followed in the mid-1960s. Since then, human rights have expanded to include "treaties on discrimination against women, racism, children, religious beliefs, and refugees, as well as institutional innovations such as the establishment in Geneva of the Office of the High Commissioner for Human Rights" (Falk 2004, 19). The ICC, which heard its first case in 2003, has the institutional responsibility for enforcing human rights when national governments cannot or do not.

Human rights are subject to glocalization; there is significant cultural variation in the expression of human rights. The reason for glocalization may in some cases be due to "propaganda ploy by leaders who seek to shield their abusive behavior from criticism" or genuine differences resulting from a mismatch of the highly individualistic view of the West and the more collectivist view of many cultures that emphasize responsibility equal to or on the same plain as rights. They may also be a reaction to "US dominance, consumerism, and the loss of tradition" (Falk 2004, 18). Even where societies are closely related, variations may lead to international court cases. The "problem is, these days human rights come in more flavors than coffee or soft drinks" (18). Every country, every culture has its own ideas. Traditional or religious practices such as "female circumcision" are abhorrent to most people, but to many women, it is a sacred religious practice. These conflicts defy resolution.

The African Charter on Human and People's Rights was adopted in June 1981 by the Assembly of the Heads of States of the Organization of African Unity and came into force in 1986. It affirms the universality of human rights as found in the UN Declaration and various human rights instruments. Planning for the document began in 1979 and was heralded as a positive step forward by accepting limits on sovereignty in recognition of individual rights and the obligations of African states toward one another. The Charter established a Commission on Human Rights to collect and disseminate information concerning human rights issues, make recommendations to governments, and develop principles and procedures to negotiate human rights concerns. It will also consider cases of violations reported by states and bring violations of human rights to resolution (ACHPR 1981). These versions of human rights adhere very closely to the Universal Declaration.

Islamic versions of human rights vary more from Western ideals, particularly in the area of individualism. These may come to have a stronger influence on how global human rights are normalized, developing a more syncretic body of human rights laws, incorporating the *ummah* and *ahimsa,* concern for the individual within the group, into European human rights constructs (Pieterese 2003 391).

Despite glocalization, the scope of human rights has expanded and human rights are being practiced in more countries, extending to about two thirds of the global population. Freedom House ratings indicate that 4 billion people live in countries that are "free" or "partly free" (Falk 2004, 19).

People also vary on how they think human rights should be enforced, whether "with sanctions, regime change, corporate window dressing, or good old-fashioned moral suasion" (Falk 2004, 18). The global issues raised by human rights concerns are turning out to be among the most volatile. It will probably not be until everyone lives in a truly free regime—a universal assumption in itself—that we can view variations on human rights as human rights.

Multiculturalism and Cosmopolitanism

The appreciation of multiculturalism went global at a particularly rapid pace facilitated by the dazzling advances in information and communication technology and decreasing cost of air travel in the 1990s (Pieterse 2007, 66). Rapidly circulating ethnoscapes and mediascapes expose people to spatially diverse and distinct cultures as they walk along most any city block. Whether you visit a restaurant run by a Vietnamese immigrant, go out to a Bollywood film, or attend a world music concert at the local community center, most urbanites can access any number of distinct foreign cultural experiences on any given day. Multiculturalism may be concentrated in cities, but ethnic, racial, and cultural diversity reaches into rural areas, if not through immigrants and live entertainment, then by television, radio, newspapers, and the Internet. The threat of national cultures becoming more like one another is in large part because each is becoming more diverse. Cities are increasingly similar in their broad menu of sights, sounds, and experiences. Expectations of finding a mix of ethnic restaurants, global hotel chains, museums, Western dress, concert halls, and fantastic buildings by internationally renowned architects are seldom disappointing. While rural areas may be less diverse, most of the global population already lives in cities and urbanization is increasing.

Although oppression of minority groups continues, respect for indigenous and minority cultures is a criterion of state legitimacy. The 2007 Declaration on the Rights of Indigenous Peoples formalized the importance of preserving multiculturalism. Increasingly, heads of state appear on the world stage to apologize, on their own behalf or that of their governments, for the inhumanities suffered by indigenous or minority groups.[3] The apologies do not always make amends; only an apology issued by a government, as opposed to a head of state, comes with compensation. The apology recognizes the legitimacy of claims made by the aggrieved groups and their rights of citizenship. This is supposed to help the country move beyond the past and into the future (Nobles 2008, 3). It also enhances the reputation of the government domestically and in the eyes of the world.

BOX 9.20   Check It Out Yourself: Test Your Cosmopolitanism

Camels' heads are a common sight in North African markets. It signifies that the butcher specializes in camel meat. How comfortable are you eating camel with the camels' head looking over your shoulder?

If you are repulsed at the thought, does that make you less cosmopolitan than someone who can adjust their menu with ease? What are the important qualities that make someone cosmopolitan?

Cosmopolitanism is "the ethical standard in a world of strangers" (Appiah 2006). Migration, within as well as among countries, of necessity or for pleasure, puts people of different cultures, religions, and lifestyles in contact more frequently. Mass communication portrays the fate of all humanity for all to see. This puts everyone in a demanding ethical position. It dissolves the distinction between in and out groups.

Cosmopolitanism is an open-minded orientation to those who are different, a willingness to interact and understand their worldview and their practices, and a competence—an ability to maneuver skillfully within cultures different than one's own. Through engaging, understanding, and developing inter-cultural skill, cosmopolitans are empowered to construct their identity selectively choosing those aspects of various cultures that appeal to them or embracing one holistically if they choose (Hannerz 1990, 239–240).

Cosmopolitanism is more than understanding other cultures. Simply understanding can lead to detachment. Commitment or a sense of belonging to the world as a whole is essential to ethical cosmopolitanism (Tomlinson 1999, 186).

Summary: Reorienting The Global Field

Cultural globalization is proceeding along two dimensions: a system that shapes discourse and interaction globally and the reorientation of cultures within societies as they are changed by and change global flows. The global system consists of elements such as rationality and science, bureaucracy and professionalism, and many cultural forms that help local content move through global spaces, facilitating communication and interaction across cultures.

Globalization calls our attention to the particulars of culture and identity. Reactions to globalization such as fundamentalisms and nationalisms are also global phenomena. They help people preserve identity in face of what some people experience as an onslaught from global and diverse cultures. Extremist versions of these reactions become dangerous if they lead to racism, ethnic hatreds, discrimination, or violent conflict.

The general tendency of the social sciences has been toward cultural relativity, accepting cultural differences non-judgmentally. Prior to the contemporary era, national sovereignty precluded countries acting against other societies on the basis of internal practices. While a practice may be repugnant in one society, such as eating mice or having more than one spouse, the general rule is to allow a culture to be the authoritative source of right and wrong within a society. Radical cultural relativists argue that the culture is the only source of validity for its moral rules. Radical universalism argues the opposite, that culture is irrelevant to what is morally valid or not. The rest of us are in between, running the gamut from strong to weak cultural relativism or universalism (Donnelly 2007). Nevertheless, globalization makes what happens in other societies everybody's business—regardless how problematic it is—when matters of human rights are at stake.

Cultural globalization has reoriented the global field, providing limits and opportunities for acceptable and unacceptable forms and behaviors—of individuals, societies, and the global systems. Cultural clashes over the content of global forms such as human rights pose dilemmas for the global community. The globalization of human rights and the accompanying obligation of everyone to protect all people, regardless of where they reside, has delegitimized the doctrine of non-interference and thrown the question of cultural relativity into sharp relief.

Questions, Investigations, and Resources

Questions

1. Debate: Do you think that traditional or indigenous cultures should be preserved or encouraged to develop?

   - If a culture wants to preserve its traditional way of life, do you think that countries should have an obligation to protect that culture? What vehicles can it use to accomplish this?
   - If a traditional way of life is likely to result in shorter life spans or harsher living conditions, should a culture be preserved?

2. Why have some people lost faith in science?

   - Is it realistic to think that because science has caused hardships that an unscientific approach to problems is better?
   - Are there ways to prevent some of the ill effects of science while preserving the benefits?

3. What changes do you think technological developments will bring in the next 25 to 50 years, within your lifetime?

4. It is probably correct that there are universal values related to preserving society. What are they? Are they reflected in the criminal codes of countries?

5. What elements of Eastern or other cultures have you or others you know adopted? To what extent does this convey greater cosmopolitanism? How have these enriched your life or the lives of others?

6. In the Internet age, it is increasingly difficult for governments to preserve their culture or limit new ideas from entering. Nevertheless, many have tried. How successful have they been, and how successful do you think they will be in the long run?

Investigations

1. Select an indigenous culture, such as Native Americans, that is a minority in its country to research.

   - Is this culture trying to preserve its traditional way of life, has it been assimilated into mainstream society, or is it vying for more autonomy or even separation?
   - How satisfied are people with their status?
   - Have they benefitted from the UN Treaty on Indigenous People?

2. See if you can map the dispersion of a cultural element from your home country or that you are familiar with that originated in another country. Using social media such as Facebook, MySpace, or YouTube, try to gauge the penetration of a cultural motif.

   - How many countries can you find represented when searching for examples of that element? For example, how many countries have someone doing a rap or hip-hop routine? Memes? What about Falun Gong groups? Or meditation, acupuncture, or other alternative therapies? To what degree do particular entertainers (Lady Gaga?) or sports stars (Michael Jordan?) have fan bases globally? TV programs? Books such as *Harry Potter* or vampire stories?
   - Map these as you find them. Can you discern a pattern?

3. Find a magazine or newspaper online from a non-Western culture. Use an English-language one if you cannot read another language. Try to find one of the leading daily newspapers for that nation.

   - Does the format resemble a U.S. newspaper or magazine?
   - What types of stories are the main headlines? Are these similar to what you would find in a U.S. newspaper?
   - How are the people dressed in the pictures?
   - Is there an entertainment section? What is written about and advertised?
   - Analyze the advertisements. Are they similar to what you would find advertised in the United States?
   - Explain evidence of cultural globalization.

4. Peter Berger (1997) described "four faces of culture" that originated in the United States, but have become independent and are now global: Davos, Faculty Club, McWorld, and Protestant

Evangelicalism (to represent social movements). Read his descriptions and see if you can find examples of each "face" in foreign magazine advertisements or articles.

5. Use the World Values Survey online analysis (http://www.worldvaluessurvey.org) to investigate cultural clash. Choose two societies whose cultures you think would clash.

- What is the basis of your choices: wealth, religions, civilization, language, level of development, educational attainment?
- Investigate the degree of similarity or dissimilarity between the countries on five questions from the world values survey. (Not all questions are asked of all countries each year.) Choose questions from different segments of the survey.

- Many of the questions are relevant to contemporary cultural debates concerning the role of women vs. men, homosexuality, abortion, freedom and equality, and human rights. Those questions might be particularly interesting to try.
- Was there more or less cultural clash than you expected? On what questions was there more convergence, on which less? Compare your results with your classmates.

Resources

World Newspapers Online http://www.world-newspapers.com

China: http://www.chinadaily.com.cn/index.html

Kenya: http://www.nation.co.ke

Morocco: http://www.map.ma/en

BOX 9.21   Check It Out: Technology Talk Answers

I've got a secret	I'm lonely	Emergency
Odds are against it	I ate	You're revolting
You're perfect	Ready to explode	I need to talk to you alone

The emoticons are probably more familiar.

You're kidding	Licking your lips	Kiss, kiss
Clowning Around	Sad	Laughing
Confused	Ill	Not funny

10

Globalization and Everyday Life

Objectives

As we move through our days, we move through a series of relationships. We go to school, work, visit (or live with) our family, cheer (or play on) our favorite sports team, go to the doctor, and so on. Despite thinking of ourselves as individuals and despite cultural diversity, many of these everyday relationships are patterned. Local and global models and norms shape how we do them and the structures in which we do them.

This chapter will help you

- analyze the role of science in molding institutional life in the take-off phase of globalization;
- understand the role of global culture, specifically rationalization, in promoting the diffusion of global models of societal institutions;
- discover similar patterns in the development of various institutions;

- understand the relationships between nationalism as ignited by globalization and expressed in institutional development; and
- assess the influence of globalization on education, health care, and sports.

The Role of Institutions in Social Life

Some of the thorniest processes of the global field are buried in the extremely intense nature of the relationship of societies to individuals. The relationships between a society and the individuals within are structured in its institutions. Individuals relate to the larger society in which they live through institutions, such as family, religion, education, medicine, the economy, polity, military, and so on. Thus, institutions are distinctively local, the place of our action in societies. At the same time, institutions are enmeshed in global systems and connect individuals to the globe. How institutions globalize has a direct effect on individuals' lives and the global order. Local, national, and global forces meet in institutions.

Globalization and Institutional Reform

Sociologists use the concept *institution* differently than other social sciences. An institution is a relatively stable pattern of social relations that fulfills important social functions. People need to eat, to reproduce members for society, and to have someone responsible for their care until they can care for themselves. They need to answer questions of good and bad and the meaning of life, to accumulate and pass on knowledge, to produce and distribute the means of survival, and myriad other activities that make life possible. Fulfilling these needs leads to relatively stable patterns of interaction and, thus, institutions—the family, religion, education, and economy, among others.

Social life is fluid, but institutions are patterns of interaction; they are social structure, and change more slowly. Globalization challenges institutions.

They may become outdated, ineffective, or out of sync with emerging ideas and values. This chapter reviews how three institutions—education, health care, and sports—were shaped by the diffusion of science and the rationalization of life that emerged during the take-off phase of globalization and the institutional reforms of the contemporary period.

The Take-Off Phase and Challenges of Rationalization

The emergence of mass society at the turn of the century in Europe and North America disrupted every dimension of social life. Newly industrializing cities grew up to 10 times their size within 50 to 60 years. Life in small towns and small communities offered little guidance for urban mass society.

Max Weber (1921/1978) assiduously documented the processes through which abstract, impersonal, and explicit rules, procedures, and principles replaced the traditional values and relationships that governed social life. Impersonality and rationality fit the anonymity, diversity, and complexity of urban life. Instrumental rationality dominated new organizational forms and changed the way that people thought about the world. Weber called this *disenchantment*: turning the world into a series of things and processes to be measured—from evolution to intelligence—and of relationships structured for efficiency and predictability—from assembly lines to classrooms. Not only science, medicine, and the economy—institutions where one might expect to find instrumentality—but also religion, art, and even family (home economics!) adopted rational models.

Rationality and science call traditional beliefs and patterns into question. Whereas traditions are bound to societies, instrumental rationality is supposed to transcend most group differences, providing a potentially universal mode of legitimacy. This brought benefits. The feminist movement advanced as traditions of patriarchy became less sustainable. This had profound impact on institutional life as women became a larger voice in every social realm and reform, from education to juvenile justice, suffrage, prisons, welfare, health care, and so on. Dramatic increases in travel, transportation, and communication demanded greater coordination across societies, and rationality overcame differences in culture and tradition. World time and the near-global adoption of the world Gregorian calendar signified that the world was fast becoming one place. In 1865, the International Telegraph Union

(now the International Telecommunications Union) became the first supranational agency, creating rules and regulations for states to follow. Rationally organized international agencies and organizations of all types proliferated.

The instrumental rational answer to establishing order seemed to work reasonably well for mass industrial societies in the West. As modernization penetrated nations and the globe, inequality decreased within nations, life expectancy increased, and morbidity and mortality decreased. Some societies on the periphery, such as the United States, grew in wealth, power, and prestige. Latin America gained independence. Others in Africa and parts of Asia did not fare as well, succumbing to colonial rule as powerful fleets with bureaucratized militaries launched the age of imperialism. Instrumental rationality became the dominant principle for organizing life, but that should not be interpreted to mean that it was either the only or best possibility for organizing mass societies.

In spite of the benefits they may bring, rational institutional structures can make the relationship between individuals and their societies problematic. The rules of efficiency and hierarchy of authority allow little room for individual expression. Weber (1921/1978) referred to the bureaucratic form of life as an *iron cage*. People had boxed themselves in by rules, regulations, and hierarchy that left little room for them to take initiative, control their work life, express creativity, or, in other words, be human. As instrumentality evolved, the social sciences, arts, and humanities took up the theme of alienation with increasing frequency.

Weber predicted that bureaucracy and the instrumental view of life would endure until the last ton of fossil fuels that fired industrialization and mass society had been burned. Events of the late 20th to early 21st centuries—repeated oil crises, pollution, severe weather and awareness of climate change, the transition to service economies, advent of information technologies, distrust of bureaucracy, and movement toward alternative energy sources—suggest that Weber was on target. However, our addiction to oil, the power of oil companies, increasing inequality within and among nations, and unrelenting poverty in many parts of the world may postpone or prevent a transition.

The Contemporary Period and the Rejection of Hyper-Rationality

From the 1920s through WWII, rationalization and bureaucratization of social life continued. The

1960s brought that to a halt. McLoughlin (1978) described the '60s as follows:

> The ferment of the sixties has begun to produce a new shift in our belief-value system, a transformation of our world view that may be the most dramatic in our history as a nation. Today the end of the world seems closer than the millennium. Scientific progress seems more often a threat than a help in adjusting to our environment. The Vietnam War has brought serious doubt about our mission and our manifest destiny. The welfare state has bogged down in inertia and bureaucracy. There is more crime and cynicism than faith and optimism. . . . Many are searching for a different order of reality than pragmatic behaviorism offers. There is a striking new interest in the wisdom of the east as that of the west loses its power to give order and meaning to life. (179–180)

Social revolutions rocked societies East and West, North and South, in rich and poor nations, in democracies and autocracies. By the mid-1960s, trust in the institutions of modern life had eroded. The sense that national and global systems were not working in the interests of the common good was pervasive. The "core features of capitalist-modernity . . . sexual repression, sexism and heteronormativity; materialism, corporate culture, and 'the achievement ethic'; consumerism, bureaucracy, and 'social control'" came under attack (Fraser 2009, 103). Rejection of the status quo was particularly vehement among young adults. This was expressed by the popular expression, "Don't trust anyone over 30." In France, Maurice Grimaud, chief of police, said that youth were refusing a "society that was decomposing." The newspaper reported that "in several weeks, everything—the old ways, habits, customs, and ideas, collapsed" (Seidman 2004, 2). That was the case, everywhere. A tipping point had been reached.

The instrumental rational model had failed to provide adequate solutions to problems within societies or to the problems of globalization. Although inequality and poverty decreased following WWII, it was apparent that women, minorities, and entire countries had been left behind. The promise of independence and democratic transitions in newly independent states of Africa and Asia gave way to dictators and sectarian conflicts. War still plagued nations long after the progress of industrialization should have ended all want.

The Cold War was heating up. Che Guevara, after aiding Castro in the communist takeover of Cuba, traveled throughout Latin America hoping to inspire revolution. Trained himself as a doctor, he preached to university students of the misery he had seen on his travels and the obligations of the educated to workers and peasants. On his capture and execution in 1967, he became a revolutionary hero; his face is still emblazoned on T-shirts as a symbol of rebellion. Oppression was the rule in the Soviet states, the Warsaw Pact countries, and most of Central and South America. In China in 1965, Mao Tse-tung declared a Cultural Revolution, closing schools and using students to root out, arrest, and imprison millions of Chinese—including in some cases their own parents and teachers—who might be dangerous to Mao's communist ideology or iron-fisted rule. Millions were killed. China, he argued, had lost its revolutionary zeal, being headed by autocrats and technocrats.

1968 was a year of revolts. Movements of students, workers, and intellectuals in the United States, Canada, Japan, Czechoslovakia, Argentina, Germany, Italy, and others led protests against their governments for activities as diverse as the Vietnam War and domestic policies of repression. There were often disastrous results. The Prague Spring reform movement in Czechoslovakia came to an abrupt end when Soviet troops invaded. Jan Palach, a student, self-immolated as protest. In Mexico, just days before the Mexico City Olympics, government troops shot into a protest of thousands of unarmed students. The death toll of this, the Tlatelolco Massacre, whether 40 documented deaths or hundreds claimed by witnesses, is still debated (Doyle 2006). Throughout the world, the role of rationality and science, the tension between the local and the global, the rights and responsibilities of individuals and authorities, the nature of freedom and equality—stimulated reform and counter-reform movements. By the 1970s, inequality, poverty, and hunger had reversed course and were on the rise in much of the world. The war in Vietnam, the violence of the Cold War, and the continuing discrimination against minorities were undermining credibility of the United States, USSR, and other developed societies—at home and abroad.

These great movements of the take-off period and contemporary periods shaped and reshaped social relations within societies.

Education

It is a global expectation that everyone goes to school. In most countries, nearly everyone does—at least through primary schooling. In countries where they do not, progress toward universal education is monitored closely. Unless people choose to pay for their own education, it is expected that governments provide for primary school—and secondary, if they are able.

BOX 10.1   Consider This: Universal Education

Formal, universal, compulsory education was instituted by the Aztecs. Boys and girls were educated differently, as were children of different classes, but everyone had to go, even children of slaves (who did not inherit their parents' positions of slavery).

What purposes could education have served in a society such as the Aztecs? How is it similar or different than education today?

The Evolution of Universal Education

People did not always assume that education should be a function of the government. Prussia was the first modern country to adopt universal education. In the early years of the 19th century, educational reformers had a difficult time convincing people to accept that anyone other than parents should pay for education. Although Prussia and the United States were very different countries in many respects, they made the same arguments to sell education. Universal education was the only way to instill strong national sentiment and character into all the people of a diverse society. Prussia and the United States both faced the task of nationalizing immigrants. Horace Mann, the most avid of the common school proponents, convinced the people of Massachusetts to pay for common schools to educate all of the children in the state, because they were all citizens of the nation. (The reformers did not accomplish all that they had set out to, rich and poor, immigrant and native born are still not educated together in the same classrooms.) As immigrants poured across borders, integrating cultures more tightly with one another, national identity needed to be bolstered and reinforced. What better way, the reformers thought, than through schools that reflected the nation's virtues—free for all children, the same for both rich and poor, and high quality? Even though U.S. reformers borrowed heavily from the Prussian system, the educational system would be copied by other nations and help cement the U.S. position in the world (Mann 1891, 2, 287).

For of what value is it, that we have the most wisely-framed government on earth. . . the wisest schemes. . . if the people have not the intelligence to understand, or the integrity to espouse them? Each of two things is necessary to our political prosperity's namely just principle of government and administration on the one side and people able to understand and resolute to uphold them on the other. (186)

Today, the importance of mass education, although not necessarily for females, is recognized all over the world in societies of all religious, ethnic, and national persuasions. A well-developed educational system is featured prominently in the global model of the modern society, propelling educational expansion from the 19th century and accelerating expansion since the 1960s. Education is a complex institution, serving individual, societal, and global functions. It is essential for individuals to make a living in a modern economy, for a society's economic development, and for the infrastructure of the global economy. Although economic functions of education seem to dominate education—people and societies expect an economic benefit for their investment in education—it has had an arguably more important role reinforcing conceptions of national identity.

Globalization has affected education in several ways:

- Demands for schooling reform reflect national identity concerns. As nations become increasingly enmeshed in the global system of societies, they expand education, and reinforcing national identity assumes an increasingly important role.
- Educational reform debates reflect competing views of national identity.
- The demands for schooling and the specific nature of schooling conform to models and developments in global culture.
- Global cultural models of schooling are based on rational principles.

The Globalization of Mass Schooling

In developed societies, primary-level mass schooling was accomplished during the incipient period of globalization in the early 18th century, and secondary schooling in the take-off phase of the early 20th. As nations integrate more fully into the global system, their educational systems expand. For example, in Latin America, Asia, and Africa, mass education is more recent concentrated in the contemporary phase of globalization.

There are not many comparative studies of the origins of mass schooling. Typically, theories relate the rise of mass schooling to the rise of industrialization and the needs of the economy. An extensive review of research in comparative education finds little evidence for those explanations (Ramirez and Meyer 1980). Mass schooling originated in Europe, the United States, and Japan before industrialization. Similarly, in the contemporary period, mass schooling is instituted irrespective of a country's level of industrialization (374).

Data support the thesis that mass schooling arose as the international system of states emerged. As states integrate into the global system, they develop mass schooling to signify good standing in the system of nation states and as a vehicle of socialization. Whether a state is strong or weak, mass schooling is instituted to teach students about the state and to socialize them in its stories, rituals, and values (376).

There are more data available to study the expansion of mass schooling than its origins. School expansion data of 120 countries from 1870 to 1980 demonstrate that as nations integrated further into the global system of societies, they tended to expand systems of mass schooling. In 1870, almost all of the developed societies had more than 10% of the 5- to 14-year-olds in school. Growth in enrollments averaged about 5% per decade before WWII. Only about 10% to 15% of the societies keeping records at this time reached 10% enrollment or beyond by WWII.

As the nation-state form spread post-WWII, mass schooling became a normative expectation, regardless of level of societal development or wealth. After WWII, the rate of enrollment increased substantially to about 12% per decade. As new states were created, school attendance jumped to 72%, then 83%, then 100% by 1980 (Meyer, Ramirez, and Soysal 1992, 137–140).

From 1970 to 2005, African and Asian (excluding China and India) educational attainment rose rapidly. (Please see Box 10.2.)

Educational growth in this period surged irrespective of societal income, contrary to popular

BOX 10.2   A Closer Look: Education and Income

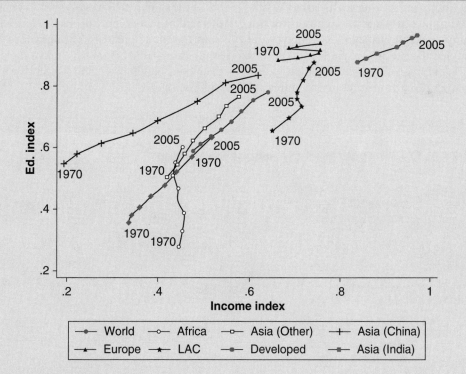

Education expanded rapidly in developing countries regardless of income growth. This is particularly evident in Africa, Latin America, and parts of Europe and Asia.

Source: Molina and Purser (2010, 34).

literature that takes for granted a relationship between educational growth and a society's labor force needs. In Africa, the education index doubled from 1970 to 2005, while income was stagnant. Latin American education growth also outstripped income, although not as dramatically. In European developing nations, education increased steadily while income fluctuated (Molina and Purser 2010, 13).

Asia and Africa have shown more growth in education than in either income or health from 1970 to 2005. Latin America has experienced more rapid growth in health. Their educational attainment expanded significantly earlier than that of developing countries in Africa and Asia. To find the same pattern of rapid educational growth outstripping income and health in Latin America, it is necessary to look further back in time. Latin America achieved independence in the late 19th century, most of Africa and Asia not until the late 20th century.

Two globalization dynamics converged to create this pattern of educational expansion. First, a number of nations became prospective or eventual candidates for statehood leading up to WWII, but that number increased dramatically after WWII. Second, the implicit normative expectation for mass schooling became an explicit requirement for legitimacy of a state in Article 26 in the UN Declaration of Human Rights. As globalization intensified, global culture pressured states to establish mass schooling. As states become embedded in a wider international system, mass education expands because the expectations for schooling increase. Mass schooling is an important norm of global culture, bestowing legitimacy internally in the eyes of citizens and externally for the global audience.

The Status of Education Globally

Basic education, primary and secondary, is now a global cultural norm, viewed as a human right that should be guaranteed by the state. The second Millennium Development Goal (MDG) is to achieve universal primary education by 2015. While many societies are close to this goal, the remaining societies with low school attendance and the remaining children who are still out of school are the toughest cases. While there is disparity by gender, the greatest inequalities in educational attainment stem from income and rural or urban living. About twice as many rural children are out of school than urban (UN 2010, 18). Urban slums are the exception. In Mumbai, the greatest numbers of school dropouts are in the slum wards. Unless there is an intervention, this will be increasingly problematic as slum populations continue to increase (Bruinius 2010). Residents in the slums of Mumbai have taken the problem into their own hands by establishing private schools for children of the slums.

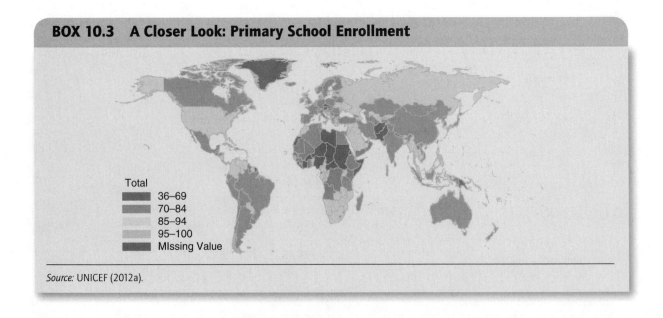

BOX 10.3   A Closer Look: Primary School Enrollment

Total
- 36–69
- 70–84
- 85–94
- 95–100
- Missing Value

Source: UNICEF (2012a).

Primary Education

Wealth inequality is the most egregious detriment to schooling. Globally, 90% of children of primary school age are in school, leaving about 67 million children out of school. As is shown on the Closer Look map in Box 10.3, most of these children are in South Asia (over 20 million), Eastern and Southern Africa (about 20 million), and West and Central Africa (over 30 million). These are the poorest areas of the world.

BOX 10.4   A Closer Look: Education, Income, and Gender

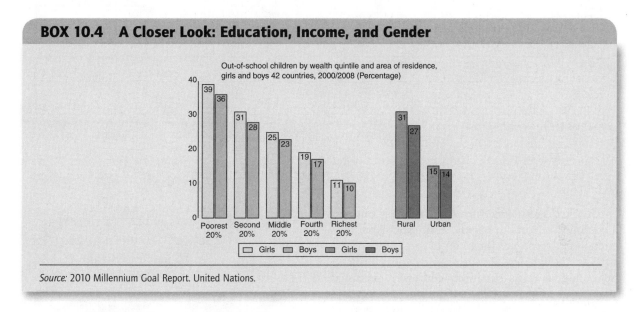

Out-of-school children by wealth quintile and area of residence, girls and boys 42 countries, 2000/2008 (Percentage)

Source: 2010 Millennium Goal Report. United Nations.

Within societies, there is also disparity by income. Thirty-six percent of girls from the poorest fifth of their country are out of school in comparison to 10% from the richest quintile. Thirty-nine percent of the poorest boys are out of school, in comparison to only 11% of the richest. As with other life chances residence also makes a difference. Thirty-one percent of rural girls and 27% of boys are out of school, whereas only 15% of urban girls and 14% of boys are out of school (UN 2011, 16–18). (Please see Box 10.4)

The likelihood that a child will be in the labor force rather than school also varies by income. About one quarter of children from the poorest quintiles of their countries in sub-Saharan Africa are in the labor force and not in school, while only 7% in the richest quintile have to forgo school for labor. The likelihood that a child will not be doing either is 10% higher in the poorest quintiles than the richest. Children in the richest quintile are almost twice as likely to attend school and not have to work as children in the poorest. (Please see Box 10.5)

BOX 10.5   Poverty, Child Labor, and Education in Sub-Saharan Africa (Percentage)

School	Child Labor	School Only	SCH & CL	CL	NSch	NCL/NSch
Poorest quintile	48.8	44.7	31.2	19.4	25.3	24.1
Second quintile	52.1	43.9	33.0	20.3	23.7	23.0

(Continued)

(Continued)

School	Child Labor	School Only	SCH & CL	CL	NSch	NCL/NSch
Third quintile	57.1	39.5	38.0	20.6	19.0	22.4
Fourth quintile	65.8	36.4	44.9	22.3	14.2	18.7
Richest quintile	78.4	23.8	61.9	16.7	7.1	14.2
Female	58.3	38.2	40.1	19.2	19.0	21.7
Male	62.4	37.9	42.8	21.1	16.8	19.3

Source: Gibbons, Huebler, and Loaiza (2005, 11, Table 4).

Conflict is also concentrated in poor regions and undermines efforts to expand education. About 43 million children, including half of those in conflict-afflicted countries, are not in school. Because schooling in crisis situations addresses emotional and social needs as well as cognitive, it is particularly important (Kirk 2008, 153–155). Refugees and internally displaced children are also likely to be skipped over for schooling. UNICEF collected data from 132 refugee camps. Only 38 camps reported that all of the children were in school. In another 32 camps, about 70% were in school, and in the remaining 62 camps, fewer than 70%. The UN estimates that among all adolescents in the camps, about 73% of girls and 66% of boys are out of school (UN 2011, 18). Only 3% of the 7 million child refugees aged 12–17 have access to schooling (Kirk 2008, 155).

Schooling serves a multitude of purposes in all societies. Education provides important social and individual benefits. In developing nations, where other institutional systems may also be weak, schools reach children on multiple levels. Even at the primary level, education helps reduce poverty, offers a safe environment, teaches life skills, and is a conduit for providing medical care such as vaccines and nutritional supplements (UNICEF 2009). While only one of these is explicitly related to the overt function of schooling, education is a pivotal institution that can meet a variety of children's needs.

BOX 10.6   A Closer Look: Primary School Students Lining Up to Get Porridge

Many students come to school without breakfast. Schools throughout the world have children's academic, mental, and physical development.

Secondary and Tertiary Enrollments

Despite progress in secondary school enrollments, it remains low. Globally, only about 55% of secondary school–aged children are in secondary school. Only 12 developing countries or territories have enrollments of 90% or more (UNICEF 2009). Enrollments vary from 92% in industrialized countries to only 23% in West and Central Africa. As with primary education, the greatest disparities are due to differences in wealth.

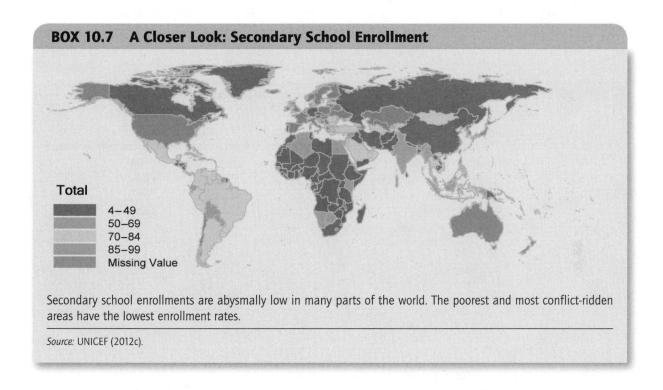

BOX 10.7   A Closer Look: Secondary School Enrollment

Total

- 4–49
- 50–69
- 70–84
- 85–99
- Missing Value

Secondary school enrollments are abysmally low in many parts of the world. The poorest and most conflict-ridden areas have the lowest enrollment rates.

Source: UNICEF (2012c).

Universal secondary education and tertiary education are not MDGs. However, there has been explosive growth in tertiary levels of education in developing countries since 1970, with the most significant surge occurring since 2000. This has resulted in a significant shift in the percentages of global enrollments from various parts of the world. The global share of tertiary enrollments from lower-middle-income countries has nearly doubled from 22% to 42%, while the share from high-income countries has decreased from 57% to 30%. Sub-Saharan Africa and Arab states have more than doubled their share, but still contribute relatively small numbers to the overall tertiary population. North American and Western Europe now contribute only 23%, down from 48% in 1970. East Asia and the Pacific now contribute 31% (UNESCO 2009, 12).

As educational levels in lower income and developing countries rise, what are the potential impacts on the global economy and the occupational structure within countries?

Gender Equity

MDG Goal Three is to promote gender equity in both secondary and tertiary education. In most developing countries, there has been significant progress toward closing the gender gap at the secondary level, with less at the tertiary level. In many of the more advanced developing countries and regions, such as Latin America and the Caribbean, Eastern Asia, and South Eastern Asia, secondary enrollment of females has surpassed that of males (UN 2010, 20). In the United States, Europe, and some of the more advanced developing countries, female college attendance has surpassed male enroll-ments. The global average indicates that tertiary enrollment of females reached parity with male enrollment in 2003 and has outpaced male enroll-ment since. The exceptions to this trend are where there are fewer spaces available or few people attend tertiary education. In such cases, women may be more reluctant to attend (UNESCO 2009, 15). Female secondary education tends to be more lim-ited in these regions as well. Global trends offering higher paying jobs for men with high school degrees than for women with college educations may encour-age males to end schooling earlier to work and women to pursue higher education.

BOX 10.8   A Closer Look: Enrollment in Post-Secondary and Tertiary Education by Gender and Region

Region	% Enrollment in Tertiary Education			% of World Tertiary Enrollment	% Enrollment in Upper Secondary Education					
					1999			2007		
	1970	2007	Male to Female		MF	M	F	MF	M	F
North America and Western Europe	30	71	F > M	23	98.2	96.8	99.7	97.7	97.3	98.1
Central and Eastern Europe	41 (2000)	62	F > M	14	80.1	80.4	79.8	85.4	88.1	82.6
Latin America and Caribbean	6	34	F > M	12	61.6	57.6	65.7	73.5	68.8	78.3
Central Asia	23 (2000)	31	F > M	2	82.8	85.6	80.0	89.2	91.1	87.2
East Asia and Pacific	3	26	F = M	31	46.3	46.9	45.8	62.9	61.9	63.9
Arab States	20 (2000)	23	F = M		46.5	48.2	44.8	52.1	53.0	51.2
South and West Asia	4	11	M > F	12	30.6	35.3	25.6	39.3	43.3	35.1
Sub-Saharan Africa	1	6	M > F	5	19.4	21.1	17.7	26.3	29.4	23.0
World	9	26	F > M	3	45.5	47.1	43.9	54.3	55.6	53.0

Source: UNESCO (2009, 12, 14, 17). The percentages of enrollments in tertiary education include a variety of types of post-secondary education, including four-year college and university.

Educational equity in primary and secondary education remains a global concern. Poverty has a direct impact on children working and the likelihood that they forgo school or combine work with school. This has long-term effects because the payoff for educating girls and women is significant:

- Increasing girls' secondary education by 1% pays off with a 3% increase in GDP.
- An extra year of schooling beyond the average for a girl increases her eventual income by 10% to 20%.
- Every extra year of a woman's schooling adds one half to one third of a year of schooling for each of her children.
- An added year of schooling avoids two maternal deaths for every 1,000 girls.
- An added year of schooling lowers the probability of child mortality by 5% to 10%.
- In Uganda, females with a secondary education are three times less likely to be HIV positive than females with no schooling.
- An increase of four years of schooling reduces a woman's fertility by one child.
- Educated women are less vulnerable to domestic violence and make more household decisions.
- Education increases the likelihood of women's participation in civic and political affairs.
- Women with an education are four times more likely to oppose female genital cutting. (Tembon 2008, 281)
- Having a mother who is educated increases a child's chance of being in school by 17%. (Gibbons et al. 2005, 13)

According to UN data, the birth rate for adolescents with a secondary or greater education is 48 per 1,000. It is 139 for a primary education and 207 when girls have had no education. Education reaps important quality of life and long-term benefits for women and their children and thus for the whole society (UN 2010, 35; LeVine 2007).

Global Pressure for Educational Quality

In OECD countries, education has a significant economic payoff. It is associated with higher income and more secure job status, even though gender, racial, and ethnic disparities in income persist at every educational level in the United States and many other rich nations. Surprisingly, educational attainment does not payoff in the same way for individuals in all societies. A UNESCO (2005) analysis of 19 developing nations discovered that with the exception of Uruguay, education did not protect an individual from unemployment. In Indonesia, education had an opposite effect: The most highly educated had the highest unemployment rate. When underemployment was considered with unemployment, people with higher levels of education were less vulnerable than those with lower educational levels but not everywhere. Peru and Indonesia were notable exceptions. The combined un- and underemployment for those with tertiary educations was 30% in Indonesia and 20% in Peru. This suggests that the labor market in some developing countries may not be able to support educational expansion (20).

The UNESCO study also raises concern about educational quality. Rapid expansion risks quality. Even in OECD countries, 34% of 15-year-olds were either not in school or had low mathematics achievement. In Brazil and Indonesia, it was 84% (2005, 39). In the mid-1990s, pressure to expand tertiary education increased secondary graduation rates, but the diversity of programs offered decreased. There has been a global movement away from vocational education in secondary schools. In China and Brazil, for example, the percentage of vocational education graduates decreased, leaving many students poorly equipped to move ahead in education or work (41–42). Some countries instituted very short programs of upper secondary education that graduated more students, but many without sufficient academic or job skills. Although these countries, notably Jamaica and Malaysia, have the highest shares of secondary graduates, they have the lowest shares of graduates prepared for tertiary education. Educational expansion needs to be more closely correlated with quality educational experiences tailored to create realistic opportunities for students.

What is the purpose of education? Is it for job opportunity, personal growth as a well-rounded individual, to develop good citizens, something else, or all of these? Depending on your answer, how

should a society structure education to achieve its objective(s)?

Rational Models of Education

Global norms prompted the expansion of mass education and also shaped the type of educational system countries developed. Rational discourse and rational models became the lingua franca of the modern age during the take-off period of globalization at the turn of the 20th century. Educational experts diffused the rational model of education as universal education became a criterion for the modern society. National models and requirements for graduation are strikingly homogenous. Educational systems are highly bureaucratized, with fine delineation of roles, from the various administrators and support staff to teacher specialties. Rules and procedures for passing from grade to grade and becoming certified with a diploma are also highly specific. The disciplinary divides that assume that knowledge can be neatly divided and parceled into courses are global. Age-based levels assume that individuals measured by age are most efficiently treated en masse and processed together through the educational system. The factory model, applied to many realms of life, was applied to schooling and continues to be applied, despite the objections of many educators and decades of experiments with other models. In most cases, schools are run much like an assembly line as students are moved through the subjects and grade levels, each teacher adding their input to the final product, the graduated student.

BOX 10.9   A Closer Look

These Victorian-era classrooms followed the factory model of schooling. Children are neatly lined in rows with lessons delivered en masse. Although the shapes of the desks may have changed, the factory model still thrives.

As new countries became integrated into the global system following WWII, international agencies and civil society helped to diffuse models of schooling. UNESCO and the World Bank are among many international organizations that promote mass schooling. As a result, education generally and mass schooling in particular are so structurally similar globally that it is possible to give a standardized test—the International Assessment of Educational Progress—that compares student performance across countries, grade levels, and subject matter. The International Association for Educational Assessment was formed in 1975 and now performs a wide array of assessments in education from primary schools through to the workplace (IAEA n.d.). International assessments further diffuse expectations about what students should be learning and when.

BOX 10.10   A Closer Look

Rational models of education prevail all over the world, including refugee camps. The students on the right are studying science in Juba, Sudan. Students on the left are in the Democratic Republic of Congo.

Acculturating people into global frameworks is a subtle function of education related to the origin and expansion of schooling. Students acquire national and global cultural capital in schools, integrating them and their society into the global system and expanding their opportunities there. It is in a society's interest to develop national citizens capable of functioning at a global level. Educational systems legitimize states on the global stage, and educational credentials establish legitimacy for individuals. Homogeneity facilitates mobility across countries for individuals, interchange among experts around the world, and communication among governmental agencies, international governmental and non-governmental organizations (NGOs), and so on. Although education does not erase all particularity, it establishes enough common ground to make the complex global system possible.

Standard forms of speech overcome the problem of diverse vernaculars—in a nation and in the globe. Learning them in school enables people to function better in the other bureaucratic structures of modern life. Education based on the global models introduces students to science as a model of legitimate knowledge, international education, rational rule systems, and rationality as a way of looking at, thinking about, and dealing with the world (Meyer 2007, 268–270; Robertson 1992, 187).

The cultural capital acquired through education is the reason that the benefits of schooling for females extend into so many dimensions of social life. Schooling prepares women to participate in bureaucracies, enabling them to access many basic services. Even a little schooling can significantly improve the health of a woman's children because she can communicate with health practitioners in the language of science and bureaucracy. In a four-nation study, LeVine (2007) demonstrated that in school students are taught an "academic register" that is different than every day conversation but typical of communication in bureaucracies. The academic register is a specialized speech code based on written text. Some of its characteristics are the use of more abstract or generalized nouns in place of the specific names of common objects and the use of explicit description. This effect occurs even in low-quality schools and is retained into adulthood. The original study was conducted in Nepal, Mexico, Zambia, and Venezuela, and replicated in Guatemala and Morocco (128–131). Having communication skills allows mothers to relay health information coherently, understand public health messages, and navigate other bureaucracies more effectively. Women without modern communication skills depend on a local vernacular and do not function as well in the many bureaucracies they encounter.

BOX 10.11   A Closer Look : Pledging Allegiance

Until granted free speech rights in schools, U.S. students could be punished if they refused to recite the pledge allegiance.

Socializing for National Identity

As nations are integrated into the global system, education becomes important as a vehicle to define and reinforce national identity. The objectives and values in education proclaim a country's national identity to its citizens and the global system. In all countries, children practice the rituals of civil religion in schools. When they sing national anthems, salute flags, or honor national leaders and historical events in pageants, children celebrate the nation and its values. Flags, pictures of national leaders, displays of national symbols (such as the Constitution, Declaration of Independence, Liberty Bell, or Statue of Liberty) are as much a part of school equipment as desks. These objects are treated reverentially, particularly the flag. They are objects with sacred status.

Educational debate often focuses on how to fashion citizens of the nation rather than the best educational practices for learning. The common school movement set about to Americanize immigrant children immersing them in American—a particular version of Protestant American—virtues. While Britain ruled Hong Kong, they used the schools and curriculum to dilute Chinese identity in Hong Kong. They were so successful that in Hong Kong, a slight majority still views themselves more as "Hong Kongers" than Chinese. To ameliorate this, the Curriculum Development Council of Hong Kong initiated a new program in morality and national development to help students in Hong Kong think of themselves as Chinese (Yeung 2011). This does not contradict that schools teach a global model also. Education into a nation occurs within the framework of global culture.

Preserving, developing, or creating shared identities depends on a sense of a shared history and the meaning of shared historical events. Formal curriculums, such as history lessons, are often used as vehicles to transmit national identity. Korostelina (2008) analyzed the history textbooks of Taiwan and North Korea and found

---

BOX 10.12   A Closer Look: Individualism in Education

Although the rational model is still dominant in education, many reform movements challenge bureaucracy in education to make it more responsive to the needs of individual children. This is not only a reaction to alienating effects of bureaucracy but also in keeping with a heightened sense of individualism.

- Some reforms reduce hierarchy to grant more decision making to teachers and principals.
- Student-centered learning puts children in charge of their own learning, while teachers facilitate by making resources available and offering guidance as needed.
- Open education classrooms break down the barriers among the disciplines and allowed children to explore solving problems and working on projects of interest to them that drew from any number of disciplinary areas.

- Experiential learning emphasized student active involvement in "learning by doing" and a very "hands-on" approach to education.
- Individualized learning allowed students to cover material at their own pace and in some programs choosing methods of learning as well, breaking down the age–grade correlations.

that history books do not present straightforward factual material or purely analytical records and interpretations of events. They propose highly colored interpretations. For example, when the Chinese Nationalist party migrated from mainland China following WWII, they dominated Taiwan. When Taiwan democratized in the mid-1980s, ethnic Taiwanese came into power. History books were reformed in the 1990s to eliminate presentations of Taiwan as Chinese and emphasize Taiwan's multicultural heritage (Dutch, Japanese, Spanish, and other Asian influences).

In North Korea, history books emphasize its true Korean heritage in contrast to South Korea, which is depicted as corrupted by imperialism and straying from their Korean values and traditions to accept the wicked ways of the West. Emphasizing national identity differentiates a people from the global system while at the same time acknowledging the nation's perceived position in the globe.

There are more subtle ways to convey national identity than through history curricula. In the United States, the practical meaning of core values of national identity such as individualism, equality, and freedom are debated in the context of educational reform. Equality has evolved over time, and this is reflected in educational reforms. The answers to questions such as who is entitled to an education, how it should be financed, and which methods should be used have changed over time and bear on what equality means in the United States.

In this contemporary period of globalization, concerns for national identity in the United States play a role in debates over the role of bilingual education, charter schools, public education and vouchers, integrating schools by race and economic class, sex education, creationism in science curriculums (also an issue during the Progressive era), back to basics math vs. new math, holistic reading methods vs. phonetic approaches, and so on. Debates about

open education and individualized instruction, qualifications of homosexual teachers, special education, and teachers' (and other public servants') right to strike reflect larger societal debates about equality and individualism.

In France, whether or not headscarves should be permitted for Muslim students caused intense debate. The issue was not how headscarves might or might not influence learning but on whether or not wearing headscarves undermined the secular nature of French society. In Italy, a parent challenged crucifixes in state-run schools. (Religious items were nixed by French courts, but Italians are allowed to keep the crucifixes. The latter was decided by the European Court on Human Rights. It ruled that as there was no European consensus, Italy should be able to do as it pleased. There was no evidence of intolerance of other religions or of compulsory teaching of religion.) Given the power of the educational system to define national identity, it is not coincidence that teachers were among Mao's priority targets during the Cultural Revolution.

Global Patterns of Health and Health Care

Health is a fundamental facet of quality of life. The expectation that a person deserves the healthiest life possible, contained in Article 25 of the UN Declaration of Human Rights, is increasingly a global norm. Globalization is related to the quality of a country's health, the rationalization and revitalization of health care, and the development of a global health regime.

The Quality of Health

How health care is accessed and distributed has a particularly poignant impact on life chances. There have been winners and losers in global health just as in other areas of globalization. Life expectancy and national income tend to rise together, tying individuals' life chances to the wealth of their country.

BOX 10.13   A Closer Look: Life Expectancy and Income

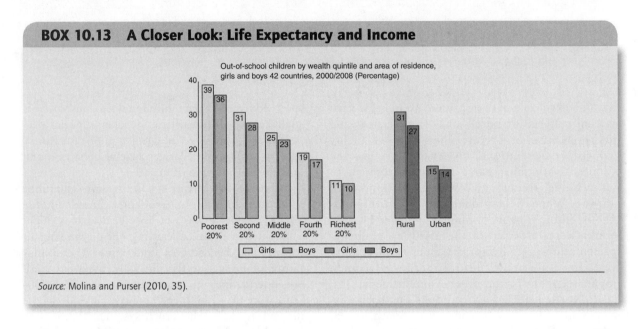

Out-of-school children by wealth quintile and area of residence, girls and boys 42 countries, 2000/2008 (Percentage)

Source: Molina and Purser (2010, 35).

Fortunately, life expectancy is not completely dependent on wealth. Life expectancy of poorer countries has risen disproportionately relative to rich countries, even though the gap in per capita incomes increased (Molina and Purser 2010, 35). This is a combined effect of factors such as increased education, better dissemination of health care information, improved water and sanitation, and the health care efforts of NGOs and international non-governmental organizations (INGOs). These are related to income but have a synergistic and exponential impact on health. This is good news and offers considerable hope; nevertheless, the indicators of the poorest nations remain dismal. Furthermore, within the richest nations, disparities related to income inequality, rural living, and minority status affect healthy living to the degree that some groups within rich nations have health statistics comparable to much poorer nations. In 2009, the United States under-five mortality rate was eight per 1,000 live births. This ranks it at 45th, behind that of all of the richest nations, tied with Latvia, and behind Cuba, Poland, Hungary, Croatia, Lithuania, Serbia, Malaysia, and Slovakia (UNDP 2011, 158–159). In 2005, the United States ranked 30th in infant mortality (under one year old) when compared to European nations with a rate of 6.9 per 100 live births, and 18th with a rate of 5.8 when very early births (under 22 weeks of gestation) were omitted. This CDC study did not include a comparison with Japan, Australia, New Zealand, and other countries with better infant mortality rates (MacDorman and Matthews 2009). This is in part due to inequality and the high rates of infant mortality among minorities in the United States.

One investigation of income and infant mortality in New York, Tokyo, Paris, and London found a significant relationship between income and infant mortality in the years 1988–1992 in New York, but not in London, Paris, or Tokyo. In the years 1993–1997, a significant relationship was found in London (at the 5% level) and New York (0.05%). Inequality in Great Britain also increased during those years. In the second period, inequality in relation to infant mortality in Paris was close to the 5% level of significance, but did not reach it. Tokyo did not have a significant difference (Rodwin and Neuberg 2005).

The health effect of income on infant mortality is complex. Some studies have found that areas of higher inequality of income within urban areas suffer poorer health than people of comparable income in areas with less inequality. A study of income inequality and infant mortality in New York found that one standard

BOX 10.14   Check It Out Yourself: Infant Mortality Among Racial and Ethnic Groups in the United States

The infant mortality rate of some minorities in the United States is higher than in many developing countries. Compare the rates to the CIA Factbook International Data. Find a country with a rate similar to each group. How do you account for the different rates?
https://www.cia.gov/library/publications/the-world-factbook/rankorder/2091rank.html

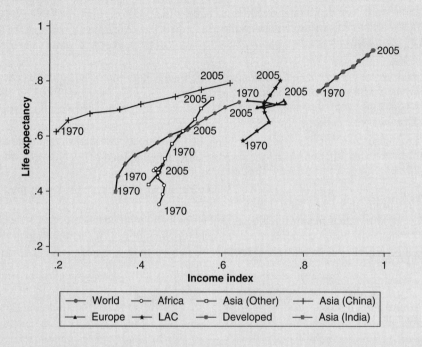

Source: MacDorman and Mathews (2011).

deviation increase in inequality is associated with a 0.8 increase in the infant mortality rate (0.080/1000) (Sohler et al., 2003). London, Paris, and Tokyo operate aggressive nationally funded programs to high-risk mothers. Mothers are closely monitored during the course of the pregnancy and after the birth. New initiatives in London and New York targeting high-risk mothers and located in high-risk neighborhoods may improve the life chances of infants in low-income areas (Rodwin and Neuberg 2005).

The MDG health-related objectives reinforce the view that the chance to fulfill one's potential for a healthy life is a human right. Many keys to basic health are tracked by the MDG indicators. Improving nutrition, ending hunger, and reducing the number of underweight children are measures under Goal One to reduce extreme poverty and hunger. Reducing child mortality, improving maternal health, and combating HIV, malaria and other diseases are Goals Four, Five, and Six. Having a safe water supply and upgraded sanitation are important indicators in Goal Seven that have direct impact on health.

Do you believe that health care is a human right? What about a civil right? Why or why not? If you answered yes to either of these, how "much" should a person be guaranteed, and whose responsibility is it to provide for it?

BOX 10.15   A Closer Look

The Millennium Development Goals Report 2010 highlights the importance of the distribution of resources within developing nations (UN 2010):

- Nearly twice as many children under five are underweight in rural areas than urban (Sec 2, 14).
- Children from the poorest households are twice as likely to be underweight than children from the richest households (Sec 2, 14).
- Of 34 countries with child death rates of 100 or more per 1,000, 33 were in sub-Saharan Africa. Afghanistan is the 34th. Most of the deaths were preventable or treatable (Sec 2, 27).
- In developing regions, only 76% of rural residents have access to an improved water source. In urban areas, it is 94% (Sec 2, 59).
- In developing regions, only 68% of residents of urban areas had improved sanitation facilities. In rural areas, it is only 40% (Sec 2, 61). Among the poorest, only 16% have improved facilities, 63% have open human sewage, and 21% have unimproved facilities. Among the richest, only 4% have open sewage and 77% have improved facilities (Sec 2, 62).
- In some developing countries, rural women are only half as likely to have professional care at childbirth. In Southern Asia and sub-Saharan Africa, poor women were only one third as likely as rich women to receive professional care (Sec 2, 32).
- Only 34% of women in rural areas received skilled care four or more times during pregnancy, in contrast to 67% of urban women (Sec 2, 34).
- The adolescent birth rate is almost three times higher for the poorest women (184/1,000) than the richest (58/1,000), and nearly twice as high for rural (149/1,000) than urban (79/1,000). The rate for women with no education is four times as high (207/1,000) as for those with secondary education or more (48/1,000) (Sec 2, 35).

While each of the indicators above is for developing countries, risks for low-income and rural residents in richer countries are also high.

As with education, lower incomes and rural residence put people at greater risk. With health the risks are earlier death, more chronic illness, and more days of illness. Again, the urban slums are exceptions. Residents of Mumbai live longer than in India as a whole, but the people in the slums of Mumbai do not. Their life expectancy is lower and their expected years of healthy life (disability adjusted life expectancies) are also lower. Despite the miserable conditions in slums, people continue intensive immigration to cities. The deteriorating impact of slums on life chances is likely to increase (UN 2010, 64).

Epidemics and Pandemics

Organisms and viruses migrate along with people and goods. Epidemics spread more rapidly due to globalization. In traveling, viruses and bacteria are likely to find new hosts, human, animal, or plant life, with little or no resistance. This can decimate a population, as happened with Native Americans, trigger an epidemic or pandemic, or wipe out crops and depleting food supplies.

Many of the health risks to human security are exacerbated by globalization. Life expectancy, infant and child mortality, and maternal mortality—fairly sensitive measures of overall health—reflect the familiar pattern of poor nations bearing an undue burden of disadvantage. Even epidemics discriminate. One of the world's most devastating influenza pandemics started in 1918. The death toll, underestimated at the time, was at least 50,000,000 but could easily have been as high as 100,000,000 (Barry 2006, 105; Johnson and Meuller 2002, 105). More people died in 25 weeks at the height of the pandemic than died of AIDS in 25 years.

Even at such high rates, death, and disease discriminated. The death rates in sub-Saharan Africa ranged from 24 to 57 per 1,000 (Johnson and Meuller 2002, 110). In the United States, a low estimate of the deaths is 500,000, but a realistic estimate is closer to 700,000. This is a rate of 6.5 per 1,000 (111). In the United States, people's acceptance of science and the expertise death and disease ready acceptance of restrictions put in place by public health officials and saved many lives. Interestingly, in the case of the 1918 influenza, people in urban areas were afforded protection by their prior exposure to similar viruses that people in remote or rural areas lacked. The earlier viruses had a more limited and different pattern of geographic spread than the 1918 strain. With the exponential increase in travel and transportation—and the movement of troops as WWI ended—influenza spread quickly to areas newly integrated into the global arena (Mamelund 2011). The pandemic spread along lines of trade and travel. Earlier globalization and exposure protected city dwellers, and increased globalization heightened risk in rural areas in this wave.

Avian flu, tuberculosis, swine flu, cholera, SARS (Toronto), and AIDS pandemics have devastated populations needlessly into the 21st century, continuing patterns of discrimination. In January 2010, Haiti was hit by a magnitude 7 earthquake that killed over 200,000 and left millions homeless (DEC 2011). The earthquake was followed by flooding and mudslides in March that brought more death and displacement. With hundreds of thousands of displaced persons and sanitation in Haiti weak to begin with, news agencies reported that the stench of human waste was overpowering. Fear of cholera and typhoid spread by contaminated water set in. The reality of cholera did not take long to materialize. In October 2010, Haiti had its first cholera outbreak in over 100 years. In November, Hurricane Tomas hit Haiti, bringing more flooding. Leogane, at the center of the January earthquake, was among the hardest hit by the flooding. Although hundreds of thousands of those whose homes were destroyed by the January earthquake were still living in camps and escaped the worst of the flooding, flooding accelerated the spread of cholera and disease.

Why Haiti? One of the poorest countries in the world, Haiti lacks the money for quake-resistant architecture. The National Palace, government buildings, hospitals, and homes crumbled, crushing people in the rubble and leaving them homeless. Was this a natural disaster? Not really; it was a disaster of poverty. Haiti lacks sewage and storm drains to handle rain and waste. It lacks a medical system that can distribute aid. Even soap was in short supply in October 2010. Hand washing, one of the simplest ways to combat cholera, was difficult. Similarly, fragile conditions throughout the poorest nations make them exceptionally vulnerable to pandemics, epidemics, diseases, and conditions conquered in the developed world.

Other epidemics manifest similar patterns. The rate of tuberculosis prevalence in Africa (475 per 100,000) is almost twice that of Southeast Asia (278). The rate in Southeast Asia dwarfs that of Europe (63) and the Americas (38) (Kaiser Family Foundation 2010b). HIV/AIDS also concentrated in Africa, which has two-thirds of the world's cases (Kaiser Family Foundation 2010a). Access to health care, inequality, low educational levels, poor nutrition, weak communication and sanitation infrastructures, and myriad other issues compromise the world's poor. Developing nations are also more likely than developed to put people at the nexus between the natural environment and human environment making them more susceptible to infection by animal-borne pathogens. Meeting the challenges of the world's health problems requires monumental global effort.

How might each of the factors listed in the paragraph above impact the spread of disease? Can you think of others?

The Rationalization of Health Care

Approaches to health care obviously change as our knowledge of health, disease, and medication increases. Health care also changes in response to the development of global culture and diffusion of practices from one culture to another. The scientifically based bureaucratic model of social organizations seems like a natural fit for medicine, marking a clear line in the sand to distinguish the snake-oil sales force, magicians, and other less than professionally trained, qualified, and certified practitioners from physicians. Controlling entry into an occupation is an essential step to professionalization. As medicine differentiated from healing, the white-coated clinician with a battery of tests to reveal or confirm a scientifically derived diagnosis was the epitome of the disinterested, scientific professional. At his (usually a "he") side, a host of white-clad nurses (usually "she's"), with distinctive caps to indicate the school at which they studied, were testament to the superiority of the rationalized, routinized, certified, medical enterprise. Although many people, at least in the United States and Europe, had a "family doctor" with whom they had a stable relationship, often, the practice of medicine in hospitals conformed closely to the factory model of production that migrated from manufacturing to food production, education, and other dimensions of institutional life.

As discussed earlier, the over-rationalization of life characteristic of the turn of the 20th century was experienced by many people just as Weber described, as an iron cage, separating them from nature, from one another, and even from their own creative and self-expressive capacities. As the 1960s approached, the white-coated clinician and the white-clad nurse began to seem old-fashioned—relics of the hyper-rationality of life. The impersonality of medical practice, the treatment of patients as illnesses, and the turn away from traditional remedies and methods was out of sync with growing concern for the humanity of patients, their rights, and the quality of their experience, not just their disease.

A 1958 article describes the bureaucratization of medicine in Israel (Ben-David, 1958). It is in the forefront of similar studies that began to appear, questioning the wisdom of bureaucratization of medicine. Hospitals in Israel expanded rapidly following WWII to accommodate the immigration of Jews from Europe. Large central clinics were established, filled with general practitioners and specialists as well as specialized equipment and facilities. Doctors were employed by the clinic on a salary basis and assigned a particular maximum number of patients they were to see each day. When patients entered the facility, they were given a ticket for a doctor. If they were lucky, they were able to see the doctor of their choice on a regular basis. If that doctor's quota was full, they took a ticket for another doctor. Follow-up house visits were tasked to another set of doctors. If the doctor needed to refer patients to a specialist, neither the patient's doctor nor patient chose the specialist. The organization made the referral.

Doctors could easily lose track of what happened to their patients. The assumption was that the doctor does not need to—the organization does. The organization has responsibility for the patient, not any one doctor. Impersonalizing medicine was thought to improve efficiency. The assumption behind this procedure is that there is no special personal bond between doctor and patient (Ben-David 1958, 256). In this system, doctors felt powerless and resented their loss of authority. They appreciated the emphasis on science and the laboratories available to them, but found that they did not have time to make use of them. To adapt, some doctors defied the institutional rules by developing private practices on the side. Others tried to develop a circle of patients that were their "own," a private practice within the clinic. Others emphasized the scientific nature of their work and gained a type of personal authority with patients through that (263–264). Doctors working in private hospitals had similar complaints of anonymity in the eyes of patients and resentment at dependence on the bureaucracy. Patients, too, seemed to suffer from the bureaucratic arrangement. In the large central clinics, they had to passively accept whatever doctor they were assigned.

The rational model—medicine and health care delivered in assembly-line fashion with patients treated as cases—was a global model, displacing traditional healing methods, remedies, and practitioners. It used to be common to hear doctors refer to patients as their diseases or operation such as "the appendectomy in Room 136." Although there have been reforms over the past decades, hospitals still tend to operate bureaucratically. A patient is admitted and processed through a series of departments, wheeled around by one person or another with little concern for continuity of care. Hospital gowns are a must for the ease of examinations and procedures such as x-rays. Schedules are arranged to meet the needs for efficiency, rather than patients' needs. All patients eat at the same time (when the cart gets to their room), are bathed when convenient for staff, and are awakened for doctors' and nurses' rounds, even if they need sleep.

Reforming Medicine and Reviving Traditional Practices

Reaction against the factory model of medicine has reaped some reforms. From midwives to Chinese herbalists, traditional practicioners were ready when the time came. One of most dramatic changes has been in the maternity wards. Childbirth has been transformed. Redesigning the experience for women and babies and giving women more control over the process was a priority goal of the feminist movement. Practices designed to create a more natural, less stressful birth process became normative. Hospitals instituted birthing rooms in which women would progress from labor through birth and recovery without moving from room to room, assembly-line style, for each step of the process. Some rooms included warm birthing tubs, so that babies would leave the warmth of the womb and slip directly into a tub of warm water, presumably lessening the trauma of birth. Natural childbirth—childbirth using breathing techniques rather than drugs—became popular. Even in-home births experienced a resurgence. Midwifery practice is now widespread. There is an International Alliance of Midwives, a Global Midwifery Council, schools that provide training and professional certifications, all in keeping with the path to legitimacy in the global system.

Some hospitals redesigned procedures. Many reorganized nurses' work so that nurses were assigned to patients rather than processes, breaking down the specialization of function. Patients are not treated by a different nurse for different procedures,

but by the same nurses, varying only by shift. This makes a more comfortable environment for patients and is more rewarding for nurses. Nurses have shed their white uniforms and caps for various colored and patterned uniforms and scrubs. As in other areas of institutional life, many of the reforms became routines, while others were discarded.

Other influences on medical practice came from the traditional remedies of Chinese and other ancient or folk medicines. Holistic treatments, treating body and mind, are the basis of many Eastern practices that migrated into the mainstream of Western culture. Contemporary statistics show that approximately 40% of people in the United States use some form of complementary (in addition to conventional) or alternative (in place of conventional) medicine (NCCAM 2011). An advertisement for the Memorial Sloan Kettering Cancer Center in a 1999 *New York Times Sunday Magazine* advertised cancer treatments that included Tibetan drum music, meditation, and other

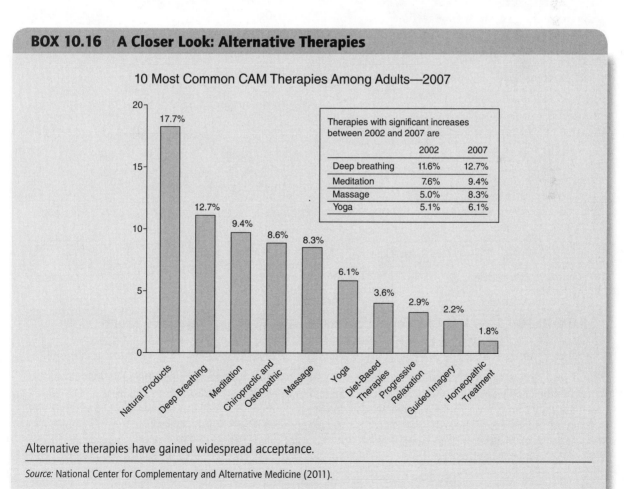

BOX 10.16   A Closer Look: Alternative Therapies

10 Most Common CAM Therapies Among Adults—2007

Therapies with significant increases between 2002 and 2007 are		
	2002	2007
Deep breathing	11.6%	12.7%
Meditation	7.6%	9.4%
Massage	5.0%	8.3%
Yoga	5.1%	6.1%

Natural Products — 17.7%
Deep Breathing — 12.7%
Meditation — 9.4%
Chiropractic and Osteopathic — 8.6%
Massage — 8.3%
Yoga — 6.1%
Diet-Based Therapies — 3.6%
Progressive Relaxation — 2.9%
Guided Imagery — 2.2%
Homeopathic Treatment — 1.8%

Alternative therapies have gained widespread acceptance.

Source: National Center for Complementary and Alternative Medicine (2011).

therapies imported from the East (see Box 10.17). In the 1950s, those would not have been available; in the 1960s and '70s, they would have been highly suspect. Now, the Integrative Medicine Service at Sloan Kettering offers a plethora of complementary therapies. Touch therapies, such as Shiatsu, Reiki, and Reflexology; and mind–body therapies, such as meditation and acupuncture, are offered alongside the traditional, scientific, chemo, and radiation therapies (Memorial Sloan Kettering Cancer Center 2010). Integrative medicine facilities and practices are now standard features at major hospitals.

BOX 10.17   A Closer Look: Enchanting Medicine

This advertisement from one of the most respected hospitals in the United States appeared in 1999, not in a "new age" magazine but in a major national newspaper. This ad would have been unthinkable in the 1950s.

Source: Memorial Sloan Kettering Cancer Center (1999).

BOX 10.18   Check It Out Yourself: Alternative Therapy, Religious Practice, or Healthful Living?

Are yoga classes, tai chi, meditation, or other classes that derive from Eastern religions offered at your university?

Are the people taking the classes religiously oriented? How about the instructors?

Try to get an interview with a yoga instructor in your town or at your university. To what extent do they view their art as religious practice? To what extent is it simply an exercise and fitness activity?

If you have health insurance, are any alternative therapies covered by your policy? What therapies are covered and for what conditions or diagnoses?

The Mayo Clinic is among many well-known and highly rated hospitals that offer acupuncture to patients. They contrast their acupuncture practice with traditional Eastern practices, but the text indicates that they are essentially translating ancient language into a more scientific sounding discourse, glocalizing it to better fit the Western medical model. Consider the Mayo Clinic's definitions of acupuncture.

- Chinese view: Acupuncture is a technique for balancing the flow of energy, or life force (*qi* or *chi*) that flows through meridian in the body. Needles inserted at specific points along the meridians rebalance the energy flow.
- Western view: Acupuncture points are places to stimulate nerves, muscles, and connective tissues.

Stimulation boosts the activity of the body's natural painkillers and increases blood flow. (Mayo Clinic 2009)

These definitions are very similar. If nerve impulses and blood flow are considered "life forces," and stimulating is considered a form of rebalancing, the definitions are the same. Qigong, from China, combines meditation, movement, and breathing. Ayurvedic, from India, combines herbs, massage, and yoga. These are holistic therapies designed to integrate the functioning of body, mind, and spirit (NCCAM 2010). Chinese herbal remedies are also mainstream. They are staples of health food stores and specialty shops but are plentiful in large chain discount and drug stores too.

BOX 10.19   A Closer Look: Universal Health Care

As in other areas of institutional life, health care has responded to globalization pressures to conform to emerging global models of what the institution should be. The movement toward universal health care emerged in the take-off phase of globalization. The earliest legislation was enacted in Germany late in the 19th century, with the passage of a series of government-sponsored insurance plans. Other countries adopted various strategies, some funding workers and others spreading coverage more broadly; Germany in 1883, Sweden in 1891, Denmark in 1892, France in 1910, and Switzerland, Austria, Hungary, Norway, Britain, Russia, and the Netherlands all followed with reforms by 1912. Japan also developed its single-payer system at this time. The UN Declaration of Human Rights mandated health care as a human right, and this started more movement toward universal coverage. It wasn't until the contemporary period that universal coverage became normative for developed countries. One of the normative questions is whether health care should be a for-profit or not-for-profit enterprise. While there are many variations in the specifics of universal coverage plans offered, they fall generally into three categories: single payer, which is the most frequent; two tier; and insurance mandates.

Religion as Fitness

Changing the meaning of an object or practice is another method of glocalization. Religious practices from the East are widely adopted as health and fitness activities in the West. Yoga, a mainstream component of the fitness movement and a $6 billion dollar industry, entered the United States during the take-off phase of globalization with the 1897 visit of Swami Vivekananda to the World Parliament of Religions (Kakutani 2010; PBS 2010). Although most instructors train at Hindu or devotional yoga training centers and consider yoga a religious practice, many yoga practitioners in the West perform yoga as part of a

stress-reduction and fitness regimen (Cadge and Bender 2004, 48). Burning incense, meditation, and the Eastern martial arts have also been popularized in the West. Incense is burned to aid relaxation. Meditation is perceived more for functionality in the West for reducing stress and improving health than as a religious journey, and martial arts are used for fitness, sport, and self-defense.

The Global Health Community

From 1990 to 2007, funding for global health assistance increased from $5.6 billion to

$22 billion. Most of the increase has been since 2000, stimulated at least in part by the adoption of the MDGs and by the entry of many new organizations and foundations into the international health field. The influx of new actors inspired a change in nomenclature from international to global health (Kruk 2010, 5).

The increase in INGOs operating in global health changed the structure of governance. The influence and role of traditional international agencies such as WHO are declining, and the new architecture of global health governance is not yet clear. Global health governance involves global, national, and local governmental organizations and NGOS. International governmental organizations include traditional actors such as the WHO and World Bank and UN agencies such as UNICEF. Countries have governmental organizations that represent their interests and commitments to global health, such as the U.S. Global Health Council and Cuba's Comprehensive Health Program. NGOs include large international organizations such as the International Red Cross and Red Crescent Societies, Doctors Without Borders, Oxfam, and the International Medical Corps, as well as many smaller ones such as the Appropriate Infrastructure Development Group (AIDG) that focuses its efforts in the United States, Haiti, and Guatemala, and had a budget of only $50,000 in 2005. Philanthropies, such as the Bill and Melinda Gates Foundation, have a significant impact on global health with large grants to partner agencies for initiatives selected by the foundation.

While epidemics and pandemics capture the public imagination, the emerging global regime is affecting a shift in the health community away from focus on disease and disaster to a comprehensive global public health policy that emphasizes promoting health and wellness. There are at least 50 multilateral agreements that support global health and health-related issues. Twenty-six of the agreements have the standing of treaties and thus are legally binding. The United States is party to 36 of the agreements, including 16 that are binding (Kates and Katz 2010, 1). These treaties and agreements are diverse, covering everything from environmental concerns (the Kyoto Protocol) and toxic weapons to the rights of women, children, and the disabled, but they are not a well-coordinated and systematic regime.

The 193 member countries of WHO adopted the International Health Regulations (IHR) in 2005 to improve coordination of health initiatives. It went into effect in 2007. The IHR require nations to improve their capacity in risk control and response to emergencies. A priority concern is improving public health surveillance to prevent health risks that have the potential to cross borders by monitoring their airports, ports, and ground crossings to limit the opportunity for disease to spread across borders (WHO 2008). The *IHR 2010 Activity Report* (WHO 2012) details the IHR Review and IHR Coordination committees' activity in helping member countries develop capacities in these areas. The main funding partners reflect the variety of actors in the global health community. They include the French government and a variety of French NGOs as well as the European Union, the Bill and Melinda Gates Foundation, USAID, and the U.S. Centers for Disease Control and Prevention.

The Global Health Initiative (GHI) coordinates most of U.S. health policy, with priorities on HIV/AIDS, malaria, tuberculosis, tropical diseases, maternal, newborn and child health, water-related diseases, and food insecurity. Over 80 partner countries in the GHI serve as testing grounds for innovative health strategies. The overarching goal is to improve health systems to conquer many health risks simultaneously, rather than disease by disease. When GHI programs are successful on a small scale, they are expanded. GHI coordinates with private foundations and NGOs as well as their partner countries.

Women's and children's health are priorities of GHI, but there is one oversight. Mental health, responsible for four of the top 10 causes of disability in women, is neglected. Psychiatric illness compounds health problems, and poor psychiatric health leads indirectly to health problems, such as increasing the likelihood of contracting AIDS and TB and stunting child growth due to maternal depression. The U.S. model of mental health is diffusing globally, but there still is not a global health model for psychiatric care (Watters 2010). About one third of countries do not have public mental health programs, and the poorest countries spend proportionately the least on mental health (Katz 2010; WHO

2008). Norms for mental health care are weak in many countries, including the United States.

Sports

They were called "too old, too small, too inexperienced," but the Japanese women's soccer team was the sports story of 2011. That summer, Japan was still reeling from a devastating 9.0 earthquake, an accompanying tsunami, and nuclear accident. As their women's team advanced in the World Cup tournament, upsetting one team after another, excitement in Japan and around the world grew. The team wanted to give hope to the people of Japan to never give up; "They can survive if they never give up," the team captain insisted. The world cheered them on and they won the cup with overtime kicks in an upset against the United States. It seemed as though the world wanted this victory for Japan.

In 1995, just a year after he came into power, Nelson Mandela used the South African rugby team to help him unite the country. The nearly all-white team, playing a white sport under the motto, "One Team, One Country," won victory after unexpected victory, singing the new national anthem, formerly the song of black revolt, and gradually won many blacks over to rugby. At the same time, whites must have come to recognize that Mandela's support of the team was a major contributor to the victories because on the day of the World Cup finals, the white audience broke out into cries of "Nelson, Nelson" when he came onto the field. It was another overtime win, but a win for the underdog and the country that needed it. The country was unified in celebration, although many struggles followed.

How did sports evolve to have such power? Athleticism and sporting games are universal dimensions of culture. Some were associated with nobility. Jousting tournaments, fencing, and archery developed from knightly practice and evolved into forms of entertainment and exercise when gunpowder made knights obsolete. An early form of tennis developed in the 14th century courts of France. Other games were available to anyone. Various forms of folk games combining balls with feet, hands, or sticks were played around the world.

From the Olympics to World Cups and cycling tours, sports are part of globalization. Global audiences share common experiences of sporting events broadcast all over the world. The migration of players is global. Global sports are a portal for newer and less powerful nations to assert themselves on the global stage. Paradoxically, despite and in part because of their extensive globalization, sports have become an important expression of national identity. Sentiments run high for home teams, and national pride competes alongside the athletes. There are hundreds of international sporting associations, and the global sports economy is hundreds of billions of dollars.

Prior to the 19th century, there were few organized sports and sport competitions, at any level. There was little time for leisure, and the bodily pleasures of sports were sinful from many, particularly Puritan, religious worldviews. In the 19th century, a complex mixture of cultural, political, and commercial interests changed how sports were viewed and how they were played. Organized sports began to spread nationally and globally in the take-off phase of globalization.

Various forces prompted the development and spread of organized sports:

- Industrialization afforded people leisure time to engage in a variety of pastimes.
- The concentration of people in urban areas provided a pool of potential participants—players and spectators.
- Rules and regulations for folk games were standardized—in keeping with developing global culture of rationalization.
- National and international associations formed, providing global legitimacy and recognition for a sport. They organized competitions and linked sports and sports teams with local and national identity.
- Mass production and technological advances made specialized sports equipment and clothing available in large quantities and brought prices down, making them more widely available. Sports became an important part of consumerist culture and profit making.
- The sports celebrity as a figure of admiration and emulation emerged. Basketball star Chuck Taylor helped to develop the Converse All Star in 1918, and the athlete endorsement as a marketing ploy began.
- The athletic body became a status symbol and symbol of individual achievement, reinforcing individualistic character of modern life.

Rationalization and Standardization of Sports

Industrialization released people from the physicality and drudgery of agricultural work; they needed new sources of physical activity and they acquired leisure time to pursue it. Rising incomes meant a bit more disposable income. Advertisements conveying the wonders and status of the latest mass-produced goods had consumers eager to try them. Urbanization conveniently concentrated people who had time and money to spend into small areas. Together, these processes created a market for sports equipment, a pool of potential sports players, and an audience for sporting events. Sports clubs began to form, and schools began sponsoring competitions among their students.

Sports modernized. Rule-less, often violent folk games became standardized, civilized, and bureaucratized in keeping with the trend of rationalization. As more people participated, written and codified rules made it possible for competitions to spread over larger areas. Governance organizations formed. Rugby Association rules were among the first codified, around 1845 at the Rugby School, in Rugby, England. Rules for association football (soccer) were written at Cambridge in 1848. Local styles and variations of all games still exist but within an increasingly complex sets of rules for competitions that govern nearly every aspect of a sport from equipment, to financial regulations, to team requirements for practices. Teams and individuals aiming for international competitions generally follow international rules and standards.

Developments in technology led to improved equipment and drove prices down to middle-class affordability. For example, better bicycle design—France is generally credited with the modern bicycle—and industrial processes combined to make bicycling the most efficient (as measured by energy expended) form of transportation and a popular sport in mid-19th century. Bicycle racers were the highest paid athletes in the United States in the early 1900s (McComb 2004, 33).

Feminists found bicycles liberating. Susan B. Anthony reportedly claimed that the bicycle did more to liberate women than any other invention. Cycling not only gave women freedom of movement but inspired changes in women's fashions, facilitating the transition from long billowing skirts to bloomers and pants. In A *Wheel Within a Wheel: A Woman's Quest for Freedom*, first published in 1895, Frances Willard wrote that the bicycle could accomplish for thousands of women what horseback riding did for the wealthy. It engages them in vigorous exercise, allows them to experience the adventure of the outdoors, and to enjoy "the swiftness of motion." It introduced them to a wider world than that to which they were relegated. The League of American Wheelmen (LAW) celebrated their female membership in their journal, promoting bicycling as a sport for the masses of women, not just the elite. "The woman who owns a bicycle also owns the many and far-reaching highways that run to the ends of the earth." They heralded the bicycle as part of women's advance in society to the point where women could share equally in the enjoyment of a sport, could enter the doors of colleges, and were creeping toward the goal of equality in churches (LAW 1899, 587).

The impact of science on sports made its way into the elementary and secondary school curriculum with the addition of physical education. Some sports—such as basketball and volleyball—were invented as a way to keep youth fit and gainfully busy while not in school or at work. The emphasis on measurement and record keeping in industry, education, and other realms of life applied to athletic achievement as well. Rationalized sports spread through various channels, first across countries, then to neighboring countries, and then across borders. European football spread in Italy along the lines of foreign capital incursion and in the Netherlands along with the expansion of the railroad (Van Bottenburg 2001, 3). Nearly everyone who traveled took sports with them. Missionaries and colonists transported its civilizing influence. Businesses and the military transported its competitive zeal, and teachers who worked abroad and students who studied abroad transported the rationalized pleasure. Sports had become all of these.

Internationalizing Sports

International Competitions

There were few international sports competitions prior to the take-off phase of globalization. An 1819 tennis match between British and French players is reportedly the first. This was followed by a Canadian–U.S. cricket match. By mid-century, there were a number of international yacht races. Boxing, according to some, emerged as the first truly global sport and did it without benefit of national or international organizations. Becoming the world boxing champion meant defeating opponents on both sides of the Atlantic (Sage 2010, 33). This was a global as opposed to international competition as boxers did not represent their countries. Others herald tennis as the first global sport. An international tournament was held in 1878 with players from England, Canada, and the United States. This was followed by the International Lawn Tennis Challenge Trophy (the Davis Cup). Players represented their nations, and the tournament was open to any country that had an official association. Tournaments spread to other countries, leading to the International Lawn Tennis Federation in 1913, now home of the Grand Slam tournaments (Smart 2007, 115). International rugby events were held in 1871, cricket in 1877, and football in 1890. The first tour de France was held in 1903. There were also international competitions in rifle marksmanship and sailing. Although each of these was a single sport competition and engaged only a few teams and countries, they were steps toward globalization and adoption of standardized models.

International competitions during this early phase of sports globalization pale in contrast to the number of contemporary competitions. As with other types of globalization, international competitions increased rapidly in the period following WWII and accelerated even further in the 1970s onward. Daniel Bell documented 1,220 international multisport competitions between 1896 and 2001. Most of them were created in the second half of the 20th century. As recently as 1959, there were only 69. By 1999, in contrast, there were over 500 competitions. Similarly, the globalization of sports is not limited to a few dozen major sports. There were over 200 different sports represented in the 1,220 multisport competitions (Bell, cited in Sage 2010, 58). New competition in the Olympics and Olympic-style games—such as the Central African Games, Asian Games, Southeast Asian Games, and Mediterranean Games—are important vehicles for new nations to promote themselves on a larger stage and reinforce their national identity. Twenty-three nations participated in the 2011 Asian Winter Games in Kazakhstan, including Near East nations of the Arab states and Far East nations, such as China. The motto of the Asian Games, "Unity of Purpose—Unity of Spirit," highlights the political importance of international games.

International Associations

As sports competitions spread across greater distances within nations and then transcended national boundaries, common understanding of rules and global governance of sporting disputes became necessary. England was the first to establish national sports organizations. By 1870, most nations had followed its lead. Women's sports associations also took off during this period. The women's field and ice hockey clubs, hundreds of women's baseball teams, the Women's French Championship, and the Ladies' Golf Union all formed before 1900. Women also competed in the Olympics in 1900 (AAUW n.d.). These developments in sports were victories in the first wave of modern feminism.

The organizations assumed the rationalized bureaucratic global models employed in governance and institutional life. The rationalization of sports exemplified the pattern of rationalization during the take-off phase of globalization. Standardized rules took the place of spontaneous recreation, and bureaucratic organizations oversaw organizations down the hierarchy, including the qualifications of players and methods of record keeping. Box 10.20 shows the periods during which various sports were standardized.

BOX 10.20   A Closer Look: Rationalization of Sports

Period	National Clubs, Regulations and/or Competitions held
Pre-1800	Horse racing, golf, cricket
1800–1840	Shooting, yachting
1840–1860	Baseball, soccer, rugby, swimming
1860–1880	Track and field, skiing, polo, cycling, canoeing
1880–1890	Football, tennis, badminton, field hockey, bandy
1890–1900	Ice hockey, gymnastics, basketball, volleyball, judo, table tennis, bowling, weight-lifting, skating
Post-1900	Squash, netball, handball, korfball, orienteering, karate, aikido, tae kwon do, among others

Source: Van Bottenburg (2001, 4).

Although there were international competitions, particularly in tennis, not many international organizations were formed in the take-off phase: two in football, one in rugby, and some amateur organizations (Smart 2007, 117). The International Olympics Committee (IOC), formed in 1894, is most responsible for the standardization of sports across countries. The modern Olympics were global from the beginning. Baron de Coubertin, the Secretary General of the French national athletic sporting society, believed that international sporting events would promote peace and understanding among nations. He proposed reviving the Olympic Games in Athens in 1896. The first IOC was restricted to 13 nations from Europe, North America, and New Zealand. There are now 205 National Olympic Committees and 103 International Sport Federations on its roster (Sage 2010, 36–37). Although not successful in establishing peace, the Olympic Games have grown into an international organization with political functions as a forum for international leaders, an alternate international competition, and, on occasion, a platform for political statements. There are now over 70 international sports organizations. Thirty-five sports have national associations in over 100 countries. Together, these form a global system of sport connecting small villages to global competitions (Van Battenburg 2001, 8).

The homogeneity across nations brought by Olympic sports applies to the games and related areas such as the expectations people have of Olympic athletes, their training, and the popularity of some events. Admission into the Olympics signifies that a game is a true global sport. It also means that teams participating must conform to the specified model of the sport. Thus, although national and local rules may vary somewhat, the Olympic model enforces a level of conformity and code of legitimacy. The IOC has been compared to the UN in its international influence over sports. As it is essential for a nation to belong to the UN and conform to certain standards, it is essential for a sports organization to belong to the IOC to be considered a genuinely global sport and for countries to have a National Olympic Committee to be a civilized sporting nation.

Idealism motivated another Frenchman, Jules Rimet, to spearhead the formation of FIFA (Fédération Internationale de Football Association). Rimet learned football (soccer) on the streets of Paris. As he developed into a professional-level player, he encouraged sports as a way to build character. With football, he saw the opportunity to build a worldwide family built on Christian principles. He viewed sports as a force for international good through healthy competitiveness (Tomlinson and Young 2006, 5). FIFA's mission remains to "[d]evelop the game, touch the world, [and] build a better future" (n.d.). With 208 associations around the world, the game has reached nearly every corner of the globe. The FIFA mission declares that

> football is no longer considered merely a global sport, but also as unifying force whose virtues can make an important contribution to society. We use the power of football as a tool for social and human development, by strengthening the work of dozens of initiatives around the globe to support local communities in the areas of peace building, health, social integration, education and more.

The globalization of sport conforms to the global cultural model of rationality that shaped institutional development within and among societies. Regardless of the country of origin or sport involved, the rationalization and standardization of sport in this early phase had several dimensions. The standardization of rules and creation of clubs and associations to govern them form a bureaucratic basis for the global spread of sport as an institution. The rationalization of play and the keeping of sports statistics started in this period. Science was brought to bear on the design and manufacture of equipment, the pursuit of excellence in sport technique, and the perfection of the athletic body. This transformed sports from folk recreation to a global institution.

Global Migration of Sports Labor

As sport became more competitive, sports clubs began recruiting outside of their immediate environment. Britain took the first step, but other nations quickly followed. Players also began a search for better playing opportunities. In this respect, sports teams are like other corporations, and players like other types of laborers.

In association football, undeniably the world's foremost sport, many professional players are not playing for their national or city team. In the UK's premier league, for example, there were 13 foreign-born players on average per team ("Where the Premier League's Players Come From" 2009). As with other forms of labor in the EU, restrictions on the number of foreign players allowed per club do not apply to other EU countries. Since 1995, players have been allowed to move freely from club to club and country to country. Free movement, even within seasons, makes it hard to pin down a foreign player figure. Rough estimates for 2007 show that the percentage of foreign players was 55% in England, 44.8% in Germany, 34.3% in Spain, 32.2% in France, and 28.9% in Italy. Within the more elite teams, the percentages are higher. About 76% of the players within the top 98 clubs in these countries were foreign born (Sage 2010, 73).

Migration of players is not random, nor is it simply a matter of economics and national laws. The best players do not necessarily go to the teams that will pay them the most. Nor are legal factors, such as immigration or association quotas, the most important factors. Migration of sports players follows patterns similar to other forms of migration. People follow pathways related to language, culture, and connections. Teams prefer to recruit foreign players that are culturally and linguistically similar to them (Rowe 2003, 287). This is reflected in the foreign population of the major European teams. In the 2005–2006 season, German leagues drew 42.8% of their foreign players from Eastern Europe. Italy (28.7%) and Spain (37.4%) drew predominantly from Latin America. France (57.2%) drew from its former African colonies, and England (51.1%) from Western Europe (Poli 2010, 498).

Migration channels (transfer networks) also influence the choices that players and clubs make. Players move from country to country according to the relationships among club officials and managers, agents, players, and private investors. The networks link the various leagues and clubs in value added chains similar to that which raw materials pass through on their way to becoming commodities (Poli 2010, 502). Each step is the result of human agency, of who knows whom, within a global structural institution. This, as Poli argues, is applicable to all globalization processes.

Sports and the Particular: Identity

National Identities and Home Teams

Sports, national identity, and individual identity exist in a complex relationship. Sport is a global institution, a vehicle through which nations represent themselves, and a celebration of individual and team achievement. Regardless of the nationality of players, people form profound attachments to local and national teams. Local teams are said to reflect the character of their cities and national teams reflect the character of their nations. (My hometown team, the Pittsburgh Steelers—from Pittsburgh, Pennsylvania—is said to win games "the hard way" through determination and a lot of sweat. This has been the case from the team's inception through the "steel curtain" days of the 1970s and the Super Bowl ring of 2009. The city was built by dangerous and hard work in coal mines and steel mills.)

People's attachment to their home team overrides the mobility of players, the mobility of franchises, and the costs of attracting or keeping a team. In the Olympics and World Cups, athletes compete for the countries of their citizenship; during the regular sport seasons, they play for the team that employs them. Annual migrations of players among teams and teams among cities fascinate millions of people globally. Even though sport is highly rationalized economic enterprise, people's attachment to it is highly emotional. Cities often make costly concessions in taxes, property rents or sales, and revenue sharing to keep or attract professional league teams. Although building a new stadium is very costly, most cities will build a new stadium rather than lose a team, even though any economic benefit is doubtful. People do not want to lose "their" team and take pride in their teams' accomplishments.

Although the decisions concerning where teams locate are commercial, when a team moves, it represents the new locale and commands the loyalty and affection of the local fans. In many league teams, except for American football, there may be few players with citizenship in the nation where they are playing. The "imaginary" is predominant in this relationship. The identification and vicarious nature of participation in winning or losing along with one's home team is striking—although the Brooklyn Dodgers seem to command the loyalty of many New Yorkers decades after they became the Los Angeles Dodgers.

Traditions of singing the national anthem and other patriotic songs at the beginning of sporting events are common, testament to the strong association between sports and national identity. The World Cup, Ryder Cup, Davis Cup, and Olympics are national competitions, not simply competitions among athletes. Sports build community as people cheer and share collectively in the victories of their teams. The unity of purpose at a live sporting event is palpable. It has been compared to the fervor and sentiment aroused by religious services. In both, people celebrate not only the object of their devotion but their solidarity and identification with the community. Wearing team colors and regalia, chanting sport songs and cheers, and participating in rituals, such as "the wave," reinforce this. Even fair-weather fans get caught up in the excitement of advancing toward a championship event. When their home team is out of play, people often adopt another favorite for the duration of the season. Identifying with a team and staking a claim to celebrate their victory or mourn their loss is an important part of spectatorship for most people.

Revival of Traditional Sports

The refinement and spread of national sports and international sports competitions are important means of establishing and reaffirming national identities in a rapidly globalizing world. Baseball—derivative of cricket—and American football—forged from accommodations of rugby and European football—helped the United States lay claim to a national tradition and identity (Guilianotti and Robertson 2007, 108). Many colonies picked up the sports of their mother countries, not only because they had to but because they could compete with their colonizer on the sports field where they could excel. An exception were the Irish who resisted the imposition of football and cricket, games of imperial Britain, and chose an indigenous Gaelic game, hurling, as their national sport. At the turn of the 20th century, activists in Ireland pushed for cultural revival, rejecting all things British, from language and literature to sports, laying the groundwork for the Irish revolution.

Globalization awakens sentiment to revitalize local sports. In many countries, contemporary movements to revive traditional sports are part of broader cultural revivals as countries integrate further into the global system. Revival of indigenous games in South Africa is part of the larger South African renaissance movement. Urbanites tend to participate in Euro-centric sports; reviving indigenous games to appeal to all of South Africa is designed to bring rural and urban areas together and celebrate the diversity of South Africa. Provinces are asked to rationalize and standardize their games by establishing a formal organization to oversee the game rules and equipment to facilitate national competitions. The first national indigenous games festival was held in 2003 (SRSA 2011). In India, sports and cultural associations promote indigenous games *tang guti, kukura juj* (cock fighting), *kalchet* (bamboo stilt racing), and *pesi ti ongpu* (tug of war) at festivals and events around the country to preserve national culture "that television has made us forget" (Kataki 2011). Similar activities are underway in Peshawar, Pakistan.

Interestingly, national revivals have internationalized, perhaps carried by migrations. The first rules of kabaddi were standardized by the Kabaddi Federation of India in 1950, and the first world championship was held in Hamilton, Canada, with five countries participating, including the United States, England, and Canada. Sepaktakraw (Takraw or Sepak takraw), a folk game of Southeast Asia, which looks like volleyball—played with a smaller ball and feet instead of hands—did not have official rules until the mid-1960s. It became a medal sport in regional competitions in 1965 at the Southeast Asian Peninsular Games. There are now teams in the United States and United Kingdom.

Sport Celebrities

A discussion of sport would not be complete without considering the celebrity player. Many fans identify with sports celebrities. This is not simply a function of contemporary mass media. Larger-than-life international sports celebrities emerged in the take-off phase of globalization. Suzanne Lenglen from France and Bill Tilden from the United States were both flamboyant and controversial. Lenglen was admired for her powerful hits and sexy tennis clothes on court. She was the Venus Williams of the 19th century. Tilden learned to capitalize on his talent, not just by winning on the court but by flouting rules against paid endorsements. Like many sport celebrities that would follow, their extraordinary physical struggles and feats engaged fans, allowing the latter to escape from the "deadliness of ordinary life . . . of what is and must be" (Charles Lemert, quoted in Hughson 2009, 138). Like other forms of globalization, transportation and communication media brought sports from all over the world to all over the world. It has allowed sports heroes to flourish on the global stage. Although teams acquire local and national loyalties, the heroes represent more than themselves and their nations. Some theorists argue that athletes represent humanity striving to overcome imperfections. They appeal to us because they rise to excellence despite being flawed or ordinary in day-to-day life (137).

BOX 10.21   A Closer Look: Sports Celebrities

People are fascinated by sports celebrities. At the turn of the 20th century, paparazzi followed Suzanne Lenglen, international tennis star.

Trading cards with sports figures began appearing in 1887. The first cigarettes sold in packs had cards with baseball and other sports heroes. The cards had pictures of the players on the front and advertisements for tobacco products or lists of players on the back. Statistics began to appear on the cards during this period as well. Individual and team statistics rationalize sports further. Measurement is essential to science, so measuring sport performance in precise detail enhances a sport's status as a serious activity. It also makes comparisons among individual athletes, teams, and countries possible.

BOX 10.22   A Closer Look: Baseball Cards

Baseball combined our fascination with celebrity and statistics. This 1887 baseball card features Adrian Anson. One card came in each box of 10 cigarettes. Later baseball cards featured athlete's statistics to the back.

The Athletic Body

Sports speak to individual identity. People connect to their bodies and prove something about themselves, to themselves, and sometimes to others, through sports. As sports developed, the image of the athletic body has transformed. The sports body is leaner and stronger, with a more clearly defined musculature. As Heywood (2007) suggests in her study of marketing sports to girls, the athletic image is promoted as power, power that is converted into success. Associating the power, discipline, and self-control epitomized by the athletic body with all kinds of success suggests that personal effort and responsibility are the keys to achievement. Achievement, effort, responsibility, and success are important dimensions of the globalizing culture. The image neglects the very real social, economic, and cultural constraints that limit not only girls' but also most people's and many countries' opportunities to succeed. It reflects and reinforces neo-liberal political and economic ideology (109). The athletic image effectively markets sporting goods and equipment as important accoutrements to self-improvement and achievement.

Sports as Big Business

Sports not only bear responsibility as vehicles of national identity and pride; sports are big business, a global industry, that includes sports teams, international and national competitions, and sports merchandise. It is fully commoditized from the marketplace for teams and players to the related competition for television coverage and advertising dollars. Teams compete for the best players, the most coverage, and thus the most advertising and promotion dollars. Estimates of the organized sports industry range from $213 billion (Markovits 2010, 505) to $285 billion (Sage 2010, 102). Expensive professional sports teams rely on the media to generate the interest in sports that supplies their audience. Fans buy team-related products and attract advertisers' money, providing corporations with a market for merchandise. Media promotion of the athletic body plays into consumerist culture. The message is that the right shoe, right clothes, right equipment can facilitate anyone's success. All they have to do is choose it (Heywood 2007, 114) or "just do it."

The Olympics alone generate fierce global competition, from hosting the games to corporate sponsorships to the athletes on the field. Cities and nations hope to benefit directly through revenue brought to the city and indirectly through enhanced reputation, even though the record suggests that cities more often lose money in the long term than gain it. Montreal reportedly had $2.7 billion of debt due to the 1976 Olympics, Barcelona $6.1 billion, and Sydney $2.2 billion in true long-term costs (Zimbalist 2009). Only with careful planning to make sure that the money spent is on long-lasting infrastructure improvements can a city hope to benefit (Barney 2009; Marshall 2009). The London Olympics in 2012 tried to do this. It has been the catalyst for a major revitalization of East London, one of the city's most depressed areas. Among the improvements brought by the Olympics are

- mixed-income housing in the Olympic Village and residential and commercial development in the Olympic Park site;
- a new wetland habitat developed from cleaning and widening waterways and canals;
- replanting of the park;
- sports facilities for the community and arenas for elite teams;
- new routes and improved transportation connecting the east to the rest of London; and

- economic transformation, and thousands of jobs during and after the Olympics (LOCOG 2010).

Sports merchandising developed in the take-off phase of globalization. Equipment and footwear became specialized for safety and performance and were mass produced. Sports manufacturing globalized relatively early. S.A.G. Spalding, a Boston Red Socks pitcher, founded Spalding in 1876, one of the earliest sporting goods companies. In 1877, Spalding designed and manufactured a baseball glove, in 1887 a football (American), in 1894 a basketball, and in 1895 a volleyball. Dunlop began making pneumatic bicycle tires in England in 1888. John Boyd Dunlop, the company founder, wanted his son to have an easier time bicycling than struggling with solid rubber wheels. In 1917, Dunlop Rubber Far East was established in Japan. In 1930, they began manufacturing Dunlop golf and tennis balls at a plant in Kobe. Wilson Sporting Goods opened in 1913 in Chicago as Ashland Manufacturing. It was the largest producer of sporting goods in the United States in the mid-20th century. It is now a subsidiary of Amer Sports Corporation, which is headquartered in Finland. As with other manufacturing, sports equipment production sites are all over the world; China is a leading manufacturer.

The history of athletic shoes demonstrates the extent and power of globalization. Nearly everyone can identify with athletic shoes, now the preferred footwear across generations globally. Many companies are so familiar that people in many different countries may think they are a domestic industry. The oldest athletic shoe manufacturer in the world is, arguably, J. W. Foster, founded in the 1890s in England. In 1958, the grandsons of the founder renamed the company Reebok. It was not until 1979 that Reebok went to the United States under the distribution license of an American, Paul Fireman. In the United States, Reebok became an industry leader and expanded its line of merchandise and its overseas market. Reebok was acquired by Adidas in 2006 (Sage 2010, 113–115). Adidas, another household name in many countries, began as a German company under the name Dassler OHG. Jesse Owens helped to popularize the brand by winning four gold medals in the Olympics track and field competition wearing its shoes. A dispute between the Dassler brothers who founded the company resulted in a split in the company shortly after WWII. Two companies emerged from the split, Adidas and Puma. Adidas was the most popular shoe choice of Olympic athletes from 1952 to 1984. Adidas bought the Saloman Worldwide Group (French) in 1997 and Reebok in 2006 (Sage 2010, 112–113).

Converse and Nike are U.S. companies. Converse was established in Massachusetts in 1908. Its famous "All Star" canvas shoe was the first mass-produced shoe in the United States. Chuck Taylor, a famous basketball star of the time, began wearing them. He helped to modify their design and then promoted them across the country. His name was added to the patch in 1923 (Smart 2007, 120). Taylor was probably the first athlete to endorse an athletic shoe. Converse remained a market leader until the mid-1980s. It was bought by Nike in 2003. The "Chuck Taylor All Star" was revived and is sold around the world.

Nike is a newcomer, founded as Blue Ribbon Sports in 1964. It was renamed Nike, after the Greek goddess of victory, in the early 1970s (Sage 2010, 116–117). Despite declines in profits and revenues from 2009 to 2010, Nike was still ahead of all other apparel industries, with over $19 billion in revenues, and was 135th among all Fortune 500 companies in the United States (CNN Money 2011). Nike has the largest share of domestic (36.3%) and global (32.2%) athletic shoe sales. Adidas, the market leader until the 1980s, is second at 8.9% and 15.5%, with Reebok third at 12.2% and 9.6%, respectively. These are followed by Puma, New Balance, ASICS, Converse, KSwiss, Vans, and then the others (Smart 2007, 120). New Balance, KSwiss, and Vans are U.S. companies; ASICS is Japanese.

Regardless of the brand, whether U.S., British, or European, whether counterfeit or genuine, manufacturing is overwhelmingly in the Far East, particularly China and Indonesia. Subcontractors for these powerhouse companies were among the global sweatshop scandals of that emerged in the 1990s and continue into the present. Christian Aid, a British INGO, commissioned a study of athletic footwear manufacturing in the mid-1990s. They reported that many competing shoe brands were manufactured in the same factories. Manufacturing made up a small portion of overall cost, and workers, including children, often worked in deplorable conditions for very low wages. In a $70.00 shoe, only about $1.66 went to labor costs (Maguire 1999, 133–134).

Extreme Sports

Coverage of the sports scene would not be complete without considering extreme sports. The definition of an extreme sport is murky, but the term is generally used to describe any sport whose objective is to test or push the athlete's endurance, strength, courage, and skill to its limits. It is not surprising that extreme sports emerged in this age of hyper-individualism.

Extreme sports have repeated the pattern of growth and development of team sports and other competitive sports. Like folk games, daredevils, the precursor to extreme sports, have been around a long time. A trip to Niagara Falls on the Canadian–U.S. border testifies to feats of the people who defied the rapids. Jean Francois Gravelet (the Great Blondin) traversed the gorge on a tightrope in 1859, including some somersaults. He made many trips across, each time a greater challenge: blindfolded, on a bicycle, pushing a wheelbarrow, stopping to cook an omelet in the center, and carrying his manager on his back—the trip that nearly killed both of them. Annie Taylor was the first to go over the falls in a barrel in 1901. Many others followed, in barrels and other containers. Masses did not participate in these activities, although they drew crowds of spectators. International celebrities such as Harry Houdini, known for life-threatening exploits of daring-do, were imitated, but did not inspire masses of people to adopt similar feats as pastimes.

Just as the industrialization brought the price of sporting goods down and technological innovation made them better, contemporary technological advances in material science and engineering of sports equipment enable levels of human performance previously thought unattainable. Good design and mass production allows many more people to play or compete at extreme levels once thought impossible or improbable for anyone. Surfboards are a good example. They were one of the last fine, handcrafted sporting goods made in the United States. New foams have made surf boards faster, more flexible, and more nimble, improving performance capabilities. The new foams make not only the best but also the cheapest board blanks. Computer-aided design enables boards to be tailored individually to a surfer's body, surfing style, and usual surfing venue. The design can be inserted into a shaping machine, and a blank can be transformed mechanically into a custom designed board. Mass production in Thailand, China, and Mexico has brought down the price. The boards can "do things we wouldn't have thought possible a few years ago" according to Jeff Bushman, a premier board designer (Scharnberg 2006, 1). Thousands of new converts are flocking to surfing, seeking to test

their limits with the thrill of an extreme sport. According to *Surf Ireland,* the 10 best surfing locations are in Tahiti; Oahu, Hawaii; Aileens, Ireland; Puerto Escondido, Mexico; Shipstern Bluff, Tasmania; Ericeira, Portugal; Ours, Australia, Newport Wedge, California; Lanzarote, Spain; and Lombok, Indonesia. Other surfing sites mention spots in Sri Lanka, South Africa, and El Salvador, among others. It is a global sport.

BOX 10.23   A Closer Look: Skateboarding

In the 1950s, skateboards were simply roller skates screwed into plywood boards—surfboards on wheels. Simple boards were manufactured in the 1960s. The advent of urethane wheels, developed in the 1970s, and the Zephyr team's (Dogtown Boys) aggressive boarding style, drawn from surfing moves, and tricks caught people's eye, but it was not enough to make it wildly popular. Skateboarding went underground, almost as a cottage industry associated with the punk movement, but skateboard design continued to evolve as small companies catered to individual skaters. It was popularized again when included in the extreme games of 1995. By this time, board and wheel design and materials had advanced, and good boards could be mass-produced.

Skateboarding has migrated across the world, from California through Asia, to the heart of Africa.

Advances in material and design and lower cost have affected all sports, but have made extreme sports—daredevil activities—popular forms of individuation. Bicycles evolved from all wood to all metal to finally metal with pneumatic tires—originally solid rubber ones. Now, ultra-light, aerodynamic, and ergonomic bikes, specialized clothing, and specialized snacks make long-distance cycling a major sporting challenge for masses, not just the elite-class athlete. Mountain and rock climbing are within the reach of the middle class with ever more sophisticated shoes, clothing, ropes, and other equipment.

Triathlons of swimming, running, and cycling have become common. While the first triathlon was held in France in 1921 and has been held annually since, it was not until the 1970s that the triathlon began to gain widespread popularity. The European Triathlon Union was established in 1984, the U.S. Triathlon Association in 1982. There are now triathlon national federations from Australia to Zimbabwe. Triathlon became an Olympic medal sport in 2000. Trimapper is an interactive website with information on triathlons around the world. In December 2011, it listed over 2,175 triathlons in 92 countries spread across six continents. There

were over 875 club listings. Ironman triathlons, the most rigorous of the triathlons (2.4 mile swim, 112 mile cycling, 26.2 mile run) are held all over the world. There is a World Championship Triathlon and national triathlon associations in many countries, as well as federations and unions in regions, such as the Asian Triathlon Confederation whose member federations include Iran, Bangladesh, Kyrgyzstan, Mongolia, Lebanon, China, Japan, Hong Kong, among others.

Media jump-started the spread of extreme sports, in contrast to team sports that were spread by missionaries, students, and other person-to-person contacts. ESPN first organized the X-Games, a global multisport competition, in 1995. The Winter X-Games were added in 1997. X-Games have been initiated in Asia, Brazil, and Europe, organized by ESPN along with local media and many corporate sponsors. The games include skateboarding, inline skating, snowboarding, surfing, free-skiing, BMX, and FMX. Pro-X Games were held in South Africa in 2009 and 2010. Red Bull, the energy drink maker, also sponsors international competitions. Their events, such as X-Fighters (motocross), Supernatural, Crashed Ice (extreme course ice racing), Dream Line (BMX), Rampage (mountain biking), and Cold

Rush (free-skiing) have their own television series as befitting their colorful names.

Extreme sports spread to China in the mid-1990s, helped along by economic growth of the period and an increased interest in sports and fitness generally. According to a Chinese rock climber, extreme sports fulfill a need that tourism and nightlife, the regular pursuits of the moneyed young in China, cannot (Jennings 2005). Even extreme sports are glocalized. The Chinese preference for group over individual activities and lack of private cars means that extreme sports promoters need to work a little harder in China. Extreme sport businesses that combine equipment sales with tours are the most successful. Organized biking and climbing events begin with bus trips taking the participants, primarily urbanites, out of the city for their activities (Jennings 2005).

What might extreme sports, the more pronounced definition of the contemporary athletic body, and the general trend toward pushing activities from workouts to sports to the extreme, indicate about contemporary life?

Summary

There is a remarkable similarity to much of everyday life in many parts of the world. The application of rational and scientific principles, standardization of forms, and spread of international—and the later development of global—agencies and organizations wrought a homogeneity of form and very often content to the institutional context of everyday life. This chapter reviewed how the development of education, health care, and sports has been shaped by globalization forces. A person from virtually any continent would recognize and be able to navigate (aside from differences in language) most classrooms, health service providers, or sporting events anywhere in the world.

Questions, Investigations, and Resources

Questions

1. Debate: How great a role should global educational models play in determining the educational needs of a country? Should everyone be encouraged to seek the highest levels of education? Should people be prepared for the job market?

2. Explain how education socializes children to be members of their society and of the globe. Provide examples from your own schooling of how you learned about your nation and its place in the world.

3. Why does the education of females tend to have a larger impact on the overall well-being of a society than the education of males?

4. How do bureaucracies both aid and hinder institutions? How could you reform institutional organization to better suit the contemporary world?

5. Summarize the role of science and technology in the development of education, health care, and sports.

6. Societal institutions based on tradition and custom have undergone significant change due to the penetration of science into institutional life. Summarize how science has changed an institution not discussed in this text.

Investigations

1. Choose an institution such as law, the military, police, industry, or family, and review the history of the institution.

   - In what ways has globalization influenced the development of the institution within countries?
   - Is there a global model that countries use to structure their own institution?
   - Consider the function and purpose of the institution. To what degree can it develop a global institutional structure, such as the global economy, or global polity?

2. **Education:** How well do you think the job structure in the United States can support college graduates? If everyone in the United States were to get a college degree, would there be enough jobs or would many be underemployed? Study the Bureau of Labor Statistics fastest-growing jobs. How many jobs will be created in fields that require advanced degrees? How many require a lower educational level? (Please see Box 4.13)

3. **Health:** Diseases that were thought conquered in developed countries are beginning to spread again. One reason is the increased travel to and from countries where vaccination rates are lower. Another is that some people in developed countries began to withhold their children from immunization. Choose a disease such as measles or whooping cough and study its prevalence globally. Can you trace the path of some outbreaks? What factors are involved in the outbreaks

4. **Sports:** Investigate one dimension of globalization as it applies to one of your favorite sports.

- To what extent has the sport penetrated globally?

  o Is it included in the Olympics competitions?

  o In how many countries is it played?

  o How many countries have an Olympic team in the sport?

  o How many associations and clubs are there?

  o Do men and women participate in the sport?

  o Are there racial, ethnic, or social class differences in participation?

- How big of a business does the sport support?

  o What are the market shares of the major suppliers?

  o Where are their headquarters?

  o Where do they manufacture?

- How diverse is the pool of players?

  o What are the percentages of foreign nationals in the leagues or on teams?

  o Are there concentrations of ethnic groups within leagues or teams?

5. Epidemiology is an important field in a global era. How disease spreads through networks of contact and transportation is a complex problem that requires sociological and demographic analytic skills as well as knowledge about diseases and viruses.

- Investigate the WHO program on epidemics and pandemics.
- What measures do they propose to reduce their spread?
- What suggestions do they propose countries follow after an epidemic?

6. Child malnutrition has serious consequences. The World Health Organization keeps a data repository of World Health Statistics. Use them to investigate children under five years old who are obese, have stunted growth, or are underweight and wasted. Go to the repository and click on "Nutrition."

- What countries are at most risk for each of the indicators?
- What does WHO say about childhood obesity globally?

Resources

UNICEF http://www.unicef.org

International Olympics Committee http://www.olympic.org/sports

List of International Sports Organizations and Links (part of a corporate website) http://www.crwflags.com/fotw/flags/int.html#sport

World Health Organization http://www.who.int/en

WHO Global Alert and Response http://www.who.int/csr/en

WHO Childhood Overweight and Obesity http://www.who.int/dietphysicalactivity/childhood/en

Levels and Trends in Child Mortality 2012 http://www.who.int/maternal_child_adolescent/documents/levels_trends_child_mortality_2012.pdf

WHO Global Database on Child Growth and Maln nutrition http://www.who.int/nutgrowthdb/en

Videos

PBS Frontline, *Sick Around the World*: A comparison of health systems of England, Japan, Germany, Taiwan, and Switzerland. This is somewhat dated but still a good reference.

http://www.pbs.org/wgbh/pages/frontline/sickaroundtheworld/

PBS Frontline, *Sick in America*: A look at people's struggles to get and pay for medical care, both with and without medical insurance. It is dated but a good look at the need for health care reform in early 21st-century United States.

http://www.pbs.org/wgbh/pages/frontline/sickaroundamerica

PBS Frontline, *God in America*: A history of religion in the United States. Interactive timeline, tape recordings of original sources.

http://www.pbs.org/godinamerica

Video Shorts

Library of Congress:

Women's Basketball at Missouri Valley College circa 1904

http://memory.loc.gov/cgi-bin/query/r?ammem/papr:@filreq(@field(NUMBER+@band(awal+1203))+@field(COLLID+workleis))

Heavyweight Championship—Squires vs. Burns, Ocean View, Cal., July 4th, 1907

http://memory.loc.gov/cgi-bin/query/r?ammem/papr:@filreq(@field(NUMBER+@band(awal+2979))+@field(COLLID+workleis))

11

Religion: Conflict and Compromise

Objectives

Religion provides us with a worldview, answering existential questions concerning the meaning of life and practical questions concerning our obligations and duties to one another as members of humanity. Religion is one of the earliest sites of globalization. It is a vast topic. This chapter focuses on the puzzles and problems that shape modern religiosity. This chapter will help you

- understand how the turmoil of intense globalization gives rise to religious questions;
- analyze the conflicts between science and faith, and the accommodations resolving them made by various religious groups;
- assess how social problems and secularization test religion, and how religions have responded to them;

- evaluate liberal, conservative, and fundamentalist approaches to religious reform; and
- identify global trends in religion and religiosity, including ecumenism and freedom of religion.

BOX 11.1 Consider This: Spiritual, but Not Religious

New Age and alternative practitioners form a loosely structured social movement that despite its image has had a great deal of success based on shrewd business practice. A 1996 U.S. survey reported that 8% of adults believe in astrology or some method of foretelling the future, 7% in the power of crystals for healing or energizing, 9% in Tarot cards, and 25% in a non-traditional conception of God (quoted in Robinson 2006). Ironically, many New Age practices and products are from ancient Asian, Native American, or other indigenous cultures.

The "alternative spirituality," New Age, and related movements in the United States, Brazil, and Europe shared common strategies in their spread into mainstream. First, by organizing into loose networks, they avoided problems of bureaucratization. Second, they achieved higher and higher profiles by extensive advertizing of a wide range of activities. Third, they used lectures and seminars, small-group study and practice sessions, bookstores, and stores for relevant material items, such as food and accessories, treatment centers, and clinics. They employed consulting firms to heighten their image and appeal to a more affluent audience. From outsider status in the 1970s and 1980s, many movements achieved mainstream success (Carpenter 2004, 222). The International New Age Trade

Shows promise metaphysical products to connect with the physical, and the New Age Wholesale Directory lists over 1,200 metaphysical distributors. Among the products is a "Wiccan Business Kit" (New Age Wholesaler 2012).

While many of these movements are not religions per se, New Age phenomenon and the preternatural seem to capture people's interest in or need for a look beyond the realm of rationality. Television programs in the United States such as *Buffy the Vampire Slayer*, *Early Edition* (a cat delivers the newspaper a day early so a man can prevent the next day's tragic headline.), *The X Files*, *Medium*, and *Charmed*, as well as a plethora of movies and novels from all over the world about angels, zombies, vampires, demons, many kinds of preternatural beings and forces, and aliens from other planets—demonstrate a fascination with the idea that there are irrational forces at work in the world, beyond those that science can comprehend—traditionally, the realm of religion.

What do you think is the significance of New Age and alternate spiritualities? Could they ever replace traditional religions?

Although many theorists predicted the demise of religions as societies modernized, religion remains a vital force in the globe today. Religion arouses intense emotional reactions, and the admonishment to avoid talking about politics and religion still applies in the 21st century. A quick search of the World Wide Web reveals advice not to discuss politics or religion at work, on a date, at the dinner table, or at the barbershop. There is even a Facebook page called "I prefer not to talk with people about politics and religion." It has only two members, and there were no posts from 2010 to April 2012. Why not? Probably it is because despite the advice, people love to talk, or very likely argue, about politics and religion.

Politics and religion are intimately connected in most societies. Although it may not be the case in every region or for every person, religion is one of the most powerful forces motivating people in the modern world. According to Huntington (1993), "what ultimately counts is not political ideology or economic interest. Faith and family, blood and belief, are what people identify with and what they will fight and die for." The contemporary world is rife with conflicts within and among religions. From the Middle East, where sects of Islam battle to control countries, to the United States where Christian sects battle in courtrooms to make their religious beliefs the law of the land, to Europe where the role of personal religious symbols in public life is controversial, religion's role in modern life is contested.

Globalization challenges people's identities, including one of the most fundamental, religious identity. Each phase of globalization raises questions of right and wrong and of good and bad, of the relationship between this world and the other, of the things of Caesar, and the things of Yahweh, Allah, or God. In

other words, each phase of globalization raises religious questions about the meaning of human life and how life is to be lived. Because religious systems are dynamic, they respond to these challenges and incursions into their domain. How they respond creates conflict. Tensions in religious organizations, between factions favoring greater integration with modern and global culture and groups resisting change, are an important dimension of the larger global dynamic. Religion is not a private matter. As with gender, the personal is political.

The germinal phase of globalization witnessed the Puritan awakening and "birth of Protestant America," the diffusion of Christianity through missions, and the expansion of Islam and the Ottoman Empire. The Treaty of Westphalia stripped public authority from empires and churches, giving the state control over religion. The incipient phase of globalization brought a wave of revival in Islam in response to the breakdown of the Muslim empires. The First and Second Great Awakenings of Protestantism in the United States helped set the stage for the American Revolution and anti-slavery movement, respectively. Although a number of religious movements are mentioned in this chapter, I concentrate on the so-called world religions: Islam, Judaism, and Christianity. This chapter picks up at the take-off phase of globalization and then jumps to the contemporary period, capturing three of the most significant dimensions in the globalization of religion:

- Religious responses to the globalization of the scientific world view and secularization
- Religious responses to the intractable social problems wrought by industrialization and modernization
- The ecumenical trends in religion and flows of religious culture east to west and west to east

Religious Issues in the Take-Off Phase, 1870–1920

Challenges to religion were plentiful in the take-off phase of globalization. The traditional prescriptions for family, education, economic, and other aspects of social life were not working. Developments in science, increasing democratization, and secularization changed how people thought about life, challenging religious and other authorities. Urbanism transformed landscapes. Poverty and other social problems were rampant with no sign of improving. All of these challenged the place of humankind and the presence of God in the world. Religions and religious people struggled to make religion relevant. Some movements modernized religion; others reinforced the fundamental orthodoxy of religious belief and practices. Some religions reached out to one another through interfaith dialog. New religions were created. The synergy of these activities generated waves of religious fervor.

Even in Japan—where membership in religious organization is traditionally low and the state usually controlled religions—dozens of new religions emerged. Japan was modernizing, industrializing, and experimenting with democracy in this period. The new religious movements reflected this. The Lotus Sutra movements, Ōmoto (dating to 1892), Ananaikyō, Seichō no Ie, and Sekaikū, in keeping with the period, adopted a very modern—rational, individualistic, and egalitarian—character, doctrine and practice (Sumimoto 2000).

Modernizing Religion: Reconciling With Science, Secularization, and Social Problems

The triple threats of secularization, science, and intractable social problems set the agenda for religious reform in the take-off phase of globalization. Each of the world religions responded similarly in that each was riddled internally with conflict and dissent. A number of strategies emerged within each religion. Each strove to make religion more relevant to social life. There is no single terminology that differentiates precisely among the various groups that arose—modernists, revivalists, fundamentalists, secularists, and so on. That holds true today. In general, liberal responses reinterpreted religious doctrine to reconcile it with

science. They sought to solve the problems of the day through reform or rejection of the social order. Conservative movements preached more individualistic solutions to problems. Fundamentalist movements rejected science and secularism and argued for literal interpretations of scriptures and for religious law to be the basis of state laws.

Islam

Social conditions in the Islamic world had deteriorated by the take-off phase of globalization. During the 19th century, the Ottoman Empire was weak, and the Middle East and Africa came under control of European powers. The imposition of Western institutions and subsequent modernization brought humiliation and soul searching in Islam, once the dominant civilization. This gave way to revivalist movements (Afsaruddin 2012).

Although religion and the state are intertwined in many countries, in Islam the foundation of the state is a religious precept. Political and religious reformers are often one and the same. Jamal al-Din al-Afghani emerged as a leader of the Modernist Islamic reform movement. Al-Afghani rejected the Islamic establishment, blaming it for the backwardness in Muslim societies. He condemned the imperialist incursions of the West into Muslim societies but blamed Islamic leaders for weakening their societies and thus making it possible for them to be overtaken. Along with Mohammad Abdu, one of his disciples, he combined political and religious objectives in his attempts to revitalize Islam. They argued that reason was the foundation of Islam and that reason and science were the very tools that the West used to overcome the Middle East. They admired the Protestant Reformation for rejecting religious absolutism and condemned Islam's turn away from reason as a pathway of learning. They called for Islam to adopt the scientific and rational values and practices that facilitated development in Europe.

There were two important objectives to this Modernist reform movement. In addition to returning Islam to its roots in reason and reconciling science with Islamic religion, they wanted to unite Islamic people. Learning of the common struggles of Muslim people while traveling the Middle East, al-Afghani was convinced that if Islamic people were united without regard to nationality, their cultural identity would be revitalized. As Muslims rediscovered their common identity, they would discover reason was the unifying thread. Al-Afghani thought pan-Islamism would reawaken the intellectual and moral greatness of the Islamic heritage (Kenney 2006, 74–75).

Rejection of the Ottoman Empire also took a determined secular turn. The Republic of Turkey, established in 1923, grew out of this movement. Mustafa Kemal Atatürk, a military leader during the war for independence, strove to create a secular state modeled after the constitutions of Western government. He rejected the caliphate, a combination of religious and political rule, and the sultanate, a form of sovereignty within the empire. In Atatürk's view, sovereignty belonged to the people through democracy. Islam had a place in Turkish society, only if it remained in the religious realm and did not interfere in the political realm or in the establishment of secular institutions. Turkey undertook massive modernizing reforms in every realm of social life, including secularizing education, the legal system, and courts, and modernizing language and the economy.

Roman Catholicism

Darwin's *The Origin of the Species* appeared during the First Vatican Council from 1868 to 1870. The Church did not take a definitive position on the relationship of evolution and creation at that time. Instead, Vatican I affirmed that reason and faith were compatible and that reason could be a tool of faith. At the same time, it warned Catholics not to accept scientific findings that contradicted Church teachings. Evolution was not specifically mentioned. Darwin's book never made it to the forbidden list, although others who tried to reconcile Darwin and the Bible were condemned. Many Catholic theologians wrestled with the role of God in evolution (O'Leary 2007). St. George Jackson Mivart, a biologist and Catholic philosopher of the 19th century, wrote that the human soul came directly from God, but the body came from animal predecessors. Although Mivart was praised and given a doctorate in philosophy by Pope Pius IX for his early work, he was ultimately disavowed by the Catholic Church. His explanation that creation applied to the soul and evolution to the body is close to that which came to be generally accepted in Catholicism.

Science was only one of the forces threatening to compartmentalize religion, severing it from social life.

For the Catholic Church, other issues proved more pressing. Differentiation of institutions and increasing secularism focused the attention of the Church on finding ways to be relevant in modern life. Toward the end of the 19th century, the Church developed a strategy of "social Catholicism" to attack the social problems of the industrial age. They established Catholic versions of social institutions such as political parties and labor unions, in addition to their schools, hospitals, and welfare agencies. Their objective was to build Catholic values into secular groups.

Inspired by the emerging social sciences, the church associated the social problems of the time with exploitation by the capitalist economic system and political systems that supported it. The conservative wing of the reform movement argued that because individuals had abandoned religious principles by becoming greedy and materialistic, the society had gone astray. Although it blamed capitalism, this Catholic response was conservative because it focused on the individual's loss of virtue and piety in the face of capitalism; thus, individuals were responsible for social ills.

More progressive and radical versions of Catholic social action viewed the inherent flaws of capitalism as the source of social problems. They established the Catholic Worker Movement at the end of the take-off phase of globalization in the 1930s. Still active, the Catholic Worker Movement continues to work for social justice among the poor. They advocate a communal, decentralized economy, preaching personal responsibility to retreat as much as possible from capitalism. They disavow individuals owning more than is needed for their survival; any surplus must be given to the poor. They operate houses of hospitality to care for the poor rather than turn the poor over to the charity of the state.

Judaism

Reform movements in Judaism also incorporated the views of science and the liberalizing views of democratization into religious practice. Reform Judaism had roots in Europe during the latter decades of the incipient phase of globalization. Rather than forge an uneasy compromise with science, the modernizers stripped Judaism of supernatural teachings and emphasized an ethical approach to religion instead. Jews immigrating to America from Germany and Bohemia brought Reform Judaism to America where it flourished. Meetings that had began in Germany in the 1840s and continued in Philadelphia in the 1860s were culminated in *The Pittsburgh Platform of 1885*. The platform reconciled historical events, science, and reason. They reached the following resolutions:

- All religions struggle to grapple with the mysteries of God and the infinite. Thus, "a hand of fellowship to all who cooperate with us in the establishment of the reign of truth and righteousness among men" should be extended.
- The Bible reflects the primitive understandings of its own age. It can be reconciled with the knowledge gained through science and reason.
- Judaism is progressive and strives to be in accord with postulates of reason.
- Mosaic and rabbinical laws serve to obstruct more than inspire piety and should be abandoned in favor of stress on moral laws.
- Jewish doctrine obliges Jews to work to solve social problems of the time.
- Judaism is not a nation but a religious community and does not expect a return to Palestine or a religious state (American-Israeli Cooperative Enterprise [AICE] 2010a).

Protestantism

Mainstream Protestant denominations accepted Darwinism and evolution. "Evolution is God's way of doing things," wrote Lyman Abbot in *The Theology of an Evolutionist* in 1891 (quoted in McLoughlin 1978, 154). Because God created nature, they reasoned, nature was a doorway to God. From this point of view, scientists were a type of theologian. As they studied nature, they got closer to God and discovering God's laws. Religion, they argued, could gain insight into moral life through the laws of science. Subjecting the Bible to "higher criticism" based on science could lead the way to deeper truths.

Three types of liberal Protestantism emerged in the take-off phase of globalization. The conservative faction retained an evangelical individualistic ethic, an emphasis on individual self-reliance and hard work. Self-control, moderation, and discipline were the ways to achieve spiritual as well as material success. In an interesting twist on evolution, individuals who remained poor were judged as evolutionarily less advanced. Moderate and radical factions proposed a "Social Gospel" and social ethic (McLoughlin 1978, 162–172). The social structure was responsible for many individual failures, not individuals themselves. Capitalism made economic success difficult (the less radical) or impossible (the most radical). The duty of the liberal Protestant was to use social action to bring about the kingdom of God on earth. They wanted to apply rationality to social affairs and use the government for rational efficient planning. Progressive humanists, such as John Dewey, sought reforms that were similar to the Christian reformers. They viewed a strong, active, and democratic state, not laissez-faire, as essential to solving the problems of urbanism. That, they argued, was what Christ would have done.

BOX 11.2   Consider This: Establishing an African Religious Identity for African Americans

Establishing or reaffirming identity is an important part of the globalization process. Asserting a religious heritage is a way to affirm and reinforce an identity. For many African Americans, practicing the Protestant religion of the slave owners denied their identity as Africans. During the take-off phase of globalization, movements among African Americans reasserted African identity by establishing Jewish and Muslim congregations (Johnson 2010).

These African American religious movements traced their genealogical roots to the ancient Falasha Jews (Beta Israel) in Ethiopia and to African Islam. Thus, they revived their deep roots of ethnicity and religion in these ancient civilizations—rather than accept the shallow heritage forced on them by slavery. Their identity in Judaism and Islam cemented their right to a true African heritage and their status as members of a world community.

African American leaders within both the Jewish and Muslim movements preached a simple lesson to attract adherents. Christianity, they claimed, was a religion of conquest, imposed on them. In contrast, Islam—according to the founders of the Moorish Science Temple of America (MSTA)—and Judaism—according to Rabbi Wentworth

Arthur Matthey, founder of the Commandment Keepers—were integral parts of an ancient racial identity and ethnic heritage that far preceded Africans forced migration to America. Christianity, in contrast, belonged to the Europeans. They condemned the slave trade and conversion to Christianity as attempt to conquer Africans, not save them. The black ethnic religions restored African Americans' ethnic and religious identity (Johnson 2010, 148).

Reaching Out to Other Faiths: Ecumenism

Science, social problems, and secularization diminished the authoritative structures of religions providing for the possibility that many religions have pathways to truth, salvation, and a better life. Ecumenical trends and religious tolerance emerged. People engaged religious ideas from other traditions to reconcile their religious differences. Religions opened themselves to mutual influences, East and West.

- The World's Parliament of Religions was held in conjunction with the World's Fair in Chicago in 1893.
- Swami Vivekananda took the World's Parliament and America by storm (Council for a Parliament of the World's Religions 2013). The Vedānta Society was established in Chicago in 1894, by Vivekananda's U.S. disciples.
- Many student and lay interfaith cooperative efforts were forged including the 1910 World Missionary Council, precursor to the World Council of Churches.
- America was introduced to Baha'i, an ancient Persian (Iranian) religion, at the 1893 Parliament. Its first community was established in Chicago. Their temple was built in 1912 (Krieger 2010).

An Early Universalistic Innovation: The Spirituality Movement

Most people are familiar with the modern sounding declaration, "Spiritual but not religious." During the take-off phase of globalization, new religious movements emerged emphasizing spirituality over particularistic religious orthodoxy and practice. People loosely identified as spiritualists sought truths that transcended religious differences. In *Restless Souls*, Leigh Eric Schmidt (2005) claims that spirituality was the most innovative religious contribution of the period (in the United States at least). While still

very localized within segments of societies in the 19th century, the movement from religions of authority to religions of the spirit began in this period. Spiritualism, tolerance, interfaith dialog and cooperation, and the cafeteria style of religious practice—borrowing from a variety of religious traditions—took root in this period.

Spirituality requires being open to experiencing or at least considering a variety of religious ways. Commitment to the idea of multiple truths and paths to truths proved difficult to maintain during this period, even within the most devoted among the spirituality movements. No one tried harder than Sarah Farmer, who founded Green Acre in 1890. Green Acre was a meeting place for all people seeking spirituality regardless of their religion. Farmer became a religious guru, turning over the sanctuary she founded to anyone who wanted to seek spiritual renewal. Many groups came to seek her guidance and her sponsorship. It was a courageous attempt, but Farmer was not able to transfer her open-mindedness and tolerance. Over time, the groups that met at Green Acre—Transcendentalists, New Thought, Vedānta, and even the Baha'i, who preached that the earth was one country and all people its citizens—became factious and sectarian. Each group wanted to prevail by getting Farmer to recognize their group's teaching as the most direct path to truth and their group the proper administrators of Green Acre. Each resented the incursions of the others (Schmidt 2005, 210).

The Fundamentalist Response

The take-off phase of globalization generated many universalizing tendencies. The adaptations to science, tackling of social problems, and acceptance of religious diversity made by mainstream denominations were not universally accepted. Not everyone was willing to accommodate religion to the increasingly pervasive role of science in the world. Not everyone was ready to accept that their religion was one among many and adopt a stance of tolerance. Not everyone was ready to accept that social structures could be the root of individual problems. Many people broke away from mainstream denominations in a flurry of sectarian movements.

The countervailing trend to modernizing religious movements was to reinforce orthodox religious beliefs. The term *fundamentalism* arose in reference to Protestants who preached strict adherence to literal interpretations of the Bible. However, every religion experienced fundamentalist reaction to the changing times. Accepting religious belief without question eliminates the anomie that accompanies rapid social change, and societies were changing rapidly. While some reformers struggled trying to establish new perspectives on right and wrong, good and bad, and how God fits or does not fit with the new realities of human life, fundamentalists turn to tradition and to strict literal interpretations of holy books. In the face of globalizing trends, fundamentalism offers a firm identity, a definitive basis for belonging, and answers to every question. It provides the sense of certainty and security in a world where everything—from the personal, such as the roles of men and women, to the political, such as the obligations of government, to the existential, such as the origin and purpose of human life—seems uncertain.

Conservative Judaism

Conservative rabbis split from reformists to pursue a more traditional religious belief and practice. In America, European Jews saw speaking and writing Hebrew as a mark of identity, distinguishing Jew from gentile. They railed against the use of English in services (Johnson 2010, 23). *Agudat Israel* denounced both Reformist Jews and Zionists, who had taken up the cause of a Jewish homeland. They argued that by denying the validity and importance of strict Biblical truth, a personal messiah, and Jewish laws, Reform Judaism integrated with modern society but denied religious orthodoxy. Zionism, they argued, denied religion altogether by pushing for a Jewish homeland granted by the international state system and secular law, rather than a state of Godly creation and religious law. The conservative movement

focused on establishing communities of orthodox Jews living and worshiping in traditional ways rather than trying to promote theocracy in Israel or to influence secularized Jews elsewhere. This effectively privatized Orthodox Judaism.

Protestant Fundamentalism

Protestant fundamentalists rejected science, calling it the enemy of God. They also rediscovered pre-millennial prophecy that argued that not all individuals could be perfected and that society would not be saved before the second coming of Christ—the end of the world. This view seemed appropriate to the bleak nature of modern society. Rather than try to reform society, their strategy was to seek inner perfection, save souls, and restrict the opportunity to sin (as in the Prohibition) so that they were prepared for the end of the world.

Political Islam

When the Ottoman Empire fell at the end of WWII many Islamic societies modernized under colonialism, adopting Western governmental forms and institutions. On independence, governments developed under the dictatorial rule of local elites who maintained many Western institutional structures, clothes, and even language. To many, they were just as objectionable as the European colonizers (Afsaruddin 2012). The Muslim Brotherhood, founded by Hasan al-Banna, emerged in Egypt at the turn of the century to fight against colonialism and Western influences. He blamed the West and secularization for degrading Islamic morals (Kurzman 2011). Al-Banna fought against colonial regimes and the governments they left behind to restore Islamic values, morals, and laws.

The original motivation of the Brotherhood was to establish Islamic states, combining political struggle including violence, religious precepts, and social work. Al-Banna favored modern social reforms such as mass education, a war on poverty, and public health. He saw an important role for science and technology in developing Muslim countries. The Muslim Brotherhood spread through the Arab world, and both fundamentalist Islam groups and more moderate reformist and modernist movements are under this loose umbrella.

Wahhabism arose in the 18th century in reaction to the secularizing trends of the Enlightenment and modernity. Mudhammad ibn Abd al-Wahhab forged an agreement with al-Saud, then just a local ruler, a tribal family. Wahhabism became the sanctioned religion of Saud territories in exchange for tithing and a military alliance. Al-Saud used Wahhabi jihad against infidenls to expand its territory trying to unify the Arabian peninsula. The al-Saud rule spread until overcome by the Ottoman Empire. At the turn of the 20th century, Wahhabi fighters helped reestablish Saud family rule. They continued to puruse jihad against non-Islamic governments and governments in Islamic countries whom they perceive as not pure enough. Al Qaeda and the Taliban are both Wahhabi movements.

The Take-Off Phase of Globalization and Colonization of Africa

The turmoil of the take-off period of globalization awakened religious zeal globally. The disruption and rapid social change of colonialism inspired religious ferment in Africa. New religious movements sought independence from the colonial religions and hoped to escape the hardships compounded by colonialism. The African Independent Churches (AIC, or African Instituted Churches) transformed Christianity, giving it an African character. The AIC is a good example of glocalization. While accepting basic tenets of Christianity, its members rejected the accompanying values that colonists and missionaries brought: individualism, secularism, consumerism, and capitalism.

BOX 11.3   A Closer Look: Religions in Africa

Predominant Religion: First Past the Post

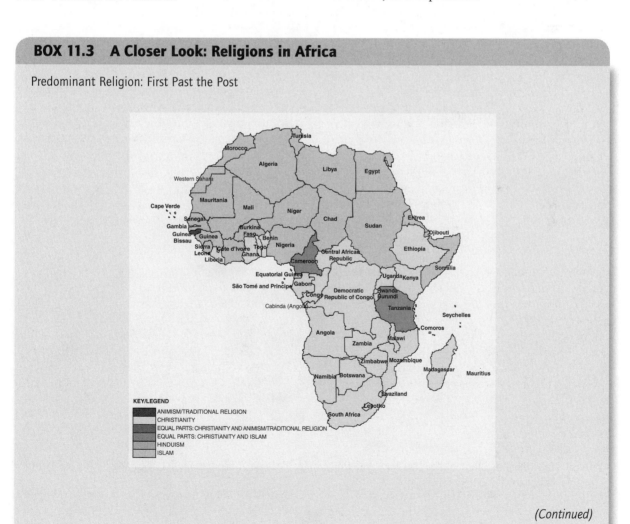

KEY/LEGEND
- ANIMISM/TRADITIONAL RELIGION
- CHRISTIANITY
- EQUAL PARTS: CHRISTIANITY AND ANIMISM/TRADITIONAL RELIGION
- EQUAL PARTS: CHRISTIANITY AND ISLAM
- HINDUISM
- ISLAM

(Continued)

(Continued)

Main Minority Religion

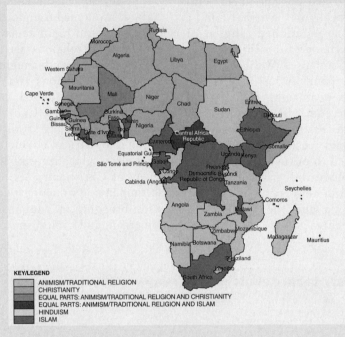

Percentage Who Practice Indigenous
Religions

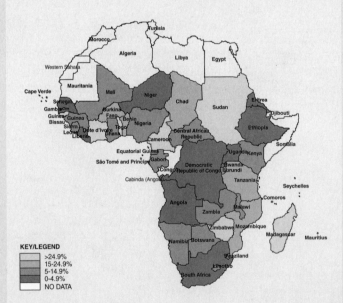

These maps illustrate that although Islam and Christianity became the predominant religions in Africa, many people still practice indigenous religions.

Case Study: The Mourimi Movement

Some new religious movements in Africa revitalized indigenous religions. Sherilynn Young (1977) recounts one such movement, the Mourimi movement in Mozambique. The Mourimi movement illustrates how one group of Africans realigned social roles and organization following the disruptions of colonization and preserved their religion. The Tsonga women, traditionally responsible for cultivation, came to dominate agriculture, and care of the family, and became the primary practitioners of indigenous religions and traditional rituals. Thus, they managed to keep their religious tradition vibrant in the private or folk realm, while men converted to Christianity in the public.

Tsonga social patterns were first disrupted in the early 19th century by Nguni incursions and rule. This was followed by Portuguese colonialism mid-century. Tsonga men, compelled by economic need or direct coercion, left homesteads to work in the mines of South Africa, colonial plantations, the military, or other Portuguese operations. Women stayed in the tribal areas, carried on their traditional roles in cultivation, and took over all the home roles of males. However, after their land was appropriated by the Portuguese, they had to pay to develop it.

The early 20th century brought intermittent flood, drought, and famine. Epidemics of measles, dysentery, pneumonia, and smallpox took thousands of lives. Managing to survive became increasingly difficult. Making payments to the Portuguese was near impossible. Some tribal women began to organize in quasi-military fashion to drive the evil spirits that were causing the havoc out of the villages. Tsonga women took a different tact. They believed that their earth god, Mwari, was angry because the Nguni king had been displaced by the Portuguese. Tsonga women sent messengers to find out from Nguni chiefs how to satisfy Mwari. They adopted a cleansing ritual and use of sacred tobacco to restore fertility to their fields and villages and, more subtly, reorganize communal responsibilities. Only those who were cleansed could perform certain duties. Men returning from the mines (where many had been unfaithful) had to be cleansed by the women before they could enter their homes. The power and influence of the chiefs over the women threatened the Portuguese. They tried to suppress it, but Mourimi continued to spread. Women took over more of the male roles, including those in religious rites and medicinal practices. Many rituals were devoted to agriculture, but many others focused on the sins committed by men. Men, working away and often living in towns while working, converted to Christianity. Men developed very separate lives in the towns, keeping their money to themselves. Women developed separate lives as well and continued to experiment with crops, developing nuts, cotton, cassava, and sufficient food for their families (Young 1977, 75–79).

Resolving the Take-Off Phase

During the take-off phase of globalization, mainstream denominations managed to accommodate religion to science, social problems, and the diversity of religious belief and practice. Fundamentalist movements experienced revival and renewed vigor by reaffirming traditional values and beliefs. This laid the foundation for so-called culture battles that continue throughout the globe today between fundamentalist and more liberal religious perspectives. Despite the efforts to spread religious tolerance, religious animosity chilled the globe during the take-off phase of globalization. Christianity was forced onto colonial populations. Pogroms in Eastern Europe and Hindu–Muslim conflict in India caused William Wallace Fenn, an analyst of the times, to pronounce in 1897 that "the idea of the 'sympathies of religion' had produced little more than 'a huge cloud of thin but amiable sentiment'" (quoted in Schmidt 2005, 117).

The Contemporary Phase, 1960s –Present

From the take-off period of globalization to the contemporary, mainstream denominations grew more bureaucratized, following rational organizational models as did other institutions. In the 1960s—a period of increasing demands for equality, self-expression and individualism, and a host of social and political rights—religious organizations that emphasized patriarchy, hierarchy, promotion of the status quo, and rigidity were out of touch with people's social experiences. In Europe, many people left mainstream religious organizations and never returned. In the United States, Africa, Latin America, and Asia, religious resurgence sent people looking for more satisfying and meaningful forms of religious involvement and answers to the social and personal ills that plagued modern life. Religious conflicts and wars have raged around the world.

Modernity did not diminish religion as much as it diminished membership in religious organizations. The secularization thesis—that religion would lose relevance as people turned increasingly to science as a path to knowledge and institutions, such as education, justice, and so on, developed their own logic apart from the religious—warrants careful examination. As Box 11.4 shows, religion is still important to many people. In this same survey, 79.6% of people said that they did not belong to a religious organization (59.5%) or were not an active member (20.1%). Nevertheless, the majority of people indicated that religion was very (49.1%) or rather (22.4%) important to them. That figure was lowest in Japan, China, Vietnam, and northern European countries.

BOX 11.4   Consider This: Religiosity Today

In the 2005–2008 World Values Survey, over 82,000 people in 57 countries were asked, "Independently of whether you go to (church) or not, would you say you are . . ." The results were that people are surprisingly religious.

	Total Sample			Europe Only	Asia Only	Asia w/o India and Indonesia
	Frequency	Percentage	Valid percentage	Percentage	Percentage	Percentage
A religious person	56,054	67.5%	70.0%	48.5%	46.6%	36.6%
Not a religious person	20,028	24.1%	25.0%	37.1%	39.3%	47.9%
A convinced atheist	3,997	4.8%	5.0%	10.9%	10.2%	13.4%
Don't know	1,852	2.2%		2.2%	3.0%	1.8%
No answer	979	1.2%		1.0%	0.8%	0.3%
Not applicable	79	0.1%		0.3%	0.2%	*
Missing; unknown	4	*			100%	100%
Total	82,992	100%	82,992	11,413	15.036	11,020

Religious sentiment was somewhat lower for the 10 developed European societies polled and lower still in the 10 Asian societies (including India). Do you think that the percentage of people indicating that they are religious would be higher or lower in the United States? Canada? Africa? South America? Explain. Do you think that eventually religion will lose meaning as the secularization thesis predicted? Why or why not?

People's religiosity has been shifting. Mainline denominations have been losing members, but formerly marginal and new religious movements have gained adherents. In the United States, for example, Evangelical Protestants are now the largest religious group, claiming 26% of religious adherents, whereas the total membership of mainline Protestant denominations is only 18% and Catholics 24% (Pew Research Center 2007, 8). Tolerance and ecumenism are strong; only 24% of people in the United States believe that their religion is the only true faith. Only in Jehovah's Witness and Mormonism do majorities hold that view (3).

In Europe, people turn to religion as a consumer choice rather than obligation (Pew 2005). A general sense of religious belonging and belief score high numbers. In a Pew poll, when people were asked if they "believe in God," 70% replied yes. Percentages are much lower as when asked a specific creedal question such as, "Is Jesus Christ is the son of God?" Similarly, not many Europeans attend religious services weekly, but they do participate in religious rites such as marriage ceremonies, funerals, and baptisms. For example, nearly all children in Sweden, Norway, and Finland—long considered among the most secular societies—are baptized (Pew Research Center 2005). In the United States, people tend to shop for a religious congregation in the same way they might shop for a barber or beautician. They switch from one organization to another until they find one that suits their style. People in these developed countries are religious but express it more personally rather than through religious organizations.

During the take-off phase of globalization, religions dealt with the global rise of science and intractable social problems in similar ways—each developed both fundamentalist and progressive strategies. Religions today remain divided among liberal and fundamentalist organizations. During the contemporary period of globalization, there are several discernible trends.

- There has been a worldwide resurgence of fundamentalism and involvement of fundamentalist movements in political affairs.
- Many new religious movements have emerged that stress global consciousness and ecumenism to overcome differences among religions.

- Purely rational understandings of life and social life are rejected by many who search for transcendent and spiritual elements of life that defy reason.
- People search for meaningful religious and spiritual experiences, such as a personal connection to God or a universal life force.
- Millennial themes concerning the end of the world have ignited religious and secular movements related to end-of-life issues such as the environment, weapons of mass destruction, pandemics, and global terrorism.

Along with the global explosion in new religions and religious movements within established traditions, there has been an exponential growth in religiously affiliated international non-governmental organizations (RINGOs). Familiar groups such as Habitat for Humanity, the Salvation Army, and those associated with world religions such as the Maryknoll Office for Global Concerns and B'nai B'rith International have expanded. There are over 300 RINGOs with consultative status at the UN (Peterse 2010). They are active agents in globalization, infusing their religious work with secular values related to poverty reduction, education, health care, and social welfare to such an extent that their aid work sometimes takes priority over their religious work (Boli and Brewington 2007, 226).

Reviving the World Religions: The Liberal Responses

Each of the world religions remains divided in its responses to global affairs. Judaism, Islam, and Christianity are decentralized. Even though the Roman Catholic Church is authoritarian, the Vatican and the laity vary in their accommodation of modern life, as do religious persons in different countries. The pattern of anomie, experiment, and liberal and conservative response characteristic of institutional reform characterizes the turn of the 20th century into the 21st.

Vatican II and Liberal Catholicism

In the early 1960s, organized religion was severely criticized for being socially irrelevant, tacitly supporting racism and economic injustice, and failing to act as a moral force (Quinley 1974, 1). In the Roman Catholic Church, Pope John XXIII was a step ahead of the critics by convening a Vatican Council in 1959 to open the Church to reform. The result was that the Church gave more latitude to diverse groups of Catholics to practice Catholicism within a more broadly defined theology.

Many reforms were particular to local contexts and preferences. Liturgies in the language of the people rather than Latin and including modern and local musical traditions into liturgies drew people closer to the Church. Charismatic Catholics brought life into deadened ritual. Women's participation expanded—although they are still excluded from the clergy—and restrictions on divorced Catholics relaxed. Many Church teachings were demystified. Nearly everything about Catholicism was called into question and debated. Meaning and ritual were revitalized. New ways of being Catholic were invited and invented.

One of the most exciting movements of liberal Catholicism was Liberation Theology in Latin America. Liberation theology combined the social ethic of Catholicism with Marxist ideology. It was shaped, on the one hand, by the globalization of values relating to freedom and equality and, on the other, by the institutional revitalization efforts of the Roman Catholic Church. Catholicism assumed a radical character: to liberate the society. Church leaders preached that poverty resulted from deliberate social oppression, not a failure of individual effort. Liberation theologians were revolutionary in calling for not just a new Church but a new society (Beyer 1994, 138). Although their political arguments were Marxist, they rejected the godlessness of communism and maintained their Catholic inspiration. Being Catholic in Latin America meant working for social justice, for equality and democracy. Rather than religion being a force of false consciousness, as Marx argued, liberation theologians used religion as a force to raise consciousness and motivate people to engage in social struggle.

As Latin America developed economically, communication and travel became easier; liberation theology diffused. Reformers became more integrated into the global Catholic networks. Missionaries who were blocked from practicing in other developing countries came to Latin America to relieve shortages of priests. Students from Latin America went to Europe to study. These migrations helped spread the reform ideas of Vatican II. International and national councils of bishops began to develop strategies and share ideas throughout Latin America (Beyer 1994, 137). Liberation theology grew as a movement, holding conferences and lectures, widely distributing publications, attracting priests and bishop internationally to the cause.

Liberation theology was not well received by the global mainstream. The Cold War was heating up. Anti-communist in religiosity and anti-capitalist in ideology, liberation theology found itself with few allies. In the late 1960s, a Rockefeller Report on liberation theology objected to its attack on capitalism. The American Enterprise Institute, the Institute of Religion and Democracy, and even the Pentagon took up the anti-liberation theology cause, issuing papers, holding conferences, and publishing books on its dangers to national security (Batstone 1997, 37). When the Vatican took a conservative turn after Vatican II, it turned against liberation theology. In the 1980s, Cardinal Joseph Ratzinger (who became Pope Benedict XVI) condemned liberation theology as a threat to the church, and Pope John Paul II pulled radical bishops from their posts and replaced them with more conservative ones (Hertzke 2009, 58).

Liberal Protestantism

Protestantism splintered further into liberal reformers and traditionalists. Methodists, United Church of Christ, Episcopalians, and Presbyterians leaned toward modernist views while Baptists and Lutherans were more traditional. Issues of abortion, homosexuality, and female clergy created deep divides between liberal and fundamentalist Protestants. Even within the mainline Protestant denominations, liberal and conservative voices clashed. In some respects, the new breed of clergy was more liberal than much of their laity (Quinley 1974).

Mainline denominations lost members to evangelical groups who stressed a personal connection to God. In 1968, 13.2% of the American population belonged to mainline Protestant churches. By 2003, only 6.8% did (Levin 2006). As liberal Protestant groups allowed women and homosexual ministers, many laity moved to more conservative churches. Some Episcopal priests left their churches over such issues as the ordination of homosexuals, abortion rights, positions on Judaism, and interpretations of the bible—and became Catholic priests. The Catholic Church made an exception for them and allowed them to keep their wives—while warning others that no priests would be allowed to marry after they joined.

Liberal Islam

Debates in Islam mirror those of the other world religions—the role of religion in politics, individual piety vs. social action, equality of genders, homosexuality, abortion, and other value clashes of the culture wars. According to Allawi (2009), modernity and secularism had crowded Islam out of the Muslim world by the 1960s. While Islam was observed in highly ritualistic form, it was ignored and marginalized by the modernizing secular factions that ruled Muslim countries. Islam was irrelevant to the Arab world organized under dictatorships and living in poverty, although Islam remained the official religion. The inner spiritual world of Islam and the outer social world had little to convey to one another. Political, militant, fundamentalist Islam emerged out of this crisis and defined resurgent Islam for the world (x–xi). The world is most familiar with fundamentalist Islam and secular dictators. These are not the only Islamic choices. There is as much, if not more, diversity within Islam as in other world religions.

Liberal Islam takes its starting point, like other liberal religious movements, in its holy book: the Qur'an. Kurzman (2011) differentiates three types of Islamic liberalism according to their view of shari'a or Islamic law. One type finds explicit liberal ideas in the shari'a. The second adopts liberal ideas where shari'a is silent, and the third argues that shari'a is subject to different interpretations. Liberal Islamic reformers use these three methods to reconcile Islam with modern life, justifying women's equality, human rights, and democracy. These strategies are akin to those of other liberal religious traditions.

There are many liberal movements in Islam and modernist Muslims. As with other religions, these are based on the idea that religious precepts and doctrines can be compatible with the modern world.

Farish A. Noor is a liberal Islamic scholar who argues for a tolerant Islam that strives for modernization, development, and the creation of a civil society to stand in opposition to the dogmatism of the mullahs. Sisters in Islam (SIS) advocates for Islamic women, justice, social equality, freedom, and democracy. They locate their activism within the "revolutionary spirit" of Islam and base their ideas on readings of the Qur'an and the participation of women in the founding of Islam. Both Noor and SIS are grounded in the Qur'an. Another liberal view within Islam argues that secular government is the best way to observe Islamic law. If there is an Islamic government, people obey laws enforced by and under coercion of the state rather than freely performing religious obligations.

To be modern or liberal, Islam does not need to conform to Western ideals. Indonesia, the largest Muslim country, is a democracy but supplements its legal system with shari'a in some cases. Some Western governments, including Britain since 2008, allow shari'a courts to decide family law and financial cases, when both parties agree. This gives Islam equal status to Anglicanism and Judaism (Johnson and Vriens 2010). Turkey, also a democracy, was founded with a strict commitment to secularism in public institutions and life. In 2002, the Justice and Development Party (AKP), an Islamic party, was elected into power and has maintained a secular rule. The party tried to lift the ban on headscarves in universities. This was denied by the Turkish Supreme Court as antisecular. While banning headscarves denies the right to freedom of religion in the United States, other democracies—such as France—justify bans on headscarves in schools on the basis of commitment to secularism.

Which is more liberal: to allow headscarves, even though they are a religious symbol, or to ban them?

In Arab Islamist politics, Rashid Al-Ghannouchi, a leader of the Al-Nahda (Renaissance) party, is considered among the most liberal reformers. He was banned from Tunisia and returned after the 2011 revolution. In a January 2011 interview, he argued for democracy, basing his position on traditional Islamic respect for religious, social, and political difference, and for varying interpretations of Islam. While not arguing for socialism, his political ideas are left leaning, supported by his interpretations of the Islamic religious obligation to equitable distribution and social justice. His vision of Islamic democracy is similar to AKP rule in Turkey. His vision of an Islamic economy is similar to the Scandinavian economic model (free trade but with substantial social welfare programs). He believes that Islamist extremists are beginning to confront the reality that they cannot rule alone and will give up their ambitions to monopolize Islam (Abedin 2011).

Reconstructionist Judaism

Rabbi Mordecai Kaplan developed Reconstructionist thinking in Judaism in 1922, toward the end of the take-off phase of globalization. Kaplan tried to bridge the divides among Reformist and Conservative Jews who saw Judaism only as a religion, and Zionists who saw it as an ethnicity. Many of his insights use sociological theory to harness the power of groups to reestablish Jewish community, identity, and civilization within the societies in which they lived, wherever they were. Kaplan envisioned Judaism as a complete civilization, with history, religion, language, organization, norms, and spiritual and social ideals, not just as an ethnicity or religion. As a civilization, Judaism would be organized on the basis of "organic communities" that joined together all of the religious and educational institutions in the community and were run by a democratically elected leadership. Belonging to the community would be the emphasis of Jewish life, not behaving to a set of rules or believing in particular doctrines (AICE 2010b).

It was not until the founding of the Reconstructionist Rabbinical College in 1968, however, that Kaplan "gave his blessing to Reconstructionism as an independent denomination," developing it along the lines of the religious organization model. At that point, congregations and membership grew rapidly (AICE 2010b). His basic tenets were highly ecumenical, rational, and democratic. He focused on salvation in this world through the continual improvement of individual personality and social order, not a later afterlife and other world.

There are five main tenets in his approach:

- Judaism as a civilization and culture is a product of human agency rather than product of divine revelation.
- The Torah is the recorded history of the people and their "search for God and behaviors that would lead to human responsibility," not inspired revelation.
- God is the sum of forces that make cosmos from chaos. There could be many conceptions of God, but it was belief in God that was the force that supports salvation—that "elicits from us the best of which we are capable."
- Kaplan rejected calling Jews the chosen people because it implies Jewish superiority, not just uniqueness as a civilization or the Jewish obligation to God or humanity.
- Like most other Americans, he supported the establishment of a homeland and the right of return of Jews (aliyah) but also saw value in the inclusion and integration of Jews in other societies.

Reconstructionist Jews began the Bat Mitzvah for girls and emphasized inclusion—of intermarried Jews, gay and lesbian Jews, and others. In the 1990s, Reconstructionists issued a new series of prayer books, which is the work of lay people as well as rabbis and academics.

The Fundamentalist Response

Periods of institutional reform typically start with a phase of liberalization. This makes sense. In expressing dissatisfaction, people throw out many old or traditional ways of doing things and try to come up with something new. This phase of experimentation is typically followed with a backlash to restore the traditional ways. For fundamentalists, traditional ways may apply in both sacred and secular realms. Drawing the line between state and religion becomes contentious during periods of fundamentalist resurgence.

Roman Catholicism

In the Catholic Church, the window of opportunity opened by Vatican II began to close just a year after it convened with the death of John XXIII.

Nevertheless, the Church would never be the same as pre–Vatican II. Local calls for reform did not stop, although the conservative faction grew very strong and came to dominate official Catholicism. John's immediate successor, Paul VI, saw Vatican II through to its close and warned the Roman Curia that the reforms of Vatican II had to be respected if the Church were to retain legitimacy. Nevertheless, later popes reinforced traditional interpretations of Catholic doctrine, diminished the role of the laity and bishops in governance, and became much more hierarchical and authoritarian. This cost them further erosion of membership in Europe and North America.

As Catholicism shrunk in Europe and North America, a wave of growth began in Africa and Asia and surged through the first decade of the new millennium. According to *Our Weekly Visitor*, a Roman Catholic newsletter, the Catholic population in Africa grew from 2 million 100 years ago to 21 million 50 years ago, to 165 million (17.4% of the population) in 2005. There has been similar growth in Asia. In India, for example, the Catholic population grew from 5 to 18.5 million in 50 years (Bunson 2011).

The Catholic Church remains conservative on social issues, condemning the use of birth control, desperately needed in many countries to curb population growth and to save women who die in childbirth. They reject women in the priesthood and do not allow priests to marry. Along with other fundamentalist religions, they condemn homosexual practice and have spread these teaching throughout Africa, supporting governments that prosecute homosexuals. They have protected priests who have sexually abused children.

Conservative Catholics have become very vocal in the political realm, denouncing candidates who are pro-choice or advocate for homosexual rights to marriage. They have also spoken out against the 2011 Affordable Care Act in the United States due to its requirement that employers offer birth control benefits in their health plans. Gaining health care coverage for birth control was a major issue of the feminist movement in the United States. The Church's interference in this regard angered many Catholic women, many of whom use birth control at some time in their lives.

How well the Catholic Church survives pulling in an opposite direction of many of its members on issues—such as the global scandal of pedophilia in the priesthood, the cover-up of the crimes by bishops and popes, the challenges of posed by women as they gain more power globally, the insistence on rejecting birth control, the condemnation of homosexuality, and the refusal to allow priests to marry or whether it will accommodate more to contemporary social life—tests its authority.

Islamic Fundamentalism

The legacy of colonialism inspired both secular democratic movements and religious movements in Islam. The religious movements used traditional religious values as a basis for uniting people in rejecting foreign influences and establishing sovereign national governments. Islamist fundamentalist revolutionaries have been among the vanguard of change. The Shi'a clerics were powerful in fighting back Western influences during the late 19th and early 20th centuries. In Iran, they helped Reza Kahn bring the Pahlavi dynasty to power, fighting to eradicate foreign influence and reassert nationhood.

Islamist movements that fuse strict interpretations of religious law and political law have become the most prominent of the fundamentalist movements in the contemporary period. Like other religious fundamentalists, Islamic fundamentalists have a long history of resisting secularizing trends of modernity and encouraging adherents to return to traditional religious beliefs and practices. The democratic revolution of the 1970s in Iran opposed the Shah's dictatorial regime and the Western governments that helped to keep the Shah in power despite oppression and impoverishment of the country. The revolutionary coalition contained secular groups and a variety of Islamic religious groups. After the revolution, fundamentalist Shi'a clerics under Ayatollah Khomeini were able to seize control, establishing a theocracy with a parliament and president elected from among candidates approved by the Guardian Council.

Islamic groups remain devoted, many violently, to their mission to establish Islamic states. The Wahhabi remain among the most fundamentalist. The Muslim Brotherhood encompasses a variety of opinions from radical to moderate. Islamic fundamentalist groups played a relatively low-key role thus far in the revolutions that began in the Arab Spring in 2011 but emerged afterward to participate in elections. The Muslim Brotherhood won the presidential election in Egypt. Whether or not the Brotherhood will abide by its promises not to try to establish a religious state in Egypt is not yet, as of this writing, known. The degree of their influence in shaping the new governments will take years to unfold.

BOX 11.5   A Closer Look: The Prosperity Gospel and the Power to Break Poverty

The Prosperity Gospel is a particular form of Evangelical Protestantism. It began in the United States but has been exported globally. The basic premise is that God gives to those who give. By giving to your church, you will get health and wealth from God—if your faith is strong enough.

There are two sides to the story. One side is that the Prosperity Gospel inspires people to take charge of their lives. It inspires people to achieve regardless of their race, income, or gender. It is a message of hope for the poor in many developing countries.

The other side is obvious. Preachers have gotten wealthy scamming their followers, who may have strong belief but haven't received payback.

When evangelical leaders from around the world were polled, 90% denied the teaching of the Prosperity Gospel that God rewards the faithful with money (Pew Research Center 2011b, 19).

Diffusion of Protestant Evangelicalism and Other Renewalists[1]

The Protestant renewal religions are the most successful contemporary movements on the global stage. The global evangelical movement is so closely associated with movements among Pentecostals and Charismatics that the terms are often used interchangeably. Pentecostals and Charismatics may also be evangelicals, but may not be. All three share an emphasis on a personal and direct experience of God: the religious experiences of being "born again" by having a personal experience of Jesus Christ or of making a "faith decision" (PBS 2004). Beyond this, Evangelicals and Pentecostals share a belief in the authority of the Bible and stress the obligation of every evangelical to spread the word of Christ. Pentecostals and Charismatics share the "gifts of the Holy Spirit" such as speaking in tongues, but are considered distinct categories. There are close to 600 million Pentecostals and Charismatics today, 26.7% of the global population (Pew Research Center 2011b).

During times of cultural reorganization, the renewal religions offer the believer a very clear set of guidelines and a religious experience that is real and immediate: the direct touch of God through miracle healings, speaking in tongues, and bearing witness (McLoughlin 1978, 153). This contrasts with the ambiguity in guidelines, routinized services, and indirect experience of God offered by the mainstream denominations.

Prior to the 20th century, only small elite groups in developing nations were Protestant. During the tail end of the take-off phase of globalization, Protestant evangelical missionaries began to make significant inroads into developing nations. Globally, evangelicals have grown from about 95 to over 298 million adherents from 1970 to mid-2012, and Charismatics have grown from about 62 million to over 612 million. The global population increased less than 100% in this same time (Center for the Study of Global Christianity 2012). Evangelical leaders in the global South (in Africa, Latin America, most of Asia, and the Middle East) are optimistic about their continued growth and influence.

The greatest proportion of Protestants in Latin America now is Pentecostal. Pentecostals and Charismatics have gone from 4% of the general population in 1970 to 28.1% in 2005 and compose 73% of all Latin American Protestants. In North America, the renewal congregations tend to be drawn from the lower socio-economic classes. In developing countries, except Chile and Guatemala, Pentecostals are fairly evenly spread across classes.

But even in Chile and Guatemala, there is not as significant an income difference and renewal congregations are more mainstream than in the global north. Their political clout is significant and growing (Pew Research Center 2006c). Within Africa, about 16% of the population, 147 million, belongs to one of the renewalist religions (Pew Research Center 2006b). They make up more than one fourth of Nigeria's population, more than one third of South Africa's, and 56% of Kenya's. In many countries, particularly in African nations, they are perceived as a threat to the state, experience oppression and violence, and are denied the right to practice.

Pentecostals have not had significant political impact in most of Asia, due to small numbers. Pentecostals are about 3.5% of the population in Asia. Japan has among the lowest percentages, where about one third of all Christians are Pentecostal or charismatic (Pew Research Center 2006c). South Korea has the largest percentage of Pentecostals in Asia—about 10% of the population. The relatively small percentage of adherents in South Korea in comparison to Latin America and Africa belies their influence. South Korea boasts the largest Pentecostal Church in the world, with 700,000 adherents. They are also among the most zealous missionaries, taking Pentecostalism into developing nations and facilitating Pentecostal growth in Africa and Latin America.

Pentecostalism influenced mainline religions as well. During the 1960s and 1970s, movements within Roman Catholicism, Episcopalians, Methodists, and Lutherans incorporated Pentecostal ideas. Although by no means widespread, speaking in tongues, miracles, prophecy, and other manifestations of the supernatural were used to restore meaning and personal spirituality to religions that some adherents found stale, cold, and ritualistic.

Case Study: Reviving an Ancient Tradition, Vodun in the 21st Century

How does a religion with roots that are potentially over 6,000 years old globalize? The revival in Benin of Vodun, a part of the Yoruba Orisa religion indigenous to Western Africa, demonstrates how adeptly even an ancient religion can accommodate modern life. Jung Ran Forte (2010) spent a year doing fieldwork in Benin and interviewed European *Vodunsi* (Vodun initiates) from France, Italy, Austria, and Germany to find out how they achieved this transformation.

From 1975 to the end of the 1980s, Benin was under communist rule. Vodun was outlawed by the government. Vodun's renaissance began in the 1990s when Benin became a democracy. The new government encouraged the revival of Vodun for political, cultural, and economic purposes. Because democracies depend on political participation and legitimacy, the religious chiefs were valuable politically as a conduit between the people and the state. Working with chiefs to revitalize the religious community helped the government secure legitimacy with civil society. The government viewed Vodun as a cultural asset as well: an important element in restoring national identity. Vodun was made an official religion equal to the foreign imports, Christianity and Islam. Economically, revitalizing traditional religion could help promote cultural heritage tourism in Benin and establish deeper transnational ties. For the religious factions within Vodun, modernization served their interests in attracting new adherents and sufficient income to allow it to flourish in the new millennium.

Through the combined interests of government and religious authorities, an international marketplace for religion grew in Benin. Vodun's prestige increased with its recognition as a significant dimension of Benin's historical heritage and folklore. With the help of the government, it developed a more sustainable set of religious practices and attracted new initiates. In 1991, the culture department of the government gathered approximately 200 religious delegates in a national symposium. The role of Vodun in Benin's development and accommodations that could be made to modernize Vodun dominated the discussions.

Three projects emerged from the symposium: a national festival, a national day of purification, and a commitment to preserve Benin's sacred places. Another step toward global legitimacy was taken later that year. A

(Continued)

(Continued)

national organization, the National Community of Beninese Vodun Cults (CNCVB), formed to present a unified modern face in the public sphere and ensure any transformations in Vodun maintained religious authenticity and legitimacy. The organization also served to take advantage of new cultural policies to secure government funding for local cults (religious groups associated with particular gods, totems, or other objects of devotion are called *cults*).

Although the CNCVB dissolved due to disputes among factions, it left a program of action through which individual cultic groups could secure benefits from the national interest in cultural heritage products. Benin built its tourist industry by promoting its cultural events throughout the country. Vodun groups secured governmental and international agency funds designated to support heritage sites and festivals. (For example, in addition to Vodun, Benin's participation in the UNESCO transnational Slave Route Project was a major cultural heritage feature.) The cultural festivities attract tourists from all over the world. Vodun leaders used this attention to attract new initiates and assure the continuation of the religion.

Although they acted autonomously, individual cults made similar accommodations to globalization. First, Vodun accepted universalism. Rather than restricting initiation to a racial or ethnic group, anyone "born" a Vodun could be a Vodunsi. As a religious leader proclaimed, "[I]f Vodun concerns the human condition, it works for everyone, no matter where people live, and the skin color does not make any difference either" (Forte 2010, 135). The feeling that one was called to Vodun was accepted as an indicator of being born to Vodun. The call could be experienced in many ways, such as an inner longing, a quest for renewal, or a search for solutions to problems. Thus, visible genetic heritage, as in race or ethnicity, was rejected as the determinant of Vodun: The inner reality, the inner genetic heritage so to speak, was accepted to make a person Vodun. Both universality and the importance of feeling or experiencing religion are themes of the global era. By preserving the idea of selection or being born to Vodun, the authenticity of the religion and religious belief were maintained, regardless of the path the initiate took to get there. The chance encounters with Vodun or other Vodunsi, unusual coincidences, past life events, and difficulties with other relationships are all interpreted as signs of destiny. "I bear the mark of Vodun within me since my birth," claimed an initiate from Europe (138).

Making Vodun life appealing to foreign visitors or those who meet Beninese Vodun in other countries and more accommodating to modern life in general was another hurdle. Vodun initiation typically requires six to nine months of reclusion in a convent to learn rituals and complete an apprenticeship. Traditionally, there are tests of physical and psychological endurance and requirements of submission and obedience to religious authorities. For the new initiates, this process was reduced to a week or, in the case of a stricter cult, one to three months, which could be broken into smaller segments. Rather than the intense discipline and tests, training concentrated on daily life practices that would be known to someone who had grown up in Vodun culture. Learning proper techniques of prayer, how to conduct incantations and offerings, and basic dance skills became the material of initiation. Secret knowledge is imparted, but only partially; the initiate learns more over time. Adapting initiation procedures is justified as legitimate because individual cultic practices have always varied somewhat and have taken the individual initiate and their specific incarnation into account as well. These accommodations were viewed as just another variation on authentic Vodun ways.

Regardless of its departure from the traditional rigor, the revised initiation does have the effect of transforming the lived experience of the initiate. By adopting the discipline of the daily routine, even though it may not be as complete as when living in Africa, initiates report that they transform themselves. They acquire a new identity, that of the specific cult into which they initiate. For example, Lakshmi (née Caroline) is a Mami Wata. Her lifestyle, worldview, habits, and social relationships are all transformed. Lakshmi, formerly an excellent swimmer who loves the water, is now forbidden to enter the sea. On Fridays, the devotional day and other specified days of prayer, sexual intercourse is forbidden. Certain foods are forbidden and others encouraged, such as salad, fruit, beans, rice, and meat from female animals. She wears white, pink, and pale blue; never red. Her long blond hair is braided; she wears jewelry and make-up, as do all Mami Wata, to please the goddess.

Ritual behavior links the initiate through their physical being to the god and the cosmological order—regardless of their physical location. "Through initiation, the body is re-signified in order to become representation and incarnation of a god. The godly essence that characterizes the individual in a distinctive and unique way is brought to the surface and turned into behaviors, looks, gestures, postures, dances, and words" (Forte 2010, 137). Caroline has become the "'re-incarnated fetish,' the princess Lakshmi" (135). As a Mami Wata, she has powers to help people with health, love, money, and social stability. She has powers to seduce men both older and younger. She brings luck to those who are close to her, which can be snatched away if they behave badly. Despite these and other powers, she is subject to bizarre behavior. Her sweet and kind disposition can give way to hasty mood shifts that the Mami Wata recognize as not coming from her, but the alien presence inside of her—the presence that must be appeased through the religious rituals and daily practices (136).

The adaptations made to survive in the 21st century—universalism, focus on experience and feeling, and streamlined procedures for initiation and practice—are all carefully crafted, as are all religious revitalizations, to retain their legitimacy as religiously authentic. Like other religious revival and reform, some practitioners have resisted change.

Vodun (Voudun) is estimated to have about 50 to 60 million adherents globally. The largest concentrations are in Benin and the Caribbean, particularly Haiti ("Vodoun" 2007). In the United States and other Western countries, people are probably more familiar with Voodoo, which is a derivative of Vodun, but should not be confused with the "real thing."

Cults and the New Religious Movements

Religious reform, revitalization, and new religious movements have been part of every period of intense globalization. The period of the 1960s differed dramatically from other periods of religious revitalization in the enormous volume of new religious movements. Counting the new religious organizations and resurgence of previously marginal religious organizations on all continents, thousands of new religious movements emerged. New religious movements seemed to erupt simultaneously in the early 1960s across the globe, and many—such as the renewal movements discussed above, Scientology, and the Unification Church—developed global appeal. Ironically, during the contemporary period of globalization, as tolerance, ecumenism, religious freedom, and individualism are being reinforced as important cultural values, some new religious movements have been vehemently demonized. The term

cult was applied pejoratively across the board to these movements.

Cult has a variety of popular meanings, none of which is very specific or useful analytically. In general, it refers to set of religious practices belonging to a smaller group that is part of a larger tradition, as in the case of the Vodun cults. A cult may be dedicated to a totem or particular god or goddess, such as "the cult of the jaguar" in Mayan religions or the "cult of Diana" in ancient Greece. Cult has also meant a religious group that rejects mainstream society, its values, and beliefs. In the 1960s, cult acquired a negative connotation in reference to new religious movements. New religious movements appeared so antithetical to mainstream beliefs and practices that people perceived them to be dangerous. Undoubtedly some groups calling themselves religious were guilty of fraud, and some were dangerous, horribly guilty of murder and neglect. Most, however, were just new religious movements, as unusual as they may have seemed.

BOX 11.6   A Closer Look: The Unification Church

The Unification Church, one of the most successful Korean new religious movements, has had considerable international success. Sun Myung Moon began preaching his brand of Christianity within the Protestant churches of Korea. Eventually, he founded "the Holy Spirit Association for the Unification of World Christianity" (aka, the

(Continued)

(Continued)

Unification Church) in South Korea in 1954. The Unification Church spread slowly through the activity of converts until its rapid expansion in the 1970s. The Unification Church attracted many youth throughout Western countries, who lived communally, made money selling flowers and candles, and were a regular sight at airports and along city streets. Reviled as the "Moonies," the Unification Church was one of the most feared new religions of the 1970s. In the early 1980s, hearings were held by the U.S. Congress to investigate the dangers of the Unification Church and other new religious movements. Moon was imprisoned on federal tax charges in 1982. Despite this, his virulent anti-communism won him power within the conservative political establishment in the United States.

One of the puzzles of the contemporary period of globalization has been why the new religious movements in general attracted so much hostility around the world given the relatively small size of their memberships and the paucity of knowledge about their actual beliefs and practices. Perhaps because most new religious movements were so different in belief and lifestyle from mainstream religions, people assumed that if someone joined a group, the person must have been taken forcibly or by brainwashing. Another factor is that the greatest achievement of the anti-cult movement was its success in changing public perception—for a time at least—of cult membership from a personal problem of families whose child may have left home to a public danger.

The dangers of cults were perceived similarly globally. Stories that circulated told of deviant sexual practices (from polygamy to pedophilia), exploitative labor of cult members for the economic benefit of their leaders, use of violence to control members, violations of human rights, physical and emotional abuse, tax and financial fraud, manipulating people by isolating them from friends and family, inciting to suicide, and even murder. All of the stories had some truth to them but were not true of all or even most religious movements. The tragic mass suicides (or suicide-murders) of People's Temple (1978), Order of the Solar Temple (multiple times and locations, 1994, 1995, 1997), Heaven's Gate (1997), and Movement for the Restoration of the Ten Commandments of God (2000) and the subway murders by Aum Shinrikyõ (1995) inspired real fear and panic globally.

The anti-cult movement was as quick to mobilize as the cults. By the end of the 1970s, a general structure and economy was in evidence. It consisted primarily of families of cult members, deprogrammers, and therapists. Pamphlets, books, courses, and workshops were offered globally to help people learn about and deal with cults. Parents hired people to kidnap their children from cults and deprogram them and restore them back to their pre-cultic selves. An industry developed around preventing children from joining cults, rescuing children who joined cults, and helping them recover, providing deprogramming or therapy after they had been rescued, escaped, or just plain returned home from cults—as most eventually did when and if they became disillusioned.

By the 1980s, the anti-cult movement had created a national organization in the United States, and there were a variety of groups throughout Europe. In the 1990s, an international anti-cult organization was formed. This industry became so extensive that the volume *Cults and New Religious Movements: A Report of the American Psychiatric Association* (Galanter 1989) was published to help psychiatrists deal with the complexity of issues from the angst of youth, search for meaning, family dynamics, individual characteristics, and characteristics of the times generally that are related to why youth might join cults. Although the report cautioned against deprogramming on both legal and ethical grounds, it acknowledged that some psychiatrists went beyond ethical boundaries by participating in involuntary interventions without evidence of psychiatric disorder or impaired judgment on the part of the cult member (9).

At a European Parliament committee meeting on cults, national representatives discussed the importance of respecting religious freedom while trying to protect citizens from predatory tactics and criminal activity of cults. Although countries declined to adopt an official definition of a cult or sect, they were believed to be increasing too rapidly for comfort in some parts of Europe. A representative from Austria claimed that in Austria, which has 12 officially recognized religions, there had been an explosion of new religious movements, and that 50,000 people were members and 200,000 others were involved with them in some way. The Italian representative noted that there were 400 new religious movements—Jehovah's Witness being the largest—in Italy, with 600,000 people involved, but Italy didn't perceive any problems with them. In Britain, immigration laws were used to restrict entry to people deemed dangerous to the public order. These had been applied at times to Reverend Moon and to members of the Church of Scientology. As with Italy, representatives from many countries, such as Spain, the Netherlands, and other Scandinavian countries, claimed that their countries had new religious movements, but they were not perceived to be problematic. A representative from France noted that he was active in a religious organization that was a cult that had succeeded—Christianity—and warned the others of undue oppression in some countries, such as denying jobs to people who were Christian Scientists. By the meeting's end, most representatives agreed on the need for countries to cooperate in sharing information and strategies for dealing with criminal activity of cults, to educate people about cults so that they make free and informed decisions, and to use existing laws against any criminal offenses that the movement or individual members may commit.

The problem of distinguishing legitimate from illegitimate religious organizations does not have an easy solution. There has not been one type of cult or cult member. Many involved group living and a substitution of cult for family, but many others did not. Similarly, some had authoritarian leaders, some not—although, to be successful, having a charismatic leader or leaders was necessary. While many people accused the cults of sexual promiscuity, many cults specifically rejected the sexual permissiveness that characterized the 1960s. New religious movements may be entirely new creations, syncretic movements that combine a variety of religious traditions, traditional religions moving into new cultures and gaining a wave of new adherents, or significant reforms of traditional religions. In each case, global movements are shaped by local circumstance or glocalized. This increases diversity exponentially, with more movements and variations on each of them.

Despite the comments of one French representative, France has been very active in official pursuit of anti-cult activities. France has refused to recognize Scientology as a religion. The Inter-Ministerial Mission for the Fight Against Sects (MILS) keeps a list of sects to watch, and Scientology is on it along with Jehovah's Witnesses, Hare Krishna, Unification Church, and Worldwide Church of God—all of which are accepted as religious organizations and have shed cult status in the United States and United Kingdom. In 2001, France passed an anti-cult law. It has tried Scientology twice under the law, in 2002 and 2009, claiming that it is a financial enterprise that keeps individuals subject through mental manipulation (Crumley 2009). The defendants were found guilty of fraud and fined, but the Church of Scientology was not banned from France.

This can be interpreted as part and parcel of the French particularization of rationality and secular thought. While the insistence on a secular state is a near global phenomenon—aside from political Islam and religious Zionists—in France, sentiment against clerical authority goes a step further and in many ways is anti-religious. In France, religion is often seen as superstitious and anti-rational, not just a-rational. Thus, religious belief is often viewed as verging on a type of brainwashing—mental manipulation. In the take-off period of globalization, France applied this same logic to some Roman Catholic priests and nuns. Their religious orders were dissolved, and they were told to go back to their families or leave France, for their own protection (Introvigne 2008, 211–212). Students were banned from wearing religious symbols in French public schools in 2004. The particular court case concerned Muslim students wearing headscarves but applies to any conspicuous religious items. This is a variation on or glocalization of global norms. Germany has also restricted headscarves. China and Russia have both cited the French example in justifying their own restrictions on religion. Cultural protectionism and secularism combine in these instances in ways that are unlikely to be justifiable in the United States.

All countries regulate religion to some extent. Associations that are recognized as religious have special privileges in most countries. They may receive tax benefits or tax exempt status. Their ceremonies, such as marriages, are usually accepted in lieu of governmental ones. Clergy have special status in law related to the confidentiality of the confessional. Sensitivity to new religious movements that may pose threats to the political order has always been a concern of states. State regulation of religion has become normatively less acceptable, although it continues. In many countries, religions have been banned, controlled, or harassed by officials or the public. The saga of new religious movements highlights the fragile balance between freedom and public order and safety. When times are relatively normal, the relationship is not problematic in a free society. However, when times are troubled and people are afraid, the relationship can become problematic very quickly and easily.

New Religious Movements in Japan: Selective Religious Amalgamation

Japanese religion reflects the same capacity to absorb foreign influence as its economy does. It has always been syncretic. What makes it uniquely Japanese is the idea that religion, indeed culture generally, should be a functional set of mix-and-match components. For most of their history, Shinto and Buddhism have been intertwined. Observing one religion is not an obstacle to observing others. This applies to the new religions as well. Many Japanese incorporate practices from several religious traditions. Practice is more important than belief, and neither Shinto nor Buddhism claims exclusivity, so adherents can incorporate other religious traditions freely. Religion, like other aspects of culture, meets a variety of functional needs; thus, different ones may be more or less appropriate for specific purposes. People generally claim to be secular, but turn to religion for life events and different religions for different events. People may turn to Shinto for weddings and births (more happy and joyous) and Buddhist ceremonies for funerals (more somber). Lately, Christian weddings have become fashionable. Many Japanese find Western ideas of religion confining (Crane 2012). Despite Japan incorporating an amalgam of religious and cultural ideas, Japanese religion incorporated very little Western religion.

Two methods of protection help retain distinction amid hybridization. Japanese use purification rituals ceremonially and in everyday practice to prevent contamination, including from ideas. Historically, the Japanese have judiciously tried to restrict the number of ideas imported, limiting their impact. Japan has carefully calibrated its periods of engagement with the world and periods, some hundreds of years long, during which it has stepped back and learned from others before it moved to adjust, change, or reform (Robertson 1992, 94–96). As with other cultures, even though it shares many cultural beliefs and practices with others, Japanese culture is constellation of elements within a framework or worldview that provides a unique context of meaning.

Japan globalized quickly following WWII, adopting a number of Western ideas. The Allies forced them to write religious freedom into their constitution and sever the ties between Shinto and the state. Given this combination of factors, it is not surprising that new religious movements emerged that were influenced by global culture, specifically rationality and ideals of freedom and individualism. The largest religious movement to emerge from this period is Risshō Kōseikai. This and two other closely related Lotus movements (Sōka Gakkai, after WWII, and Reiyūkai, the oldest) combine rational principles and religious ideas. A practice of Risshō Kōseikai, called hōza (dharma session—note the Indian influence), is akin to a group therapy or self-help session. Hōza groups apply rational understanding of Buddhist principles to understanding the life problems they discuss. Discussion of personal problems such as why a husband is drinking or why children are not doing well in school helps participants identify the cause of such behaviors (Pye 2010, 505). The Tenrikyō, the "Teaching of Divine Reason," is a principle tenet of Sōka Gakkai. Each of the religions is a lay movement which reinforces modern ideas of individualism and egalitarianism. Sōka Gakkai International was established in 1975 and has adherents in over 100 countries. Reiyūkai has adherents in the United States, Latin America, and Asia (Inoue 2007, 461).

After the terroristic subway bombings in 1995, the group responsible, Aum, was quickly labeled a cult, and the anti-cultic movement gained momentum in Japan. These were supported by a fearful majority of the Japanese, as they were in the United States and Europe. Actions against new religious movements intensified. Japan became part of the lecture circuit of touring Western anti-cultists. Although Sōka Gakkai also became feared as a cult, most groups labeled cultic were imports. Japan began labeling any religious organization that violated traditional family values by requiring the believers to live apart from their families a cult (Reader 2004, 196–197).

Despite some religious fervor following the war, Japan remains ambivalent toward religion and religious freedom (Sumimoto 2000). Only about 10% of Japanese are members of new religious movements. Christianity has not attracted many adherents in Japan or China, despite its long history there. Membership is under 1% of the Japanese, with 20% of the 1% being Jehovah's Witnesses (Inoue 2007, 455). About 5% of Chinese are Christian (Pew Research Center 2011a).

Diffusion of Buddhism to the West

Whereas Western religions have had relatively little influence in the East, Eastern religions have had impact in the West. Europeans visiting Asia during the take-off phase of globalization brought Buddhism home with them. It remained an esoteric practice and interest until the contemporary period. During the 1960s, along with other Eastern religions, Buddhism enjoyed success as a religious practice, a spiritual practice, and a healthful practice. The quest for a meaningful spirituality, increasing ease of travel and communications, and the emergence of lifestyles devoted to health and fitness prompted people in Western nations to seek out experiences with Asian religions.

Buddhism has a significant presence in Western nations. In 2007, about 0.7% of the United States was Buddhist, about 0.6% Muslim, and about 0.4% Hindu. While the majority of Hindus (80%) and Muslims (66%) are immigrants, most of the Buddhists (75%) are converts (Pew Research Center 2007, 8). In the United States, the number of Thai Buddhist Temples increased from fewer than five in 1975 to more than 80 in 2000. Teaching and meditation

centers doubled just from 1987 to 1997. Many Buddhist temples and teaching centers have two sets of services on Sundays in the language of its Asian congregation and one on Saturdays for English speakers. Called "parallel congregations," services are led by the same monks. In some centers, there is more mixing of the congregations, and the teachings are delivered in English and the congregation's Asian language at the same time (Cadge and Bender 2004, 47-48).

The impact of Buddhism in Western societies goes beyond converts. The most significant impact is on people who have been influenced by Buddhism, even though they are not religious adherents. A 2003 national study in the United States found that a significant number of people claim to have been influenced by Buddhist teachings or practices. Those who are younger, majored in the Humanities or Social Sciences in college, had contact with converts to Buddhism, were influenced by New Age movements or alternative medicine and holistic health practices, and have taken interreligious classes are more likely to have been influenced by Buddhism than others.

These influences are possible because of the opportunity to develop cultural capital and move in diverse circles (Wuthnow and Cadge 2004, 375). Being more "available" religiously and not participating regularly in any religious tradition also make people more likely to be influenced by Buddhism (177). The Pew Forum on Religion and Public Life reports that about 39% of the population in the United States meditates, which could also be Hindi, at least weekly. Since Buddhists account for less than 1% of the population, this is a significant integration into the mainstream. While this is less than the number who prays at least once a week (75%), it shows a significant impact of Asian religions, even though meditation is used more for health and relaxation than religion (Pew Research Center 2007, 13).

BOX 11.7   A Closer Look: Buddhist Tourism

A Buddhist tourism website provides links to Buddhist tourism sites in 19 Asian countries, along with European, North and South American, and African locales. Vipassana meditation, an ancient Indian technique, rediscovered by Gotma Buddha over 2,000 years ago, is offered at centers in dozens of countries, 15 U.S. states, and 6 Canadian provinces. It is promoted as non-sectarian and handed down by an unbroken chain of teachers.

One such Buddhist Tourism site is located at this URL:
http://www.buddhist-tourism.com

People generally have a positive view of Buddhism, whether or not they have been influenced by it. People associate Buddhism with words like *tolerant* and *peace loving* and would welcome a stronger Buddhist presence in the United States (Wuthnow and Cadge 2004, 365). Buddhism is compatible with other religious beliefs, which is another factor in its appeal. At the Millennium World Peace Summit in 2000, S. N. Goenka, the leader of Vipassana meditation, offered classic Buddhist ecumenical perspective: "'Rather than converting people from one organized religion to another organized religion,' said Mr. Goenka, 'we should try to convert people from misery to happiness, from bondage to liberation and from cruelty to compassion'" (Higgins 2000).

Whether Buddhism, Confucianism, Shinto, and some other Eastern religions are better categorized as philosophies or religions is often discussed. They do not conform to most Western ideas of religion as they do not have gods and do not worship a superior being. They do offer a program of teachings and practices to help guide and manage daily life. They do not claim exclusivity but open their ideas to those of other religions. This has facilitated their incorporation into the worldviews and practice of adherents of other religions as well as those who consider themselves atheists. In the modern period, the influence of Asian religions on Western thought is evident in the transcendentalist and New Age movements.

Hinduism has also been influential. Mahesh Prasad Varma (Maharishi Mahesh Yogi), a leader in the Transcendentalist meditation movement, and the International Society for Krishna Consciousness (Hare Krishna) were both influential in the West—helped along with their association with the Beatles. They helped popularize meditation, burning incense, yoga, and related spiritual experiences, as well as the rhetoric of the peace and justice movements. Those born since the 1970s may not recognize the Eastern influences on the Western world. Incense burning, mediation, and yoga are so common that they may seem Western in origin.

Religion and Freedom: The Right to Religion

Many new religious movements are global. The Unification Church, the Prosperity Gospel, and Scientology, while relatively small, have near-global reach. Even fundamentalisms, which are by definition particularistic, have gone global. There has probably never been as large a marketplace for religious and quasi-religious ideas at any other time in world history. China's huge population and recently liberalized attitude toward religion forms a market of approximately 1.3 billion people. The Eastern European and former Soviet Union nations released from communist prohibition of religion are another large market, although they have stronger religious traditions. The United States, with a large population that views itself as religious and undergoing reorganization related to globalization, is also a ripe market, as are Latin America and Africa for much the same reason. Immigrants are bringing religion to Western and Northern Europe, the least religious of the globe's regions. As discussed above, societies have found a number of subtle ways to address new religions. The fright that some new religions or religions new to a society inspire is a powerful motivator for people to accept restrictions on their freedoms and the freedom of others.

Article 18 of the Universal Declaration of Human Rights states,

> Everyone has the right to freedom of thought, conscience and religion; this right includes freedom to change his [sic] religion or belief, and freedom, either alone or in community with others and in public or private, to manifest his [sic] religion or belief in teaching, practice, worship and observance.

At the World Conference in Vienna in 1993, over 150 countries reaffirmed their commitment to human rights. Establishing these rights has been a major triumph of cultural and political globalization. Enforcing them and having countries respect them, however, is not as far advanced.

A Pew Research Center (2009) study of 198 countries covering 99% of the global population found that 70% of humanity is denied the right to religious practice even though all but 4% of the Constitutions of the 198 countries provide for religious freedom. Seventy-four percent of countries have some restriction on or qualification of that freedom. Some countries have vague restrictions that could be enforced against any religious group the state finds offensive or threatening. The qualifier that religious freedom extends only to the point where public morality is not offended is one such restriction. In other countries, the exercise of religious freedom may not contradict a secular law. The study is not clear how a country such as the United States would rate, where a number of religious practices, such as polygamy of the Mormons, Jehovah's Witness parents refusing a blood transfusion for their child, and use of drugs in some Native Americans rituals are unlawful. How and when a country chooses to invoke these rules will vary by how the religion is viewed at any point in time rather than by an objective criterion.

The Pew study also found that in many societies religious groups suffer from intimidation or harassment by various layers of government, such as the local police or school officials. Only one third of the countries had no harassment documented. Similarly, in other measures, such as favoritism in funding, banning of certain religions, and allowing in foreign missionaries, about 60% of countries had low restrictions; 20% percent were rated high, and 20% moderate. When adjusted for proportion of people living under such conditions—which is not as much of a measure of globalization as of the quality of life of humanity—57% of people live in highly restrictive countries. Although there is not universal respect for religious freedom, the normative forces of globalization have been at least moderately effective.

New religious movements may pose challenges to both the state and personal identity. Russia and France view many new religious movements as American imperialism, and thus the movements become the incidental victims of political power struggles. Profoundly secular states such as France react with hostility to new religious movements that they see as "abusing their sacred doctrines of rationality and rights" (Beckford 2004, 256). From the persecution of Falun Gong in China to the much publicized threat of Qur'an burning in Gainesville, Florida, in 2010, religious revival and reform seem to generate controversy and tension, whether deliberately or accidently, when confronting both official and personal worldviews and power structures.

Freedom of Religion in China

Religious organizations do not automatically acquire recognition as a religion in any country. Scientology, for example, is a recognized religion in some countries, such as the United States, but not in others, such as Germany. China and many formerly communist societies tend to be particularly restrictive. There are only five approved religions in China: Buddhism, Daoism, Catholicism, Christianity, and Islam. Groups within these religions must register with the state and operate within state guidelines. Among those guidelines is the requirement to associate with and support a patriotic organization. Not all groups register. Leaders of unregistered groups are routinely arrested and their meetings shut down (Lowe 2004, 186). They are not permitted to travel abroad for training or anything else. Despite these restrictions, jailing, and harassment, they continue to meet and practice. Not all adherents join the state-sponsored religious organizations. This makes membership statistics difficult to interpret. A 2010 U.S. State Department report on religious freedom in China estimated that in 2007, about 31.4% of Chinese citizens over 16 were religious believers.

Religious groups viewed as threatening to the state, because of hierarchical structures or lifestyles thought not compatible with good Chinese citizenship, are banned or have strained relationships with the state. China's relationship with Catholicism, for example, is strained. China wants to appoint bishops and mistrusts the rigid hierarchy of Rome. Some religious groups, such as those in the Qi Gong movement (the broad group of mind and body meditative practices) as well as many Protestant organizations, are also frowned upon. As happened in Europe, the Americas, and other Asian societies in the 1970s and 1980s, as counter-cultural religious movements arose, groups deemed dangerous were labeled cults and accused of brainwashing, among other evils. Although Tibet is a deeply religious Buddhist nation, Chinese oppression in Tibet is high, particularly repression of religion. Tibetan monks are not trusted. The Dalai Lama, the highest of monks and the religious leader, traditionally ruled Tibet. The current Dalai Lama was forced into exile in 1959. Despite assurances from the Dalai Lama that he advocates only more autonomy for Tibet, the Chinese government fears his power to provoke independence movements. The crackdown on Tibetan protestors leading up to the 2008 Beijing Olympics led to major protest demonstrations globally. Buddhist monks, who originated self-immolation as protest during the Vietnam War, reactivated this form of protest against the oppression by China in 2011.

The Case of Falun Gong (Falun Dafa)

Politics and religion often clash, sometimes in highly volatile ways. In July 1999, Amy Lee was arrested as part of a crackdown on Falun Gong. Practicing in the park, she complained to the arresting police officer,

> "There are other people in the park doing Tai Chi exercises, why don't you arrest them? With Falun Gong, you move your hands up and down. With Tai Chi you move your hands side to side. Is side to side legitimate and up and down against the law?" (quoted in Lehrer and Sloan 2003, 46)

Ms. Lee reported that 3,000 people were arrested within three days. She was beaten, tortured for 11 days, sent to a detention facility, and then sent to a facility to be "brainwashed." When finally released on bond, she escaped surveillance and fled, eventually to settle in Queens, New York. Human rights groups have documented many similar stories. Tens of thousands of religious devotees have been killed or imprisoned.

Falun Gong was founded in 1992 when the Chinese government encouraged a return to all things Chinese and a rejection of foreign influences (such as democracy). Falun Gong is syncretic, combining Buddhism, Taoism, Qi Gong, Chinese medicine and exercise, and other traditional beliefs and practices. Li Hongzhi was praised by the Chinese government and recognized with the Award for Achievement in the Science of the Mind and Metaphysics when he founded Falun Gong. He registered with the Chinese government, as required, and had a loosely organized hierarchical structure mirroring the Chinese Communist party structure.

Falun Gong shares the characteristics of the new religious movements. Its focus is spirituality rather than theology. Falun Gong does not claim exclusivity. Adherents may practice any religion along with Falun Gong. Rather than constituting a well-defined organization of local groups, as most traditional religious organizations, Falun Gong is a loosely organized network. Its objective is to heal the mind–body connection (Lum 2006, 2–3). In these respects, Falun Gong satisfies the modern desire to escape hyper-rationality and connect to spirituality and deeper meaning. It offers a foundation for ethics and morality without a rigid set of beliefs, a conception of God as a person, or a theocentric worldview. It does not reject rationality. Its practices are not scientifically derived but claim to be a window "beyond science."

Falun Gong is also characteristic of the globalized reaction to the impersonality of rationalized medical care. The modern or Western model treats patients as cases and relies on the doctor as the dispenser and dictator of care. Falun Gong, like other alternative therapies (some new, some derived from Chinese and other traditional cultures), is personalized. It makes the individual responsible for their own care, connects the person with collective forces and flows of life, and removes many of the strictures of hyper-rational priorities on efficiency.

Falun Gong went from being praised in the early 1990s to being looked on with suspicion in the mid-1990s to being condemned in the late 1990s. It became the victim of its success. Qi Gong religions, of which Falun Gong is one, grew very quickly into a mass movement of local associations and organizations, possibly the largest in Chinese history. Although registered with the state, it is not controlled by the state (McDonald 2006, 152–153). The number of adherents, as with many religions is difficult to determine. One resource ("Falun Gong" 2007) cites several reports placing it at about 70 million adherents in the 1990s. It rivals and, according to some counts, surpasses the Chinese Communist party in membership. (Falun Gong has several thousand members in the United States as well as other countries with large ethnic Chinese populations.)

The Chinese government began to view the philosophy of Falun Gong and the Qi Gong religions as dangerous. By imagining illness as a reflection of social problems, their teaching could be interpreted as a diagnosis against the Chinese state for causing the individual ailments of the practitioners. There were no direct indictments or attacks against the government, but the teachings and lectures of Li Hongzhi became increasingly explicit. Depression, fatigue, and dizziness were all caused by the conditions of the world. Following the "characteristics of the universe," truth, kindness, and forbearance, rather than of ordinary people, was necessary to restore health. These teachings reflected a world out of balance, a world that—like Chinese society—was increasingly unequal (McDonald 2006, 154–155).

The government cracked down on practitioners of these new movements. In April 1999, 10,000 people participated in a silent protest directed against the official newspapers for their remarks disparaging Falun Gong. Because the government did not know of the protest in advance, they called it a threat to national security (Jacobs 2009). The official crackdown began in July 1999. Amnesty International (2000) reported that within one year, there were over 20,000 arrests of Falun Gong and Qi Gong practitioners, along with those of other religions such as Lingling Jiao, Mentu Hui, Chongsheng Pai, Donfang Shandian, and Yilya Jiao. The Congressional Executive Commission on China's (2012) report counted over 3,500 deaths since the persecution began in 1999.

Falun Gong practitioners around the world are extremely active lobbying for and trying to gain freedom of information for adherents in China. U.S. Congressional representatives have made public statements on behalf of Falun Gong. The U.S. Congress has passed resolutions, including a 2006 resolution that condemned the brutality and escalating persecution of Falun Gong. The U.S. Department of State repeatedly labels China "a country of particular concern" for human rights violations, specifying the persecution of Falun Gong, among others. The U.S. government has supported Internet companies started by Falun Gong to give Chinese citizens free access to websites, including Voice of America and Radio Free Asia. At least one federal court (in San Francisco) upheld a lawsuit against Chinese government officials (the mayor and Communist party secretary in Beijing) for violating human rights and Chinese law (Lum 2006, 8).

Summary

The take-off period of globalization confronted religion with three primary dilemmas: the role of science as a source of knowledge when it contradicted religious teachings, secularization and the differentiation of institutions from religious world views, and the social problems confronting a rapidly industrializing world. Religions responded in similar fashion, each one being riddled with internal dissent. Some factions accommodated science and modernization, while others rejected science and remained focused on literal translations of religious truth and traditional values and norms. Some factions emphasized the individual's responsibility for his or her experience of social problems, while others located the source of the problems in the social structure and saw individuals as victims. All religions struggled to make themselves relevant to the laity.

The contemporary period confronts religion with dissatisfaction with over rationalized institutions, increasing inequalities, and anomie related to the meaning of life, and how to live the good life. One response has been diminishing memberships in the developed world and renewed religious fervor in the developing world. Mainstream denominations lost much of their appeal as people search for more meaningful, more personalized, and less ritualistic ways to experience the supernatural. Many people turned to fundamentalist, evangelical, and new religious movements. Tolerance for diverse beliefs and acceptance that there may be many paths to spirituality prompted ecumenical movements and inter-faith dialogs at the same time that dissent over issues such as abortion and women or homosexual clergy have resulted in splintering within religious groups. "Spiritual but not religious" has become a common sentiment as people reject formal religious organizations and seek individualistic, less authoritative, and less theocentric worldviews.

Religion is increasingly recognized as a right. All nations officially grant religious freedom, although approved or official religions are tightly regulated in several countries and religions deemed dangerous to the state are persecuted. Religion remains a dynamic force in individuals' personal lives, the political life of nations, and global geo-politics. The consequences if religion continues to evolve in two opposing directions—the intense belief structures of fundamentalism and evangelicalism, on the one hand, and the much looser "spiritual but not religious," on the other—are potentially devastating if the current global tensions across civilizational and economic divides persist.

Questions, Investigations, and Resources

Questions

1. Debate: What is the future of religion and religiosity? Will the developing nations in Latin America and Africa follow in the more secular pathways of wealthier societies such as Europe and Japan and lose adherents to religious organization, or continue to be highly religious societies?

2. What do the new religious movements and alternative and less organized forms of spirituality offer to people that makes them attractive?

3. The intersection of religion and politics as institutions is problematic. Choose a country with a secular government and strong religiosity (such as the United States or Egypt) or low religiosity with religious minority groups (such as France or Scandinavian countries).

    a. What tensions have arisen between religion and state?

    b. How do they get resolved?

    c. What have been some of the resolutions achieved?

    d. Are people happy with the resolutions, or do they remain contentious?

4. Explain how different religions have accommodated or resisted reason and science with faith.

Investigations

1. Using the World Values Survey, investigate religion in Asian countries. Find data for the following questions:

    - Is religion important in your life?
    - Do you consider yourself a religious person?
    - Are you a member of a religious organization?

    How do you explain the discrepancy between the answers to the first two questions and the third?

2. Human Rights Watch reports persecution all over the world. What do recent publications report for religious persecution? You can search for religious freedom and religious persecution.

3. The U.S. Department of State publishes the *Report on International Religious Freedom* each year. In 2011, the State Department specified Burma, China, Eritrea, Iran, North Korea, Saudi Arabia, Sudan, and Uzbekistan as countries of particular interest. Choose one of these countries and investigate its actions and policies pertaining to religion.

4. Update your knowledge of religion in Islamic societies, particularly those affected by the Arab Spring. How many majority-Muslim societies are now democratic? What role do Islam and Islamic political parties play in these societies?

Resources

Amnesty International http://www.amnestyusa.org

Pew Forum on Religion and Public Life http://religions.pewforum.org

Pew Global Attitudes Project: Importance of Religion http://www.pewglobal.org/subjects/importance-of-religion

Pew Forum on Religion and Public Life, World Religion Interactive Database http://features.pewforum.org/africa/question.php?q=1&r=Not+too+%2F+not+at+all+imp

U.S. Department of State: *2010 Report International Religious Freedom* http://www.state.gov/j/drl/rls/irf/2010/index.htmhttp://www.state.gov/j/drl/rls/irf/2010/index.htm

World Values Survey http:www.worldvaluessurvey.org

Pew Forum on Religion and Public Life, *Religion and the Millennials* *http://www.pewforum.org/Age/Religion-Among-the-Millennials.aspx*

Transborder Threats to Human Well-Being: Inequality and Migration

Objectives

While many global forces are promising, such as continuing waves of democracy and concern for human rights, globalization is also fraught with problems that transcend borders. This chapter examines the risks and problems of inequality related problems of migration. After reading it, you should be able to

- explain the risks associated with inequality in the contemporary world;
- summarize how economic and political factors influence inequality among and within nations;
- explain the effects of poverty in people's lives, particularly for children;

- evaluate programs and policies designed to alleviate poverty and inequality;
- compare and contrast the costs of different types of migration to host and home countries;
- evaluate the brain drain on developing countries; and
- assess countries' responsibilities to migrants and refugees.

"What the whole world wants is a good job. That is the single biggest discovery that Gallup has ever made (Clifton 2007, 3).

Risk and Uncertainty

The risks that humans suffer today are largely of human creation. Famines are due to depleted soil and the inability to distribute surplus. People do not die of hunger because there is no food; they die because they have no money to buy food (Khondker 2010, 234). Poisons seep into water supplies from chemicals used in agriculture. Smog produced by our fossil fuel addiction subjects us to aggravated asthma and bronchitis, killing tens of thousands of people prematurely

each year. Humans create the conditions of their own insecurity.

Social location is an important factor determining security. Where people live has a lot to do with how secure they feel and how secure they are. There are bad neighborhoods within cities, within countries, and within the world. Bad neighborhoods are characterized by poverty, violence, crime, poor health, and chronic stress from exposure to constant insecurity. Social location means more than just geographic location. Social location may be income level, gender, race, or ethnicity—any characteristic that has the power to constrain or enhance a person's opportunities for a life of quality.

Problems of human insecurity are aggravated by globalization. The connectedness of the globe means that the dynamics within one country impact others. Environmental pollution and epidemics do not respond to guards at borders, and political boundaries do not mean anything to them. Criminals and terrorists are anti-social. They operate in spite of and in defiance of states. They do not stop at borders either. Advanced technologies of travel and communication and networks of business and finance make it easier for any of these forces to travel the globe. Everyone is vulnerable to the threats to human security. Social location simply makes some people more vulnerable than others. Threats cross the boundaries of both class and countries. They are transborder problems.

In 1997, George Tenet, then acting Director of the U.S. Central Intelligence Agency (CIA), warned of five serious threats global security. The threats that he listed continue to destabilize the world.

- The continuing transformation of Russia and China
- States whose policies can undermine regional security, such as Iraq, Iran, and North Korea
- Transnational issues that cut across nations and regions, such as terrorism
- Proliferation of weapons of mass destruction, international drug trafficking, international organized crime, and threats to information systems
- Regional hot spots in the Middle East and South Asia
- States and regions buffeted by human misery and suffering on a large scale; states involved in or unable to cope with ethnic or civil conflict, forced migration, refugee flows, resulting in the potential for disease and destruction (Tenet 1997, 1)

BOX 12.1   Check It Out Yourself: Global Indicators

The UC Atlas of Global Inequality is an interactive website that allows you to investigate the risks and uncertainties—the transborder problems that confront the globe.

You can search by country or geographic region for data on income, education, health, gender, environment, population, technology, and other issues. You can also search for data back to 1960, the beginning of the contemporary period of globalization. The program creates maps, charts, and graphs illustrating these relationships.

What questions do you have about the risks faced in different parts of the world? Make good use of this site to get a closer look at the threats to human security as you progress through Chapters Twelve, Thirteen, and Fourteen.

http://atlas-dev.ucsc.edu/howto.html

The 2010 threat assessment to the U.S. Congress by Dennis Blair, then Director of National Intelligence, added the financial crisis and global financial contagion, energy security, strategic health challenges, nuclear proliferation, cyber crime, and other threats to cyber infrastructure (Blair 2010).

While this is a diverse list, the issues are related. Economic globalization has made people vulnerable to financial insecurity, with which this chapter opens. Poverty makes people more vulnerable to health crises, international crime, and civil conflict. Conflict creates a lawless environment and haven for terrorism. Weak or failed governments allow environmental destruction and corrupt business and political processes. All of these lead to failing states. Failing states make for bad neighborhoods. Shared risks to human well-being require collective or at least collaborative problem solving. However, national and international constraints impede developing global policies. This chapter and the next two discuss six interrelated threats to human security: inequality, migration, food, the environment, violent conflict, and crime. As you read about these problems, recall the theories that help illuminate the sources of the problems

- How have historical forces of colonialism and the Cold War made some societies more vulnerable to risk than others?
- How do economic policies exacerbate poverty?
- In what ways can better global governance alleviate risks?
- What are our shared responsibilities, as members of wealthy societies and of humanity, to solve problems of risk to the most vulnerable and humankind generally?

Inequality: The Global Pyramid

The function of an economy is to produce and distribute necessities of survival. How successful is the global economy?

Here are some clues. About 25,000 people die of hunger every day. About 29,000 children under five years old die daily, mostly due to preventable causes; about 5,000 die from lack of clean water alone. Children die from respiratory infections, diarrhea, malaria, measles, tetanus, whooping cough, and myriad illnesses that were conquered generations ago. More than half of these children could be saved by very inexpensive, low-tech treatments (UNICEF 2006b).

We tend to think of these problems as health issues. We send mosquito nets, antibiotics, and nutritional supplements. Undoubtedly, this has saved hundreds of thousands, if not millions, of lives. Yet treating these problems only as health issues will never solve them.

These problems are issues of sewage, sanitation, agriculture, and food—issues that are fundamentally systemic and economic. Until there is significant systemic change, all the mosquito nets in the world will not make the problems disappear. Whether or not the change will come through the global economic system as it is structured or through some alternative is one of the most critical issues facing humankind. Our survival is at stake.

BOX 12.2   Global Distribution of Income

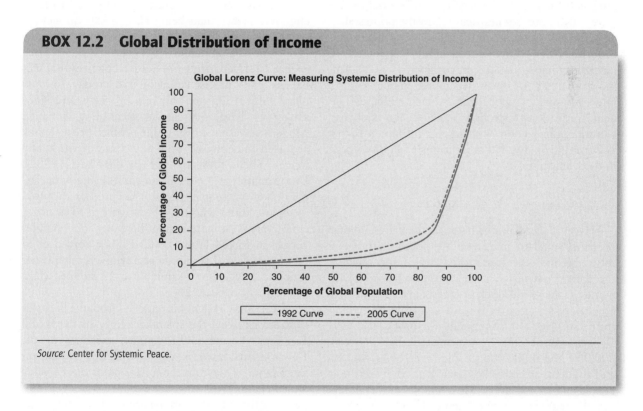

Source: Center for Systemic Peace.

Global Inequality: Income and Wealth

The resources in the world are plentiful enough to satisfy people's material needs. The problem is allocating resources. One measure of inequality is the Gini coefficient, or Gini ratio. A Gini coefficient is a number from zero to one. Zero would be absolute equality. Every 1% of people in a population would have 1% of the money. One is absolute inequality.

One person would have all the money. Global inequality stands at about .65 (A). This is greater than inequality within most societies, including those most unequal, South Africa and Brazil. To understand what this means, imagine all of global income as $1.00. The richest 5% of the society receives about $0.33. The top 10% gets $0.50. The bottom 5% gets only 0.2 of one penny, and the bottom 10% only 0.7 of one penny of the world's income. It takes a year for the poorest to earn what the richest earn in two days (Milanovic 2006, 9).

Global inequality of wealth is even more skewed than income. The most thorough study of global wealth to date found that in 2000, the richest 10% of people possessed 85% of all of the wealth in the world. In a population of 100, if one person possesses $900 and the remaining 99 people each have about $1, the distribution would have a Gini coefficient of about 0.892, the approximate measure of global inequality of wealth in 2000 (Davies et al. 2008, 7).

The global expansion of capitalism changed the relationships among societies. As the Industrial Revolution began in the mid-19th century, there was much less inequality across countries. The richest 10 were only about 6 times richer than the poorest 10; now, they are about 42 times richer. From this broad historical perspective, globalization has increased inequality among nations. In considering inequality, most analyses focus on economic globalization. However, political globalization, such as increasing democratization or stronger social welfare systems; cultural globalization, with respect of human rights and the rule of law; and other forms of globalization impact inequality.

The Most Indigent Group: Slaves

Slavery is illegal everywhere. Yet there are millions of slaves. Some toil in many of the poorest nations of the globe, and others are tucked away, imprisoned in the damp basements of the most exclusive town-homes in the world's richest cities. Slaves are of two types. One set of slaves is trafficked from one country to another, as a commodity for profit. The U.S. Department of State has estimated that between 700,000 and 4,000,000 people (over 80% women and children) are trafficked each year. Many of these people end up in slavery. Most females and children become sex workers or domestic slaves, or work in sweatshops. Males tend to be used in agricultural and other labor contexts (2008, 7). Thousands of these slaves are in the United States.

Many people are enslaved in their homeland. Employment in many societies is scarce, particularly in rural areas. Forced migration, due to economic hardship, leaves people vulnerable to enslavement. Debt bondage is a centuries-old practice. While not all debt bondage results in slavery, much does. People desperate for work fall victim to schemes where they work in agricultural or extremely low-level and dangerous manufacturing enterprises. Often, the jobs are located in desolate places that are well guarded. Once there, they may be paid less than they are charged for their very meager shelter and daily rations. They become increasingly indebted to their employer rather than being able to save money or send any home. Escape is difficult and often deadly. People may be hunted down if they manage to flee.

The U.S. Department of State recognizes that it is hard to get a precise count of slaves today. In most places, slaves are not valuable property, and since slavery is illegal, no careful accounting is made. Modern slaves are "disposable people" because they are used and abused until they cannot work any longer. Then, they are left to die (Bales 2002). Unfortunately, there seems an endless supply of desperately poor people who can be lured or captured to replace those who have been worked to death. A conservative estimate is that there are "12.3 million people in forced labor, bonded labor, forced child labor, and sexual servitude at any given time; other estimates range from 4 million to 27 million" (U.S. Department of State 2008, 7).

Slavery may appear far removed from the lifestyles of those enjoying the splendid luxury of the World Economic Forum (WEF) annual meetings at the Davos resorts; however, the suffering and uncompensated labor of slaves is the lowest point on the value added chain. Their servitude accounts for significant profit of those further up the economic pyramid.

BOX 12.3   A Closer Look: Anna's Story

Anna is young woman living in a shelter. She is only 15 years old, with a tattoo of a butterfly on her back and an innocent smile. In her room at the shelter, there are toys, stuffed animals, dolls, fairy-tale books—all the objects of a lost childhood. Anna left home at age 12 and slept on the stairs of an apartment building. Looking for a job, she stumbled upon a woman who promised her a brighter future. In reality, the woman was part of a trafficking network, and Anna was soon forced to become a prostitute.

At age 14, Anna was given a passport and sent to Turkey, where she was caught by the police and sent back home. But back in Romania, the same woman was waiting for her and sent her to Spain. There, she was locked up in a house during the day and forced to go out with clients at night. Finally, she found help and was able to escape home to Romania (UNICEF 2004).

Anna was saved. Most are not. With the collapse of the Eastern European economy in the 1990s, sex trafficking became a lucrative business for global organized crime syndicates. Thousands of girls and young women are lured by the promise of domestic service or nanny jobs in the developed world.

"Bottom of the Pyramid"

There are people in the bottom, middle, and top of the pyramid in every region of the world.

Seventy percent of the global poor live in "middle income" countries. Many of the middle class in the United States and other rich nations are quite well-to-do by global standards: "[T]he poorest 5% of Frenchmen have a mean income which places them in the 72nd percentile of the world income distribution; the richest 5 per cent have incomes which place them in the top percentile of the world" (Milanovic 2006, 10).

BOX 12.4   A Closer Look: Global Pyramid of Wealth and Income

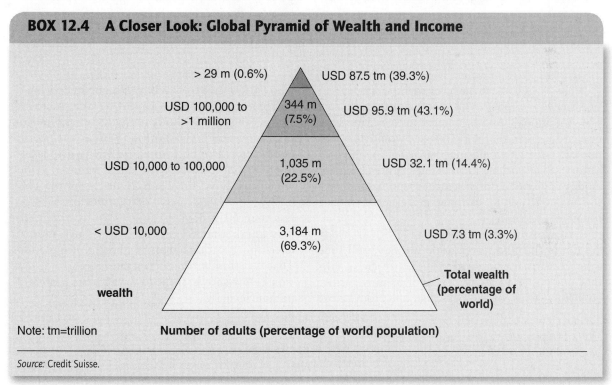

Wealth range	Number of adults (percentage of world population)	Total wealth (percentage of world)
> 29 m (0.6%)		USD 87.5 tm (39.3%)
USD 100,000 to >1 million	344 m (7.5%)	USD 95.9 tm (43.1%)
USD 10,000 to 100,000	1,035 m (22.5%)	USD 32.1 tm (14.4%)
< USD 10,000	3,184 m (69.3%)	USD 7.3 tm (3.3%)

Note: tm=trillion

Source: Credit Suisse.

The WEF reports that about 3.7 billion people (half of the world's population) live on under $8 a day. Over half of those, about 2.6 billion people, live on less than $2 a day. Almost half of those, 1.1 billion, live on less than just $1 a day. Although the cost of living varies dramatically between and within countries, global poverty is severe by any measure.

- 1.1 billion $2–$8 per day
- 1.6 billion $1–$2 per day
- 1 billion $1 per day (WEF 2009a, 2)

Having an income this low makes it near impossible to survive, let alone accumulate wealth. As we have seen, inequality of wealth is even greater than of income. It takes extra income in order to be able to save or invest money.

In 2012, global household wealth was about $223 trillion, up from $113 trillion in 2000 (Keating et al. 2012, 9). The bottom half of the pyramid—50% of the world's adult population—shared barely 1.0% of the world's wealth, one penny of every dollar, down from 1.1% in 2000 (13). Not everyone in the bottom half had assets. For example, in the United States, the bottom 20% of people as a pool have more debt than the total value of the things that they own.

BOX 12.5   A Closer Look: People Living on Less Than $1 a Day

Poverty is not evenly spread over the world. Poverty is most concentrated in sub-Saharan Africa and South Asia.

People Living on Less Than $1 a Day (in $US)	Sub-Saharan Africa	South Asia	Europe and Central Asia	East Asia and Pacific	Middle East and North Africa	Latin America and Caribbean
% Chronically Poor Over Five Years (estimate)	40	31	15	22	12.5	35
Number in Millions (estimate)	354	496	17.8	302	23.5	49

Source: Chronic Poverty Research Center (n.d.).

What does it mean to have so little money? In subsistence economies, not much money is needed. The traditional Amish community—before they needed to enter the marketplace—would fall into this category, as would most societies for most of history. When societies turn to agriculture as a commodity rather than for sustenance, and industrialize the manufacture of clothing and shelter, money becomes a necessity.

It is plausible that those earning $1–$2 a day are not in the labor force or do not have full-time jobs. Nevertheless, they do. There are many jobs that pay under $1 a day. Those of us in wealthier countries, with better jobs, benefit from those who earn only $1–$2 a day. No one further up on the economic pyramid would be able to live as well as they do without the work of the bottom of the pyramid: the bottom half of the world's population. The bottom half of the world is productive, but they acquire little value for their work and have little job security. As the chart below illustrates, many of the world's jobs pay less than $1 a day; many jobs are insecure. You may think that $1 or $2 a day buys more in developing nations than it does in rich nations. That is certainly true. Nevertheless, as the discussion below shows, these low wages are a threat to human security.

BOX 12.6   A Closer Look: Poverty and Employment

Most of the poor work. However, their jobs are often insecure and pay very low wages.

	Sub-Saharan Africa	Southern Asia	Oceania	Southeast Asia	Eastern Asia	Latin America and Caribbean
% of the Employed Earning Under $1/day	51.4	31.5	21.6	24.1	8.7	8.0
% in Unstable and Insecure Jobs	64	73	63	56	52	33

Source: UN (2008, 9).

The Quality of Life for the Very Poor

Poverty places severe limitations on the quality and texture of life. The lives of the very poor are similarly difficult wherever they live. *The United Nations Millennium Development Goals Reports* (UN 2008, 2010a) detail progress toward the goal of reducing global poverty by half by 2015 and of alleviating the conditions under which the poor suffer. Unfortunately, it looks as though many of the goals will not be met by their target date of 2015.

BOX 12.7   A Closer Look: Micronutrient Malnutrition

- Maternal and child under-nutrition micronutrient deficiency causes a million child deaths (under age five) and 100,000 preventable birth defects.
- Zinc deficiency contributes to over 800,000 child deaths per year.
- Malnutrition contributes to over half of the 10.6 million deaths of children under five each year in developing countries (WHO 2005, 106).
- Vitamin A deficiency contributes to child mortality, anemia, and night blindness. Studies have reported a decrease in child mortality from diseases such as malaria and measles. Vitamin A supplementation is one of the most efficient child and maternal survival interventions (WHO 2009, 2).
- Over 1.62 billion people—including over 293 million, or 47.4%, of pre-school children globally—are anemic (i.e., iron deficient). This affects global productivity, mental and physical development, as well as mortality (WHO 2008, 7).
- Vitamin A deficiency affects approximately 25% of the developing world's pre-school students. It is associated with blindness, susceptibility to disease, and higher mortality rates. It leads to the death of approximately 1 to 3 million children each year (WHO 2009).
- Iodine deficiency is the greatest single cause of developmental disability and brain damage. Worldwide, 1.9 billion people are at risk of iodine deficiency, which can easily be prevented by adding iodine to salt (WHO 2008).

For more hunger statistics, refer to the sites linked from the World Food Programme. http://www.wfp.org/hunger/stats

---

Childhood Poverty

The risk poverty poses to human security is best illustrated by its impact on the most vulnerable of humanity: children. There are 2.2 billion children in the world. About half of them, 1 billion, are living in poverty. More than 30% of the world's children live on less than US$1 a day (UNICEF 2006a). In 2007, 18% of children in the United States lived in poverty, the highest rate in the developed world. Child poverty brings myriad serious health consequences, including early death, stunted growth, and stunted brain development. The social consequences are as profound, including child labor and limited educational and employment opportunities. Despite the passage of the UN Convention on the Rights of the Child in 1989, poverty jeopardizes and diminishes the quality of life for children the world over.

Food Insecurity

About, one sixth of the world's population is chronically undernourished. Many of the poor who eat enough calories have diets that do not have sufficient protein or micronutrients. Micronutrients such as iodine, Vitamin A, and iron play vital functions in growth and development. Deficiencies cause blindness, loss of IQ points, physical and mental disability, in addition to early death. Micronutrients provide for higher quality of life, greater productivity in life, and for life itself. Box 12.7 details some of the effects of malnutrition.

Globally, approximately, 888 million people are undernourished, 868 in developing regions. This is down from 1 billion in 1990–1992 (FAO 2012). There are close to 20 million more in developed nations (FAO 2010). Recent inflations in food prices—one spike in 2003–2005 followed by another sharp spike in 2007—stalled progress in many parts of the world, bringing hunger reduction essentially to a standstill. Many Asian nations averted the worst impacts of the recession, and hunger reduction increased. In Latin America, it stalled. Africa felt the full effects of the recession, and hunger worsened (FAO 2012, 10–11). Rising

food prices escalate the price of all goods. This could force as many as 100 million more people into extreme poverty (UN 2008, 6).

- One third of children in the developing world were underweight in 2006. More than half of them are in Southern Asia (UN 2008, 10–11).

BOX 12.8   A Closer Look: Number of Undernourished People in the World by Region in Millions

India	Sub-Saharan Africa	Asia and Pacific*	China	Latin America and Caribbean	Near East and North Africa	Developed Countries
231	212	189	123	45	33	16

Source: Food and Agricultural Organization (2008, 12). *Excluding India and China, which are listed separately.

Water and Sanitation

The data on water and sewage may surprise you. Lack of sanitation and access to clean water is a major cause of death for children in the developing world (UN 2010a, 57–60). As many as 5,000 children die every day from water-related illnesses.

One billion people do not have safe drinking water. Who has it and who does not is another function of social location. Only 50% of the people in Oceania have access to safe water. About 2.8 billion people, 40% of the world's population, live in areas with water scarcity.

About 47% of the world's population lacks adequate sanitation. This percentage is highest in sub-Saharan Africa and Southern Asia, where 64% and 69%, respectively, have inadequate sanitation facilities. Globally, almost 25% of people have no form of water sanitation. This is highest in Southern Asia, where 44% have no alternative to open defecation. In developing regions, 35% of people do not have facilities that ensure separation of human waste from human contact. They are vulnerable to diarrhea, cholera, hepatitis, and worm infestation. Children are especially vulnerable.

- **Twenty percent of children still have no access to safe water (UNICEF 2006a).**

Health

Childhood mortality, the number of children who die before their fifth birthday, is a very sad yet sensitive measure of health of a population. The child mortality rate in the developing regions of the world is 80 per 1,000. Malnutrition causes about one third of these early deaths. Diseases that are easily prevented or treated in the developed world, such as measles, malaria, diarrhea, and pneumonia, kill many children in poor nations (UN 2008, 20–21).

Ninety-nine percent of women who die of childbirth-related causes are in the developing regions of the world, primarily sub-Saharan Africa and Southern Asia. In sub-Saharan Africa, 900 women die for every 100,000 pregnancies. The overall rate for developing regions is 450 for every 100,000 pregnancies (UN 2008, 25). Much of this death is caused by the lack of access to health care workers and facilities.

- **One seventh of children do not have access to health services (UNICEF 2006a).**

Housing

Slum housing is defined by lack of access to clean water, sanitation, durable housing, and sufficient living space. The percentage of the global population living in slums has decreased from

46.1% in 1990 to 32.7% in 2010, but slum populations grew by several hundred thousand people since 1990 (UN 2010a, 62). In sub-Saharan Africa, the percentage is as high as 62%. If we count the people living in housing with one or more slum characteristics, the percentage rises to 94% in sub-Saharan Africa (64).

- **Over one third of children in developing countries live in severe deprivation of without adequate shelter—this is about 640 million (UNICEF 2005, 1, 19).**

Education

One of the most promising statistics in the human development report is that close to 90% of primary school–age children are enrolled in school in the developing regions of the world. Less heartening is that only 54% of appropriately aged children are in secondary school. Another 19% of secondary-aged children are in primary school. Twenty seven percent of children are not in school. Whether or not children go to school depends a lot on urban or rural location, but it depends even more on their parents' income. Eighty-eight percent of children in the richest quintile of the poorer regions of the world are in primary school; only 65% of the poorest quintile are in school. This changed little by 2010 data (UN 2008, 13–14; 2010a, 18). The gender gap is significant in primary and secondary enrollment; girls in the poorest households have the least likelihood of being in school. This is more pronounced in rural than urban areas (2010a, 18, 21).

Child Labor

In the mid-19th century, early compulsory schooling laws in the United States mandated that children had to be in school or at work. Now, children are required to be in school until at least 16 years old in most states of the United States and cannot work for wages without permits stating the explicit nature of the work.

Most laws globally restrict work for children to jobs that do not threaten their health or safety. Although all countries now have child labor laws, children still labor in nearly every country. The

International Labor Organization (ILO) Convention 182 calls for the elimination of the worst forms of child labor. It was ratified by 186 countries. The worst forms of child labor are listed as follows:

- Slavery and practices similar to slavery, including sale and trafficking of children, debt bondage, serfdom, any forced labor, and compulsory recruitment to armed forces
- Use of children in any way in pornography or prostitution
- Using children in any illegal activities such as drug trafficking
- Any work that can harm the health safety or morals of children (USDOL 2009, xlii)

BOX 12.9   A Closer Look : Child Labor

This young Latina does not fit many people's picture of a miner.

International and most national laws permit light work for children as young as 12 but not to the extent that it interferes with compulsory schooling (USDOL 2009, xliv). Despite international conventions and protocols, many children work in the worst forms. In Albania, for example, hundreds of children are trafficked domestically and internationally. They work in chromium mines and as drug runners. They work on farms and as sheep herders, street vendors, and beggars (4–5). UNICEF estimates that there are 158 million children working in conditions that do not meet international standards (2009, 24). The young girl pictured in Box 12.9 works in Latin America with many other young children, mining.

Bolsa Familia is a Brazilian program that provides stipends to parents who keep their children in school. It has been successful in combating child labor, reaching about 15.5% of Brazilian children between five and 17. School attendance is 10.8% higher among families who receive the stipend than among those who do not ("Brazil's Foreign-Aid Programme" 2010). Similar programs are spreading globally. Brazil is investing millions of dollars aiding the poorest countries such as Haiti to adopt similar programs. This investment in the developing world will pay off in security, not just for Haiti but also for Brazil and the entire region.

Any program that improves the lives of children improves human security everywhere. The World Bank is also using stipends to send girls to school. Girls in rural areas of poorer regions have an out-of-school rate of 31% in comparison to the 27% rate for boys. In urban areas, the ratio is much closer: 15% of girls out of school and 14% of boys (UN 2010a, 18). Education for girls has a ripple effect in postponing their having children, lessening their poverty rates as adults, and improving the health and overall life chances of their children.

The 51st–90th Percentiles

In the middle of the pyramid is the global middle class. The global middle class is difficult to imagine. Every country has a middle class, the purchasing power of which varies dramatically from one country to another and within countries. The middle of the global pyramid is poor by the standards of the developed world, and many of the global middle class suffer many conditions described for the bottom of the pyramid. The middle-class portion of the global pyramid is generally able to meet the needs of survival; however, their status is fragile, particularly when they live in developing countries.

In the global middle class, most of the wealth that people hold is in the assets they use regularly, such as their homes and the tools and equipment that they use to make a living. They do not have excess of fluidity or spendable cash. An annual income of $3,000 puts a person in the top half of the world's population in income. This is earnings of about $8 to $10 a day. The upper threshold of the middle class is about $20 per day (adjusted for local prices in 2000). As you might expect from the low wages, 56% of the global middle class lives in developing countries.

To make it over the threshold of poverty into the top half of the global distribution of wealth, only $2,129 was required in 2000 (Davies et al. 2008, 7). The share of wealth of the 60th through to the 90th percentiles—up to $61,000 in assets at the 90th percentile—of the world's adult population is just 13.8% of the total wealth of the world (Milanovic 2006). By 2012, it took $3,700 to make it to the top half of the global population, and $71,000 was the threshold into the top 10%. The share of wealth of the middle class, the 60th through 90th percentiles, declined to about 13% of the global wealth (Keating et al. 2012, 13). The good news was that the global middle class was growing rapidly—until the recession of 2007. This progress has stalled due to declines in employment. Before the recession, the World Bank projected that by 2030, the global middle class would exceed 1 billion—16.1% of the world population—up from 400 million in 2005.

Families of four in that class earn between $16,800 and $72,000 in purchasing power parity (PPP) dollars. Attaining global middle-class status puts most individuals in developing nations in the upper deciles of their national economies (World Bank 2007, 69–73). Whether or not this goal is met depends on how quickly the global economy can catch up with the projected growth rates.

Top of the Pyramid: The Top 10% and Top 1%

To belong to the top 10% of the global population in wealth, you would have to own roughly $71,000 in assets (Keating et al. 2012). This may not sound like a lot of money. Keep two things in mind. First, most of the world's population is poor, which dramatically lowers the wealth threshold of the top 10% of the global population. Second, incomes are higher and wealth is concentrated in the United States, Europe, and some parts of Asia. Global wealth thresholds within rich countries are much higher than the wealth thresholds of the total global population. This is evident in the comparison of wealth thresholds in the United States and the world in the Box 12.10.

BOX 12.10   A Closer Look: Thresholds of Wealth

How much does it take to get into the top 10% or 1% of the richest people in the United States and in the world?

	Top 10%	Top 1%
Globe		
2000	$61,536	$512,386
2012	$71,000	$710,000
United States 2004	$827,000	>$6,000,000

Sources: Davis et al. (2008, 8) and Keating et al. (2012, 13); United States: Frank (2007).

Where They Live	Top 10%	Top 1%
United States	25%	37%
Japan	21%	27%
Europe	36%	26%

Source: Davies et al. (2008, 12, 15).

Many adults in the United States, 45.5%, are in the top 10% of the global population in wealth. Like the global middle class, most of their wealth is in their home. Before the recession, 67% of Americans owned their home, and taking into account the amount they owe on it, its average value as an asset was $59,000 (Kay 2006). The poorest 20% of Americans have no wealth; they are in debt. Like the poorest segment of the global population, they are working and have income. Their income amounts to about 4% to 5% of the total income of the United States, but as a group, their debts exceed their assets.

The richest 10% of adults globally own 85% of the wealth; 5% own 71%, 2% of global adults own more than half and the top 1% owns 40%. To be in the top 1% in 2000, it took $512,000 in assets. (Davies et al. 2008, 7)

The top 10% of the global pyramid earns one half of the global income.

BOX 12.11   A Closer Look: Wealth Distribution and Distribution by Type of Asset, United States, 2010.

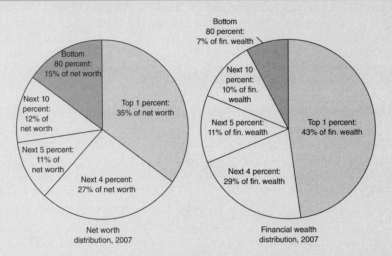

Net worth distribution, 2007

Financial wealth distribution, 2007

It takes money to make money. The very rich own nearly all of the money making assets in the United States. Investment income is taxed at a lower rate than ordinary income, enhancing their ability to make even more money.

Source: Domhoff (2013).

Why is inequality of wealth so much more skewed than income inequality? The answer is a cliché, yet accurate: "It takes money to make money." The rich make money through investment, which earns "capital gains." The upper class of the United States, the top 1% of earners, received 21.3% of the income in 2006. But you can see from Box 12.11 that in 2007, they held 43% of the money-making assets. Additionally, they held twice the business equity (62.4%) and over 1.5 times the financial securities (60.6%) of even the next highest 9%, who owned 30.0% and 37.9% of those respective assets. The bottom 90% (next 10% and bottom 80% combined) held very few money-making assets, only 17% (Domhoff 2013).

At the top of the pyramid, wealth creates capital gains—a form of income that is taxed in the United States at a lower rate than income earned through work. Capital gains are converted into more wealth. The proportion of capital income going to the top of the pyramid has been increasing. In the United States,

in 2003, just 1% of all households—those with after-tax incomes averaging $701,500—received 57.5% of all capital income, up from 40% in the early 1990s. In contrast, the bottom 80% received

only 12.2% of capital income, down by nearly half since 1983, when the bottom 80% received 23.5%. (Domhoff 2013, 9)

In 2007 there were 10.1 million high-net-worth individuals (HNWI) globally: 3.3 million live in North America, 3.1 million in Europe, 2.8 million in the Asia-Pacific region, 400,000 in Latin America and the Middle East, and 100,000 in Africa. This wealth class experienced the strongest growth in the period 2005–2007, accounting for 14.5% of economic growth and only 8.8% of population growth (Capgemini and Merrill Lynch 2008).

Where a person or a country falls in the global economic pyramid affects the quality of life in nearly every aspect of human security—exposure to violent conflict, environmental toxins, crime, and overall health.

The Cost of the Global Recession: Update on the Eight Millennium Development Goals

The 2000 UN Millennium Declaration was a breakthrough in international relations. The world agreed that there were some things to which all people had rights, and it was the responsibility of all nations to provide them. Nations agreed to cooperate on eight goals, divided into 21 targets, measureable by 60 indicators.[1] The target date for achieving them is 2015. The goals are to eradicate extreme poverty and hunger; achieve universal primary education; promote gender equality and the empowerment of women; reduce child mortality; improve maternal health; combat HIV/AIDS, malaria, and other diseases; ensure environmental sustainability; and develop a global partnership for development.

BOX 12.12   Consider This: The Human Cost of the Global Economic Crisis

The World Bank estimated that "[t]he global economic crisis will cause an additional 22 children to die per hour throughout all of 2009" (Kristof 2009)—that is, 192,720 children added to the mortality list in 2009.

To what extent are those whose actions precipitated the financial crisis responsible for the deaths that will result?

Could they have foreseen that their actions would endanger human life?

The global recession of 2007 exacerbated inequality. The poor got poorer as the rich got richer. In 2010, the World Bank issued a report assessing progress toward the goals. The global financial crisis, not surprisingly, has stalled progress toward the goals. Food consumption, vital to the current and future health (physical and economic) of societies, took a beating. In Turkey, for example, 53% of families decreased their food consumption; in Armenia, 41% did; and in Montenegro, 31% (World Bank 2010, 53).

BOX 12.13   Check It Out Yourself: MDG Progress

The Millennial Development Goals Interactive database allows you to check the progress of each country. Are the World Bank's predictions concerning the effects of the global recession holding true?
  http://mdgs.un.org/unsd/mdg/Default.aspx

Poverty reduction, one of the baseline pathways to a healthier life, will take considerably longer than hoped. In 2015, the global poverty rate will be about 15% rather than the anticipated 14.1%. That means an additional 64 million people over the anticipated rate will be left in extreme poverty at the end of 2010. By 2020, an additional 71 million will still suffer extreme poverty. Thirty-eight percent of sub-Saharan Africa will still be in extreme poverty, rather than 36%. While the percentage may seem low, the loss in quality of life is enormous.

The impact of the crisis on infant mortality is that an additional 55,000 infants and 260,000 more children under age five might die in 2015, for a total of 265,000 infants and 1.2 million children for the years 2009–2015. Completion of elementary school will be sacrificed for an additional 350,000 students in 2015. One hundred million more people will be without an improved water supply than if the crisis hadn't happened (World Bank 2010, 103).

The crisis has been a setback—one with deadly results.

BOX 12.14   Consider This: Sharing Technology

Benefits of the new technologies must be shared by all of humanity. This was stressed by some of the governmental leaders present at the WEF.

(Continued)

(Continued)

Article 27 of the Universal Declaration of Human Rights is quoted in the Annual Report stressing the right of everyone "to share in scientific advancement and its benefits" (WEF 2009b, 23–24).

To what extent do richer nations owe it to poorer to share environmentally clean technologies, the best medical care, prescription drugs, agricultural techniques, and other technologies? How do history and the current economic relationships among countries bear on your answer?

Case Studies to Alleviate Poverty

Is there a way to reconcile global capital and economic development of the poorest of humanity? Developing the bottom of the pyramid can improve the health of the global economy. The programs presented here do not address some key issues of the global economy, problems of regulating global capital and finance, or alternate visions of globalization. They are programs that work at the level of individuals, to help them better their lives. They offer promise to mitigate some of the worst effects of the global recession, and stimulate economic growth. It is very important to note that they are not a substitute for macro-level solutions to global economic inequality and insecurity. They are an important complement.

Strategies for Bottom of the Pyramid (BOP)

Stimulating growth and profit in the developing world has been one of the most intractable problems of the contemporary era. A strategy emerged from the 2009 WEF meeting to meet the issue head-on by aligning the needs of the poorest 3.7 billion people on the planet with the needs of global capital. It is an intriguing proposition. What could be the common interests shared by the most desperately poor and most extravagantly rich?

The obvious answer is money. As we have seen, the poor work hard and have an income. There is $2.3 trillion of annual income shared among the poorest of the world's population. Globally, it is growing at a much faster rate than other population segments, at 8% in recent years leading up to the recession. This may be the most promising and fruitful growth opportunity in the world today.

The BOP is a fast-growing consumer market, an underutilized productive sector, and a source of untapped entrepreneurial talent. "Engaging the 'next billions' at the BOP as producers, consumers and entrepreneurs is therefore key to both reducing poverty and driving broader economic growth" (WEF 2009a).

Two issues complicate this scenario: Can it be done, and will the BOP really benefit if it is done? Aid agencies and civil society organizations have tried to unleash the potential of the poorest for decades without great success. However, the global environment may very well have changed. Aid agencies and civil society groups struggled uphill— underfunded, pushing against the oppression of dictatorial regimes and the interest of global capital. Their efforts were neither well coordinated nor integrated sufficiently into the global economy. Much of the investment was wasted through corrupt regimes that made no investment in growth opportunities for the poor. The days of dictators are over in many places. The days of global capital acting with impunity, stripping the BOP of resources and labor as cheaply as possible, may also be numbered, if not over. Despite the recession, global capital is not underfunded. It has means and mechanisms of integration and coordination. Directing flows of capital within developing countries and developing strong laws to protect the poor from exploitation are keys to success.

How can we ensure that people are rewarded for their resources, labor, and talent, and that development is a vehicle to autonomy? This depends on the political will of the global community. As discussed earlier, countries that controlled the flows of finance and investment fared much better in their dealings in the global economy. This requires that strong systems of national and global governance be built.

Partnering Global Capital and the BOP

Opportunities providing mutual benefit for global capital and the poor lie where there is the most need and the most potential for growth. A healthy food sector is one such opportunity. The poor spend most of their money on food, consuming as much as half of a family's budget in the poorest areas of the world.

BOX 12.15   A Closer Look: Business of Farming

One of the fundamental successes of the USAID/Olam partnership is the change in how smallholders view farming. The first year of the USAID/Olam partnership helped over 10,000 farmers secure markets, commercial financing, and technical assistance.

Farm productivity increased almost 260%, and farmer net income more than doubled.

The WEF approach to food security relies on the cultivation of private enterprise, private markets, and linkages between local farmers in developing nations and the global market. There are several model programs that reportedly have succeeded in building these capacities for the mutual benefit of the poor and a multinational corporation. Most of these partnerships involve governmental or civil society groups as well. In Nigeria, local farmers team with a multinational to produce high-quality rice. The farmers' yields grew 75%, and incomes grew 155% in the first two years. Olam Nigeria (a division of the multinational Olam, a food producer) worked with USAID and others to develop a supply chain from grower to market. In 2006, the project provided over 10,000 growers secure access to secure markets. This program is providing a high-quality food product and entrepreneurial opportunities for thousands of people. Olam Nigeria Limited won one of the 2008 World Business and Development Awards sponsored by United Nations Development Program (USAID Nigeria 2009).

Non-food agricultural products are another opportunity. Unilever developed a vegetable oil from allanblackia seeds in Africa and designed a supply and processing chain for the product (Adams 2009). The Novella African Initiative (NAI) is a partnership of Unilever and a variety of government and local organizations. Unilever has committed to moving out of the supply chain and leaving it to local governments and collectives of growers when it can stand on its own. It appears to be sustainable and could contribute about $175 annually to a small grower's income. The supply chain offers other opportunities for entrepreneurship and employment. This program is operating in Cameroon, Nigeria, Ghana, Liberia, and Tanzania. The allanblackia oil is used in products such as soap and edible spreads. It is primarily an export product (NAI 2011).

Strong governmental apparatus is needed to ensure that the objectives of private industry complement those of their partners. Governmental infrastructure is also needed to ensure that the bulk of the benefits of such programs reach those who are working in partnership with private industry and lead to self-sufficiency, not dependency, as have some past agricultural programs in which farmers had to pay yearly for patented seeds or chemical fertilizers.

Information and money—technoscapes and financescapes—need to travel for agricultural programs to succeed. Communication infrastructure is often weak in developing societies. BT, Cisco, and OneWorld developed a telecom- and Internet-based information service for farmers, Lifelines India, which provides access to information that farmers need. It has increased participating farmers' productivity by 20% to 30%. Cell phones have become financial tools used to receive and make payments very simply and safely. It is a cell-phone version of an online system such as PayPal, bypassing the need—at least temporarily—for a sophisticated banking system. It enables the chain of transactions to proceed smoothly.

Low-cost housing is another market of opportunity.

> With the drop in demand for luxury housing due to the financial crisis, there is an opportunity to address an ignored market segment: low-income housing in developing countries. Until now, developers have focused on the richest 20% of the world's population, ignoring a vast market segment. Private sector developers are needed to invest in projects once considered unattractive and the domain of governments. (Bianchi et al. 2009)

Transfer of land rights and local needs related to housing were addressed at the WEF meeting by a civil society representative from Architecture for Humanity (United States).

These projects offer promise because they are partnerships. Private enterprise brings research, investment money, technical skills, and established channels through the global economy to the projects. They make a profit and improve their reputations in return. (Whether or not the profit is shared fairly is, of course, a central question.) Government agencies, such as USAID, and international civil society agencies, such as the World Conservation Union (ICUN), have been used to provide oversight, evaluative capacity, community building, and democracy-building strategies and experience. Local government agencies and civil society organizations are strengthened by their participation, and provide oversight and development activities. The local entrepreneurs are being trained in business and will eventually take over the projects, expand them, and add new ones.

Microloans

Finding capital for startup enterprises is difficult anywhere. It is particularly difficult if you have no money, no collateral, no credit history, and not even a bank account. That is the situation for many of the world's poor. It is a market that is not served by traditional banks and financial institutions. Microfinance institutions (MFIs) have filled this void.

Consider microloans. A microloan is a small loan, as little as $100 and rarely over $1,500. A microloan may enable a person to buy something like a sewing machine, a truck, or a refrigerator to help start a small business. Microloans are a substitute for direct grants and bank loans, which are not available to the very poor. They are not handouts and must be paid back.

Microloans have helped millions of people, particularly women, and have benefits beyond the people who acquired the loan. For example, one study reported that at a UNFPA conference reported that 40 women clients of a microbank in South Asia employed their husbands in their enterprises. This took the husbands out of the local job market, which caused an increase in the wages of other men in their towns (UNFPA 2006a). That is 80 new jobs created and 120 people employed rather than 40. When more people have income, it means more spending to meet their life needs. As demand rises, it increases the potential and allure of the area for more hiring and more new enterprises. The record of microloans, done honestly, is impressive.

BOX 12.16   A Closer Look: Microloans

Bulgaria, a small grant for economic development in areas with high ethnic minorities enabled this sewing company to build its capacity.

Grameen Bank (2011) was the first MFI, founded in 1976, in Bangladesh. Grameen and other MFIs provide loans, checking and savings accounts, and a range of financial services not usually available to the poor. Their central function, however, is to provide small loans—the average size of Grameen bank loan is $398—for small start-up enterprises. The largest loan made was $23,209. Grameen, the first of the MFIs, has a number of loan programs for everything from housing to student loans and interest-free loans to beggars. It provides scholarships and has made a profit in every year except three. Traditional banking wisdom is that this risky population would have a high rate of default. The loan recovery rate of Grameen is 97.38%.

Grameen Bank established itself with private resources—donations, grants, and loans. It has not needed any new donations since 1995. Nor does it take out any loans. As people repay their loans, the money is cycled back into more loans. It is now totally supported by loan repayment of its members. Its borrowers are the members and owners of Grameen.

Grameen Bank provides a number of financial and related services, helping people develop the knowledge and skills for a sound financial lifestyle. Financial literacy courses are compulsory for members. They are required to keep savings accounts and make regular deposits. They must send their children to school, keep their homes in good repair, grow and eat vegetables, and sell the surplus. Initial and ongoing financial education is also required. Borrowers start businesses serving local markets, providing goods and services that help to improve the quality of life in their communities. Grameen affords help in every step of establishing and maintaining a business.

Although Grameen is not registered as a bank in the United States, it has expanded its microloan program there. It has branches in Atlanta, Boston, Charlotte, Indianapolis, San Francisco, Tampa, and Washington, DC. They loan to individuals making under $15,000 annually. This is a group not served by traditional business loans in the United States. Loans are kept small, usually under $1,500. The intent is to get people their first few dollars of financing, which are usually impossible for the poor to find.

The founder of Grameen, Muhammad Yunus, and Grameen Bank won the Noble Peace Prize in 2006. He was awarded the Medal of Freedom by President Barak Obama in 2008.

There are over 7,000 MFIs, and they have loaned billions of dollars to millions of the poor. Grameen charges about 20% on loans for opening businesses— with cheaper loans for education and housing. Some predatory for-profit MFIs have taken advantage of the microloan movement and vulnerability of its clients to charge exceptionally high rates and plunge borrowers into over-indebtedness. More responsible investors offer more reasonable rates with a long period for repayment. They still make a profit and the borrower has an opportunity to grow. Until these legitimate MFIs can make their services widely available—MFIs may be reaching only 15% of those who could use them—illegitimate lenders can exploit the poor through predatory practices. This is another example of the need for strong governments to develop strong economies.

Patient Capitalism

Hot money that is put into a country for short-term profit and then removed quickly has exacerbated poverty. Patient capitalism, the strategy of the Acumen Fund, has the opposite approach. A venture capitalist fund for the poor, it invests over the long term, helping to build capacity before expecting a return. It was founded by Jacqueline Novogratz in 2001. Novogratz has spent decades combating poverty in Africa. She helps local people develop entrepreneurial ventures to meet local needs such as affordable housing, water, energy, and health. As of 2007, Acumen had invested $20 million in 20 enterprises and had created about 20,000 jobs and tens of millions in services (Novogratz 2007). The Acumen Fund finances not-for-profits, small- to medium-sized businesses, and specific units of larger businesses committed to serving the poor. Acumen invests from $300,000 to $2,500,000 per project with payback expected within five to seven years. They have at times worked with Grameen Bank to secure portions of the financing.

BOX 12.17   Consider This: What Is a Legitimate Wage?

Some corporations that invest in the Third World to make a social investment in the country also pay very low wages. If the market for labor in a country or region is $0.50 or $1.00 a day, is creating more jobs at $1.50 a day a benefit?

Is a low wage better than no wage? Are the prices we pay for products from the Third World too low? Would fewer people in the developed world buy products of developing countries if they were more expensive? Would that help the poor? Those that had low-paying jobs making these commodities might be out of work. These questions are hard to answer.

When the company that pays low wages is started by a poor entrepreneur in the developing country and is owned by the poor in the country, does that make a difference? These are the types of companies that Novogratz works to get up and running.

Finding a middle way may be essential.

Acumen also works with local banks by guaranteeing investments in locally owned enterprises (Acumen Fund n.d.). It concentrates on models of poverty alleviation that are scalable and sustainable. Although Acumen relies on market mechanisms, it supplements the market with technical advice, networking, management, and support necessary for these fledging enterprises to succeed. Like Grameen, it supplies not only financial capital but also the cultural capital necessary for success. The key to the Acumen strategy is helping people do for themselves. This is patient capitalism because it supports investments over the long term and does not chase quick returns. Novogratz looks for investors and projects that combine social need with striving for success (Novogratz 2007).

All three of these models are examples of capitalist enterprises that work for reasonable profits. They have rejected the ethic of seeking the most profit, which led to many unstable practices and global crises. Much of the profit is invested back into new enterprises and shareholders are reasonably paid. These programs are important for alleviating suffering in poorer segments of the world though the benefits are shared globally. They expand productive forces and the global market; more importantly, they help achieve global economic and political stability. Two of the richest men in the world, Warren Buffet and Bill Gates, both promote development aid. Gates delivered a 75-minute talk at the 2011 G20 meetings to encourage a "Robin Hood" tax on financial transactions; Buffet has consistently supported development aid and harshly criticized the U.S. tax code, which, he reported, taxed him at a 17% rate in 2010, lower than most low- and middle-income Americans.

Migration

People migrate for a variety of reasons. Most are related in one way or another to inequality. Many choose to emigrate from their homeland for economic opportunity or to escape persecution based on their ethnicity, religion, or political or sexual orientation. Others leave to escape environmental catastrophe or violent conflict. Some are forced to leave, expelled from their homeland. Although migration may have benefits for both host countries and migrants, it is also implicated in human security issues in a number of interrelated ways.

- Human economic, political, and social insecurities push migrants out of their homelands.
- Waves of migration can place temporary—until immigrants adjust and become economically integrated—pressures on host countries and increase actual or perceived insecurity in those counties.
- Refugees often live in conditions of extreme economic and social insecurity in host countries. Many groups live as refugees for generations,

impeding their own future welfare as well perhaps of their homeland and host country.

- Refugees from conflict-torn countries may carry that conflict across borders and destabilize countries with a similar ethnic mix or tensions, or use border countries to stage incursions into their homeland.
- Networks connecting migrant communities may facilitate ethnically based organized crime movement of money or goods globally.
- When waves of migration reach a level that citizens in a host country perceive as threatening to their economic, cultural, or other interests, discrimination, hate crime, and other reactionary activities rise.

Refugees

Migrants are classified in a number of ways. A *refugee* is someone who cannot live in safety in his or her homeland. Refugees have the right to international protection. When there is a mass movement of migrants fleeing conflict or natural disaster, their status as refugees is clear. Where people are fleeing individually or as a small group, they are not automatically designated refugees. No country is obliged to accept any migrants, but all have the obligation to accept refugees. If persons are already in the country where they wish to reside or at a port of entry, they are considered asylum seekers. They must meet refugee status.

Box 12.18   Largest Number of Asylum Claims by Selected Characteristics

# of Asylum Seekers		# per 1,000 Inhabitants 2006–2010	# per $US1 GDP Per Capita 2006–2010
United States	55,000	Cyprus 24.2	United States 5.6
France	47,800	Malta 19.3	France 5.4
Germany	41,300	Sweden 15.2	United Kingdom 3.9
Sweden	31,800	Liechtenstein 14.2	Sweden 3.8
Canada	23,200	Norway 11.1	Canada 3.7
United Kingdom	22,100	Switzerland 8.8	Germany 3.7
Belgium	19,900	Austria 7.8	Turkey 3.5
Switzerland	13,500	Greece 7.5	Greece 2.7
Netherlands	13,300	Belgium 6.8	Italy 2.7
Greece	10,300	Luxembourg 5.4	Poland 2.0

Source: UNHCR (2011).

In 2010, 358,800 people sought asylum, primarily in the North America and Europe. Asylum seekers come from many countries; it is a different list than the countries with large numbers of refugees. The asylum seeker may be suffering religious persecution, such as members of Falun ong in China. They may be targeted victims of political persecution if they are members of an opposition group in a country with an oppressive regime, or homosexuals in a country where same-sex sexual orientation is considered deviant or criminal. Once these persons' asylum application is accepted, they become refugees. This may take years, and there are close to a million people globally who are in asylum-seeking status (UNHCR 2009, 151).

BOX 12.19   A Closer Look: Refugee Camps

School children in Kakuma refugee camp, Kenya.

Between 2000 and 2009, over 42 million people were uprooted by conflict or persecution (UN 2010a, 15). Some are displaced temporarily, but for many, refugee status may last a lifetime. As of 2007, there were 8,525,500 people living in refugee populations of 10,000 or more for more than 10 years. There are 14,047,300 officially recognized refugees and asylum seekers globally (USCRI 2008, 30–31). Most seek refuge close to home, in neighboring countries. They are limited to where they can walk—a walk, for some, of thousands of miles.

In 2007, over 1 million refugees fled their homelands. This was the highest number since 2001. A large number, over half in 2007, continue to flee from Iraq. In 1991, 2 million Kurds streamed out of Iraq into Turkey and Iran, where there are significant Kurdish populations subject to extreme discrimination. Turkey, fearing both the cost of providing for the refugees and the possibility of Turkish Kurds mobilizing against Turkey, closed its borders. Streams of families went back through the snow and mountains into Iraq. Britain and the United States responded to the crisis by creating a "no fly" zone in northern Iraq that provided safe haven. Similar situations of economic burden combined with potential upsets of racial or ethnic relations existed between Rwanda and Burundi, and the Democratic Republic of Congo and surrounding states. In these cases, combatants sought refuge in ethnic enclaves, and conflicts ricocheted back and forth across borders, prolonging and expanding conflicts. Corrupt government in host countries, corrupt leaders, and sometime corrupt relief workers, particularly in conflict zones, may try to manipulate and control supplies coming for refugees from humanitarian organizations (MacFarlane 2000).

Hundreds of thousands of refugees return home each year. Sometimes, they return because conditions have improved, sometimes due to the oppressive conditions of life in camps (USCRI 2008, 28). Not only are conditions in camps deplorable because of lack of basic needs for survival, lack of opportunity for employment, and other indignities, but people in refugee camps are also more subject to natural disasters such as the floods that ravaged Pakistan in 2010. They swept through Azkhel Village established 30 years ago as a refugee camp for Afghans escaping one war after another. It had evolved into a village of grandparents, their children, and children's children. The camp was flattened by the flooding. Mosquitoes—which spread malaria and a variety of deadly viral diseases—followed, preying on families living in the open until enough tents could be distributed.

The security of refugees does not depend on the wealth or democratic leanings of a country. Ironically, Iraqi refugees found better treatment in Syria than in they did in most other countries. Treatment of refugees depends primarily on shared characteristics between refugee and host: physical, ethnic, religious, language, and other common bonds. Where there is less commonality, there is less humane treatment (Límon 2008, 2). All nations that accept refugees make sacrifices to do so. When the nation is poor, they cannot create secure environments or maintain their own security without significant international aid.

Refugees have recognized status and rights globally, such as freedom of religious practice and the right to food and secure shelter. Rights beyond the minimum stipulated in international law vary widely by host country. The care of refugees is a shared global responsibility. Two primary documents—the 1951 Convention Relating to the Status of Refugees

BOX 12.20   A Closer Look: Seeking Asylum

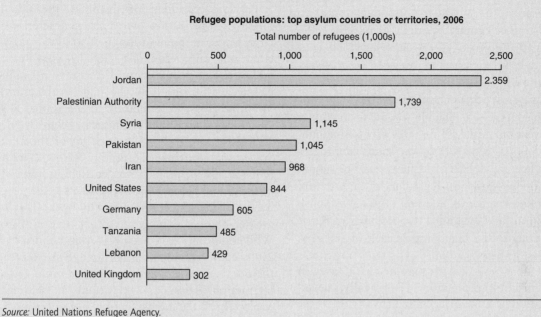

Refugee populations: top asylum countries or territories, 2006

Total number of refugees (1,000s)

Jordan	2.359
Palestinian Authority	1,739
Syria	1,145
Pakistan	1,045
Iran	968
United States	844
Germany	605
Tanzania	485
Lebanon	429
United Kingdom	302

Source: United Nations Refugee Agency.

BOX 12.21   A Closer Look: Al Salaam Refugee Camp

New arrivals at Al Salaam camp, in Sudan's North Darfur region, make temporary shelters out of household goods they were able to carry with them.

and the 1967 Protocol Relating to the Status of Refugees—outline states' obligations to refugees. Under the terms of Article 3 of the Convention, refugees are not to be subject to "discrimination as to race, religion or country of origin" (UNCHR 2007, 19). The 1967 Protocol, due to changing global conditions and very clearly in response to evolving global norms, revised the original convention in several ways. Article I eliminates the 1951 date for qualifying refugees as eligible for treatment under the convention. Article II requires states to submit regular reports to the UN on the status of refugees they are hosting. Article III requires states to submit their national legislation regarding refugees to UN review (49). The convention and protocol establish global norms and the global responsibility of signatory nations to the humane treatment of refugees, regardless of their location.

Permanent resettlement may occur in cases of people needing protection. Historically, developed countries have accepted most of these migrants. Australia and Canada have accepted the greatest ratio of refugees in proportion to their population. The United States has accepted by far the greatest number, although only about one third of the proportion of Australia.

Previous periods—for example, the take-off phase of globalization—were also characterized by large waves of immigration. Industrialization escalated not only economic globalization but the movement of people as well. Close to 50 million people left Europe from the mid-19th century to WWI, headed predominantly to the United States and, second, to South America. From 1850 to 1930, the foreign-born population of the United States soared from 2.2 million to 14.2 million (Gibson and Lennon 1999). In 2010, about 3.1% of the global population, over 213,943,812 people, lived outside of their country of birth. This is a greater number than at any other time in history. While rates may have been higher at the turn of the 20th century, population density and size increases the number, variety, and intensity of cross-cultural interaction. These are important in helping to explain both the intensification and uncertainty of globalization effects characteristic of the contemporary period.

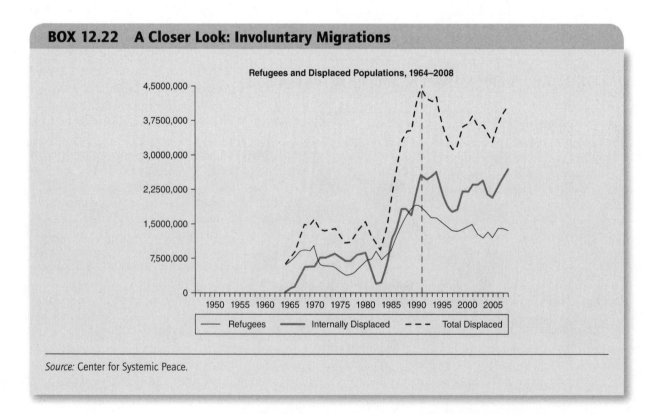

BOX 12.22   A Closer Look: Involuntary Migrations

Refugees and Displaced Populations, 1964–2008

Refugees — Internally Displaced — — Total Displaced

Source: Center for Systemic Peace.

Internally Displaced Persons

Internally displaced person (IDP) is another category of migrant. About 27.1 million people were living outside of their homes, but in their homeland, in 2009. This was an increase of about 1 million in a year. Six countries have over 1 million IDPs—Sudan, Colombia, Iraq, Congo, Somalia, and Ethiopia (IDMC 2010a, 8). About half of these are displaced due to internal war, others due to natural disasters and human rights violations, among other causes. For example, before the independence movement in Bosnia-Herzegovina, the city of Sarajevo was a mosaic of Muslim, Croat, and Serbian mixed neighborhoods. The war devolved into genocide. The term *ethnic cleansing* emerged in reference to Bosnia-Herzegovina. People were forced from their homes into segregated ethnic neighborhoods, and some fled the country. The war created a massive refugee and IDP crisis, with 2.3 million fleeing violence. By the end of 2009, 15 years later, 114,000 people remained IDPs. The first wave of those who returned home returned to areas where they were in the ethnic majority. As the years progressed, the numbers of returnees dwindled. The last returnees returned to their homes in neighborhoods where they were the ethnic minority where they have suffered hardship and discrimination. Bosnia-Herzegovina and neighborhoods within Sarajevo remain segregated. A plan to create three ethnically based territories within the country was developed in 2009. There is one territory for each ethnic group, and Sarajevo is mixed with three segregated ethnic areas within. Croatian and Serbian nationalists still hope the territories will split and join with Croatia, on the one hand, and Serbia, on the other (Woehrel 2010, 4).

The number of IDPs in Bosnia-Herzegovina is relatively small and has persisted over a relatively short time in comparison to other countries. In many countries, millions have lived in displacement for generations. Sudan has the largest internally displaced population: 4.9 million. Armed conflict has been near constant since independence in 1956. Oppression of religious and racial minorities by an Arab government spawned rebellions in South, West (Darfur), and Eastern Sudan. Sudan is home to two UN peacekeeping forces, one in the South and one in Darfur. Over 4 million people fled Southern Sudan alone. With the peace treaty signed in 2005, returnees started to flow back into Southern Sudan. About 2 million refugees and IDPs have returned as of 2009. As part of the peace agreement, Southern Sudan was given steps to independence, one of those being the referendum on independence in January 2011, which passed with 98% approval. Independence day was July 9, 2011. After years of displacement, the society will be hard to rebuild. War between Sudan and the new South Sudan continues over borders and control of oil. In the meantime, people's homes have been destroyed; water, land, and health and education services are sparse (IDMC 2010b, 18–19).

The 1951 UN Convention on Refugees did not address IDPs. The responsibility for IDPs is left to the very governments who in many cases bear at least some of the responsibility for their displacement. In 1998, a group of international experts drafted "Guiding Principles" to consolidate and clarify existing international laws. The principles now serve as a blueprint for the treatment of internally displaced persons and reaffirm their rights as humans and reinforce that internally displaced persons are owed the same rights as any other citizen of the country, their homeland. Regional alliances have encouraged member states to develop national laws based on the principles. The Organization of American States (OAS) and Council of Europe, among others, have mandated that any signatories incorporate the principles into their domestic law (Great Lakes Protocol on the Protection and Assistance Internally Displaced Persons in Africa). The guidelines stress a country's obligation to prevent displacement and start planning durable solutions if it occurs. Prevention efforts are to include effective disaster risk reduction, emergency preparedness, and effective conflict prevention. Ending displacement as expediently as possible requires early recovery strategies. This requires partnerships among governments, civil society organizations, and development agencies (Couldrey and Henson 2008, 7).

In 2008, an assessment of the principles demonstrated that they had served as a valuable guide for countries that developed domestic policies and laws based on them. The guidelines are also used effectively to guide the action of humanitarian agencies (Couldrey and Henson 2008).

Burma (Myanmar) is an example of a country where the "Guiding Principles" have done little to achieve relief for IDPs. International laws and principles apply to people whether they have been forced from their homes by violence and abuse, fear of the government, the government, or a combination of coercive and economic factors. In the case of Burma, the government that came to power through a military coup in 1988 caused most of the displacement through "land confiscation, asset stripping, forced procurement policies that impose political conditions on contracts, agricultural production quotas, forced labour, arbitrary taxation, extortion and restrictions on access to fields and markets" (Thailand Burma Border Consortium 2008, 2). The burden of these policies has fallen heavily on those communities that are perceived to oppose the state. International principles did not result in the government acknowledging their role in causing displacement or their responsibilities to displaced persons.

The enforcement of the principles in Burma grew to be a responsibility of the international community, clarified as they are in international law (Thailand Burma Border Consortium 2008, 15). How the international community can force governments to conform to international law remains problematic. Burma had been subjected to economic and political sanctions from Western nations since 1997. Sanctions have had little to no effect on the activity of the government. The constructive engagement of ASEAN, of which Burma is a member, namely, continuing to deal with them while encouraging them to change, had not improved the situation either. China, Burma's ally, often acted as a buffer, providing extensive aid and vetoing UN Security Council proposals.

BOX 12.23   Check It Out Yourself: Ethnicity in Burma

Stimson, a non-partisan, not-for-profit institute devoted to peace studies, has an interactive map that shows the locations of Burma's major ethnic groups and provides background on each.
    The map can be found at http://www.stimson.org/programs/myanmar-map.

About 3 million Burmese are in refuge in neighboring countries. Despite democratic reforms instituted beginning in 2010 (see Chapter Eight), Burmese military continues to fight rebel groups, and inter-ethnic violence continues. In June 2012, a 17-year cease fire with the Kachin, primarily Christian, rebel group broke down, sending thousands into China and displacing tens of thousands more, some of whom are living in government-run camps (Wong 2012). Fighting between Buddhist Rakhine and Muslim Rohingya sent thousands more refugees into Bangladesh. Thousands arriving in boats to Bangladesh have been turned away.

The new government has asked for international help in dealing with the crisis of refugees and IDPs.

The problems of IDPs highlight the tensions between a global community that increasingly recognizes global norms to which all states are to be held accountable and states that see many of these norms as purely internal matters, matters over which they hold sovereignty. The states that recognize the rights of the global community to protect all of humanity,

and those that resist global norms, vary by issue. The international guidelines have had particular success in places where they have served as "best practice" models. In disaster response, such as to Typhoon Durain in the Philippines in 2006, the training provided based on the principles resulted in coordinated, targeted assistance. The cooperation among government, NGOs, the community, and private sector was very successful in mitigating the effects of the typhoon and facilitating recovery (McHattie 2008, 30).

Brain Drain and Brian Gain

Among the voluntary migrants are people who are looking for better economic opportunities or to join their families. Most developed countries have special immigration statuses for these migrants. When employers want to bring in highly skilled employees, they apply for a special visa. They are usually limited in number and controversial. Canada is considering dropping the number of high-skilled visas by 20% from the 2010 number. This has created an uproar. Many high-skilled workers claim that the visas provide a vehicle for bringing cheaper labor into the country. Many business enterprises claim that there are not enough native workers with the right education to do the job.

The *State of the World Population 2006* report of United Nations Population Fund (UNFPA) provides a thorough analysis of emigration and immigration issues. Most migration is to developed countries. The most popular destination is Europe, which accounts for about one third of immigration, and about one fourth is to North America. Migration is almost always from developing societies to those where there is more opportunity or freedom. But, with the exception of those who are just crossing a border, it is not the least educated and least skilled of nationals who leave their homeland. It generally costs money to immigrate. From professionals to manual laborers, those who emigrate tend to be better educated or have more skills than those who stay behind.

This is a double-edged dilemma for the developing country: a "brain drain" in the upper echelon of the educated class and a skill drain within the working classes. There is also a loss of the investment a country made in educating these workers. From 1990 to 2003, about 20,000 highly educated Africans left the continent each year (Mutume 2003). The brain drain is most acute in the health care industry. Sub-Saharan Africa has about 25% of the world's cases of infectious disease, but only 1.3% of the world's health care practitioners. Only 50 of 600 physicians trained in Zambia are still practicing there. In Manchester, England, there are more doctors from Malawi than are practicing in Malawi. This drain of the health care industry is devastating. In some of the smallest least developed countries, as many as 70% of the most highly educated population has left. Overall, about 10% of those with a college or higher education have left the developing world (UNFPA 2006b).

That 10% makes a difference. Twenty-five years ago, economists predicted that the economy of Japan would grow to about $5 trillion and Germany's to $4.5 trillion. They thought the U.S. economy would fall behind them and clock in third at $3 trillion. Japan did grow to $4.5 trillion and Germany to $4 trillion. The economists were close. Overlooking human behavior and migration patterns of the world's most talented people, the predictions on the U.S. economy were far off. The U.S. economy grew to over $13 trillion, thanks at least in part to talented and hard-working immigrants (Clifton 2007).

There are seven important conditions for attracting talent: law and order, food and shelter, work, economics, health, well-being, and citizen engagement—the conditions of human security (9).

Migration is not only a global flow of people, or remittances, discussed below; it is also an important source of the globalization of ideas. Females are now about 50% of migrants. Females are more likely to bring knowledge that can help further a country's development back home with them and diffuse it among family and communities (UNFPA 2006a, Chapter 1).

Destabilization

Waves of migrants can destabilize the countries receiving them. They may create pressures on social services, resources, and the environments of local areas when migrants concentrate in particular areas.

There are dangers to host countries that offer refuge. Refugees are likely to be burdensome to neighboring states, often themselves poor. Stretching resources too thinly is likely to create tensions between the displaced population and the host community. Sharing the cost of integrating migrants with global and multilateral organizations and NGOs is necessary to mitigate this impact.

Ethnic and racial balances in host states may also be tipped. Refugees may use neighboring states to launch military actions across the border. This may bring retaliation and may even escalate conflicts. Each of these possibilities brings destabilization and potential for further conflict. These dangers may cause host states to manipulate access to refugee communities and redirect the aid from humanitarian agencies (MacFarlane 2000). Global flows of refugees also provide cover for terrorists and transnational criminals who move across borders with them.

Where a dispersed community has had success, they may be mobilized on behalf of the homeland. A World Bank study found that the financial support coming from abroad can perpetuate conflict. Settled conflicts were 6 times more likely to be reignited if there was a significant community of migrants from a country in conflict supporting the conflict from abroad. This occurred in Kosovo, Turkey, Sri Lanka, and the Sudan (Adamson 2006, 192).

Minimizing the problems of migration and maximizing the potential seems to require nothing less than creating a world in which people were not "pushed" by events and opportunities out of their homelands. This is not to say that emigration and immigration should be stopped. It is rather that there are fewer problems associated with voluntary migrations. As the standard of living in Mexico and Central America increases, as it is doing, there will be less push out of these countries. Emigration rates from South America, where conditions are much better, is much lower. Improving the living conditions and providing for the security of people in developing nations would allow the world to have open borders.

Responding to Risks

The responses to the risks posed by inequality and migration presented here all fit into the current political and economic orders. Most alternate or utopian visions of globalization suggest a world that conforms more closely to socialist principles.

The Efficacy of Aid for Development Security

A debate has been brewing over the last two decades: Does aid help or hinder development? The answer seems to be that it is capable of either. Money thrown at a problem is not enough. It has to be well targeted, and there must be sufficient readiness to make use of the aid. Conditions of aid and conditions of the receiving country both impact the effect of aid on development.

A 1997 Congressional Budget Office (CBO) report on aid and development outlined a set of conditions for successful development efforts.

- A high measure of political stability and social order

- The less corrupt and self-serving a developing country's government, the more likely it is to achieve long-term development
- The means to protect property rights and maintain an efficient economic system, such as a fair and impartial judicial system or a finance ministry and central bank
- Investment in elementary education

Democracy does not appear to be necessary for development, though it may be important in some countries (CBO 1997, xiii).

In 2008, USAID reiterated similar findings: Successful development is linked to countries where there are strong commitments to good governance, education, and health, adding sound economic policies that emphasize entrepreneurship and enterprise (1–2). A report of aid in fragile states, the most difficult cases, found that governance issues were particularly important. It also found that working through the national governments was often more effective than working through civil society. This was because, however weak, national and local governments reach into more local areas and had more resources than civil society. The report stressed consideration of local governments in addition to national and the importance of fostering local preferences, which can lead to greater legitimacy for national governments. Donors should work on influencing governments in small projects at first in order to establish legitimacy and trust. Mainstream bureaucratic agencies can be rebuilt in this way, as well as connections between local and national, and government and civil society. Leaving government at any level out of the picture would leave them out of rebuilding a new, stronger social order (Manor 2007).

BOX 12.24   A Closer Look: Aid and Development

The motivation behind development aid is not above question. Many accuse rich nations of using aid in ways that benefit themselves more than it does developing countries. Several critiques by both independent researchers and the UN have criticized aid, stating that it may actually do more harm than good. Critiques make these points:

- Aid is often wasted on conditions that the recipient must use overpriced goods and services from donor countries.
- Most aid does not actually go to the poorest who would need it the most.

- Aid amounts are dwarfed by rich country protectionism that denies market access for poor country products, while rich nations use aid as a lever to open poor country markets to their products.
- Large projects or massive grand strategies often fail to help the vulnerable; money can often be embezzled away. (Shah 2013)

The Reality of Aid Network (2010), a "North–South" non-governmental network, analyzes and addresses aid issues as they affect poverty eradication, the presumed goal of global aid and institutions such as the World Bank. It has found that despite pledges to correct the misguided and wasteful use of aid, it continues. Specifically, it reports that the focus on poverty reduction resulted in only 42% of new aid dollars being spent on that goal. The amount of aid spent on the public goods targets of the Millennium Development Goals has not changed since 1995 (as measured using proxy indicators for years prior to 2000). Technical assistance, programming, and leadership on aid decisions are still donor driven, allowing for little local ownership or leadership. Aid is still coming with conditions established by the IMF and World Bank rather than policy dialog (150–151). Not only might aid be misdirected, critiques charge, but the amount of aid per capita donated has also shrunk as a proportion of gross national income (GNI) per capita (158).

The U.S. Foreign Operations Budget includes several categories that are classified as forms of aid.

South to South Aid Flows

Bolstering human security has become a global priority. One of the most recent trends is the significant increase in "South–South" aid flows. India, China, Brazil, and, to a lesser extent, Venezuela have become significant donors, equaling or exceeding the aid given by some of the richer countries of the world.

The People's Daily Online, English edition, reports that 2010 is the 60th anniversary of the People's Republic of China's participation in foreign aid, donating to 120 countries and 30 international and regional organizations. Most of the aid goes to Latin America and Africa. This aid has ranged from over 200 disaster relief projects in just the last six years, to interest-free loans, sustainable development projects, scholarships, training, medical care, and equipment. China is sending youth volunteers to provide services that include teaching Chinese language, traditional Chinese medicine, and agricultural science. It has canceled 380 debts (Jun 2010).

A U.S. Congressional Research Service report tallies China's global aid contribution in 2007 to have been about $25 billion (Lum et al. 2009, 5). If it were even half that amount, considering that this number may be inflated,[2] this puts China among the largest donors and signals China's evolving position in the political and economic global community. It also demonstrates how much China has been changed by globalization.

There are three global forces at work, one acknowledged by the Chinese government and two alleged by the Congressional Research Service. Jun's (2010) article in the *People's Daily* opens with the statement that China's aid is to "make contributions to the development of human society," among other reasons such as friendly relations. It closes on the note that

when providing assistance, China fully respected the recipient countries' sovereignty and wishes, did not interfere with their internal affairs, did not seek any political privileges, sincerely helped them to improve their self-independent capacity and won recognition and high appraisal from them.

These statements emphasize China's acknowledgment of its need for legitimacy and acceptance by the global community. It signifies that it is willing to adjust to global norms and standards: non-interference, not using aid for privilege, respecting of a country's wishes. This is not to say that China does not pick and choose which global norms it acknowledges and accepts. China is very selectively observant. China does not publicize the volume of its foreign assistance. Speculation is that because China still receives aid, it does not want its population to know how much it is investing abroad. China does not keep centralized records, and a lot of aid is given out ad hoc through a variety of government agencies and is not included in the overall aid record (Lum et al. 2009, 1).

The U.S. Congressional Research service reports that, like other countries, China uses foreign assistance strategically in its economic interest and to make allies. Infrastructure projects, resource production and extraction, telecommunications, and hydropower are its primary financing targets for loans and investment. Most of its infrastructure investments have been in countries with oil fields (Lum et al. 2009, 10–12). These supply resources and markets for China's own development. Despite its size, China recognizes that it cannot advance further without interdependence with other nations.

Juxtaposing its influence against Taiwan's is another major factor in distributing aid. In 2007, China offered Malawi $6 billion in aid and investment, and in 2008, Malawi switched its diplomatic relations away from Taiwan to the People's Republic. China has invested heavily in Africa, and only four African Nations still maintain diplomatic relations with Taiwan (Lum et al. 2010, 9). In Southeast Asia—although Thai steel and Philippine, Vietnamese, and Burmese ores are important to China—diplomacy may be China's primary motivation for assistance, rather than their economic interest. Chinese aid in these countries is diversifying, particularly in using youth volunteers to combat human and drug trafficking.

China celebrates its agreement signings with great fanfare and publicity in the host countries as demonstrations of friendship between China and the other countries. China accumulates influence with these soft power techniques. Counterbalancing the influence of the West and the United States in particular has been an important goal of China and other emerging powers trying to secure a greater voice in global affairs. Chinese investments and loans are secured by bilateral agreement and carry very little short-term risks for the host. They are offered without the environmental, political, and social safeguards and conditions of Western donor countries—concessions that may cost the host country in the long run.

China also invests in countries that other countries sanction. China's investments in military and humanitarian assistance in places such as Burma and Sudan strengthened and emboldened these murderous regimes for decades. A 2003 $200 million loan to Burma followed swiftly on the heels of U.S. sanctions. A $2.1 billion aid package to Cambodia was announced the day following the forceful deportation of ethnic Uighurs seeking asylum. The joint Burmese–China dam project in northern Burma has been a source of conflict with the Kachin ethnics living there, adding fuel to the ongoing conflict (Weston, Campbell, and Koleski 2011, 13). In September 2011, Thein Sein, president of Burma, halted the dam project because it was "against the will of the people." Although risking angering China, it demonstrated the growing Burmese commitment to reform and Burma's opening to other countries.

Brazil is also becoming one of the top donors of international aid. Like China, most of the aid does not go through the central aid agency. The budget of the Brazilian Cooperation Agency (ABC) was $30 million, but it is estimated that Brazil's actual aid—including loans, money to the World Food Program, a large commitment to Haiti, and other forms of aid—could be as much as $4 billion ("Brazil's Foreign-Aid Programme" 2010, 42). Brazilian aid is more concentrated in social programs than in economic interests. Financing the global export of the Bolsa Familia model of paying parents to send children to school is one of their major initiatives. Brazil supports and promotes the global diffusion of tropical agricultural research, agricultural programs, and HIV/AIDS treatments. These programs extend Brazilian influence, an exercise in soft power. Along with China, Brazil has been lobbying to secure a permanent seat on the UN Security Council. Being a good neighbor and global citizen helps it lay claim to such a prestigious and powerful role.

Venezuela, flush with oil money, has also used aid to promote itself. Foreign aid and foreign investment increased dramatically under the Hugo Chávez presidency. Direct investments rose from roughly 3% of its GDP annually from 1990 to 2000, to 8% in 2006. The per capita investment is higher than that of either Mexico or Brazil. From 1999 to mid-2007, Chávez made foreign commitments of about $43 billion: 17% was social investment or development assistance; the rest was a combination of direct and indirect investments. Programs for education, health care, and housing in Haiti, medical equipment and supplies in Nicaragua, and oil subsidies in many countries, including heating oil subsidies to 1 million U.S. consumers, are among the many development efforts (Corrales 2009, 76). Because many Venezuelan interests are national, not private, investments made by the government of Venezuela are similar to those that would be made by multinational corporations from the United States and other countries. They include many joint ventures in China, Iraq, and Brazil, among many other countries. Like China, there are no conditions placed on these ventures.

Among the revelations of Wikileaks' release of U.S. Department of State documents was confirmation that the latter believed that Chávez sent suitcases of about $500 million in cash to President Ortega of Nicaragua via Venezuelan diplomats, a figure that some people thought the Department had exaggerated. The money was to be used in a variety of ways to boost the power of Ortega's ruling party ("Wikileaks and Nicarauga" 2010). Chávez used aid as an alternative to the IMF and other sources that require conditions placed on how the aid was spent or accounted for, swaying them away from incorporating more free market principles or indebtedness to the global community (Corrales 2009, 77). Competing for strategic advantage through aid and investment is no longer just a tool of the superpowers.

Remittances

Remittances, the money that nationals working abroad send home to their families, are also a source of aid. Remittances have significant impact on development. In 2007, recorded remittances were $240 billion, twice the amount of official development aid. Remittances can help stabilize an economy. People send more money to friends and relatives when a country experiences economic hardship or natural disaster. This prevents the economy from slowing and stalling to the degree that it otherwise would (Ratha and Mohapatra 2007, 3). In these cases, remittances act as a stimulus package.

Remittances rose 40% in response to the economic and food crises. In 2008, remittances were topped $340 billion, three times the amount of Overseas Development Assistance of rich countries. Although it dropped to $317 billion in 2009, it is still a significant response to the crisis (Mousseau 2010, 11). The macro impact of remittances on societies is debated, but the positive impacts on individuals' lives are significant and measurable. While some of the richest developing countries receive larger dollar amounts of remittances, poor countries make a larger portion of their GDP through remittances. In Tajikistan and Moldova, for example, the remittances received in 2006 were 36.2% of their GDP (Ratha and Mohapatra 2007, 1–2).

BOX 12.25   Consider This: Empowering Women

A number of security efforts, in poverty reduction, agricultural sustainability, and conflict resolution, are now targeting women. The traditional roles of women in agriculture, household production, civil society, and care of children are directly related to security. Benefits that accrue to women are a direct benefit to children as well. Some areas where women are of particular importance are microloans, government, education, and agriculture.

Many of these are discussed in later chapters. How have women advanced in richer nations? In what ways has this promoted the welfare of the society as a whole?

Remittances, because they are gifts, are used however the receiver desires. Poverty rates, health, and education all improve when a family receives remittances. Research in Mexico, Guatemala, Nicaragua, and Sri Lanka shows higher birth weights and better health in households that receive remittances than in those that do not. In El Salvador and Sri Lanka, studies have shown lower drop-out rates. Small business investments are made possible with remittances, as they do not come with the high interest rates of microloans. Poverty reductions were found in cross-country comparisons and upward social mobility in middle-income groups (Ratha and Mohapatra 2007, 3–4).

One caution is that for societal development, the evidence is mixed. The loss of skilled workers to migration may slow growth and development. Some studies show that remittances may affect the exchange rate and make a country's exports more costly and less competitive. Generally, economic policy can be adjusted to maximize the benefits of remittances and mitigate the consequences. This is an example of ways in which the needs of societies and individuals are not always compatible.

The Global Compact

The Global Compact is an agreement to abide by ethical business practices. It was initiated in 2000 by 40 corporations joined by some influential civil society and labor organizations. It now has 6,000 corporate members from 135 different countries, as well as 2,000 civil society, labor, and other organizations.

The mission of the compact is even more pressing today than when it began 10 years ago. The need for stronger ethics, "better caretaking of the common good and more comprehensive management of risks" is more broadly understood following the financial crisis of 2007–2008 (Kell, quoted in UN 2010b).

The Global Compact has standards in 11 topical areas: human rights, labor, environment, anti-corruption, development, peace, investment, business education, expansion to more businesses and organizations in domestic locations, responsibilities for communicating on progress in these areas, and UN-business collaboration. Corporate responsibility can mitigate risk significantly. Six thousand corporations after 10 years may not be very impressive; there certainly is a long way to go. However, increasing the accountability of corporations is an important aspect of global governance.

Other forms of corporate voluntary governance organizations, such as ISO 14000, which upholds a set of environmental standards for businesses, also exert influence in compelling corporations to take responsibility for meeting corporate objectives in socially responsible ways.

Summary

Globalization has changed relationships among elements of the global field resulting in risks related to inequality and migration as well as prospects for ameliorating them.

Relationships of societies to the global system: The expansion of capitalism has increased inequality among societies. The legacy of colonialism and the Cold War left societies vulnerable and allowed core societies to concentrate power and wealth, as World Systems Theory would highlight. The distribution of wealth within societies, as well as regular meetings of elites, suggest a global elite class is emerging that has been successful in promoting their interests. Global economic and political systems make it challenging, if not impossible, for states to manage the welfare of their citizens.

Limited access to technology restricts the development of many societies. Intellectual property and patent rights exercised by powerful nations, and corporations are increasingly questioned and modified by a developing global political system that engages all countries, as well as civil society groups more than in the past.

Relationships of societies to individuals: Institutional failures within societies abound. Traditional institutions and ways of life are no longer feasible for most of the world's poor. Poor states cannot manage basic sanitation and health services. Economies are short on jobs, and many have extremely low wages. Large numbers of children are not enrolled in school. Food, even when sufficient in caloric content, is often lacking in proper nutrients.

Relationships of global system to humanity: Responsibility of the global community for providing a minimal quality of life has been recognized through the Millennium Development Goals. Treaties such as the International Covenant on Civil and Political Rights, Refugee Convention and Protocol acknowledge all societies' obligations, the obligation of global governance to assure a minimal level of security and relief to suffering of humanity by providing refuge regardless of national origin.

Agreements promising more socially responsible behavior on the part of powerful actors in the global economy are minimally an acknowledgment of corporate responsibility to humanity. These result from developments in global culture.

Individuals to the global system: Inequality within societies has grown over the course of capitalist expansion as well. Elite and disadvantaged exist within all societies. As global systems theory suggests, this may be a function of sorting individuals into classes within the global economy.

Whether inequality is an inherent characteristic of capitalist expansion or a result of the particular ways that capitalism has evolved remains to be see. If the reforms promised by the WEF, G20, and individual governments raise the quality of life for the BOP and poor within wealthy nations, capitalism may persevere. In the meantime, the global community has pledged to protect individuals and the dignity of each individual, as best it can, from threat, regardless of its source.

Questions, Investigations, and Resources

Questions

1. Debate: Do the rich nations of the world have a moral or ethical responsibility to help the developing world alleviate poverty and its related problems?

   - Do the richer nations of the world have a moral and ethical responsibility to help the developing world achieve a standard of living equivalent to the developed world?

2. Who or what bears the most responsibility for the lack of development in many countries: the country itself for poor leadership, corruption, and so on, or the global system for the legacy of colonialism, the Cold War, and multinational corporations?

3. What programs and policies show promise to lift countries out of extreme poverty?

4. Debate the responsibilities that governments should have toward each group of migrants:

   a. Economic migrants looking for a better life
   b. Politically persecuted ethnic, religious, or sexual orientation minorities
   c. Migrants fleeing violent conflict

Investigations

1. Investigate the Human Development Report Index Trends. http://hdr.undp.org/en/data/trends/

   - Which nations have the lowest human development scores?
   - Select "Hybrid: HDI Value." Examine the range of countries in each region. Find the highest and lowest in each region. What are some factors that account for this variation within region? Some sources of information to investigate the these countries are listed below:
   - CIA World Fact Book: https://www.cia.gov/library/publications/the-world-factbook/index.html
   - Country Profiles on the Human Development Index site: http://hdr.undp.org/en/countries
   - World Bank database (to investigate some of the differences among them): http://data.worldbank.org/country

2. In the United States, average weekly wages reached their peak in value in 1973 and began to decline. At the same time, the economy grew from almost $4 trillion to over $13 trillion. The general trend during these years has been for the share of income of the bottom 80% of society to decrease, while the top 20%, particularly the top 10% and 1%, increased their share.

BOX 12.26 Check It Out Yourself

The table below has the percentage share of the total income in the United States received by quintile of households and the top 5% from 1967 to 2008.

	Bottom 20	40	60	80	Top 20	Top 5	Upper Limit of Each Fifth 2008
1970	4.1%	10.8%	17.4%	24.5%	43.3%	16.6%	At the 20%ile $20,712
1980	4.2%	10.2%	16.8%	24.7%	44.1%	16.5%	40%ile $39,000
1990	3.8%	9.6%	15.9%	24.0%	46.6%	18.5%	60%ile $62,725
2000	3.6%	8.9%	14.8%	23%	49.8%	22.1%	80%ile $100,240
2008	3.4%	8.6%	14.7%	23.3%	50.0%	21.5%	Top 5% $180,000

How would you use this table to decide whether or not income inequality is increasing or decreasing in the United States?

Go to Table 666 of the Statistical Abstracts. How much has the GDP of the United States grown from 1970 to 2009? Look at both current and chained dollars. Compare this to growth in income in each category.

Source: U.S. Census Bureau (n.d.).

3. Investigate the host and home countries of international migrants. Use the UN Statistics Division *Demographic Yearbook* to find the countries that are the major contributors to population flows and the countries that are the major recipients of the flows.

- Where does the United States rank?
- What are the five highest and lowest ranking countries in each category?
- What factors contribute to their rankings?

4. Investigate immigration to the United States.

- What special categories of people are offered humanitarian assistance and protection by the U.S. Citizen and Immigration Service? Describe each category.
- How many people applied for immigration benefits during 2011?
- What is the H-IB alien status? How many people come to the United States under this status in the most recent year reported? What are their characteristics? You can find this information in the Annual Report on H-1B Petitions and the Characteristics of Specialty Occupation Worker Report.

Resources

Inequality

CIA World Factbook https://www.cia.gov/library/publications/the-world-factbook/index.html

Human Development Report Index Trends http://hdr.undp.org/en/data/trends/

World Bank Country Database http://data.worldbank.org/country

Migration

Population Reference Bureau http://www.prb.org/pdf11/2011population-data-sheet_eng.pdf

http://www.prb.org/DataFinder.aspx

U.S. Citizenship and Immigration Services (USCIS) Report on H-1B and Specialty Workers http://www.uscis.gov/portal/site/uscis/menuitem.eb1d4c2a3e5b9ac89243c6a7543f6d1a/?vgnextoid=9a1d9ddf801b3210VgnVCM100000b92ca60aRCRD&vgnextchannel=9a1d9ddf801b3210VgnVCM100000b92ca60aRCRD

USCIS Report on Petitions for Immigration Benefits http://www.uscis.gov/portal/site/uscis/menuitem.eb1d4c2a3e5b9ac89243c6a7543f6d1a/?vgnextoid=34d7898cf7927210VgnVCM100000082ca60aRCRD&vgnextchannel=34d7898cf7927210VgnVCM100000082ca60aRCRD

Humanitarian Programs http://www.uscis.gov/portal/site/uscis/menuitem.eb1d4c2a3e5b9ac89243c6a7543f6d1a/?vgnextoid=194b901bf9873210VgnVCM100000082ca60aRCRD&vgnextchannel=194b901bf9873210VgnVCM100000082ca60aRCRD

International Organization for Migration http://www.iom.int/jahia/Jahia/lang/en/pid/1

International Migration Institute at Oxford http://www.imi.ox.ac.uk/

Migration Policy Institute http://www.migrationpolicy.org/

The Bradshaw Foundation Interactive Trail http://www.bradshawfoundation.com/journey/ Based on mitochondrial DNA and Y chromosome evidence, this interactive map depicts human migration from a presumed single originating spot in East Africa.

Demographic Yearbook: Volume Three International Migration Characteristics http://unstats.un.org/unsd/demographic/products/dyb/dybcens.htm#MIGR

13

Transborder Threats to Human Well-Being: Violent Conflict and Crime

Objectives

This chapter will help you

- differentiate types of intra-state conflicts;
- analyze causes of intra-societal conflict related to the historical development of global systems, the political legitimacy of states, and workings of the global economy;
- provide examples of how international and global processes such as liberalization contribute to violent conflict;

- explain the costs of war to women and children;
- assess the role of the UN and other international bodies in conflict situations and in peace-building policies and programs;
- analyze how globalization has contributed to crime;
- cite the risks and costs of global crime; and
- discuss proposals to mitigate against global crime.

In 1985, the administration of Ronald Reagan secretly defied the arms embargo against Iran that was instituted in 1979 after the U.S. embassy was seized and 52 American hostages held for over a year. The Reagan administration offered arms to Iran in return for their help securing the release of American hostages being held in Lebanon. In this action, the administration defied their own frequently repeated policy not to deal with terrorists and condemnation of Iran as a state sponsor of terrorism. At the time, Iran was engaged in war with Iraq, who was receiving support from the U.S. military (Wines and McManus 1986).

On November 25, 1986, Reagan announced that the profits from the weapons sale were used to buy arms for the contras—counter-revolutionaries fighting in Nicaragua—in defiance of a congressional act, which explicitly forbade the administration to supply weapons to the contras. In supporting the contras, the administration supported terrorist activity, participated directly in a Cold War conflict, undoubtedly prolonging it, and assisted in the attempt to overthrow a democratically elected government.

This was a complicated affair of Cold War intrigue involving flights diverted to Israel from their originally logged destinations and shipments of U.S. planes through the Netherlands. The level of Reagan's personal involvement in the "Iran-Contra Affair" remains unknown. Through this action, government agents became a link in the underground networks that connect violent conflict and crime, and legal and illegal activity flows of money and weapons. In addition, the arms supplied to Iran undoubtedly made their way to other conflicts in parts of the world where they could have been used against American interests. Government agents participated in illegal arms trade with a country condemned by the United States as a state sponsor of terrorism, including terrorism against the United States, and used the profits to arm a terrorist group against its government (Byrne, Korbluh, and Blanton 2006).

The Challenge of Violent Conflict

"If we make peaceful revolution impossible, we make violent revolution inevitable."

John Fitzgerald Kennedy

Violent conflict, unfortunately, seems a universal of the human social condition. Wars between two or more countries and international terrorism seem to get the most attention from global audiences, but most violent conflict and terrorist activity are within countries—intra-state war and domestic terrorism. As you read about the violent conflicts that blanket the world, consider how theories of globalization might explain the conflicts and their historical roots, how the global economy contributes to the conflict, and how state and global governance have failed to maintain a stable society.

Today's wars are different than those of other eras. Violent conflict between states became a rarity following WWII. Europe became a "zone of peace" by extending and expanding integration through trade, treaty, and ultimately incorporation into the European Union. Even during the Cold War period, in which intra-state violent conflicts were fueled by the rivalry between the United States and the USSR, most states avoided direct confrontation with one another. From WWII to the present, conflicts between two or more states accounted for no more than about one fourth of wars.

BOX 13.1   A Closer Look: Armed Conflict by Type, 1946–2010

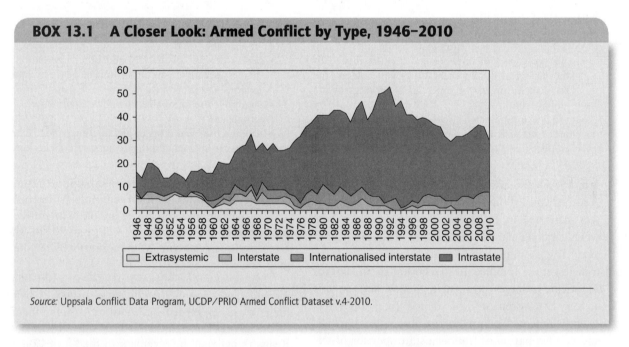

Source: Uppsala Conflict Data Program, UCDP/PRIO Armed Conflict Dataset v.4-2010.

In contrast, from WWII to the end of the Cold War, conflict within states mounted steadily. By the end of the 1970s, the vast majority of conflicts (about 95%) were intra-state ethnic and revolutionary wars. Today's wars are "globalized interstate-civil wars" (Kaldor, quoted in Shaw 2010, 324), an apparent oxymoron. These wars engage ethnic or religious groups within the same country (who see themselves as distinct from one another) in violent conflict. The groups became locked into the same state by the contemporary system of nation-states. Political borders drawn by colonialism or war settlements overlooked, or deliberately violated, the territorial integrity of religious and ethnic groups. The wars are motivated by revolution of one group who is ruled by the other, the desire for independence of one group from another, or for more autonomy within the state.

Contemporary warfare is often called *irregular warfare* because there is no clear theater of war; an entire country or region may be a battleground. There is no clear delineation of soldiers or military. Combatants may be any citizen. Entire populations may be demonized by the enemy, not just combat groups. Rwanda's Hutu majority was called to arms to rid Rwanda of the cockroaches—every Tutsi man, woman, and child. In Sudan, al-Bashir repeatedly referred to Southern Sudanese as insects, and since South Sudan's independence, has threatened to overthrow the "insect government." While war crimes are part of every war, war crime such as rape and the deliberate massacres of innocents are increasingly war tactics rather than a latent dysfunction (White 2008).

BOX 13.2   Check It Out Yourself: Violent Conflict Database

Uppsala University Department of Peace and Conflict Resolution is a valuable resource for violent conflict and peace studies. The Conflict Data Program (UCDP) has a number of interactive databases. The link below takes you to a map set where you can view a map of the world for any year from WWII to the present and display the location of violent conflicts by type of conflict. While at the site, explore the other resources that are available for your use.
http://www.ucdp.uu.se/gpdatabase/search.php

Early indicators of vulnerability to violent conflict include a number of social, political, and economic variables: political processes that are closed to discourse and opposition party participation; groups that are excluded from mainstream development; unemployed youth; impoverishment; declining public services and employment opportunities; human rights violations and other sources of indignities; and economically or politically motivated migratory flows (OECD 2001, 32).

International organizations are woefully inadequate in these vulnerable countries both in preventing conflict from erupting and in establishing a stable peace once they do. Many intra-state conflicts persist for decades. In many cases, a fragile peace is attained that breaks down months or year later, and violent conflict resumes. When warfare persists for generations, it becomes a way of life. The costs are high. From 1989 to 2000 alone, "more than 4 million people are estimated to have perished in violent conflicts . . . and 37 million people have been displaced as refugees, either inside or outside their countries" (World Bank, quoted in Gupta et al. 2004). These armed conflicts are a major threat to human well-being in their own right and a major impediment to achieving the Millennium Development Goals (UN 2010, 4).

Intra-societal violence poses thorny problems for the global community. The first is determining global responsibility for mediating the violence and ensuring the rights of people engaged in conflict.

A second is mediating the spillover effects and preventing destabilization in surrounding countries, that is, bad neighborhood effects. The third is the question of determining legitimacy—who has the authority to speak for and act on the behalf of the groups engaged in conflict? In the case of combatant groups, they may be loosely affiliated networks. One faction within a group may want to negotiate a peace, while another wants to continue fighting.

Another dilemma is ridding a country of a tyrant who has lost the confidence of the people. It used to be that whoever held power was the legitimate representative of the state. That is no longer accepted as the basis of legitimacy. Some leaders do not accept this. In nations where violent oppression is practiced, heads of state have lost legitimacy to the domestic or global audience, yet have refused to give up power. Qaddafi of Libya was brutally murdered in crowd violence during the Arab Spring uprising. In Zimbabwe, the dictator Mugabe was forced to share power after refusing to leave office when he lost elections. In Sudan, Omar al-Bashir continues a reign of terror and genocide. In Ivory Coast, Alassane Ouattara is recognized by the UN as the legitimate head of state. He won the right to rule by election in November 2010. Laurent Gbagbo, who has clung to power years longer than his term of office allows, lost the election but refused for months to give up power, returning the country to the throes of civil war. Violent conflict between forces loyal to each continued into 2011. The Ivory Coast is not a stranger to violence. Decades of violence have plagued the country. In effect, it is two nations, a Muslim north, home to Ouattara and a Christian south, home of Gbagbo. In April 2011, Gbagbo finally surrendered, after thousands of lives were lost. The UN and regional alliances such as NATO and the African Union have assumed obligations of peacemaking and conflict resolution. These are difficult roles to play without becoming party to the conflict.

Globalization is forcing the international community to intensify its role with respect to warfare within and among nations. Among the challenges is addressing historic, ongoing, and evolving injustices before they erupt into violence. This is achieved through negotiating peace in crisis situations but most importantly in building conditions for future peace. The factors relating to violent conflict are distinguished for the purposes of analysis; however, many are likely to be implicated in any one violent conflict.

Globalization and the Roots of Violent Conflict

State Fragility

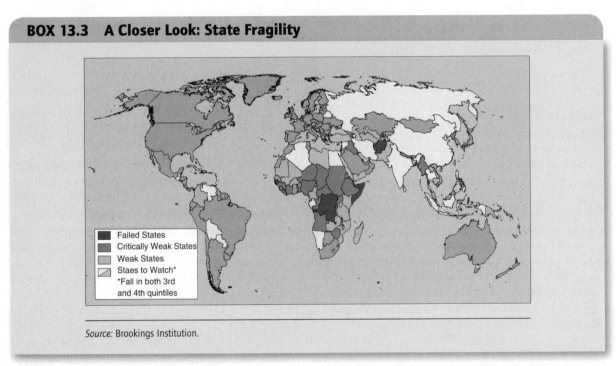

BOX 13.3   A Closer Look: State Fragility

Failed States
Critically Weak States
Weak States
Staes to Watch*
*Fall in both 3rd and 4th quintiles

Source: Brookings Institution.

Of three general governmental forms—democracy, anocracy (an unconsolidated democracy or mix of democratic and authoritarian characteristics and institutions), and autocracy—the anocracy is the most likely to dissolve into war (Marshall and Cole 2009, 17). Its institutions may not be developed sufficiently to resolve conflicts in ways perceived as legitimate. Societies that have forged a peace may revert to war if economic and political institutions cannot settle people's grievances or satisfy their demands. New democracies are also fragile. Weak institutional structures make them vulnerable to war or devolution into

anocracy. Leaders may find ways to seize more power than their post allows by circumventing or abolishing institutions (such as judiciaries or legislatures).

The Center for Global Policy and Center for Systemic Peace have been ranking societies according to their fragility, since 1995. Fragility is a fourfold function of a state's capacity

- to manage conflict, make and implement public policy and deliver essential services;
- to maintain system coherence, cohesion, and quality of life;

- to respond effectively to challenges and crises; and
- to sustain progressive development (Marshall and Cole 2009, 31).

The Brookings Institution uses a 20-point matrix ranking of 141 developing countries. Their index includes indicators in four categories:

- Economic (income and GDP)
- Security (conflict and human rights)
- Political (rule of law)
- Social welfare (human development)

Countries that do the best on these measures have good governance and enable them to overcome legacies of exploitation by colonialism and the multinational corporations. A 2008 UN Conference on "The Governance Challenge in Africa" concluded that good governance is the foundation of development and capacity building.

BOX 13.4   A Closer Look: A More Stable World

Since 1995, the world as a whole has been significantly less fragile. The greatest overall gains were in the former Soviet states and in Latin America. The countries that improved the most, by group, were Bosnia, Latvia, Croatia, and Estonia in Eastern Europe; Mexico, Guatemala, and Peru in Latin America; Equatorial Guinea, Madagascar, and Togo in Africa; and Mali, Bangladesh, and Bhutan in Asia. Mali devolved into civil war in 2012–2013, involving government troops, a separatist rebel group that seized control of the northern territory, Islamic groups who took control of the territory from them, and thousands of French and West African troops who have intervened (Seay 2013). The most improvement among these countries has been in the political dimension, reflecting democratization following the Cold War (Marshall and Cole 2009, 17–22). However, in the case of Mali, improvements may reverse if not accompanied by developments in all critical areas.

Good governance does not ensure global prosperity or security. Nevertheless, warfare rarely breaks out in stable democracies (or in stable autocracies). The most stable states are democracies that have achieved at least a lower-middle-class standard of living. "A democracy has statistically *no chance* of collapsing in a country with a GDP of at least $6,000 per capita. The democratic institutions are safely locked in place" (Kuper 2004, 10, emphasis original). Note that this is no *statistical* chance. It could happen, but it is unlikely.

Many fragile states do not have the capacity to overcome their deficiencies on their own. It is in the interests of the global community to assist. When countries cannot maintain a democratic transition or regain ground after receding, global well-being is threatened. Further improvements in global stability require more determined effort, rejection of unrealistic demands, and more patience on the part of the stable donor nations (Marshall and Cole 2009, 27).

The social structural roots of violence—whether violent crime or violent conflict and war—are failing institutions: an economy that does not supply jobs, weak government and rule of law, poor educational systems, family stressors, discrimination, and inequality. The reasons for these failures are complex. Whether within or among societies, the roots lie in globalization processes and their consequences. Interference that prevented societies from developing strong and legitimate governments are among the roots.

War and Poverty

Violent crime is the most feared characteristic of a bad neighborhood, and violent conflict is one of the most feared characteristics of a bad region of the world.

As indicated in Box 13.5, Asia and Africa account for nearly all of the armed conflict since WWII. Within these continents, it is the poorest areas where the most conflict is found. An International Peace Research Institute study of armed conflict showed that in 1993, 65 of 126 developing countries experienced war or sub-war (less than 1,000 people killed annually) violence (Smith 1994, 32–33). Violent conflict was concentrated in the poorest of the poor: 31 of these countries were in the poorest third of developing nations and 24 in the middle third.

BOX 13.5   A Closer Look: Armed Conflict by Region, 1946–2010

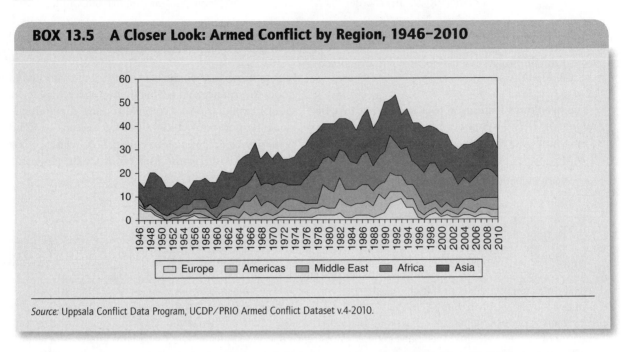

Source: Uppsala Conflict Data Program, UCDP/PRIO Armed Conflict Dataset v.4-2010.

Among the roots of violent conflict are the forces of globalization that support poverty and inequality within societies. Violent conflict is rarely contained within societal walls. It is contagious. For example, refugees from countries in conflict spill over borders, bringing economic hardship and environmental stress to host countries. Warring parties often find refuge in neighboring countries and exacerbate tensions among states. It appears that weapons from the revolution in Libya made their way to Mali to fuel violence there (Johnson 2012). Violent conflict can spread quickly across the poorest regions of the world.

Liberalization and Violence

Ironically, violence often escalates along with liberalizing political transitions. While waves of democracy are welcome, states are more subject to conflict and war increasing the likelihood of conflict and the potential intensity of ethno-political conflicts. We saw this as the level of warfare increased dramatically after WWII and spiked at the end of the Cold War.

During the Cold War, intra-state conflicts tended to be ideological in nature between groups that leaned left toward socialist economic systems and those that leaned right to free-market systems. At the end of the Cold War, ideologically rooted conflicts declined precipitously and ethnically rooted violent conflicts erupted worldwide, taking hundreds of thousands of lives and devastating countries.

In both cases, global forces were at work. During the Cold War, groups jockeying for power were able to strengthen their position by aligning with one of the super powers. If the government of a country aligned left, the opposition aligned right, and vice versa. Insurgency and conflict ensued regardless of who was in power. When the Cold War ended, ethnic groups that had been disempowered under Cold War regimes fought back.

Consider the situation of Africa depicted in Box 13.6. Interstate conflicts have been infrequent and few. Nevertheless, war has been a chronic condition for many African states. Since independence in the 1960s, most countries have experienced upheaval and instability. About half of the anti-colonial wars turned into civil wars following independence. During the Cold War, Africa averaged about 10 countries engaged in intra-state war every year. These were political wars, ideologically based. After the Cold War, the average number of conflicts rose annually, peaking at 18 in 1993. This was driven by a rise in ethnic conflicts. As ethnic conflicts subsided, declining to eight by 2004, more directly political conflicts took their place (Marshall 2005, 4).

Globalization is implicated in myriad ways. Inequality along ethnic lines that resulted from colonialism, the spoils of the world wars, political and economic interference during the Cold War, and community breakdown due to industrialization, structural homogenization, and immigration

BOX 13.6   A Closer Look: Armed Conflict in African Countries 1946–2004

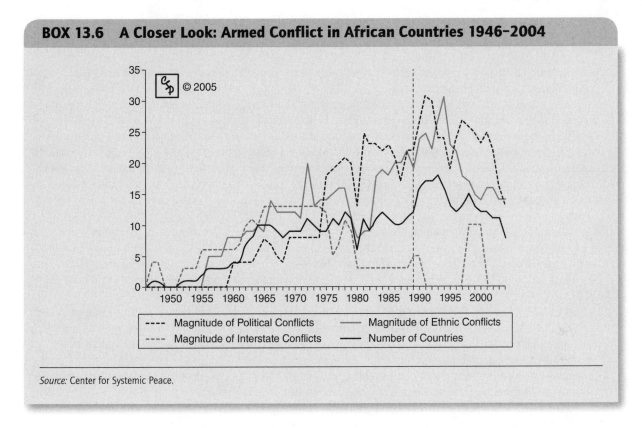

Source: Center for Systemic Peace.

pose threats and stimulate conflict (Conversi 2010, 349). Americanization, or the perception of it, also catalyzes conflict. Resistance to Americanization may reflect cultural protectionism that feeds nationalism and ethnic conflict (362).

Liberalization can bring conflict even without ethnic strife. Historically, conflicts do not occur when times are at their worst; they occur when people see that things can be different. Democratic processes following periods of autocratic rule shake up the system, leaving a power vacuum that competing groups try to fill. Without strong legitimate institutions to mitigate conflict—political parties, elections, a judiciary, and so on—conflict turns violent. This is evident in the patterns of warfare in Africa, Asia, and Eastern Europe. Two periods of liberalization, independence and the end of the Cold War, spiked not only the level of war but of violent conflict in general. The Arab Spring is the latest demonstration of this globalization effect.

BOX 13.7   A Closer Look: Genocide Post-WWII

Contemporary genocides have been too frequent. Following their communist revolution in Cambodia, the Khmer Rouge violently oppressed anyone who could be the slightest threat to their power, killing and imprisoning millions. In Rwanda, decades of armed struggle between Hutu and Tutsi followed independence from Belgium. In 1994, when the Hutu president negotiated a power-sharing agreement with the Tutsi, Hutu downed his plane, blaming Tutsi. It set off a genocidal war that some Hutu military and insurgents had been planning. Over 800,000 people were slaughtered in a matter of months.

In Sudan, violent oppression by the Arab government of the African Christian and animist southern and western regions has claimed millions of lives. Genocide continues in the Darfur region. Although Southern Sudan won

(Continued)

(Continued)

independence in 2011, war between north and south continues. Al-Bashir, president of Sudan, has vowed to wipe out the "insects" of Southern Sudan.

The objective of genocide is to "substantially destroy the real or putative social power" of a group; it includes any form of coercion and violence to this objective, not just mass killing, rape, and torture (Shaw 2010, 313). It is clear that genocide is not a rare phenomenon in the global age. The globalization of democracy has, unfortunately, escalated genocidal violence. Global norms require that governments legitimize their rule. The need to win elections inspires nationalistic fervor to eliminate or severely suppress opposition. Violence to expel or minimize opposition group(s) makes an election a predictable win (324). It also consolidates support within the dominant group. The argument made in cases of genocide, "If you aren't with us, you are against us," convinces many of those opposed to the violence to engage in the atrocities.

Perceived threats from international surveillance and intervention may also inspire genocidal violence. The power-sharing agreement between Hutu and Tutsi in Rwanda was perceived as a threat to Hutu power. The NATO intervention in Kosovo threatened Serbian control and led to an increased slaughter of ethnic Albanians there. The U.S. invasion of Iraq led to Sunni violence against Shi'a as Sunni foresaw the erosion of their power (Shaw 2010, 324–325).

Despite the number of brutally violent genocidal wars, there is evidence that this trend is waning. The number of violent conflicts, after spiking at the close of the Cold War, decreased sharply within a few years. The ethnic violence in Eastern Europe that followed the Cold War has been largely managed, although not particularly well, by the international community. The Global South, in contrast, is captive to the collusion of global forces. Diffusion of the ideal "nation state model, confusion of demos and ethnos, rise of fundamentalism, weakening of liberalism and socialism, decline of class politics, the globalization of democracy, the requirement of global legitimating leave multiethnic societies vulnerable" (Shaw 2010, 325–326).

Ethnicity and Nationalism

Nationalism accompanied the waves of independence that birthed dozens of new nations during the 1960s with the end of colonialism and new democracies in the 1990s with the end of the Cold War. Nationalistic fervor has also given rise to groups seeking their own nation, to take over the country in which they live, or more control over their own affairs within existing countries. There are about 70 active separatist movements in Africa, Asia, Central Asia, Europe, and the Americas (Beary 2008, 87). Many of these groups engage in violent conflict at least sporadically and some are engaged in outright war.[1]

BOX 13.8   A Closer Look: The Red Garden

In Sri Lanka, children played a tragic role in the rebel movement. Children who have lost their parents are taken from camps to "the Red Garden, the University of the Tamils" hidden in the jungle. There the children are trained to be "Black Tigers," human bombs. The children don't know anything of the war, only their leader. They are not dying for a cause or independence for the Tamils. They are dying for their leader and will be heroes. Once chosen, they have no choice. Once they put on the jacket, they cannot turn back. They have to go and die (Manorajan 2002).

The conflict in Sri Lanka was among the longest. It began with oppression of the Tamil minority following independence in 1948. In 1976, the Liberation Tigers of Tamil resistance group was formed. The first phase of ethnic war formally began in 1983. Despite peace talks and a cease-fire in 1985 and

2002, the war continued until 2009. The Tamil Tigers made liberal use of child soldiers, particularly as suicide bombers—recounted in the story of the Red Garden. After the war, over 11,000 rebel forces surrendered, including many child soldiers. As in many instances where rebel factions do not agree on the terms of peace, this peace is not yet complete.

Some movements are revolutionary. In these cases, they do not want to establish a new country but want to govern the country. Other nationalistic conflicts rage not over separation or revolution but autonomy. Autonomy gives a group more control over their own region and affairs. They do not want to conduct foreign policy independently or have their own currency. They want significantly more sovereignty as a politically defined unit within the country.

Some analysts view movements toward separatism or autonomy as "tearing at the . . . political foundations of the nation-state" (Gilpin 2002, 239). An alternate view is to see politically active ethnic movements as further globalization of the system of nation-states. These movements reaffirm the importance of states to people. They attempt to create nation-states closer to the ideal of a nation-state as a self-governing people. If external threats or violence (real or imagined) are necessary to give rise to the solidarity of the nation-state, then the division of ethnic nations by colonialism, their enclosure within multination boundaries, and the systematic positioning of one group against the other by colonial powers created a situation of the threat coming from within (Katongole 2005).

BOX 13.9   A Closer Look: The Democratic Republic of Congo

With borders porous to refugees fleeing violence and ethnic groups divided across and among nations, one country's violence spills over to its neighbors, usually of a similar ethnic mosaic. Power relations in one country are disrupted when rebels from another find sanctuary among their ethnic supporters and launch attacks on home governments from camps in neighboring countries.

Despite the brutal slaughter of civilians, the world watched in 1997 as Laurent Kabila led a Zairian Tutsi militia (backed by the Rwandan Tutsi government, Uganda, and Angola) in a successful rebellion against the self-aggrandizing, thoroughly corrupt dictatorship of Mobutu Sese Seko. The Democratic Republic of the Congo was reborn. This success came after almost 40 years of Mobuto rule and 40 years of ethnic and civil strife, which had often erupted violently.

Peace was short-lived. The Rwandan and Ugandan forces did not leave Congo. They were intent on rooting out Hutu who fled to the Congo, taking government positions in Congo and enriching themselves with the Congo's precious minerals. Kabila, fearing internal insurrection because of the foreign forces and his own corruption, tried to force them out. Rwanda, Uganda, and Burundi joined with Congolese rebel groups and mounted an insurrection against Kabila. Angola, Namibia, Chad, and Zimbabwe joined in the fight to support Kabila. With eight countries fighting in the Congo and millions of lives lost, it became known as Africa's First World War. (Kabila was assassinated in 2001 and succeeded in the presidency by his son, who was then democratically elected in 2006.) A truce was signed in 2003, but fighting continues among armed groups of nearly every faction. The corrupt Congolese army rapes, pillages, and kills routinely. Over 20,000 UN peacekeepers were in the Congo as of May 2010. The Congolese government views this as a violation of their sovereignty and wants the troop level reduced dramatically. In May 2010, the UN agreed to reduce their force by 2,000 (Gettleman 2010). The UN secured another truce agreement in 2013, but this saga is far from resolved.

The end of the Cold War released countries from their role as strategic pawns of the superpowers. It also meant the loss of superpower support, which dissipated the power of dictators. Many, if not most,

African nations have been subject to a similar pattern of violence, driven by ethnic or communal division. Since 1990, armed rebellions involving communal minority groups have occurred in 25 African nations.

Box 13.10   Armed Conflict in Asian Countries, 1946–2006

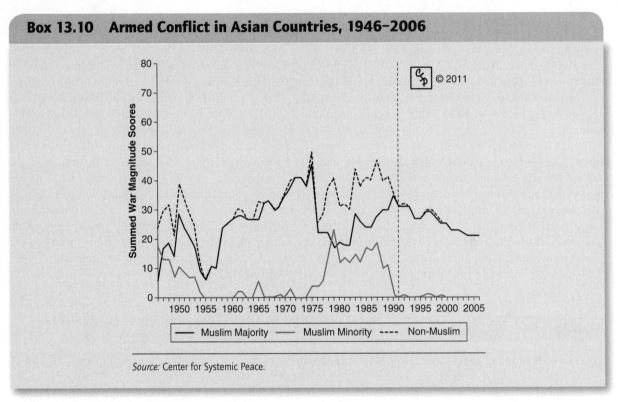

Source: Center for Systemic Peace.

South Asia, East Asia, and the subcontinent did not fare much better. The independence movement of Kashmirs against India began immediately after India got independence from Britain and has not ended. One of the few interstate protracted conflicts, there have been three wars between Pakistan and India over Kashmir. There have been countless acts of terrorism and violence. Other ethnic groups within India have also rebelled.

Eastern Europe and Central Asia have also been hot spots. With the fall of communism, the Soviet republics and Warsaw Pact countries gained independence from Soviet domination. Some escaped ethnic violence, but for many of these new states, violence is ongoing. Yugoslavia came into existence as a multiethnic kingdom after WWI and a state of six socialist republics of different ethnicities—Croatia, Macedonia, Montenegro, Serbia (Kosovo, Vojvodina, and Serbia), Bosnia-Herzegovina, and Slovenia—following WWII.

The breakup of Yugoslavia, following the fall of the Iron Curtain, reignited hostilities among these groups, some ancient, others the legacy of WWI, and some related to genocidal activities during WWII. Slobodan Mileosevic issued violent reprisals as republics tried to secede. Only Macedonia and Slovenia were able to break away without much bloodshed. The secession of Croatia cost thousands of lives and caused massive displacement and migration of Serbs in Croatia to Serbia. The separation of Bosnia-Herzegovina triggered extreme violence, classified officially by the UN as genocide. Serbian genocide against Croats and Muslims in Bosnia-Herzegovina resulted in over 250,000 deaths, massive internal displacement, and refugee migration. The Dayton Accord, negotiated in 1995, divided Bosnia-Herzegovina into four sections: one for each ethnicity, and a mixed Sarajevo. It remains very fragile. Ethnic groups are largely segregated and the presidency rotates among the three groups.

BOX 13.11   A Closer Look: The Kurds

Bridging Eastern Europe and Central Asia sits Kurdistan. It is the home of about 1 million Kurds. The Kurds are the largest ethnic group fighting for independence (Beary 2008, 98) and a homeland. Kurdistan is not a country, but a geo-cultural area. Kurdistan is dispersed through Turkey, Iraq, Iran, and Syria. Kurds are a minority in every state where they exist. The treaties following WWII almost granted them statehood but ultimately left them divided. They are a people divided across nation-states. People still determine their fundamental interest the basis of an *ethnie,* or ethnic community—people with a common history and heritage. Kurds, like hundreds of ethnic groups who correctly perceive themselves as oppressed minorities without a state, are not a *demos*—a public with a common interest—nor are they included as part of a larger one. The defeat of Iraq following its invasion of Kuwait led to the establishment of an autonomous Kurdistan Region in northern Iraq. This is the closest the Kurds have to a homeland.

In 1990, Kosovo—a supposedly autonomous region of Serbia—declared its independence. It was not recognized nor addressed by the Dayton Accords. Kosovars themselves were divided between those favoring peaceful or armed resistance to Serbia's continued rule. The violence escalated in 1996, and Serbia also unleashed genocidal violence against Kosovo. The international community finally stepped in with NATO airstrikes in 1999, forcing Serbia to withdraw after over two months of strikes. Kosovo was administered by the UN from 1999, with its independence in question until the International Court of Justice ruled in 2010 that its 2008 declaration of independence, while not official, was not illegal. As of July 2012, Kosovo does not have a seat at the UN, and its status as independent is not recognized by all nations. It is recognized by the United States, most of NATO, and most of the European Union.

Milosevic's genocidal violence resulted in his indictment in 1999 and arrest in 2000. He was held in the Hague to be tried by the International Criminal Tribunal for crimes against humanity in the case of Kosovo. This was the first time that an indictment was issued against a sitting head of state. Later, indictments for his actions in Croatia and Bosnia-Herzegovina were added. (The indictment of Pinochet came from European Courts when he was no longer head of state, but was very significant for establishing universal jurisdiction for crimes against humanity.)

The breakup of the Soviet Union into 15 republics, beginning peacefully by declaration, led to brutal ethnic violence within and among some of the newly independent states. Georgia declared independence

from Russia in 1991. Two ethnically Russian provinces of Georgia, Abkhazia and South Ossetia, declared independence from Georgia, engaging in on-again, off-again provocations with Russian support and assistance. In 2008, Georgia moved militarily into the South Ossetia, and Russia responded militarily. In 2013, Russia provoked Georgia by installing barbed wire fences extending into Georgian territory. Georgia and most of the world considers them occupied by Russia. Like Kosovo, this is a situation where the question, "Who has the right to declare a nation independent?" affects the lives of hundreds of thousands of people.

Armenia and Azerbaijan, two former soviets that are now independent, have fought continuously with one another since 1988. Their argument is over Nagorno-Karabakh, an area assigned to Azerbaijan by Moscow in the early part of the 20th century. It is ethnically Armenian. This conflict has hampered the economic and political development of each country. At the current time, Nagorno-Karabakh and some surrounding areas of Azerbaijan are controlled by Armenian separatists. This situation is similar to the India–Pakistan longstanding conflict over Kashmir—part of India officially but Muslim, not Hindu—and the conflict over Kosovo, which is ethnically Albanian.

Although liberalization can ignite violence, few ethnic conflicts turn violent in stable democracies. The Basques straddling the border between France and Spain, the Flemish and French in Belgium, and the Sardinians in Italy have behaved violently in the past yet rarely do in the contemporary era. Northern Ireland is an exception.

BOX 13.12   A Closer Look: Ethnic Conflict in Western Asia

The news on Monday June 14, 2010, brought word of increasing violence in Kyrgyzstan, where Kyrgyz and Uzbeks had been had been warring for about five days. Estimates of deaths range from about 120 to 200, with 1,000–2,000 injuries in just that short time ("Thousands Flee" 2010). Women and girls were raped. Uzbek towns were leveled by fire. In some areas, Kyrgyz homes were marked with spray paint and left standing while all around them homes were burnt to the ground ("Uzbek Leader" 2010). Reportedly 100,000 fled within days.

(Continued)

(Continued)

Some people were being shot en route and arriving in Uzbekistan wounded, where a "humanitarian catastrophe," according to the Red Cross, unfolded. It was the worst violence there since 1990 ("Thousands Flee" 2010).

Background: Both the Uzbek and Kyrgyz are Sunni Muslim. In Kyrgyzstan, Uzbek who own many businesses tend to be better off than the Kyrgyz. In April, President Bakiyev, who was widely accused of gross corruption, was overthrown in a coup. He had a broad base of Kyrgyz support in the south. Uzbek supported the interim government that replaced him. The new government was scheduled to hold a referendum. Some accused Bakiyev supporters and Kyrgyz of starting the violence to block the referendum needed to legitimize the government. Uzbek accused the military of condoning the violence. Surrounding states have similar ethnic mixes. Violence in Kyrgyzstan could become tinder to light a much bigger fire throughout the "neighborhood."

The former states in the USSR are referred to as *states in transition* because they are transitioning from one political form to another. During this process, governments are likely to have some features of democracy along with autocratic features. They are likely to fluctuate back and forth. Some may stay in this inchoate state. As demonstrated in this vignette, political transitions are fragile. Recently, overall, there have been fewer failures of anocratic (mixed democratic and autocratic) regimes than historically (Marshall and Cole 2009, 12).

Fundamentalism and Religious Violence

One of the most vigorous responses to globalization has been the worldwide resurgence of fundamentalism that emerged in the late 1960s and early 1970s. Religious affiliation functions similarly to ethnicity, as a source of identity and group cohesion. It is not surprising that violence has broken out along religious as well as ethnic fault lines. Fundamentalist religious views tend to gain traction in times of political and social uncertainty. Defined by intolerance of ambiguity, fundamentalism offers an uncompromising world view. As such, it affords people a clearly defined identity and protection from threats to identity. Fundamentalisms do not recognize secular and religious differentiations, favoring political rule based on religious precepts. Because of their fervor, fundamentalists—Christian, Jewish, and Islamic—often exercise a considerable level of political muscle. Political crusades of fundamentalists are imbued with religious, even divine, fervor. This has been true of the far right globally, who claim their political practice serves the will of God, and secular fundamentalists of the far left, who in the case of communism substitute political ideology for God.

Christian fundamentalists in America and American political fundamentalists invoke emotionally charged images—such as the "real America" and "America as a Christian nation"—to infuse politics with very particularistic world views. Protecting the U.S. national identity from globalization gives political positions an aura of religious righteousness. Most of the battles of fundamentalists in wealthy nations are fought in courtrooms. However, when groups feel that they have no recourse, they may turn to violence. "Soldiers in the Army of God," who advocate killing doctors who perform legal abortions and whose members have killed medical personnel and injured many more, and Christian Identity, a white supremacist group also responsible for murders, are on the FBI's terrorism list.

The global resurgence of Islamic fundamentalism in the mid-1970s led to a rapid rise in armed conflict in Muslim societies. Prior to that, violence in non-Muslim societies was greater than that of majority-Muslim countries or countries with a significant Muslim minority population. From 1979 to about the late 1990s, violence in majority-Muslim countries has exceeded that in non-Muslim societies. At times, the conflict is between Shi'a and Sunni, or sects within these major divisions. In these cases, it is usually because one sect represents a secular government, which the other wishes to overthrow in favor of a religious government, political Islam.

The most significant Islamic fundamentalist victory is the 1979 revolution in Iran. Secular and religious groups—some fundamentalist and some not—joined to overthrow the Shah. They were fueled by decades of oppression, energized by months of strikes and violent clashes with army and police forces loyal to the Shah, and hungry for the promises of democracy. The radical Islamic Shi'a faction was able to wrest power from the other revolutionary groups. This was the first successful replacement of a secular government by a political Islamist movement.

BOX 13.13   A Closer Look: Technology and War

High technology fuels the most primitively armed and brutally violent wars. Precious minerals are responsible for the performance qualities that make cell phones, MP3s, cameras, computers, and other devices "high" tech. Ironically, The Congo, with the second lowest per capita income in the world and victim to one of the most savage and deadly wars of the contemporary era, is cursed rather than blessed with the wealth of these minerals. Control and sale of these minerals are fueling the atrocities of the decades-long war.

Children are called into conflict as soldiers, couriers, and sex slaves. One of the oldest weapons of war, rape of women and children, is common. Efforts to end trafficking in these minerals to pay for this war require coordination by governments, the high tech industry, the corrupt army, and us, consumers of the high-tech devices who potentially have blood on our hands every time we use one of these devices.

The Taliban, members of the fundamentalist Wahhabi sect of Sunni Islam, gained control of most of Afghanistan during its civil war. Afghanistan had been weakened by a decade of Soviet invasion and war. Civil war among groups of warlords followed. The Taliban emerged as the most successful, capturing control of all Afghanistan except the northern provinces. Leaders among the Taliban coalition were not all religious extremists. Many groups who joined the Taliban were not ideological and joined for practical reasons as the Taliban grew more successful. Recently released U.S. Department of State documents indicate that the United States was acutely aware of the diversity among the leadership and Osama Bin Laden's growing influence on Mullah Omar, the top Taliban leader at the time. This caused dissention among their leaders because many wanted to purge the Taliban of connection to terrorist Osama bin Laden. Those leaders were purged from the Taliban. The Taliban was never recognized as the official government of Afghanistan by the UN.

Ironically, from these anti-globalization roots, political Islam emerged as a force of globalization. Unlike American Christian fundamentalism, Islamic fundamentalism transcends nationalism. Islamists advocate a "pan-Islamic" identity that would unite people of Islamic religion, language, and culture from all over the world.

BOX 13.14   A Closer Look: Armed Conflict in Muslim Countries, 1946–2010

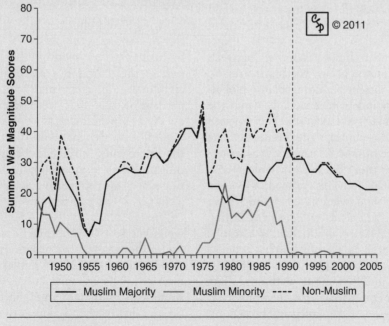

Source: Center for Systemic Peace.

As shown in Box 13.14, conflict within majority-Muslim countries began to subside in 2000. It increased again after a year or so. The revolutionary turmoil across the Arab nations beginning in 2011 spiked the level of violence in majority-Muslim countries. The 2011 protests and uprisings in Arab nations are not religiously motivated, nor have religious opposition groups played lead roles in the revolutions, although they are actively participating in elections. Whether the revolutions will result in majority-Muslim democracies such as in Turkey or Indonesia, further violence as the states try to establish stable democracies, the establishment of more Islamist states if political Islamists take control of any new governments, or an unstable condition of fragility and conflict emerges—will take decades to unfold.

The Irish independence movement began as a movement for more autonomy during the take-off phase of globalization, a period that also sparked waves of nationalism. Religion and nationality intersected to produce strong sentiments on both parts. When home rule was granted, British Protestants concentrated in Northern Ireland formed an armed resistance to Irish autonomy, prompting the Irish Catholic majority to form a paramilitary organization, leading eventually to a war for Irish independence. Independence gave the Irish their own nation, but partitioned the Protestant British Northern Ireland and preserved it as an autonomous part of the United Kingdom. This suited Britain, because the industrialized north was the richest part of Ireland and the northerners, but not the Catholics living in Northern Ireland.

Nationalistic and religious conflict between Catholics and Protestants in Northern Ireland flared again in the current period of intense globalization, along with independence movements the world over. From 1963 to 1985, waves of violence erupted, naming that period "The Troubles." The armed groups of the turn of the century became terrorist groups. Since the 1998 accord, violent conflict in Northern Ireland has calmed; however, splinter groups remain dangerous. The groups have resisted giving up their arms to cement a lasting peace. In 2002, IRA activists crucified a Catholic man (Donovan 2002). In March 2009, Catholics killed two soldiers and a policeman. Several car bombs detonated in 2009–2010, without killing anyone. As in other countries, youth unemployment may be the real trigger of the violence. Throughout its history, the violence in Northern Ireland has resulted in many occasions where Britain has imposed direct rule.

The Israeli–Palestinian conflict has cost many more lives than the Irish conflict. Considered a religious war by most, this intra-state war pits a country, Israel, against a minority group within, the Palestinians, who have lived without a homeland since the end of WWII. Conflict over the small parcel of land that both Israelis and Palestinians claim is at the center of global geopolitics. Iran, for example, has repeatedly pledged to seek the destruction of Israel. Support of the Western democracies for Israel, a democracy, is one of the reasons for their tension with Middle Eastern countries.

Global norms that guide the development of new constitutions call for "constraining majority rule with rights and review" (Sweet 2008, 235). Minority rights are recognized as human rights. Certainly, these will influence new governments as they are formed. Whether they will prevent further bloodshed remains to be seen. Even where constraints are written into constitutions, states are plagued with religious and ethnic fault lines where minority rights have not been upheld and constitutional democracy or rule of law has failed to take root. This leads to violence.

Women and Children in War

Women and children bear the greatest casualties of contemporary warfare, including as combatants and as victims. In irregular warfare (where the war is not segregated from society), civilian casualties are high (White 2008). Seventy percent of casualties are women and children on average (Mayanja 2010).

Children are particularly vulnerable. Despite the increasing influence of global norms and international treaties, the use of child soldiers increased dramatically after the Cold War, although it has probably declined since its height. Estimates place at least 250,000 and probably well over 300,000 children in warfare by 2002—a figure thought to have grown by 2006 (Achvarina and Reich 2006, 128). Whereas global norms and international law are successfully constraining some aspects of human rights abuses, they have broken down when it comes to child soldiers. It is

BOX 13.15   A Closer Look: Child Soldiers

These boys fought in the Democratic Republic of the Congo.

used boy and girl child soldiers to fight in the Democratic Republic of the Congo and allowed their sexual abuse. From the issuance of the arrest warrant in 2006, international justice moved very slowly, causing people to question whether or not there would ever be justice. In 2012, he was finally sentenced to 14 years in prison. Both the prosecution and defense are appealing as of this writing. The prosecution wants a longer sentence, and the defense wants to present new evidence. In the meantime, the use and abuse of child soldiers continues in the Congo and elsewhere.

Structural features of societies are certainly the underlying reason for child soldiering. Poverty, the increasing number of orphans, and smaller, lighter weaponry have increased the use of child soldiers. In poor countries, children are breadwinners—soldiering is one way that they can make money. Children without parents find a substitute family in the armed groups. In some cases, parents are shot when they refuse to conscribe their children. Children can bear small arms, although they cannot necessarily use them well. Each of these factors plays a role, but each is part of a much larger problem, and none of them provides insight into child soldiering in particular. Their chief failure is that they do not differentiate the many countries that have these characteristics, are at war, and do not have high numbers of child soldiers from those that do (Achvarina and Reich 2006, 133–138).

not just rebel groups or insurgent factions using children in war. States are responsible as well. In Liberia 30% of the children in conflict were engaged by the government. In Sudan in 2004, 76% were in government forces and in Angola as many as 33% are employed by the government (Achvarina and Reich 2006, 129).

The trial of Thomas Lubanga Dyilo was the first trial of the International Criminal Court. Lubanga

BOX 13.16   A Closer Look: Laptops for Children in Conflict Regions

On a bright note, the "One Laptop per Child" program has targeted children in war zones. One of the priceless disasters in war is human intellectual capital. The loss of years of education impedes a person and a society for generations into the future. "The XO laptop has a special place in children's education in regions that are disrupted by ongoing violence," said Nicholas Negroponte, founder of the organisation ("One Laptop per Child" 2010).

Achvarina and Reich (2006) compared the rates of child soldiers to rates of poverty and orphans, for 19 African conflicts. Africa was chosen because they had the highest concentrations of both conflicts and of child soldiering since 1975. In the 1990s, about 40% of child soldiers globally were in Africa. The average age of child soldiering in some African con-

flicts has dropped to 10 or 11 years old (130–131). Their analysis shows no relationship between either poverty rates or rates of orphans and child soldiers (144–147). They found a striking correlation between attacks on refugee and internally displaced persons camps and rate of child soldiers. The lack of protection for refugees in camps is a significant reason why there is child soldiering in some conflicts but not in others. A regression analysis of poverty, orphans, and access to camps by belligerents shows that only access to the camps is related to the rate of child soldiers (147–150).

The global community can do something about this. While the level of poverty, arms trafficking, and the persistent conflicts are long-term concerns for the global community, use of children for soldiering, sex, support, and suicide bombers in armed conflict can be mitigated in the short run. As it is now, many people are gathered in unprotected camps, including children without parents or with parents who can do little to protect them against armed militants and government troops. Ironically, being in the camp puts them at greater risk. Camps are attractive targets. Gathering a group of children who are congregated in a camp is easier than if they were scattered.

Sexual violence has long been war tactic. Now, however, it violates global norms and international law. Like many dimensions of international law, prior to the contemporary period of globalization, there were only a few weak means of enforcement. When sanctions are used, their effect can be diminished by states eager to take advantage of the situation for their own economic or strategic benefit. Militaries have not been held accountable for the sexual violence of their soldiers. A review of nearly 300 peace accords from 1998 to 2009 showed that only 18 mentioned the sexual violence known to

have occurred (Goetz and Jenkins 2009). Over 60,000 women were raped in Bosnia, and approximately 64,000 incidents of sexual violence occurred in Sierra Leone from 1991 to 2001. These are not unusual. This is typical of violent conflict. "The bodies of women and girls have become battlegrounds" (Mayanja 2010).

The UN Security Council Resolution (SCR) 1325 (2000) on women, peace, and security has done little to curb violence against women, although many activities have been undertaken. Follow-up SCR 1888 (2008) and 1820 (2009) put stronger accountability and enforcement measures into practice. Two days before the passage of SCR 1820, a peaceful demonstration in Guinea was suppressed by violence. One hundred and nine women were raped in public, in the stadium where the demonstration was held. The new resolutions call for more monitoring and reporting, training of peacekeepers, and more accountability for the activity of military. The resolutions also require involving more women in peacekeeping, peace building, and post-conflict deliberations, and, perhaps most importantly, they call for making prosecution of offenders a priority (Goetz and Jenkins 2009).

The obligation to protect women and children falls squarely on the international community. Global norms concerning conflict and human rights require global governance to reach into state boundaries to protect the vulnerable, particularly in conflict-ridden areas.

BOX 13.17   Consider This: State Terrorism

Robespierre, one of the revolutionary heroes of France turned despotic, justified terror as a domestic policy in the time of revolution to protect the virtue, liberty, and equality of the people. This justification of terror to protect the state has been repeated throughout history. Nazi Germany and the Soviet Union under Stalin terrorized their citizens to establish control. More recently, Pinochet in Chile, Milosevic in the former Yugoslavia, al-Bashir in Sudan, Qhaddafi in Libya, among many others have used similarly terroristic tactics against citizens. Global norms now condemn and put state terror on trial as crimes against humanity. When terror is used by a state as a tactic against citizens of other nations, it is considered a war crime.

Terrorism

For most of human history, fortifying the territorial perimeter was a viable defense against threats of violence. That defensive posture became meaningless with the advent of the intercontinental ballistic

missile in the 1950s. Contemporary terrorism erodes the relationship of territoriality and the threat of violence altogether.

Each country has defined terrorism on its own terms. Thus, there are hundreds of definitions, and the United Nations has been stymied for years trying to establish a common definition. The definition of the U.S. FBI calls terrorism

> a violent act or an act dangerous to human life, in violation of the criminal laws of the United States or of any state, to intimidate or coerce a government, the civilian population, or any segment thereof, in furtherance of political or social objectives.

Domestic terrorism is carried out by citizens or residents of a country against a target (governmental, military, or civilian) of their same country. They are based and operate entirely within one country. International terrorism is "committed by a group or individual who has some connection to a foreign power or whose activities transcend national boundaries" (FBI 1999, ii).

BOX 13.18   A Closer Look: Muslim Extremism

It is important to note that there is little support for terrorism in the Muslim world. In Lebanon, terrorism is most widely accepted among those nations polled. There, 39% said that terrorism was sometimes or often justified. In Jordon, it was 20%, Pakistan 8%, Indonesia 15%, Turkey 6%, Nigeria 34%, and Egypt 20% (Pew Research Center 2010, 65). Suicide bombing was also rated very unfavorably, ranging from a high of 39% in Lebanon down to only 6% in Turkey. Support for terrorism has been on a downward trend since 2002 in all the countries polled (66). In no country was there a majority with a favorable view of Osama bin Laden or al-Qaeda (67).

Similarly, there is little support for Hezbollah or Hamas (the political branch of Hezbollah). The exceptions are in Palestinian territories, where 61% have a favorable view of Hezbollah, and Jordan, where 51% do. For Hamas in Jordan, 56% have a favorable view, and Egypt 52% (Pew Research Center 2010).

These definitions are problematic. Terrorism is a form of violent conflict and, as such, is difficult to distinguish from war when over 1,000 people are killed in a year or a lower level conflict between otherwise warring parties. The deliberate killing of innocent civilians may be the defining characteristic of terrorism, but even that is murky, as civilian casualties are a given in irregular warfare, so almost any violent act could be said to deliberately target civilians. Terrorist groups finance themselves in many ways, including trafficking in arms, drugs, or people. Olson, Director of the National Counterterrorism Center (NCTC), noted that many groups are multidimensional, being terrorists, insurgents, and criminal gangs (2012, 2).

The era of contemporary terrorism began in the late 1960s (FBI 1999, 15). There have been shifting patterns of terrorism, resulting from various combinations of global events. The wave of terrorism in the 1960s was spawned by transitions in power and struggles between adherents of left and right ideologies over the control of governments. This era of terrorism was closely related to the global Cold War that transformed the world into a struggle for ideological influence and strategic allies.

Another distinguishing feature of this period was that through to the 1980s, terrorism was dominated by formal groups such as FARC (Colombia), Hezbollah

(Lebanon), Shining Path (Peru), Abu Nidal (aka Fatah, Palestinian), and Tamil Tigers (Sri Lanka). Hezbollah has cells in the United States to raise money and conduct intelligence, but their main supporter has always been Iran. Other groups were also sponsored by states. States also committed terrorist acts, such as the 1988 bombing of Pan Am Flight 103 by Libya. During the Cold War, both the United States and USSR sponsored terrorism by supplying arms, training, and other forms of support to guerilla groups who often used terrorist tactics. This is hardly distinguishable from international—state-sponsored—terrorism.

Within the United States and globally, most terrorism in the early decades was domestic terrorism of the left. Groups associated with radical movements such as Weather Underground in the United States and the Red Brigade in Italy acted to bring radical change to their own countries. As the Cold War wound down, domestic terrorist attacks came more often from the right of the political spectrum. The FBI's first recorded domestic attack by a right-wing anti-government group in the United States was a 1983 attack by the Posse Comitatus (FBI 1999, 17). Through the 1990s, these anti-government groups and coalesced around the militia and patriot movements, focusing on the illegitimacy of the U.S. government (30). Domestic terrorist groups of the right have also had a racist agenda, such as

World Church of the Creator and Aryan Nations. Special interest groups such as the anti-abortion group Soldiers in the Army of God also arose in this period. These domestic terrorists have an international agenda as well. Although there are many different beliefs that feed terrorism, one of the common ones among anti-government groups is that the U.S. government is conspiring with the UN (and sometimes Russia) to form a new world order or world government.

BOX 13.19   A Closer Look: Types of Attack

The Global Terror Database catalogs terrorist incidents from 1970 to 2011—with periodic updates. Each incident is categorized by the country attacked, region, nationality of target, type of attack, and type of weapon. You can create stacked charts for visual representations of the data. Colored layers for each variable are stacked on one another, giving an "at a glance" depiction of the overall volume of attacks in a given year and the volume of each type. Changes in the patterns of incidents are easily discernible. Elements within each category, such as attacks against the United States or bombings can be examined individually. Data can also be examined by year. Below is the aggregate data by type of attack.

Type of Attack	Total 1970–2007
Bombing/Explosion	44,777
Armed Assault	26,038
Assassination	14,273
Facility/Infrastructure Attack	7,134
Hostage Taking	5,189
Unknown	2,595
Unarmed Assault	640
Hijacking	436

The URL for the interactive database is http://www.start.umd.edu/gtd.

Most terrorist groups are not global in their targets. Most have specific grievances against either a government or a particular group. Historically, the greatest proportion of terrorist attacks globally has been domestic. In 2002–2005, for example of the 24 incidents in the United States, 23 were domestic acts of anti-government and anti-abortion groups. In the United States, most recent domestic terrorism has been acts of religious fundamentalists (NCTC 2010, 22). There were several terrorist acts by Islamist extremists in 2009. They resulted in two fatalities and are the most significant incidents since 2001. Attacks within the United States have similar roots to those globally. Religious fundamentalist terrorist groups fight against encroachment on their religious identity by secularism that is growing globally. Other domestic terrorists, such as many in the militia movements, fear a global government, led by the UN—this is also seen as a threat to U.S. identity. Racist groups see African Americans, Hispanics, Asians, or others as a threat to "real America."

International terrorist groups, such as al-Qaeda, that target Western countries have similar objectives, resisting the loss of their cultural identity to modernization, secularization, and Westernization. Sunni Islamist extremists were identified with about one half of all attacks globally in 2009. This must be interpreted with caution. Most of these attacks were in Iraq and Afghanistan. They were the deadliest group, followed by Al-Shabaab and al-Qaeda (NCTC 2010, 9). Like poverty, warfare, and crime, terrorism is concentrated into few geographic areas.

Only 20 countries account for 71.93% of terrorist attacks from 1970 to 2007. The United States ranked 20th on the list, with about 1.6% of attacks. The United States ranked 15th in fatalities, due to the September 11, 2001, attacks. Without this tragedy, the United States would have dropped from the list. U.S. targets abroad were attacked, the most devastating being the 1983 attack on the Marine barracks in Lebanon. Colombia, Peru, El Salvador, India, and Northern Ireland suffered the most attacks, and Iraq the most fatalities (LaFree 2010).

Advances in communication technology and the ease of travel have enabled new forms of terrorism to emerge, increasing the threat of international terrorism in Western Europe and the United States. The pattern of terrorism shifted in the 1990s. Rather than terrorism by formal groups, it is now conducted by loosely affiliated networks rather than formal organizations and states (FBI 1999, 35). Infiltration of terrorist groups is more difficult because of sleeper cells—small groups of terrorists who may live in a target country for years while they make preparations. Plans are made far in advance, money is put in place, and communication with the larger terrorist organization is infrequent, if it occurs at all.

Mass communication and delivery of pro-terrorist messages have made "self-radicalization" more common. Rather than terrorists being recruited in person and educated person to person in the ways of terrorism, young people are visiting websites to learn the motivation for and techniques of terror. Networks of non-state actors, along with some

states who sponsor them, direct terrorism through flows of money, people, and communications. Therefore, they are able to choreograph violence anywhere in the world, from anywhere in the world.

The threat of terrorism to states, particularly democratic states, is severe. The availability of tools of mass destruction, hatred for the Western world, and the ease of entry into democratic states make them highly vulnerable. Furthermore, punishment has no deterrent effect on use of violence when suicide is the vehicle for delivering the weapon. Information gathering is difficult when contemporary communications make the flow of information and money logistically easier for the terrorist and harder for intelligence and law enforcement to detect (Keohane 2001).

Tactics shifted as well. Aside from the tragedy of the September 11, 2001, attack on the United States by al-Qaeda, airplane hijacking and hostage taking diminished. In their place are much more deadly bombings. A tactic that emerged in the 2000s is the "secondary attack," an attack on the responders to an initial attack. "Person-borne improvised explosive devices" diminished in use while suicide-vehicle attacks have increased. This shift is occurring faster in Africa and somewhat slower in Afghanistan and Pakistan, each ending 2008 with almost equal numbers of each type of attack. In Iraq, suicide vehicular attacks were significantly greater than person-borne suicide attacks. They were about equal numbers of each in 2008 (NCTC 2010, 13).

BOX 13.20   Consider This: Terror and Justice

Terrorists claim supreme authority: the right to use violence on the basis of an authority superior to both the states' authority and the authority of the global system of states. Terrorists are the only direct challenge to the authority of states. Other global actors—international non-governmental organizations, multilateral organizations, multinational corporations, transnational capitalism—generally operate within the confines of state authority and the global system of states, regardless of the power and influence that they exert on it. None claims the authority to use violence, not even global crime groups, although they do use it.

Is the use of terror ever just? Who has the right to declare it just? What criteria constitute the just use of violence? What influenced your decision? Do other voices seem legitimate?

It is worth mentioning that hate crime is similar to terrorism in several respects. Its objective is to intimidate and scare, even when it ends in death. Hate crimes and terrorism are violations of criminal codes.

Unlike common crimes, hate crimes and terrorism are not motivated by the usual desire for money or goods. They are not motivated by rage, anger, or any other emotion directed to a specific person. Hate crimes and terrorism are politically motivated. They are directed at a group or category of people to intimidate and oppress or weaken. Both are problems globally. The revival of hate groups shares some common roots with terrorism; both come from fear of threats to national, ethnic, racial, or religious identity as well as worsening economic conditions. Although the United States and Europe are relatively resistant to terrorist acts, hate crimes are problematic in each.

Terrorism is a challenge to "national sovereignty as the locus of the exclusive right to employ terrorizing violence against a foreign foe" (Buck-Morss 2009, 47). Many of the forces that give rise to terrorism are the result of globalization, and some are reactions to globalization. Ironically, terrorism advances globalization by highlighting the mutual contingency of states. Terrorism is undoubtedly a global phenomenon. Terrorists build global networks using very modern technologies: the Internet, cell phones, and press releases in audio and videotaped messages to the mass media. With the constant news coverage of terrorism, it is easy to lose sight of the important parameters of terrorism that belie some of the popular images. It is important to remember them.

Among the factors that give rise to terrorism are

- prolonged unresolved conflicts;
- dehumanization of victims of terrorism in all its forms and manifestations;
- lack of the rule of law and violations of human rights;
- ethnic, national, and religious discrimination;
- political exclusion; and
- socio-economic marginalization and lack of good governance (UN General Assembly 2006).

Resolving these requires global effort. States are rendered more interdependent in combating the rise of terrorism and providing security in the face of terrorism. They are required to be more responsive generally to partner nations, international institutions, and multilateral policy making (Keohane 2001). Mutuality is required in more than the direct fight against terrorism; it is required in every aspect of international relations. States need to cultivate allies so that they can count on them when they are needed.

Global governance has taken up the issue of combating terrorism. There are 16 universal anti-terrorist instruments, as well as relevant UN Security Council resolutions. The *United Nations Global Counter-Terrorism Strategy* was adopted by member states in

2006. It outlines a three-pronged approach. First, it promises the resources of the UN to combat the conditions that promote terrorism These are long-range strategies such as negotiating conflicts; promoting dialog to foster tolerance; strengthening a culture of peace and international law; prohibiting incitement to terrorism; achieving development goals, including youth in society through employment; strengthening rule of law, human rights, and good governance efforts; and creating, where they are desired, victim assistance systems.

Second, states promise to cooperate meaningfully in a global counter-terrorism effort. Some of the measures that states promise are to refuse to harbor or support terrorists, to prosecute and extradite terrorists and help bring them to justice, and to cooperate on timely information exchange. They promise the cooperation of their law enforcement agencies across borders on matters of terrorism and on crime fighting linked to terrorism, such as drugs and arms trafficking, money laundering, and smuggling of nuclear and other deadly materials. They also pledge to reinforce the protection of vulnerable targets. There are many more specifics.

Third, the parties to the treaty pledge to help build the capacity of individual states and the UN to combat terrorism. This strategy, along with the laws that develop, is a step in the development of a global anti-terrorist regime (UN General Assembly 2006).

Sanctions, Strikes, and Rogue States

Traditional international law calls for respect of the sovereignty of states by other states. First strike could be justified as a defensive act, if and only if an attack was imminent. This was articulated by U.S. Secretary of State Daniel Webster in 1837. A first strike must be necessary and in proportion to the threat. In contrast, the UN Charter authorizes pre-emptive use of force even more restrictively: only when authorized by the Security Council. It is less clear about the consequences of pre-emptive strikes without Security Council sanction (Welsh 2003).

Pre-emptive strikes as a "coalition of the willing," in Secretary of Defense Rumsfeld's words, became part of U.S. military strategy following the U.S. attack on Iraq in 2003. It was incorporated into doctrine in 2004 as part of the five-year review of strategic plans (Hendren 2005). In a speech at West Point, Bush reiterated his pre-emptive strike policy and defined it as part of his legacy for fighting terrorism. "'If we wait for threats to fully materialize, we will have waited too long. So we made clear that hostile regimes sponsoring terror or pursuing weapons of mass destruction would be held to account'" (quoted in Dinan 2008). The United States reconsidered the pre-emptive strike and in the end withdrew its most aggressive statement from its military strategy.

Japan is considering the pre-emptive option. North Korea and Iran have nuclear ambitions. When North Korea tested ballistic missiles in 1998, Japan opened discussions with the United States to develop a missile defense system. In 2003, Japan decided to adopt a system in conjunction with the United States and opened the door to consideration of pre-emptive strikes. North Korea continues to provoke Japan and the international community with nuclear tests in 2006 and 2009, firing missiles over Japan, and the sinking of a South Korean warship, despite UN Security Council warnings and sanctions. Despite sanctions having exacted a heavy toll—North Korea's economy shrank 9.7%, and they were expected to run out of food in June 2010—they remain unresponsive (Toki 2009). Floods that followed a devastating drought in 2012 brought food aid to North Korea, which remains heavily reliant on food aid and continues to risk aid by defying international calls to stop uranium enrichment. Over 24 million North Korean suffer from chronic food shortages ("UN: North Korea" 2012). North Korea launched a missile in December 2012, bringing further condemnation from the international community and sanctions against its leaders, including freezing the assets of several of its institutions.

In the meantime, China has helped North Korea weather international sanctions. China, which has historic ties with North Korea, and whose old guard considers it an ally, avoids confrontation with North Korea and in so doing hopes to avoid conflict on the peninsula. It also hopes to avoid the fall of the North Korean regime, which could send millions over the border into China. It has participated in the "Six-Party Talks" along with United States, South Korea, Russia, Japan, and North Korea, and signed off on the Security Council sanctions. Still, China continues to negotiate the balance between its role on the Security Council, its increasing ambition to be a world leader, and its support for North Korea. It is marketing its economic transactions with North Korea as economic development and humanitarian assistance (Bajoria 2010).

Iran has also been the target of frequent sanctions by the UN Security Council despite frequent reluctance from China and Russia. The sanctions have affected the Iranian people yet have done little to persuade the Iranian government to give up its nuclear ambitions. The president of Iran, Ahmadinejad, accepted a deal from the United States and its allies in October 2009 but reneged when he came under fire from his domestic opposition. He made a separate similar agreement with President Lula of Brazil and Prime Minister Erdogan of Turkey in May 2010. By this time, Iran had been able to increase its uranium supply, rendering the agreement of little value, according to the UN Security Council. The latter moved ahead with sanctions in June 2010. Although China has joined in the sanctions, it has prevented sanctions against Iranian oil, which China needs. With China's oil hunger making up for some of the losses due to sanctions, there is not any obvious way to force Iran to the negotiating table. The June 2010 sanctions could also be interpreted as giving "a green light to a US-NATO-Israel military alliance to threaten Iran with a pre-emptive punitive nuclear attack using the Security Council as a rubber stamp" (Chossudovsky 2010).

The problem for global governance is figuring how to make a safer, more secure world in light of global threats from states—on either end of a pre-emptive strike—that escape sanctions or allow their people to suffer them.

Peacemaking and Peace Building

The Cold War determined the global structure and balance of power that has shaped the flux and flow of war and peace from WWII through to the present. The UN Peacekeeping Force was created during the Cold War specifically to mitigate violence erupting throughout Latin America, Africa, and Asia. As permanent members of the UN Security Council, the United States and the Soviet Union had the capacity to block UN action on these and other global issues. Even though each used its veto liberally to keep the UN from intervening in conflicts where its interests were at stake, the UN established 13 peacekeeping operations during the Cold War. The peacekeeping operations are credited with containing "dangerous conflicts which might otherwise have escalated into nuclear East-West confrontation" (UNDPI 1998).

BOX 13.21   A Closer Look: Sri Lanka

The USAID mission in Sri Lanka tries to build bridges across ethnic groups through cooperative projects such as the People's Forum, rebuilding "Peace Road," which borders Singhale and Tamil communities, and engaging Tamil and Singhalese youth in distributing mosquito nets.

The missions were concentrated in the Middle East, beginning with overseeing a truce between Israel and Palestine in 1948. Others included several involving Israel and Egypt, Syria, or Lebanon. Two involved India and Pakistan. All of these remain hot spots today. In these missions, the main function of the UN forces was to help reach agreements, supervise withdrawals and cease-fires, and to act as a buffer. In some cases of intra-societal strife such as in the Congo in 1960, the UN acted in support of the government, at the government's request, to prevent civil war. But their golden rule was neutrality and non-interference in support of victims.

With the end of the Cold War, the nature of the conflict changed, and the UN changed its mission. The UN was pulled into the internal affairs of states to fulfill its mandate to secure peace and justice. The mission changed

from traditional military peacekeeping tasks to multidimensional operations which involved political and humanitarian work such as the supervision of elections, verification of human rights practices or the delivery of humanitarian relief. Many of these new missions were inserted into internal conflicts and major humanitarian crises in "failed" and disintegrating States. (UNDPI 1998)

Peace building came to include conflict prevention.

The number of peace-building missions has remained steady from about 15 to 17 annually since the end of the Cold War. However, the number of uniformed troops deployed has risen dramatically. After a surge in the mid-1990s, the number of troops dropped to below 20,000. By 2009, it was just over 98,000 and in 2010 rose to over 120,000 (UNDPI 2011, 81). The number of peacekeepers deployed continues to rise.

Building Peace

The challenges of building peace in impoverished societies wracked by conflict are severe.

BOX 13.22   A Closer Look: Reconciliation

Shoghla, 19, teaches ex-mujahideen commanders who fought the Soviets for 10 years, and then fought each other. They have now laid down their arms and are being trained under a USAID program to use computers, write and edit documents, surf the Internet in Dari and Pashtu, and prepare for jobs in the peacetime economy.

De jure power sharing has been one method of forging peace in deeply divided societies. South Africa, Bosnia-Herzegovina, Fiji, Northern Ireland, Sierra Leone, Liberia, and Iraq all accepted negotiated power sharing to escape, or attempt to escape, years (often decades) of devastating internal conflict and war. This *consociational* model of governing has become a normative standard to escape winner-take-all majority rule (Reynolds 2006, 20). Nevertheless, power sharing along lines of religious and ethnic divides may exacerbate differences rather than ameliorate them. Candidates need only appeal to their own constituency to win office. Extreme candidates tend to win over moderates. Polarization is a likely and frequent outcome. Those states that have instituted power-sharing arrangements tend to remain divided and fragile. For example, in Bosnia-Herzegovina, 15 years after the genocidal conflict between Serbs and the Croatian and Muslim groups ended, reconciliation is evasive. Efforts of the international community working with civil society groups have made little progress in creating a stable state structure or integrating ethnic groups. The country is divided into three administrative units and segregated into ethnic enclaves. A rotating three-person presidency—one Serb, one Croat, and one Bozniak—remains, as do desires on the part of many for separation of the ethnic territories and unification with their ethnically homogenous neighbors, Serbia and Croatia.

Strategically designed electoral systems show promise for resolving some of these difficulties. Systems that require candidates to appeal across ethnic and communal fault lines may help ameliorate them. Where ethnic divides run deeply, electoral fixes to include both sides in government, even moderates, will probably not be enough. Establishing democratic governments after lengthy histories of colonialism, violent oppression by dictators, or violent conflict among ethnic or religious groups requires complex processes of reconciliation. These processes may take decades and experience varying levels of success.

- In cases such as Bosnia-Herzegovina, where three ethnic territories in a conflict-ridden state lie beside states of the same ethnicities, should maintaining the state be the priority of the global community? What might be the result of annexing ethnic territories to the contiguous states of the same ethnicity? What problems might be solved? What problems might be created?

Global civil society organizations and international organizations are instrumental in facilitating reconciliation. Partnerships among domestic civil society groups and the international community are essential to success. Their efforts are not always effective, but there are a number of promising strategies. Reconciliation efforts in Southern African countries are instructive. The lessons below are drawn from case studies in Malawi, Mozambique, Namibia, South Africa, and Zimbabwe. They are discussed collectively below as Southern Africa (Colvin 2007).

In these Southern African countries, domestic and global civil society organizations played a pivotal role. They provided services directly and indirectly by pressuring governments on behalf of victims. Trauma counseling, victim-support services, demobilization, meaningful memorials, and reparations were all part of the reconciliation efforts (Colvin 2007, 326). The complex problems victims confront from poverty to ill health to lack of education must be sorted out and incorporated into reconciliation. Rather than bureaucratic processes driven from the top down, the involvement of civil society made victim centered reconciliation possible. When states make reparations or policies to help victims, these should be victim-driven. Victims know what they need and what their priorities are, and will have ideas for designing constructive interventions. Usually these processes are taken out of the hands of victims. This marginalizes and disempowers them.

Local culture needs to be respected, as well. Reconciliation built on local customs, religious preferences, local authority, and decision making will be more easily integrated into the fabric of victims' lives. In Southern Africa, a holistic approach, offering medical, educational, financial, legal, institutional, and legislative aid, was necessary. Reforms were integrated with one another through partnering of civil society groups and government. Typically, as in Southern Africa, relations between civil society and government are strained. More and better government involvement is needed, particularly if domestic civil society organizations in these conflict-ridden countries is weak.

One way to forge a linkage is through women. This accomplishes several interrelated goals. In the Southern African conflicts, as in most others, women and children suffer disproportionately as victims; they need to be made the first priorities. Their resources for coping are severely limited. Because women are responsible for social reproduction—child birth, child rearing, maintaining households,

and much agricultural labor—every benefit to them goes directly into strengthening the community generally. Women are also very involved in civil society. Therefore, prioritizing their needs and the needs of their children fosters social stability. At the same time, it makes the important link between civil society and government in a way that has a good chance of being perceived as legitimate and effective.

In December 2011, the United States announced a National Action Plan on Women, Peace, and Security. Where women have full rights and opportunity, societies are more peaceful. Thus, the plan institutes a gender-responsive approach that emphasizes strengthening women's rights; their access to health, education, and other services needed for healthy development; building their leadership and problem-solving capacities; and getting them into more roles in government and security related decision making bodies (U.S. Department of State [USDOS] 2011).

Allowing conflicting groups to work together has also been valuable in Southern Africa. This allows them to practice interacting with one another in a limited forum. People can get a sense of what reconciliation might "feel like." In addition to the large-scale institutional level formal changes, informal interventions should be cultivated as well. "Less planned, more local, and non-state contexts" can integrate those on the margins and provide opportunities for mixing. While informal programs of civil society groups are sometimes criticized for being inefficient and unaccountable, they have proven necessary in the Southern African experiences of reconciliation (Colvin 2007, 332–335).

Despite the importance and success of grassroots design and organization of reconciliation, it will take global efforts to accomplish reconciliation among the many warring factions. International legal and human rights principles need to be strengthened and invoked. A vast amount of financial and human capital aid must be donated globally, then directed and coordinated holistically and locally. States need to apply pressure to other states so that they will implement the processes of reconciliation in earnest. Global civil society organizations need to facilitate strong local participation in decision making, instead of taking over the processes. This is a restorative approach to conflict resolution, making the society whole.

Transnational Organized Crime (TOC)

How do insurgent or terrorist groups get the supplies that they need to wage war against a country? How do impoverished groups make a living in a country where they are denied opportunity? States are, after all, the determinants of who gets what and, conversely, who does not. We have seen the impact of this state power on world poverty, how some groups literally starve in lands of plenty. Another area where this is relevant is in global crime. People can be determined to get what they need and sometimes what they merely want. Others get what they need by supplying others with what they want—sometimes illegally. The haves and have-nots and the local and global connect through crime in complicated ways.

One of the darker globalization effects is transnational crime and the easier movement of criminals and criminal contraband. Global crime syndicates exploit labor in developing countries to counterfeit everything from prescription medications to movies. Counterfeiters make billions of dollars annually. We may buy counterfeit products not considering how we are contributing to exploiting labor or the thousands of legitimate jobs lost to counterfeiting. Use of illegal drugs puts people on the receiving end of criminal networks that stretch from small farmers in developing nations barely making a living, to rebel or terrorist farms hidden in mountains and forests, to international criminal organizations that participate in terrorism and human trafficking.

Opportunities for crime, motivation for crime, and vulnerability to crime have all coalesced to heighten the dangers of crime. More open borders, more efficient transportation and communication, and the ease of moving people, goods, services, and information around the world provide as abundant opportunities for criminal activity as for legitimate activity. Increasing global disorder, particularly in corrupt and failing states, makes for weak law enforcement and good hideouts. Along with strife and disorder which create lawless territories, the globalization of crime has become one of the most severe threats to national and global security. International crime is as threatening to human well-being as political conflict and war (Stepanova 2010, 5).

Opportunities for new forms of crime and cross-border coordination of age-old crimes come from increasing technology, enabling swifter travel, transport, and instantaneous global communication. Counterfeiting and forgery are relatively old crimes. But imagine the array of crime made possible just through breakthroughs in more sophisticated copying techniques—music and movies on audio and video tapes have given way to CDs and DVDs that are cheaper to produce, easier to transport, and provide a higher quality copy. Easy online access to detailed imagery of brand products makes them easier to copy precisely. Whereas a fake Gucci used to be relatively easy to spot, it now takes an expert. Cybercrimes reduce the risk to the criminal and open up opportunities for crimes such as financial fraud and embezzlement that used to be available only to white-collar criminals. Even more tragically, Internet communications open a world of child targets to pedophiles and other predatory criminals. Increased vulnerability makes for easier targets as well. The elderly and the poor are frequent targets of Internet scams. Men, women, and children trying to escape desperate poverty or persecution make easy targets for human trafficking.

Although there will always be some level of crime, increasing motivation comes from the global proportions of economic distress. Somali pirates, working off the coast of arguably the "most failed" of the failing states, reportedly started to ply their extremely risky trade not to get rich but to survive. They have, for the most part, conducted their piracy as business executives, taking hostages but usually treating them well in exchange for ransom. They have rarely killed, although 2011 may mark a turning point in their strategy. It may be a response to the 33-year sentence of a pirate the week before—who had not killed. At least one pirate reported that from now on, he would kill hostages before being captured. Anyone who tries to rescue hostages will only find dead ones (Associated Press 2011). But another turning point may also have been reached. The number of successful attacks and attempts has decreased. The business of pirating may no longer be as lucrative given the increased international naval patrols and more vigilance on the part of the shipping industry (Anyimadu 2013).

Coca, poppy, and marijuana growers find drugs more lucrative than food crops—although coercion is also used to get people to grow illegal crops. Without the drug trade, some local economies may crash. The inability of some governments to pay living wages or sometimes any wages to police and some public servants also makes crime an attractive alternative survival strategy. Not every criminal needs money for survival. As materialism spreads globally, so does the attitude that there is no amount of money that is enough money. It seems as though greed has no limit. This escalates crime and corruption among police, politicians, and business executives. State officials aid and abet international crime through corrupt practices such as issuing falsified licenses and documents or aiding in money laundering. Some states sponsor terrorism and some are associated with international crime through the drug and arms trades in particular. Sometimes states act like organized criminal gangs. North Korea has long supplemented its national budget through counterfeiting and drug sales.

The EU Organized Crime Threat Assessment cautions that the consequences of the global economic crisis may result in conditions favorable for TOC expansion. There may be more market for counterfeit and smuggled products. TOC may supply irregular or undeclared labor for legal enterprises trying to cut costs. Unfair competition may deprive law-abiding businesses of business. Loan sharking may increase as entrepreneurs in serious financial difficulty may cooperate with TOC for advantage. TOC may be able to penetrate further into the legitimate world. Combating international crime during an economic crisis requires more coordination among jurisdictions and homogeneity in approaches world over (Europol 2009, 59).

Most global crime, because of its complex nature obtaining, transporting, and distributing goods and services, is organized crime. In 2000, the UN adopted the Convention Against Transnational Organized Crime to which three protocols—on human trafficking, arms trafficking, and migrant smuggling—have been added. The Convention defines a TOC group as "three or more persons, existing for a period of time and acting in concert with the aim of committing one or more serious crimes or offenses . . . in order to obtain directly or indirectly, a financial or material benefit" (UN 2004, 5). This definition is less restrictive than that used by the U.S. FBI in defining organized crime in United States.

TOC groups tend to be defined ethnically. With modern technology, ethnically based criminal networks in different countries can ally with one another, forming migration-based networks (Adamson 2006, 194). These are among the most truly global systems. Although as individuals, each criminal presumably has a citizenship, it is not related to the criminal process. They owe no allegiance, nor do most pay taxes to any country. (Profits from criminal activity are taxable in U.S. law although not many are collected.) They by definition are not bound by any domestic laws. If caught, they could be tried in any number of domestic courts, as well as the International Criminal Court for their crimes against humanity.

Combating international crime begins with international cooperation and justice in stopping crime at its source in underdevelopment, failed states, and zones of conflict. But intensive cross-border coordinated efforts of monitoring, intelligence, and operations are also needed. States too often view sharing information, resources, and policing as a threat to sovereignty. It should be viewed as a way of strengthening it. Police activities are stopped at borders, but criminals are not. That is the real loss of sovereignty.

The UN Security Council has urged international cooperation in combating TOC. At a Security Council meeting in February 2009, Antonio Maria Costa, the Director of the UN Office on Drugs and Crime (UNODC) said the best antidotes to international crime are development and security. Crime, development, and violent conflict overlap. Unfortunately, international crime fighting networks are not as organized as the criminals are.

Some steps that he recommended are as follows:

- Greater participation and implementation by states in the Convention against Transnational Organized Crime, not yet ratified by about one third of member states
- Upgrading criminal justice systems in vulnerable countries
- Investigation of how crime networks operate
- Developing a way to measure progress

- Plugging the "black holes" in financial systems, such as "informal money transfers (hawala), offshore banking, recycling through real estate and liquid assets" that allow money laundering
- Eliminating corruption, which allows crime to prosper (UNODC 2010)

Interpol (International Criminal Police Organization) is an independent multilateral organization with 188 member states. It is trying to better coordinate cooperation with and among national police to share information, investigations, police training, and international policing activity. It is not a political or a military organization and does not participate in political activity or war (Interpol 2010). Interpol's six priority crime areas are drugs and criminal organizations, public safety and terrorism, financial and high tech crimes, fugitives, trafficking in human beings, and corruption. They also investigate crimes against humanity, crimes against children, environmental crimes, and intellectual property crimes.

Organized crime has costs far beyond the economic. Violence accompanies organized crime. It can corrupt global civil society. Networks that build an international public sphere provide opportunities for illicit activities. The involvement of UN staff and military acting under their command are painful examples of this. Organized crime challenges and sometimes conquers weak and failing states or portions of them. Dependence on transnational crime networks can develop, as it does in states with weak institutions and poor economies, creating severe security issues (Adamson 2006, 194).

There are too many places in the world that are

> out of government control and too scary for investors and tourists. Those were precisely the places where smugglers, insurgents and terrorists operated. Unperturbed and undetected, they ran fleets of ships and planes, trucks and containers, which carried tons of drugs and weapons. Their activities were mostly discovered by chance: a crash of a phantom plane; a drug ship short of fuel; a fortuitous seizure of an illicit cargo. (Costa, quoted in UN Security Council, 2010)

Covering the array of global crimes is beyond the scope of this book. Each criminal activity discussed below highlights not just a different type of crime, but also a different aspect of the problem, establishing an international protocol and standards, getting goods to markets, and potential threat and costs.

Human Trafficking

Human trafficking is a human rights issue, an international crime issue, and a migration issue. It is one of organized crime's largest revenue generators, generating about $9.5 billion annually. About 600,000 to 900,000 people are trafficked across borders annually, and in combination with domestic trafficking (which could well involve TOC), the total is between 2 and 4 million (Wagley 2006, 5). The Protocol to Prevent, Suppress, and Punish Trafficking in Persons, Especially Women and Children is Annex II of the UN Convention Against Organized Crime (UN 2004). Even some of those who are voluntarily trafficked, often for the promise of a job, end up in slavery. The USDOS reports that there are about 12.3 million adults and children globally in some form of slavery or forced servitude (2010, 7). Until the UN Convention, there had been little state or international prosecution of human trafficking action and no international activity (359).

Trafficking is related to all of the problems of vulnerability: poverty, conflict, the desire for cheap labor, the status of women and children, and corruption. Persons are trafficked for slave labor, child soldiering, drug running, prostitution, and domestic service. Some are kidnapped. Others are lured or tricked into bondage with offers of good jobs or even marriage. Some go voluntarily, their best chance at survival. There is very little risk for the traffickers. Laws are often weakly enforced or not enforced at all. Even though the UN Protocol expressly states that initial consent is irrelevant where exploitive tactics are subsequently used, the victims are often treated as criminals if they turn to the legal system because they came into a country illegally, they were acting as prostitutes, or they were involved in other illegal activities such being a drug "mule" (UN 2004, 43).

Article 2 states the purpose of the protocol is to bring nations together to prevent and prosecute human trafficking, protect the victims, and promote cooperation in the endeavor (UN 2004, 42). As of 2010, 116 nations had created or changed national laws to combat human trafficking. Although these are steps forward toward a global regime to address the problem, prosecution has been weak. There were only about 4,166 successful prosecutions worldwide in 2009 (USDOS 2010, 7). In the United States, USDOS is required by congressional order to report how countries are meeting their obligations to combat human trafficking. These reports set forth a set of normative guides to help countries develop successful policies and pressure them to enact effective laws and institute programs. Under the act authorizing the reports, the U.S. president is given the authority to sanction governments not meeting minimum standards (Wagley 2006, 8). This could be an important strategy to encourage states to comply with the UN Convention and prosecution of traffickers.

The guidelines for good law include

- a broad definition of coercion that would include all forms—financial, physical, reputational, or anything that would compel a person to continue in their activity to avoid harm;
- a well-articulated definition of trafficking, to include all forms, not just recruitment and transportation;
- provision for the complete care of the victim—mental, physical, and legal;
- immigration relief for victims regardless of their legal or illegal status; and
- legal services to address financial compensation for the crimes committed against them (USDOS 2010, 13).

The standards for evaluating countries are specific relating to how seriously and diligently they try to prevent trafficking through such means as educational campaigns about the dangers and techniques of trafficking; whether the laws treat trafficking as seriously as comparably serious crimes; the vigor with which they investigate, charge criminals, and prosecute them or extradite them, if appropriate; whether they cooperate with other countries in investigations and prosecutions; whether the government monitors its efforts; and whether or not it has made serious efforts to reduce demand (USDOS 2010, 366–367).

The articulation of global norms is a first step in establishing effective programs. A well-articulated set of laws not only enables individual countries to address the issue, but also allows for much better coordination. Like other areas of international law, these standards may be used as means of reputational accountability, to generate compliance from allies in informal quid pro quo, or to apply sanctions if deemed appropriate.

Countries that rank poorly in human trafficking prevention and enforcement are rife with other problems as well. Weak or corrupt governments, little freedom and civil liberties, and poor economies increase vulnerability to trafficking and erode societal or governmental capacity to deal effectively with organized crime in its many manifestations. A USDOS (2010) comparison of rankings on human trafficking standards found the "trafficking in persons scores" ranked very similarly to Freedom House civil liberties scores and Transparency International's corruption index. Weak human trafficking programs, low civil liberties, and high corruption are, not surprisingly, found together (29–30). It will take coordinated transnational public, private, and NGO activity to help these countries.

BOX 13.23   A Closer Look: Anti-Trafficking

Actress Lucy Liu collaborated with USAID and the MTV Foundation on the documentary "Traffic" for the EXIT campaign.

Anti trafficking efforts include providing support for survivors and potential victims. Gainful employment opportunities are an important dimension of global efforts.

USAID programs have targeted countries where human trafficking is most severe. It has worked in over 70 countries combating human trafficking. USAID works with governments, NGOs, and the private sector to strengthen each element's capacity to prevent and combat trafficking. The USAID approach is multifaceted. Attacking the problem from all angles—root causes, weak government, lack of knowledge about trafficking, enforcement, and victim's services—is one key. The other key element is working on the ground, to strengthen local capacity and the collective efficacy of the area. This is in keeping with USAID decentralization projects that build people's capacity through strengthening local governments and civil society. Efforts to strengthen countries' capacity to combat human trafficking include

- strengthening government surveillance and monitoring capacity;
- monitoring private contracts with the government to ensure adequate labor standards;
- working on legislative reform, including training prosecutors and judges;
- raising public awareness of techniques of traffickers and safe migration practices by mobilizing community resources for awareness campaigns, including neighborhood watch campaigns;
- working to develop local capacity for helping victims, including work with NGOs to establish reintegration and rehabilitation programs for victims, including shelter, health care, and psychological counseling; and
- providing literacy, life skill, self-esteem, and vocational programs for victims (USAID 2006, 10–23).

In 2004, USAID partnered with MTV to create an ongoing campaign, MTV EXIT (End Exploitation and Trafficking; mtvexit.org). Using rock, movie, and television stars, MTV and USAID are producing a wide variety of activities and events. In the summer of 2010, a series of concerts in Indonesia and Vietnam attracted over 400,000 people by midseason. Hundreds of thousands more will see the concert broadcasts. MTV EXIT produces films and music throughout Asia and Europe. In addition to its online website, broadcasts can be found on social networking sites and YouTube.

Victims of human trafficking are often inserted into the supply chains of legitimate businesses. This makes private partnerships important in fighting human trafficking. The fruits of forced labor become part of the supply chain of everyday products. One of the largest human trafficking investigations of the FBI convicted sweatshop operators to life in prison for human trafficking. They were supplying clothes for Walmart, Target, Sears, and J.C. Penney, among others. Some of these companies have promised restitution to the victims (National Labor Committee 2003). Subcontractors for Toyota are alleged to have forced labor trafficked from China, Vietnam, Indonesia, Philippines, Brazil, and Thailand. Workers are stripped of passports and threatened with deportation if they try to leave. Toyota has promised a full investigation (National Labor Committee 2008). Corporations need to make the extra effort to secure their supply chain, from the source of raw materials, the component parts, assembly, and transport. This has become an important focus of USDOS efforts. The 2010 *Trafficking in Persons Report* calls for corporate responsibility and holding corporations accountable for complying with local laws and international standards, developing security procedures, holding employees accountable, and paying restitution where trafficking is found (USDOS 2010, 30). The USAID programs also perform audits of government subcontractors to guarantee the supply chain is free of forced labor.

UN personnel and military under UN command, unfortunately, have participated in drug trafficking, human trafficking, black market distribution of food and medical aid, and sexual exploitation in countries where they have been deployed. In 2003, the UN adopted a "no tolerance" policy and series of reforms to prevent and combat sexual exploitation by anyone working under UN aegis, as contractor, volunteer, staff, or military force. In 2009, there were 112 sexual exploitation and abuse allegations. Thirty-nine new and pending cases were investigated with 21 deemed credible. There are 98 cases pending (USDOS 2010, 368). NATO and OSCE have adopted similar policies, although there are no known allegations in those groups.

Drug Trafficking

It is hard to fathom the global drug problem. The UNODC estimates between 155 and 250 million people, aged 15 to 64, used illegal drugs at least once in 2008. While most of these are cannabis users, there are estimated to be about 16 and 38 million problem users considered drug dependent, and only about 12% to 30% of those received treatment (2010, 12). The opiate industry is arguably the most deadly and destabilizing. More users die from heroin than any other illegal drug, including people who use, people in the drug trade, law enforcement, and innocent bystanders. The opiate and cocaine trade are ravaging countries, adding to problems of political corruption and instability, in developed and developing countries. From growers to users, illicit drugs create havoc at every step in the chain. The drug trade would not exist without the drug market. Heroin alone is a $55 billion dollar market; the other opiates add on another $10 billion (UNODC 2010, 35). Most heroin comes from Afghanistan. About 20% of the global heroin flow is intercepted en route (46). Eighty percent of heroin from Afghanistan takes a route from Afghanistan to Iran, Pakistan, and Turkey, then through the Balkans into Europe. About 40% of heroin seizures are in Iran, Pakistan, and Turkey. Even with the 20% loss, heroin is so lucrative that the routes continue to be used. In heroin trafficking, more foreigners than citizens tend to be arrested in European countries. But aside from Pakistan, which acts as a hub, the majority of people arrested on the eastern side of the drug seizures are domestics; for example, groups seized in Iran are Iranian nationals. Ethnic Kurdish groups seem to handle the border crossings between Iran and Turkey. The Balkans organized crime groups are particularly hard to penetrate because they are clan based. There are very few seizures once the drugs have passed through Turkey (57). Burma (Myanmar) has heroin production as well. It exports primarily to the regional and Chinese market. West Africans, particularly Nigerians, are pivotal in both heroin and cocaine trafficking. In Pakistan, as many Nigerians are arrested as Pakistanis, each accounting for 32% of the heroin traffickers arrested (62).

The value of the global cocaine market shrunk more than half from 1995 to 2008. UNODC estimates the market was $88 billion in 2008, a substantial decrease from $177 billion (in 2008 dollars) in 1995 (2010, 69).

Cocaine trafficking originates in the Andes region of South America. Organized crime is very adaptable, and often enforcement efforts seem like two steps forward, one step back. From WWII into the late 1970s, most of the cocaine consumed in North America was grown in Peru and Bolivia, and refined in Colombia. Enforcement efforts began shutting down the air traffic in coca leaves between Peru and Colombia. Peruvian farmers began growing other crops. Gradually, cultivation in Colombia increased, and in 1997, Colombia surpassed Peru in production. Gradually Peruvians developed technology for refining the coca leaves and their farmers started growing coca again. Next, large-scale eradication programs, many cooperative between the United States and Colombia, cut Colombian cultivation by 58% between 2000 and 2009. Peru and Bolivia were able to make up for some of the decline, but overall supply from the region is down 28% (UNODC 2010, 65).

Most cocaine traffic travels up through Central America to North America. As the North American market decreased, whether by increased enforcement, less demand, or both, traffic through the Caribbean and West Africa to Europe increased (UNODC 2010, 70). The major traffic route into Europe is by sea and enters in Spain and Portugal, where there are close cultural and ethnic ties to Latin America. It enters Belgium and Netherlands further north (83). Over 50% of sea traffic leaves South America through Venezuela. Colombia is still the major producer, but is losing importance as Bolivia and Peru are picking up more business, being the sole suppliers for some of the smaller markets (84).

One of the most worrying connections in security issues is the relationship between insurgency, terrorism, and drug trafficking. The Taliban protect drug routes through parts of Pakistan and Afghanistan. Al-Qaeda also benefits from the heroin drug trade. Illicit drugs are grown in the Global South, in poor, developing countries. An FBI report (Medford 2003) to the U.S. Senate described several of these relationships. FARC is the oldest terrorist group still operating. It is a Marxist domestic terrorist organization, fighting American oil, the Colombian government, and the paramilitaries that protect Colombian business interests. They fund their terrorist activity through kidnapping, extortion, protection, and drug trafficking. Some analysts argue that FARC has lost much of its revolutionary zeal and is more drug trafficker than revolutionary, a "hybrid" organization. It operates flights for drug traffickers and shoots down surveillance planes to protect cocaine operations. In July 2010, Gerardo Aguilar Ramirez, a FARC commander, was sentenced to 27 years in prison for a cocaine operation that sent "ton quantities" of cocaine into the United States ("Top FARC Commander" 2010). Even Hezbollah—which condemns drug use on religious grounds, is supported by Iran, and fights trafficking through interceptions—may have links to the drug trade. In testimony to the Senate Judiciary Committee, Steven McCraw, assistant director of intelligence for the FBI, detailed some al-Qaeda and FARC drug activities. He also reported on the activities of drug traders with suspected ties to Hezbollah who directed drug money to them (McCraw 2003).

The violence and destabilization associated with the drug trade is primarily in the trafficking. UNODC reports that any change in trafficking disrupts the system and results in violence (2010, 26). Ironically, the decrease in the U.S. cocaine market may be responsible for the increase in violence as organized crime groups fight for larger shares of the shrinking market. Violence in Guatemala, El Salvador, and Honduras threatens governance. The concomitant increase in the European market has increased violence in the Caribbean, along the new cocaine flow. The violence is not in the cities but in the areas most affected by drug trade: ports and border areas. In Mexico, extreme violence is a result of government crackdowns on drug cartels that began in 2006. This violence may be transitory. It may be shifting the balance to the government's side (27). In 2012, cartel-related homicides decreased in Mexico (T. Johnson 2012).

Rerouting of the drug trade has also brought drug traffic to West Africa. Drug traffic comes to West Africa by sea and by air, in bulk. Guinea-Bissau is often the destination. A country with little money, and with scores of islands on its coast, it is near tailor-made for organized crime. The social environment is even more important than the physical. Since independence from Portugal in 1974, Guinea-Bissau has suffered coups, civil wars, and assassinations. It is another lawless territory, a failing state. The drug trade provides much more income than the cashews it exports. Guinea-Bissau corruption is so rife that it appears that the government and drug traffickers are one and the same. When the drug trade came to Guinea-Bissau, it went to the military. With control of the air and the seas, the military was in a perfect position to assure the safety of drug shipments by plane or boat. Military officers have unloaded planes, have been arrested in seizures, and have had standoffs with the police.

Judiciary police trying to combat the trafficking have been forced to turn over seizures of drugs and traffickers to other government branches, only to have the arrestees released and drugs disappear (Traub 2010). Once arrested, traffickers are often released. Death threats have been received by journalists, activists, the attorney general, and minister of justice for their apparent interest in stopping the drug traffic (UNODC 2010, 242). The heads of the army and navy were involved with the threats. The former was killed in 2009, and within hours, the president—Joao Bernardo Vieira, the longstanding dictator ousted by a military uprising and civil war in 1999 but re-elected president in 2005 for promising reform—was also assassinated, either in retaliation or perhaps by forces in the military responsible for killing both (Traub 2010). The head of the navy fled but returned in 2010 to help depose the prime minister and head of the military (UNODC 2010, 243).

Trafficking seemed to decrease, at least temporarily, in Guinea-Bissau, but increased in neighboring countries. Mauritania, Mali, Guinea, Senegal, the Gambia, Cape Verde, Sierra Leone, Ghana, Togo, and Benin are all involved. West Africa is a hub on the drug-trading route from South America to Europe, although in May 2010, four tons of Colombian cocaine presumably headed for the United States were seized in Liberia ("West Africa Drugs" 2011). There are so many lawless areas from which to operate that organized crime can adapt quickly, as it did in the problems with coca cultivation in South America.

Drug trade along the border of the United States and Mexico makes it one of the most dangerous places on earth. It is again the drug appetite of North America that feeds this violence, along with the firearms trade, and import of American-manufactured guns. "La Barbie," a blond-haired, green-eyed Texan, was arrested in Mexico in August 2010. One of the most powerful and vicious drug lords in Mexico, Edgar Valdez Villarreal rose to the top of the Mexican organized crime cartels through savagery, beheading, mutilation, and videotaping victims in attempts to intimidate enemies, techniques he allegedly copied from Islamist terrorists (McKinley and Malkin 2010).

In Mexico, where gun control laws are strong, there are only 6,000 legally registered weapons in private hands. In the first half of 2007 alone, 11,000 weapons were seized coming into Mexico from the United States. Since the expiration of the assault rifle ban in the United States, more assault weapons are flooding the Mexican market. They are used not only in inter-cartel killings but also to make more efficient and deadly attacks on Mexican police and military (Nevaer 2007). The illegal arms trade, although a fraction of the drug trade in dollar value, is a deadly threat to human security that exacerbates and escalates the dangers from other forms of international crimes, among them drugs, human trafficking, counterfeiting, and piracy.

Drugs are commodity crops, grown for export. When the price of a food commodity is better than the drug commodity, growers will switch. Many growers of illicit crops are regular farmers. They make very little from their crop. Decreasing demand for drugs in rich nations and increasing the prices farmers can get for growing food may be the best way to combat illegal drug trafficking.

Cybercrime Grows Up

Crime breeds in lawless places. Perhaps no place is as lawless as cyberspace (Lewis 2010, 4). Like the frontier of the Wild West, there are few laws in cyberspace and particularly few in global cyberspace. Creating order in cyberspace will take coordinated international effort to define responsible behavior for states and for individuals within them.

Cyberspace presents unique opportunities for criminals and difficulties for law enforcement. In addition to the host of new crimes that technology makes possible, cyberspace enlarges the neighborhood for crime to include the world as a potential target. Cybercriminals engage online in traditional crimes, such as extortion and pornography, on a greatly expanded scale. The Nigerian letter scam that asks people for their bank account information so that a wealthy heir can put their inheritance in a safe place did in fact come from Nigeria and targets millions of people all over the world. Sending the e-mail costs little. It only takes one response for the fraud to pay off for the cybercriminal. Crimes can be committed across national borders or from different continents. Criminals do not need to be physically present to commit the crime. This reduces the risk of capture and prosecution, and makes the job of law enforcement that much harder (McAfee 2005, 8).

A new class of cybercriminal has emerged, more sophisticated and systematic than earlier generations: the amateur cyber-"delinquent" has joined a criminal gang. While, in 2000, most cybercriminals acted alone, organized cybercrime is rapidly developing. Cybercriminals are collaborating across countries. Tracing a scam through cyberspace may be impossible when the trail bounces from one country to another until its origin is obscured. Another twist is that traditional organized crime is acquiring cyberskills and expanding into cyberspace (McAfee 2005, 5).

The boundary between cybercrime and cyberwar is strained. Some states do not prosecute cybercriminals, allowing them to hone their skills in the event they will eventually need them to conduct cyberattacks. Others actively collaborate with them. Russia, for example, launched a denial of service attack on Estonia during a dispute. Russia overloaded their websites with traffic, causing them to collapse. The Center for Strategic and International Studies (CSIS) maintains that the Russians enlisted patriotic Russian hackers and cybercriminals through e-mails and chat rooms to carry out the attack for them (Lewis 2007, 1). This gives the Russian government deniability—the attacks did not come from their computers. Before the Iraqi War, the Bush administration planned cyberattacks on the Iraqi financial system, including Saddam Hussein's bank accounts (McAfee 2009, 15). Beginning in the Bush administration, the United States launched cyberattacks—an operation called Olympic Games—on Iran's nuclear facilities to disrupt their operations and slow their progress. Attacks intensified during the Obama administration and continued even after becoming public in 2010 when the computer worm Stuxnet escaped Iran and traveled the globe through computer networks.

Attacks on other nations invite retaliation, if the nation is capable. The possibilities for cyberattacks are limitless. Lewis (2010), of CSIS, believes that the United States faces four types of cyberthreats. These would apply around the world.

- Economic espionage—collecting information about various companies and other business information
- Political and military espionage—a technological update of traditional spying about military capabilities, a country's intentions, and so on
- Cybercrime against the financial system for money as opposed to information
- Cyberwar

Most of these threats can be encompassed within existing international law. Economic espionage is a trade issue. It often goes unnoticed, but when discovered, corporations usually hide it to protect stock prices or brand. While the United States, for example, has pressured China to prosecute its extensive counterfeiting and piracy industry, the same pressure has to be applied to theft of intellectual property in cyberspace (Lewis 2007, 2).

Similarly, political and military espionage could be treated under the existing rules. Additional punitive measures—such as public embarrassment, warrants for arrest, expelling attachés, and so on—could be applied to increase the cost associated with cyberespionage (Lewis 2007, 2).

Global culture lags far behind technological capabilities and events with respect to cybercrime. Cybercrime needs international clarification, such as an international agreement that countries are responsible for the cybercrimes of individuals operating in their territory. As in the Russian case, a country could not dismiss the crime as the work of overzealous patriots. Penalties making it more difficult for them to connect to the global network or having their networks monitored may prevent crimes and prevent nations from harboring cybercriminals

(Lewis 2007, 3). Common understandings on laws of cyberwar, escalation in cyberconflict, responsibilities before and after cyberwars, and consequences for different levels of hostility need definition with respect to specific threat as well as general principles.

Many states have the capability for cybercrime and cyberwar. Two global trends that increase interconnectivity of information systems and efficiency increase vulnerability at the same time. Network convergence merges all communication types (voice, data, video, etc.) over a common network. Channel consolidation concentrates data on users. While these technologies will improve efficiency, they expose information systems to more security breaches (Blair 2010, 3).

Most countries' defenses, like those of the United States, are weak. There have been several infiltrations of U.S. government databases. In 2007, hackers stole information from government agencies. The data stolen was greater than the total Library of Congress collection, but they extracted the data indiscriminately. It ranges from the very mundane, such as lunch menus, to much more sensitive security issues. Richard Clarke, a chief national security officer in the Clinton and George W. Bush administrations, argues that the likelihood of a cyberwar or attack is inevitable and that states most likely to attack are those such as North Korea, whose infrastructure has little interconnectivity with the Internet. If they launched a cyberattack, they would have little to fear from a cyberretaliation for their first strike.

Cooperatively developed and internationally adopted norms, as well as strategic understandings, about what is or is not permissible, and the consequences or retaliations likely to apply, are necessary (Lewis 2010, 3). Negotiating rules of cyberwar poses more difficulty than conventional warfare. There are no political boundaries in cyberspace. Places where people and servers are physically located are likely far from where they conduct operations. The Council of Europe Cybercrime Convention showed how difficult this is. The Convention was entered into force in 2002. The United States ratified it in 2004 (Lewis 2004). Although the objective of preventing and punishing cybercrime was shared, cultural clashes over the terms of acceptable or unacceptable behaviors ran deeply. Core cultural values—privacy vs. freedom, due process vs. security—create huge rifts in international negotiations (3).

As noted earlier, determining when an act was instigated by a rogue individual or an individual acting at the bequest of a government is another difficulty. An act of a rogue individual would not be considered an act of war, whereas the same act by a country would be. Distinguishing acts of war from crime is just one problem. Distinguishing legal acts of war from illegal acts of war is another. Attacks on civilian targets would be against the rules of war, but not attacks on military targets. However, military and civilians share the same cyberspaces, and their information travels over the same networks (Gjelten 2010b).

Determining how and when to enforce international law may be difficult. In the case of the Stuxnet computer worm, it escaped from Iran and traveled all over the world, including back to the United States. Programmed for a specific target—the Iranian nuclear centrifuges—it reportedly traveled harmlessly through computer networks. However, it underscores the potential for similar attacks to create havoc beyond the intended target. The worm found its way deep into control systems and could have adjusted valves, changed monitor readings, and caused significant damage in any number of ways, including causing gas lines to explode or nuclear plants to malfunction (Gjelten 2010a). How and to what degree the offending countries should be held responsible for unintended consequences is a matter of debate.

Responding to Risks

Global Aid for Global Security

Historically, aid has been viewed as critical to both the security of donor nations and receiving nations. Although there was not much development aid before WWII, people recognized that it was necessary if Europe was to rebuild after the war. The massive investment in the Marshall Plan and the development of the multilateral institutions were designed to stabilize Europe, prevent pro-communist sentiment from gaining more ground, and ensure that Europe could aid in its own defense. When Truman initiated aid to developing countries in the 1950s, it was to develop the skills and knowledge needed for growth. Food aid also solved problems of distributing surplus agricultural product and maintaining prices. Aid was deliberately directed to countries friendly to the United States, maintaining, as stated by President Kennedy in 1961, that "development assistance was security assistance" (CBO 1997, 11). Following this logic, military assistance ranks as the primary category of aid. As Europe recovered, it achieved enough prosperity to contribute to the growth of less fortunate nations. One Organization for Economic Co-operation and Development (OECD) charge is to coordinate aid and development efforts of the world's rich nations. This set up a global system of giving and receiving, with rights and responsibilities on the part of those countries with recognized status as donors, and those countries with recognized status as recipients. Despite this, aid remains associated primarily with countries' strategic and economic interests. The poorest nations do not necessarily receive the most funds. For example, until the war in Iraq, Israel and Egypt were the primary recipients of U.S. foreign assistance. Most of the aid has been military aid, and it remained relatively stable while military aid to other countries decreased. Multilateral organizations, such as the World Bank and the variety of UN programs, have concentrated primarily on developing nations, although the strategic interests of donor nations influences their aid programs as well (16).

States' interests continue to dominate aid programs. Support for Eastern European Democracy Act of 1989 and the Africa Conflict Resolution Act of 1994 are especially geared toward promoting democratization. While these offer promise to strengthen governance and grant people rights they would not otherwise have, the strategic importance of democracy in Eastern Europe to global stability cannot be underestimated (Ehrenfeld 2004).

BOX 13.24   A Closer Look: Food for Drugs

Farmers in Ecuador are harvesting cacao beans for chocolate. Legitimate crops are encouraged and supported to take land out of coca-production.

With assurance of a healthy, sustainable food crop and a reliable market for the crops, farmers can alleviate poverty and hunger along with freeing themselves from growing drugs for global drug trafficking.

Combating Transnational Crime

Transnational crime respects no borders, so crime fighting efforts must also transcend borders. UN experts contend that there is no substitute for coordinated international action. That said, transnational crime is a tightly woven network of local to global connections. Local reforms are essential to mitigate the problems at their source. Weak and failing states—states wracked by poverty and conflict—have little chance against well-funded, well-equipped crime cartels.

Strong local governments—at the community level—are a defense against corruption and can deter criminal practices. This is one approach championed by USAID in their decentralization efforts. In Peru, USAID's "decentralization program focuses nationally on policy reform and locally in the key coca-growing regions" (USAID 2012). Strong local governments can mitigate drug trafficking, terrorism, and other crimes by responding effectively to citizen needs. By strengthening political parties and anti-corruption strategies such as transparency, accountability, and generating greater citizen participation in government and crime fighting programs, local governments can reduce people's motivation to cooperate with criminal activity.

Global crime fighting has to evolve from the local to the global level, as it evolved in the United States from local to national levels. While crime and criminals traveled at will across the country, the United States was confronted with developing a criminal justice system that transcended the borders of the 50 states, forming a national crime-fighting system. Two primary strategies are homogenizing criminal justice systems, including conforming laws across borders and regularizing relationships among crime fighting agencies. Convergences of structure, function, and policy occur to a certain degree as bureaucratic forms and models globalized. To fight transnational crime, homogenization needs to be deliberate and much more thorough in the key areas of global crime.

In some areas, such as the treaties and regimes condemning slavery, there is significant homogenization. However, there are many areas of contradiction and conflict in law across states. States that allow secret bank accounts, for example, aid criminals hiding illegal sources of cash. Switzerland has begun to reverse some financial policies that allow international criminals—including white-collar criminals and political figures—to hide money in the infamous Swiss bank accounts. Similarly, where countries do not criminalize tax evasion, money laundering, and insider trading in their own borders, they often fail to extradite to countries that do. Where states have similar laws but sanction offenses differently—as with the death penalty—it also aids and abets criminality (Andreas and Nadelmann 2009, 29).

Regularizing laws across borders is often a matter of power relations. Stronger states typically are able to force weaker states to conform to their laws; the reverse is less often true. Thus, throughout Latin America, the drug program of the United States has resulted in significant changes in criminal justice. The pleas of Mexico to the United States to conform their gun laws to Mexican standards by tightening controls have been largely ignored. Many of the firearms used in the Mexican drug wars, and a majority of some frequently used models, are manufactured and distributed from the United States (Andreas and Nadelmann 2009, 28).

Relations within criminal justice systems also require institutionalization and coordination. As fighting crime is ultimately the responsibility of policing and prosecutorial functions, regularizing formal and informal relations to achieve a seamless process across borders is critical. The duty to protect citizens and the singular right of a state to use coercive measures is directly related to state sovereignty. States' concern for their sovereignty inhibits global crime fighting. Cooperative relations allowing more joint investigation and prosecution is necessary. (Within the United States, relations across systems are not perfectly regularized. When various local jurisdictions or local and federal jurisdictions have claims on a case, there may be conflict over lead and backup roles.)

Professional associations, international training programs, bilateral and multilateral working groups, joint investigations, and international meetings facilitate forming an international law enforcement community. These help to overcome political tensions and jurisdictional territorialism to establish formal and informal norms of team building to create the cooperation essential in crime fighting.

Questions, Investigations, and Resources

Questions

1. Debate: Who should decide whether or not a people who declare independence as a sovereign state are officially recognized: the people themselves or an international body?

2. Throughout the discussion of violent conflict, states have been implicated in the causes of violence. How have states and state structures contributed to violent conflict? How can it be rectified?

3. Why are countries in transition fragile? How can transitions from autocracy to democracy be made more stable and peaceful?

4. What are the risk factors for violent conflict?

5. To what extent do you think that video games present war as entertainment? Do video games have a larger role in making war seem more a fact of life than an anomaly?

6. How is poverty related to global crime?

7. What role does technology play in global crime?

8. Explain some of the programs that you think are most promising for dealing with global risks to human security.

Investigations

1. Update your knowledge of global conflict.

   - Use the Center for Systemic Peace Website (http://systemicpeace.org) or Uppsala Conflict Data Program (http://www.pcr.uu.se/research/UCDP/) to find out what conflicts are occurring in the world today.
   - Go to the CIA World Factbook (https://www.cia.gov/library/publications/the-world-factbook/index.html) to investigate the countries where there is warfare. What factors reported in the country profiles that might be indicators of a high-conflict or fragile state?

2. Investigate the peacekeeping missions of the UN: http://www.un.org/en/peacekeeping. Choose one of the oldest missions to investigate in depth.

   - How successful has the UN been in maintaining peace?
   - What factors are aggravating the peace process?
   - How many peacekeepers are on the mission, and what is the range of responsibilities of the UN peacekeepers?
   - Have the peacekeepers been accused of any wrongdoing?
   - What countries have contributed troops to the UN mission in each country?

3. Global crime is a serious threat to world security. Terrorism, cybercrime, counterfeiting, and drug and arms trafficking cost the world trillions of dollars and harm hundreds of thousands of lives yearly. You can investigate the cost of these crimes, where they occur, and what is being done to combat them. The websites listed below will give you a good start in your investigation.

Resources

Violent Conflict

Center for Systemic Peace http://systemicpeace.org

Uppsala Conflict Data Program http://www.pcr.uu.se/research/UCDP/

CIA World Factbook https://www.cia.gov/library/publications/the-world-factbook/index.html

International Peace Institute http://www.ipacademy.org/

Global Terrorism Database: Information on 98,000 terrorist events from 1970 to the present http://www.start.umd.edu/gtd/features/GTD-Data-Rivers.aspx

Crime

Human Trafficking

- CIA: https://www.cia.gov/library/publications/the-world-factbook/fields/2196.html

- UNDOC: http://www.unodc.org/unodc/en/human-trafficking/index.html
- U.S. State Department "2007 Trafficking in Persons Report": http://www.state.gov/g/tip/rls/tiprpt/2007/

Drug Trade

- UN Office on Drugs and Crime: http://www.unodc.org/unodc/index.html
- *New York Times* Topics: http://topics.nytimes.com/top/news/international/countriesandterritories/mexico/drug_trafficking/index.html

Piracy on the High Seas:

- International Chamber of Commerce, International Crime Center: http://www.icc-ccs.org/index.php?option=com_fabrik&view=visualization&controller=visualization.googlemap&Itemid=219
- *New York Times* Topics: http://topics.nytimes.com/top/reference/timestopics/subjects/p/piracy_at_sea/index.html

14

Transborder Threats to Human Well-Being: Food and the Environment

Objectives

This chapter reviews the related problems of food security and environmental degradation. After studying this chapter, you should be able to

- understand hunger as a manufactured risk;
- compare and contrast the successes and failures of the green revolution in fighting hunger;
- evaluate the benefits and disadvantages of several major food policies;
- analyze the factory model of food production and weigh its benefits and harm in crop, poultry, and livestock production;

- describe new trends in agriculture toward more sustainable farming;
- identify environmental risks to land, water, and air;
- relate environmental risks to the production of food; and
- assess the impact of modern life on the capacity of the earth's environment to sustain it.

Earth's ability to feed its population and the health of its environment are intimately related. Degrading the environment by depleting or polluting resources or warming the earth's atmosphere by even a few degrees cripples the capacity of the earth to feed its people. Excessive use of fossil fuels in transportation and industrialization are culprits, but oft-overlooked culprits are unsustainable farming and food-production methods that deplete the soil of its nutrients and deplete and pollute water supplies. Modern seed that is expensive to buy and grow because of patents or the need for special fertilizers and pesticides puts many small or subsistence farmers out of business, pollutes soil and water, and compounds problems of food supply.

This chapter cannot detail the science of food production or environmental threats. There are many

good sources in the scientific literature. Instead, I focus on how policies and programs diffused by governments, intergovernmental organizations, and corporations exacerbated food crises in many parts of the world. The related environmental damage threatens all of humanity. The chapter concludes with programs and policies undertaken to combat the problems.

A World of Contrast: Starving on a Planet of Plenty

How could people be starving in countries where there are agricultural exports? The idyllic view of farming is that it is one of the most wholesome of human activities, but unsustainable agricultural practices and trade in food cause hunger and environmental destruction. Each of these presents myriad issues for our analysis. First, how do theories of comparative advantage, which have to do with trade, apply to food and the possibility of hunger?

- If a food staple, such as corn, rice, or wheat, can be produced more cheaply by another country, should a country buy it from the other, rather than grow it itself? It seems reasonable, but is there a possible downside?
- When a food donor country purchases food from its own farmers to supply food aid in other countries, is it more likely to increase or decrease hunger in the long run? If food aid undermines the market for local farmers, putting them out of business, whom does it really aid?
- Do genetically modified foods present an opportunity or further constraint to food security? The Zambian government, pressured by farmers, has refused to accept free genetically modified (GM) maize. It will prevent them, they believe, from ever achieving food independence from multinationals—their grain, fertilizers, and pesticides. Is GM food aid really aid, or is it the seed of future hunger? Is GM food safe? What should Zambian farmers do?
- Women, who have traditionally farmed Africa and produced most of the food, are resisting the World Bank's efforts to commercialize farming. Displacing subsistence farming, they believe, has caused food deficiency in Africa. Women are trying to return to variations of their "cooking pot economics," in urban as well as rural areas (Gibson 2004, 2). Is this a good idea, or could highly productive commercial farms feed more people more nutritiously than small sustenance farms?

None of these questions is easy to answer. Food and globalization are linked in many ways. Culturally, cuisine is a way of creating identity or establishing an identity in a new land. It may also be used to resist changes in identity. Politically, globalization is relevant to where and how foods are produced and distributed, how they are regulated, and the environmental degradation that poor agricultural practices create. Economically, food is relevant in global trade patterns, prices of food commodities, subsidies, multinational agribusiness, and so on. Even in criminology, food topics are relevant, in particular when considering the risk of genetic pollution, demise of alternative farming techniques, bio-piracy, and exploitation by larger corporations. Globalization affects whether people are well fed or starving and why.

The Food Regime: Food Markets and Food Policy

Population growth, urbanization, increasing wealth, and information about health and nutrition change how much food the world needs and what types people want. Filling global demands for sufficient and affordable food has been a global challenge for a long time. Producing enough food of nutritional quality in an environmentally sustainable way is the most recent challenge. As with other forms of globalization, global flows in culture, particularly rationalization and uncritical pursuit of the fruits of science, trade policies, technological products, consumer tastes, and many others relevant to agriculture produce different results in different countries as they diffuse throughout the globe. Varying local conditions, such as climate, irrigation potential, population density, infrastructure for transportation to markets, and access to finance, determine who can benefit from changing technologies and tastes in food.

For most of human history, societies produced their own food. Feast or famine was determined by how well the hunting, gathering, and growing went. To insure against hunger, societies developed elaborate norms of reciprocity and production. Some of these relied on forms of community ownership of the fruits of labor; some involved inter-group reciprocity (or raids). Food shortages were primarily a function of local conditions of the natural environment: the season, the rainfall, the nature of the land, and people's skill in obtaining what they needed. Many production practices were sustainable, but if the environment could no longer support them, people moved. They moved with the seasons or when they had used land beyond its ability to produce. When the environment recovered, they could return, or different people could move in. This has changed. Now, there is plenty of food, but humans' relations with each other and their environment prevent many of the world's people from getting enough. As in other areas, people have collectively manufactured the risk of hunger.

Where different foods are grown and what they cost is not random. Policy choices of governments, non-governmental organizations, and corporate incentives determine what foods are grown in which countries. Government policies also determine how food is distributed, whether through free markets or state regulation. As in other areas of trade, where there is a dominant nation, it typically has the most influence in setting the parameters, for instance, by setting tariffs to make imported food more expensive or subsidizing its farmers to make their goods cheaper on the global market. Its policies are influenced by interest group lobbying within countries and global politics. A complex interplay of national and global factors and coalitions determine how the rules are set. The stakes in food regimes are high. They directly influence life or death for millions of people (Winders 2009, 134). Understanding the globalization of food production and distribution is critical.

The Development of Specialized Niches

Food was the earliest widely traded commodity. Trade in spices, sugar, tea, and coffee, particularly between Asia and Europe, grew dramatically between 1500 and 1700. But food staples were produced close to home. From the mid-19th century until WWI, a massive transformation in agriculture changed that. Agriculture mechanized, allowing for large-scale production. Regional specialties began to develop, and countries carved out market niches for their produce. For example, throughout Southeast Asia, British, French, Chinese, American, Thai, and Portuguese farmers began commercial rice cultivation. This

changed food production. Rather than cultivate small plots close to where foods would be consumed, new areas of land were opened in export zones. Instead of growing a variety of rice strains on a single plot, new techniques of mono-cropping—planting only one rice variety—were introduced. New irrigation techniques, such as controlled flooding, were used. Hundreds of thousands of workers migrated from rural areas into the new rice exporting zones that spread across Southeast Asia. It changed the dynamic of agriculture. Similar phenomenon occurred over the world (Kratoska 2008).

Attracting workers from rural areas to the rice plantations took them away from indigenous crops and subsistence agriculture. Farmers who did not move to the rice zones invested in lucrative cash crops, such as tea, rubber, tobacco, oil palm, coconuts, and fruits. Many food-rich areas that used to grow a variety of foods became dependent on imported foods (Kratoska 2008, 78–81). This trend toward increasing specialization, large farm size, and more dependence on exports was global. The charts in Box 14.1 track changes in the United States. Farms decreased in number over time as they increased in size became specialized and came to rely more on export.

BOX 14.1   A Closer Look: Consolidation in Agriculture

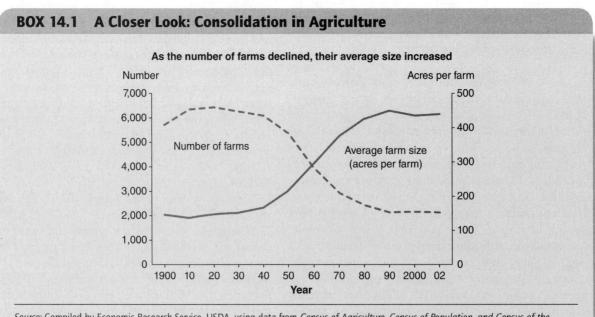

As the number of farms declined, their average size increased

Source: Compiled by Economic Research Service, USDA, using data from *Census of Agriculture, Census of Population, and Census of the United States.*

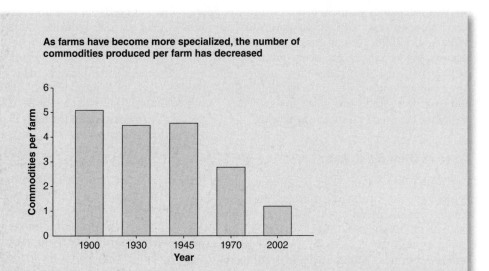

As farms have become more specialized, the number of commodities produced per farm has decreased

Source: Compiled by Economic Research Service, USDA, using data from *Census of Agriculture, Census of the United States*, and Gardner (2002).

Note: The average number of commodities per farm is a simple average of the number of farms producing different commodities (corn, sorghum, wheat, oats, barley, rice, soybeans, peanuts, alfalfa, cotton, tobacco, sugar beets, potatoes, cattle, pigs, sheep, and chickens) divided by the total number of farms.

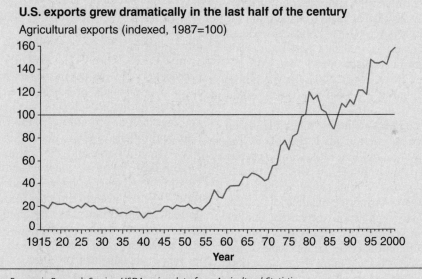

U.S. exports grew dramatically in the last half of the century

Agricultural exports (indexed, 1987=100)

Source: Compiled by Economic Research Service, USDA, using data from *Agricultural Statistics.*

Note: Standard techniques were used to combine four series of data for quantity of goods exported.

Regional economies based on specialization and export worked well as long as the supply and demand for the crop—in the case of Southeast Asia, rice; in the United States, corn and wheat—were balanced. Those who grew an export crop had money to import other foods, and those who grew other things could afford to buy the exports. It seemed to make sense. Global trade in food rose sharply. By the early 20th century, 80% of the world's rice was produced in the commercialized areas of Southeast Asia (Kratoska 2008, 77). The 3.44% annual growth in food trade from 1850 to 1913 dwarfed all previous rates of growth. By 1913, food trade accounted for 27% of world exports (Nützenadel and Trentmann 2008, 5). It was the first time that staples, people's survival needs, were shipped and traded at competitive prices (Nützenadel 2008, 153). In America, exports brought farmers higher prices for their produce, and the period 1910–1914 became the "golden age" of American agriculture" (Dimitri, Effland, and Conklin 2005, 7). But would this work for everyone? What are the best strategies to feed the world?

World Wars and Famine

No one foresaw the disruption caused by WWI. Famine spread throughout Europe. European agriculture was disrupted by the war, and the supply of grain from Russia was also shut off. In response, countries tried to coordinate food production and stabilize markets (Nützenadel and Trentmann 2008, 11). This was an early step toward global governance of food. However, the negotiated balance between supply and demand did not hold. After the war, oversupply, climate, and the Depression interfered. World market prices dropped in the 1920s. In the United States, industrial and agricultural interests' pressure for protective tariffs resulted in the 1930 Smoot-Hawley Act. Other countries reacted with similar protectionist policies, and food trade shrank. Agricultural exports dropped 20% from the preceding decade (Dimitri et al. 2005, 7). The global depression killed markets. Global food trade would not rise significantly until the 1960s.

Rice harvests had become more vulnerable. Using one variety of rice in a field made it easier for large scale commercial planting, harvesting, and processing. But this has disadvantages as well. With one variety, one pest or disease could wipe out an entire season's yield. When a farmer plants multiple varieties, one pest or disease may spoil one variety, but not all of them. Also one variety means one concentrated harvest. Different varieties of rice have different harvesting cycles. Planting more than one variety means crops could be harvested over a much longer period, and in some areas throughout the year, not in only one season. These advantages were lost with mono crop commercialization. In Southeast Asia, Thailand (then Siam) lost much of its rice crop and could not export. This caused prices to rise and made rice hard to secure.

In their quest for resources, Japan's expansionism—into China, Manchuria, and Russia—posed a severe threat across Southeast Asia, spreading uncertainty and fear (Kratoska 2008, 82–83). With their invasion of Vietnam in 1940, they controlled all the rice producing areas of Southeast Asia. With the war raging, food could not be moved to where it was needed. Farmers planted less, reducing output to subsistence levels. During WWII in Vietnam, it did not pay to grow rice. Farmers made more money working building armaments for the Japanese. This posed great hardship for food deficient countries, and starvation ensued. The French claim that about 700,000 Vietnamese died. The Vietnamese claim the number was closer to 1.5–2 million. By either account, the carnage was astronomical (84). Europe faced the same hardships; hunger and starvation stalked the continent.

Managing a global food supply has proven difficult. Food has to be profitable enough for farmers to want to grow, but it has to be affordable. If supply exceeds demand, profits drop; farmers may stop growing and supply shrinks. To try to resolve the difficulties of WWI and the Depression, the United States began instituting supply management through supply controls and price supports. Supply controls allow for the government to buy surplus and hold it until supplies drop; then the surplus goes back into the domestic and global market, or they can pay farmers not to grow as much. Price supports set a minimum price and compensate farmers if the price drops below the minimum. These prevent oversupply. Farmers do not need to plant extra to attain their income target if prices begin to fall.

In theory, controls and supports make sense; in practice, supply management has had only limited success. Oversupply of wheat, rice, and other commodities continuously threatened to drive prices down and farmers out of business in the United States and Europe through the 1950s and 1960s (Winders 2009, 130). Great Britain and the European Community faced hunger following the wars and became acutely aware of the danger of their dependence on imported food. They too instituted supply management policies and increased production, becoming net exporters along with the United States, Australia, and South Africa (Winders 2009, 146, 154).

Supply management was the cornerstone of U.S. agricultural policy from the 1930s to 1996. It should be noted that these farm policies came into being with other social welfare programs of the Great Depression such as social security, unemployment insurance, and collective bargaining, and was retrenched at the same time as welfare (Aid for Families with Dependent Children) reform in 1996 (Winders 2009, xvii). Although supply management may have made sense for U.S. farmers and consumers by keeping prices more predictable, it under-priced U.S. products on the global market. Supply management—along with trade liberalization and farm subsidies in the United States (and Europe)—set up an unfair competition between farmers in the United States and Europe, and small-scale farmers in developing nations. According to the International Assessment of Agricultural Science and Technology for Development (IAASTD), it has resulted in "'long term negative effects for poverty, food security and the environment.' Many of the worst of these effects have been borne by the most economically and socially disadvantaged sections of rural society, in particular women and indigenous communities" (quoted in Brandon 2008).

Revolutions in Agriculture

Increasing populations were already straining food supplies in the 1960s. The "green revolution" was the first globalized food trend in the contemporary period of globalization. A number of globalization factors coalesce in the story of the green revolution: the preference for science over traditional knowledge and technique, the rationalization of production processes—in this case, agriculture—transforming small farm enterprises into big business, the activity of non-governmental agencies in policy making, and the diffusion of innovation by countries jumping on the bandwagon.

The Green Revolution

Science was brought to agriculture in Mexico through the professionalization of the *agronomists*—the *agrónomos*—beginning in the 1920s. Science as an objective disinterested source of specialized knowledge was going global. To be modern was to accept the validity of science. It became a universal way of attaining legitimacy. Agronomists wanted to establish themselves as scientific professionals and therefore the experts in agriculture. The new revolutionary government of Mexico wanted to establish domestic and international legitimacy and bring prosperity to its people. Elevating the *agrónomos* was part of their larger cultural campaign to introduce science and specialized professional knowledge into many practices, such as medicine, law, and education. The government's agenda and the agronomists' agenda complemented one another (Cotter 2003).

The green revolution began after WWII in Mexico with an "agricultural miracle." The Rockefeller Foundation pursued an ambitious program of agricultural science in Mexico, producing new seeds, chemicals for fertilizers and pesticides, and developing modern farming techniques. With their enhanced stature, *agrónomos* took on political appointments within the government bureaucracy, furthering their rise in the

political and social structure. They used this to cement their position as the experts in the agricultural sector of the country. Gradually, the science of agriculture displaced most of the traditional agricultural and plant-breeding techniques of the peasants and the hacienda owners. Traditional techniques produced good yields, but not the largest possible yields. Traditional crops were also reliable. Potato, corn, tomato, and tropical crops that had been bred and cultivated over centuries survived the storms and frosts that destroyed hybrid breeds of the Rockefeller Foundation's agricultural program (Cotter 2003). Nevertheless, the traditional gave way to the modern and scientific.

The value of the green revolution was judged by only one measure: the immediate increase in yields. Mexico experienced an agricultural miracle. The new scientific techniques produced dramatic increases. The program looked ready to go global. In 1961, figuring that what worked in Mexico would work everywhere, the Rockefeller Center with help from the World Bank, USAID, and multinational corporations diffused the green revolution. A network of research facilities were established worldwide. Seed varieties and technologies, some of which were developed for Mexico, were packaged and exported to developing nations through Latin America and Asia. Policies and practices of the green revolution diffused globally through the work, advice, and encouragement of agricultural science experts, and the financial backing of the international financial institutions. They did not account for the different environmental and social contexts of different countries or any of the less obvious or potential long-term consequences.

In Asia, the green revolution focused on high-yielding rice. The green revolution brought new seeds, fertilizers and machinery, and irrigation and production methods to developing countries such as India, Pakistan, the Philippines, Sri Lanka, and Indonesia. The goal was to make them self-sufficient, particularly with respect to staple crops. Massive programs of aid—money to buy the new seeds and other products of the green revolution—were implemented. Yields increased 300% from 1970 to 2006. Hunger decreased from 34% to 16% in the same time. In India and through Southeast Asia, agricultural output surged increasing cereal yields, reducing food prices, and decreasing poverty. Undoubtedly, thousands of lives were saved.

The glow of modernity—rationalized business practice, scientific products and techniques, and the promise of food abundance—had near universal appeal. In contrast, small-scale subsistence farming and traditional seed, crops, and methods seemed antiquated. Even the best-intentioned people were blinded to the detrimental effects of green revolution polices on the social structure of these societies and the long-term costs to food security.

Unintended Consequences of the Green Revolution

The long-term and less obvious costs of the green revolution were not considered when it was heralded a success. The social and environmental costs, as well as costs in food security, were severe. There is an extensive literature on the problems caused by the green revolution. Only a few are reviewed here.

Social Costs

Most peasants, who had received little land in the redistribution of the revolution, could not afford to purchase the seed. Rather than relying on one year's crop to produce next year's seed, new seed had to be bought annually. Pesticides, fertilizers, and irrigation systems were also expensive. Small farmers were left out of the green revolution, increasing inequalities in wealth.

Women's contributions to agriculture were devalued because they could not be traded on the international commodities market. Women took advantage of the local environments to forage for medicines and foods. They kept the soil healthy restoring it with agricultural by-product. Large farming enterprises left little land in a natural state available for foraging indigenous plants. Industrialized pesticides and fertilizers displaced their soil-enrichment efforts. Women, without education and often without the right to own property, became more marginalized and poor (Brandon 2008).

Aid flowing to subsidize large-scale factory farming disrupts markets and undercuts competition from smaller growers. Even small growers who borrowed money to purchase the tools of the green revolution were not able to repay their debt and went bankrupt. People were replaced by machines in agriculture and were forced to urban areas, where many people now make a living picking refuse from garbage fills. Slums of makeshift housing, with open ditches for sewage and no running water or electricity, grew up around cities. The peasants who stayed to work on farms for wages became a rural proletariat (Real-Cabello 2003, 131).

Costs to Crops

When the green revolution reduced the variety of crops grown, it increased the vulnerability of a farm's yield to disease. On traditional farms, planting varieties of a crop prevents an outbreak of a pest or disease from affecting an entire harvest. On the new farms, one pest or disease could wipe out an entire year's produce.

On traditional farms, different varieties of a crop or a variety of crops grown are ready for harvest at different times. This ensures a steady food supply. Using mono-cropping, the entire crop is ready at the same time, affecting the cycle of supply.

The traditional practice of rotating varieties enriches the soil as different varieties consume different combinations of nutrients. Mono-cropping drains the soil of the very nutrient needed for the next farm cycle.

To combat these effects, the green revolution depended heavily on chemical pesticides, fertilizers, and irrigation. When the energy crisis of the 1970s hit and oil prices soared, everything related directly or indirectly to oil cost more. The cost of fertilizers and pesticides, which are petroleum based; irrigation, which consumes energy to operate; and transportation of produce to market became much more expensive. Food costs rose, exacerbating hunger.

Environmental Costs

Other indirect costs became apparent as well. The heavy irrigation required for the new seeds and fertilizers depleted groundwater supplies rapidly. Water thought to be a renewable resource became scarce. Aquifers and other fresh water supplies shrank and became polluted faster than they could be replenished. Fertilizers and pesticides diminish the quality and capacity of soil, disturb ecosystems, and harm plant and animal species.

In Bali, runoff from fertilizers to grow miracle rice destroyed many of the coral reefs in Bali Barat National Park. Pesticide use killed birds and spiders that were the natural predators for the pests found on rice (Wijaya 2008). The high-yield hybrids developed for the green revolution were very high maintenance. The costs of the high maintenance have been severe, hampering our capacity to produce food for the foreseeable future and perhaps destroying some environments beyond repair. Traditional farming methods avoided these catastrophic costs and more typically enriched rather than ravaged the environment.

After the Green Revolution

The green revolution increased the food supply in many countries despite the costs to farmers and long-term costs to the environment. Nevertheless, in 1970, hunger threatened the world again. In Afghanistan, Bangladesh, Chad, Ethiopia, Kenya, Senegal, Somalia, and other nations—an estimated 32 countries in all—populations were threatened with starvation. Pockets of hunger became obvious in the United States and other rich nations. The Department of Agriculture estimated 400,000,000 people globally faced the very real possibility of starvation (Winders 2009, 129–130). The population explosion in the developing world was an important factor in the crisis. Climate was another; both flood and drought resulted in poor harvests in many nations. But with stockpiles of staples on hand, explanations beyond the obvious must apply (153).

When global trade in agriculture began to rise again in the 1970s, farmers took advantage of more open markets to export as much as they could. Adjustments in exchange rates and the Soviet Union's demand for imported grain helped increase the rate of exports rapidly (Dimitri et al. 2005, 7). That does not mean that all was well. Governments had to subsidize the surplus and try to get rid of it through export. Managing the ever-increasing surplus strained government budgets (Winders 2009, 153, 155). When governments released surplus into the market, they flooded and prices dropped.

Do these repeated crises in the global food supply mean that no food should be imported, that everything needs to be grown locally? Probably, it does not. But a reasonable balance needs to be found between domestic and export markets. Food need not be grown only where and when it can be most cheaply produced (Allen and Wilson 2008, 535). Like poor countries, developed countries that depend too heavily on food imports suffer shortages when the sources of their imports dry up. When a new wave of agricultural globalization hits, global output soars, as it did in the 1990s. As more countries adopt new agricultural technologies, exports flood the market, and competition for international markets drives prices down and trade down (Dimitri et al. 2005, 8). In the United States, government subsidies to growers keep profits up so that they can sell cheaply on the domestic and global markets.

Are U.S. agricultural products really cheap? Are large commercial farms really the most efficient and effective growers?

The question of how cheap industrialized food stuffs are does not have a straightforward answer. You cannot determine cost by looking at the price on the shelf or in the commodity exchanges. If the costs of production are being transferred from producers to others, the commodity may not be as cheap as it appears. The same is true if it is of poorer quality. If we are getting poor quality for our money, it is not cheap, regardless of what it costs.

In the United States, agriculture has tremendous costs that are born by others, by non-producers. One cost is the subsidies paid to agribusiness. In 2009, farm subsidies were about $15 billion. Of this sum, 90% went to agribusiness, large farming corporations. Much of the 90% was for animal feed, cotton, and other industrial use products, not food (Picard 2010). Another cost is water pollution (Wise 2010, 3). In the Mississippi Gulf, there is a "dead zone," 6,000 to 7,000 square miles where nothing much grows except algae. It is one of the largest dead zones in the world. The algae overgrowth is caused by agricultural runoff of fertilizer and pesticides from the Mississippi basin (Allen and Wilson 2008; Bruckner 2008). The crops that are produced so cheaply are not cheap if all the costs of production are included. The long- and short-term costs of the dead zone and the loss to the fishing industry are immeasurable.

A third cost is to domestic farmers in poorer nations. For example, at times, corn from the United States outsells Mexican corn not only in the United States; it outsells it in other countries and even in Mexico. Subsidies to U.S. farms allow them to sell corn very cheaply. Mexican producers are being put out of business. In the meantime, Mexican farmers have been maintaining biodiversity in their corn supply, which makes their corn cost more. Biodiversity has value. When the world needs crops that can cope with climate change, pesticide-resistant pests, and any number of unpredictable risks, current crops lacking diversity will not meet the challenges. But not many people seem willing to pay for the value of biodiversity (Wise 2010, S3).

The Global Food Crisis of 2008

Rising energy costs, increased demand for grain-fed meat, global warming, and corn-based bio-fuels pushed food prices up in 2008 (Allen and Wilson

BOX 14.2   A Closer Look: The Cost of Food Aid

Food aid is clearly one of the most important forms of aid, but it has been widely criticized. Food aid has been a way for richer nations to ensure that their food products are sold. Aid money is used to buy surplus product in richer nations, which is then distributed in poorer nations. This undermines local agriculture and ensures the profits of agribusiness.

Recognizing this, a new World Bank program for investment in agriculture in poorer nations was designed on the heels of the global food crisis of 2008. The program, part of the "New Deal on Global Food Policy," has, allegedly, backfired. The International Finance Corporation, a private sector branch of the World Bank, created foreign direct investment financial tools that have been characterized as "land grabs," allowing foreign investors, including Morgan Stanley and Goldman Sachs, to acquire land cheaply without making any long-term commitments in jobs or agricultural development. The World Bank reported this in one of its own reports (Daniel and Mittal, 2010).

The World Food Programme (WFP), headquartered in Rome, redesigned its food aid. In 2008, WFP

- purchased 72% of its food in developing countries, boosting the development of agriculture there;
- gave cash and voucher assistance to over 1 million individuals to purchase food locally; and
- launched the Purchase for Progress Program (P4P) to procure food from small farmers in the poorest countries and connect them to larger markets.

These programs will help to build the agricultural capacity of poorer nations toward food security and provide jobs and livelihoods as well (Mousseau 2010).

2008; "World Food Crisis" 2010). Corn, a staple in much of the world, doubled in price from 2006 to 2008. In the United States, where about 16% of the budget of a poor family is spent on food, this caused a rush to food banks. The price of food imports for developing countries increased 25% from 2007 to 2008. In countries like Nigeria, where 73% of a family's budget is for food, or Vietnam, where it is 65%, it creates more than rush to food banks; it brings disaster.

From 2008 to 2009, the World Bank food benchmark index increased again, up 23%. It began to settle at a point that was less than the 2008 peak but still considerably higher than 2007. Some countries saw their main staple crops—which are significant proportions of their diets, such as sorghum, maize, rice, and cassava—increase as much as 61% (World Bank 2010, 2).

If farmers stop growing food and cannot afford to buy it, their families have nothing to eat. In the recent food crisis,

> countries like the Philippines could not get the rice they needed. They had stopped producing enough rice to protect themselves from such a market shock and they could not get anyone to sell it to them because governments were concerned about feeding their own people first. (Wise 2010, 2)

This was a repeat of a story often told.

The global food market is failing. Poverty among food producers is increasing, along with increased food dependence and increased hunger. The quest for cheap food is the main culprit in food crises (Wise 2010, 3). Export-oriented agriculture worked for some countries. But there was a fallacy at work. It turns out that what works for one country might not work for all. Countries flocked to the export markets after WWII, encouraged by the World Bank, IMF, and donor countries. Rice, sugar, and coffee were all subject to this rush to export, flooding the market. This is a classic case of how diffusion of a model becomes dysfunctional when everyone jumps on the bandwagon. Now the rush is to cut flowers (Polaski, in Schalatek 2008, 5).

It is ironic that in Asia, the majority of starving people live in rural areas where farmers are producing for export and buying food for themselves. Importing food consumes most of these families' budgets: 71% in Cambodia, 70% in Tajikistan and Burma, 64% in Georgia, 60% in Azerbaijan, and 59% in Nepal (Macan-Markar 2010). This is true of many other countries as well. There are agricultural exports, whether coffee, sugar, rubber, wood or some other agricultural product, but not enough food.

BOX 14.3   A Closer Look: Food for Fuel

Using food crops for fuel has set food prices skyrocketing. Ethanol, a gasoline additive and alternative, can be processed from corn and other food crops. When crops are grown for the fuel market, the prices that they command cannot be matched in the food market. In the second half of 2010, corn prices in the United States soared 73%, in significant part due to increased use of corn in ethanol. Food and fuel competition over palm oil contributes to hunger in the Middle East, where protests over food prices are toppling governments and challenging others.

Now, cassava has entered the fuel market. Thailand is the world's largest cassava exporter. Cassava is source of animal feed and a backup human food in Asia. It is a staple in Africa. China's fuel hunger consumed 98% of Thailand's cassava exports, which has grown fourfold and doubled in price from 2008 through 2010.

This is likely to increase the price of meats and contribute to hunger in Asia and potentially Africa if China's appetite for cassava-based fuel turns to African producers, or if others acquire the taste (Rosenthal 2011).

New varieties of many crops are low in nutritive content. Although food production increased in 2009, ranging from 17% to 18%, the food crisis is complicated by lack of micronutrients. More than half of the hungry live in Asia, and the majority of the 15,000 children who die every day from hunger are in Asia. The problem is not the number of calories that they consume, but the lack of vitamins and minerals. Their immune systems are weak (Makan-Markar 2010). (You can read more about micronutrient malnutrition in Chapter Twelve.)

In the long run, the advice of the experts, the scientific advances in food production, and attempts to balance supply and demand in the global market failed to end hunger. Complicating this, strategic behavior on the parts of a few firms with oligarchies in seed and fertilizers created dependence on expensive technologies, pricing many small farmers out of business and ruining soil with overuse and chemical overload. Water supplies depleted through inefficient irrigation and pollution. The factory model and cheap food approach to agriculture are more costly than they appear.

The Livestock Revolution

As global income increases, demand for meat, poultry, fish, eggs, and milk increases. The factory model—large-scale efficient production—that dominates farming dominates the livestock industry as well. Agricultural methods, designed to appeal to the developing tastes for well-marbled meats and plump chickens—combine sciences of genetics, feed, and medicine to produce cheap meat. Increasing demand led to intensified meat production, quickly processing more cattle and poultry from gestation to slaughter to packaging in highly rationalized ways, as products on an assembly line.

Like the green revolution in produce, the livestock revolution is resource and energy intensive. The estimates vary by source, but they agree that livestock production is grossly inefficient, even when compared to other meats. Some estimates are that cattle consume from 50% to 80% of the grain grown in the United States. Beef consumption in the United States consumes 57,172 gallons of water per capita per year. Another is that half of the water used in the United States is used to grow grain to feed cattle, and that the water consumed in producing 10 pounds of steak is equivalent to a family's consumption in a year (Barclay 2012; Fischetti 2012; IPACC 2007; John Robbins 2001). On average, each quarter pound hamburger requires 6.7 pounds of feed, 58.2 gallons of water, 74.5 square feet of land, and 1,036 btus of energy (Barclay 2012). Meat consumption in the United States has contributed to fuel shortages, food shortages, and land degradation. Production methods are associated with illnesses among livestock, some of which have been passed onto humans.

In Mexico, like many other developing countries, the science of genetics and the technologies related to production, such as seed, facilities, medicine, and inoculations, have come from the United States and Europe. In turn, farmers deliver a product that meets the specifications of agribusiness. This creates market for U.S. and European technologies and provides a supply of cheap food to meet the tastes of consumers in the United States, Europe, and the expanding global middle class. Like the manufacture of products along the border, the maquila model applies in the poultry industry as well. The component parts—chickens, feed, incubators, and so on—are imported to the factory. The product—chickens and eggs—are created and shipped back. In Mexico, only about 30% of poultry comes from traditional producers (Real-Cabello 2003, 136).

A New Revolution? Countervailing Trends

The factory model emphasizes efficient production techniques by harvesting large parcels of land with one crop or treating animals like just another assembly-line product, using whatever means will produce the most volume in the short run. Long-term costs, resource depletion, environmental degradation, and health concerns have not been factored into the costs (John Robbins 2001, 227). As other countries emulate the factory model and the Western diet, health and environmental effects also diffuse.

BOX 14.4   A Closer Look: Paying for Quality

Everyone knows that fair trade means that workers are getting a decent wage for their work. Because these goods usually cost a bit more than others, we assume we are getting quality, too. In reality, fair trade has nothing to do with quality.

Intelligentsia, a coffee company, believes we should pay fairly for quality as well. Rather than pay a fair trade price for mediocre coffee beans, Intelligentsia pays a premium price. Its founder spends considerable time and money, about $200,000 annually, traveling in coffee-growing countries seeking out coffee competition winners and establishing relationships with individual coffee growers. He wants them to understand the Intelligentsia point of view and trust him to pay a fair price for high quality.

His price offers and quality demands were so premium that Intelligentsia was a bit of a joke in the coffee business. Not any longer. His growers are happy. His company is growing. He is cultivating a culture of quality (Weissman 2008).

Very recently, countervailing trends may be shaping a new revolution. Agriculture became a focus of the environmental movement in the 1980s, and new approaches have been diffusing slowly. The primordial and symbolic importance of food and the countryside have been powerful images in mustering support for environmental and related food issues (Buttel 1995, 11).

Concern for hunger, healthy food, and the health of the environment has raised concern for sustainable agriculture. The increasing awareness of health risks associated with agricultural technologies from the fertilizers and pesticides to the hormones and antibiotics given meat products, and filthy conditions of livestock, the market for organic foods is growing. Agricultural programs have grown beyond soil conservation to consideration of air and water quality, wildlife and landscape protection, and animal welfare (Dimitri et al. 2005, 7).

The World Food Programme (WFP 2012) has been steadily increasing its practice of buying local foods. In 2010, it purchased over 80% of its food aid—$1.25 billion—from local purveyors in developing countries. This promotes sustainable agriculture in developing nations. It also lowers the cost of foods by saving on transportation, and it tailors food aid to local tastes. Where local purchasing programs are in place, they help protect local consumers from the global rise in food prices. The WFP has launched a program—Purchase for Progress (P4P)—to help small farmers secure reliable markets for staple commodities at a fair price. By providing local to global collaboration in skill development for every step in the agricultural process, from the business end (accessing seed, financing, marketing, pricing, packaging) to the agricultural, and with particular attention to enabling women, P4P offers promise for building a country's self-sufficiency and contribution to a healthier, more abundant global food supply.

The Global Horticultural Revolution

Tastes are changing in the developed world and in urban areas the world over. Demand is increasing for fruits and vegetables and decreasing for grains and tubers. People want fresh produce, year-round, and a wide variety of products. This is part of the healthy lifestyle trend. People also want environmentally friendly and fair trade produce. These trends result from the increasing global concern for human rights, environmental protection, and health. To differentiate this movement from agriculture as it is practiced, the term *horticulture* has come into play. Although there is certainly overlap, the primary distinctions are the emphases on plants and trees—fruits and vegetables in particular—the nutritional value of produce, and environmentally friendly growing—although this may involve controlled environments such as high tunnels for protection from climate factors such as temperature extremes, wind or rain, or pests ("Environmental Horticulture" 2011).

Low consumption of fruits and vegetables is among the 10 top risk factors for death (Weinberger and Lumpkin 2005, 4). In 2002, the global fruit and vegetable supply was 173 kg per capita (3), but consumption varies widely. In the developed world, it is about 200 kg per capita. In Asia, supply has grown to 180 kg, now outpacing Africa, which lags at 106 kg. However, wide variations exist within each region and by gender and age. In some areas of Eastern Europe, Latin America, and South Asia, consumption is as low as 54 kg to 75 kg for young women.

The horticultural revolution increased the production of fruits about 3.6% a year and vegetables about 5.5% a year from 1980 to 2004. Fifty-eight percent of the increase came from China, 38% from all other developing countries, and only 4% from the developed countries (World Bank 2007, 58). Trade in fruits and vegetables increased fivefold from 1961 to 2001 (Weinberger and Lumpkin 2005, 7).

Those countries that take advantage of this global shift can realize dramatic profits. As the Closer Look box indicates, horticulture has a much greater return, about tenfold, than cereals. It is also more labor intensive, so has a more dramatic impact on employment—particularly the employment of women—throughout the production chain from farm, through processing,

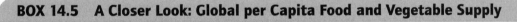

BOX 14.5   A Closer Look: Global per Capita Food and Vegetable Supply

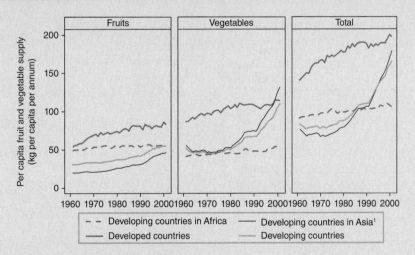

[1] Upward trend of vegetables largely influenced by changes in China.

FAOSTAT data, 2004.

Source: Weinberger and Lumpkin (2005, 4).

packing, and marketing (Weinberger and Lumpkin 2005; World Bank 2007, 58).

For poorer, developing countries to take advantage of the economic and health benefits of horticultural agriculture, several systemic problems need to be addressed. Horticulture is a more risky venture than cereals. It requires much more pesticide, which is an area where research is needed. There is an investment period of several years with some fruits before a yield is seen. There is also more price volatility. Most growers will need credit to participate in the market. Better quality seed is needed for production in some local environments in poorer countries. A Box14.6 and 14.7 of post harvest improvements are also necessary. Fragility of produce requires better facilities for processing or getting fresh produce to market (Weinberger and Lumpkin 2005, 14). The accessibility to markets varies significantly. Improving access to markets to reduce perishing is important for countries to take advantage of opportunities in horticultural markets.

Storage, transportation, price information, traceability to ensure food safety, quality control, and standardization for supermarket chains and large processors are all areas where small growers in developing countries will need training (Weinberger and Lumpkin 2005, 14–15). Programs such as the P4P are trying to fill these needs.

Growing food for local consumption is also an important part of the horticultural revolution. Home gardens, community gardens, and farmers markets for urbanites are an important segment of the market for fresh produce. Well-done urban gardens can have a vital role in household food security. Urban poor who participate in urban farming eat more fresh vegetables than other families in the same income category (Weinberger and Lumpkin 2005, 15).

There is danger that the local food movement ignores and sometimes perpetuates food inequalities (Allen and Wilson 2008). By focusing on individual consumption practices, neo-liberal assumptions are not challenged. Agriculture is not significantly

BOX 14.6 A Closer Look: Cereal and Vegetable Production

Average number of labor days for production of cereals and vegetables in Asia

	Cereals	Vegetables
Bangladesh	133	338
Cambodia	81	437
India	80	124
Lao PDR	101	227
Philippines	93	185
Vietnam (northern)	216	468
Vietnam (southern)	111	297

Sources: Bangladesh: Ali and Hau (2001); Cambodia: Abedullah et al. (2002); India: Joshi et al. (2003); Lao PDR: Siphandouang et al. (2002), Philippines: Francisco (2004); Vietnam (northern): Thuy et al. (2002); and Vietnam (southern): Hau et al. (2002).

BOX 14.7 A Closer Look: Net Farm Income per Family Member of Horticultural Versus Non-Horticultural Smallholder Farms

Horticultural farms net smallholder farms much more income per family member than non-horticultural farms, as shown in this chart.

% Difference in Country Farm Income

Kenya	497
Bangladesh	29
Cambodia	117
Lao PDR	380
Vietnam (northern)	20
Vietnam (southern)	189

Source: Weinberger and Lumpkin (2005, 10).

BOX 14.8   Distance to Markets

Road rehabilitation in Madagascar facilitates community access to both the Health Center and Market, improving people's chance to develop income-generating activities.

changed. Slow Food USA celebrates "good food" at fairs, carnivals, and tastings. It is all very upscale but not very helpful to local poor who cannot afford them. In my own city, Pittsburgh, there is still a paucity of fresh produce, even supermarkets, in urban areas. Those that are located in the inner city tend to cater to a trendy crowd that is gentrifying the city. Some localities are enriched by the local movement, while others suffer. "Buy Local" food movements vary considerably from their historical predecessors, the "Buy Union" and "Buy Black" movements, that addressed inequalities directly (537).

The food sovereignty movement was formally organized at a 1996 World Food Summit by Via Campesina, an international coalition. It stresses local control of food supply from production through consumption. It is different than the simply Buy Local movements. Food sovereignty proclaims the right of all people for safe, nutritious, and culturally appropriate food (Allen and Wilson 2008, 537). It is a holistic approach that recognizes that protecting land, water, seed, ecosystems, and local growing and harvesting methods is necessary for sustainable agriculture—what they term *agroecological production*. The factory model of grain, produce, and livestock production is rejected, and the movement goes a step further by trying to heal the earth of harm done by decades of unsustainable practices. Trade is not rejected, but trade practices must be scrutinized to ensure that practices are fair—not food aid dumping or unfair subsidies that

undermine local producers—and encourage healthy and sustainable production. The movement has grown into a network of global alliances, partnering groups from developed and developing countries in pursuing the common food sovereignty agenda.

The Buy Local movement in the United States might serve as a springboard for social justice if it can awaken people's consciousness—and consciences. The ethics of consumption can be extended to embrace fair trade standards here in the United States. The organic food movement might lead to greater attention to food quality, the nature of factory food systems, and the commoditization of food, and to rejecting the notion that food should be industrialized and cheap. Developing a sense of locality can be generalized to other localities and other places. Local should not be read as good, and global as bad. Partnering with other regions and localities, globally, may lead to more just policies and practices (Allen and Wilson 2008, 538). It is certainly possible that buying globally can be every bit as good for the environment, our health, and social justice as buying locally.

Africa: The New Green Revolution and Sustainability

Salzburg Global Seminars gather leaders from around the world to develop solutions for pressing global problems. The first green revolution largely bypassed Africa. The new green revolution for Africa was among the subjects of the Salzburg

Global Seminar session in 2008, a year of global food crisis. Kofi Annan (2008) explained the strategy of the Alliance for the Green Revolution in Africa to avoid the mistakes and reverse some of the policies of the first green revolution. He identified six primary action items, all of which place the small farmer in a central role.

The first recommendation is to transform institutional support for agriculture by establishing a grassroots network of farmers to direct research and technology needs. This would be funded through private and government sources. It requires significant reappraisal and revision of education, research, and funding. Small farmers, rather than being an afterthought, would be the focus of the "new green." It should concentrate on improved varieties of traditional crops, taking into account the varied climate conditions of Africa. In some ways, the baseline assumption is the same: African agriculture can be transformed through science, technology, and innovation. This remains a major theme of contemporary globalization (Annan 2008). Nevertheless, it is modified by a more mature view of science that moderates the zeal for scientific progress with concern for social and environmental priorities and progress.

A 2010 evaluation of the Alliance for a Green Revolution in Africa (AGRA) warned that small farmers were still not getting enough public funds. Small farmers who could not afford the seed and technology were left out of the last green revolution. They are in danger of being left out again. This time, they are left out for a different reason. Most funding is going to farmers who own their land. Commercialization of agriculture eroded traditional systems of communal land sharing and left many farmers, particularly women, without land. Women are the bulk of small farmers, and the most likely to rent their land. Many of them are missed by the grants. Leaving them out eliminates a considerable portion of the small farming population (AGRA 2010, 13). There needs to be a solution to reinvigorate small farming.

Another weakness in AGRA is that the concentration has been on training crop scientists and not social scientists. Agriculture is more than a technical process; it is a complicated social process. The unanticipated effects of past policies on practice have been devastating. Vigilance in understanding and monitoring the relationships and effects of the dynamics between small farmers and technology emanating from transnational corporations is important to guarantee the survival of small farms and their knowledge of sustainable farm practice. In India, high-yielding rice and wheat were substituted for indigenous varieties. In traditional practices, crops produced more than food. There was absolutely no waste of plant material. Important biological by-products—what others might have seen as waste—were used by women farmers as fodder, fertilizer, fuel, and fiber (Pande 2007, 137). Changing the farm crops and processes meant that more products had to be bought as commodities, pricing small farmers out of business. This was an unforeseen cost of commercialization. Traditional methods were more efficient.

In the Philippines, 7,000 rice varieties were replaced with mono-cropping of green revolution rice. Local small farmers there become dependent on buying seed, fertilizers, and pesticides, which harmed the land. Another unaccounted cost was unemployment. Commercialized agriculture adds to job loss. Farm labor is an important source of employment. In Africa, most people are still employed in agriculture. There are very limited opportunities in both rural and urban areas, and job loss has serious ramifications (AGRA 2010, 14), as happened in other green revolution countries that experienced very rapid urbanization.

Genetically Modified (GM) Seed

Genetically modified (GM) seed is controversial on many grounds, from the point of its production, through its use, to the health of the food grown from it. One of the main controversies concerning the production of GM seeds is who owns the genetic

---

BOX 14.9   A Closer Look: Disaster Risk Management in Food and Agriculture: The Challenge

The number of reported disasters increased significantly from 1987 to 2006—particularly hydro-meteorological hazards (such as droughts, floods, tropical storms, and wild fires)—averaging 195 per year in 1987–1998 and 365 per year in 2000–2006—with the likelihood that the trend will continue in coming years.

- Every year, more than 230 million people on average were affected by disasters between 2000 and 2007.
- Disaster losses are steadily increasing due to a number of factors such as increased extreme weather events associated with climate change, population growth, unplanned urbanization and environmental degradation.
- The Intergovernmental Panel on Climate Change (IPCC 2007) Fourth Assessment report points to a future where climate induced hazards and disasters will further increase.
- The possible breakdown of agricultural systems due to climate change, such as increased exposure to drought, rising temperatures, and more erratic rainfall, could result in malnutrition for an additional 600 million people.
- Disasters undermine development progress, constrain economic growth, and threaten food production. Systematic disaster risk management—as an integrated component of development—plays a critical role in assuring future agricultural production and access to food and water by the world's most vulnerable people.

Source: RPDRM (n.d.).

material in the seed. When local seed bred over centuries by farmers is taken, given a new genetic trait, patented, and sold back to farmers, it is stealing the genetic material over which the farmers once had control. Despite the reforms in agriculture, this threat is still looming in Kenya (Bornstein 2012).

Proprietary rights to seeds do not benefit small farmers because they are controlled by private enterprises. Intellectual property rights to seed derived from local knowledge and public institutional research are poorly, if at all, protected. Once these rights fall into agribusiness control, farmers and local communities are forced into expensive arrangements (AGRA 2010, 14). Farmers cannot use seed from one year's crop to plant the following year. They must buy new, expensive seed every year, a costly proposition. The patents prevent farmers from producing their own seed for the following year from this year's crops. Eventually, local maize would be lost (Gibson 2004, 3).

According to a host of researchers, multinational corporations are establishing proprietary rights to traditional and local remedies and medicines as well. This practice, called *bio-prospecting*, has been going on for years. In 2009, India licensed 200,000 of its local treatments as public property. This move was motivated after Indian researchers found that foreign companies had patented 5,000 "medicinal plants and traditional systems," over 2,000 of which are components of Indian medicinal systems (Ramesh 2009).

Chemical companies reap huge profits through genetically modified seed engineered to complement their pesticides, herbicides, and fertilizers. When genetically modified seed is grown, it often has specific requirements regarding fertilizers and pesticides. For example, Monsanto, a leader in the industry, has engineered one of its seeds to pair with its popular herbicide, Round-Up. Not only are farmers forced by government policy or intergovernmental

BOX 14.10   Consider This: Patenting Living Organisms

In 1930, The U.S. Congress passed the Plant Patent Act that allowed for patenting asexually reproducing plant species. In 1970, the Plant Variety Protection Act allowed the patenting of some sexually reproducing plants (but excluded bacteria).

In 1980, The U.S. Supreme Court ruled that a live, human-made organism could be patented. The case involved a genetically engineered bacterium that could do what no known bacteria could do—break down crude oil. It was according to the court a product of human ingenuity—a "manufacture" and "composition of matter" as specified by Congress, not a product of nature (http://laws.findlaw.com/us/447/303.html).

Organic Farmers vs. Monsanto

What happens if genetically modified seed blows into an organic field and contaminates the crop? Farmers will not be able to certify that their crop is organic or that milk from cattle that feed on contaminated alfalfa crops is organic,

(Continued)

(Continued)

ruining people's livelihoods. Whereas a lower court banned the sale of Monsanto's GM alfalfa seed until its safety could be further studied, the Supreme Court overruled the decision (Dickenson 2011). In the United States, some farmers have given up their farms, unable to ensure the purity of their crop.

Another issue, however, is whether or not the farmers could be sued for patent infringement. In 2011, a group of farmers sued Monsanto for refusing to sign agreements not to sue them if Monsanto seed contaminated their crops.

Traditional Breeding Methods

Farmers have bred seeds for thousands of years. By selecting the best specimens from each year's crop to plant the next year, they continuously upgrade the species. They may select specimens on the basis of drought resistance, the volume of food, pest resistance, or, most likely, the chosen seed came from plants that demonstrated all of the above.

The lineage of some species goes back thousands of years. These are true heirloom plants.

organizations to use the seed, but they must then also use the other products to grow the seed.

The majority of the traditional agricultural workforce is women. Women are big losers in the globalization of agriculture. Higher capital intensity and the mechanization of commercial commodity production have displaced women. Women's connection to family welfare and security is significant. A greater portion of women's income goes to family welfare than does men's. Women's incomes translate more directly into child health and nutrition. The loss of women's place in agriculture jeopardizes families. Privatization has pushed many of them from rural to urban areas for employment and has contributed to their pauperization. It is also costly in terms of losing specialized knowledge that women have developed. In low-input agriculture and agriculture-related forestry, women's knowledge of the relationships among forest, farm trees, fields, and the uses of biomass contains many of the secrets of sustainable small farm subsistence agriculture (Pande 2007, 138).

Last is the issue of food safety. Many people fear that GM foods may be toxic or may cause resistance to antibiotics (which is certainly a problem in the United States; however, whether GM foods contribute to it has not been demonstrated). In the United States, there are no regulations governing growing, importing, or labeling of foods made with genetically modified seed. They as well as foods produced with them are assumed to be safe. In the EU, approval must be granted to sell or grow GM seed or use it in feed or food. Seed and genetically grown plants must be handled in such a way as to prevent any mixing with conventional seed or products. Foods must be labeled so that consumers can make informed decisions (GMO Compass 2006). Actual labels as of 2007 were still hard to find. Fearing dropping sales, producers were finding alternatives to GM ingredients. Indirect use of GM, however, might be present such as in meat fed with GM feed or cheeses or wines fermented with GM microorganisms (GMO Compass 2007).

Facing food crises in 2002, governments in Southern Africa came face to face with the dilemma: accept food aid, which undoubtedly contained some GM grain because much came from the United States, or risk starvation for many people. Their primary fear was safety. Zimbabwe refused the grain. Zambia locked up what it had already accepted. Extra care must be taken not to repeat mistakes of the past green revolution in leaving countries export heavy and food short.

Threats to the Natural Environment

We have seen how humanity's food platform rests on the earth's environment. So does humankind's health and general welfare. The earth's support of human life is referred to as *ecosystem services*. We are just now beginning to realize the many services that nature provides and the delicate balance in the systems of nature.

Environmental depletion and degradation through pollution and misuse are among the most serious issues facing humanity. Encroachments into the natural environment have unleashed epidemics. Chemicals, mono-cropping, and other poor agricultural techniques have leeched nutrients from once arable land

and depleted it. Some farm-suitable land is held hostage to landmines. The supply of potable water once thought to be a renewable resource has been diminished, and much has been destroyed by pollution. Air pollution was so dense in Mexico City and Beijing that dark clouds shrouding the landscape were visible in satellite photos. Natural weather events such as hurricanes, droughts, and heat waves have been exacerbated due to climate change.

Whether one accepts that global climate change is caused by human action, primarily burning of fossil fuels, as nearly all scientists agree, or one believes that it is a natural cycle, it is vital to reduce any contribution that people make. The environment enjoins all of humanity and is the platform that supports all life. The environment binds humanity to a common fate. But it does not impact everyone in the same way. Like other aspects of globalization, social location and local context shape globalization effects.

Globalization and environmental issues are related in several ways. Most obviously, the environment is a shared resource, and everyone depends on its health. Globalization exacerbates environmental problems as trade increases, transporting goods and people all over the world. Economic growth demands industrialization and increased production and consumption. Among the costs of production is environmental damage through the release of toxic chemicals into land, water, and air. Continuous consumption and the spread of consumerism as a global value fill dumpsites and oceans with products that are rendered obsolete—many of them harboring toxic chemicals. Feeding over 6 billion people with unsustainable globalized agricultural strategies poisons the environment. Environmental problems are global problems that must be dealt with collaboratively. Global environmental problems cause national and global security risks, among them the following:

- Conflict over water exacerbates international conflicts.
- Depleted land strains global food supplies.
- Synergy among environmental problems may threaten human security long after the original sources have diminished (in this case, threats to the earth's protective ozone layer).
- Climate change intensifies weather events, leading to humanitarian emergencies.

Existing problems related to poverty, social tensions, ineffectual leadership, and weak political institutions will be heightened and contribute to interstate conflict and state instability (Blair 2010, 39).

The range of environmental issues and the science of environmental issues cannot be reviewed in this chapter. There are many good resources that cover these in depth. In deciding what issues to write about, I chose topics that would best illustrate the role of globalization in causing a problem or the importance of managing the problem globally. I also wanted to choose problems that may not get as much attention as some others and cover at least one water, land, and air quality issue. Economic growth and environmental health are pitted against one another as though one has to be chosen over the other. But this may be a false choice. Sustainable development, along with sustainable agriculture, is theme that is gaining traction globally.

Water Issues

On July 28, 2010, the UN General Assembly declared that access to safe and clean drinking water and sanitation is a human right. This is a tall order to fill. Over 880 million people lack access to safe drinking water, and more than 2.5 billion people do not have access to basic sanitation. One and one half million children under the age of five die every year because of water- and sanitation-related diseases, and children lose 443 million school days (UN News Center 2010). Disease and health issues due to water pollution are important human security issues in developing countries. However, severe water problems are not confined to the developing world.

Despite the laws of the seas, water does not respect political boundaries. Waste put into water flows across borders and into seas and oceans, leaving dead zones—hypoxic areas—such as those in the Chesapeake Bay, the Gulf of Mexico, and many other bodies. Many river basins and aquifers span several countries, creating conflicts over sharing a resource that in many countries is more precious than oil.

The Ogallala, one of the world's largest aquifers, is in the Great Plains of the United States. It feeds one third of the nation's corn crop and supplies drinking water to seven states. It has enough water to flood the entire United States under 1.5 feet of water. While it is large, it may well be the most rapidly diminishing aquifer as well.

Ulysses, Kansas, where wells used to draw from the Ogallala, is oil rich but water poor. Rivers have turned to gravel and streams have dried up. The water table there dropped 25 feet, and drought has deprived crops

BOX 14.11   A Closer Look: Water Consumption

This map indicates the degree of oversubscription of a country's water supply. Countries are coded according to the percentage of their territory in which over 40% of available water is consumed. According to this measure, the United States, densely packed European countries

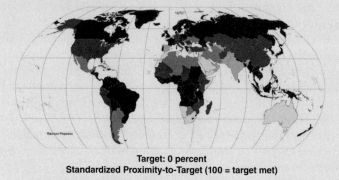

Target: 0 percent
Standardized Proximity-to-Target (100 = target met)

| 100 – 80 | 80 – 60 | 60 – 40 | 40 – 20 | 20 – 0 | no data |

Source: United Nations Environment Programme.

of sky-fed free water. Farmers are switching to cotton, and the town is looking to buy millions of dollars of water to drink (U.S. Water News Online 2006). Water in aquifers, like the Ogallala, is not renewable, but is recharged slowly as water diffuses through the ground. For now, water quality in the Ogallala is of good quality for drinking, irrigation, and livestock watering. Shallow areas of the aquifer and more southerly sources reveal contamination as water used in irrigation, laden with chemicals, seeps underground (Gurdak 2010b). Water from rain rarely reaches the aquifer, evaporating before it can diffuse down (Gurdak 2010a). "'Out here, water is like gold,' said Ulysses' mayor, 'without it we perish'" (quoted in U.S. Water News Online 2006).

Water scarcity due to overuse, contamination, and decreasing rainfall plagues every region and most countries. Satellite images of Lake Chad and the Aral Sea shockingly illustrate the environmental destruction. In the case of the Aral Sea, its desertification has left behind a salt bed carried by the wind to pollute plant life and starve animal life within a 300 km area surrounding it. The water left is so salty that there are no fish. It is contaminated with bacteria and not potable. It is a health risk to the surrounding population, which suffers from anemia, cancer, tuberculosis, typhoid fever, viral hepatitis, and throat cancer at levels as great as 3 times the national average (Bomford 2006; UNEP 2008).

To feed their booming population, Chinese farmers added an extra planting of water-intensive winter wheat to their rotation of crops. Groundwater usage doubled every year since 1970, lowering the water table. Scientists predict the aquifers below the North China plains will be drained within 30 years, unless water habits change. The once lush region is parched. Natural streams have disappeared, and once-navigable rivers are mostly dust. Water treatment is poor, and wastewater often goes right back into the supply. There is no uncertainty in this prediction (Yardley 2007). Trained as engineers, not ideologues, China's current leadership is trying to correct some excesses of the past, but they still put economic growth first.

Aquifers in other countries face the same problem. Over use, over contamination, and lower rainfall deplete and destroy what was once thought to be an abundant and renewable resource. Because aquifers are out of sight, they have not received the same level of attention in international politics as river basins or the seas. Laws of the Seas are over a hundred years old. Laws of river basins were hammered out through the 1980s and 1990s. Laws of aquifers, the purist of earth's waters, are in their infancy.

In the Israel-Palestinian conflict over settlements, most of the public attention is drawn to land disputes. But underneath the land are three important aquifers. Some of the most challenging international management problems involve water sharing, such

BOX 14.12   A Closer Look: Water Depletion

What has happened...

In 1989–1990, the Aral Sea separated into two parts: the 'Large Aral' and the 'Small Aral'

1957 from a map

1977 from satellite images

1982 from satellite images

1984 from satellite images

1993 from a map

November 2000 from satellite images

What could happened...

Between November 2000 and June 2001, Vozrojdeniya Island joined the mainland to the south

November 2007 from satellite images

PHILIPPE REKACEWICZ
FEBRUARY 2008

Sources: Nikolai Denisov, GRID-Arendal, Norway (especially for the graphics below); Scientific Information Center of International Coordination Water Commission (SIC ICWC); International Fund for Saving the Aral Sea (IFAS); The World Bank; national Astronautics ans Space Administration (NASA); United States Geological Survey (USGS), *Earthshots: Satellite images of environmental change*, United States Department of the Interior, 2000.

The salt, contamination, pesticides, and heavy metals left in the dry bed of the Aral Sea cause disease and death to humans and livestock.

Lake Chad is only about one fifth the size it was in 1963. About 50% of the decrease in size is due to human water use.

Source: United Nations Environment Programme.

Issues on Land

There are many issues of land use that disrupt the ecological balance. Several of these were detailed in our discussion of food and the environment. Changes in land use and disruptions in ecological balances pose a severe threat to humans beyond food shortages. Loss of forest diminishes the earth's capacity to absorb carbon, exacerbating global warming caused by burning fossil fuels. People are increasingly pushed into areas once inhabited and

as the Jordan River basin shared among Israel, the Palestinian territories, Syria, and Lebanon, and the Mountain aquifer shared by Israel and the Palestinians.

less arable. This erodes the land further, making it even less serviceable to human needs.

Deforestation

Forests are critical to global growth and global health. Deforestation threatens both. Historically, subsistence agriculture has been the primary cause of deforestation. More recently, globalization has accelerated depletion of forestland. Roads and railroads to meet the transportation needs of growing economies opened previously inaccessible areas of forest to development and exploitation. From 1990 to 2005, forestlands diminished at an average annual pace of 13 million hectares. Every day, the equivalent of 18,100 soccer playing fields is lost

BOX 14.13   A Closer Look: Transboundary Aquifers

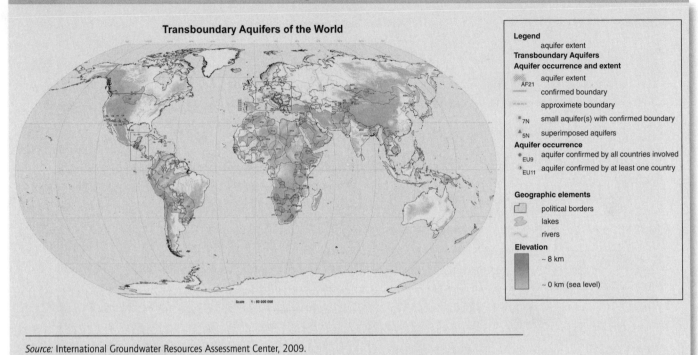

Transboundary Aquifers of the World

Source: International Groundwater Resources Assessment Center, 2009.

(UNEP n.d.). Global demands for exotic woods, increased meat consumption, and food demands have led to industrial cattle ranching, cultivating exotic woods, and factory farms in forestlands. Unmanaged, or improperly managed, each of these diminishes the economic value of the forests and its capacity to support human well-being.

Forests provide an irreplaceable array of services. Water issues are exacerbated by deforestation as trees return water vapor to the atmosphere. Forests are often referred to as the lungs of the planet, absorbing greenhouse gases. They house much of the earth's biodiversity—uses for hundreds of species we are just discovering.

BOX 14.14   A Closer Look: Primary Drivers of Zoonotic Pathogens

Rank	Driver
1	Changes in land use or agricultural practice
2	Changes in human demographics and society
3	Poor population health
4	Hospitals and medical procedures
5	Pathogenic evolution (i.e., drug resistance)
6	Contamination of food sources or water supplies
7	International travel
8	Failure of public health programs
9	International trade
10	Climate change

Source: Woolhouse and Gowtage-Sequeria (2005, 1843).

A less well-known risk is the emergence of new infectious diseases. Rather than the burden of infectious diseases decreasing and eventually disappearing, they have quadrupled over the last 50 years. A 2005 review of the research identified 177 emerging or reemerging pathogens (13% of human pathogens). The majority (73%) of these pathogens originate in wildlife, in contrast, only 58% of all known human pathogens are zoonotic (Woolhouse and Gowtage-Sequeria 2005, 1844). Approximately 15% of newly emerging pathogens have direct association with forests. Others originated in the forests but have become independent of them (Wilcox and Ellis 2006). The newly emerging pathogens are taking advantage of every new opportunity for transfer to human hosts. We are just beginning to understand how human alterations of natural environments introduce new pathogens and thus new infectious diseases into the human population. Changes in land use and agriculture are the most frequently cited drivers of these pathogens into human populations. Most of the other causes are also related to globalization (Woolhouse and Gowtage-Sequeria 2005).

Wildlife populations serve as natural host reservoirs for any number, perhaps thousands, of viruses, bacteria, and other pathogens. Natural hosts suffer little or no harm from them. As human habitats expand, they intrude into wildlife habitats, force wildlife to move closer to humans and other animals, and may destroy the natural predators of a pathogen's host population. Some pathogens that the wildlife carry have shown remarkable resilience, crossing species barriers to find new host populations. Some enter other animals; others may transfer straight to humans. Some dead-end with one host; others spread like weeds, passing through animal or human populations or both, causing serious illness and death. They take advantage of nearly any change in human ecology to find new opportunities for transmission. Global travel and trade can spread these pathogens all over the world, resulting in epidemics and pandemics (Woolhouse and Gowtage-Sequeria 2005).

BOX 14.15   A Closer Look: Zoonotic Diseases

Fruit bats hang upside down eating fruit, chewing on the pulp and spitting out juice and seeds. Occasionally, the bats catch something like a cold, from the hendra or henipah virus. If the bat spittle does not come into contact with other species, there is not much harm done.

In Australia, however, suburbanization spread too close to the bats' natural habitat. It spread to horses and people. Four people and dozens of horses died. In Malaysia, 276 people became infected, and 106 of them died. The outbreak was traced to a pig pen located in a forest. At least a dozen smaller outbreaks occurred in South Asia. Due to loss of habitat, poor nutrition, or some unknown cause, bats in suburban and urban areas are now more likely to become infected, thus more able to spread the disease to people (Jim Robbins 2012, 6–7).

HIV/AIDS, severe acute respiratory syndrome (SARS), H5N1 avian influenza, mad cow disease, and H1N1 are but a few of the zoonotic pathogens that moved from their animal hosts to humans (USAID 2009). The potential number of pathogens that may emerge as new infectious diseases from human alteration of wildlife environments is infinite—both because there are so many and because they can adapt, becoming new strains, very quickly.

Geographic hotspots for these man-made epidemics are in tropical areas of developing countries. There people's daily lives put them in closer contact with domestic and wild animals and the natural environment.

Land Desertification and Degradation

The globe's drylands are home to about 2.1 billion people. These are productive lands that support agriculture and livestock. Desertification in the drylands is claiming about 12 million hectares yearly—enough land to grow 20 million tons of grain. Land degradation is a broader problem, threatening over 1 billion hectares. About 24 billion tons of fertile soil are lost annually (IFAD 2002).

Although climatic factors—drought and high temperatures such as experienced through parts of the United States in 2012—contribute to land degradation, arid, semiarid, and dry sub-humid ecosystems are very vulnerable to exploitation. Over-grazing, over-farming, deforestation, using wood for fuel, global warming, industrialization, and urbanization hasten what has been a much slower process for over a millennium. As land becomes desert, people are forced to migrate—environmental refugees. This put increasing pressures on new areas for food and habitation. It also contributes to a loss of biodiversity.

There is good news as well, though. Studies of biomass volume indicate that some regions of the globe have "greened" over the period from roughly the 1980s to early 2000s. One such study (Helldén and Tottrup 2008) looked at biomass growth in six regions. As you can see in Box 14.16, the most greening was in West and East Africa, then the Mediterranean and East Asia. South Africa and South America growth was weak compared to the other regions.

BOX 14.16   A Closer Look: Biomass Rejuvenation and Rainfall

The Normalized Difference Vegetation Index is used to estimate depletion and rejuvenation. Overall, the trend it toward increasing biomass, a greeing of the earth (z scores of 0.075 to 0.15). This is most pronounced in West and East Africa, the Mediterranean region, and East Asia.

The lower set of maps indicates that there is a strong relationship between rainfall and increased greening. However, there are sufficient anomalies to suggest that other factors are also at work. Among them might be that increased temperatures have created a longer growing season in some areas, increased carbon dioxide may be acting as a fertilizing agent, people may have migrated from some areas reducing the stress on the land, and land management practices and governmental policies to reverse have had good effects.

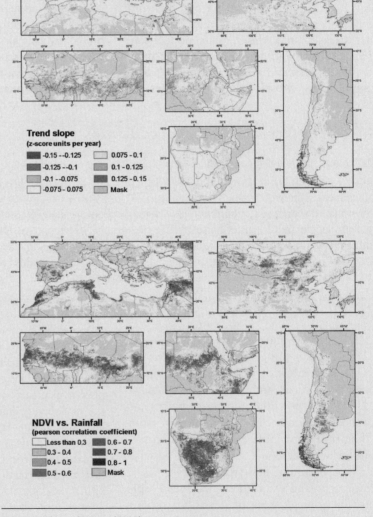

Trend slope
(z-score units per year)

-0.15 - -0.125	0.075 - 0.1
-0.125 - -0.1	0.1 - 0.125
-0.1 - -0.075	0.125 - 0.15
-0.075 - 0.075	Mask

NDVI vs. Rainfall
(pearson correlation coefficient)

Less than 0.3	0.6 - 0.7
0.3 - 0.4	0.7 - 0.8
0.4 - 0.5	0.8 - 1
0.5 - 0.6	Mask

Source: Helldén and Tottrup (2008).

Explaining the increase in vegetation requires multiple factors. In some of the areas (West Africa, Syria, and Mongolia), greening was explained by rainfall. West Africa, for example, had a return to pre-drought levels of rainfall. Other regions require different explanations. Higher concentrations of atmospheric CO_2, while dangerous for global warming, may enhance plant growth. Increased temperatures may prolong the growing season. Urbanization and abandonment of dryland agriculture in favor of opportunities in the cities, changes in the types of vegetation, payoffs from land management and anti-desertification strategies, and the introduction of large-scale irrigation projects and small-scale farmer initiated irrigation are all plausible explanations for the increases in one or more of the regions studied (Helldén and Tottrup 2008). Whether or not the new biomass is of the same quality as what was lost, or whether revitalized land can support the same quality of growth, is being studied.

Land destruction has multiple causes, in addition to desertification: Industrial waste discharge, nuclear waste disposal, off-road vehicles, landmine fields, landfills, and rising ocean levels all result in loss of arable and habitable land.

Climate Change

The World Bank's *World Development Report 2010* found that the most significant factors of vulnerability to climate change are socially created. Higher income countries are less dependent than lower income ones on the natural environment. Richer societies have more capacity to adapt their food production and living conditions to environmental change. Poorer countries are physically and economically precarious. They have little financial and institutional capacity to adapt (World Bank 2010b, 5).

The effect of climate change may have dire consequences for human security. The effects in Northern Africa

are likely to exacerbate existing threats to the region's water and food resources, economies, urban infrastructure, and sociopolitical systems. Cities will probably face deteriorating living conditions, high unemployment, and frequent civil unrest. Climate stress coupled with socioeconomic crises and ineffective state responses could generate localized social or governmental collapses and humanitarian crises. Climate change will likely increase the already substantial emigration of North Africans to Europe. The region also will serve as a route for transmigration if Sub Saharan Africans flee severe climatic stress. North Africa will absorb an increasing proportion of Europe's attention and resources. (Blair 2010, 40)

Other vulnerable regions will experience similar crises. Aside from Vietnam and Indonesia, Southeast Asia has done little to address climate change. Corruption, weak governance, and vested economic interests dampen state capacity to deal with it. Agriculture, fisheries, and human habitation are threatened by dam building on the Mekong River Basin. Along with migration from distressed areas to cities and to other countries, climate change is likely to exacerbate tensions among ethnically diverse groups.

Food, water, and health are all affected by climate change. Extreme weather events are more common. In two decades, natural disasters doubled from an average of about 200 per year to 400. Seventy percent of natural disasters in recent decades have been climate related. The number of people suffering from these disasters yearly has tripled; 211 million people are directly affected. Looking at this as a "moving average," it is clear that these numbers are increasing. In the decade 1998 to 2007, 2.2 billion people were affected, compared to 1.8 billion in the previous decade (UNFPA 2009, 30). Our response to climate change has potential to revolutionize social and economic development.

The entire nation of Kiribati may have to relocate. A country of small atolls, barely 10 feet above sea level in the Pacific Ocean, Kiribati's people are adding sand to their floors and building sea walls to keep dry and preserve their homes from the rising seas. They have no high ground to which to retreat. In all likelihood, they will have to leave or, as their president so bluntly puts it, they will drown. Unless they move en masse to land that is very like their own—and that is donated to them—they will lose their state and much of their culture. Some Kiribati have already lost their battle with the sea. Entire villages have gone underwater (UNFPA 2009, 30). As extreme weather pushes people from disaster-prone areas to more secure areas, their migration is likely to heighten environmental degradation, setting up a vicious feedback loop.

Traditional Knowledge and Environmental Health

Most of the environments in which modern people live are unnatural. Cities, with air conditioned skyscrapers, processed foods, and water filled with chemicals, are manufactured environments. For most of us to live in comfort, nature must be conquered and defied. Development efforts have threatened and displaced customary ways of life. New development efforts will have to respect livelihoods of traditional societies. Indigenous people traditionally have lived in relatively sustainable relationships with the environment. They have accumulated a wealth of knowledge and strategies for everything from natural building materials, to techniques for cooling and heating their homes (although not indoor fires), to planting and harvesting. One of the rights sought by indigenous populations is the right to live in ways compatible with their cultural heritage. The United Nations has delineated expectations for respecting this right (UNDP 2001). In most cases, this means accommodating their return to living in direct relationship with the natural environment, if so desired. These eco-friendly efficiencies can be incorporated into modern design.

Traditional knowledge of habitats and resources is being incorporated into conservation, biodiversity, agriculture, and resource management strategies. Adobe architecture is a good example of the incorporation of indigenous knowledge into mainstream development. Modern societies are beginning to see the value in the knowledge that indigenous cultures have of using nature without abusing it. As mentioned earlier in the chapter, some private enterprises are exploiting and patenting the technologies they have learned from indigenous groups, but governments are still making too little use of their knowledge.

A 2008 sampling of country reports for progress on the UN Millennium Development Goals (MDGs) noted with disappointment that only two of the 10 reports made consistent mention of including indigenous people in their planning toward meeting the MDGs. Nor was there much evidence that indigenous peoples were included in development planning generally. Three reports mention indigenous people with respect to environmental sustainability (Hartley 2008, 35).

Women had also been left out of environmental planning. This seems a gross oversight given women's close association with the environment in most traditional societies. Also, the payoff for including women in the action on many development issues, from microloans to agriculture to environmental issues, has obvious potential. Bringing the knowledge and experience of women and indigenous peoples into the environmental equation is a necessity. It is tragically ironic that for centuries of colonization, the knowledge of indigenous people and of women in particular—recall the burning at the stake of witches—was dismissed. Now that science recognizes the value of traditional practices and knowledge, such as in medicine, much of it is being commoditized—packaged, patented, and controlled by transnational corporations.

Summary: Risk and the Global Field

Problems of food security and the environment are intimately related. The quest to feed booming populations quickly and an unshakeable trust that scientific methods must be better than traditional have created severe environmental damage to land, water, and air. Ironically, this has crippled our capacity to grow sufficient and sufficiently healthy food in areas where it is most needed. Environmental damage exacerbates problems of poverty and pollution, and depletion of resources pushes people from their homelands, often into near equally desperate countries. Depleted and polluted resources shared across political border house the possibility of violent conflict, if environmental remediation and global negotiations are not successful.

What makes you feel secure? A full stomach, warm and dry shelter, a stable job, a loving family, and sleeping peacefully at night are basic elements of human security. Clean water to drink and bathe in, clean air to breathe, and food that is nutritious, not just filling, can make the difference between life and death. Being able to send your children to school, or go to school yourself; living without fear of gunfire, rocket fire, or bombing—most of the world cannot take these simple aspects of security for granted. Most people do not have them.

In Chapters Twelve, Thirteen, and Fourteen, we reviewed six risks to human well-being and security. General awareness of the severity of environmental problems, the intractable nature of modern violent conflicts, the depth of poverty, international crime, and other shared security issues has provoked a greater sense of urgency in globalization debates. Each of them is a "manufactured uncertainty"

BOX 14.17   A Closer Look: Reviving Degraded Land

The beginnings of reformation—turning a desert into grasslands: Villagers carry seedlings to start re-plantation activities that will turn a desert into grasslands.

(Beck 2009) in the world of risk in which we live. Each is related to global forces and is shared in one way or another by everyone on the globe.

The common fate of humanity as a whole was awakened in the 1960s. Civil rights and other reform efforts of that time evolved into human rights reforms with demands that individuals be treated as humans first, members of particular societies, races, religions, or classes second. These presaged the broader demands for human rights that permeate every human security issue. Perhaps more than other issues, transborder problems focus attention on the shared vulnerability of individuals as humans, an objective condition of globalization, and thus consciousness of humanity as a whole, the subjective reality of globalization.

Questions, Investigations, and Resources

Questions

1. Debate: Is food security a human right?

2. How would you prioritize the problems of food and environment that confront the world? Should environmental quality to meet the immediate needs of starving people? Can this choice be avoided?

3. How have domestic and international policies and programs contributed to the world's hunger problem? What policies and program have helped mitigate the problem of hunger?

4. What types of food regimes show the most promise for feeding the world? Are local approaches best? Can we combine local and global, scientific management, and traditional practices?

5. Discuss ways in which the horticultural revolution and livestock revolutions could alleviate some world hunger or make world hunger worse.

6. How has overpopulation contributed to environmental issues? Discuss with respect to water, land, and air.

7. To what extent are the problems that confront human well-being interrelated? Are there ways in which two or more problems can be tackled through a single reform?

Investigations

1. The UNDP's *Human Development Report 2011 Sustainability and Equity: A Better Future for All* focuses on the environment. The report is a wealth of informative discussion of trends and possibilities for a

more sustainable future. Table 6 of the Statistical Annex contains extensive data on environmental sustainability by country.

- Do countries seem to share similarities based on their level of human development?
- Make a list of the 10 best performing and 10 worst performing countries on the following variables or variables of your choice. Do your lists reveal any general trends?

    i. The percentage of energy that they get from renewable

    ii. Per capita carbon dioxide emissions

    iii. Green house gas emissions

2. Table 7 of the *Human Development Report 2011* details some of the human development effects of environmental threats. You can investigate within the report to answer these questions.

- Which threats appear to be higher in the higher development countries, and which in the lower?
- What may be responsible for these differences?

3. How safe is your local environment? *Scorecard* uses Environmental Protection Agency data to calculate the exposure to environmental risks for every county in the United States.

- Use the *Scorecard* site to discover the major pollutants in your county.
- How does your county rank in each category?
- How does the risk for each of these threats vary by income level and race?
- What are the major sources of pollution?

4. Project Predict is a collaborative effort among governmental organizations and NGOs to catalog and study the pathogens carried by wildlife to predict where the next emerging infectious diseases will originate and what they will be. They have programs operating in 20 countries, the globe's hot spots. Project Predict's website has an interactive health map showings the countries in which it is working and information concerning emerging infectious diseases, by region and country.

USAID Healthmap: http://www.healthmap.org/predict

- Choose a region and sort the information by disease. Rank the diseases by severity according to the numbers of human deaths and the number of human cases. Are the rankings the same? If the rankings are different, how might you explain it?
- Are the rankings for animals different?
- If possible, compare rankings across the regions? Which diseases appear in the most regions? How would you rate their severity?

Investigate the most deadly pathogen for your country or region and determine its natural host and how it was transmitted into human or other animal populations. Was globalization implicated? If so, how is it related?

Resources

Food

The World Food Program http://www.wfp.org/

Food and Agriculture Organization of the United Nations http://www.fao.org/

World Food Programme Videos http://www.wfp.org/videos

Environment

Human Development Report 2011: Sustainability and Equity: A Better Future for All http://www.beta.undp.org/content/dam/undp/library/corporate/HDR/2011%20Global%20HDR/English/HDR_2011_EN_Complete.pdf

Scorecard

http://www.scorecard.org

Food and Agriculture Organization Climate Change http://www.fao.org/climatechange/en

USAID Predict (interactive map tracking epidemics) http://www.healthmap.org/predict

World Wildlife Fund Alternative Energy Report http://www.worldwildlife.org/climate/Publications/WWFBinaryitem19481.pdf

World Wildlife Fund http://www.worldwildlife.org/home-full.html

World Resources Institute http://www.wri.org

15

Global Trajectories: The City

Objectives

Most people are now living in cities. Thus, the future security and health of humankind will depend on how creative we are in creating livable cities—or alternatives. This chapter will help you to

- understand the relationship among cities and nations, and the constraints and opportunities that nations present to cities;
- analyze the role of globalization on migration to cities and the subsequent connections among cities and countries from which migrants come and to which they go;
- assess common problems of urbanization and the diffusion of proposed solutions to city problems;

- distinguish between global and mega cities and assess the role of each in modern life;
- compare a variety of indices for city assessment and the implications for models of city life that they represent;
- analyze the global political, economic, and other social networks that coalesce in cities; and
- recognize the importance of communities within cities.

The Nature of Cities

Ancient Cities

Over half of the world's population lives in cities. Both the prospects and the problems of globalization are most pronounced in the world's cities. Cities have been central to globalization processes from the earliest phases, shaping and being shaped by globalization forces. Cities form and inform networks across regions and civilizations. Nowhere is this more clearly demonstrated than in the ancient trade routes from Central Asia through the Middle East to the Mediterranean, which in the 19th century came to be called "the Silk Road." The Silk Road connected cities along its main arterial routes, forming global markets and connected cities tangential to the road from which people and goods arrived

to the markets. Along with the varied products—silk, rice, gems, metals, spices, gunpowder, and animals—disease, languages, religions, and genes also traveled the Silk Road. Great cultures were created along these roads, and variations of older cultures emerged. For hundreds of years, numerous empires and kingdoms, including the Persians, Indians, Greeks, Romans, Chinese, and Mongols, influenced and were influenced by the development of the area and the civilizations east and west of them. Although trade through the area was much older, Greek colonization laid the foundation of the Silk Road. Roadways built for conquer attracted merchants and settlers to the cities along the routes, fusing Greek (Hellenic) culture with local cultures, giving rise to Hellenistic variations throughout the Near and Middle East. Greek and Buddhist cultures merged to form Ghandara. Ancient Greek and

Roman religions, Buddhism, Daoism, Hindu, and later Christianity and Islam—spread along these routes. Languages and cultures blended as people traveled some of the most physically demanding terrain in the world. Although not many people traveled the entire route, products, ideas, and other cultural forms did as they flowed from one city into the next. Migrants were the lifeblood of the Silk Road cities as they moved from one to another nourishing and transforming the places through which they passed and to which they headed. Like more contemporary patterns of global interaction, activity on the Silk Road was frequently disrupted by war and invasions and therefore waxed and waned over the course of its long history from about the 2nd to the 15th century.

The Silk Road cities were the nexus of trans-civilizational and trans-ecological exchanges. While some flourished due to their position astride the juncture of civilizations, others flourished at the juncture of ecological divides, such as rural and urban or mountain and flatland (Christian 2000, 9). This is the essence of the city as a social structure. Cities are bridges, hubs, and cogs. They facilitate exchange of what one has for what one does not. Cities become centers and celebrations of diversity, not just economic but cultural and political as well.

Cities of the ancient empires reflected the underlying values or cosmos of their cultures, belief systems, and codes (Gottdiener and Hutchison 2010, 27). Their development and growth was controlled by the ruling classes. In Athens, the center of the city was the community center, the agora, the public hearth of the city of the world. All houses were equidistant from the center, built in a radial pattern, reflecting the equality of the citizens, the golden mean used to bring balance.

Ancient Rome was initially built on a human scale and stressed social interaction and public life. As the empire grew, the look of the city changed to grandeur and dominance, reflecting the power of the state, and the forum became the city center. Rome lived off the wealth that poured into it from ever-more far-flung regions and became known for its decadence. Inequality increased and with it all of the problems that plague modern cities (Gottdiener and Hutchison 2010, 29).

Cities of the empires were political administrative centers built to control the territories and commerce of the empire. This made them dependent on the areas surrounding and connected to them. For most of history, the largest cities were in the Middle and Far East. From 1100 to 1850, the largest cities were almost exclusively in China, reflecting their dominance in commerce.

BOX 15.1   Consider This: Cityscapes

How do the physical characteristics reflect of a city reflect its character, or that of the region or nation where it resides?

For instance, what does it suggest when a city has run-down parks, schools, roads, and other public areas that are surrounded by lavish gated communities, private clubs, and exclusive restaurants suggest?

What message do well-lighted, clean, neat, and well-kept public areas convey?

Are there back stories to the architectural mix of cities?

The Industrial City

The dominance of East over West changed abruptly. With industrialization, the center of production and commerce shifted to Europe. European cities grew exponentially, and all of the ills familiar to modern cities grew with them. London grew 300% in 30 years and at the turn of the 19th century was the world's largest city with a population of over 2 million. City life and social life adjusted to conform to the needs of the emerging industrial

capitalist economy (Gottdiener and Hutchison 2010, 35–38). For better or worse, institutions formalized and bureaucratized to handle the sheer volume of people in mass society. Globalization caused agglomeration of industries, and cities developed specialties as manufacturing centers clustered.

For the classical social theorists Adam Smith, Karl Marx, Ferdinand Toennies, Emile Durkheim, Georg Simmel, and Max Weber, the qualitative shift from the small town to industrial city was palpable.

It was the best and worst of times. The productive power that fossil fuels and capitalism unleashed could provide a life of comfort for every child, woman, and man on earth. Instead, many people were left behind in more dire straits than they experienced under feudalism.

Life in the city also gave birth to the modern individual. Internal migration and immigration changed the faces, colors, sights, sounds, and smells of urban life. The ever-increasing division of labor required people to cultivate their distinctions and difference. The cities freed individuals. It released people from the unjust inequality imposed by traditional and arbitrary authorities, and from the prejudices of the small town. But freedom has dangers. In "The Metropolis and Mental Life," Simmel (1903/1971) observed that within the city, the vast quantity of stimulation posed a danger to the psyche. He claimed that the overstimulation of the city caused people to screen and attend only to the most personal or relevant. The blasé attitude of reserve was the affected adaptation.

Did this blind us to others and their problems? Could the blasé attitude of indifference be the germ of today's "cosmopolitanism"? How are they similar or different?

BOX 15.2 Consider This: Cities and Creativity

Contemporary social theorists credit the city with encouraging creativity. Jane Jacobs inspired decades of controversy with her 1961 book *Death and Life of Great American Cities*. Jacobs argued that the animation of city streets—the constant flow people, sights, sounds, smells, and tastes—was invigorating and spawned innovation. Diversity, difference, and strangers are all inescapable in cities. They force us to open our minds and are essential for stimulating new ideas.

Cities agglomerate people; the more people, the more they inspire one another. Observing the postwar urban renewal projects bulldozing poor neighborhoods, she was appalled at the lack of attention to the attractiveness of the new projects to people. Rather than sanitizing cities through urban renewal and creating what she called a *pretended order*, Jacobs advocated city streets that were crowded with the animated and diverse activities that made human life full and colorful.

Freedom may also exert a price in the loss of informal social controls. When traditional norms and values are not replaced by new ones, their breakdown leaves a society without strong guideposts and leaves many people floundering for answers to the question of how to live the good life. Immigration and transience also produce conflicting norms between homeland and adopted country norms. This conflict may be particularly poignant for children of immigrants. The rapidity of social change wrought by urbanization challenges norms on both these fronts, delegitimizing traditional norms before new norms can evolve. This, according to Durkheim (1893/1964), creates anomie. Among the costs of anomie to society and people are increased crime, suicide, family dysfunction, institutional dysfunction generally, and poverty.

On the side of urban advantages, extreme individuation leads to the massive production of culture in art, institutions, and comforts. But this also can have costs. During the take-off phase of globalization, Simmel (1903/1971) worried about the need to become a specialist, an extreme individualist. He questioned the endurance of the well-rounded individual. Would the individual personality become increasingly one-sided, allowing some aspects of an individual's personality to fall into neglect? Was this the beginning of later dissatisfaction with "the organizational man" or a life where one complains of living to work, rather than working to live, or a life so disenchanted that meaning and fulfillment are aspirations out of reach for many?

For better or worse, the city "was one of those great historical structures in which conflicting life embracing currents find themselves with equal legitimacy" (Simmel 1903/1971, 339). For all of the qualitative differences of ancient and modern cities, they share essential structural qualities that have characterized cities for nearly a millennium. Like the Silk Road city, the industrial city stood at the nexus, connecting civilizations through commerce, connecting ecological niches—primary commodity production of the countryside, forest, fishery, or mine in industrializing and non-industrialized nations—with manufacturing centers, bridging for migrants and nomads the places from where they came with the places to where they are going, and serving for the individual as the nexus of constraint and freedom.

Contemporary Cities

Cities today are larger and busier, with more diversity and more objective culture than Simmel might have imagined. At the turn of the century, it made sense to talk of cities as relatively discrete locations, but by mid-20th century, cities had spilled over their political boundaries and become "metropolitan regions" with much of the industry and manufacturing moving into outlaying areas. The cities of the turn of the 20th century were centers of manufacturing and commerce. They were very often filthy from burning fossil fuels, lack of sewage and sanitation, and homelessness. As manufacturing moved from many cities, aggregating or disaggregating in nearly any region of the world, cities became visibly cleaner. At the beginning of the 21st century, global cities gleam, at least in their imagined and stylized form.

The contemporary city is a complicated social structure. Cities serve as a nexus, but they are strategic rather than manufacturing centers. Corporate headquarters and those that serve them agglomerate in cities. They bridge the advanced economic zones and sectors and the backward zones and sectors (Sassen 2011). They former is made up the well-paid officers and professionals of multinational corporate offices and the consulting, actuarial, insurance, advertising, investment, wealth management, legal, accounting, and other firms and agencies that service them. The janitors, taxi drivers, dry cleaners, and other attendants that serve the advanced zones are the poorly paid and work in what are referred to as *backward zones and sectors*. Amid these extremes, a new population is reentering and perhaps reinventing segments of the city. Young, avant-garde and creative classes are drawn to cities. Artist, designers, skilled craft artisans, even craft brew masters are finding opportunities serving the corporate economy without becoming part of it. Demand for their goods and services attract the young to the old industrial cities of the North and even to the slums of the mega and global cities of the South.

Amassing people in cities has long been credited with producing economies of scale. It takes less infrastructure and resources, such as roads, sewer systems, and power grids, to support a concentration of people than to support the same number of people dispersed. The costs of production and transport decline. Income, health care, and educational levels rise with urbanization, and fertility levels decline. This should raise the quality of life. Still, as in ancient Rome, cities remain the nexus of extreme wealth and extreme poverty. The stark contrasts of prosperity for some with displacement for others are among the accelerants of the "Occupy" movements and protests against austerity in social welfare spending that have spread globally. Protests are likely to be a permanent part of the political landscape of the global era.

BOX 15.3   Consider This: Iconic Architecture

Shanghai by night.

To testify to their stature and importance, global cities are home to "iconic architecture." Architectural firms of global fame build iconic, one-of-a-kind buildings in global cities. The buildings are stunning, designed to inspire awe. They often bear remarkably little relation to the cities in which they are found. Iconic architecture gives the skylines of global cities a fantasy-like quality. What do you suppose it means? Does it reflect the power and importance of cities? Could the fantastic element represent the playland of capitalism? Is the homogenization of cities a feature of universalism? Is it desirable?

At what point do cities become too large, so that they are unlivable and unsustainable? How can the quality of life be enhanced for all of the cities' inhabitants to take advantage of economies of scale? Is there an optimal level for centralization in cities after which decentralization is the wiser route?

Global Cities

Inhabiting Global Cities

The concept of the world city was initiated by Hall (1966) and elaborated by Friedmann and Wolff (1982). *World city* designated a particular type of city that emerged with globalization. They are not necessarily the largest cities, nor are they necessarily capital cities. The outstanding characteristic of a world city is its role as a hub of power—political and economic, national, and international—and the extent to which it is integrated with other hubs of power. As globalization advanced and control of production, consumption, finance, and commerce from around the world became more concentrated in particular cities, the term *global city* (Sassen 1991) replaced world city.

Global cities are dense with influential global economic, political, and cultural transactions. During the industrial era, different types of manufacturing tended to concentrate in different cities, where they found comparative advantage, however defined. Global cities are still sites of agglomeration. As manufacturing dispersed, cities acquired new specialized roles, crystallizing as command centers for far-flung production, commercial, and financial enterprises. Able to communicate with managers at sites in remote locations, corporate executives found more value in being located centrally rather than near one facility or another. Just as cities tended to specialize in discrete forms of manufacturing, command centers for certain commodity, production, or service processes tended to concentrate in particular cities. The advanced services—financial planners, accountants, stockbrokers, tax attorneys, marketing gurus, business consultants, and the like—cluster near the headquarters of firms, wherever they are located, creating an effervescence or synergy by concentrating the knowledge and information networks.

These wealthy and elite groups—commanders and their advisors—depend on others for their basic needs. Particularly in two-working-professional partner families, they rely on the intimate services of myriad low-paid service workers (often migrants) to clean their homes, cook their food, wash their clothes, and watch their children. They have assumed the role of wife in professional households. Global staffing companies have added home care services to accommodate the mother and wife roles (Sassen 2009, 3).

Other low-wage workers clean the offices, drive the cars, and ferry the elite in taxis. They work in hotels, groceries, dress shops, dry cleaners, laundries, and so forth. The elite class also demands a culturally rich life of restaurants, film, theater, and activities, although this seems significantly different from the high culture of the industrial era, which supported world-class symphonies, ballets, and opera. These audiences are declining in many cities. Sassen points out that the services demanded by the elite classes are labor intensive. French hand laundries employ more people than the laundry to which middle-level managers might take their shirts and blouses to be thrown into a huge washing machine and ironed with presses. Diners at expensive restaurants may be tended by three or more servers dedicated to their table alone. The personal services demanded by the elite class accounts for 30% to 50% of the global economic infrastructure, according to her calculations. Personal service is a class primarily of immigrant, female, low-level workers.

The juxtaposition of the most powerful classes and the least powerful in the world's cities forms the basis of the global economic, political, and cultural infrastructure. The flow of people, money, and communication via intimate connections with one another and their connections outward to the rest of the world makes the global city the global nexus. These classes are probably the two largest global networks. They are both migrant classes. The elite migrate for politics and business, jetting all over the world for both work and play. Their interests, in business, finance, and fun, span the globe. Their command reaches all corners of the globe. The poorest migrate for work, but not for play. Their interests also span the globe. They send money home. Often, they may return home to be with family or eventually to stay. They bring family and friends to join them in their new homelands along well-traveled routes, forged by global forces of colonialism, war, language, or cultural similarities. They serve the wealthy in their home countries, as tourism is a major industry of the developing world.

Connections within and among global cities are plentiful and complex. Interrelations among city residents and those outside the city span every aspect of life. Executives control manufacturing and distribution centers from strategic locations. Communications technologies connect migrants with relatives in homelands. A mother from the Dominican Republic living as a housekeeper in New York or a Thai mother working in Tokyo, although separated from their families, may still be the command centers of their families, sending money, giving advice, supervising activities, and making rules for those she left at home. These global migrants also consume city services, furnished by other migrants or low-level workers. Each of these women may belong to a religious organization along with immigrants from many other countries. Each may buy food at a farmer's market and a farmer who is part of the Women, Food, and Agricultural Network, a global organization, or the Buy Local global movement. Each may dine at an ethnic restaurant run by recent immigrants who are sending money back to their homeland. Each is connected in myriad ways to global networks that weave their way through the flux and flow of city life.

Many theorists of the city argue that we are moving away from the age of nations, to the age of cities. In a way reminiscent of Marco Polo's enthusiasm for the Silk Road cities he traveled, it is not the powerful empires, but the powerful cities that are striking in their vibrancy. Some theorists maintain that cities will become islands of governance replacing nations as the most critical political unit (Khanna 2010, 122).

A global city is distinguished by the extent of its influence around the world, not the size of its population. Global cities structure the basic architecture of the globe, connecting the world through transactions: formal, informal, personal, and impersonal. Images of global cities are abundant—"chain of nodes," "Global Commodity Chain," "Global Value Chain," "Global Production Network," "networks of information flows," and the "World City Network" are some of the ways people have described them and their relationship to one another. Understanding how cities function in the global system, how they are transformed by their roles in global networks, and how their institutional and social fabrics transform the global networks is central to understanding the impact of globalization on people's everyday lives (Derudder and Witlox 2010, 3).

Whether or not networks agglomerated in global cities are replacing states as global political and economic command centers is dependent on agency. Friedmann (1986), in his early formulation, distinguished the city as a place from the concept of actor. For example, nation-states have agency, the capacity to commit to international and multinational treaties, go to war, command taxes, deny people liberty through imprisonment, and so on.

Do cities or the networks among them have, or will they ever have, this same degree of agency?

If global cities are the nodes and hubs of networks, undoubtedly actors within the networks have agency. The extent of the global economy and deregulation of many economic processes enables them to bypass the nation-state. Many of these actors are also very powerful in controlling corporations, finance, information, influencing political decisions, and so on. Even networks of NGOs, also concentrated in cities, are powerful through their global and local influence on people, corporations, and governments. The networks are global. But networks themselves do not have a collective decision-making body or capacity. Even when they coalesce and concentrate in cities, they do not decide; they are amalgams of decisions of many actors.

As political units, the agency of city governments is limited, even though city administrators typically work closely with the decision makers in the economic command nodes. Control of command centers is oriented in two directions. In one direction, actors orient to the specific operations over which they have control. In this sense, cities as places are indeed global command centers. On the other hand, even the most powerful actors are oriented to states. Their range of control, for example is still determined by states. Enacting or eliminating regulation expands or contracts the range of control of a command center. Corporate "command centers," whether oriented to production or servicing production, still operate within the "spaces" and "places" and under the guidelines as defined by state parliaments, legislatures, executives, and judiciary, as well as the international groups of states. In this sense, globalization has not yet, and may never, overcome space.

Ranking and Rating Global Cities

Cities are distinct as particular locations and places. Although the population of the global elite or transnational capitalist class is drawn from every country, cities reside within countries, and despite the globalization of many attitudes and values, global cities may retain cultural distinctions in how decisions are made and the priorities on which they are based. This raises the issue of the influence of global cities on the values and lifestyles of people and the structure and decisions of states. The "Global Cities Index 2010" (Foreign Policy 2010) finds that the most influential cities are trending

Asian, as they did in the centuries before the Industrial Revolution. Of the top 10 global cities on the 2010 list, half are Asian: Tokyo, Hong Kong, Singapore, Sydney, and Seoul. Only three are in the United States: New York, Chicago, and Los Angeles. Two—London and Paris—are European. Eight of the next 10 are Western, either European or North American. Whether this, and the growing wealth of Asian nations, portends a shift "eastward" in the concentration of power is an interesting question.

BOX 15.4   A Closer Look: The Diversity of Toronto

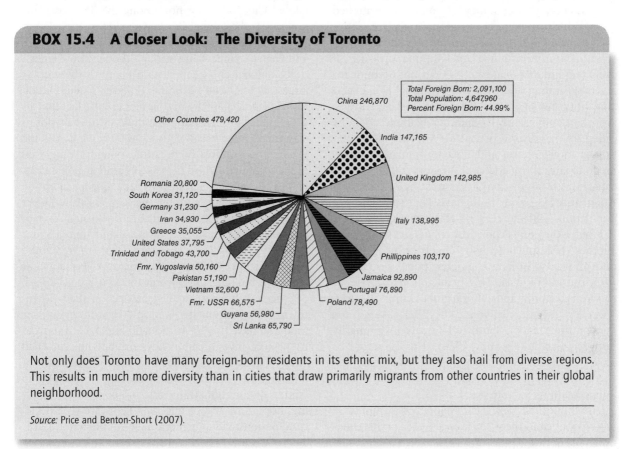

Not only does Toronto have many foreign-born residents in its ethnic mix, but they also hail from diverse regions. This results in much more diversity than in cities that draw primarily migrants from other countries in their global neighborhood.

Source: Price and Benton-Short (2007).

The Global Cities Index 2010 (Foreign Policy 2010) uses 25 criteria in five categories to measure the most global, or widely connected, cities. The categories and a sample of the criteria are

- business activity, such as such as the number of Fortune 500 companies headquartered there and the size of capital markets;
- how well it attracts diverse and talented people, such as the number of immigrants, international schools and universities;

- information exchange, such as number of news bureaus and level of censorship;
- cultural experience, such as number of sporting events, performing arts venues, and restaurants; and
- political engagement, that is, the number of embassies, political organizations, and think tanks.

Like other indices, the Global Cities Index reduces qualitatively distinct criteria—such as the production of culture and number of financial transactions—into quantitative rankings. As with any composite score, the differences among criteria are obscured. Even though connections may be weighted differently, a single score is difficult to interpret.

Hong Kong and Singapore are rated 5 and 8 on the Global Index. Do they have the influence of New York, London, or Paris—numbers 1, 2, and 4—or of San Francisco (12), Madrid (17), Los Angeles (7), Toronto (14), Boston (19), or Frankfurt (20)? Both Hong Kong and Singapore are important financial centers, but they do not produce the quantity of culture, science, or technology of some lower ranked cities. Which set of measures is more likely to influence global affairs such as global governance?

In measuring cultural strength, the measure of attracting international tourists does not account for diversity among tourists. Tokyo, Hong Kong, and Singapore are not, at least not yet, magnets for diverse groups of immigrants. Toronto, for example, could be called a hyper-diverse city. About 44% of its population is foreign born, and no one immigrant group predominates (Price and Benton-Short 2007). Tokyo's foreign-born population, in contrast, is 2.4%. Hong Kong and Singapore both have large foreign-born populations, 38% and 18.3%, respectively. However, in Hong Kong, 86% come from mainland China, and another 11% from other Asian countries. In Singapore, only about 3% of its foreign-born population comes from outside of Asia. This highlights the difference between economic and cultural globalization (Benton-Short, Price, and Friedman 2005, 952). Overall, the immigration trend in South and East Asia is primarily intra-regional immigration (956). This is bound to have a different effect on global development than more the much more broadly based international immigration to Toronto (see Box 15.4).

Although the index was developed in conjunction with global cities theorists, it obscures the differentiation most of these theorists make between comprehensive global cities like London, Paris, and New York, and niche cities like Tokyo, Hong Kong, and Singapore, which are much more specialized in function. So while there is a final list of the most global, none of the cities dominates the index in most categories.

The Global Power Cities Index, based in Japan, ranks 35 cities on 69 indicators that represent six categories: economy, research and development (R&D), cultural interaction, livability, ecology and natural environment, and accessibility. Although some of the same advisors serve on both, the indicators vary somewhat. The purpose of the power index is to ferret out urban strategies for Tokyo and other cities to "attract creative people and excellent companies" (Mori Memorial Foundation 2009, 1). The rankings are derived from four groups of global actors; managers, researchers, actors, and visitors, and one local group, residents and what they want in a city (Mori Memorial Foundation 2009, 10). Ratings on the indicators may be compared to see where a city is weak and what it needs to do to become stronger. The top 20 cities on the two lists are similar. They differed on eight. Chicago, San Francisco, and Washington were in the Global City Index but not among the 35 chosen for ranking in the Global Power City Index. Included in the power index were Amsterdam, Zurich, Copenhagen, and Geneva, somewhat smaller although dense cities.

The global cities, along with many of the world's largest cities—Seoul, Mumbai, Jakarta, Delhi, Osaka/Kobe, and Shanghai—may leverage globalization to spur Asianization. Money that flows into Asia tends to stay there. Inter-Asian trade exceeds trade across the Pacific and low cost carriers transport to Asian cities of the second and third tiers. Deals among global cities within the Asian nations bypass European cities. Among developing nations, the same is true. Direct flights such as Doha to Sao Paulo or Buenos Aires to Johannesburg bypass the European and United States international airports. The port cities are free zones with efficient re-export without red tape. Persian Gulf cities are building their center cities at record speed, offering tax breaks and fast services in their downtowns. They are buying land in Africa to grow their food and have private armies and intelligence services to protect investments. They are building planned "smart cities," not haphazardly as the old cities of industrialization were built. They aim to be smart in land use, sanitation, transport, and community building, hoping to attract migrants from Western developed nations with a higher quality of life and tax-free environment (Khanna 2010, 123).

While global clout may very well follow the rise of the new global cities moving from West to East (Foreign Policy 2010), the numbers bear closer inspection. This is not to say that there is inevitability or desirability to political, economic, or cultural influence remaining rooted in the West. But analysis and projections of the most influential networks have more to take into account than the numbers of connections and the current rate of economic growth. There are many questions whose answers will influence the dynamics of the new urban age.

The Global Economic Power Index (Florida 2011) uses economic, financial, and innovative power to rank cities. Their ranking is substantially different than the prior two. Including innovation may be responsible for the difference, pushing more U.S. cities into the top 10.

What are the consequences of rapidly aging populations in Europe and much of Asia, including China?

Are cultural opportunities growing along with the growing productive capacity of the global cities? (They seem to be in Beijing, Shanghai, and Singapore.)

What is the quality of life in the global cities? Will the lack of freedoms in Asian societies ultimately limit their development?

Another question is whether making Tokyo more like London makes it more desirable, powerful, or in any way a better city—or will it just advance in the list of indicators?

Within the older global cities, not just production but also creative services are locating along the borders. Urban populations in the North are stabilizing

---

BOX 15.5   A Closer Look: Global Cities, Global Power Cities, and Global Economic Power Cities

Compare and contrast the three global cities indices. How different are they, and how might you account for the similarities and differences?

		Global Cities Index 2010		Global Power City Index 2010	Global Economic Power Index
Rank	City	Rank by Population	Rank by GNP	Rank 1–10	Rank 1–10
1	New York	6	2	New York	Tokyo
2	London	28	5	London	New York
3	Tokyo	1	1	Paris	London
4	Paris	20	6	Tokyo	Chicago
5	Hong Kong	31	14	Singapore	Paris
6	Chicago	25	4	Berlin	Boston
7	Los Angeles	12	3	Amsterdam	Hong Kong
8	Singapore	38	23	Seoul	Osaka
9	Sydney	43	24	Hong Kong	Tied at 9th Washington DC and Seoul
10	Seoul	22	19	Sydney	

Sources: Florida (2011); Foreign Policy (2010); Mori Memorial Foundation (2009).

---

and in many cases shrinking. Suburbs have given way to exurbs. Silicon Valley in California and Lincolnshire outside of Chicago seem to suggest that there are healthier ways to grow than urbanizing. After all, much of the urban growth of the late 20th and early 21st centuries has been to urban slums.

Mega Cities

The global population reached 7 billion on or around October 31, 2011. Approximately 3.5 billion,

or half of the people on earth, live in cities. This could rise to as many as 70% by 2050. Most of this growth will be in developing nations. This presents opportunities and challenges. One the one hand, urbanization can mean more efficient production of goods and delivery of services from health care to education. On the other, population growth can exceed the capacity of the urban infrastructure leaving people in squalor. Already 1 billion people, over 25% of the people in cities, are living in slums.

Most of the largest cities in the world are not global cities. Most cities of 10 million are not centers of command and control. They are just big. Rather than being hubs of command, they are hubs of humanity: incredibly dense populations of people. People congregate in and near them seeking economic opportunities that are more available in cities than rural areas (World Bank 2009, xix).

BOX 15.6   A Closer Look: Urban Slums

This barrio is outside of Bangladesh. In many global and mega cities, the slums are well established. In Rio de Janiero, when people able to acquire ownership of their land, they made improvements. High rents in the rest of the cities push more people, including middle class, into slums.

Mega cities share some features with the global cities, notably crime, congestion, and pollution. Together, they house the greatest densities of the poor (World Bank 2009). They are characterized by "a low standard of living and little strategic influence" (Kotkin 2010, 129). In Mumbai, the majority of people now live in slums (130). Global and mega cities share the extremes of inequality signified by the horrible squalor of slums without sewage systems that sprawl at the feet of gated communities housing private schools, grocery stores, and manicured parks. The residents of the gated communities never have to face the poor surrounding them as they pass through the slums in sleek cars with darkened windows or over them by helicopter (126). If this is the face of the future, it is not very pretty.

BOX 15.7   A Closer Look: Mega Cities

1.	Tokyo, Japan	32,450,000
2.	Seoul, South Korea	20,550,000
3.	Mexico City, Mexico	20,450,000
4.	New York City, USA	19,750,000
5.	Mumbai, India	19,200,000

6.	Jakarta, Indonesia	18,900,000
7.	São Paulo, Brazil	18,850,000
8.	Delhi, India	18,680,000
9.	Osaka/Kobe, Japan	17,350,000
10.	Shanghai, China	16,650,000

Source: WorldAtlas (2012).

Estimates and Projections of Numbers of Slum Dwellers by Region

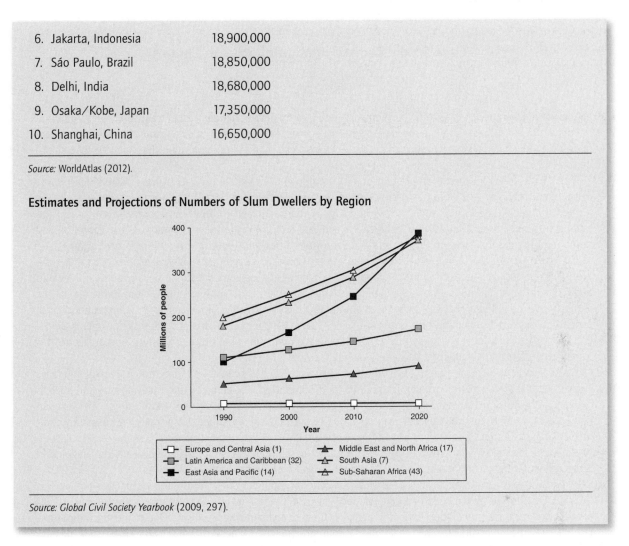

Source: Global Civil Society Yearbook (2009, 297).

The large cities of the advanced world, New York, Tokyo, London, and Paris, are situated in declining domestic economies. The other large cities are in poor or developing economies. The scenario of increasing inequality and exodus of the middle class suggests that the new age of the city may be "an era of unparalleled human congestion and gross inequality" (Kotkin 2010, 129).

The problems that plague the megacities are complex. Environmental degradation is one of the most severe. Physical security is threatened by the location of squatter communities on floodplains or hillsides, adjacent to dangerous industries. Diseases spread opportunistically through open sewage, dirty water, and polluted air (Perlman 1990, 5).

Yet, even in the poorest cities, opportunity outstrips that of the countryside. Productivity and thus jobs, if they are to be found, are found in the cities. The World Bank (2009) identifies three dimensions of economic geography that account for some regions, such as Western Europe or Southeast Asia, doing well: high density population as in the growth of cities, shorter distances between home and work, and fewer, more permeable economic borders. Each of these will keep cities growing. Unless there is intervention, urbanization is expected to continue, resulting in 27 cities of over 10 million by 2050. While many welcome this projection, this could create more catastrophe than opportunity, unless cities are well managed.

Case Study: Growth of Middle Cities in China

Much of the literature on globalization and urbanization has focused on global and mega cities. Urbanization in China has taken a different tact, particularly since the late 1970s. As urbanization progressed in China, the flow of people was deliberately channeled by government policy to a number of middle-level or peripheral cities. Although the middle cities of China have enormous problems, the concept has promise. The cultivation of middle cities could be a successful strategy in ameliorating the negative consequences of rapid urbanization that tends to concentrate people and overburden infrastructure.

From 1978 to 2004, the urban population of China grew from 12.8% to 41% (Airriess, 2008, 136). Most of the growth was not in its largest cities, but in the middle cities. In 1978, 52% of industrial output was found in municipalities—the largest cities. By 2002, it had decreased to only 22%. Industrial output in the middle cities increased from 47% in 1978 to 75% in 2002. Unlike other developing countries, China pursed a deliberate strategy of growing its second- and third-tier cities and limiting most of its largest cities.

The study by Christopher Airriess (2008) demonstrates how China used middle-city development to shape the economic and social changes wrought by globalization. Whereas China is the most populous country in the world and 41% of its population is urban, only one of its cities is in the top 10 most populous cities in the world. The success of China in the global economy raises questions about the wisdom of increasing agglomeration in cities to reap comparative advantage or economy of scale (138). To structure his analysis, Airriess documents demographic and economic changes to identify trends statistically, then, going back through historical record, correlates trends with shifts in governmental policy and global forces.

Strategic and ideological issues motivated China to cultivate its mid-sized cities rather than its capital and large cities in its first wave of urban reform. From 1945 to 1965, Cold War strategy dictated placing mass production securely in the country's interior and close to energy sources. This put them in second- and third-tier cities, encouraging their growth. During the Cultural Revolution, the second wave of reform, neither primary nor secondary cities grew. Chinese communism faulted cities as systems of exploitation. Cities did not produce but survived by consuming and appropriating wealth produced by others. Youth were sent into rural areas to get a peasant's education and protect them from the corrupting influence of capitalism and materialism found in the cities.

A third wave of reform began in 1978. Massive economic, political, social, and cultural changes occurred as China opened to the West. Urban growth exploded when the Chinese government welcomed foreign investment and allowed capital accumulation under the aegis of "Chinese-style market socialism." One of the most important reforms was the reorganization of the administrative structure of Chinese provinces and cities. New policies expanded the boundaries of urban areas to include quasi-rural areas and several towns into a single administrative unit. China now has four tiers in its urban administrative rankings. National cities are the most powerful. They are not incorporated into provinces in the way that U.S. cities, no matter how large, are part of states. They stand alone and fall directly under the federal government. They are, in effect, provinces. Sub-province cities, prefecture cities, and county-level cities each exist within provinces. The territories of the new cities were expanded to include some of the peri-urban or hinterland that surrounds them as well as small towns and townships nearby, blurring the distinction between rural and urban. This expands the city's tax base and provides for a larger more integrated regional economy. Some U.S. cities have reorganized along similar lines, joining with the surrounding county in an administrative unit. Many U.S. suburban communities resist joining with cities because many suburban residents migrated from the cities to escape crowding and crime. In China, some rural residents resented the unification with the city calling it a "city-extorting-counties" system (Airriess 2008, 137).

Along with expanding the categories of administrative ranks and the territories encompassed, China increased decentralization: More administrative responsibility transferred to local levels and more places gained political and economic autonomy. The cost of autonomy is more responsibility for generating revenue rather than depending heavily on the national or provincial governments. Heightened responsibility sent the cities out looking for investment opportunities.

BOX 15.8   A Closer Look: Urban Administrative Structure in China

Type of Administrative Unit	Number of units in China	Description
National Cities	4	Fall directly under the federal government and have status equal to a province Beijing, Chongqing, Shanghai, Tainjin
Sub-Province Cities	15	Located within provinces, some are the provincial capital
Prefecture Cities	282	Administer an urban core and surrounding districts and wards
County-Level Cities (Sub-Prefecture Cities)	374	Smaller towns and rural township counties

Source: Airriess (2008).

The government designated specific territories for particular economic functions. In 1978, China created four Special Economic Zones (SEZs); each incorporates a middle-sized city and its surroundings. In 1984, China designated 14 open coastal cities to be similar to the SEZ. These zones channel and disperse foreign direct investment throughout the area. Township and village enterprises (TVEs) were also encouraged. The TVE is a partnership between domestic private enterprise and local Communist party officials or foreign investors. These are located around the perimeter of cities, not quite rural and not quite urban, but close to urban markets. Each of these designations presents an area with a specific set of designated opportunities.

Changes in migration policy allowed more people to take advantage of the opportunities. In the mid-1980s, some restrictions on migration within China were lifted and people began more intensive migration from rural areas for better opportunities in the cities. These reforms resulted in dramatic growth in medium- and small-sized cities. Larger cities grew much less. (Note: The Hukou, or household registration system in China, set up in the 1950s, limited people's movement. The registration system is generally criticized for discriminating against rural citizens and ethnic minorities. People only received social services such as education and health care within the area of their registration. This system kept people within the area in which they were born, although moving among rural areas was not too difficult. Marriage and university

study were among the few ways to move into the cities. Hukou was reformed in phases beginning in 1978 but still restricts and controls people's movements. In 1995, to limit migration to Shanghai and Beijing, rules required that rural to urban migrants brought their ID cards, apply for a Temporary Residence Card, and use that to apply for a work permit. Then, the administrative unit would decide what type of employment the migrant could seek. See the Congressional-Executive Commission on China (2011) for more details on contemporary hukou.

Airriess' (2008) study examines the effects of these reforms on two prefecture level cities, Dongguan and Suzhou. Dongguan is in the Pearl River Delta and lies close to Hong Kong, and Suzhou is in the Yangtze River Delta (YRD), bordering Shanghai. They differ in many respects and have many problems, but each is a success story when measured by economic growth and urban transition.

Dongguan has four urban areas and 28 other towns within its administrative purview. It is known as "the city of migrants" because its population of 6.64 million was 73% migrants in 2000. By 2005, its population grew to 7.5 million. Dongguan's first growth spurt came through the activity of the TVEs, industrialization from below. State owned and collective enterprises dominated. In the mid-1980s, foreign investment from Hong Kong became a critical segment of Dongguan's economy. Dongguan and Hong Kong enjoy close ties. Most of

Hong Kong residents originate from the Guangdong province. Until 1984, when border controls were intensified, migration in both directions across the border was common. The social relationships between the two made Dongguan a suitable destination for Hong Kong's offshoring of land and labor-intensive manufacturing. Hong Kong accounted for about 96% of Dongguan's foreign investment in 1990 (Airriess 2008, 140).

Industries dispersed within Dongguan. Good communications and road networks facilitated the spread of factories throughout the prefecture. The four urban areas of Dongguan accounted for only 6.2% of its export value in 2005, whereas four other counties within Dongguan had higher shares of exports than the cities. Wanting to attract higher level industrial work rather than the low-level manufacturing of textiles, shoes, toys, and furniture Hong Kong was sending, Dongguan set up nine industrial technology parks with help from the province and federal government. The parks were a strategic move. First, parks attract cleaner, higher quality manufacturing. Second, rather than scattering similar industrial factories throughout the prefecture, the parks design agglomerates specific high-tech industries in one area, making them more attractive to investors. The nine parks were spread throughout the prefecture: three in Dongguan city and the other six in six different towns. The transformation was a success. Taiwan is now its largest investor, accounting for 30% of the export volume. Electronics products are 60% of Dongguan's total export value, and Dongguan now produces 95% of the parts for final assembly of products for Nokia, Samsung, IBM, and other multinational corporations (142).

Suzhou has the largest non-agricultural population of all the prefectures in the YRD, with the exception of the large cities. Even before the reforms of 1978, it was economically robust, having textile production, banking, finance, and rural and small town craft industries. Following the reforms, Shanghai was designated as a modern SEZ. Many state-owned enterprises of lower quality migrated from Shanghai to the YRD in the early 1980s, followed by foreign and domestically owned labor-intensive industries through the 1990s.

The Suzhou Industrial Park (SIP), developed by national and local governments in conjunction with Singaporean firms, opened in 1994. Along with the Suzhou New District, 5,500 foreign high-technology industries were attracted to the prefecture (145). Singapore's interest in the SIP gives them needed access to new markets and high income employment opportunities for Singaporean nationals. Taiwan has also entered Suzhou with R&D, in addition to manufacturing. As the area has grown, some of the assembly work has dispersed to smaller YRD cities while tertiary industries stayed in Suzhou. The net benefit has been that from the late 1990s to 2002, state-owned and collective enterprise share of industrial output dropped from close to 60% to under 10%, FDI climbed to over half (144). From 1985, the primary industry share of its domestic product dropped from almost 20% to about 2%, a 90% reduction. The share in secondary industry rose to 65.7%, and the share in tertiary industry grew to 32.1%. Tertiary industry was the highest growth area. Suzou became a competitor to Shanghai. In 2002, its GDP per capita was 88% of Shanghai's, and its FDI was almost equal to Shanghai's, US$48 billion in comparison to US$50 billion (143). As industries dispersed, other counties within the prefecture established industrial parks. Even though Suzhou city's GDP per capita is higher by 6% than the overall prefecture, there are two counties whose GDPs are higher. They are also strong enough to compete with Shanghai (145).

Airriess's (2008) studies of China's middle cities demonstrates how forces of globalization—including the dispersion of manufacturing, the demand for and development of the high-tech industry, export trade, and migration—and urbanization can be steered by domestic policy. Through its reform initiatives, China was able to direct and shape many forces of globalization related to urbanization. Whereas other developing nations experienced relentless flows of people into one or two major—mega—cities, China used policy and regulation to disperse flows of people and foreign investment and build a variety of urban areas rather than simply swell existing ones.

Despite these successes in channeling development, China's urban problems are far from solved. Inequalities continue to grow. The research of Zheng et al. (2009) is instructive. Beijing and other cities, including middle cities, have slums that rival those of any mega city. Urban villages, rural villages swallowed by urbanization policies, exist as pockets of poverty within the cities. Over a hundred urban villages may be nestled in the shadows of the buildings in large cities such as Guangzhou. Remnants of traditional lifestyles, they offer a stark contrast to the skyscrapers surrounding them. Unable to secure housing in the formal or government subsidized housing market, about 80% of migrant workers find homes in the villages. Renting to migrants has replaced agriculture as the villagers' chief source of income. They build onto their houses, often with disregard for fire and other building codes. Housing is dense. Units are one room. Over 90% have no bath or kitchen. Migrants use public facilities. The urban villages are plagued by the social problems typical of slums: crime, drugs, and poverty. They are a public security issue.

On the other hand, research (Zheng et al. 2009) in the villages indicates that under current conditions, migrants do not want to spend on rent. The rules governing migrants are still oppressive and still discriminate against people with rural residential registration in housing, employment, and social services such as education of their children. Migrants face social discrimination as well. Most intend to return home. They view the city as a place to work, not live. China has a circulatory pattern of migration rather than one way to the city. Money is sent home, not spent on rent or in the city. Migrants would spend more on housing to improve their living conditions, if other life conditions were improved and the price of rent were low enough to help them meet their long-term goals. Policies to improve the social and job security of migrants enabling them to accumulate human capital such as education, qualify for high-skill jobs, and increase social integration would encourage them to stay and spend more money in the cities, helping to solve the slum problem of urban villages (443).

There are alternatives to mega cities for developing nations. Although many would not tolerate the level of regulation that China has imposed to achieve decentralization, incentive packages may help create healthier urban patterns. In the United States, the population is already trending toward moving to smaller cities. Some of the most popular cities, such as Santa Fe (population 62,000 in 2007) have populations well under 100,000. At the same time, city centers of big and mid-sized cities that have used urban planning to create the amenities of neighborhoods in their downtown areas are attracting new residents and restoring vitality to city centers. However, in 2000, the 44 largest U.S. downtowns still had only about 1 million people, 0.3% of the U.S. population (Rybczynski 2010, 174–178). The study of urban migrants (Zheng et al. 2009) points the way to potential reforms to improve city life in other developing countries.

Creative Cities

Urban studies encompass sociology, geography, history, economics, political science, and a host of disciplines. What diverse theorists from these disciplines agree on is that because cities all over the world are so intimately connected through flows of people and production, they are the primary location of competition for the economic and human capital resources that drive economic, cultural, and social development. To attract these resources, cities need to be creative.

Measuring and indexing cities has become an industry. The CCI Creative City Index includes 23 such indices that collectively measure approximately 16 dimensions—cultural tourism, creative industries, cultural capital, government, business and economy, entrepreneurship, innovation and research, technology and ICT, and environment—(Hartley, Potts, and MacDonald 2012, 11). The CCI Creative City Index (CCI-CCI) tries to capture the factors that account for the competitive advantage that attracts and retains people in a city and gives them the wherewithal to build a great city.

BOX 15.9   Consider This: The Creative Class

Is the vitality of a city dependent on its ability to attract the creative class—people who have new ideas and can turn them into creative enterprises? There is a creative class in every industry and typically includes scientists and engineers, artists, entertainers, journalists, university professors, high techies—anyone who innovates and turns ideas into cutting-edge opportunities is a member.

According to Richard Florida (2002), the creative class is about 35% of the workforce. Some cities are becoming centers for the creative class, while others have attracted few. Florida argues that cities with a good share of the creative class are likely to thrive, others will not. To attract the creative class, a city has to make them feel comfortable, and this depends on visible diversity. The creative class values creativity, individuality, and merit. They look for lifestyle options that generally include a thriving art and music scene, cultural diversity,

(Continued)

(Continued)

outdoor recreation, nightlife. This is similar to Jane Jacobs (1964) prescription of diversity and an animated and diverse street life to create livable cities.

Florida's Creativity Index rates cities on four factors: the percentage of the labor force belonging to the creative class, the high-tech industry, innovation, and openness (encouragement of diversity). These are the three Ts—talent, technology, and tolerance.

Attracting the creative class does pose dangers as well. Florida has cautioned that the creative class can drive the price of housings and other amenities up. Cities must plan to raise wages of other workers to compensate for this and create a livable city.

Similar indices are the Vitality Index and Creative City Index.

The Creative City index measures institutional, cultural, social, and physical factors and, following Jane Jacobs's lead, processes of experimentation, adaptation, and learning (Hartley et al. 2012, 31). The assumption behind that approach is that cities are dynamic. They grow through the efforts of those who live and work there—not from top-down planning. Nevertheless, the indices provide best practices and benchmarks to guide government funding and policy makers "by providing robust, efficient, evidential data to measure comparative changes over time (127). It can be thought of as investing in setting the conditions for innovation and success, rather than investing in particular projects such as sports stadiums.

Because the Creative Cities Index is an amalgam of many others, its factors are identified here, along with some indicators. The factors that are unique to this index are the indicators that capture the engagement and creative activity of the general citizenry. Microproductivity captures social networking and producing cultural content—for example, you do not have to be employed in the creative industries to upload a clip to YouTube. The indicators related to civic engagement and youth culture are scattered throughout the dimensions. Something like references in *Lonely Planet* travel book series might capture youth tourism and also be indicative of social and cultural capital. Eight dimensions and over 200 measures were included when the index was piloted. In cross-cultural applications, some indicators—such as uploads to specific sites such as Photobucket or Flickr—need to be replaced with equivalent local indicators.

The eight dimensions and some sample indicators are as follows:

- **Creative Industries, Scale, Scope, and Employment:** overall activity in the creative industries (such as film, theater, television, design, architecture, etc.)
  - People employed in creative industries
  - Number of firms
  - Millions of dollars represented by the industry

- **Microproductivity:** user-created content and computer-enabled and other social networks
  - Uploads to YouTube, Flickr, Photobucket
  - Music profiles uploaded to the Internet
  - Image uploads, tags, and blogs

- **Attractions and Economy of Attention:** the number of tourist and cultural attractions and the coverage of the city in a variety of media
  - Number of concert halls, hotels, cinemas, libraries, theaters, museums
  - Pages in *Lonely Planet*, entries in Wikipedia, references in books, Google trends, films with the city as presumed setting, films filmed in the city

- **Participation and Expenditure:** attendance and expenditures at cultural events
  - Admissions to facilities and events such as museums, libraries, galleries, cinema, theater, concerts
  - Household expenditure on cultural events

- **Public Support:** governmental financial support
  - Per capita government cultural funding at local, state, and federal levels

- **Human Capital and Research:** quality of labor force for R&D, products of R&D
  - University graduates
  - Places of cultural education
  - Patents per capita

- **Global Integration:** connections of the city to the rest of the world

- ○ International airport traffic
- ○ Total migration and population turnover
- ○ Globalization, connections to world's largest law, financial services, advertising, and accounting firms (glamour sector firms)
- **Openness, Tolerance and Diversity**: how accepting of difference, outsiders, non-traditional or dissenting views and lifestyles, the level of civic engagement and dynamic of its demographics
  - ○ Number of foreign-born and variety within the foreign population
  - ○ Voter registration
  - ○ Youth population
  - ○ Income inequality Hartley et al. 2012, 81–123

Note that these indicators are not all directly related to creativity, but they are signs that an area is more welcoming to diversity and likely to tolerate or nurture new ideas. Creative cities are thought to offer more promise for a higher quality of city life than is now evident in most of the world's cities. They are presumed to have an edge over other cities in attracting and retaining the talented individuals capable of keeping up in a rapidly changing and globalizing world.

Cities and the Quality of Life

Is it a human right to live in decent surroundings where attention has been paid to livability? If so, millions of people are denied this basic right. Their living conditions are not of their making, and the stress created by the chronic conditions in which they live—of noise, filth, and crime—takes a serious toll on both physical and mental health.

Cities, like other living systems, have life cycles. As they grow, develop, and change, they require care and maintenance. They need to be rebuilt and renewed periodically. Cities in even the richest nations are home to slums, crime, and disease. Global economic restructuring and privatization policies have had different impacts in developing and developed societies. In a pattern somewhat the reverse of developing societies, urban areas of developed societies decayed from within, as manufacturing left the cities and industry declined. Middle- and working-class jobs were lost to the suburbs, to other countries, and to technology. A polarized job structure of elite and low-level service jobs eventually replaced them. When manufacturing left the cities, the blue-collar neighborhoods within cities were decimated, and decades later, many have still not recovered.

Poor urban planning was not the primary cause of cities' ill fortunes post-WWII, but it aggravated the cost of decline. New highways and low-income loans lured the middle class, industry, and jobs to the suburbs. Initial urban renewal efforts in the United States and Europe consisted mainly of slum clearance (Grebler 1962). In the United States, low-interest loans were available to developers who would create new projects in distressed neighborhoods. Because developers were not required to rebuild the area with low- or mixed-income housing, many inner city properties on the edge of downtowns that house viable interracial neighborhoods were torn down and replaced with luxury developments, from apartment complexes to entertainment facilities. Urban poor were displaced, often without compensation or relocation assistance. The supply of low income housing shrunk as demand was increasing.

BOX 15.10   A Closer Look: Urban Redevelopment in Pittsburgh, PA

Hundreds of people and businesses on the edge of the city center were displaced to make way for the Mellon Arena (formerly Civic Arena and home of the Pittsburgh Penguins) and adjacent Chatham Center, an upscale shopping and entertainment development. Parts of the area have since been rebuilt to accommodate mixed-income housing.

Government-owned or -subsidized projects did not fare well. Vertical high-rise apartment buildings isolated and concentrated the poor with little or no greenery, noise amplified by concrete, and very few public amenities. Many became havens for predators. Pruitt-Igoe, in St. Louis—built in 1956 and razed in 1972 and 1973—has become an urban legend, hard to distinguish fact from fiction concerning its demise, but many cities built similar and similarly disastrous projects that had to be destroyed.

Often, areas that were designated as blighted and thus subject to renewal were stable neighborhoods without much physical deterioration. Still, they were destroyed. In Pittsburgh, Pennsylvania, for example, more than 1,500 businesses and 5,000 families were uprooted from low-income, mixed race neighborhoods. Often, when viable racially mixed areas were torn down, residents moved into established areas with people of their own race, further segregating the city. Many who would have stayed in the city left for the suburbs, where housing was more plentiful. Following the disasters of slum clearance and neighborhood redevelopment, the federal government turned to the less politically sensitive task of commercial, as opposed to residential, displacement. Urban renewal left the United States short of low-income housing and long on abandoned city areas where neighborhoods used to be.

BOX 15.11   A Closer Look: Jane Jacobs

Decades ahead of her time, Jane Jacobs condemned bulldozing neighborhoods and replacing them with high-rises under the guise of urban planning. She advocated starting at the grassroots—allowing a community to actively plan its own development. She compared cities to living organisms, needing a diversity of systems to thrive. Mixed-use neighborhoods—combining retail, residential, businesses, parks, and schools in one area bringing people of different ages, incomes, ethnicities, and professions into contact—was the key to community vitality. Rather than seeing high density as detracting from city life, she saw that a critical mass of people—different than overcrowding—was necessary for city vitality. Social interaction, and lots of it, was the key to good health, personal and urban. She developed a four-part prescription for cities: mixed use; short blocks to encourage people's paths crossing; diversity in building age, condition, and use; and population density (1961/1992, 196–197).

Housing for the poor faced similar problems in Europe. High rises (tower blocks), built for public housing in England, suffered a similar fate, with many being torn down after they had deteriorated substantially. As in the United States, one root of the problems was bad design. Lack of play space; lack of community facilities such as shops, parks, and entertainment; isolation of the poor; poor maintenance of buildings; the cost of rubbish removal; noise; and insecurity due to fear of crime or fire all contributed to the demise of the "estates" (Spicker n.d.).

The social protests of the 1960s promoted community-directed development efforts in residential areas. In the United States today, displacement policies require that federal units taken from the housing inventory must be replaced. There must also be relocation assistance. The Model Cities Program, first established in 1966, now requires local planning of renewal efforts, partnering with local and private sources, and social needs for education, health, and employment (Koebel 1996, 19). Vouchers for private housing stock rather than government-owned inventory are recognized as a better solution to low-income housing. The federal government aids families directly with housing grants that enable them to move into any community where there is approved housing. The units must meet standards set by the federal government. An important note, however, is that landlords do not have to participate in the federal housing programs, so there may be long waiting lists for housing, and there may be a very limited pool of housing in mixed-income areas. Many state and local jurisdictions have similar policies.

After nearly 50 years, the inner city neighborhoods of many cities may be reviving. Mixed-income housing and more neighborhood-friendly housing have replaced concentrations of low-income housing. Businesses are moving in. There seems to be a revival in even some of the hardest-hit cities. Detroit's population shrank by 25% in the first decade of the 21st century. But the number of college educated residents under 35 increased by 59% (Conlin 2011). While homes in the outer suburbs were in high demand in the 1990s, the center city and inner suburbs seem to be the most desirable areas of the 21st century. People are looking for walkable, centrally located areas. Areas that were considered slums not too long ago, such as Capitol Hill in Seattle, German Village in Columbus, and Logan Circle in Washington, have gentrified and are now among the most expensive neighborhoods in their areas (Leinberger 2011).

A new generation of approaches to urban renewal is taking shape in Europe as well. European cities experienced declines similar to the United States in inner city manufacturing and quality of life. Creative Urban Renewal in NW Europe (CURE) is a transnational effort funded by the EU. The current project partners are Germany, Belgium, France, the Netherlands, and the United Kingdom. CURE developed a "Creative Zone Innovator" model to attract creative and entrepreneurial businesses to mid-sized cities. The LUDA Project (Improving the Quality of Life in Large Urban Distressed Areas) is supported by the EU to develop and disseminate knowledge about regenerating distressed areas of cities. A *large distressed urban area* is defined as a significant portion of the city that harms the city as a whole. It suffers multiple deprivations such as degraded housing, sub-standard facilities, derelict industrial sites, environmental risks, unattractive and disconnected urban structures, high unemployment, and weak social cohesion. The LUDA Project generated 12 reference case models and long-term implementation plans for sustainable redevelopment in the six partner cities. A 2010 LUDA update stressed the importance of establishing relationships between researchers, local authorities, and stakeholders to develop the give and take necessary to help local policy makers understand the contributions of the research and allow local stakeholders to direct the course of research toward important objectives (Berni 2010, 12–13).

Best practices gleaned from European regeneration efforts reflect emerging global themes related to human rights, autonomy and decentralization,

sustainability, and diversity. Best practices likely to achieve sustainable regeneration of distressed areas can be gleaned from a review of redevelopment projects, models, and assessment indices. Policies that minimize involuntary displacement of residents and their activities will be most successful. Other guidelines for successful redevelopment are as follows:

- Empower all the local inhabitants and stakeholders—including immigrants and ethnic groups, and private, public, and non-governmental organizations—through a decentralized governance structure from the beginning of the process.
- Develop a holistic plan by integrating all sectors, the economic, political, and cultural; all levels of governance, from local to national; and all policy areas, such as equal opportunity policies and strategic land use, environmental and demographic policies.
- Project a strong brand and identity to attract newcomers and outside investors.
- Coordinate investment in infrastructure, such as schools, hospitals, and roads, with spatial context so that the right investments get to the right people in the right way.
- Assess different outcomes in terms of their own time scales and cycles. (Colantonio and Dixon 2011, 244–249)

They have found that regeneration projects can make a difference in virtually all aspects of city life: demographic change (ageing, migration, mobility), education and skills, employment, health and safety, housing and environmental health, identity, sense of place and culture, participation, empowerment, access, social capital, social mixing and cohesion, well-being and happiness, and quality of life (Colantonio and Dixon 2011, 241).

Transferring policies and programs from country to country or from developed to developing countries may pose challenges. Can these best practices be applied to developing societies? What obstacles may be encountered? How can they be overcome?

With rapid growth and rapid change, innovation must exceed decay. Ideas for humanizing cities have not kept up with the growth of cities. Several different approaches have emerged in the last decades to address this condition.

BOX 15.12   A Closer Look: Creative Entrepreneurship

This boy contributes to his family income by collecting and reselling the throwaways of richer lives.

More Than Just a Slum

People see different things when looking from different perspectives. Many of the neighborhoods torn down in the United States by urban redevelopment may have looked shabby to an outsider but were viable neighborhoods where many people lived happy and productive lives. Looking at the slums of Mumbai or Rio de Janiero, it may be hard to imagine that good things are happening and viable communities are growing within. Nevertheless, the resilience and creativity of people can flourish, against all odds, in even the direst circumstances. The world's slums house many viable communities not built by governments, but rather by the creative, talented, and determined people who live within them.

The *New York Times* (Yardley 2011) ran an investigative series about one such remarkable place. Dharavi is one of the world's most famous slums—star of a movie (*Slumdog Millionaire*), subject of a Harvard Business School case study, and puzzle to urban planners from Europe to Japan. Like the urban villages in China, it sits as a city within a city, having been surrounded by the growth of Mumbai. Dharavi is home to about 1 million people in 60,000 structures in an area not as large as New York's Central Park. Yet, within Dharavi, small shops and industries have built an economy estimated to be between US$600 million and US$1 billion. Dharavi's economy exists in the shadows of the formal economy, part of India's vast informal economy. While the government of India concentrated on developing the high-tech sector, people took it on themselves to develop lower level manufacturing. And they did it well. Goods from the Dharavi slum industries are sold in India's most exclusive shops and are exported around the world.

Dharavi qualifies as a slum as determined by the quality of its housing stock. Open channels carry sewage and garbage through the streets. Water comes from taps that serve ten families each and operate about three hours daily. Communal toilets are available for a charge. However, there is little crime, and people talk of their work more than their misery. There is plenty of work. Not hampered by government regulation, Dharavi residents are limited only by their ingenuity and ambition. USAID has documented 500 large garment shops, having 50 or more sewing machines, and 3,000 smaller shops. There are 5,000 leather shops. Printmakers, embroidery shops, snack food processors, and many large plastic recycling operations find home in Dharavi.

And there are schools in Dharavi. Like millions of Indians, who view education as the hope for their children's future, they are avoiding government schools and sending their children to the private schools that are spreading in both rich and poor neighborhoods. For Dharavi's children, there was little choice. Dharavi children are discriminated against in schools outside the slum, often because they are from the untouchable caste or are Muslim, so parents began their own schools. Parents save and sacrifice to send their children to private schools set up in the slums where they can learn English—unlike most government schools. While some schools are run by Muslims and enroll primarily Muslims, in most of the schools, Hindu and Muslim children learn just as they live, side by side.

Dharavi's magnetism is the availability of work and the word of its success stories. Following channels of migration along kinship and village ties, people continue to flow into Dharavi, hundreds a day. Many come alone and send the largest part of their earnings home. Dharavi is so successful that it has become a training incubator. Some migrants come as apprentices to learn a trade or skill that they take with them to another slum where they will set up their own shops.

Dharavi is now attracting redevelopment planners. The property on which Dharvi lies is now in the middle of Mumbai and is valuable. Most of the residents are squatters, without title to the property on which they live and work. The land could be used for luxury apartments and office buildings. The fate of Dharavi is locked in bureaucratic fighting.

How might India as a whole benefit from the initiative and innovation shown by Dharavi residents and the industries of the slums? Can the slums and their residents be integrated into mainstream Indian society and reap benefits of water, sewage, education, and other government services? Can Dharavi be developed to bring a better quality of life for residents of Dharavi and ensure that the lives—including the work, production, and sales chains, which people have built—will not be destroyed?

What can the developing world learn from the redevelopment successes and failures of the developed nations?

Innovative Approaches to City Life

Large-scale social changes are needed to solve the problems of cities. However, there are many innovations that can make life a lot better. Many of these can be implemented through local coalitions. The innovative models I discuss here can be replicated.

Putting Globalization to Work: The Mega-Cities Project

The Mega-Cities Project could be replicated in any city for local and global renovation. It is notable for its intensive process. Replication is how they define success. Megacities exhibit problems common to all cities—just in exaggerated form. That makes megacities a good choice for research and testing innovations. If an innovation works in a megacity, it is likely to work in smaller cities as well. The project has found hundreds of innovative strategies people use to better city life. They scaled up and transferred 40 of them to new cities, working through a network of project teams, located in 22 cities. Some of their innovation development and transfer successes include the following:

- "Magic Eyes" in Bangkok uses a number of media to teach children not to litter. It transferred to Los Angeles and Rio de Janeiro.
- The "surface metro" is a clear cylinder in which people queue for the bus, paying in advance while in the tube. When the bus comes, the passengers board quickly. This innovation, transferred from Curitiba, Brazil to New York, saves on traffic congestion and pollution.
- "Alert II" is a program that closes select city streets on dangerously smoggy days. It transferred from Sáo Paulo to New York.
- In Cairo, a program to allow trash pickers to convert trash to sellable products has been replicated in Manila and Bombay and is being transferred to Los Angeles.
- "City Harvest" began in New York, "harvesting" unused food from restaurants and serving it up in soup kitchens. It transferred to Sáo Paulo and Rio de Janeiro.
- In Bombay, children are trained as "mini-doctors" to teach friends and families how to prevent health problems and cure some. This "Child-to-Child" community health care program is being transferred to Rio de Janeiro (Mega-Cities Project 2010).

Their approach is not top down. Like other successful regeneration projects, it invests in developing local ideas and local leaders, including and giving voice to marginalized people. It develops partnerships with public and private sectors, research centers, media, grassroots groups, and other institutions, and coordinates their activity. There are seven policy areas on which megacity focuses:

- Income generation and jobs
- Food and energy

- Water and sanitation
- Transportation and communication
- Education and training
- Public health and safety

One of the major problems of innovation is the time it takes for an innovation or discovery to be implemented, and even longer for the innovation to be diffused and adopted in other locales. The Mega-Cities Project is a vehicle to facilitate each step of the process. Despite the differences in the cities in which they have worked, the project discovered several common themes that can guide the diffusion of innovation.

- Environmental and poverty problems were critical in all of the cities.
- The richest sources of innovation were NGOs and, second, local governments; the closer the source of the innovation is to the client group, the more likely it is to succeed.
- Innovations that have the acceptance of local government are more likely to succeed.
- Structural innovations that change power relationships lead to more innovations.
- The group that initiates an innovation may be very vulnerable within bureaucracies in the early stages of an innovation (Perlman 1990, 13).

The process of transferring innovation is important to success. As we have seen in our study of how policies and programs diffuse, it is often hasty and does not involve reflection or learning. The Mega-Cities Project found that in transferring innovations, it is better if innovations, or parts thereof, are imported (chosen) rather than exported (imposed). This is a recurrent theme of successful problem solving. Although it should not need repeating, the tendency remains to impose solutions. Transferring programs successfully requires partnering between peers from the source of the innovation to the new locale, allowing the group to think through what they are trying to solve and how the innovation will meet their needs, keeping very close watch on the process to ensure that needed resources—financial as well as knowledge based—are in place, rewarding local partners through recognition and publicity, involving as many layers of the community as possible, using media coverage to create interest and acceptance

among the public, clearly stating what is being changed, and celebrating success (Perlman 1990, 14–15). These repeated themes—participatory, democratic, reflexive, well-supported processes (financial, expertise, and knowledge)—are the central features of the successful programs.

There are a number of other organizations for working on solutions to city problems. "Polis" is a network of European cities and regions tackling transportation problems. The network identified quality of life concerns affected by transportation issues such as environmental, health, mobility, traffic efficiency, economics, safety, and security (Polis 2010). The CLIP (Cities for Local Integration Policy) is a network of 30 cities that are trying to solve the problems of migrants. They have identified four main areas of concern: housing, equality and diversity in employment and in government services, intergroup relations and intercultural policies, and ethnic entrepreneurship (CLIP 2010).

Rebuilding Cities for the Poor

Unfortunately, gentrification is often a consequence of urban renewal, displacing many poor. Low-income housing makes way for luxurious townhouses or money-making center city cultural activities, creating shortages of low-income housing and exacerbating homelessness. There has been some attention to the plight of the poor in developing more humane public housing in place of the high-rises common to many cities, most of which themselves have been torn down. These often involve dislocating people from their neighborhoods.

Some architects are taking up the challenge of renewing the landscape of poverty in inner cities and rural areas. It does not involve tearing down neighborhoods or displacing residents. It revitalizes urban low-income areas without disrupting them. A 2010 exhibit at the Museum of Modern Art (MOMA) in New York documented 11 projects from different parts of the world that are part of a movement to enrich people's lives through good design; something that has always been available to the more wealthy. This revisits a theme of architecture in the first half of the 20th century—social consciousness—that had been all but forgotten during the post-war opulence (Ouroussoff 2010). The message is clear: Poverty does not have to be ugly, nor does the uplifting nature of art need to be grossly expensive and available only to the well-to-do. The projects in the show include urban and rural landscapes from a remote village in Burkina Faso to Skid Row in Los Angeles and the poor and working class area of Paris.

Design With the Other 90%: Cities celebrates simple but elegant solutions to daunting urban problems. This exhibition, which was hosted by the UN in 2011, showcases 60 projects that brought inventive designers together with people who needed their services. Many of these projects are in the informal settlements surrounding cities. The designs acknowledge that despite the problems, people have created viable neighborhoods and communities. By helping people solve problems in their communities, they build social capital along with physical improvements. Innovations have been as inexpensive but chemically sophisticated as a $35 two-bucket water filter that removes arsenic and other contaminants from groundwater drinking supplies. One filter can serve a family of five for 14 years. Larger filters are available for community water supplies and smaller for table top use (Design 2011, SONO Water Filter). People in the informal settlements northeast of Cape Town are micro-farming organic vegetables. This effort has been so successful that it not only serves subsistence needs but also provides a livelihood for 3,000 micro-farmers and supplies vegetables to local schools (Design 2011, Abalimi Bezekhaya). In Nairobi, Solidarités International developed "gardening in a sack." On average, households using the sacks grow enough vegetables for about four meals a week. Sixty community groups are now doing sack gardening, and 40 of them are earning incomes in addition to feeding themselves (Design 2011, Garden in a Sack). Digital drums, computers in waterproof easily transported oil drums, are bridging the digital divide, bringing the national school curriculum, public health campaigns, and public service announcements to cities and villages in Uganda (Design 2011, Digital Drums).

How many other problems can be solved if we learn to approach them simply one at a time, rather than looking for only "the big idea" or total solution? To what extent can these simple solutions have larger impact?

The Charter City

The Charter City is a very unique approach. It gives people the chance to start fresh in clean and safe surroundings. Charter cities are created as complete communities with schools, jobs, grocery stores, banks—all of the prerequisites for a modern, comfortable life. Only those people, corporations, and investors who agree to be bound by a charter of rules and regulations would be permitted to live, work, or do business there.

The premise of charter cities is that cities with good rules and good enforcement work better. Crime is lower, streets are clean, schools provide good educations, and jobs are available. Among the most important criteria for investment are a willing and able work force and the rule of law. People and investment will flow to a charter city if these are guaranteed. Good governance is the guarantee.

Those kinds of cities exist, but most people do not have the opportunity to move to places with better rules. Whether due to distance, immigration rules, or cost, most people have little choice but to live in or move to places that are overcrowded and strife with poverty, crime, and illness. Charter city advocates argue that reforming cities that are already established and operating poorly is more difficult than creating new ones. With large-scale migrations expected to continue, people will choose better places to go if such places are available. Establishing these better places requires an empty piece of land and a set of rules.

Charter cities would need a partner to guarantee good governance. In some cases, such as India, the national government could be the partner. In other countries with weaker national governments or national governments with weaker rule of law, another country could be the partner. The partner would enforce the charter for the city.

Population density is a concern for city manageability. The suggested size for a charter city is a population density of 17,000 per square kilometer, about 10 million people per 1,000 square kilometers. This is about 60% the density of Manhattan (Charter Cities n.d.).

Hong Kong is cited as an example of a charter city. Although not designed as such, it nevertheless followed the formula. China provided the space and Britain provided the rules. Pennsylvania is also an example of a state created by charter. William Penn was provided the land, and he wrote a charter, providing in particular for freedom of religion that attracted migrants to Pennsylvania (Charter Cities n.d.).

BOX 15.13   A Closer Look: The Cities That Oil Built

Abu Dhabi.

The tallest building in the world at 2,717 ft/828 meters, the Burj Khalifa dwarfs other buildings in Dubai.

"If you build it, they will come" seems to be the theme of the cities grown out of the desert of the United Arab Emirates (UAE). The emirates are building, hoping to reestablish the Middle East as the nexus of East and West as it was at the height of the Silk Road. Until 1971–1972, when they gained in dependence from the British, the emirates were sparsely populated, even though oil had been discovered in parts of Dubai and Abu Dhabi decades earlier. Now they are attracting tourists, Western business, and workers. About 85% of the population is foreign workers building the cities. They compose 99% of the private (non-governmental) workforce.

These cities have set a standard for lavish displays of the grandest urban spectacles. Nowhere else is there the vast reservoir of disposable wealth that differentiates the cities of the oil rich Arab states from every other city. The strategy of using iconic architecture as spectacle to attract investment, tourists, and ultimately new wealthier residents is global, but nowhere has it achieved the superlatives that have been the mark of Dubai. Dubai has been accused of using the symbols of significance to try to force itself into significance. The "only way it can create this significance is by exaggeration…irrespective of any relation to local context" (Elsheshtawy 2010, 135). One of the first iconic buildings in Dubai was the Burj Al Arab Hotel. From its beginning, it was planned to be out of reach of ordinary people, being built on a manufactured island that is reached by helicopter or guarded bridge. The lobby has an atrium that extends through to the roof, gold-coated pillars in the lobby, a cantilevered restaurant, fountains, and very upscale shops. Entry is limited to hotel guests and those with a reservation for one of the shops. The cost of a night of luxury at the Burj is from

The cranes atop the buildings are evidence of the intense rate of construction in Dubai.

US$2,000–5,000 (Elsheshtawy 2010, 137–138). The Burj Khalifa, also in Dubai, is the tallest building in the world.

Dubai Under Construction

How it was built and how it operates, however, is far from enchanted. Dubai is one of the largest employers of modern day slavery. Migrant workers from India, Pakistan, Nepal, and Bangladesh pay an agent for the trip to Dubai. There, they are housed and fed in camps built for them (and by them) that are far from the glamour and hidden from tourists' view. They are transported to their work site each day. Investigative journalists who visited camps of several companies found the situation the same in them all. The camps are filthy and overrun with sewage; meals are paltry. Workers work 12 hour days for little pay. Leaving can be impossible, because workers cannot pay back the debt they owe to agents who brought them to the jobs and confiscated their passports. Many are without even this forced labor, being left go after the recession. They now live on the streets (Allen 2009; Simpson 2011).

The suicide rate among these workers is high. One estimate puts it at seven per week.

A 2012 Human Rights Watch report focused on the development of Saadiyat Island in Abu Dhabi. The island is being developed as a cultural Mecca. There will be a branch of the Louvre and Guggenheim Museums and a campus of New York University, among other performing arts and cultural attractions. Although there had been some improvements in wages and living conditions of some workers, most of the promises made by the developers were being ignored. Most workers were still laboring under abusive conditions. Recruitment fees, and confiscation of passports was continuing. Many workers had the terms of their contracts changed when they arrived.

There are few legal protections or legal avenues for these workers to pursue. In these cases, NGOs such as Human Rights Watch can play a major role. The responsibility of institutions such as NYU and the museums needs to be clarified and enforced.

Is Smaller Better?

The idea of decentralization of city life was proposed by EF Schumacher in the 1970s. With increasing foreign oil dependence, increasing pollution, and the need for growth, he thought the only sensible solution was to move jobs and industry to where people were, not to continue to congregate people in increasingly crowded, dirty, unsustainable industries and cities. Although more people are now living in urban areas than out of them, his question resounds today with even more urgency. "What can be done to bring health to economic life outside the big cities, in the small towns and villages which still contain—in most cases—eighty to ninety percent of the total population"? (Schumacher 1973/2010).

Schumacher's prescription has four very basic elements.

- Workplaces need to be created where people are living, not in urban areas where they tend to migrate. In some cases, this may need to be revised to pull people out of cities.

- The workplaces need to be cheap enough so that many can be created.
- Production methods need to be relatively simple. Intermediate technologies allow the poor to help themselves.
- Production should be from local materials and for local use.

With everyone chasing high technology as the wave of the future, Schumacher's prescription may seem old-fashioned or even ignorant of the times, written as it was almost half a century ago. However, the modern economy, as Schumacher predicted, has not been able to absorb everyone. Could intermediate technologies fill the chasm that has developed between the highly educated, highly skilled, and high-technology sectors, and the poverty waged service sectors that characterize the contemporary job structure? His prescription seems particularly applicable in the economic climate of poor nations, poor regions of wealthy nations, and any nation recovering from severe economic recession.

BOX 15.14   A Closer Look: Red River Valley and Interstate Cooperation

Source: Red River Valley Research Corridor.

One region of the United States finding success in the manner that Schumacher advocated is the economic development of the Red River Valley. Running along the borders of North and South Dakota with Minnesota, the Red River Valley has been reinventing itself as a high-tech research and development corridor. Since 2002, North Dakota has achieved 14.1% growth in employment with 30.3% growth in the technology related fields (RRVRC 2010). The activity is concentrated in North Dakota but impacts other states, as does one of their projects, the "Northern Tier Network," an alliance created to improve internet capability in North Dakota, South Dakota, Minnesota, Montana, Nebraska, Wisconsin, Michigan, Iowa, Idaho, Wyoming, Washington, and Alaska (Schill 2010). The area has been recognized as a hub for R&D and has brought thousands of jobs. Those jobs run the range from those requiring advanced graduate degrees to associate degrees and skilled labor. Although growth in the area has been accelerated by an oil boom, there is a commitment to develop a diversified economy including farming and ranching.

Other dimensions of Schumacher's prescription are being revived, although not usually as a comprehensive set. Despite the rapid growth of the megacities, the percentage of the world's population that is living in the 100 largest megacities has decreased from about 30% to about 25%. Eighty percent of metropolitan growth since 2000 has been in suburbs not cities, and population density in cities has declined since the 19th century (Kotkin 2010, 131). Big cities dominated urban life for most of urban history. By 1970, in the United States, slightly more people lived in small cities of 25,000 to 250,000 than in cities over 250,000. By 2006, 50% more people were living in small to mid-sized cities. Since 1970, the proportion of people living in large cities has steadily declined (Rybczynski 2010, 172–173).

Despite these trends, spontaneous dispersion of people from cities facilitated by worker mobility is unlikely in cities where inequality is increasing and more people are more downwardly than upwardly mobile. In these circumstances, it seems as though people are pushed from rural areas to large urban centers and become trapped, resulting in mega-city growth.

Summary

The future of globalization is intimately bound to the future of cities. Flows of people, of finance, of production, and of information pass through cities, changing the lives of people everywhere as they do. The more people aggregate in cities, the more intense these flows become, and the more quickly change comes. Managing the macro-global systemic flows and the micro-level flows of individuals, communications, jobs, and so forth through global and local neighborhoods is a necessity and a responsibility for cities of all sizes. How we nurture cities and how cities nurture humanity will determine the quality of people's lives.

As at the time of the Industrial Revolution, the world is at a turning point. Whereas the classical social theorists of the Industrial Age observed the chaos of societies and asked, "What makes society possible?" the question confronting the world now is, "What makes the globe possible?" Globalization has changed the nature of the relationship between individuals and the systems within their societies—the economy, polity, and community of that society. It has changed the relationships among societies of the world as overarching global systems—the global economy, global governance, global civil society, and global culture—emerged. It has also changed the relationship and responsibilities of individuals, societies, and the emerging global systems to humanity.

To the degree that the challenges of globalization are met with innovative and pragmatic policies aimed at the greatest common good rather than dictated by ideology, the challenges may be well met. There are, of course, no guarantees. Just as societies are very fragile while in transition, so is the globe.

Questions, Investigations, and Resources

Questions

1. Debate: Because urban life can be crime ridden, poverty ridden, and in other ways detrimental to health and well-being, should we devote more time, energy, and resources to decentralizing the population, or should we create better cities?

2. What aspects of life are influenced or controlled by the activities that go on in the global cities? How are the economic activities of global cities related to political activity of capital cities (some of which are also global cities)?

3. Consider the Global Power City Index. Is London the model of what a city should be? New York ranks first on nearly every list and on many of the indicators. Would the world be better if every city were like New York?

4. Is the agglomeration of command, control, and people into global cities necessary for creativity and effervescence, or is there a better way to do city life?

5. How may the rights and needs of city residents be reconciled with the need for cities to rejuvenate?

6. Can cities afford to make concessions to attract jobs?

7. How can the mistakes made and lessons learned—and still being learned—by developed countries help negotiate the millions in slums of developing world?

Investigations

1. Study the Global Cities Index and Global Power Cities Index measures. What characteristics make an ideal city and how should each be weighed? Would your measures and priorities change the rankings of any of the cities?

2. How are other developing countries working with urban slums to integrate people into the wider benefits of citizenship?

   Investigate proposals and bids for slum development. Which conform to the best practices suggested in the chapter?

   a. This is a request for bids for slum development in Rajasthan, India. http://ppp.rajasthan.gov.in/Slum_Development_PolicyJune2010.pdf
   b. This first section of this reading describes development in Sankalitnagar, Juhapura, India. The second section is a proposal for development in Ahmedabad.

      http://www.mapsofindia.com/maps/rajasthan/
   c. There are some newspaper articles about Sankalitnagar.

      http://articles.timesofindia.indiatimes.com/keyword/juhapura/featured/4

3. Investigate the ingenious projects undertaken in the *Design With the Other 90%: Cities.* Find three projects that would help solve a problem in another city. To what cities would you export them? How would they alleviate a problem in that city?

   http://designother90.org/cities/solutions

4. The Migration Policy Institute Global City Migration map provides data on the total number of foreign-born residents in a city and the proportion of migrants from different global regions. Which do you consider more important in measuring the global reach of a city: the number of foreign-born residents or the diversity of the areas from which those foreign-born residents originate? Based on your answer, which are the top 10 ranking global cities? Provide the data as evidence.

http://www.migrationinformation.org/datahub/gcmm.cfm#map1

Resources

The China Boom Project   http://chinaboom.asiasociety.org/period/reckoning/0/124

The Creative Cities index http://www.charleslandry.com/index.php?l=creativecityindex

Global Cities Index http://www.city-infos.com/global-cities-index-2010/

Life in Favela of Rochina, Rio de Janiero: a first-hand account of life in the favela by a man defending his neighborhood http://lifeinrocinha.blogspot.com/2010/04/living-in-favela.html

Mori Memorial Foundation (MMF)

- MMF Institute for Urban Development

http://www.mori-m-foundation.or.jp/english/research/development.shtml

- MMF Institute for Urban Strategies

http://www.mori-m-foundation.or.jp/english/research/strategies.shtml

- MMF Global Power Cities Index

http://www.mori-m-foundation.or.jp/english/research/project/6/pdf/GPCI2011_English.pdf

UN Global Compact Cities Programme http://citiesprogramme.com/

The Urban Age Project https://www.lse.ac.uk/collections/urbanAge/index.html

Vitality Index http://www.creativecities.org/vi.html

Migration Policy Institute Data Hub http://www.migrationinformation.org/datahub/comparative.cfm

Video

Conditions of Dubai's Immigrant Workers, *BBC News Middle East*, John Simpson reporting http://www.bbc.co.uk/news/world-middle-east-12246979

Notes

Chapter 1

1. If you have never seen this famous picture, it can be found in many online sites. Search under her name: Kim Phúc Phan Thị (Phan Thị Kim Phúc). Kim Phúc was rescued by the photographer who took the famous photo. He took her immediately to a hospital where his status as a media reporter facilitated her getting treatment. She now lives in Canada.

2. *Organization Man,* a study of CEOs in major U.S. corporations, was written in 1956 by William Whyte. The phrase *organizational man* became widely used to describe bureaucratic workers. It symbolized the loss of individuality and creativity working in a bureaucracy. *Rational man* captures the assumption that people have free will and deliberately calculate the costs and benefits of their actions.

3. In the 1960s, alienation and anomie made older political, economic, cultural, and social scripts obsolete. The structure of social life and the principles on which it was organized increasingly failed more people in more societies. Ultimately, the status quo became untenable. Globalization as a process of contemporary social change is analogous to a Kuhnian "revolution." Part and parcel of the rationality and legitimation crises facing nations, it also provides the reference for a new framework, a new organizing principle for social life and social relations, a way out of the anomie that it—at least in part—created.

Chapter 2

1. Recent research has suggested that we are becoming addicted to extra-sensory environments.

2. The page numbers used in the text are from the article as it appeared on Douglas Kellner's website.

3. Rodrik borrows this term and concept from the work of Thomas Friedman (1999).

4. Wallerstein is neither a globalization theorist nor, as he admits, a theorist of any type; instead, he is a historian. Other world systems thinkers have promoted a world systems theory and view of globalization.

5. The volume of international trade would be expected to increase steadily as societies grow in population and develop. They require more resources, goods, and markets. In some measures of globalization, satisfying these needs internally is debited from external trade. Increasing globalization is only indicated if the volume of across-border trade increases more than within-border trade. Other researchers have used measures of globalization based on external trade only. It is a straightforward indicator of interaction. The crux is whether globalization is wrought by increasing interaction or only by increasing the amount of external in relation to internal interaction. Interaction across borders still requires the same degree of order, regardless of the interaction within borders. Total volume of trade, without modification, should be considered a valid measure of globalization. Increasing outside interactions has significant consequences, even if internal interactions increase at the same rate.

Chapter 3

1. The East India Company colonized and administered India until the company was dissolved in the late 19th century. The British government took over, bolstered by the continued large military presence.

2. Sweden gave (some) women the right to vote in the 18th century; New Zealand and a few others in the 19th. It was not until 1868 that the 14th Amendment to the Constitution proclaimed that justice should extend to all citizens (not all people) in the United States. Women were not given the right to vote in national elections until 1920 with passage of the 19th Amendment.

3. Markoff (1999) points out that there were some "prototypical" constitutions before the U.S. Constitution. The centerpiece of Markoff's study is that constitutional and democratic innovation arose in semi-peripheral societies, not the central powers of the era. This is similar to world systems theory theses concerning economic innovation arising from the periphery.

4. These are now housed in the United Nations Treaty Collection (UN 2010).

Chapter 4

1. Protectionism does not necessarily inhibit trade flows and liberalization does not necessarily increase it.

2. The most basic definition of *liberalization* is opening a country's trade and financial markets to foreign competition,

investment, and influence—allowing them to operate freely, with few if any national barriers to economic activity among actors, individual or corporate.

3. *Neo-liberalism* and *Washington Consensus* came to be used interchangeably. John Williamson, who identified the trend in policies and named them the Washington Consensus, did not intend them to be a blueprint to be followed in every country. He simply identified them.

4. There is disagreement as to whether inequality among nations has been increasing or decreasing. Most of the disagreement results from different methods of measuring and comparing income. For an excellent review of these debates, see Svedberg (2004).

5. The OECD has developed a lengthy list of economic indicators of globalization, clustered into four categories: multinational activity, foreign direct investment, capital flow, and internationalization of technology.

Chapter 5

1. Adam Ferguson is credited with coining the term *civil society* in 1767 (Roginsky and Shortall 2009, 474).

2. There is not a clear delineation between INGO and NGO. Many NGOs get involved in global governance, some through their states and some in partnership with or as local or domestic affiliates of INGOs.

3. Senator Patrick Leahy remained very active in the landmine ban movement. The ICBL continues its work as well. On May 18, 2010, over two thirds of U.S. Senators signed a letter to President Barack Obama asking him to finally sign the Ottawa Convention.

4. These countries had a significant intellectual heritage associated with liberal ideas whereas in other bloc countries intellectuals were more nationalistic in focus. Hungary already enjoyed significantly more cultural freedoms and experienced little mobilization at this time.

5. Charter 77 took its name from the year, 1977, which was proclaimed the Year of the Political Prisoner (Manifesto of Charter 77).

Chapter 6

1. According to Mauro Guillén's "Indicators of Globalization," in 2009 there were 241 international organizations and 7,752 non-governmental organizations (Guillén 2010). There are other much higher estimates.

2. Tilly differentiates three periods of globalization, 1500, 1850–1914, and 1950 onward. The period 1950 onward, he argues, is strikingly different from other periods in many ways, notably in being global.

3. A 2010 decision by the U.S. Supreme Court cemented the free speech right of corporations as individuals and eliminated the cap on contributions to political parties. Many people viewed this as reinforcing the role of corporations in governance and increasing the democratic deficit in governance.

Chapter 7

1. This is not to say that they did not interfere in the inner workings of other states. States regularly interfered, supporting revolutions, advancing coups, assassinating foreign nationals.

2. The 22 member states of the League of Arab States are Jordan, United Arab Emirates, Bahrain, Tunisia, Algeria, Djibouti, Saudi Arabia, Sudan, Syrian Arab Republic, Somalia, Iraq, Oman, Palestine, Qatar, Comoros, Kuwait, Lebanon, Libyan Arab Jamahiriya, Egypt, Morocco, Mauritania, and Yemen.

3. These terms are all used in this text in accordance with the usage of the analyst under discussion.

Chapter 8

1. A number of surveys—World Values Survey, Global Attitudes Project, and Afrobarometer, among others—show that support for democracy is strong globally.

2. The world's countries increased in number from 151 to 194 during these years.

3. One major exception to this pattern is China, reporting 74.4% have a "great deal" or "quite a lot" of confidence in their government and less (37.1%) in the UN.

4. The Polity Index runs from –10 to +10. "A "+10" *democracy* . . . has institutionalized procedures for open, competitive, and deliberative political participation; chooses and replaces chief executives in open, competitive elections; and imposes substantial checks and balances on the powers of the chief executive. Countries with *Polity* scores from +6 to +10 are counted as democracies (Marshall and Cole 2009, 9).

5. East Asian countries included are Japan, Mongolia, South Koreas, Taiwan, Hong Kong, China, the Philippines, Thailand, Vietnam, Cambodia, Singapore, Indonesia, and Malaysia.

6. South Asian countries included are India, Pakistan, Bangladesh, Sri Lanka, and Nepal.

7. See Ames, Reno, and Rodrigues (2003) for a discussion of diffuse support, specific support, and commitment to democracy.

8. Albania, Armenia, Azerbaijan, Belarus, Bosnia, Bulgaria, Croatia, Czech Republic, Estonia, Georgia, Hungary, Kazakhstan, Kosovo, Kyrgyzstan, Latvia, Lithuania, Macedonia, Moldova, Montenegro, Poland, Romania, Russia, Serbia, Slovakia, Slovenia, Tajikistan, Turkmenistan, Ukraine, and Uzbekistan.

Chapter 9

1. Anomie, Durkheim taught us in *Suicide*, was the underlying cause of suicide. When meaning drains from life, life does not seem worth living. Rapid social change can render many ways of life meaningless, such as in the transition from agricultural to industrial society. Strong systems of meaning can protect individuals from anomie. That is one of the reasons that charismatic leaders and fundamentalist groups have such broad appeal in times of rapid change.

2. Interconnectivity, mobility, and security are three of five elements of global culture discussed by Paul James (2004).

3.   South Africa (1993), Australia (1992, 1995), Canada (2002, to Acadians), Great Britain (1995, to Tainui of New Zealand), New Zealand, the United States (1993, to Hawaiin natives), and Pope John Paul II (1995, to women) made public apologies (PNC 2003). In March 2010, Michele Bachelet, the outgoing president of Chile, apologized for the treatment of the indigenous Kawesqar. The Mapuche of Chile, however, still feel like "prisoners of war" and called for an end to the discriminatory treatment (MRG 2007).

Chapter 11

1.   This report depends very heavily on the Pew Forum on Religion and Public Life reports on Pentecostalism (2006a, 2006b, 2006c). Although Charismatics may belong to a mainstream Protestant or Catholic denomination, the Pew report lumps them together into a "renewalist" category. Any people who speak in tongues, call themselves charismatic, or call themselves a pentecostalist but do not belong to a Pentecostal denomination are considered charismatics.

Chapter 12

1.   A list of the goals, targets and indicators can be found at the UN statistics site: http://unstats.un.org/unsd/mdg/Host.aspx?Content=Indicators/OfficialList.htm.

2.   The Congressional Research Service Report notes that in the accounting, some projects which span several years may have been included as one year. Some obligation not fulfilled may have been counted. Some projects may have been counted in more than one category. In other cases, the value of projects may be underestimated because the costs of Chinese materials and labor were not included (Lum et al. 2009, 4).

Chapter 13

1.   The most frequent differentiation between violent conflict and war is the level of intensity. If a conflict results in 1,000 or more deaths within a year, it is called a war.

References

Chapter 1

Angang, Hu, Hu Linlin, and Chang Zhixiao. 2003. *China's Economic Growth and Poverty Reduction (1978–2002)*. Washington, DC: International Monetary Fund. http://www.imf.org/external/np/apd/seminars/2003/newdelhi/angang.pdf.

Appadurai, Arjun. 1996. *Modernity at Large: Cultural Dimensions of Globalization*. Minneapolis: University of Minnesota Press.

Barry, Ellen. 2009. "Protests in Moldova Explode, With Help of Twitter." *New York Times,* April 7, A1.

Beck, Ulrich, and Christoph Lau. 2005. "Second Modernity as a Research Agenda: Theoretical and Empirical explorations in the 'Meta-Change' of Modern Society." *The British Journal of Sociology* 56 (4): 525–557.

Brown, David L., Sanjeev Khagram, Mark H. Moore, and Peter Frumkin. 2000. "Globalization, NGOs and Multi-Sectoral Relations." Working Paper No. 1, Hauser Center for Nonprofit Organizations and Kennedy School of Government, Harvard University. http://www.hks.harvard.edu/hauser/PDF_XLS/workingpapers/workingpaper_1.pdf.

Castells, Manuel. 1996. *The Rise of the Network Society*. Oxford: Blackwell.

Chase-Dunn, Christopher, Yukio Kawano, and Benjamin D. Brewer. 2000. "Trade Globalization Since 1795: Waves of Integration in the World-System." *American Sociological Review* 65 (1): 77–95.

Davies, Phil. 2007. "'Nostalgia Tourism' Uncovered as New Trend." *Travel Mole*. http://www.travelmole.com/news_feature.php?id=1124918.

DeMarco, Anthony. 2011. "China Leads World in Luxury Spending." *Forbes*, October 14. http://www.forbes.com/sites/anthonydemarco/2011/10/14/china-leads-world-in-luxury-spending.

Dickens, Charles. 1859/1999. *A Tale of Two Cities*. Mineola, NY: Dover Publications.

Donnelly, Jack. 2007. *International Human Rights*. Boulder, CO: Westview Press.

Drori, Gili S., John W. Meyer, and Hokyu Hwang. 2009. "Rationalization and Actorhood as Dominant Scripts." In *Institutions and Ideology,* edited by Renate E. Meyer, Kerstin Sahlin, Mark J. Ventresca, and Peter Walgenbach, 17–43. Vol. 27 of *Research in the Sociology of Organizations*. Bingley, UK: Emerald.

Durkheim, Emile. 1933/1964. *The Division of Labor in Society*. Translated by George Simpson. New York: The Free Press.

Fiss, Peter C., and Paul M. Hirsch. 2005. "The Discourse of Globalization: Framing and Sensemaking of an Emerging Concept." *American Sociological Review* 70 (1): 29–52.

Giddens, Anthony. 2003. *Runaway World: How Globalization Is Reshaping Our Lives*. New York: Routledge.

Goldstone, Jack A. 2010. "The New Population Bomb." *Foreign Affairs* 89 (1): 31–43.

Hasija, Namrata. 2011. "Rising Suicide Rates Among Rural Women in China." Paper 3466, Institute of Peace and Conflict Studies, New Delhi. http://www.ipcs.org/article/china/rising-suicide-rates-among-rural-women-in-china-3466.html.

Hannerz, Ulf. 1990. "Cosmopolitans and Locals in World Cultures." In *Global Culture: Nationalism, Globalization and Modernity,* edited by Mike Featherstone 237-251. London: Sage.

Keane, John. 2003. *Global Civil Society?* Cambridge: Cambridge University Press.

Keohane, Robert O., and Joseph S Nye, Jr. 2000. "Globalization: What's New? What's Not? (And So What?)" *Foreign Policy* 118 (Spring): 104–199.

Kristofferson, Kris, and Fred Foster. 1969. "Me and Bobby McGee." Recorded by Roger Miller. On *Roger Miller 1970* [vinyl album] Nashville: BNA 69035.

Landler, Mark. 2009. "French Official Indicates Reluctance on a Possible Blockage of Gasoline for Iran." *New York Times,* September 22, A10.

Landler, Mark, and Clifford J. Levy. 2009. "Russian Minister Rejects Iran Sanctions." *New York Times,* October 14, A4.

Meyer, John W., John Boli, George M. Thomas, and Francisco O. Ramirez. 1997. "World Society and the Nation State." *The American Journal of Sociology* 103 (1): 144–181.

O'Hearn, Denis. 2009. "The Anthropology of Globalization or the Globalization of Anthropology." *Identities* 16 (4): 492–510.

Putnam, Robert D. 1995. "Bowling Alone: America's Declining Social Capital." *Journal of Democracy* 6 (1): 65–78.

Putz, Ulrike. 2009. "Neda, Is She Iran's Joan of Arc?" *ABC News,* June 22. http://abcnews.go.com/International/story?id=7897043&page=1.

Richburg, Keith B. 2012. "Getting Chinese to Stop Saving and Start Spending Is a Hard Sell." *Washington Post,* July 5. http://articles.washingtonpost.com/2012-07-05/world/35488534_1_savings-rate-chinese-consumers-china-market-research-group.

Ritzer, George. 2004. *The Globalization of Nothing*. Thousand Oaks, CA: Sage.

Robertson, Roland. 1990. "Mapping the Global Condition: Globalization as the Central Concept." In *Global Culture: Nationalism, Globalization and Modernity*, edited by Mike Featherstone, 15–30. London: Sage.

———. 1992. *Globalization: Social Theory and Global Culture*. London: Sage.

———. 2007. "Global Millennialism: A Post-Mortem on Secularization." In *Religion, Globalization and Culture*, edited by Peter Beyer and Lori G. Beaman, 9–34. Leiden, the Netherlands: Koninklejke Brill, NV.

Robertson, Roland, and JoAnn Chirico. 1985. "Humanity, Globalization and Worldwide Religious Resurgence." *Sociological Analysis* 46 (3): 219–242.

Scholte, Jan Aarte. 2000. *Globalization: A Critical Introduction*. New York: St. Martin's Press.

Schwartz, John. 2009. "Two German Killers Demanding Anonymity Sue Wikipedia's Parent." *New York Times*, November 13, A13.

Simmel Georg. 1908/1971. "Freedom and the Individual." In *Georg Simmel: On Individuality and Social Forms*, edited and translated by Donald N. Levine, 217–226. Chicago: University of Chicago Press.

Sklair, Leslie. 2002. *Globalization: Capitalism and Its Alternatives*. New York: Oxford University Press.

Smith, Adam. 1776/1991. *The Wealth of Nations*. Amherst, NY: Prometheus Books.

Thompson, Ginger. 2009. "White House's New Sudan Strategy Fits Envoy's Pragmatic Style." *New York Times*, October 19, A12.

Tsing, Anna. 2000. "The Global Situation." *Cultural Anthropology* 15 (3): 327–360.

Wadhwa, Vivek, AnnaLee Saxenian, Ben A. Rissing, and Gary Gereffi. 2007. "America's New Immigrant Entrepreneurs: Part I." Duke Science, Technology & Innovation Paper No. 23. http://papers.ssrn.com/sol3/papers.cfm?abstract_id=990152.

The World Bank. 2010. "Defining Civil Society." August 4. http://go.worldbank.org/4CE7W046K0.

World Public Opinion (WPO). 2004. "19 Nation Poll on Global Issues." June 4. http://www.worldpublicopinion.org/pipa/articles/btglobalizationtradera/90.php?nid=&id=&pnt=90.

World Values Survey (WVS). 2010. *WVS 2005–2008*. Online Data Analysis. World Values Survey Association. Stockholm, Sweden. http://www.wvsevsdb.com/wvs/WVSAnalizeSample.jsp.

Chapter 2

Anderson, Lisa, Meghnad Desai, John J. Mearsheimer, Felix Rohatyn, and Leslie Sklair. 2002. "Perspectives of Globalization: A Roundtable Discussion." School of International and Public Affairs at Columbia University. http://www.fathom.com/feature/122547.

Amin, Samir. 1974. *Accumulation on a World Scale*. New York: Monthly Review Press.

Appadurai, Arjun. 1996. *Modernity at Large: Cultural Dimensions of Globalization*. Minneapolis: University of Minnesota Press.

Arrighi, Giovanni. 1978. *The Geometry of Imperialism*. London: NLB.

Beck, Ulrich. 1992. *Risk Society*. London: Sage.

———. 2005. *Power in the Global Age: The New Global Political Economy*. Cambridge: Polity.

———. 2006. *Cosmopolitan Vision*. Translated by Ciaran Cronin. Cambridge: Polity.

Beck, Ulrich, and Edward Grande. 2006. *Cosmopolitan Europe*. Cambridge: Polity.

Beck, Ulrich, and Natan Sznaider. 2006. "Unpacking Cosmopolitanism for the Social Sciences: A Research Agenda." *The British Journal of Sociology* 57 (1): 1–23.

Bunker, Stephen G., and Paul S. Ciccantell. 2005. "Space, Matter, and Technology." In *The Historical Evolution of World Systems*, edited by C. C. Dunn and E. N. Anderson, 174–210. New York: Palgrave.

Chase-Dunn, Christopher. 2006. "World Systems Theory." In *Handbook of Sociological Theory*, edited by Jonathan H. Turner, 589–613. New York: Springer.

Chase-Dunn, Christopher, Yukio Kawano, and Benjamin D. Brewer. 2000. "Trade Globalization Since 1795: Waves of Integration in the World-System." *American Sociological Review* 65 (1): 77–95.

Drori, Gili S., John W. Meyer, and Hokyu Hwang. 2009. "Rationalization and Actorhood as Dominant Scripts." In *Institutions and Ideology*, edited by Renate E. Meyer, Kerstin Sahlin, Mark J. Ventresca, and Peter Walgenbach, 17–43. Vol. 27 of *Research in the Sociology of Organizations*. Bingley, UK: Emerald.

Elkins, Zachery, and Beth Simmons. 2005. "On Waves, Clusters, and Diffusion: A Conceptual Framework." *Annals of the American Academy of Political and Social Sciences* 598 (2005): 33–51.

Frank, Andre Gunder. 1969. *Capitalism and Underdevelopment in Latin America*. New York: Monthly Review Press.

Friedman, Thomas L. 2011. "Out of Touch, Out of Time." *New York Times*, February 11, A27.

Giddens, Anthony. 1990. *The Consequences of Modernity*. Cambridge: Polity.

———. 2003. *Runaway World: How Globalization Is Reshaping Our Lives*. New York: Routledge.

Huberman, Bernardo A., Daniel M. Romero, and Fang Wu. 2009. "Social Networks That Matter: Twitter Under the Microscope." *First Monday* 14 (1). http://firstmonday.org/htbin/cgiwrap/bin/ojs/index.php/fm/article/viewArticle/2317/2063.

Jorgenson, Andrew W., and Edward Kick, eds. 2006. *Globalization and the Environment*. Leiden, the Netherlands: Brill.

Kellner, Douglas. 2002. "Theorizing Globalization." *Sociological Theory* 20 (3): 285–303. http://gseis.ucla.edu/faculty/kellner/papers/theoryglob.htm.

Melman, Seymour. 2001. *After Capitalism: From Managerialism to Workplace Democracy*. New York: Alfred A. Knopf.

Meyer, John W. 2007. "Globalization: Theory and Trends." *International Journal of Comparative Sociology* 48 (4–5): 261–273.

Meyer, John W., John Boli, George M. Thomas, and Francisco O. Ramirez. 1997. "World Society and the Nation State." *The American Journal of Sociology* 103 (1): 144–181.

Robertson, Roland. 1992. *Globalization: Social Theory and Global Culture*. London: Sage.

Robertson, Roland, and JoAnn Chirico. 1985. "Humanity, Globalization and Worldwide Religious Resurgence." *Sociological Analysis* 46 (3): 219–242.

Robinson, William I. 2007. "Beyond the Theory of Imperialism: Global Capitalism and the Transnational State." *Societies Without Borders* 2 (1): 5–26.

Robinson, William I., and Jerry Harris. 2000. "Towards a Global Ruling Class? Globalization and the Transnational Ruling Class." *Science and Society* 64 (1): 11–54.

Rodrik, Dani. 2002. "Feasible Globalizations." NBER Working Paper 9129. http://www.nber.org/papers/w9129.pdf.

———. 2011. *The Globalization Paradox.* New York: W.W. Norton.

Simmons, Beth, Frank Dobbin, and Goeff Garrett. 2006. "Introduction: The International Diffusion of Liberalism." *International Organization* 60 (4): 781–810.

Sklair, Leslie. 1999. "Competing Conceptions of Globalization." *Journal of World-Systems Research* 5 (2): 143–163.

———. 2002. *Globalization: Capitalism and Its Alternatives.* New York: Oxford University Press.

———. 2004. "The End of Capitalist Globalization." In *Rethinking Globalism,* edited by Manfred B. Steger, 39–49. Lanham, MD: Rowman and Littlefield.

———. 2005. "Generic Globalization, Capitalist Globalization, and Beyond: A Framework for Critical Globalization Studies." In *Critical Globalization Studies,* edited by R. Applebaum and W. Robinson, 55–64. New York: Routledge.

Tabb, William K. 2009. "Globalization Today: At the Borders of Class and State Theory." *Science and Society* 73(1): 34–53.

Takhteyev, Yuri, Anatoliy Gruzd, and Barry Wellman. 2012. "Geography of Twitter Networks." *Social Networks* 34 (1): 73–81.

Wallerstein, Immanuel. 1974. "The Rise and Future Demise of the World Capitalist System: Concepts for Comparative Analysis." *Comparative Studies in Society and History* 16 (4): 387–415.

———. 2005. "After Developmentalism and Globalization, What?" *Social Forces* 83 (3): 1263–1278.

———. 2007. "Northeast Asia and the World System." *The Korean Journal of Defense Analysis* 19 (3): 7–25.

World Values Survey. 2011. *World Values Survey 2005 Official Data File v.20090901, 2009.* Online Data Analysis. World Values Survey Association. Madrid: ASEP/JDS.

Chapter 3

Acemoglu, Daron, Simon Johnson, and James Robinson. 2002. "Reversal of Fortune: Geography and Institutions in the Making of the Modern World Income Distribution." *The Quarterly Journal of Economics* 117 (4): 1231–1294.

———. 2005. "The Rise of Europe: Atlantic Trade, Institutional Change and Economic Growth." *American Economic Review,* 95 (3): 546–579.

Aivazovsky. 2008. "Cold War Map." University of Notre Dame OpenCourseWare. http://ocw.nd.edu/physics/nuclear-warfare/images-1/Cold-War-Map.jpg/view.

Bhavagan, Manu. 2010. "A New Hope: India, the United Nations and the Making of the Universal Declaration of Human Rights." *Modern Asia Studies* 44 (2): 311–347.

Bland, Ben. 2012. "Asean Chief: South China Sea Risks Becoming 'Asia's Palestine.'" *CNN,* November 28. http://edition.cnn.com/2012/11/28/business/south-china-sea-asia-palestine/index.html.

Blinder, Alan S. 2006. "Offshoring: The Next Industrial Revolution?" *Foreign Affairs* 85 (2): 113–128.

"Deep Waters Slowly Drying Up." 2010. *Economist* October 7, 86–87. http://www.economist.com/node/17199914.

Donnelly, Jack. 2007. *International Human Rights.* Boulder, CO: Westview Press.

Falk, Richard. 2006. "International Law and the Future." *Third World Quarterly* 27 (7): 727–737.

Frank, Andre Gunder. 1998. *ReOrient: Global Economy in the Asian Age.* Berkeley: University of California Press.

Frankema, E. 2006. "The Colonial Origins of Inequality: The Causes and Consequences of Land Distribution." Groningen, the Netherlands: University of Groningen, Groningen Growth and Development Centre. http://siteresources.worldbank.org/INTDECINEQ/Resources/1149208-1147789289867/IIIWB_Conference_ColonialOrigins_of_InequalityREVISED.pdf.

———. (2010) "The Colonial Roots of Land Distribution: Geography, Factor Endowments or Institutions?" *Economic History Review* 63 (2): 418–451.

Gavison, Ruth. 2003. "Constitutions and Political Reconstruction? Israel's Quest for a Constitution." *International Sociology* 18 (1): 53–70.

Giddens, Anthony. 1987. *Social Theory and Modern Sociology.* Stanford, CA: Stanford University Press.

Greenfield, Gerard. 2004. "Vietnam and the World Coffee Crisis: Local Coffee Riots in a Global Context." PROBE International. http://journal.probeinternational.org/2009/10/27/vietnam-and-world-coffee-crisis-local-coffee-riots-global-context.

Held, David. 2000. "The Changing Structure of International Law." In *The Global Transformations Reader,* edited by David Held and Anthony McGrew, 162–172. Cambridge: Polity Press.

International Criminal Court (ICC). 2012. "ICC-The State Parties to the Rome Statute." The Hague, the Netherlands: International Criminal Court. http://www.icc-cpi.int/en_menus/asp/states%20parties/Pages/the%20states%20parties%20to%20the%20rome%20statute.aspx.

Joyner, Christopher C. 1991. "Sanctions, Compliance and International Law: Reflections on the United Nations' Experience Against Iraq." *Virginia Journal on International Law* 32 (1): 1–46.

Kaldor, Mary. 2003. *Global Civil Society: An Answer to War.* Cambridge: Polity Press.

Landes, David S. 1999. *The Wealth and Poverty of Nations: Why Some Countries Are So Rich and Some Are So Poor.* London: W.W. Norton.

Mann, Michael. 2003. "The End of the Rise of the Nation State." In *The Global Transformation Reader,* edited by David Held and Anthony McGrew, 135–146. Cambridge: Polity Press.

Markoff, John. 1999. "Where and When Was Democracy Invented?" *Comparative Studies in Society and History* 41 (4): 660–690.

Meyer, John W. 2000. "Globalization: Sources and Effects on National States and Societies." *International Sociology* 15 (2): 233–248.

Meyer, John W., John Boli, George M. Thomas, and Francisco O. Ramirez. 1997. "World Society and the Nation-State." *The American Journal of Sociology* 103 (1): 144–181.

Murphy, Joseph. 2009. "Environment and Imperialism: Why Colonialism Still Matters." Leeds, UK: University of Leeds Sustainability Research Institute (SRI). http://www.see.leeds.

ac.uk/fileadmin/Documents/research/sri/workingpapers/SRIPs-20_01.pdf.

Nandan, Satya N., Michael W. Lodge, and Shabtai Rosenne (General Editor). 2002. *The Development of the Regime for Deep Seabed Mining.* The Hague, the Netherlands: Kluwer Law International; Charlottesville: University of Virginia, Center for Oceans Law and Policy, University of Virginia. http://www.isa.org.jm/files/documents/EN/Pubs/Regime-ae.pdf.

Painter, David S. 2007. "The Global Cold War: Third World Interventions and the Making of Our Times Roundtable *Review*" [Review of *The Global Cold War: Third World Interventions and the Making of Our Times,* by Odd Arne Westad]. In *H-Diplo Roundtable Reviews* 3 (12). http://www.h-net.org/~diplo/roundtables/PDF/GlobalColdWar-Painter.pdf.

Picco, Ginadomenico. 1994. "The UN and the Use of Force." *Foreign Affairs* 73 (5): 14–18.

Scholte, Jan Aarte. 2000. *Globalization: A Critical Introduction.* New York: St. Martin's Press.

SIPRI. 2010. *SIPRI Arms Transfer Database.* Stockholm: Stockholm International Peace Research Institute. http://www.sipri.org/databases/armstransfers.

Smith, Keri E Iyall. 2008. "Comparing State and International Protections of Indigenous Peoples' Rights." *American Behavioral Scientist* 51 (12): 1817–1835.

Stiglitz, Joseph E. 2002. *Globalization and Its Discontents.* New York: W.W. Norton.

———. 2006. *Making Gobalization Work.* New York: W.W. Norton.

Sweet, Alec Stone. 2008. "Constitutions and Judicial Power." In *Comparative Politics,* edited by Daniele Caramani, 217–239. Oxford: Oxford University Press.

Thacker, Strom Cronan. 1999. "The High Politics of IMF Lending." *World Politics* 52 (1): 38–75.

Topik, Steven. 2005. "When the Periphery Became More Central: From Colonial Pact to Liberal Nationalism in Brazil and Mexico, 1800–1914." LSE Research Online. London: London School of Economics. http://www2.lse.ac.uk/economicHistory/Research/GEHN/GEHNPDF/Conf7_Topik.pdf.

United Nations (UN). 1960. "Declaration on the Granting of Independence to Colonial Countries and Peoples." http://www.un.org/en/decolonization/declaration.shtml.

———. 2006. "Growth in United Nations Membership, 1945–Present." http://www.un.org/en/members/growth.shtml.

———. 2010. *Charter of the United Nations.* New York: United Nations. http://www.un.org/en/documents/charter/index.shtml.

United Nations Division for Ocean Affairs (UNDOA). 2007. *The United Nations Convention on the Law of the Seas: A Historical Perspective.* New York: UNDOA and the Law of the Sea, Office of Legal Affairs. http://www.un.org/Depts/los/convention_agreements/convention_historical_perspective.htm#Historical Perspective.

United Nations Information Service (UNIS). 2006. "Together, United Nations, Non-Aligned Movement Can Make Real Difference in Lives of Those Who Need It Most, Says Secretary-General to Malaysia Meeting." Vienna, Austria: UNIS.

Van Maarseveen, Henc, and Ger van der Tang. 1978. *Written Constitutions: A Computerized Comparative Study.* Dobbs Ferry, NY: Oceana Publications.

Weber, Max. 1921/1978. *Economy and Society.* Berkeley: University of California Press.

Wells, H. G. 1920/1956. *The Outline of History: Being a Plain History of Life and Mankind.* Garden City, NY: Garden City Books.

Chapter 4

Alderman, Liz. 2011. "In Ireland, a Boom Is Quickly Becoming a Painful Memory." *New York Times,* May 7, B1.

Allegretto, Sylvia. n.d. *Basic Family Budgets: Working Families' Incomes Often Fail to Meet Living Expenses Around the U.S.* Washington, DC: Economic Policy Institute. http://www.epi.org/page/-/old/briefingpapers/165/bp165.pdf.

American Pet Products Association (APPA). 2012. *Industry Statistics and Trends.* http://www.americanpetproducts.org/press_industrytrends.asp.

Andrews, Edmund. 2008. "Greenspan Concedes Error on Regulation." *New York Times,* October 23. http://www.nytimes.com/2008/10/24/business/economy/24panel.html.

Army Information School. 1946. *United Nations Monetary and Financial Conference at Bretton Woods. Summary of Agreements. July 22, 1944.* Carlisle Barracks, PA: Book Department, Army Information School. http://www.ibiblio.org/pha/policy/1944/440722a.html.

Arruda de Almeida, Monica. 2005. "National Government Policies." In *Globalization Encyclopedia of Trade, Labor, and Politics,* edited by Ashish K. Vaidya, 203–211. Santa Barbara, CA: ABC-CLIO.

Associated Press. 2012. "Spain Under Scrutiny After ECB Bond-Buying Plan." *The Huffington Post.* September 7. http://www.huffingtonpost.com/huff-wires/20120907/eu-spain-financial-crisis.

Bajaj, Vikas, and David Leonhardt. 2008. "The Reckoning Tax Break May Have Helped Cause Housing Bubble." *New York Times,* December 18, A1.

Baldwin, Richard. 2006. "Globalisation: The Great Unbundling(s)." Prime Minister's Office: Economic Council of Finland: Globalisation Challenges for Europe and Finland Project. http://graduateinstitute.ch/webdav/site/ctei/shared/CTEI/Baldwin/Publications/Chapters/Globalization/Baldwin_06-09-20.pdf.

Bhattacharya, Amar. 2009. "A Tangled Web." *Finance and Development* 46 (1). http://www.imf.org/external/pubs/ft/fandd/2009/03/bhattacharya.htm.

Blinder, Alan S. 2006. "Offshoring: The Next Industrial Revolution?" *Foreign Affairs* 85 (2): 113–128.

"BRICs Emerging Markets and the World Economy: Not Just Straw Men." 2009. *Economist,* June 18. http://www.economist.com/world/international/displaystory.cfm?story_id=13871969.

Center on Budget and Policy Priorities. 2011. *Chart Book: The Legacy of the Great Recession.* Washington, DC: Center on Budget and Policy Priorities. http://www.cbpp.org/cms/index.cfm?fa=view&id=3252.

China View. 2009. "Hu's Proposals Play Important, Constructive Role at G20 Summit." http://news.xinhuanet.com/english/2009-04/04/content_11129260.htm.

Coe, David T. 2008. "Jobs on Another Shore." *Finance and Development* 45 (1). http://www.imf.org/external/pubs/ft/fandd/2008/03/coe.htm.

Cohen, Benjamin J. 2001. "Bretton Woods System." In *Routledge Encyclopedia of International Political Economy*, edited by R. J. Barry Jones. New York: Routledge. http://www.polsci.ucsb.edu/faculty/cohen/inpress/bretton.html.

Coster, Helen A. 2010. "How We All Spend Our Money." *Forbes,* December 6. http://www.forbes.com/2010/12/06/how-the-world-spends-its-money-entrepreneurs-finance-ask-an-expert-10.html.

Das, Satyajit. 2009. "Lessons of the Global Financial Crisis: 3. Built to Fail." *EuroIntelligence,* August 5. http://www.eurointelligence.com/eurointelligence-news/archive/single-view/article/lessons-of-the-global-financial-crisis-3-built-to-fail.html.

Doh, Jonathan P. 2005. "Offshore Outsourcing: Implications for International Business and Strategic Management Theory and Practice." *Journal of Management Studies* 43 (2): 695–704.

Dore, Ronald. 2000. "Making Sense of Globalization." London School of Economics Center for Economic Performance. http://cep.lse.ac.uk/pubs/download/occasional/OP016.pdf.

Eichengreen, Barry, Rachita Gullapalli, and Ugo Panizza. 2009. "Capital Account Liberalization, Financial Development and Industry Growth: A Synthetic View." University of California, Berkeley, Department of Economics. http://www.econ.berkeley.edu/~eichengr/capital_account_2-10-09.pdf.

Estrada, Daniela. 2009. "We Need to Let the World Social Forum Evolve." *OpenSpaceForum.* http://www.openspaceforum.net/twiki/tiki-read_article.php?articleId=797.

Eurostat. 2012. "Unemployment Statistics." European Commission. http://epp.eurostat.ec.europa.eu/statistics_explained/index.php/Unemployment_statistics.

Friedman, Benjamin M. 2009. "The Failure of the Economy & the Economists." *New York Review of Books.* May 28. http://www.nybooks.com/articles/archives/2009/may/28/the-failure-of-the-economy-the-economists.

G20. 2009a. "London Summit—Leaders' Statement." April 2. http://www.imf.org/external/np/sec/pr/2009/pdf/g20_040209.pdf.

———. 2009b. "Progress Report on the Economic and Financial Actions of the London, Washington and Pittsburgh G20 Summits." Prepared by the UK chair of the G20. http://www.g20.utoronto.ca/2009/2009progressreport1107.pdf.

———. 2009c. "Russian Proposals to the London Summit." http://archive.kremlin.ru/eng/text/docs/2009/03/213995.shtml.

———. 2010. "The G20 Seoul Summit Leaders' Declaration." Seoul Summit of the G20, Seoul, Republic of South Korea, November 11–12. http://www.consilium.europa.eu/uedocs/cms_data/docs/pressdata/en/er/117705.pdf.

"G20 Summit: Nicolas Sarkozy and Angela Merkel Demand Tough Market Regulations." 2009. *The Telegraph,* April 20. http://www.telegraph.co.uk/finance/g20-summit/5090442/G20-summit-Nicolas-Sarkozy-and-Angela-Merkel-demand-tough-market-regulations.html.

Galperin, Hernán, and Judith Mariscal. 2007. "Mobile Opportunities: Poverty and Telephony Access in Latin America and the Caribbean." DIRSI Regional Report v 1.0, November. Lima, Peru: DIRSI: Regional Dialogue on the Information Society. http://www.dirsi.net/files/REGIONAL_FINAL.pdf.

"The Globalization Index." 2007. *Foreign Policy,* November–December: 69–76. http://www.globalpolicy.org/images/pdfs/11globindex.pdf.

Goldman, David. 2009. "Worst Year for Jobs Since '45." *CNN Money,* January 9. http://money.cnn.com/2009/01/09/news/economy/jobs_december/?postversion=2009010908.

Gonyea, Don, and Renee Montagne. 2009. "Obama Gets Down to Business Before G-20." *National Public Radio,* April 1. http://www.npr.org/templates/story/story.php?storyId=102590403.

Gowing, Nick, Anand G. Mahindra, Maria Ramos, and Jeroen van der Veer. 2009. *The Global Agenda for 2009: The View From Davos, February 1.* www.weforum.org/pdf.php?download=59836.

Greenhouse, Steven. 2003. "I.B.M. Explores Shift of White-Collar Jobs Ovreseas." *New York Times,* July 22. http://www.nytimes.com/2003/07/22/technology/22JOBS.html.

Gregg, Samuel. 2008. "No Morality, No Markets." *Acton Commentary,* September 30. http://www.acton.org/commentary/478_no_morality_no_markets.php.

Harrison, Anne E., and Margaret S. McMillan. 2006. *Outsourcing Jobs? Multinationals and US Employment.* NBER Working Papers 12372. Cambridge, MA: National Bureau of Economic Research.

Hawksworth, John, and Gordon Cookson. 2008. *The World in 2050: Beyond the BRICs: A Broader Look at Emerging Markets Growth Prospects.* London: PricewaterhouseCoopers UK. http://www.pwc.com/gx/en/world-2050/pdf/world_2050_brics.pdf.

Helleiner, Gerald Karl. 2000. "Markets, Politics and Globalization: Can the Global Economy Be Civilized?" Tenth Raúl Prebisch Lecture, Palais des Nations, Geneva, December 11. CIS Working Paper 2000-01. http://www.utoronto.ca/cis/working_papers/2000-1.pdf.

Holusha, John. 1981. "G. M. Shift: Outside Supplies." *New York Times,* October 14. http://www.nytimes.com/1981/10/14/business/gm-shift-outside-suppliers.html.

Holzner, Burkart, and Leslie Holzner. 2006. *Transparency in Global Change.* Pittsburgh, PA: University of Pittsburgh Press.

Hutton, Will. 2011. "Ireland's Austerity Plan Is Self-Defeatingly Harsh." *Guardian,* February 18. http://www.guardian.co.uk/commentisfree/2011/feb/18/ireland-austerity-measures-irish-labour-party.

Institute for Innovation in Social Policy. n.d. *The Index of Social Health.* Poughkeepsie, NY: Institute for Innovation in Social Policy, Vassar College. http://iisp.vassar.edu/ish.html.

International Monetary Fund (IMF). 1997. "Good Governance: The IMF's Role." http://www.imf.org/external/pubs/ft/exrp/govern/govern.pdf.

"Japan, Facing Its Worst Economic Times in 35 Years Announced a $150 Billion Stimulus." 2009. *The Economic Times,* April 9. http://economictimes.indiatimes.com/News/International-Business/Japan-set-for--150-bn-stimulus-spending/articleshow/4378743.cms.

Kirk, Alejandro. 2009. "WSF Ends With Political Resolutions and a Plan of Action." Share the World's Resources (STWR), London. http://www.stwr.org/the-un-people-politics/world-social-forum-and-davos-at-the-crossroads.html#plan-of-action.

Krugman, Paul. 2007. "The Housing Bubble Has Burst." *New York Times,* July 27. http://krugman.blogs.nytimes.com/2007/07/27/the-housing-bubble-has-burst/

———. 2011. "Keynes Was Right." *New York Times,* December 30, A23. http://www.nytimes.com/2011/12/30/opinion/keynes-was-right.html?_r=0

Krugman, Paul, and Anthony J. Venables. 1995. "Globalization and the Inequality of Nations." *The Quarterly Journal of Economics* 110 (4): 857–880. http://www.jstor.org/stable/2946642.

Labaton, Stephen. 2009. "Bill Shields Banks and Review." *New York Times,* October 16. http://query.nytimes.com/gst/fullpage.html?res=9902E4DF1F31F935A25753C1A96F9C8B63&ref=stephenlabaton&pagewanted=2.

Levy, David L. 2005. "Offshoring in the New Global Political Economy." *Journal of Management Studies* 42 (3): 685–693.

Lewin, Tamar. 2009. "Recession Makes the Frozen North More Appealing." *New York Times,* June 2. http://thechoice.blogs.nytimes.com/2009/06/02/canada.

Martin, Andrew, and Louise Story. 2009. "Banks Brace for Fight Over an Agency Meant to Bolster Consumer Protection." *New York Times,* June 18, B1.

Meltzer, Allan H. 2001. "A Report of the International Financial Institution Advisory Commission: Comments on the Critics." In *Reforming the Architecture of Global Financial Institutions,* edited by C. Gilbert, J. Rollo, and D. Vines. Cambridge: Cambridge University Press. http://www.gsia.cmu.edu/afs/andrew/gsia/meltzer/Spanishedition3.doc.

Milanovic, Branko. 2006. *Global Income Inequality: What It Is and Why It Matters?* DESA Working Paper No. 26 Series 3865. New York: United Nations. http://www.un.org/esa/desa/papers/2006/wp26_2006.pdf.

Milner, Helen V., and Keiko Kubota. 2005. "Why Move to Free Trade? Democracy and Trade Policy in the Developing Countries." *International Organization* 59 (1): 107–143.

Organization for Economic Co-operation and Development (OECD). 2005. *OECD Handbook on Economic Globalisation Indicators.* Paris: OECD Directorate for Science Technology and Industry. http://www.oecd.org/document/44/0,3343,en_2649_34443_34957420_1_1_1_1,00.html.

OECD/WTO. 2007. *Aid for Trade at a Glance 2007: First Global Review.* http://www.oecd.org/dataoecd/24/63/39638213.pdf.

———. 2009. *Aid for Trade at a Glance 2009: Maintaining Momentum.* http://www.wto.org/english/res_e/booksp_e/aid4trade09_e.pdf

Ott, Mack. 2002. "Foreign Investment in the United States" *The Concise Encylcopedia of Economics.* Indianapolis, IN: Liberty Fund Inc. http://www.econlib.org/library/Enc1/ForeignInvestmentintheUnitedStates.html.

Pfanner, Eric. 2008. "Iceland, in Financial Collapse, Is Likely to Need I.M.F. Help" *New York Times,* October 9. http://www.nytimes.com/2008/10/10/business/worldbusiness/10icebank.html.

Pleyers, Geoffrey. 2009. "World Social Forum 2009: A Generation's Challenge." *Democracy News Analysis,* January 30. http://www.opendemocracy.net/node/47232/pdf.

Plunkett, Jack W. 2012. "Introduction to the Offshoring and Outsourcing Industry." Plunkett Research, Ltd. http://www.plunkettresearch.com/outsourcing-offshoring-bpo-market-research/industry-trends.

Relinger, Rick. 2010. "NAFTA and U.S. Corn Subsidies: Explaining the Displacement of Mexico's Corn Farmers." *Prospect: Journal of International Affairs at UCS.* http://prospectjournal.ucsd.edu/index.php/2010/04/nafta-and-u-s-corn-subsidies-explaining-the-displacement-of-mexicos-corn-farmers.

Rodrik, Dani. 2000. "Development Strategies for the Next Century." Research Paper. Harvard Kennedy School, Cambridge, MA. http://www.hks.harvard.edu/fs/drodrik/Research%20papers/devstrat.PDF.

Sahni, Diksha. 2011. "Bankers to Occupy India's Wall Street." *The Wall Street Journal: India Real Time,* November 3. http://blogs.wsj.com/indiarealtime/2011/11/03/role-reversal-bankers-occupy-indias-wall-street/?mod=google_news_blog.

Sanger, David, and Mark Landler. 2009. "In Europe, Obama Faces Calls for Rules on Finances." *New York Times,* April 2, A1.

Schwab, Klaus. 2008. "Global Corporate Citizenship: Working With Governments and Civil Society. *Foreign Affairs* 87 (1), 107–118. http://www.foreignaffairs.com/articles/63051/klaus-schwab/global-corporate-citizenship.

———. 2009. *Global Competitiveness Report 2009–2010.* Geneva: The World Economic Forum. http://www.weforum.org/pdf/GCR09/GCR20092010fullreport.pdf.

Schwartz, Nelson D., and Matthew Saltmarsh. 2009. "Emerging Countries May Also Be Driving the Global Economy." *New York Times,* June 25, A1.

Serrin, William. 1989. "The Mobility of Capital Disperses Unisons' Power." *New York Times,* March 21. http://select.nytimes.com/1982/03/21/weekinreview/the-mobility-of-capital-disperses-unions-power.html.

Shierholz, Heidi. 2011. *Unemployment Rises, Recovery Remains on Pause.* Washington, DC: Economic Policy Institute.

Simmons, Beth, and Zachary Elkins. 2005. "On Waves, Clusters, and Diffusion: A Conceptual Framework." *Annals of the American Academy of Political and Social Science* 2005 (598): 33–51.

Sindzingre, Alice. 2005. "Reforms, Structure or Institutions? Assessing the Determinants of Growth in Low-Income Countries." *Third World Quarterly* 26 (2): 281–305.

Stiglitz, Joseph E. 2002. *Globalization and Its Discontents.* New York: W.W. Norton.

———. 2006. *Making Globalization Work.* New York: W.W. Norton.

Tabb, William K. 2009. "Globalization Today: At the Borders of Class and State Theory." *Science and Society* 71 (1): 34–53.

Thomas, Landon, Jr. 2009. "In Britain, an Aversion to Rules from Europe." *New York Times,* June 18, B7.

United Nations Conference on Trade and Development (UNCTAD). 2009. *Trade and Development Report 2009.* Geneva: United Nations. http://www.unctad.org/en/docs/tdr2009_en.pdf

U.S. Bureau of Labor Statistics. 2009. "Occupational Employment Projections to 2018." http://www.bls.gov/opub/mlr/2009/11/art5full.pdf.

U.S. Census Bureau. 2012. Table 694: Share of Aggregate Income Received by Each Fifth and Top 5 Percent of Households: 1970 to 2009. In *Statistical Abstract of the United States.* Washington, DC: U.S. Census Bureau Department of Commerce. http://www.census.gov/prod/www/abs/statab2011_2015.html.

U.S. Department of Treasury. 2007. "Fact Sheet: An Open Economy Is Vital to United States Prosperity." May 10. http://www.treas.gov/press/releases/hp395.htm.

Varian, Hal R. 2007. "An iPod Has a Global Value. Ask the Many Countries That Make It." *New York Times*, June 28.

Weisbrot, Mark. 2007. "How Argentina Jump-Started its Economy." *Los Angeles Times*, October 27. Reproduced by Center for Economic and Policy Research (CEPR), Washington, DC. http://www.cepr.net/index.php/op-eds-&-columns/op-eds-&-columns/how-argentina-jump-started-its-economy.

Westad, Odd Arne. 2005. *The Global Cold War: Third World Interventions and the Making of Our Times*. Cambridge: Cambridge University Press.

Williamson, John. 2004. "A Short History of the Washington Consensus." Barcelona: Fundación CIDOB for a conference "From the Washington Consensus towards a new Global Governance." September 24–25, 2004. http://www.iie.com/publications/papers/williamson0904-2.pdf.

World Bank. 2007. *World Development Indicators 2007: Section 4 Economy*. Washington, DC: The International Bank for Reconstruction and Development/The World Bank. http://siteresources.worldbank.org/DATASTATISTICS/Resources/WDI07section4-intro.pdf.

———. 2008. *World Bank Annual Report 2008: The Year in Review*. Washington, DC: The International Bank for Reconstruction and Development/The World Bank. http://siteresources.worldbank.org/EXTANNREP2K8/Resources/YR00_Year_in_Review_English.pdf.

———. 2009. *World Development Report 2009: Reshaping Economic Geography*. Washington, DC: The International Bank for Reconstruction and Development/The World Bank. http://econ.worldbank.org/WBSITE/EXTERNAL/EXTDEC/EXTRESEARCH/EXTWDRS/EXTWDR2009/0,,contentMDK:21955654~pagePK:64167689~piPK:64167673~theSitePK:4231059,00.html.

———. 2010. *Global Monitoring Report 2010: The MDGs After the Crisis*. Washington, DC: The International Bank for Reconstruction and Development/The World Bank.

World Economic Forum (WEF). 2009a. "Putin Vows Cooperation in Tackling Crisis, Decries State Interference in Business." WEF News Release, February 1. http://www.weforum.org/node/65910.

———. 2009b. *Shaping the Post Crisis World*. Davos-Klosters, Switzerland: World Economic Forum Annual Meeting 2009. January 28–February 1. http://www3.weforum.org/docs/WEF_AM09_Report.pdf.

———. 2009c. "What Global Challenge Most Threatens Economic Recovery?" Davos-Klosters, Switzerland: World Economic Forum Annual Meeting 2009, January 28–February 1. https://members.weforum.org/pdf/AnnualReport/2009/economic_recovery.htm.

———. 2009d. "What Industry Must Do to Prevent a Broad Social Backlash." Davos-Klosters, Switzerland: World Economic Forum Annual Meeting 2009, January 28–February 1. https://members.weforum.org/pdf/AnnualReport/2009/print_social_backlash.htm.

———. 2012a. "The Global Competitiveness Index 2012–2013 Data Platform." Geneva, Switzerland: WEF. http://www.weforum.org/issues/competitiveness-0/gci2012-data-platform.

———. 2012b. *Global Competitiveness Report 2012–2013*. Geneva, Switzerland: WEF. http://www.weforum.org/issues/global-competitiveness.

World Social Forum (WSF). 2002. *World Social Forum Charter of Principles*. São Paulo: Fórum Social Mundial. http://www.forumsocialmundial.org.br/main.php?id_menu=4&cd_language=2.

World Trade Organization. 2008. *World Trade Report 2008: Trade in a Globalizing World*. http://www.wto.org/english/res_e/publications_e/wtr08_e.htm.

Ydstie, John, and Steve Inskeep. 2009. "G-20 Leaders Set Out to Tackle Global Recession." *NPR*, April 2. http://www.npr.org/templates/story/story.php?storyId=102634925.

Chapter 5

Aldashev, Gani, and Thierry Verdier. 2009. "When NGOs Go Global: Competition on International Markets for Development Donations." *Journal of International Economics* 79 (2): 198–210.

Anderson, Kenneth, and David Rieff. 2004. "Global Civil Society: A Skeptical View." In *Global Civil Society 2004/2005*, edited by Helmut Anheier, Marlies Glasius, and Mary Kaldor, 26–40. London: Sage.

Andonova, Liliana B. 2009. "International Organizations as Entreprenuers of Environmental Partnerships." In *International Organizations in Global Environmental Governance*, edited by Frank Biermann, Bernard Siebenhüner, and Anna Schreyögg, 195–222. London: Routledge.

Anheier, Helmut K. 2007. "Reflections on the Concept and Measurement of Global Civil Society." *Voluntas* 18 (1): 1–15.

Anonymous. 1977. Appendix D: Manifest of Charter 77—Czechoslovakia. http://lcweb2.loc.gov/frd/cs/czechoslovakia/cs_appnd.html.

Ayers, Jeffrey M. 2003. Review of *The Politics of Globalization in the United States* by Edward S. Cohen. *Perspectives on Politics* 1 (1): 182–193.

Berry, Craig, and Clive Gabay. 2009. "Transnational Political Action and 'Global Civil Society' in Practice: The Case of Oxfam." *Global Networks* 9 (3): 339–358.

Biermann, Frank, Bernard Siebenhüner, and Anna Schreyögg. 2009. "Setting the Stage." In *International Organizations in Global Environmental Governance*, edited by Frank Biermann, Bernard Siebenhüner, and Anna Schreyögg, 1–16. London: Routledge.

Bob, Clifford. 2001. "Marketing Rebellion: Insurgent Groups, International Media, and NGO Support." *International Politics* 38: 311–334.

———. 2002. "Merchants of Morality." *Foreign Policy* 129 (March–April): 36–45.

Brauman, Rony, and Joelle Tanguy. 1998. "The MSF Experience." *Médecins Sans Frontières*. http://www.doctorswithoutborders.org/work/field/msfexperience.cfm.

Club of Rome. 2009. "The Story of the Club of Rome." http://www.clubofrome.org/?p=375.

Davies, Thomas Richard. 2008. "The Rise and Fall of Transnational Civil Society: The Evolution of International Non-Governmental Organizations Since 1839." Working Paper.

London: City University for International Politics. http://www.city.ac.uk/intpol/dps/WorkingPapers/T_Davies%20The%20Rise%20and%20Fall%20of%20Transnational%20Civil%20Society.pdf.

Donnelly, Jack. 2003. *Universal Human Rights in Theory and Practice* (2nd ed.). Ithaca, NY: Cornell University Press.

———. 2007. *International Human Rights*. Boulder, CO: Westview Press.

Durkheim, Emile. 1915/1965. *The Elementary Forms of the Religious Life*. New York: The Free Press.

Global Environmental Facility (GEF). 2013. "What Is the GEF?" http://www.thegef.org/gef/whatisgef.

Grant, Ruth, and Robert O. Keohane. 2005. "Accountability and Abuses of Power in World Politics." *The American Political Science Review* 99 (1): 29–43.

Hails, Chris. 2013. "WWF's Approach to Conservation From Its Inception to 2006." *WWF International*. http://wwf.panda.org/who_we_are/history/wwf_conservation_1961_2006.

Held, David. 2004. *Global Covenant: The Social Democratic Alternative to the Washington Consensus*. Cambridge: Polity.

Hubert, Don. 2000. "The Landmine Ban: A Case in Humanitarian Advocacy." Occasional Paper No. 42. Providence, RI: The Thomas J. Watson Institute, Brown University. http://www.watsoninstitute.org/pub/op42.pdf.

International Campaign to Ban Landmines. 2010. *Landmine Monitor 2010*. Canada: International Campaign to Ban Land Mines. http://www.the-monitor.org/lm/2010/resources/Landmine_Monitor_2010_lowres.pdf.

Kaldor, Mary. 2003. *Global Civil Society: An Answer to War*. Cambridge: Polity.

Keane, John. 2003. *Global Civil Society?* Cambridge: Cambridge University Press.

Keohane, Robert O., and Joseph S. Nye, Jr. 2000. "Globalization: What's New? What's Not? (And So What?)" *Foreign Policy* 118 (Spring): 104–119.

Koch, Dirk-Jan. 2008. *A Paris Declaration for International NGOs?* Policy Insights No. 73. Paris: OECD Development Centre.

Landmine Monitor. 1999. "Americas." *Human Rights Watch*. http://www.hrw.org/reports/1999/landmine/WEBAM1.html.

Laxer, Gordon, and Sandra Halperin. 2003. *Global Civil Society and Its Limits*. Basingstoke, UK: Palgrave Macmillan.

Long, Graham. 2008. "Justification and Legitimacy in Global Civil Society." *Journal of Global Ethics* 4 (1): 51–66.

MacFarlane, Neil S. 2000. Preface to *The Landmine Ban: A Case in Humanitarian Advocacy*, by Don Hubert, ix–xv. Occasional Paper No. 42. Providence, RI: The Thomas J. Watson Institute, Brown University. http://www.watsoninstitute.org/pub/op42.pdf.

Mangaliso, Mzamo P. 1997 "South Africa: Corporate Social Responsibility and the Sullivan Principles." *Journal of Black Studies* 28 (2): 219–238.

McDonald, Kevin. 2006. *Global Movements: Action and Culture*. Malden, MA: Blackwell.

Meyer, John, David John Frank, Ann Hironaka, Evan Schofer, and Nancy Brandon Tuma. 1997. "The Structuring of a World Environmental Regime, 1870–1990." *International Organization* 51 (4): 623–651.

Putnam, Robert D. 1995. "Bowling Alone: America's Declining Social Capital." *Journal of Democracy* 6 (1): 65–78.

Roberts, Shawn, and Jody Williams. 1995. *After the Guns Fall Silent: The Enduring Legacy of Landmines*. Washington, DC: Vietnam Veterans of America Foundation.

Roginsky, Sandrine, and Sally Shortall. 2009. "Civil Society as a Contested Field of Meanings." *International Journal of Sociology and Social Policy* 29 (9–10): 473–487.

Ronfeldt, David, John Arquilla, Graham Fuller, and Melissa Fuller. 1998. *The Zapatista Social Netwar in Mexico*. Santa Monica, CA: RAND. http://www.rand.org/content/dam/rand/pubs/monograph_reports/1998/MR994.pdf.

Rutherford, Kenneth R. 2000. "The Evolving Arms Control Agenda: Implications of the Role of NGOs in Banning Antipersonnel Land Mines." *World Politics* 53 (1): 74–114.

Seidman, Gay W. 2007. *Beyond the Boycott: Labor Rights, Human Rights, and Transnational Activism*. New York: Russell Sage Foundation.

Sikkink, Kathryn. 2005. "Patterns of Dynamic Multilevel Governance and the Insider-Outsider Coalition." In *Transnational Protest and Global Activism*, edited by Donatella Della Porta and Sidney Tarrow, 155–173. Lanham, MD: Rowman and Littlefield.

Simmel, Georg. 1908/1971. *On Individuality and Social Forms*. Chicago: The University of Chicago Press.

Slim, Hugo. 2011. "International NGOs: A Necessary Good." *Global: The International Briefing*. http://www.global-briefing.org/2011/10/a-necessary-good.

Thomas, Daniel C. 2001. *The Helsinki Effect*. Princeton, NJ: Princeton University Press.

Thurow, Roger. 2000. "Ten Years After: South Africans Who Fought for Sanctions Now Scrap for Investors—but They Find Luring Back Capital Is a Lot Harder Than Was Chasing It Out." *The Wall Street Journal* (Eastern edition), February 11, A1.

Traer, Robert. 2009. *Doing Environmental Ethics*. Boulder, CO: Westview Press.

Trzyna, Ted. 2008. "About Environmental Organizations & Programs." California Institute of Public Affairs, Sacramento, California. http://www.interenvironment.org/wd1intro/aboutorgs.ht.

United Nations Environment Program (UNEP). n.d.-a. *Chronological List of Environmental Agreements*. http://www.unep.org/Law/Law_instruments/index_complete_list.asp.

UNEP. n.d.-b. *Organizational Profile*. Nairobi, Kenya: UNEP. http://www.unep.org/PDF/UNEPOrganizationProfile.pdf.

Weber, Clare. 2002. "Women to Women: Dissident Citizen Diplomacy in Nicaragua." In *Women's Activism and Globalization*, edited by Nancy A. Naples and Manisha Desai, 45–63. New York: Routledge.

WWF. 2012. *History*. http://www.worldwildlife.org/about/history.

———. 2013a. "The 2000s." In *50 Years of Achievements*. http://wwf.panda.org/who_we_are/history/50_years_of_achievements.

———. 2013b. *WWF in Brief*. http://wwf.panda.org/wwf_quick_facts.cfm#initials.

Worth, Owen, and Karen Buckley. 2009. "The World Social Forum: Postmodern Prince or Court Jester." *Third World Quarterly* 30 (4): 649–661.

Yang, Tongjin. 2006. "Towards an Egalitarian Global Environmental Ethics." In *Environmental Ethics and International Policy*, edited by Henk A. M. J. ten Have,

23–45. Paris: UNESCO. http://publishing.unesco.org/chapters/978-92-3-104039-9.pdf.

Zelli, Fariborz. 2008. "Regime Conflicts in Global Environmental Governance: A Framework for Analysis." Global Governance Working Paper No 36. Amsterdam: The Global Governance Project. http://www.glogov.org/images/doc/WP36.pdf.

Chapter 6

African Union. 2010. *AU in a Nutshell*. Addis Ababa, Ethiopia: The African Union Commission. http://au.int/en/about/nutshell.

Ames, Barry. 2002. *The Deadlock of Democracy in Brazil*. Ann Arbor: The University of Michigan Press.

Appadurai, Arjun. 1996. *Modernity at Large: Cultural Dimensions of Globalization*. Minneapolis: University of Minnesota Press.

Barkun, Michael. 1990. "Racist Apocalypse: Millennialism of the Far Right." *American Studies* 31 (2): 121–140.

Barnett, Thomas P. M. 2006. *Blueprint for Action: A Future Worth Creating*. New York: The Berkley Books.

Bartlett, Bruce. 2009. "Who Saw the Housing Bubble Coming?" *Forbes*, January 2. http://www.forbes.com/2008/12/31/housing-bubble-crash-oped-cx_bb_0102bartlett.html.

Bloom, Paul. 2010. "The Moral Life of Babies." *New York Times Sunday Magazine*, May 9, MM4.

Bob, Clifford. 2002. "Merchants of Morality." *Foreign Policy* 129 (March–April): 36–45.

Boseley, Sarah. 2008. "Mbeki AIDS Denial Caused 300,000 Deaths." *Guardian*, Wednesday 26. http://www.guardian.co.uk/world/2008/nov/26/aids-south-africa.

Brooks, David. 2008. "Missing Dean Acheson." *New York Times*, August 1, A23.

Bush, George W. 2001. "President Bush's Address on Terrorism Before a Joint Meeting of Congress." *New York Times*, September 21.

Chase, Kerry A. 2005. "Introduction." In *Trading Blocs: States, Firms, and Regions in the World Economy*, 1–14. Ann Arbor: University of Michigan Press. http://www.press.umich.edu/pdf/047209906X-ch1.pdf.

Chopra, J. 2000. "The UN's Kingdom of East Timor." *Survival* 42 (3): 27–39.

Consumer Reports. 2010. "Don't Buy: Safety Risk—2010 Lexus GX 460." April 13. http://news.consumerreports.org/cars/2010/04/consumer-reports-2010-lexus-gx-dont-buy-safety-risk.html

Dalby, Simon. 2007. "Regions, Strategies and Empire in the Global War on Terror." *Geopolitics* 12 (4): 586–606.

"Economics and the Rule of Law: Order in the Jungle." 2008. *Economist*, March 13. http://www.economist.com/node/10849115.

Etzioni, Amatai. 2004. *From Empire to Community*. New York: Palgrave Macmillan.

European Commission. 2009. *The Europeans in 2009: Special Eurobarometer 308*. Brussels: The European Commission of the European Union.

Falk, Richard. 2005. "Reimagining the Governance of Globalization." In *Critical Globalization Studies*, edited by Richard P. Appelbaum and William I. Robinson, 217–226. New York: Routledge.

———. 2006. "International Law and the Future." *Third World Quarterly* 27 (7): 727–737.

Fishkin, James S. 2002. *Deliberative Polling: Toward a Better Informed Democracy*. The Center for Deliberative Democracy, Stanford University, Palo Alto, CA.

Fishkin, James S., Baogang He, Robert C. Luskin, and Alice Siu. 2010. "Deliberative Democracy in an Unlikely Place: Deliberative Polling in China." *British Journal of Political Science* 40 (2): 435–448.

Freedom House. 2009. *The UN Human Rights Council Report Card: 2007–2009*. Washington DC: Freedom House. http://www.freedomhouse.org/uploads/UNHRC_Report_Card.pdf.

Gilpin, Robert. 2002. "A Realist Perspective on International Governance." In *Governing Globalization: Power, Authority and Global Governance*, edited by David Held and Anthony McGrew, 237–248. Cambridge: Polity Press.

Gongloff, Mark. 2012. "Apple, Google, Microsoft Avoid Taxes by Keeping Billions in Profits Offshore: Senate Report." *Huffington Post*, September 20. http://www.huffingtonpost.com/2012/09/20/microsoft-taxes-profits-offshore_n_1901398.html.

Goodhart, Michael. 2005. "Civil Society and the Problem of Global Democracy." *Democratization* 12 (1): 1–21.

Grant, Ruth W., and Robert O. Keohane. 2005. "Accountability and Abuses of Power in World Politics." *The American Political Science Review* 99 (1): 29–43.

Grim, Ryan. 2010. "Greenspan Wanted Housing-Bubble Dissent Kept Secret." *Huffington Post*, July 3. http://www.huffingtonpost.com/2010/05/03/greenspan-wanted-housing_n_560965.html.

Guillén, Mauro. 2010. "Mauro Guillén's Indicators of Globalization, 1980–2010." Wharton's Management Department, University of Pennsylvania. http://www-management.wharton.upenn.edu/guillen/2010-docs/Global_Table_1980-2010.pdf.

Habermas, Jurgen. 1984. *Theory of Communicative Action*. Translated by Thomas McCarthy. Boston: Beacon Press.

Held, David. 2004. *Global Covenant*. Cambridge: Polity Press.

———. 2007. "Reframing Global Governance: Apocalypse Soon or Reform!" In *Globalization Theory: Approaches and Controversies*, edited by David Held and Anthony McGrew, 240–260. Cambridge: Polity Press.

International Court of Justice (ICJ). 2010. *Accordance With International Law of the Unilateral Declaration of Independence in Respect of Kosovo, Advisory Opinion, I.C.J. Reports 2010*, 403–453. http://www.icj-cij.org/docket/files/141/15987.pdf.

Jackman, Simon, and Lynn Vavreck. 2010. "Cosmopolitanism." Unpublished paper. http://jackman.stanford.edu/papers.

Joyner, Christopher C. 1991. "Sanctions, Compliance and International Law: Reflections on the United Nations' Experience Against Iraq." *Virginia Journal of International Law* 32 (1): 29–33.

Kaldor, Mary. 2003. *Global Civil Society: The Answer to War*. Cambridge: Polity Press.

Keohane, Robert O. 2001. "The Globalization of Informal Violence, Theories of World Politics" and 'the Liberalism of Fear.'" *Social Science Research Council*. http://essays.ssrc.org/sept11/essays/keohane2.htm.

Keohane, Robert. 2002. "Governance in a Partially Globalized World." In *Governing Globalization: Approaches and*

Controversies, edited by David Held and Anthony McGrew, 325–348. Cambridge: Polity Press.

———. 2005. "Abuse of Power: Assessing Accountability in World Politics." *Harvard International Review* 27 (2): 48–53.

Koenig-Archibugi, Mathias. 2002. "Mapping Global Governance." In *Governing Globalization: Approaches and Controversies*, edited by David Held and Anthony McGrew, 46–69. Cambridge: Polity Press.

Kuper, Andrew. 2004. "Democracy and Rule of Law Endangered." In *Promoting Democracy Through International Law*, edited by Richard Goldstone, Andrew Kuper, and Aryeh Neier, 9–12. New York: Carnegie Council on Ethics and International Affairs.

———. 2007. "Reconstructing Global Governance: Eight Innovations." In *Globalization Theory: Approaches and Controversies,* edited by David Held and Anthony McGrew, 225–239. Cambridge: Polity Press.

Landes, Richard. 2004. "Millennialism." In *The Oxford Handbook of New Religious Movements*, edited by James R. Lewis, 333–358. Oxford: Oxford University Press.

Maynard, Michelene. 2010. "Apology From Toyota's Leader." *New York Times*, February 25, B1.

Pfanner, Eric. 2012. "Starbucks Offers to Pay More in British Taxes Than Required." *New York Times*, December 7, B3. http://www.nytimes.com/2012/12/07/business/global/07iht-uktax07.html.

Putnam, Robert D. 2000. *Bowling Alone: The Collapse and Revival of American Community*. New York: Simon and Schuster.

Quinn, Andrew, and Brian Ellsworth. 2010. "U.S. Rift With Brazil and Turkey Deepens." *Reuters*, May 28. http://www.reuters.com/article/idUSTRE64R66G20100528.

Roberts, Susan, Anna Secor, and Matthew Sparke. 2003. "Neoliberal Geopolitics." *Antipode* 35 (5): 886–897.

Roginsky, Sandrine, and Sally Shortall. 2009. "Civil Society as a Contested Field of Meanings." *International Journal of Sociology and Social Policy* 29 (9–10): 473–487.

Rosenau, James N. 2002. "Governance in a New Global Order." In *Governing Globalization: Approaches and Controversies*, edited by David Held and Anthony McGrew, 70–86. Cambridge: Polity Press.

Sang-Hun, Choe. 2010. "Hyundai to Recall Some 2011 Sonatas." *New York Times*, February 24. http://www.nytimes.com/2010/02/25/business/global/25hyundai.html?scp=1&sq=hyundai%20recall&st=cse.

Sikkink, Kathryn, and Margaret E. Keck. 1998. *Activists Beyond Borders*. Ithaca, NY: Cornell University Press.

Sklair, Leslie. 2002. "Democracy and the Transnational Capitalist Class." *Annals of the American Academy of Political and Social Sciences* 581 (2002): 144–157.

Steans, Jill. 2002. "Global Governance: A Feminist Perspective." In *Governing Globalization: Approaches and Controversies*, edited by David Held and Anthony McGrew, 87–108. Cambridge: Polity Press.

Stiglitz, Joseph. 2006. *Making Globalization Work*. New York: W.W. Norton.

Tabb, William K. 2009. "Globalization Today: At the Border of Class and State Theory." *Science and Society* 73 (1): 34–53.

Tilly, Charles. 2004. *Social Movements 1768–2004*. Boulder, CO: Paradigm.

World Public Opinion. 2005. "23 Nation Poll Finds Strong Support for Dramatic Changes at UN." Report of BBC World Service Poll, March 21. http://www.worldpublicopinion.org/pipa/articles/btunitednationsra/72.php?lb=btun&pnt=72&nid=&id=.

———. 2006. "UN Continues to Get Positive, Though Lower, Ratings With World Public." Report of a BBC World Service Poll, January 24. http://www.worldpublicopinion.org/pipa/articles/btunitednationsra/163.php?lb=btun&pnt=163&nid=&id=.

———. 2007. "World Public Favors New Powers for the UN." Report of a Chicago Council Poll, May 9. http://www.worldpublicopinion.org/pipa/articles/btunitednationsra/355.php?lb=btun&pnt=355&nid=&id=.

Yoon, Sangwon. 2013. "Kim Signals Warmer North Korea Ties With South." *Bloomberg*, January 2. http://www.bloomberg.com/news/2013-01-01/north-korea-picks-stronger-economy-south-ties-as-top-2013-tasks.html.

Chapter 7

Ahearn, Raymond J. 2010. "Globalization, Worker Insecurity, and Policy Approaches." CRS Report for Congress, RL 34091. Washington, DC: Congressional Research Service.

Ames, Barry. 2002. *The Deadlock of Democracy in Brazil*. Ann Arbor: University of Michigan Press.

Ayers, Alison J. 2006. "Demystifying Democratisation: The Global Constitution of (Neo)Liberal Polities in Africa." *Third World Quarterly* 27 (2): 321–328.

Barboza, David, and Miguel Helft. 2010. "China Renews Google's License." *New York Times*, July 9, B1.

Baiocchi, Gianpaolo, and Sofia Checa. 2009. "Cities as New Spaces for Citizenship Claims: Globalization, Urban Politics, and Civil Society in Brazil, Mexico and South Africa in the 1990s." In *Democracy, States and the Struggle for Global Justice,* edited by Heather Gautney, Omar Dahbour, Ashley Dawson, and Neil Smith, 131–151. New York: Routledge.

Beard, David. 2012. "Roundup of Vote Irregularities." *Washington Post*, November 4. http://www.washingtonpost.com/blogs/post-politics/wp/2012/11/04/roundup-of-vote-irregularities.

Bird, Karen. 2003. "The Political Representation of Women and Ethnic Minorities in Established Democracies: A Framework for Comparative Research." Working paper presented for the Academy of Migration Studies, Aalborg University, Denmark.

Boone, Catherine. 2003. "Decentralization as a Political Strategy in West Africa." *Comparative Political Studies* 36 (4): 355–380.

Brinks, Daniel, and Michael Coppedge. 2006. "Diffusion Is No Illusion." *Comparative Political Studies* 39 (4): 463–489.

Carter Center. 2009. "Waging Peace Through Elections." http://www.cartercenter.org/peace/democracy/observed.html#table.

———. 2012. "Democracy Program." http://www.cartercenter.org/peace/democracy/index.html.

Castle, Stephen, and Steven Erlanger. 2010. "Vote Widens Divide Between Flemish- and French-Speaking Regions." *New York Times*, June 13, A4.

"Change You Can Believe In? The Prime Minister Calls Frankly for Political Reform." 2010. *Economist*, August 26, 35.

"China: The Debate Over Universal Values." 2010. *Economist,* September 30, 43.

CIA World Factbook. 2013. "China." https://www.cia.gov/library/publications/the-world-factbook/geos/ch.html.

Common Cause. 2012. *Deceptive Election Practices and Voter Intimidation: The Need for Voter Protection.* Washington, DC: Common Cause. http://www.commoncause.org/atf/cf/%7Bfb3c17e2-cdd1-4df6-92be-bd4429893665%7D/DECEPTIVEPRACTICESREPORTJULY2012FINALPDF.PDF.

Connerley, Edwin. 2009. *Democratic Decentralization Programming Handbook.* Washington, DC: USAID. http://transition.usaid.gov/our_work/democracy_and_governance/publications/pdfs/DDPH_09_22_09_508c.pdf.

Council of the League of Arab States. 1994. "Arab Charter on Human Rights." Reprinted in 18 Hum. Rts. L.J. 151 (1997). http://www1.umn.edu/humanrts/instree/arabcharter.html.

Dahlerup, Drude, and Lenita Freidenvall. 2009. "Gender Quotas in Politics—A Constitutional Challenge." In *Constituting Equality. Gender Equality and Comparative Constitutional Law,* edited by Susan H. Williams. Cambridge: Cambridge University Press.

Donno, Daniela. 2013. *Defending Democratic Norms: International Actors and the Politics of Electoral Misconduct.* New York: Oxford University Press.

"Economics and the Rule of Law: Order in the Jungle." 2008. *Economist,* March 13. http://www.economist.com/node/10849115.

Eichengreen, Barry, and David Leblang. 2006. "Democracy and Globalization." BIS Working Papers, No. 219. Basel, Switzerland: Monetary and Economic Department of the Bank for International Settlements.

Elkins, Zachary, and Beth Simmons. 2005. "On Waves, Clusters, and Diffusion: A Conceptual Framework." *Annals of the American Academy of Political and Social Science* 598 (2005): 33–51.

EuropeNews. 2007. "Human Rights in Islam?" December 1. http://europenews.dk/en/node/3847.

Falk, Richard. 2002. "The First Normative Global Revolution? The Uncertain Political Future of Globalization." In *Globalization and Civilizations,* edited by Mehdi Mozaffari, 51–70. New York: Routledge.

Freedom House. 2009. *Undermining Democracy.* Washington, DC: Freedom House, Radio Free Europe/Radio Liberty and Radio Free Asia. http://www.freedomhouse.org/sites/default/files/inline_images/Undermining%20Democracy.

Freidman, George. 2010. "Europe, Nationalism and Shared Fate." *Stratfor Global Intelligence.* http://www.stratfor.com/weekly/20100510_europe_nationalism_and_shared_fate.

Gates, Scott, Håvard Hegre, Mark P. Jones, and Håvard Strand. 2006. "Institutional Consistency and Political Stability." *American Journal of Political Science* 50 (4): 893–908.

Gleditsch, Kristian Skrede, and Michael D. Ward. 2006. "Diffusion and the International Context of Democratization." *International Organization* 60 (Fall): 911–933.

Grant, Ruth W., and Robert O. Keohane. 2005. "Accountability and Abuses of Power in World Politics." *American Political Science Review* 99 (1): 29–43.

Ha, Eunyoung, and George Tsebelis. 2010. "Globalization and Welfare: Which Causes Which?" Unpublished manuscript.

http://politicalscience.stanford.edu/sites/default/files/workshop-materials/cp_tsebelis.pdf.

Han, Dongfang. 2010. "China's Workers Are Stirring." *New York Times,* June 17. http://www.nytimes.com/2010/06/17/opinion/17iht-edhan.html?_r=1&scp=1&sq=%22china%27s+workers+are+stirring%22&st=nyt.

Held, David. 2004. *Global Covenant.* Cambridge: Polity Press.

Helleiner, Gerald Karl. 2000. "Markets, Politics and Globalization: Can the Global Economy be Civilized?" Paper delivered at the 10th Raúl Prebisch Lecture, Palais des Nations, Geneva, December 11. http://www.utoronto.ca/cis/working_papers/2000-1.pdf.

Herkenrath, Mark, Claudia König, Hanno Scholtz, and Thomas Volken. 2005. "Convergence and Divergence in the Contemporary World System: An Introduction." *International Journal of Comparative Sociology* 46 (5–6): 363–382.

Holmes, Leslie. 2009. "Good Guys, Bad Guys: Transnational Corporations, Rational Choice Theory and Power Crime." *Crime, Law and Social Change* 51 (3–4): 383–397.

Huntington, Samuel. 1993. *The Third Wave: Democratization in the Late Twentieth Century.* Norman: University of Oklahoma Press.

International Council on Human Rights Policy (ICHRP). 2002. *Local Rule: Decentralization and Human Rights.* Versoix, Switzerland: ICHRP. http://www.ichrp.org/files/reports/13/116_report.pdf.

Inter-Parliamentary Union. 2012. "Women in National Parliaments." http://www.ipu.org/wmn-e/world.htm.

Kaufmann, Daniel, Aart Kraay, and Massimo Mastruzzi. 2009. "Governance Matters VIII: Aggregate and Individual Governance Indicators, 1996–2008." World Bank Policy Research Working Paper No. 4978. http://papers.ssrn.com/sol3/papers.cfm?abstract_id=1424591.

Levy, Clifford J. 2010. "Russia Uses Microsoft to Supress Dissent." *New York Times,* September 12, A1.

Leyenaar, Monique. 2008. "Challenges to Women's Political Representation in Europe." *Journal of Women in Culture and Society* 34 (1): 1–7.

Meyer, John W., Francisco O. Ramirez, and Yasemin Nuhoglu Soysal. 1992. "World Expansion and Mass Education, 1870–1980." *Sociology of Education* 65 (2): 128–149.

Motha, Stewart. 2010. "Neo-Nationalism Threatens Europe." *Guardian,* September 7. http://www.guardian.co.uk/commentisfree/2010/sep/07/neo-nationalism-threatens-europe.

National Endowment for Democracy (NED). 2006. *The Backlash Against Democracy Assistance: A Report Prepared by the National Endowment for Democracy for Senator Richard G. Lugar, Chairman Committee on Foreign Relations United States.* Washington, DC: NED. http://www.ned.org/docs/backlash06.pdf.

OECD. 2010a. "OECD Anti-Bribery Convention: Entry into Force of the Convention." http://www.oecd.org/document/12/0,3343,en_2649_34859_2057484_1_1_1_1,00.html

———. 2010b. *Working Group on Bribery Annual Report 2009.* http://www.oecd.org/dataoecd/23/20/45460981.pdf.

Reynolds, Andrew. 2006. *Electoral Systems and the Protection and Participation of Minorities.* London: Minority Rights Group International.

Saine, Abdoulaye. 2008. "The Gambia's 'Elected Autocrat Poverty, Peripherality, and Political Instability,' 1994–2006: A Political Economy Assessment." *Armed Forces & Society* 34 (3): 450–473.

Simmons, Beth, Frank Dobbin, and Geoffrey Garrett. 2006. "Introduction: The International Diffusion of Liberalism." *International Organization* 60 (Fall): 781–810.

Smith, Keri E. Iyall. 2008. "Comparing State and International Protections of Indigenous Peoples' Rights." *American Behavioral Scientist* 51 (12): 1817–1835.

Transparency International (TI). 2009. *Global Corruption Barometer 2009*. Berlin: Transparency International. http://www.transparency.org/whatwedo/pub/global_corruption_barometer_20091.

———. 2010. *Transparency International Corruption Perceptions Index*. Berlin: Transparency International. http://www.transparency.org/cpi2010/results.

Westervelt, Eric. 2011. "Critics Fear Democracy Is Eroding in Hungary." *National Public Radio*, January 15. http://www.npr.org/2011/01/15/132964317/Critics-Fear-Democracy-Is-Eroding-In-Hungary.

Whitton, Evan. 2007. Kickback: Inside the Australian Wheat Board Scandal." *The Australian*, May 17. http://www.theaustralian.com.au/news/kickback-inside-the-australian-wheat-board-scandal/story-e6frg8no-1111113542684.

Wong, Edward. 2010. "As China Aids Labor, Unrest Is Still Rising." *New York Times*, June 20, A1.

World Bank. 2011. "What, Why and Where." In *Decentralization & Subnational Regional Economics*. http://go.worldbank.org/D0CZQ5IFM0.

Chapter 8

Afrobarometer. 2002. "Islam, Democracy, and Public Opinion in Africa." Afrobarometer Briefing Paper No. 3, September. Michigan State University, East Lansing, MI. http://afrobarometer.org/files/documents/briefing_papers/AfrobriefNo3.pdf.

———. 2009. "Neither Consolidating Nor Fully Democratic: The Evolution of African Political Regimes, 1999–2008." Afrobarometer Briefing Paper No. 67. Michigan State University, East Lansing, MI. http://www.ireep.org/i/files/doc_afrobarometer/survey2009/AfrobriefNo67.pdf

———. 2013. "Afrobarometer Round 5 (2010–2011)." Michigan State University, East Lansing, MI. http://afrobarometer-online-analysis.com/aj/AJBrowserAB.jsp.

Al-Khalidi, Suleiman. 2012. "Our Revolution Has Been Stolen, Say Libya's Jihadists." *Reuters*, October 2. http://www.reuters.com/article/2012/10/02/us-libya-jihadists-id USBRE8910K620121002.

Ames, Barry. 2001. *The Deadlock of Democracy in Brazil*. Ann Arbor: University of Michigan Press.

Ames, Barry, Andy Baker, and Lucio R. Renno. 2009. "Split-Ticket Voting as the Rule: Voters and Permanent Divided Government in Brazil." *Electoral Studies* 28 (1): 8–20.

Ames, Barry, Lucio Reno, and Francisco Rodrigues. 2003. "Democracy, Market Reform, and Social Peace in Cape Verde." Afrobarometer Paper No. 25. http://pdf.usaid.gov/pdf_docs/Pnadf456.pdf.

Appadurai, Arjun. 2007. "Hope and Democracy." *Popular Culture* 19 (1): 29–34.

Bajunid, Omar Farouk. 2001. "Islam and Civil Society in Southeast Asia: A Review." In *Islam and Civil Society in Southeast Asia*, edited by Mitsuo Nakamura, Sharon Siddique, and Omar Farouk Bajunid, 177–202. Tokyo: Sasakawa Peace Foundation.

Bamyeh, Mohammed. 2011. "The Egyptian Revolution: First Impressions from the Field." Sociology of Islam & Muslim Societies, College of Liberal Arts & Sciences. Portland, OR: Portland State University. http://www.pdx.edu/sociologyofislam/egyptian-revolution-first-impressions-field-mohammed-bamyeh.

Bilefsky, Dan. 2010a. "Communists Could Gain in Czech Vote." *New York Times*, May 28, A4.

———. 2010b. "Czech Court Bans Far Right Party, Calling It Xenophobic and a Threat to Democracy." *New York Times*, February 19, A12.

Bilefsky, Dan, and Jan Krcmar. 2009. "Czech Wounds Still Open, Communists Face a Ban." *New York Times*, December 27, A10.

Blair, Dennis C. 2010. "Annual Threat Assessment of the US Intelligence Community for the Senate Select Committee on Intelligence." Washington, DC: Office of the Director of National Intelligence. http://intelligence.senate.gov/100202/blair.pdf.

"Bloodless Regime Change: A Rainbow of Revolutions." 2006. *Economist*, January 19. http://www.economist.com/node/5408104.

Boone, Catherine. 1995. "The Social Origins of Ivoirian Exceptionalism: Rural Society and State Formation." *Comparative Politics* 27 (4): 445–463.

Boone, Catherine. 2003. "Decentralization as Political Strategy in West Africa." *Comparative Political Studies* 36 (4): 355–379.

Bratton, Michael, and Wonbin Cho. 2006. "Where Is Africa Going: Views From Below." Afrobarometer Working Paper No. 60. Michigan State University, East Lansing, MI. http://www.sarpn.org/documents/d0002243/Afrobarometer_Africa_May2006.pdf.

Bujaric, Bojan. 2008. "Populism, Liberal Democracy, and the Rule of Law in Central and Eastern Europe." *Communist and Post-Communist Studies* 41 (2): 191–203.

Carver, Richard. 1993. "Deadly Marionettes: State-Sponsored Violence in Africa." *Article 19*. http://www.article19.org/pdfs/publications/africa-deadly-marionettes.pdf.

Castle, Stephen. 2011. "Hungarian Leader Takes On Foreign Critics." *New York Times*, January 7, A9.

Center for Systemic Peace. 2011. "Coups d'Etat, 1960–2011." *Armed Conflict and Intervention (ACI) Datasets*. http://www.systemicpeace.org/inscr/inscr.htm.

"China: A Lot to Be Angry About." 2008. *Economist*, May 1, 49.

Chinaka, Chris. 2013. "Mugabe Buries Deputy Nkomo, Urges Peaceful Zimbabwe Poll." *Reuters*, January 21. http://www.reuters.com/article/2013/01/21/us-zimbabwe-mugabe-id USBRE90K0IV20130121.

Chu, Yun-han, Min-hua Huang, and Yu-tzung Chang. 2008. "Quality of Democracy and Regime Legitimacy in East Asia." Paper prepared for delivery at an Asian Barometer Conference on "The State of Democratic Governance in Asia" organized by Program for East Asia Democratic Studies of the Institute for Advanced Studies in Humanities and Social Sciences, National Taiwan University, and co-sponsored by the Asia Foundation and Institute of Political Science at Academia Sinica, June 20–21, Taipei, Taiwan. http://www.asianbarometer.org/newenglish/publications/conferencepapers/2008conference/sec.1.2.pdf.

Collier, Paul. 2012. "Guinea's Battle Against Corruption: Which Side Is the West on?" *Guardian*, November 15. http://www.guardian.co.uk/commentisfree/2012/nov/15/guinea-corruption-which-side-is-west-on.

Corrales, Javier. 2009. "Venezuela Petro-Politics and the Promotion of Disorder." In *Undermining Democracy: 21st Century Authoritarians*. Freedom House, Radio Free Europe/Radio Liberty and Radio Free Asia, 65–80. Washington, DC: Freedom House.

"Direct Democracy in Germany: When Voters Want a Say." 2008. *Economist*, May 1. http://www.economist.com/node/11293654.

Dunning, Thad. 2008. *Crude Democracy*. Cambridge: Cambridge University Press.

Doorenspleet, Renske. 2000. "Reassessing the Three Waves of Democratization." *World Politics* 52 (3): 384–406.

Fishkin, James S. 2003. "Deliberative Polling: Toward a Better-Informed Democracy." Palo Alto, CA: Center for Deliberative Democracy, Stanford University. http://cdd.stanford.edu/polls/docs/2003/executivesummary.pdf.

——— 2011. "Deliberative Polling: Executive Summary." The Center for Deliberative Democracy, Stanford University. Palo Alto. http://cdd.stanford.edu/polls/docs/summary.

Fishkin, James S., Baogang He, Robert C. Luskin, and Alice Siu. 2010. "Deliberative Democracy in an Unlikely Place: Deliberative Polling in China." *British Journal of Political Science* 40 (2): 435–448.

Freedom House. 2008. *Freedom in the World 2008: China*. Washington, DC: Freedom House. http://expression.freedomhouse.org/reports/freedom_in_the_world/2008/china.

———. 2010. "Freedom of Assembly Under Assault in Russia." Press Release. Washington, DC: Freedom House. http://www.freedomhouse.org/template.cfm?page=70&release=1130.

———. 2012. *Freedom in the World 2012: The Arab Uprisings and Their Global Repercussions*. Washington, DC: Freedom House. http://www.freedomhouse.org/report/freedom-world/freedom-world-2012.

Fukuyama, Francis. 2008. "Poverty, Inequality, and Democracy: The Latin American Experience." *Journal of Democracy* 19 (4): 69–79.

Gates, Scott, Håvard Hegre, Mark P Jones, and Håvard Strand. 2006. "Institutional Consistency and Political Stability." *American Journal of Political Science* 50 (4): 893–908.

Gettleman, Jeffrey. 2008. "Death Toll in Kenya Exceeds 1,000, but Talks Reach Crucial Phase." *New York Times*, February 6. http://www.nytimes.com/2008/02/06/world/africa/06kenya.html?_r=0.

———. 2010. "Rwanda's Mix: Order, Tension, Repressiveness." *New York Times*, May 1, A1, A7.

Gibbs, Nancy, Clive Mutiso, Andrew Purvis, Thomas Sancton, and Ann M. Simmons. 1994. "Why? The Killing Fields of Rwanda." *Time*, May 16. http://www.time.com/time/magazine/article/0,9171,980750,00.html.

"Guinea's Elections: A General Insists They Must Be Fair." 2010. *Economist*, June 17, 51.

Halliday. Terence. 2009. "Recursivity of Global Normmaking: A Sociolegal Agenda." *Annual Review of Law and Social Science* 5: 263–289.

Hirshman, Michael. 2009. "Gene Sharp: Theoretician of the Velvet Revolution." Prague, Czech Republic, Radio Free Europe/Radio Liberty, November 27. http://www.rferl.org/content/Gene_Sharp_Theoretician_Of_Velvet_Revolution/1889473.html

"Honduras Truth Commission Rules Zelaya Removal Was Coup." 2011. *BBC*. http://www.bbc.co.uk/news/world-latin-america-14072148.

Hovannisian, Garin. 2010. "Waiting for Armenia." *New York Times*, September 22. http://www.nytimes.com/2010/09/22/opinion/22iht-edhovannisian.html.

Human Rights Watch. 2012a. "Iran Fair Vote Impossible: Opposition Imprisoned, Barred from Running in Parliamentary Elections." http://www.hrw.org/news/2012/03/01/iran-fair-vote-impossible.

———. 2012 b. "Torture Archipelago: Arbitrary Arrests, Torture, and Enforced Disappearances in Syria's Underground Prisons, Since March 2011." http://www.hrw.org/node/108415/section/2.

Huntington, Samuel. 1993. *The Third Wave: Democratization in the Late Twentieth Century*. Norman: University of Oklahoma Press.

Kaldor, Mary. 2003. *Global Civil Society: The Answer to War*. Cambridge: Polity Press.

Keane, John. 2009a. "Bad Moons, Little Dreams." http://www.thelifeanddeathofdemocracy.org/resources/excerpt/jkeane_life_and_death_democracy_intro.pdf.

———. 2009b. "¿Democracia monitorizada? La historia secreta de la democracia desde 1945." Talk delivered at the the Universitat Jaume I, Castelló de la Plana, Spain, February 5. http://www.thelifeanddeathofdemocracy.org/videos/videos_monitory_democracy_castellon.html.

———. 2009c. "Glossary: Monitory Democracy." http://www.thelifeanddeathofdemocracy.org/glossary/glossary_monitory_democracy.html.

"Kenya's Constitutional Referendum: Stoking Up Violence." 2010. *Economist*, June 17. http://www.economist.com/node/16381138.

Khalid, Adeeb. 2007. *Islam After Communism: Religion and Politics in Central Asia*. Los Angeles: University of California Press.

Kramer, Andrew E. 2010. "Kyrgyz Voting Calm After Violence." *New York Times*, June 28, A7.

Kuran, Timur. 2012. "The Economic Roots of Political Underdevelopment in the Middle East: A Historical Perspective." *Southern Economic Journal* 78 (4): 1086–1095.

Lacey, Marc. 2010. "Latin America Still Divided Over Coup in Honduras." *New York Times*, June 6, A10.

Larraín, Jorge. 2000. *Identity and Modernity in Latin America*. Cambridge: Polity Press.

"Libya's Election: A Big Step for a Battered Country." 2012. *Economist*, July 14. http://www.economist.com/node/21558634.

Lindberg, Staffan I. 2006. *Democracy and Elections in Africa*. Baltimore: The Johns Hopkins University Press.

Mainwaring, Scott, and Aníbal Pérez-Liñan. 2003. "Level of Development and Democracy: Latin American Exceptionalism, 1945–1996." *Comparative Political Studies* 36 (9): 1031–1067.

———. 2005. "Why Regions of the World Are Important: Regional Specificities and Region-Wide Diffusion of Democracy." Working Paper No. 322. The Helen Kellogg Institute for International Studies, Notre Dame, IN. http://kellogg.nd.edu/publications/workingpapers/WPS/322.pdf.

Marshall, Monty G., and Benjamin R. Cole. 2009. "Global Report 2009: Conflict, Governance and State Fragility." Center for Systemic Peace and Center for Global Policy, George Mason University. http://www.systemicpeace.org/Global%20Report%202009.pdf.

McCauley, John F., and E. Gyimah-Boadi. 2009. "Religious Faith and Democracy: Evidence From the Afrobarometer Surveys." Working Paper No. 113. http://afrobarometer.org/papers/AfropaperNo113.pdf.

McNeil, Donald G. 1999. "Romania's Revolution of 1989: An Enduring Enigma." *New York Times*, December 31. http://www.nytimes.com/1999/12/31/world/romania-s-revolution-of-1989-an-enduring-enigma.html.

Nachawati, Leila. 2012. "Misrepresenting the Syrian Revolution." Zurich, Switzerland: Center for Security Studies. http://www.isn.ethz.ch/isn/Digital-Library/Articles/Detail/?id=150955.

Nichol, Jim. 2012. "Russian Political, Economic, and Security Issues and U.S. Interests." CRS Report for Congress, RL33407. Washington, DC: Congressional Research Service. http://www.fas.org/sgp/crs/row/RL33407.pdf.

Nossiter, Adam. 2010. "As Guinea Moves Forward, the Old Order Has Its Defenders." *New York Times*, July 9, A6.

———. 2012. "Soldiers Overthrow Mali Government in Setback for Democracy in Africa." *New York Times*. March 22. http://www.nytimes.com/2012/03/23/world/africa/mali-coup-france-calls-for-elections.html.

———. 2013. "On the Ground in Mali, French and Local Troops Confront Islamist Forces." *New York Times*, January 16. http://www.nytimes.com/2013/01/17/world/africa/france-mali-intervention.html?hp.

Pan, Philip P. 2010. "Drop in U.S. Aid Hits Democracy Efforts in Ukraine, Which Heads to Polls Today." *Washington Post*, February 7. http://www.washingtonpost.com/wp-dyn/content/article/2010/02/06/AR2010020602045.html.

Pérez, Orlando J. 2009. "Crime and Support for Coups in Latin America." AmericasBarometer Insights No. 32. Latin American Public Opinion Project. http://sitemason.vanderbilt.edu/files/ebuddC/I0832Crime%20and%20Support%20for%20Coups%20in%20Latin%20America.pdf.

Pérez-Liñan, Anibal. 2006. *Presidential Impeachment and the New Political Instability in Latin America*. Cambridge: Cambridge University Press.

Pew Global Attitudes Project. 2009. *End of Communism Cheered but Now With More Reservations: The Pulse of Europe 2009: 20 Years After the Fall of the Berlin Wall*. Washington, DC: Pew Research Center. http://www.pewglobal.org/files/2009/11/Pew-Global-Attitudes-2009-Pulse-of-Europe-Report-Nov-2-1030am-NOT-EMBARGOED.pdf

———. 2012. "Most Muslims Want Democracy, Personal Freedoms, and Islam in Political Life." http://www.pewglobal.org/2012/07/10/most-muslims-want-democracy-personal-freedoms-and-islam-in-political-life.

Politzer, Patricia. 1989. *Fear in Chile: Lives Under Pinochet*. New York: New Press.

Puddington, Arch. 2010. "Freedom in the World 2010." http://www.freedomhouse.org/report/freedom-world/freedom-world-2010.

———. 2011. "Freedom in the World 2011: The Authoritarian Challenge to Democracy." http://www.freedomhouse.org/report/freedom-world/freedom-world-2011.

———. 2013. "Freedom in the World 2013: Democratic Breakthroughs in the Balance." http://www.freedomhouse.org/sites/default/files/FIW%202013%20Booklet%20-%20for%20Web.pdf.

Rettig, Jessica. 2012. "Death Toll of Arab Spring." *US News and World Report*. http://www.usnews.com/news/slideshows/death-toll-of-arab-spring.

Reuters. 2010. "UPDATE 1-Nigeria's Ruling Party Appoints New Chairman." June 17. http://af.reuters.com/article/nigeriaNews/idAFLDE65G1XX20100617.

Reynolds, Andrew. 2006. "Electoral Systems and the Protection and Participation of Minorities." *Minority Rights Group*. http://www.minorityrights.org/1075/reports/electoral-systems-and-the-protection-and-participation-of-minorities.html.

Romero, Simon. 2009. "Rare Hemisphere Unity in Assailing Honduran Coup." *New York Times,* June 28, A6.

Ross, Michael L. 2001. "Does Oil Hinder Democracy?" *World Politics* 53 (3): 325–361.

Saine, Abdoulaye. 2008. "The Gambia's 'Elected Autocrat Poverty, Peripherality, and Political Instability,' 1994–2006: A Political Economy Assessment." *Armed Forces & Society* 34 (3): 450–473.

Schraeder, Peter T. 1995. "Understanding the 'Third Wave' of Democratization in Africa." *The Journal of Politics* 57 (4): 1160–1168.

Schriefer, Paula. 2010. *The UN Human Rights Council Report Card: 2009–2010*. Washington, DC: Freedom House. http://freedomhouse.org/images/File/Full%20Report%20Card%20Final.pdf.

"Seven More Years (at Least): President Nazarbaev Wins Again." 2005. *Economist*, December 8. http://www.economist.com/node/5284866?zid=309&ah=80dcf288b8561b012f603b9fd9577f0e.

Shkolnikov, Vladimir D. 2009. *Nations in Transit 2009: Democracy's Dark Year*. Freedom House. http://www.freedomhouse.org/report/nations-transit-2009/overview-essay.

Silva, Eduardo. 2004. "Authoritarianism, Democracy and Development." In *Latin America Transformed: Globalization and Modernity*, edited by Robert Gwynne and Cristóbal Kay, 141–156. London: Edward Arnold.

Silva, Patricio. 2004. "The New Political Order: Toward Technocratic Democracies?" In *Latin America Transformed: Globalization and Modernity*, edited by Robert Gwynne and Cristóbal Kay, 157–170. London: Edward Arnold.

Stiglitz, Joseph. 2006. *Making Globalization Work*. New York: W.W. Norton.

Stolberg, Sheryl Gay. 2011. "Shy U.S. Intellectual Created Playbook Used in a Revolution." *New York Times*, February 17, A1.

Sulami, Mishal Al. 2005. "Democracy in the Arab World: The Islamic Foundation." *openDemocracy*. http://www.opendemocracy.net/author/Mishal_Al_Sulami.jsp.

Sweet, Alec Stone. 2008. "Constitutions and Judicial Power." In *Comparative Politics*, edited by Daniele Caramani, 217–240. Oxford: Oxford University Press.

"The Swiss Minaret Ban." 2009. *Economist,* November 30. http://www.economist.com/blogs/charlemagne/2009/11/_normal_0_false_false_6.

Tar, Usman A. 2009. *The Politics of Neoliberal Democracy in Africa: State and Civil Society in Nigeria.* New York: Palgrave Macmillan.

Tavernse, Sabrina. 2008. "With a Collective Shrug, Azerbaijan Votes for Its Leader." *New York Times*, October 15, A10.

Temple-Raston, Dina. 2012. "U.S. Sees Signs of Al-Qaida Arm in Syria." *National Public Radio*, August 3. http://www.wbur.org/npr/157932381/u-s-sees-signs-of-al-qaida-arm-in-syria.

Van Maarseveen, Henc, and Ger van der Tang. 1978. *Written Constitutions: A Computerized Comparative Study.* Dobbs Ferry, NY: Oceana Publications.

Walker, Christopher. 2010. "Nations in Transit 2010: Democracy and Dissent." *Freedom House.* http://www.freedomhouse.org/report/nations-transit-2010/overview-essay.

Walker, Christopher, and Sylvana Habdank–Kołaczkowska. 2012. "Nations in Transit: Fragile Frontier: Democracy's Growing Vulnerability in Central and Southeastern Europe." *Freedom House.* http://www.freedomhouse.org/report/nations-transit-2012/overview-essay.

Wallerstein, Immanuel. 1995. *After Liberalism.* New York: New Press.

Chapter 9

Adams, Beatrice. 2007. "McDonald's Strange Menu Around the World." *Thrifter*, July 19. http://trifter.com/practical-travel/budget-travel/mcdonald%E2%80%99s-strange-menu-around-the-world.

Adams, Laura L. 2008. "Globalization, Universalism, and Cultural Form." *Comparative Studies in Society and History* 50 (3): 614–640.

African Commission on Human and Peoples' Rights (ACHPR). 1981. *African Charter on Human and Peoples' Rights.* Nairobi: African Commission on Human and Peoples' Rights. http://www.achpr.org/english/_info/charter_en.html.

Albrow, Martin, John Eade, Neil Washbourne, and Jorg Durrschmidt. 1994. "The Impact of Globalization on Sociological Concepts: Community, Culture and Milieu." *Innovation: The European Journal of the Social Sciences* 7 (4): 371–389.

Andrews, Edmund L. 2005. "Snow Urges Consumerism on China Trip." *New York Times*, October 14. http://www.nytimes.com/2005/10/14/business/14yuan.html.

Appadurai, Arjun. 1996. *Modernity at Large: Cultural Dimensions of Globalization.* Minneapolis: University of Minnesota Press.

Appiah, Kwame Anthony. 2006. *Cosmopolitanism: Ethics in a World of Strangers.* New York: W.W. Norton.

Beck, Ulrich. 2004. "The Truth of Others: A Cosmopolitan Approach." *Common Knowledge* 10 (3): 430–449.

Berger, Peter. 1997. "Four Faces of Global Culture." *National Interest* 49: 23–29.

Biodrowski, Steve. 2008. "Remaking Asian Horror: A Brief History." *Cinefantastique Online.* http://cinefantastiqueonline.com/2008/02/remaking-asian-horror-a-brief-history.

Boli, John. 2005. "Contemporary Developments in World Culture." *International Journal of Comparative Sociology* 46 (5–6): 383–404.

Castells, Manuel, Mireia Fernandez-Ardevol, Jack Linchuan Qiu, and Araba Sey. 2007. *Mobile Communication and Society: The Global Perspective.* Cambridge, MA: MIT Press.

Chan, Stephanie. 2008. "Cross-Cultural Civility in Global Civil Society: Transnational Cooperation in Chinese NGOs." *Global Networks* 8 (2): 223–252.

Cumming-Bruce, Nick, and Steven Erlanger. 2009. "Swiss Ban Building of Minarets." *New York Times*, November 29, A6. http://www.nytimes.com/2009/11/30/world/europe/30swiss.html.

Donnelly, Jack. 2007. "The Relative Universality of Human Rights." *Human Rights Quarterly* 29 (2): 281–306.

Drori, Gill S., John W. Meyer, and Hokyu Hwang, eds. 2009. *Globalization and Organization.* Oxford: Oxford University Press.

"Drucker in the Dug-Out: A Japanese Book About Peter Drucker and Baseball Is an Unlikely Hit." 2010. *Economist*, July 3. http://www.highbeam.com/doc/1G1-230274176.html.

Erlanger, Steven. 2010. "Sarkozy Wants Ban of Full Veils." *New York Times*, April 21. http://www.nytimes.com/2010/04/22/world/europe/22france.html.

Falk, Richard. 2004. "Think Again: Human Rights." *Foreign Policy* 141 (March/April): 18–26.

Featherstone, Mike. 1990. "Global Culture: An Introduction." In *Global Culture: Nationalism, Globalization and Modernity*, edited by Mike Featherstone, 1–14. London: Sage.

Fisher, Ian. 2008. "Is Cuisine Still Italian Even if the Chef Isn't?" *New York Times*, April 7. http://www.nytimes.com/2008/04/07/world/europe/07food.html?_r=1&ref=Tunisia.

Frank, Andre Gunder. 1998. *ReOrient: Global Economy in the Asian Age.* Berkeley: University of California Press.

Giddens, Anthony. 1990. *The Consequences of Modernity.* Cambridge: Polity Press.

———. 2003. *Runaway World: How Globalization Is Reshaping Our Lives.* New York. Routledge.

Gilroy, Paul. 2008. "Race, Rice and the Info War." In *Cultural Politics in a Global Age*, edited by David Held and Henrietta L. Moore, 196–203. Oxford: One World Publications.

Hannerz, Ulf. 1990. "Cosmopolitans and Locals in World Culture." In *Global Culture: Nationalism, Globalization and Modernity*, edited by Mike Featherstone, 237–251. London: Sage.

———. 1992. *Cultural Complexity.* New York: Columbia University Press.

Herkenrath, Mark, Claudia König, Hanno Scholtz, and Thomas Volken. 2005. "Convergence and Divergence in the Contemporary World System: An Introduction." *International Journal of Comparative Sociology* 46 (5–6): 363–382.

Huntington, Samuel. 1993. "The Clash of Civilizations?" *Foreign Affairs* 72 (3): 22–49.

Jacobs, Andrew, and Miguel Helft. 2010. "Google, Citing Attack, Threatens to Exit China." *New York Times*, January 12, A1.

James, Paul. 2004. "The Matrix of Global Enchantment." In *Rethinking Globalism*, edited by Manfred B. Steger, 27–38. Lanham, MD: Rowman and Little field.

Keeler, Ward. 2009. "What's Burmese About Burmese Rap?" *American Ethnologist* 36 (1): 2–18.

Kehrer, Micheala. 2007. "Transnational Consumer Goods Corporations in Egypt: Reaching Towards the Mass Market." *Research in Economic Anthropology* 25: 151–172.

Khondker, Habibul Haque. 2004. "Glocalization as Globalization: Evolution of a Sociological Concept." *Bangladesh e-Journal of Sociology* 1 (2): 12–20.

Kim, Doo-Sub. 2009. "The 1997 Asian Economic Crisis and Changes in the Pattern of Socio-Economic Differentials in Korean Fertility." In *Ultra-Low Fertility in Pacific Asia: Trends, Causes and Policy Issues*, edited by Gavin Jones, Paulin Tay Straughan, and Angelique Chan, 110–131. Abingdon, UK: Routledge.

Kristof, Nicholas D. 1997. "Stateside Lingo Gives Japan Its Own Valley Girls." *New York Times*, October 19, A3.

La Franiere, Sharon. 2011. "For Many Chinese, New Wealth and a Fresh Face." *New York Times,* April 24, A6.

Lane, Charles. 2005. "5–4 Supreme Court Abolishes Juvenile Executions." *Washington Post*, March 2, A1.

"Legal Confusion on Internet Piracy: The Clash of Data Civilisations." 2010. *Economist*, June 17. http://economist.com/node/16377097.

Livingston, Gretchen. 2011. "In a Down Economy, Fewer Births." *Pew Social & Demographic Trends*, October 12. http://www.pewsocialtrends.org/files/2011/10/REVISITING-FERTILITY-AND-THE-RECESSION-FINAL.pdf.

Mäkelä, Janne. 2007. "Foreign Issues: The National and International in 1960s Finnish Popular Music Discourse." *Journal of Interdisciplinary Music Studies* 1 (1): 51–62.

Matejowsky, Ty. 2006. "Global Tastes, Local Contexts: An Ethnographic Account of Fast Food in San Fernando City, the Philippines." In *Fast Food/Slow Food: The Economic Anthropology of the Global Food System* (Society for Economic Anthropology Monograph Series 24), edited by Richard Wilk, 145–159. Walnut Creek, CA: Altamira Press.

McDonald's. 2007. "Global Stars." In *The McDonald's Electronic Press Kit.* http://mcdepk.com/globalcastingcall/stars.html.

———. 2011. "Getting to Know Us." http://www.aboutmcdonalds.com/mcd/our_company.html.

Meyer, John W., John Boli, George M. Thomas, and Francisco O. Ramirez. 1997. "World Society and the Nation-State." *The American Journal of Sociology* 103 (1): 144–181.

Minority Rights Group (MRG). 2007. "Chile Apologizes for Treatment of Indigenous Groups but Communities Call for End to Discriminatory Treatment." http://www.minorityrights.org/?lid=9780.

Nobles, Melissa. 2008. *The Politics of Official Apologies.* Cambridge: Cambridge University Press.

Nye, Joseph S., Jr. 2004. *Soft Power*. New York: Public Affairs.

———. 2008. "Recovering American Leadership." *Survival* 50 (1): 55–68.

Onishi, Norimitsu. 2008. "Thumbs Race as Japan's Best Sellers Go Cellular." *New York Times*, January 20. http://www.nytimes.com/2008/01/20/world/asia/20japan.html.

Ouane, Adama, and Christine Glanz. 2010. "Why and How Africa Should Invest in African Languages and Multicultural Education." UNESCO Institute for Lifelong Learning, in collaboration with the Association for the Development of Education in Africa (ADEA).

Penn National Commission on Society, Culture, and Community (PNC). 2003. "Political Apologies: Chronological List." University of Pennsylvania. http://www.upenn.edu/pnc/politicalapologies.html.

Pieterse, Jan Nederveen. 1994. "Globalisation as Hybridity." *International Sociology* 9 (2): 161–184.

———. 2003. *Globalization and Culture: Global Mélange.* Lanham, MD: Rowman and Littlefield.

———. 2007. "Global Multiculture, Flexible Acculturation." *Globalizations* 4 (1): 65–79.

Richburg, Keith B. 2012. "Getting Chinese to Stop Saving and Start Spending Is a Hard Sell." *Washington Post*, July 5. http://articles.washingtonpost.com/2012-07-05/world/35488534_1_savings-rate-chinese-consumers-china-market-research-group.

Ritzer, George. 1993. *The McDonaldization of Society*. London: Sage.

Robertson, Roland. 1992. *Globalization: Social Theory and Global Culture*. London: Sage.

———. 1994. "Globalisation or Glocalisation?" *Journal of International Communication* 1 (1): 33–52.

Robertson, Roland, and JoAnn Chirico. 1985. "Humanity, Globalization and Worldwide Religious Resurgence." *Sociological Analysis* 46 (3): 219–242.

Scholte, Jan Aarte. 2000. *Globalization: A Critical Introduction.* London: Macmillan.

Simmons, Beth, and Zachary Elkins. 2004. "The Globalization of Liberalization: Policy Diffusion in the Political Economy." *The American Political Science Review* 98 (1): 171–189.

Stamberg, Susan. 2010. "Blue and White and Mad All Over: 'Chinamania.'" *NPR*, August 26. http://www.npr.org/templates/rundowns/rundown.php?prgId=3&prgDate=8-26-2010.

Stearns, Peter N. 2006. *Consumerism in World History: The Global Transformation of Desire*. New York: Routledge.

Steger, Manfred B. 2009. "From 'We the People' to 'We the Planet': Neoconservative Visions of a Global USA." In *Politics of Globalization*, edited by Samir Dasgupta and Jan Nederveen Pieterse, 65–81. London: Sage.

Tomlinson, John. 1999. *Globalization and Culture.* Chicago: University of Chicago Press.

Tschofen, Bernhard. 2008. "Of the Taste of Regions: Culinary Practice, European Policy and Spatial Culture—A Research Outline." *Anthropological Journal of European Cultures* 17: 24–53.

UNESCO. 2009. *UNESCO World Report: Investing in Cultural Diversity and Intercultural Dialog.* Paris: France. http://unesdoc.unesco.org/images/0018/001852/185202E.pdf.

Wallerstein, Immanuel. 1995. *After Liberalism*. New York: New Press.

Watters, Ethan. 2010. "The Americanization of Mental Illness." *New York Times*, January 10, MM40. http://www.nytimes.com/2010/01/10/magazine/10psyche-t.html.

Wells, H. G. 1920/1956. *The Outline of History: Being Plain History of Life and Mankind.* Garden City, NY: Garden City Press.

World Health Organization (WHO). 2008. "Scaling Up Care for Mental, Neurological, and Substance Use Disorders." WHO Mental Health Gap Action Program. Geneva, Switzerland.

World Values Survey. 2011. *World Values Survey 2005 Official Data File v.20090901, 2009.* Online Data Analysis. World Values Survey Association. Madrid: ASEP/JDS.

Chapter 10

American Association of University Women (AAUW). n.d. "Women in Sports Timeline." In *Women's History of Sports*. St. Lawrence County, NY: St. Lawrence County Branch AAUW. http://www.northnet.org/stlawrenceaauw/timeline.htm.

Barney, Robert K. 2009. "Planning Makes the Difference." *New York Times* October 2. http://roomfordebate.blogs.nytimes.com/2009/10/02/do-olympic-host-cities-ever-win.

Barry, John M. 2006. "The Effects on Society at Large." In *Pandemic Influenza: Past, Present, and Future. Workshop Proceedings*, 5–8. Washington, DC: U.S. Department of Health and Human Services, Centers for Disease Control and Prevention. http://www.flu.gov/pandemic/workshop.pdf.

Ben-David, Joseph. 1958. "Professional Role of the Physician in Bureaucratized Medicine: A Study in Role Conflict." *Human Relations* 11 (3): 255–274.

Bruinius, Harry. 2010. "Megacities of the World: A Glimpse of How We'll Live Tomorrow." *Christian Science Monitor*, May 5. http://www.csmonitor.com/World/Global-Issues/2010/0505/Megacities-of-the-world-a-glimpse-of-how-we-ll-live-tomorrow.

Cadge, Wendy, and Courtney Bender. 2004. "Yoga and Rebirth in America: Asian Religions Are Here to Stay." *Contexts* 3 (1): 45–51.

CNN Money. 2011. "Fortune 500: Our Annual Ranking of America's Largest Corporations." http://money.cnn.com/magazines/fortune/fortune500/2011/industries/4/index.html.

Disaster Emergency Committee (DEC). 2011. "Haiti Earthquake Facts and Figures." http://www.dec.org.uk/haiti-earthquake-facts-and-figures.

Doyle, Katie. 2006. "The Dead of Tlatelolco: Using the Archives to Exhume the Past." *The National Security Archive*. Washington, DC: George Washington University. http://www.gwu.edu/~nsarchiv/NSAEBB/NSAEBB201/index.htm.

FIFA. n.d. "Mission and Statutes: Our Brand, Our Commitment." http://www.fifa.com/aboutfifa/organisation/mission.html.

Fraser, Nancy. 2009. *Scales of Justice: Reimagining Political Space in a Globalizing World*. New York: Columbia University Press.

Gibbons Elizabeth D., Friedrich Huebler, and Edilberto Loaiza. 2003. *Child Labour, Education and the Principle of Non-Discrimination*. New York: UNICEF. http://www.childinfo.org/files/Childlabour_GibbonsHueblerLoaiza_2005.pdf.

Giulianotti, Richard, and Roland Robertson. 2007. "Forms of Glocalization: Globalization and the Migration Strategies of Scottish Football Fans in North America." *Sociology* 41 (1): 133–152.

Heywood, Leslie. 2007. "Producing Sport: Empire, Girls and the Neoliberal Body." In *Physical Culture, Power, and the Body*, edited by Jennier Hargreaves and Patricia Anne Vertinsky, 101–120. New York: Routledge.

Hughson, John. 2009. "The 'Global Triumph' of Sport." *Sport in Society: Cultures, Commerce, Media, Politics* 12(1): 134–140.

International Association for Educational Assessment (IAEA). n.d. "About Us." http://www.iaea.info/about.aspx.

Jennings, Ralph. 2005. "Extreme Sports Battle for Business." *Asia Times*, November 2. http://www.atimes.com/atimes/China_Business/GK02Cb05.html.

Johnson, Niall P. A. S., and Juergen Mueller. 2002. "Updating the Accounts: Global Mortality of the 1918–1920 'Spanish' Influenza Epidemic." *Bulletin of the History of Medicine* 76 (1): 105–115.

Kaiser Family Foundation. 2010a. "Fact Sheet: The Global HIV/AIDS Epidemic." http://www.kff.org/hivaids/upload/3030-15.pdf.

Kaiser Family Foundation. 2010b. "Fact Sheet: The Tuberculosis Epidemic." http://www.kff.org/globalhealth/upload/7883-03.pdf.

Kakutani, Michiko. 2010. "Where the Ascetic Meets the Athletic." *New York Times*, July 29. http://www.nytimes.com/2010/07/30/books/30book.html?_r=0&gwh=01B6FD8BD23CB445B3FBB6064EA4F2EB.

Kataki, Rupamudra. 2011. "Revival Time for the Games People Played—North East Zonal Cultural Centre Plans to Promote Indigenous Sports in Events Across the Country." *Telegraph* (Calcutta, India), June 14. http://www.telegraphindia.com/1110615/jsp/northeast/story_14113024.jsp.

Kates, Jen, and Rebecca Katz. 2010. *US Global Health Policy: US Participation in International Health Treaties, Commitments, Partnerships and Other Agreements*. Menlo Park, CA: The Henry J. Kaiser Family Foundation.

Katz, Craig L. 2010. "Mind the Global Health Care Gap." *Huffington Post*, August 2. http://www.huffingtonpost.com/craig-l-katz-md/mind-the-world-health-gap_b_667943.html.

Kirk, Jackie. 2008. "Addressing Gender Disparities in Education in Contexts of Crisis, Postcrisis, and State Fragility." In *Girls' Education in the 21st Century: Gender Equality, Empowerment, and Economic Growth*, edited by Mercy Tembon and Lucia Fort, 153–180. Washington, DC: World Bank. http://siteresources.worldbank.org/EDUCATION/Resources/278200-1099079877269/547664-1099080014368/DID_Girls_edu.pdf.

Korostelina, Karina. 2008. "History Education and Social Identity." *Identity: An International Journal of Theory and Research* 8 (1): 25–45.

Kruk, Margaret E. 2010. *Globalization and Global Health Governance: Implications for Public Health*. The Changing Landscape of Global Public Health Conference, October 24–26, Columbia University, New York. http://www.globalpublichealthconference.org/_downloads/bg/BackgroundPaper_Kruk_BKA_15OCT_C.pdf.

League of American Wheelmen (LAW). 1899. "Women and the League." *L.A.W. Bulletin and Good Roads*, April 28, 587. http://www.proteanpaper.com/scart_results.cgi?comp=howiebik&framed=0&part=Women-009&scat=1&scatord=desc&scatall=no&skey=norm&srkeyall=&srkeywords=&srcateg=00000000000000000311.

LeVine, Robert A. 2007. "The Global Spread of Women's Schooling: Effects on Literacy, Health, and Children." In *Learning in the Global Era: International Perspectives on Globalization and Education*, edited by Marcelo M. Suárez-Orozco, 121–136. Berkeley: University of California Press.

London Organising Committee of the Olympic Games (LOCOG). 2010. "Legacy." http://www.london2012.com/about-us/legacy.

MacDorman, Marian F., and T. J. Mathews. 2009. "Behind International Rankings of Infant Mortality: How the United States Compares With Europe." NCHS Data Brief No. 23, November. Washington, DC: National Center for Health Statistics, Centers for Disease Control and Prevention. http://www.cdc.gov/nchs/data/databriefs/db23.pdf.

———. 2011. "Understanding Racial and Ethnic Disparities in U.S. Infant Mortality Rates." NCHS Data Brief No. 74, September. Washington, DC: National Center for Health Statistics, Centers for Disease Control and Prevention. http://www.cdc.gov/nchs/data/databriefs/db74.htm.

Maguire, Joseph. 1999. Global Sport. Malden, MA: Blackwell.

Mamelund, Svenn-Erik. 2011. "Geography May Explain Adult Mortality from the 1918–20 Influenza Pandemic." Epidemics 3 (1): 46–60.

Mann, Horace. 1891. Life and Works of Horace Mann. 2 vols. Edited by Mary Tyler Peabody Mann. Boston: Lee and Shepard.

Markovits, Andrei S. 2010. "The Global and the Local in Our Contemporary Sports Cultures." Society 47 (6): 503–509.

Marshall, Dashi. 2009. "A Renaissance for Atlanta." New York Times October 2. http://roomfordebate.blogs.nytimes.com/2009/10/02/do-olympic-host-cities-ever-win.

Mayo Clinic Staff. 2009. "Acupuncture Definition." Rochester, MN: Mayo Clinic. http://www.mayoclinic.com/health/acupuncture/MY00946.

McComb, David G. 2004. Sports in World History. New York: Routledge.

McLoughlin, William G. 1978. Revivals, Awakenings, and Reform. Chicago: University of Chicago Press.

Memorial Sloan Kettering Cancer Center. 1999. Advertisement in The New York Times Sunday Magazine. New York: Memorial Sloan Kettering Cancer Center.

Memorial Sloan-Kettering Cancer Center. 2010. "Integrative Medicine." New York: Memorial Sloan Kettering Cancer Center. http://www.mskcc.org/mskcc/html/1979.cfm.

Meyer, John W. 2007. "Globalization: Theory and Trends." International Journal of Comparative Sociology 48 (4): 261–273.

Meyer, John W., Francisco O. Ramirez, and Yasemin Nuhoglu Soysal. 1992. "World Expansion and Mass Education, 1870–1980." Sociology of Education 65 (2): 128–149.

Molina, George Gray, and Mark Purser. 2010. Human Development TrendsSsince 1970: A Social Convergence Story (Human Development Reports Research Paper 2010/02). New York: United Nations Development Programme. http://hdr.undp.org/en/reports/global/hdr2010/papers/HDRP_2010_02.pdf.

National Center for Complementary and Alternative Medicine (NCCAM). 2011. The Use of Complementary and Alternative Medicine in the United States. Washington, DC: National Institutes of Health. http://nccam.nih.gov/news/camstats/2007/camsurvey_fs1.htm.

PBS. 2010. "God in America." On Frontline, October 11. Arlington, VA: Public Broadcasting Service. http://www.pbs.org/godinamerica.

Poli, Raffaele. 2010. "Understanding Globalization Through Football: The New International Division of Labour, Migratory Channels and Transnational Trade Circuits." International Review for the Sociology of Sport 45 (4): 491–506.

Ramirez, Francisco, and John W. Meyer. 1980. "Comparative Education: The Social Construction of the Modern World System." Annual Review of Sociology 6: 369–399.

Robertson, Roland. 1992. Globalization: Social Theory and Global Culture. London: Sage.

Rodwin, Victor G., and Leland G. Neuberg. 2005. "Infant Mortality and Income in 4 World Cities: New York, London, Paris, and Tokyo." American Journal of Public Health 95 (1): 86–90.

Rowe, David. 2003. "Sport and the Repudiation of the Global." International Review of the Sociology of Sport 38 (3): 281–294.

Sage, George H. 2010. Globalizing Sport: How Organizations, Corporations, Media, and Politics are Changing Sports. Boulder, CO: Paradigm.

Scharnberg, Kirsten. 2006. "Going Down the Tube: Surfing's Popularity, Extreme Sports, Technology and Globalization, Dude, Are Pushing American Boardmakers Toward a Major Wipeout." Knight Ridder Tribune Business News, July 30, 1.

Seidman, Michael M. 2004. The Imaginary Revolution: Students and Workers in Paris in 1968. Oxford: Berghahn Books

Smart, Barry. 2007. "Not Playing Around: Global Capitalism, Modern Sport and Consumer Culture." Global Networks 7 (2): 13–134.

Sohler, Nancy L., Peter S. Arno, Chee Jen Chang, Jing Fang, and Clyde Schechter. 2003. "Income Inequality and Infant Mortality in New York City." Journal of Urban Health 80 (4): 650–657.

Sport and Recreation South Africa (SRSA). 2011. "Indigenous Games." SA Sports Awards. http://sasportsawardsblog.weebly.com/indigenous-games-sa.html.

Tembon, Mercy. 2008. "Conclusions and Recommendations for the Way Forward." In Girls' Education in the 21st Century: Gender Equality, Empowerment, and Economic Growth, edited by Mercy Tembon and Lucia Fort, 279–305. Washington, DC: World Bank. http://siteresources.worldbank.org/EDUCATION/Resources/278200-1099079877269/547664-1099080014368/DID_Girls_edu.pdf.

Tomlinson, Adam, and Christopher Young. 2006. "Culture, Politics, and Spectacle in the Global Sports Event—An Introduction." In National Identity and Global Sports Events: Culture, Politics, and Spectacle in the Olympics and the Football World Cup, edited by Alan Tomlinson and Christopher Young, 1–14. Albany: State University of New York Press.

United Nations (UN). 2010. The Millennium Development Goals Report 2010. New York: United Nations. http://www.un.org/millenniumgoals/pdf/MDG%20Report%202010%20En%20r15%20-low%20res%2020100615%20-.pdf.

———. 2011. The Millennium Development Goals Report 2011. New York: United Nations. http://www.un.org/millenniumgoals/11_MDG%20Report_EN.pdf.

United Nations Development Programme (UNDP). 2011. Human Development Report 2011: Sustainability and Equity: A Better Future for All. New York: United Nations. http://hdr.undp.org/en/media/HDR_2011_EN_Contents.pdf.

UNESCO. 2005. Education Trends in Perspective: Analysis of the World Education Indicators, 2005 Edition. Montreal,

Canada: UNESCO Institute for Statistics. http://www.uis
.unesco.org/Library/Documents/wei05_en.pdf.

———. 2009. *The Global Education Digest*. http://www.uis
.unesco.org/Library/Documents/ged09-en.pdf.

UNICEF. 2009. "Child Info: Monitoring the Situation of Women
and Children: Statistics by Area/Education: Challenge." http://
www.childinfo.org/education_challenge.html.

———. 2012a. "Child Info: Monitoring the Situation of Children
and Women: Statistics by Area/Education: Overview." http://
www.childinfo.org/education_1055.htm.

———. 2012b. "Child Info: Monitoring the Situation of
Children and Women: Statistics by Area/Education:
Primary School Participation and Survival." http://www
.childinfo.org/education_1056.htm.

———. 2012c. "Child Info: Monitoring the Situation of Children
and Women: Statistics by Area/Education: Secondary School
Participation." http://www.childinfo.org/education_1057
.htm.

Van Bottenburg, Maarten. 2001. *Global Games*. Urbana:
University of Illinois Press.

Watters, Ethan. 2010. "The Americanization of Mental Illness."
New York Times, January 10, MM40. http://www.nytimes
.com/2010/01/10/magazine/10psyche-t.html.

Weber, Max. 1921/1978. "Bureaucracy." In *Economy and Society:
An Outline of Interpretive Sociology*, Vol. 2, 956–1005.
Edited by Günther Roth and Claus Wittich. Berkeley:
University of California Press.

"Where the Premier League's Players Come From." 2009. *BBC*,
August 17. http://news.bbc.co.uk/sport2/hi/football/eng_
prem/8182090.stm.

World Health Organization (WHO). 2008. "What Are the
International Health Regulations?" http://www.who.int/
features/qa/39/en/index.html.

———. 2012. *IHR Activity Report 2011*. Geneva, Switzerland:
World Health Organization, International Health Regulations
Coordination Department. http://www.who.int/ihr/public
ations/activity_report_2011/en/index.html.

Yeung, Joseph C. K. 2011. Building National Identity Is Core of
National Education." *China Daily*, June 25, 3. http://www
.chinadaily.com.cn/hkedition/2011-06/25/content_12773736
.htm.

Zimbalist, Andrew. 2009. "Not a Rosy Picture." *New York
Times* October 2. http://roomfordebate.blogs.nytimes.
com/2009/10/02/do-olympic-host-cities-ever-win/.

Chapter 11

Abedin, Mahan. 2011. "Tunisia: The Advent of Liberal Islamism—
An Interview With Rashid Al-Ghannouchi." *Religioscope*,
January 30. http://religion.info/english/interviews/
article_516.shtml.

Afsaruddin, Asma. 2012. "Revivalism and Reform." University of
Notre Dame OpenCourseWare. http://ocw.nd.edu/arabic-
and-middle-east-studies/islamic-societies-of-the-middle-
east-and-north-africa-religion-history-and-culture/
lectures/lecture-9.

Allawi, Ali A. 2009. *The Crisis of Islamic Civilization*. New Haven,
CT: Yale University Press.

American Israeli Cooperative Enterprise (AICE). 2008. "Revisionists,
Zionist." In *Jewish Virtual Library*. http://www.jewishvirtual-
library.org/jsource/judaica/ejud_0002_0017_0_16687.html.

———. 2010a. "The Pittsburgh Platform." In *Jewish Virtual Library*.
http://www.jewishvirtuallibrary.org/jsource/Judaism/pitts
burgh_program.html.

———. 2010b. "Reconstructionism." In *Jewish Virtual Library*.
http://www.jewishvirtuallibrary.org/jsource/judaica/
ejud_0002_0017_0_16541.html.

Amnesty International. 2000. "China: The Crackdown on Falun
Gong and Other So-Called 'Heretical Organizations.'"
http://www.amnesty.org/en/library/info/ASA17/011/2000.

Batstone, David B. 1997. *Liberation Theologies, Postmodernity,
and the Americas*. London: Routledge.

Beckford, James. 2004. "New Religious Movements and
Globalization." In *New Religious Movements in the 21st
Century: Legal, Political, and Social Challenges*, edited by
Phillip Charles Lucas and Thomas Robbins, 253–264. New
York: Routledge.

Beyer, Peter. 1994. *Religion and Globalization*. London: Sage.

———. 2010. "Religion Out of Place?" In *The Routledge
International Handbook of Globalization Studies*, edited
by Bryan S. Turner, 269–286. New York: Routledge.

Boli, John, and David V. Brewington. 2007. "Religious Organizations."
In *Religion, Globalization, and Culture*, edited by Peter Beyer
and Lori Beaman, 203–231. Leiden, the Netherlands: Brill.

Bunson, Matthew. 2011. "Where in the World Are Today's
Catholics." *OSV Newsletter* http://www.osv.com/
DesktopModules/EngagePublish/printerfriendly.aspx?itemI
d=5709&PortalId=0&TabId=7621.

Cadge, Wendy, and Courtney Bender. 2004. "Yoga and Rebirth in
America: Asian Religions Are Here to Stay." *Contexts* 3 (1):
45–51.

Carpenter, Robert T. 2004. "The Mainstreaming of Alternative
Spirituality in Brazil's Religious Marketplace." In *New
Religious Movements in the 21st Century: Legal, Political
and Social Challenges in Global Perspective*, edited by Phillip
Charles Lucas and Thomas Robbins, 173–186. New York:
Routledge.

Center for the Study of Global Christianity. 2012. *Status of
Global Mission*. South Hamilton, MA: Gordon-Conwell
Theological Seminary. http://www.gordonconwell.edu/
resources/documents/StatusOfGlobalMission.pdf.

Congressional Executive Commission on China. 2012. *Congressional Executive Commission on China Annual Report
2012*. Washington, DC: U.S. Congress. http://www.gpo.
gov/fdsys/pkg/CHRG-112shrg76190/pdf/CHRG-
112shrg76190.pdf.

Council for a Parliament of the World's Religions. 2013. "Our
History." Chicago: Council for a Parliament of the World's
Religions. http://www.parliamentofreligions.org/index.
cfm?n=1&sn=4.

Crane, Lauren Shapiro, Jessica L. Bruce, Ptamonie Y. Salmon, R.
Tony Eich, and Erika N. Brandewie. 2012. "Blending
Buddhism, Shinto, and the Secular: Japanese
Conceptualizations of the Divine." *Journal of Ethnographic
and Qualitative Research* 6 (2): 76–89.

Crumley, Bruce. 2009. "Scientology Trial in France: Can a
Religion Be Banned?" *Time World*, May 28. http://www
.time.com/time/world/article/0,8599,1901373,00.html.

"Falun Gong." 2007. http://www.adherents.com/Na/Na_285.html#1563.

Forte, Jung Ran. 2010. "Black Gods, White Bodies: Westerners' Initiations to Vodun in Contemporary Benin." *Transforming Anthropology* 18 (2): 129–145.

Galanter, Mark. 1989. *Cults and New Religious Movements: A Report of the American Psychiatric Association.* Washington, DC: Committee on Psychiatry and Religion of the American Psychiatric Association.

Hertzke, Allen D. 2009. "The Catholic Church and Catholicism in Global Politics." In *Routledge Handbook of Religion and Politics*, edited by Jeffrey Haynes, 48–63. London: Routledge.

Higgins, Bill. 2000. "S. N. Goenka Adresses Peace Summit." Reproduced from *Belief Net* on *Vipassana Meditation.* http://www.dhamma.org/en/goenka.shtml.

Huntington, Samuel. 1993. "If Not Civilizations, What? Paradigms of the Post-Cold War World." *Foreign Affairs* 72 (5): 186–194.

Inoue, Nobutaka. 2007. "Globalization and Religion: The Cases of Japan and Korea." In *Religion, Globalization, and Culture*, edited by Peter Beyer and Lori Beaman, 453–472. Leiden, the Netherlands: Brill.

Introvigne, Massimo. 2008. "Something Peculiar About France: Anti-Cult Campaigns in Western Europe and French Exceptionalism." In *The Oxford Handbook of New Religious Movements*, edited by James R. Lewis, 206–220. Oxford: Oxford University Press.

Jacobs, Andrew. 2009. "China Still Presses Crusade Against Falun Gong." *New York Times*, April 28, A4.

Johnson, Sylvester A. 2010. "The Rise of Black Ethnics: The Ethnic Turn of African American Religions, 1916–1945." *Religion and American Culture: A Journal of Interpretation* 20 (2): 125–163.

Johnson, Toni, and Lauren Vriens. 2010. "Islam: Governing Under Shari'a." In *Campaign 2012.* New York and Washington: Council on Foreign Relations. http://www.cfr.org/religion/islam-governing-under-sharia/p8034.

Kenney, Jeffrey T. 2006. *Muslim Rebels: Kharijites and the Politics of Extremism in Egypt.* Oxford: Oxford University Press.

Krieger, Hilary. 2010. "In Chicago, A Host of Sacred Places." *Washington Post*, August 20. http://www.washingtonpost.com/wp-dyn/content/article/2010/08/20/AR2010082003978.html?wprss=rss_religion.

Kurzman, Charles. 2011. "Islamic Reform—Bibliography." In *Science Encyclopedia.* http://science.jrank.org/pages/8030/Islamic-Reform.html.

Lehrer, Warren, and Judith Sloan. 2003. *Crossing the Blvd.* New York: W.W. Norton.

Levin, Steve. 2006. "Mainline Denominations Losing Impact on Nation." *The Pittsburgh Post-Gazette*, July 17. http://www.post-gazette.com/pg/06198/706415-84.stm#ixzz1TplCJV3B.

Lowe, Scott. 2004. "Religion on a Leash: NRMs and the Limits of Chinese Freedom." In *New Religious Movements in the 21st Century: Legal, Political, and Social Challenges*, edited by Phillip Charles Lucas and Thomas Robbins, 179–190. New York: Routledge.

Lum, Thomas. 2006. "China and Falun Gong." CRS Report for Congress, RL 33437. Washington, DC: Congressional Research Service. http://fpc.state.gov/documents/organization/67820.pdf.

McDonald, Kevin. 2006. *Global Movements.* Malden, MA: Blackwell.

McLoughlin, William G. 1978. *Revivals, Awakenings, and Reform.* Chicago: University of Chicago Press.

New Age Wholesaler. 2012. "The Wiccan Business Kit CD 2012 Edition." http://www.newagereseller.com/wiccan-business-kit.html.

O'Leary, Don. 2007. *Roman Catholicism and Modern Science: A History.* New York: Continuum.

PBS. 2004. "The Jesus Factor." On *Frontline*, April 29. Washington, DC: Public Broadcasting Service. http://www.pbs.org/wgbh/pages/frontline/shows/jesus.

Peterse, Marie Juul. 2010. "International Religious NGOs at the United Nations: A Study of a Group of Religious Organizations." *Journal of Humanitarian Assistance*, November 17. http://sites.tufts.edu/jha/archives/847.

Pew Research Center. 2005. "Believing Without Belonging: Just How Secular Is Europe?" [Event transcript]. Washington, DC: The Pew Forum on Religion and Public Life. http://pewforum.org/Politics-and-Elections/Believing-Without-Belonging-Just-How-Secular-Is-Europe.aspx.

———. 2006a. "Many Americans Uneasy With Mix of Religion and Politics" Press release, August 24. Washington, DC: The Pew Forum on Religion and Public Life. http://people-press.org/reports/pdf/287.pdf.

———. 2006b. "Overview: Pentecostalism in Africa." Washington, DC: Pew Forum on Religion and Public Life. http://www.pewforum.org/Christian/Evangelical-Protestant-Churches/Overview-Pentecostalism-in-Africa.aspx.

———. 2006c. "Overview: Pentecostalism in Asia." Washington, DC: The Pew Forum on Religion and Public Life. http://www.pewforum.org/Christian/Evangelical-Protestant-Churches/Overview-Pentecostalism-in-Asia.aspx.

———. 2006d. "Overview: Pentecostalism in Latin America." Washington, DC: The Pew Forum on Religion and Public Life. http://pewforum.org/Christian/Evangelical-Protestant-Churches/Overview-Pentecostalism-in-Latin-America.aspx.

———. 2007. US Religious Landscape Survey: Summary of Key Findings. Washington D.C.: The Pew Forum on Religion and Public Life. http://religions.pewforum.org/pdf/report2religious-landscape-study-key-findings.pdf.

———. 2009. "Global Restrictions on Religion." [Event transcript]. December 17. Washington DC: The Pew Forum on Religion and Public Life. http://pewforum.org/Government/Global-Restrictions-on-Religion-Roundtable-Event.aspx.

———. 2011a. "Global Christianity: A Report on the Size and Distribution of the World's Christian Population." Washington, DC: The Pew Forum on Religion and Family Life. http://www.pewforum.org/Christian/Global-Christianity-exec.aspx.

———. 2011b. "Global Survey of Evangelical Leaders." Washington, DC: The Pew Forum on Religion and Public Life. http://www.pewforum.org/uploadedFiles/Topics/Religious_Affiliation/Christian/Evangelical_Protestant_Churches/Global%20Survey%20of%20Evan.%20Prot.%20Leaders.pdf.

Pye, Michael. 2010. "New Religions in East Asia." In *The Oxford Handbook of New Religious Movements*, edited by James R. Lewis, 491–513. Oxford: Oxford University Press.

Quinley, Harold E. 1974. *The Prophetic Clergy*. New York, CA: John Wiley and Sons.

Reader, Ian. 2004. "Consensus Shattered." In *New Religious Movements in the 21st Century: Legal, Political, and Social Challenges*, edited by Phillip Charles Lucas and Thomas Robbins, 191–202. London: Routledge.

Robertson, Roland. 1992. *Globalization: Social Theory and Global Culture*. London: Sage.

Robinson, B. A. 2006. "New Age Spirituality." Ontario Consultants on Religious Tolerance, Ontario, Canada. http://www.religioustolerance.org/newage.htm.

Schmidt, Leigh Eric. 2005. *Restless Souls: The Making of American Spirituality*. San Francisco: Harper One.

Sumimoto, Tokihisa. 2000. "Religious Freedom Problems in Japan: Background and Current Prospects." *The International Journal of Peace Studies* 5 (2). http://www.gmu.edu/programs/icar/ijps/vol5_2/sumimoto.htm.

U.S. Department of State. 2010. "China." In *2010 Report on International Religious Freedom*. Washington, DC: United States Department of State. http://www.state.gov/g/drl/rls/irf/2010/index.htm.

"Vodoun." 2007. http://www.adherents.com/Na/Na_661.html#4165.

Wuthnow, Robert, and Wendy Cadge. 2004. "Buddhists and Buddhism in the United States: The Scope of Influence." *Journal for the Scientific Study of Religion* 43 (3): 363–380.

Young, Sherilynn. 1977. "Fertility and Famine: Women's Agricultural History in Southern Mozambique." *In Roots of Rural Poverty in Central and Southern Africa: Volume 1*, edited by Robin H. Palmer and Neil Parsons, 66–81. Berkeley: University of California Press.

Chapter 12

Acumen Fund. n.d. "Investment Discipline." http://www.acumenfund.org/investments/investment-discipline.html.

Adams, Mark. 2009. "Base of the Pyramid Innovations Offer Growth Opportunities for Business and Communities." World Economic Forum. http://www.weforum.org/en/media/Latest%20Press%20Releases/PR_BSSFP.

Adamson, Fiona B. 2006. "Crossing Borders: International Migration and National Security." *International Security* 31 (1): 165–199.

Bales, Kevin. 2002. *Disposable People: New Slavery in the Global Economy*. Berkeley: University of California Press.

Blair, Dennis C. 2010. *Annual Threat Assessment of the US Intelligence Community for the Senate Select Committee on Intelligence*. Washington, DC: Office of the Director of National Intelligence. http://www.au.af.mil/au/awc/awcgate/dni/threat_assessment_2feb10.pdf.

Bianchi, Stefania (moderator). 2009. "Opportunity for Growth: Low-Cost Housing" [Summary]. World Economic Forum, Dead Sea, Jordan, May 15. https://members.weforum.org/pdf/Middle_East/2009/summaries/15_May_low_cost_housing.pdf.

"Brazil's Foreign-Aid Programme: Speak Softly and Carry a Blank Cheque." 2010. *Economist*, July 15. http://www.economist.com/node/16592455.

Capgemini and Merrill Lynch. 2008. "Capgemini and Merrill Lynch Release 12th Annual World Wealth Report." http://www.capgemini.com/m/en/n/pdf_Merrill_Lynch_and_Capgemini_Release_12th_Annual_World_Wealth_Report.pdf.

Chronic Poverty Research Center. n.d. *The Chronic Poverty Report 2008–2009: Escaping Poverty Traps*. Manchester, UK: The Chronic Poverty Research Center.

Clifton, Jim. 2007. "Global Migration and Problems of Job Creation." White Paper, Gallup World Poll, Washington, DC.

Congressional Budget Office (CBO). 1997. *The Role of Foreign Aid in Development*. Washington, DC: U.S. Congress, Congressional Budget Office. http://www.cbo.gov/sites/default/files/cbofiles/ftpdocs/0xx/doc8/foraid.pdf.

Corrales, Javier. 2009. "Venezuela Petro-Politics and the Promotion of Disorder." In *Undermining Democracy: 21st Century Authoritarians*, 65–80. Freedom House, Radio Free Europe/Radio Liberty and Radio Free Asia. http://www.freedomhouse.org/sites/default/files/inline_images/Undermining%20Democracy.pdf.

Couldrey, Marion, and Maurice Herson. 2008. "Achievements, Challenges and Recommendations: Summary of the Outcomes of the GP10 Conference." In *Ten Years of the Guiding Principles on Internal Displacement*, edited by Marion Couldrey and Maurice Herson. Special issue, *Forced Migration Review*, December: 6–8.

Davies, James B., Susanna Sandström, Anthony Shorrocks, and Edward N. Wolff. 2008. "The World Distribution of Household Wealth." Discussion Paper No. 2008/03, United Nations University, World Institute for Development Economics Research, Helsinki, Finland.

Domhoff, G. William. 2013. "Wealth, Income, and Power." Sociology Department, University of California at Santa Cruz. http://sociology.ucsc.edu/whorulesamerica/power/wealth.html.

Food and Agricultural Organization of the United Nations (FAO). 2008. State of Food Insecurity in the World: High Food Prices and Food Security—Threats and Opportunities. Rome: FAO. ftp://ftp.fao.org/docrep/fao/011/i0291e/i0291e00.pdf.

———. 2010. State of Food Insecurity in the World: Addressing Food Insecurity in Protracted Crises. Rome: FAO. http://www.fao.org/docrep/013/i1683e/i1683e.pdf.

———. 2012. State of Food Insecurity in the World: Economic Growth Is Necessary but Not Sufficient to Accelerate Reduction of Hunger and Malnutrition. Rome: FAO. http://www.fao.org/docrep/016/i3027e/i3027e.pdf.

Frank, Robert. 2007. "The Wealth Report: Rich-O-Meter 2.0." *Wall Street Journal Blogs*, February 1. http://blogs.wsj.com/wealth/2007/02/01/rich-o-meter-20.

Gibson, Campbell, and Emily Lennon. 1999. "Historical Census Statistics on the Foreign-Born Population of the United States: 1850–1990." Population Division Working Paper No. 29. U.S. Bureau of the Census, Washington, DC. http://www.census.gov/population/www/documentation/twps0029/twps0029.html.

Grameen Bank. 2011. "Grameen Bank at a Glance." http://www.grameen-info.org/index.php?option=com_content&task=view&id=26&Itemid=175.

International Displacement Monitoring Center (IDMC). 2010a. *Internal Displacement: Global Overview of*

Trends and Developments in 2009. Geneva, Switzerland: IDMC.

———. 2010b. "Southern Sudan: Overcoming Obstacles to Durable Solutions Now—Building Stability for the Future." IDMC Briefing Paper, August. http://www.internal-displacement.org/8025708F004CE90B/(httpDocuments)/B2779194 AE4ED824C1257791004EEA8B/$file/Sudan-Southern_Aug2010.pdf.

Jun, Laing. 2010. "China Granted Foreign Aid to 120 Countries in 60 Years." *People's Daily*, August 12. http://english.people daily.com.cn/90001/90776/90883/7102941.html.

Kay, Joe. 2006. "Report Documents Extreme Levels of Global Wealth Inequality." *World Socialist Website*, December 8. http://www.wsws.org/articles/2006/dec2006/ineq-d08.shtml.

Keating, Giles, Michael O'Sullivan, Anthony Shorrocks, James B. Davies, Rodrigo Lluberas, and Antonios Koutsoukis. 2012. *The Global Wealth Report 2012.* Zurich, Switzerland: Credit Suisse Research Institute.

Khondker, Habibul. 2010. "Globalization, Disasters and Disaster Response." In *The Routledge International Handbook of Globalization Studies*, edited by Bryan S. Turner, 227–244. New York: Routledge.

Kristof, Nicholas D. 2009. "At Stake Are More Than Banks." *New York Times*, April 2, A27.

Límon, Lavinia. 2008. "The Race to the Bottom." In *World Refugee Survey 2008.* Arlington VA: United States Committee on Refugees and Immigrants (USCRI). http://www.refugees.org/article.aspx?id=2114&subm=19&ssm=29&area=About%20Refugees.

Lum, Thomas, Hannah Fisher, Julissa Gomez-Granger, and Anne Leland. 2009. "China's Foreign Aid Activities in Africa, Latin America, and Southeast Asia." CRS Report for Congress, R40361. Washington, DC: Congressional Research Service. http://www.fas.org/sgp/crs/row/R40361.pdf.

MacFarlane, Neil S. 2000. "Preface." In *The Landmine Ban: A Case in Humanitarian Advocacy*, by Don Hubert, ix–xv. Occasional Paper 42. The Thomas J. Watson Institute, Brown University, Providence, RI. http://www.watsoninstitute.org/pub/op42.pdf.

Manor, James. 2007. Aid That Works: Successful Development in Fragile States. Washington, DC: World Bank.

McHattie, Sara. 2008. "Guiding Principle 27 and Philippine Typhoon Response." In *Forced Migration Review Special Issue: Ten Years of the Guiding Principles on Internal Displacement*, edited by Marion Couldrey and Maurice Herson, 30. http://fmreview.nonuniv.ox.ac.uk/FMRpdfs/GP10/GP10.pdf.

Milanovic, Branko. 2006. "Global Income Inequality: What It Is and Why It Matters?" UN/DESA Working Paper No. 26. http://www.un.org/esa/desa/papers/2006/wp26_2006.pdf.

Mousseau, Frederic. 2010. *The High Food Price Challenge: A Review of Responses to Combat Hunger.* Oakland, CA: The Oakland Institute. http://www.scribd.com/doc/47960521/The-High-Food-Price-Challenge.

Mutume, Gumisai. 2003. "Reversing Africa's 'Brain Drain'." *Africa Recovery* 17 (2): 1.

Novella African Initiative (NAI). 2011. "The Supply Chain." http://www.allanblackia.info/?q=node/17.

Novogratz, Jacqueline. 2007. "Jacqueline Novogratz on Patient Capitalism." *TEDGlobal 2007.* http://www.ted.com/talks/jacqueline_novogratz_on_patient_capitalism.html.

Ratha, Dilip, and Sanket Mohapatra. 2007. Increasing the Macroeconomic Impact of Remittances on Development. Washington, DC: Development Prospects Group/The World Bank. http://siteresources.worldbank.org/INTPROSPECTS/Resources/334934-1110315015165/Increasing_the_Macro_Impact_of_Remittances_on_Development.pdf.

Reality of Aid Network (RoA). 2010. *Aid Development and Effectiveness: Towards Human Rights, Social Justice and Democracy.* Quezon City, Philippines: Reality of Aid Network. http://www.realityofaid.org/roa-reports/index/secid/375/Aid-and-Development-Effectiveness-Towards-Human-Rights-Social-Justice-and-Democracy.

Shah, Anup. 2013. "Foreign Aid for Development Assistance." *Global Issues*, April 8. http://www.globalissues.org/article/35/foreign-aid-development-assistance.

Tenet, George. 1997. "Current and Projected National Security Threats: Statement by Acting Director of Central Intelligence George J. Tenet Before the Senate Select Committee on Intelligence Hearing on Current And Projected National Security Threats to the United States." February 5, CIA, Washington, DC. https://www.cia.gov/news-information/speeches-testimony/1997/dci_testimony_020597.html.

Thailand Burma Border Consortium (TBBC). 2008. *Internal Displacement and International Law in Burma.* Bangkok: Thailand Burma Border Consortium. http://www.tbbc.org/idps/report-2008-idp-english.pdf.

United Nations. 2008. *Millennial Development Goals Report: 2008.* New York: United Nations. http://www.un.org/millenniumgoals/2008highlevel/pdf/news room/mdg%20reports/MDG_Report_2008_ENGLISH.pdf.

———. 2010a. *The Millennium Development Goals Report: 2010.* New York: United Nations. http://www.un.org/millenniumgoals/pdf/MDG%20Report%202010%20En%20r15%20-low%20res%2020100615%20-.pdf.

———. 2010b. *United Nations Global Compact Annual Review—Anniversary Edition June 2010.* New York: United Nations Global Compact Office. http://www.unglobalcompact.org/docs/news_events/8.1/UNGC_Annual_Review_2010.pdf.

UN High Commissioner on Refugees (UNHCR). 2007. *Convention and Protocol Relating to the Status of Refugees.* Geneva, Switzerland: UNHCR Media Relations and Public Information Service. http://www.unhcr.org/3b66c2aa10.html.

———. 2009. *Global Report.* Geneva, Switzerland: UNHCR. http://www.unhcr.org/gr09/index.html.

———. 2011. *Asylum Levels and Trends in Industrialized Countries 2010.* Geneva, Switzerland: UNHCR. http://www.unhcr.org/4d8c5b109.html.

UNICEF. 2004. "Voices of Youth: Child Living in Poverty, Anna's Story." http://www.unicef.org/voy/explore/sowc/explore_1659.html.

———. 2005. *State of the World's Children 2005: Childhood Under Threat.* New York: UNICEF. http://www.unicef.org/sowc05/english/sowc05.pdf.

———. 2006a. "UN Millennium Project Goal: Eradicate Extreme Poverty and Hunger." http://www.unicef.org/mdg/poverty.html.

———. 2006b. "UN Millennium Project Goal: Reduce Child Mortality." http://www.unicef.org/mdg/childmortality.html.

———. 2009. State of World's Children Special Edition: Celebrating 20 Years of the Convention on the Rights of the

Child. New York: United Nations Children Fund. http://www.unicef.org/rightsite/sowc/fullreport.php.

United Nations Population Fund (UNFPA). 2006a. "Gender Equality: From Microfinance to Macro Change: Highlights from the Panel Discussion." http://www.unfpa.org/gender/micro.htm.

———. 2006b. *State of the World Population 2006: A Passage to Hope Women and International Migration*. New York: United Nations. http://www.unfpa.org/upload/lib_pub_file/650_filename_sowp06-en.pdf.

U.S. Agency for International Development (USAID). 2002. *Trafficking in Persons: USAID's Response*. Washington DC: United States Agency for International Development. http://pdf.usaid.gov/pdf_docs/PDACH052.pdf.

———. 2008. "Paris Declaration and Accra Agenda for Action." http://www.oecd.org/dac/aideffectiveness/34428351.pdf

USAID Nigeria. 2009. *Rice Farmers: Making Money, Feeding The Country*. http://transition.usaid.gov/stories/nigeria/ss_nga_rice.html.

U.S. Census Bureau. n.d. "Income, Expenditures, Poverty, & Wealth: Household Income." http://www.census.gov/compendia/statab/cats/income_expenditures_poverty_wealth/household_income.html.

U.S. Committee for Refugees and Immigrants (USCRI). 2008. *World Refugee Survey 2008*. Arlington, VA: USCRI. http://www.refugees.org/article.aspx?id=2114&subm=19&ssm=29&area=About%20Refugees.

U.S. Department of Labor (USDOL). 2009. *2008 Findings of the Worst Forms of Child Labor*. Washington, DC: US Department of Labor's Bureau of International Labor Affairs. http://www.dol.gov/ilab/programs/ocft/PDF/2008OCFTreport.pdf.

U.S. Department of State. 2008. *Trafficking in Persons Report 2008*. Washington, DC: U.S. Department of State. http://www.state.gov/g/tip/rls/tiprpt/2008.

Weston, Jonathan, Caitlin Campbell, and Katherine Koleski. 2011. "China's Foreign Assistance in Review: Implications for the United States." Washington, DC: U.S.–China Economic and Security Review Commission Staff Research Backgrounder. http://www.uscc.gov/researchpapers/2011/9_1_%202011_ChinasForeignAssistanceinReview.pdf.

"Wikileaks and Nicaragua: A Novel Mechanism for Foreign Aid." 2010. *Economist*, December 8. http://www.economist.com/blogs/americasview/2010/12/wikileaks_and_nicaragua.

Woehrel, Steve. 2010. "Bosnia and Herzegovina: Current Issues and US Policy." CRS Report for Congress, R40479. Washington, DC: Congressional Research Service. http://www.fas.org/sgp/crs/row/R40479.pdf.

Wong, Edward. 2012. "An Ethnic War Is Rekindling in Myanmar." *New York Times*, January 20, A1.

World Bank. 2007. *Global Economic Prospects: Managing the Next Wave of Globalization*. Washington, DC: The International Bank for Reconstruction and Development/The World Bank. http://www-wds.worldbank.org/external/default/WDSContentServer/IW3P/IB/2006/12/06/000112742_20061206155022/Rendered/PDF/381400GEP2007.pdf.

———. 2010. *The MDGs After the Crisis* (Global Monitoring Report 2010). Washington, DC: The International Bank for Reconstruction and Development/The World Bank. http://www-wds.worldbank.org/external/default/WDSContentServer/WDSP/IB/2010/05/11/000333037_201005110017 00/Rendered/PDF/544380PUB0EPI01BOX0349416B01PUBLIC1.pdf.

World Economic Forum (WEF). 2009a. "The Next Billions: Unleashing Business Potential in Untapped Markets" [Executive summary]. http://www.weforum.org/pdf/BSSFP/ExecutiveSummaryUnleashingBusinessPotential.pdf.

———. 2009b. *Shaping the Post Crisis World*. Davos-Klosters, Switzerland: World Economic Forum. http://www.weforum.org/en/events/ArchivedEvents/AnnualMeeting2009/index.htm.

World Health Organization (WHO). 2005. *The World Health Report 2005—Make Every Mother and Child Count*. Geneva, Switzerland: World Health Organization. http://www.who.int/whr/2005/en/index.html.

———. 2008. *Worldwide Prevalence of Anaemia 1993–2005*, edited by Bruno de Benoist, Erin McLean, Ines Egli, and Mary Cogswell. Geneva, Switzerland: World Health Organization. http://whqlibdoc.who.int/publications/2008/9789241596657_eng.pdf.

———. 2009. "Global Prevalence of Vitamin A Deficiency in Populations at Risk 1995–2005." *WHO Global Database on Vitamin A Deficiency*. Geneva, Switzerland: World Health Organization.

Chapter 13

Achvarina, Vera, and Simon F. Reich. 2006. "No Place to Hide: Refugees, Displaced Persons, and the Recruitment of Child Soldiers." *International Security* 31 (1): 127–164.

Adamson, Fiona B. 2006. "Crossing Borders: International Migration and National Security." *International Security* 31 (1): 165–199.

Andreas, Peter, and Ethan Nadelmann. 2009. "The Internationalization of Crime Control." In *Crime and the Global Political Economy*, edited by H. Richard Friman, 21–33. Boulder, CO: Lynne Rienner.

Anyimadu, Adjoa. 2013. "Notorious Somali Pirate Quits: Now Is Shipping Safe?" *CNN*, January 11. http://www.cnn.com/2013/01/11/opinion/somalia-pirate-retires.

Associated Press. 2011. "Somali Pirates Threaten to Murder More Hostages After Deaths of Four Americans." *Guardian*, February 23. http://www.guardian.co.uk/world/2011/feb/23/somali-pirates-american-hostages-trial.

Bajoria, Jayshree. 2010. "The China–North Korea Relationship." *Backgrounder*, October 7. Council on Foreign Relations, New York and Washington, DC. http://www.cfr.org/publication/11097/chinanorth_korea_relationship.html.

Beary, Brian. 2008. "Separatist Movements: Should Nations Have a Right to Self-Determination?" *CQ Global Researcher* 2 (4): 85–144.

Blair, Dennis C. 2010. "Annual Threat Assessment of the US Intelligence Community for the Senate Select Committee on Intelligence." Statement for the Record, Office of the Director of National Intelligence, Washington, DC. http://www.isisnucleariran.org/assets/pdf/2010_NIE.pdf.

Buck-Morss, Susan. 2009. "Sovereign Right and the Global Left." In *Democracy States and the Struggle for Global Justice*, edited by Heather Gautney et al., 45–61. New York: Routledge.

Byrne, Malcolm, Peter Kornbluh, and Thomas Blanton. 2006. "The Iran-Contra Affair 20 Years On: Documents Spotlight Role of Reagan, Top Aides." The National Security Archive, Washington, DC. http://www.gwu.edu/~nsarchiv/NSAEBB/NSAEBB210/index.htm.

Chossudovsky, Michel. 2010. "UN 'Green Light' for a Pre-Emptive US-Israel Attack on Iran? Security Council Resolution Transforms Iran Into a 'Sitting Duck.'" *Global Research*, June 11. http://www.globalresearch.ca/index.php?context=va&aid=19670.

Colvin, Christopher J. 2007. "Civil Society and Reconciliation in Southern Africa." *Development in Practice* 17 (3): 322–337.

Congressional Budget Office (CBO). 1997. *The Role of Foreign Aid in Development*. Washington, DC: Congressional Budget Office.

Conversi, Daniele. 2010. "Globalization, Ethnic Conflict, and Nationalism." In *The Routledge International Handbook of Globalization Studies*, edited by Bryan S. Turner, 346–363. New York: Routledge.

Dinan, Stephen. 2008. "Bush Defends Pre-emptive Strike Doctrine." *Washington Times*, December 9. http://www.washingtontimes.com/news/2008/dec/09/bush-defends-pre-emptive-strike-doctrine.

Donovan, Gill. 2002. "Priest Says Man's Crucifixion Was a Sectarian Attack." *National Catholic Reporter* 39 (5): 10. http://www.highbeam.com/doc/1G1-94873012.html.

Ehrenfeld, Daniel. 2004. " Foreign Aid Effectiveness, Political Rights and Bilateral Distribution." *The Journal of Humanitarian Assistance*, February 1. http://sites.tufts.edu/jha/archives/75.

Europol. 2009. *OCTA 2009: EU Organized Crime Threat Assessment*. The Hague, Netherlands: Europol. https://www.europol.europa.eu/sites/default/files/publications/octa2009_0.pdf.

Federal Bureau of Investigation (FBI). 1999. *Terrorism in the United States 1999: 30 Years of Terrorism*. Washington, DC: FBI.

Gettleman, Jeffrey. 2010. "U.N. to Pull 2,000 Peacekeepers From Congo, Draft Resolution." *New York Times*, May 27. http://www.nytimes.com/2010/05/28/world/africa/28congo.html.

Gilpin, Robert. 2002. "A Realist Perspective on International Governance." In *Governing Globalization: Power, Authority and Global Governance*, edited by David Held and Anthony McGrew, 237–248. Cambridge: Polity Press.

Gjelten, Tom. 2010a. "Cyberworm's Origins Unclear, but Potential Is Not." *National Public Radio*, September 27. http://www.npr.org/templates/story/story.php?storyId=130162219.

———. 2010b. "Extending the Law of War to Cyberspace." *National Public Radio*, September 22. http://www.npr.org/templates/story/story.php?storyId=130023318.

Goetz, Anne-Marie, and Rob Jenkins. 2009. "Sexual Violence as a War Tactic—Security Council Resolution 1888: Next Steps." *UN Chronicle*. http://www.un.org/wcm/content/site/chronicle/cache/bypass/home/archive/issues2010/empoweringwomen/sexualviolencewartacticscr1888.

Gupta, Sanjeev, Benedict Clements, Rina Bhattacharya, and Shamit Chakravarti. 2004. "Fiscal Consequences of Armed Conflict and Terrorism in Low- and Middle-Income Countries." *European Journal of Political Economy* 20 (2): 403–421.

Hendren, John. 2005. "Preemptive Strikes Become Policy." *Los Angeles Times*, March 18. http://articles.latimes.com/2005/mar/19/nation/na-defense19.

Interpol. 2010. "Interpol: An Overview Factsheet." http://www.interpol.int/pv_obj_cache/pv_obj_id_EBBBC4A5ADD7EFA75F9222C01F60A40434F80200/filename/GI01.pdf.

Johnson, Glen. 2012. "Libya Weapons Aid Tuareg Rebellion in Mali." *Los Angeles Times*, June 12. http://articles.latimes.com/2012/jun/12/world/la-fg-libya-arms-smuggle-20120612.

Johnson, Tim. 2012. "Mexico: Sharp Fall in Drug Violence Inspires New Optimism." *Christian Science Monitor*, November 6. http://www.csmonitor.com/World/Americas/2012/1106/Mexico-Sharp-fall-in-drug-violence-inspires-new-optimism.

Katongole, Emmanuel M. 2005. "Violence and Christian Social Reconstruction in Africa: On the Resurrection of the Body (Politic)." *The Other Journal* 6. http://theotherjournal.com/2005/08/08/violence-and-christian-social-reconstruction-in-africa-on-the-resurrection-of-the-body-politic.

Keohane, Robert O. 2001. "The Globalization of Informal Violence, Theories of World Politics and 'the Liberalism of Fear.'" Social Science Research Council. http://essays.ssrc.org/sept11/essays/keohane2.htm.

Kuper, Andrew. 2004. "Promoting Democracy Through International Law." Second Report of the Democracy and Law Project, Carnegie Council on Ethics and International Affairs, New York. http://www.carnegiecouncil.org/publications/articles_papers_reports/4423.html/_res/id=sa_File1/4423_Prom_Dem_Thru_Intl_Law.pdf.

LaFree, Gary. 2010. "The Global Terrorism Database: Accomplishments and Challenges." *Perspectives on Terrorism* 4 (1). http://www.terrorismanalysts.com/pt/index.php/pot/article/view/89.

Lewis, James A. 2004. "The Council of Europe Cybercrime Convention Entered Into Force January 2004." Center for Strategic and International Studies. http://csis.org/files/media/csis/pubs/060804_coecybercrime.pdf.

———. 2007. "Commentary: Cyber Attacks Explained." Center for Strategic and International Studies, Washington, DC, June 15. http://csis.org/files/media/csis/pubs/070615_cyber_attacks.pdf.

———. 2010. "The Cyber War Has Not Begun." Center for Strategic and International Studies. http://csis.org/files/publication/100311_TheCyberWarHasNotBegun.pdf.

Manoranjan, S. 2002. "The Making of a Suicide Bomber." Interview with Rohan Gunaratna. *Frontline*. Arlington, VA: Public Broadcasting Service. http://www.pbs.org/frontlineworld/stories/srilanka/feature.html.

Marshall, Monty G. 2005. *Conflict Trends in Africa, 1946–2004: A Macro-Comparative Perspective*. Report prepared for the Africa Conflict Prevention Pool, Government of the United Kingdom. http://www.systemicpeace.org/Conflict Trends in Africa.pdf.

Marshall, Monty G., and Benjamin R. Cole. 2009. *Global Report 2009: Conflict, Governance, and State Fragility*. Center for Systemic Peace and Center for Global Policy, School of Public Policy. http://www.systemicpeace.org/Global%20Report%202009.pdf.

Mayanja, Rachel. 2010. "Armed Conflict and Women: 10 Years of Security Council Resolution 1325." *UN Chronicle*, February

25. http://www.un.org/wcm/content/site/chronicle/cache/bypass/home/archive/issues2010/empoweringwomen/armedconflictandwomenscr1325.

McAfee. 2005. *Virtual Criminology Report: North American Study Into Organized Crime and the Internet.* Santa Clara, CA: McAfee. http://www.softmart.com/mcafee/docs/McAfee%20NA%20Virtual%20Criminology%20Report.pdf.

———. 2009. Virtual *Criminology Report: Virtually Here: The Age of Cyber Warfare.* Santa Clara, CA: McAfee. http://img.en25.com/Web/McAfee/VCR_2009_EN_VIRTUAL_CRIMINOLOGY_RPT_NOREG.pdf.

McCraw, Steven. 2003. "International Drug Trafficking and Terrorism." Testimony before the Senate Judiciary Committee, May 20. http://www.fbi.gov/congress/congress03/mccraw052003.htm.

McKinley, James C., Jr., and Elisabeth Malkin. 2010. "U.S. Student Became Mexican Drug Kingpin." *New York Times,* September 9, A21.

Medford, Larry A. 2003. "Testimony." Before the United States Senate Terrorism, Technology and Homeland Security Subcommittee, June 27, 2003. Washington, DC: Federal Bureau of Investigation. http://www.fbi.gov/news/testimony/the-state-of-the-terrorist-threat-facing-the-united-states.

National Counterterrorism Center (NCTC). 2010. *2009 Report on Terrorism.* Washington, DC: Office of the Director of National Intelligence National Counterterrorism Center.

National Labor Committee. 2003. "Sweatshop Owner Convicted of Human Trafficking." Institute for Global Labour and Human Rights, Pittsburgh, PA. http://www.globallabourrights.org/alerts?id=0112.

———. 2008. "The Toyota You Don't Know: The Race to the Bottom in the Auto Industry." Institute for Global Labour and Human Rights, Pittsburgh, PA. http://www.globallabourrights.org/reports?id=0503.

Nevaer, Louis. 2007. "American Weapons Flood Mexico, Fueling Violence." *New America Media,* July 11. http://news.newamericamedia.org/news/view_article.html?article_id=ae0f349b5a2797fa94e4da7f5022104f.

"One Laptop per Child Reaches Gaza Strip." 2010. *BBC,* April 29. http://news.bbc.co.uk/2/hi/middle_east/8651580.stm.

Organisation for Economic Co-operation and Development (OECD). 2001. *The DAC Guidelines: Helping Prevent Violent Conflict.* Paris: OECD Publications. http://www.oecd.org/dataoecd/15/54/1886146.pdf.

Olsen, Matthew. 2012. "The Evolving Terrorist Threat and the NCTC Mission." Remarks Prepared for Delivery by the Director of the National Counterterrorism Center to the American Bar Association Standing Committee on Law and National Security, May 16, Washington, DC. http://www.nctc.gov/press_room/speeches/20120516_Director_Olsen_ABA_Remarks.pdf.

Pew Research Center. 2010. *Muslim Publics Divided on Hamas and Hezbollah.* Washington, DC: Pew Research Center, Global Attitudes Project. http://www.pewglobal.org/files/2010/12/Pew-Global-Attitudes-Muslim-Report-FINAL-December-2-2010.pdf.

Reynolds, Andrew. 2006. *Electoral Systems and the Protection and Participation of Minorities.* London: Minority Rights Group.

Seay, Laura. 2013. "Mali is not a Stan." *Foreign Policy,* January 30 http://www.foreignpolicy.com/articles/2013/01/30/mali_is_not_afghanistan_france_africa.

Shaw, Martin. 2010. "Genocide in the Global Age." In *The Routledge International Handbook of Globalization Studies,* edited by Bryan S. Turner, 312-327. Abingdon Oxon: Routledge.

Smith, Dan. 1994. "War, Peace and Third World Development." Occasional Paper No. 16, International Peace Research Institute, Oslo. http://hdr.undp.org/docs/publications/ocational_papers/oc16.htm.

Stepanova, Ekaterina. 2010. "Armed Conflict, Crime and Criminal Violence." In *SIPRI Yearbook 2010: Armaments, Disarmament and International Security.* Stockholm: Stockholm International Peace Research Institute. http://www.sipri.org/yearbook/2010/files/SIPRIYB201002.pdf.

Sweet, Alec Stone. 2008. "Constitutions and Judicial Power." In *Comparative Politics,* edited by Daniele Caramani, 217–240. Oxford: Oxford University Press.

Toki, Masako. 2009. "Japan's Evolving Security Policies: Along Came North Korea's Threats." Nuclear Threat Initiative, June 4. http://www.nti.org/e_research/e3_japan_north_korea_threats.html.

"Thousands Flee Ethnic Violence in Kyrgyzstan." 2010. *CNN,* June 14. http://ac360.blogs.cnn.com/2010/06/14/thousands-flee-ethnic-violence-in-kyrgzstan/?iref=allsearch.

"Top FARC Commander Sentenced to 27 Years in Cocaine Conspiracy." 2010. *CNN,* July 22. http://www.cnn.com/2010/CRIME/07/22/farc.cocaine.prison/index.html.

Traub, James. 2010. "Africa's Drug Problem." *New York Times Sunday Magazine,* April 11, MM42.

"UN: North Korea Seeks Immediate Food Aid After Floods." 2012. *BBC,* August 2. http://www.bbc.co.uk/news/world-asia-19107049.

United Nations (UN). 2000. "Security Council Resolution 1325." http://www.un.org/events/res_1325e.pdf.

———. 2004. *United Nations Convention Against Transnational Organized Crime.* Vienna: United Nations Office on Drugs and Crime. http://www.unodc.org/unodc/en/treaties/CTOC.

———. 2008. "Security Council Resolution 1820." http://www.state.gov/documents/organization/106577.pdf.

———. 2009. "Security Council Resolution 1888." http://www.unrol.org/files/N0953446.pdf.

———. 2010. *The Millennium Development Goals Report: 2010.* New York: United Nations. http://www.un.org/millenniumgoals/pdf/MDG%20Report%202010%20En%20r15%20-low%20res%2020100615%20-.pdf.

UN Department of Public Information (UNDPI). 1998. "50 Years of United Nations Peacekeeping 1948–1998." Panel Discussion, June 11, New York.

———. 2011. "United Nations Peace Operations: The Year in Review." New York: UNDPI Peace and Security Section. http://www.un.org/en/peacekeeping/publications/yir/yir2010.pdf.

UN General Assembly. 2006. *United Nations Global Counter-Terrorism Strategy.* New York: United Nations. http://www.un.org/terrorism/strategy-counter-terrorism.shtml.

UN Office on Drugs and Crime (UNODC). 2010. *World Drug Report 2010.* Vienna: UNODC. http://www.unodc.org/documents/wdr/WDR_2010/World_Drug_Report_2010_lo-res.pdf.

UN Security Council. 2010. "Security Council Calls for Strengthened International, Regional Cooperation to Counter Transnational Organized Crime, in Presidential Statement." Press release, February 24. http://www.un.org/News/Press/docs/2010/sc9867.doc.htm.

U.S. Agency for International Development (USAID). 2006. *Trafficking in Persons: USAID Response.* Washington, DC: USAID. http://pdf.usaid.gov/pdf_docs/PDACH052.pdf.

———. 2012. "Latin America and the Caribbean: Peru Overview." Lima, Peru: USAID. http://transition.usaid.gov/locations/latin_america_caribbean/country/peru.

U.S. Department of State. 2010. *Trafficking in Persons Report: 10th Edition.* Washington, DC: U.S. Department of State. http://www.state.gov/documents/organization/142979.pdf.

———. 2011. "Fact Sheet: The United States National Action Plan on Women, Peace, and Security." December 19. http://transition.usaid.gov/our_work/cross-cutting_programs/wid/peace/Fact_Sheet_NAP_peace.pdf.

"Uzbek Leader: 100,000 Flee Kyrgyzstan Violence." 2010. *National Public Radio,* June 14. http://www.npr.org/templates/story/story.php?storyId=127826482.

Wagley, John R. 2006. "Transnational Organized Crime: Principle Threats and US Responses." CRS Report for Congress, RL33335. Washington, DC: Congressional Research Service. http://www.fas.org/sgp/crs/natsec/RL33335.pdf.

Welsh, Steven C. 2003. "Preemptive War and International Law." International Security Law Project, Center for Defense Information. http://www.cdi.org/news/law/preemptive-war.cfm.

"West Africa Drugs Trafficking 'Increasingly Sophisticated.'" 2011. *BBC,* June 21. http://www.bbc.co.uk/news/world-africa-13852399.

White, Jeffrey B. 2008. "Some Thoughts on Irregular Warfare." CIA Center for the Study of Intelligence. https://www.cia.gov/library/center-for-the-study-of-intelligence/csi-publications/csi-studies/studies/96unclass/iregular.htm.

Wines, Michael, and Doyle McManus. 1986. "US Sent Iran Arms for Hostage Releases; Weapons Were Supplied for Aid in Freeing 3 in Lebanon, Government Sources Say." *Los Angeles Times,* November 6. http://articles.latimes.com/1986-11-06/news/mn-16560_1_iran-several-times.

Chapter 14

Allen, Patricia, and Alice Brooke Wilson. 2008. "Agrifood Inequalities: Globalization and Localization." *Development* 51 (4): 534–540.

Alliance for a Green Revolution in Africa (AGRA). 2010. *AGRA in 2010: Driving Real Change.* Nairobi, Kenya: AGRA. http://www.agra-alliance.org/AGRA/en/our-results/annual-reports.

Annan, Kofi A. 2008. "Forging a Uniquely African Green Revolution." Address at Salzburg Global Seminars, Austria, April 30. http://www.future-agricultures.org/pdf%20files/Salzburg_KA_speech_final.pdf.

Barclay, Eliza. 2012. "A Nation of Meat Eaters: See How It All Adds Up." *National Public Radio,* June 27. http://www.npr.org/blogs/thesalt/2012/06/27/155527365/visualizing-a-nation-of-meat-eaters.

Beck, Ulrich. 1992. *Risk Society.* London: Sage.

Blair, Dennis C. 2010. "Annual Threat Assessment of the US Intelligence Community for the Senate Select Committee on Intelligence." Washington, DC: Office of the Director of National Intelligence. http://www.dni.gov/testimonies/20100202_testimony.pdf.

Bomford, Andrew. 2006. "Slow Death of Africa's Lake Chad." *BBC,* April 14. http://news.bbc.co.uk/2/hi/4906692.stm.

Bornstein, Daniel. 2012. "Technological Fixes to Food Insecurity Lose Sight of Farmers' Rights." *Dartmouth Business Journal,* June 8. http://dartmouthbusinessjournal.com/2012/06/technological-fixes-to-food-insecurity-lose-sight-of-farmers-rights.

Brandon, Josh. 2008. "The Green Revolution Revisited." *Canadian Dimension* 42 (4): 25–27.

Bruckner, Monica. 2008. "The Gulf of Mexico Dead Zone." *Microbial Life.* http://serc.carleton.edu/microbelife/topics/deadzone.

Buttel, Fredrick H. 1995. "Twentieth Century Agricultural-Environmental Transitions: A Preliminary Analysis." *Research in Rural Sociology and Development* 6: 1–21.

Cotter, Joseph. 2003. *Troubled Harvest: Agronomy and Revolution in Mexico, 1880–2002.* Westport, CT: Praeger.

Daniel, Shepard, and Anuradha Mittal. 2010. *Mis(Investment) in Agriculture: The Role of the International Finance Corporation in Global Land Grabs.* Oakland, CA: The Oakland Institute. http://media.oaklandinstitute.org/node/2622.

Dimitri, Carolyn, Anne Effland, and Neilson Conklin. June 2005. "The 20th Century Transformation of U.S. Agriculture and Farm Policy." Economic Information Bulletin 3, U.S. Department of Agriculture, Economic Research Service. http://ageconsearch.umn.edu/bitstream/59390/2/eib3.pdf.

"Environmental Horticulture." 2011. Clemson University, School of Agricultural, Forest, and Environmental Sciences, Clemson, SC. http://www.clemson.edu/cafls/departments/horticulture/index.html.

Fischetti, Mark. 2012. "How Much Water Do Nations Consume?" *Scientific American,* May 21. http://www.scientificamerican.com/article.cfm?id=graphic-science-how-much-water-nations-consume.

Gibson, Nigel C. 2004. "Africa and Globalization: Marginalization and Resistance." *Journal of Asian and African Studies* 39 (1–2): 1–28.

GMO Compass. 2006. "Genetic Engineering, Plants, and Food: The European Regulatory System." http://www.gmo-compass.org/eng/regulation/regulatory_process/156.european_regulatory_system_genetic_engineering.html.

———. 2007. "GMO Labeling: Labelled Goods Hard to Find." http://www.gmo-compass.org/eng/regulation/labelling/92.gmo_labelling_labelled_goods.html/.

Gurdak, Jason. 2010a. "The High Plains Aquifer: Part One." *Prairie Fire,* May. http://www.prairiefirenewspaper.com/2010/05/the-high-plains-aquifer-part-one.

———. 2010b. "The High Plains Aquifer: Part Two." *Prairie Fire,* June. http://www.prairiefirenewspaper.com/2010/06/the-high-plains-aquifer-part-two.

Hartley, Bonney. 2008. "MDG Reports and Indigenous Peoples: A Desk Review." No. 3, February. Prepared for the Secretariat of the UN Permanent Forum on Indigenous Issues. http://www.un.org/esa/socdev/unpfii/documents/MDG_Reports_and_IPs_2008.pdf.

Helldén, Ulf, and Christian Tottrup. 2008. "Regional Desertification: A Global Synthesis." *Global and Planetary Change* 64 (3–4): 169–176.

Intergovernmental Panel on Climate Change (IPCC). 2007. *Climate Change 2007: Synthesis Report.* Contribution of Working Groups I, II and III to the Fourth Assessment Report of the Intergovernmental Panel on Climate Change. Geneva, Switzerland: IPCC. http://www.ipcc.ch/pdf/assessment-report/ar4/syr/ar4_syr.pdf.

International Fund for Agricultural Development (IFAD). 2002. *Desertification: A Global Issue.* Rome: International Fund for Agricultural Development. http://www.ifad.org/events/wssd/gef/GEF_eng.pdf.

Kratoska, Paul H. 2008. "Commercial Rice Cultivation and the Regional Economy of Southeast Asia: 1850–1950." In *Food and Globalization: Consumption Markets and Politics in the Modern World,* edited by Alexander Nützenadel and Frank Trentmann, 75–92. Oxford: Berg.

Macan-Markar, Marwaan. 2010. "Green Revolution Has Little to Offer New Hungry Mouths." *Inter Press Service Agency,* June 5. http://ipsnews.net/news.asp?idnews=51729.

Mousseau, Frederic. 2010. *The High Food Price Challenge: A Review of Responses to Combat Hunger.* Oakland, CA: The Oakland Institute. http://www.scribd.com/doc/47960521/The-High-Food-Price-Challenge.

Nützenadel, Alexander. 2008. "A Green International? Food Markets and Transnational Politics c. 1850–1914." In *Food and Globalization: Consumption Markets and Politics in the Modern World,* edited by Alexander Nützenadel and Frank Trentmann, 153–172. Oxford: Berg.

Nützenadel, Alexander, and Frank Trentmann. 2008. "Introduction: Mapping Food and Globalization." In *Food and Globalization: Consumption Markets and Politics in the Modern World,* edited by Alexander Nützenadel and Frank Trentmann, 1–20. Oxford: Berg.

Pande, Rekha. 2007. "Gender, Poverty and Globalization in India." *Development* 50 (2): 134–140.

Picard, Joseph. 2010. "Small Farms Get Small Help Compared to Subsidies to Big Business." *International Business Times,* June 4. http://www.ibtimes.com/articles/26961/20100604/farming.htm.

Ramesh, Randeep. 2009. "India Moves to Protect Traditional Medicines From Foreign Patents." *Guardian,* February 22. http://www.guardian.co.uk/world/2009/feb/22/india-protect-traditional-medicines.

Real-Cabello, Gaspar. 2003. "The Mexican State and the Agribusiness Model of Development in the Globalisation Era." *Australian Journal of Social Issues* 38 (1): 129–139.

Robbins, Jim. 2012. "News Analysis; Man-Made Epidemics." *New York Times Sunday Review,* July 15, P1.

Robbins, John. 2001. *The Food Revolution: How Your Diet Can Help Save Your Life and Our World.* San Francisco, CA: Conari Press.

Rome Partnership for Disaster Risk Management (RPDRM). n.d. *Disaster Risk Management in Food and Agriculture* [Brochure]. Rome, Italy: Food and Agricultural Organization, World Food Programme and International Fund for Agricultural Development of the United Nations. http://home.wfp.org/stellent/groups/public/documents/communications/wfp201794.pdf.

Rosenthal. Sharon. 2011. "Rush to Use Crops as Fuel Raises Food Prices and Hunger Fears." *New York Times,* April 7, A1.

Schalatek, Linda (Moderator). 2008. "The Global Food Crisis: Sustainable Agriculture Policy Alternatives." Carnegie Endowment for International Peace Panel. Transcript by Federal News Service, Washington, DC.

UN Development Programme. 2001. "UNDP and Indigenous Peoples: A Practice Note on Engagement." http://www.undp.org/content/dam/aplaws/publication/en/publications/poverty-reduction/poverty-website/undp-and-indigenous-peoples/UNDP%20and%20Indigenous%20People.pdf.

UN Environmental Programme (UNEP). n.d. *Terrestrial Ecosystems.* Nairobi, Kenya: UNEP. http://www.unep.org/ecosystemmanagement/UNEPsWork/TerrestrialEcosystems/tabid/436/Default.aspx.

———. 2008. *Vital Water Graphics.* Nairobi, Kenya: UNEP. http://www.unep.org/dewa/vitalwater/index.html.

UN News Centre. 2010. "New UN Report Calls for 'Green Revolution' by Africa's Small Farmers." http://www.un.org/apps/news/story.asp?NewsID=34751.

UN Population Fund (UNFPA). 2009. *State of the World's Population. Facing a Changing World: Women, Population, and Climate.* New York: UNFPA. http://www.unfpa.org/swp/2009/en/pdf/EN_SOWP09.pdf.

U.S. Agency for International Development (USAID). 2009. "USAID Launches Emerging Pandemic Threats Program." Press release, October 21. http://www1.usaid.gov/press/releases/2009/pr091021_1.html.

U.S. Water News Online. 2006. "World's Largest Aquifer Going Dry." http://www.uswaternews.com/archives/arcsupply/6worllarg2.html.

Weinberger, Katinka, and Thomas A. Lumpkin. 2005. *Horticulture for Poverty Alleviation: The Unfunded Revolution.* Taiwan: AVRDC–The World Vegetable Center. http://www.zef.de/module/register/media/b099_weinberger_lumpkin_2005.pdf.

Weissman, Michaele. 2008. "A Coffee Connoisseur on a Mission: Buy High and Sell High." In *Contemporary Readings in Globalization,* edited by Scott Sernau, 23–25. Thousand Oaks, CA: Pine Forge Press.

Wijaya, Sidarta. 2008. "Through the Eyes of Researcher: 'Miracle Rice' Unwittingly Destroys Bali's Coral Reefs." May 14. http://blog.baliwww.com/environment-nature/1421.

Wilcox, Bruce A., and Brett Ellis. 2006. "Forests and Emerging Infectious Diseases of Humans." *Unasylva* 224. http://www.fao.org/docrep/009/a0789e/a0789e00.htm.

Winders, William. 2009. *The Politics of Food Supply: U.S. Agricultural Policy in the World Economy.* New Haven, CT: Yale University Press.

Wise, Timothy A. 2010. "The True Cost of Cheap Food." *Resurgence and Ecologist* 259 (March–April). http://www.resurgence.org/magazine/article3035-the-true-cost-of-cheap-food.html.

Woolhouse, Mark E. J., and Sonia Gowtage-Sequeria. 2005. "Host Range and Emerging and Reemerging Pathogens." *Emerging Infectious Diseases* 11 (12): 1842–1847. http://wwwnc.cdc.gov/eid/article/11/12/pdfs/05-0997.pdf.

World Bank. 2007. *World Development Report 2008: Agriculture for Development.* Washington, DC: The World Bank Group. http://web.worldbank.org/WBSITE/

EXTERNAL/EXTDEC/EXTRESEARCH/EXTWDRS/0,,c
ontentMDK:23092267~pagePK:478093~piPK:477627~th
eSitePK:477624,00.html.

———. 2010a. "Food Price Watch." Poverty Reduction and
Equity Group. Poverty Reduction and Equity Management
(PREM) Network, the World Bank, Washington, DC. http://
siteresources.worldbank.org/INTPOVERTY/Resources/
335642-1210859591030/FINAL_Food_Price_Watch_
Feb2010.pdf.

———. 2010b. *World Development Report 2010: Development
and Climate Change*. Washington, DC: The World Bank.
http://web.worldbank.org/WBSITE/EXTERNAL/
EXTDEC/EXTRESEARCH/EXTWDRS/0,,contentMDK:2
3062354~pagePK:478093~piPK:477627~theSit
ePK:477624,00.html.

"The World Food Crisis." 2010. *New York Times*, April 8. http://
www.nytimes.com/2008/04/10/opinion/10thu1.html.

World Food Programme (WFP). 2009. "Number of World's
Hungry Tops a Billion." June 19. http://www.wfp.org/stories/
number-world-hungry-tops-billion.

———. 2012. "Our Work: P4P Overview." http://www.wfp.org/
purchase-progress/overview.

Yardley, Jim. 2007. "Beneath Booming Cities, China's Future Is
Drying Up." *New York Times*, September 28, A1.

Chapter 15

Airriess, Christopher. 2008. "The Geographies of Secondary City
Growth in a Globalized China: Comparing Dongguan and
Suzhou." *Journal of Urban History* 35 (1): 134–149.

Allen, Lila. 2009. "Dark Side of Dubai Dream." *BBC News
Magazine*, April 6. http://news.bbc.co.uk/2/hi/uk_news/
magazine/7985361.stm.

Benton-Short, Lisa, Marie D. Price, and Samantha Friedman.
2005. "Globalization From Below: The Ranking of Global
Immigration." *International Journal of Urban and Regional
Research* 29 (4): 945–959.

Berni, Marta. 2010. "Making Research Work for Local
Sustainability." Informed Cities Forum, Newcastle, England,
April 14–16. http://informed-cities.iclei-europe.org/fileadmin/
template/projects/primus/files/images/ICleaflet_web.pdf.

Charter Cities. n.d. "Charter Cities FAQs." http://chartercities.org/
faq/11/faq.

Christian, David. 2000. "Silk Roads or Steppe Roads? The Silk
Roads in World History." *Journal of World History* 11 (1):
1–26.

Colantonio, Andrea, and Tim Dixon. 2011. *Urban Regeneration
and Social Sustainability: Best Practice from European
Cities*. Oxford: Wiley Blackwell.

Cities for Local Integration Policy (CLIP). 2010. "European
Network of Cities for Local Integration Policies for Migrants
(CLIP)." *Eurofound*. http://www.eurofound.europa.eu/areas/
populationandsociety/clip.htm.

Congressional Executive Commission on China. 2012.
*Congressional Executive Commission on China Annual
Report 2012*. Washington, DC: U.S. Congress. http://www.
gpo.gov/fdsys/pkg/CHRG-112shrg76190/pdf/CHRG-
112shrg76190.pdf.

Conlin, Jennifer. 2011. "Detroit Pushes Back With Young Muscle."
New York Times, July 3. http://www.nytimes.com/2011/07/03/
fashion/the-young-and-entrepreneurial-move-to-downtown-
detroit-pushing-its-economic-recovery.html.

Derudder, Ben, and Frank Witlox. 2010. "World Cities and Global
Commodity Chains: An Introduction." *Global Networks* 10
(1): 1–11.

Design. 2011. *Design With the Other 90%: Cities*. New York: The
Smithsonian, Cooper Hewitt, National Design Museum.
http://www.designother90.org/cities/home.

Durkheim, Emile. 1893/1964. *The Division of Labor in Society*.
New York: The Free Press.

Elsheshtawy, Yasser. 2010. *Dubai: Behind an Urban Spectacle*.
London: Routledge.

Florida, Richard. 2002. *The Rise of the Creative Class*. New York:
Basic Books.

———. 2011. "The 25 Most Economically Powerful Cities in the
World." *The Atlantic*, September 15. http://www.theatlanticcities
.com/jobs-and-economy/2011/09/25-most-economically-
powerful-cities-world/109.

Foreign Policy (with A. T. Kearney and the Chicago Council on
Global Affairs). 2010. "The Global Cities Index 2010."
Foreign Affairs, November–December. http://www.foreign
policy.com/articles/2010/08/11/the_global_cities_index_2010.

Friedmann, John. 1986. "The World City Hypothesis."
Development and Change 17 (1): 69–83.

Friedmann, John, and Goetz Wolff . 1982. "World City Formation:
An Agenda for Research and Action." *International Journal
of Urban and Regional Research* 6 (2): 309–344.

Gottdiener, Mark, and Ray Hutchinson. 2010. *The New Urban
Sociology*. Boulder, CO: Westview Press.

Grebler, Leo. 1962. "National Programs for Urban Renewal in
Europe." *Land Economics* 38 (4): 293–304.

Hall, Peter Geoffrey. 1966. *The World Cities*. London: Weidenfeld
and Nicholson.

Hartley, John, Jason Potts, and Trent MacDonald. 2012. "The CCI
Creative City Index." *Cultural Science Journal* 5 (1): 1–144.
http://cultural-science.org/journal/index.php/culturalscience/
article/view/51/133.

Human Rights Watch. 2012. "UAE: Saadiyat Workers Better
Protected but Gaps Remain." http://www.hrw.org/
news/2012/03/21/uae-saadiyat-workers-better-protected-gaps-
remain.

Jacobs, Jane. 1961/1992. *The Life and Death of Great American
Cities*. New York: Vintage Books.

Khanna, Parag. 2010. "Beyond City Limits: The Age of Nations Is
Over: The New Urban Era Has Begun." *Foreign Policy* 181
(September–October): 120–123, 126–128. http://www.foreign
policy.com/articles/2010/08/16/beyond_city_limits.

Koebel, C. Theodore. 1996. "Urban Redevelopment, Displacement
and the Future of the American City." Report for Community
Affairs Office, Federal Reserve Bank of Richmond, Richmond,
VA. http://www.vchr.vt.edu/pdfreports/redevelopment.pdf.

Kotkin, Joel. 2010. "Urban Legends: Why Suburbs, Not Cities,
Are the Answer." *Foreign Policy* 181 (September–October):
128–131. http://www.foreignpolicy.com/articles/2010/08/16/
urban_legends?page=0,0.

Leinberger, Christopher B. 2011. "The Death of the Fringe Suburb."
New York Times, November 26. http://www.nytimes.com/
2011/11/26/opinion/the-death-of-the-fringe-suburb.html.

Mega-Cities Project. 2010. "International Transfers." http://www.megacitiesproject.org/trans_1.php.

Mori Memorial Foundation. 2009. *Global Power City Index 2009*. Tokyo: The Institute for Urban Strategies. http://www.mori-m-foundation.or.jp/english/research/project/6/pdf/GPCI2009_English.pdf.

Ouroussoff, Nicolai. 2010. "Real Life Design: Erecting Solutions to Social Problems." *New York Times*, October 15, C25.

Perlman, Janice E. 1990. "A Dual Strategy for Deliberate Social Change in Cities." *Cities* 7 (1): 3–14. http://www.megacitiesproject.org/pdf/dual_strategies.pdf.

Polis. 2010. "Polis EU Projects." http://www.polisnetwork.eu/eu-projects/eu-projects-2.

Price, Marie, and Lisa Benton-Short. 2007. "Counting Immigrants in Cities Across the Globe." Migration Policy Institute, Washington, DC. http://www.migrationinformation.org/Feature/display.cfm?ID=567.

Red River Valley Research Corridor (RRVRC). 2010. *Impact: Milestones and Horizons 2002–2010*. Fargo, ND: RRVRC. http://theresearchcorridor.com/sites/default/files/Research_Corridor_IMPACT_booklet.pdf.

Rybezynski, Witold. 2010. *Makeshift Metropolis: Ideas About Cities*. New York: Scribner.

Sassen, Saskia. 1991. *The Global City: New York, London, Tokyo*. Princeton, NJ: Princeton University Press.

———. 2009. "The Other Workers in the Advanced Corporate Economy." *Scholar and Feminist Online* 8 (1). http://sfonline.barnard.edu/work/sassen_01.htm.

———. 2011. "The Global City and the Global Slum." *Forbes*, March 22. http://www.forbes.com/sites/megacities/2011/03/22/the-global-city-and-the-global-slum.

Schill, Mark. 2010. "Northern Tier Broadband Network Supports RRVRC Research Activity." RRVRC. http://www.theresearchcorridor.com/content/00106-northern-tier-broadband-network-supports-rrvrc-research-activity.

Schumacher, E. F. 1973/2010. *Small Is Beautiful: Economics as if People Mattered*. New York: HarperCollins.

Simmel, Georg. 1903/1971. "The Metropolis and Mental Life." In *Georg Simmel: On Individuality and Social Forms*, edited by Donald N. Levine, 324–339. Chicago: University of Chicago Press.

Simpson, John. 2011. "Conditions of Dubai's Immigrant Workers Highlighted" [Video]. *BBC News Middle East*, January 20. http://www.bbc.co.uk/news/world-middle-east-12246979.

Spicker, Paul. n.d. "Housing and Urban Policy." Working Paper. The Robert Gordon University Centre for Public Policy and Management, Aberdeen, Scotland.

WorldAtlas. 2012. "Largest Cities of the World." http://www.worldatlas.com/citypops.htm.

World Bank. 2009. *World Development Report 2009: Reshaping Economic Geography*. Washington, DC: The International Bank for Reconstruction and Development/The World Bank. http://go.worldbank.org/FAV9CBBG80.

Yardley, Jim. 2011. "India's Way: In One Slum, Misery, Work, Politics and Hope." *New York Times*, December 29, A1.

Zheng, Siqi, Fenjie Long, C. Cindy Fan, and Yizhen Gu. 2009. "Urban Villages in China: A 2008 Survey of Migrant Settlements in Beijing." *Eurasian Geography and Economics* 50 (4): 425–446.

Photo Credits

6: Courtesy of Antonio Rosa (left and right); 7: Courtesy of Antonio Rosa (left and right); 9: United Nations Photo/Sylvain Liechti; 14: NASA/Visible Earth; 18: Wikimedia; 20: Courtesy of JoAnn Chirico; 35: USAID; 43: The Council of Europe; 71: Courtesy of Kristin Park; 86: World Economic Forum (top left), Courtesy of Lauren Langman (bottom left and right); 144: Peter Turnley/CORBIS; 152: NASA/Visible Earth; 157: Wikimedia; 165: United Nations Photo; 174: USAID; 177: United Nations Photo/JC McIlwaine; 194: USAID/M. Taft-Morales; 216: USAID (left and right); 217: Mosa'ab Elshamy for Getty Images; 244: USAID; 255: Courtesy of Laura Lucadomo Scott; 266: Flickr/Photo by glenmcbethlaw; 273: Courtesy of JoAnn Chirico; 282: Courtesy of Barry Ames; 292: UNECSO/ G. Leite Soares; 296: Library of Congress (left and right); 297: ©UNESCO/B. Desrus (left), ©UNESCO/D. Willetts (right); 298: Library of Congress; 315: Library of Congress; 316: Library of Congress; 359: Courtesy of Antonio Rosa; 365: USAID/ Jide Adeniyi-Jones; 366: USAID; 370: ©UNESCO/D. Willetts; 371: USAID; 397: USAID; 404: USAID; 405: USAID; 410: USAID; 417: USAID; USAID (left and right); 445: USAID; 450: Courtesy of Lars Plougmann; 456: Courtesy by Mark Knobil; 463: Courtesy of Joseph Lee Novak; 466: Antonio Rosa; 470: Allan Baxter/Getty Images (left), Corbis (right); 471: Courtesy of Lars Plougmann.

Index

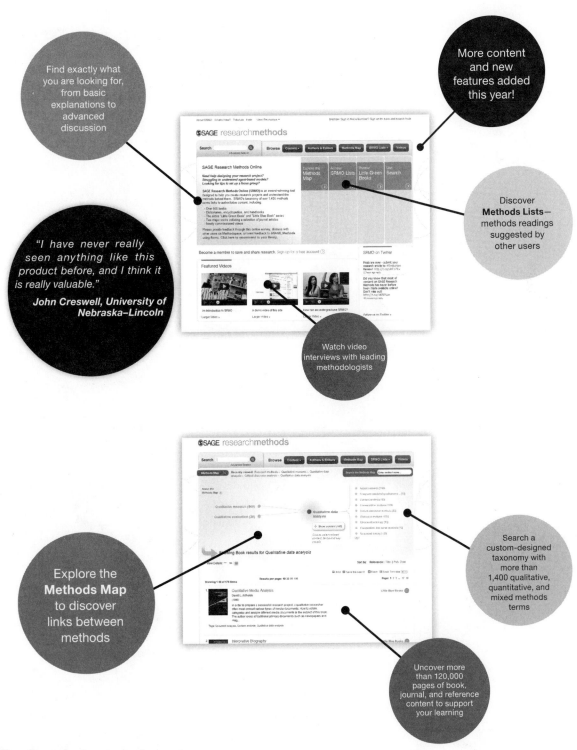

⑤SAGE research**methods**

The essential online tool for researchers from the world's leading methods publisher

Find exactly what you are looking for, from basic explanations to advanced discussion

More content and new features added this year!

"I have never really seen anything like this product before, and I think it is really valuable."

John Creswell, University of Nebraska–Lincoln

Discover **Methods Lists**— methods readings suggested by other users

Watch video interviews with leading methodologists

Explore the **Methods Map** to discover links between methods

Search a custom-designed taxonomy with more than 1,400 qualitative, quantitative, and mixed methods terms

Uncover more than 120,000 pages of book, journal, and reference content to support your learning

Find out more at
www.sageresearchmethods.com